the cooking book

the cooking book

Editor-in-chief
Victoria Blashford-Snell

London, New York, Melbourne,
Munich, and Delhi

ed,

Film Production **Spicer and Moore** www.spicerandmoore.com
DVD Production **Pink Pigeon** www.pinkpigeon.net

First published in Great Britain in 2008
by Dorling Kindersley Limited
80 Strand, London WC2R 0RL

Penguin Group (UK)

Copyright © 2008 Dorling Kindersley Limited

2 4 6 8 10 9 7 5 3 1

A CIP catalogue record for this book
is available from the British Library

ISBN 978-1-4053-3222-4

Colour reproduction by Alta Image, UK

Printed and bound in China by Leo Paper Group

Discover more at
www.dk.com

Contents

STARTERS AND LIGHT BITES 14

Foreword

I am passionate about cooking and eating, and thoroughly enjoy all that goes with it. Reading about food, researching and purchasing ingredients, choosing recipes old and new, thumbing through magazines and books, and talking to fellow enthusiasts are among my favourite activities. I enjoy experimenting with much-loved family dishes, finding new ways for them to "hit the spot", but I do love to make something different when I have friends around.

I run a catering business, teach, and write about food, and like many, have a family to look after, so although I would be happy to be pottering about in the kitchen all day, I do not have all that much time to spare, so organization is essential in planning my menus, especially if I want to include something to please everyone. There can be as many as seven people most days for lunch in our home, so I need to feed everyone quickly.

For these reasons and many others, I am thrilled to be involved with the creation of this book, as I believe it is essential for helping other modern busy people like myself. The book makes it easy for us to prepare nutritious and healthy meals simply by following clearly laid-out recipes, each accompanied by a tempting photograph. There are hundreds of superb ideas for everyday family food, and others for more formal entertaining, and a comprehensive collection of recipes from all over the world includes the classics of fine dining, and modern variations to spice up one's everyday repertoire.

The book is so full of special features, that it is certain to please every level of cook, from the beginner, to the more adventurous. The wealth of cooking expertise on offer is truly exceptional. Enjoy!

Introduction by Victoria Blashford-Snell

Becoming a confident cook is all about producing delicious meals consistently. This book has been designed to help you do just that.

As you become familiar with the contents of this book, you will benefit hugely from the range of recipes that will enable you to create a multitude of imaginative and delicious meals. Whatever the occasion – from everyday sandwich lunches to elegant party fare – and whatever it is you want to achieve – from serving up healthy everyday dinner dishes cooked in as little time as possible, to mastering the classic dishes of international cuisine – this book will enable you to achieve great results. It contains a marvelous collection of recipes from the ever-more familiar world of international cookery. Recipes that were once eaten only in exotic restaurants can now be served successfully at home alongside family favourites. Furthermore, many recipes have variations, which means that having mastered one, you can very easily make another along similar lines.

Most lives today are busy ones, so all the recipes have preparation and cooking times and, where applicable, instructions on preparing ahead and freezing. Any requirements for special equipment and/or advance preparation are flagged, and when a dish is low fat or low GI, there is an icon to point it out, making this book unusually helpful.

Recipe Choosers with photographic galleries of dishes suitable for specific occasions make your meal planning easier. At a glance you'll be able to see many different possibilities for main meals under 30 minutes, meat-free dishes, or a weekend brunch or dinner party.

Special Features look more closely at the preparation of certain key dishes, such as roasting the most flavoursome chicken, making different types of omelettes, cooking the perfect steak, and perfecting your pastry skills.

Techniques demonstrate step-by-step how to work with a wide range of ingredients including vegetables, fruits, nuts, eggs, seafood, pasta, and rice.

Plan

Leafing through the pages of this book, there's no doubt that your appetite will be whetted to try out various dishes, simply because they look so delicious. However, the choice of what to cook can arise from a number of other things. You may choose to cook a dish because of its main ingredient – you liked the look of fresh fish in the market, or a neighbour gave you some freshly picked vegetables. Or, you may want to cater for a specific occasion, such as a breakfast or lunch. Sometimes there will be particular circumstances – you've invited vegetarian friends over for brunch or you are hosting a cocktail party. Time or equipment may be other factors; what can you get on the table in under an hour, is there something you can prepare the night before, and what tastes good grilled outdoors?

Your budget and how many are eating need to be considered. You may decide to splurge on lobster for an intimate dinner for two, but a casserole will be a cheaper and easier choice when cooking for a large number of guests (see Cook for a Crowd, far right).

Another consideration when menu planning should be to provide varied textures, colours, and tastes – all of which work well together. This will come with practice; the more you cook, the faster you will learn what works with what, and why. These days it is not usually necessary to serve a three-course meal. For everyday dining, a substantial main course with a salad and/or vegetables could be followed by fruit or a simple dessert, and this book helps you to choose with Recipe Choosers in each main section, and an image for every recipe in the book.

Shop

Shopping, rather than being a chore, should be about buying the freshest ingredients available without having to visit too many different shops, therefore not having to take a lot of time and travel. Shop at good quality shops to avoid the disappointment of aisles of limp, colourless vegetables or tired old fish, and whenever possible, shop locally. The choice of ingredients may be smaller, but their freshness and quality will make up for it. Always attempt to buy meat from a good quality butcher, and fish from similar fishmonger; supporting small local shops is essential to the future of quality ingredients. To save time, know how many you're cooking for, make a list, and pre-order important ingredients.

Tips for Quantities

There are times when a recipe does not yield the right quantity of food for the number of people you plan to serve, and altering the quantities can become confusing. When halving, doubling, or serving more than one course, consider the following weights before shopping for ingredients:

- **175g (6oz) per person** when serving one meat or fish main course dish
- **115g (4oz) per dish per person** when serving two courses
- **85g (3oz) per dish per person** when serving three courses

Store

Once the shopping is done, it is important to store the ingredients properly to avoid food spoiling. Be careful not to place tender lettuce and herbs at the back of the refrigerator where they are at risk of over chilling and possibly freezing. All dried, tinned, and boxed products should be stored in a cool and dark place. Root vegetables should be stored in a cool, well-ventilated place, but not necessarily the refrigerator. Certain foods, like tomatoes, are best kept in the light, i.e. a basket or bowl on the windowsill.

Soft fruit, such as berries, will keep for several days if kept dry and cool. Store hard fruit, such as apples, pears, or pineapple, for up to a week in a cool place out of direct sunlight, which will keep them from becoming over-ripe.

Meat and fish should be stored on a plate, loosely covered with cling film, in the refrigerator for 1–2 days. Be careful not to store any meat or fish that may drip above dairy foods or vegetables.

Dairy products such as cream, butter, and yogurt need to be refrigerated, but soft cheeses must be kept at room temperature to ripen before serving. Hard cheeses can be kept in a cool place or chilled. Eggs should be kept in a cool place, pointed end downwards, to keep the yolk central in the white.

Freeze

If you are not planning to use ingredients right away, they should be frozen when fresh, and as quickly as possible. Freezing is useful to preserve leftovers for last-minute meals.

Keep a thermometer in your freezer, to maintain the temperature at -17°C (0°F).

For even freezing, keep the freezer only three-quarters full.

Make sure all food is properly covered, labelled, and sealed before freezing to avoid the food drying out and becoming ruined or unidentifiable at a later time.

Milk and cream do not freeze well, as they often curdle when defrosted.

Don't freeze dishes that contain mayonnaise or raw eggs.

Never refreeze defrosted food.

De-frost food slowly, ideally in the refrigerator or overnight somewhere cool, never near direct heat.

Cook for a Crowd

Many cooks find cooking for a large number of people daunting. The important thing is to keep things simple. Do not over-stretch yourself; plan around what space you have to store dishes, as well as the facilities you have to prepare them in. Here are some tips for success:

When multiplying a recipe, be careful not to over-season, add too much liquid, or over-cook.

A casserole for six people and one for twelve will take approximately the same amount of time to cook, even though you may have doubled the weight of the ingredients.

Preparing too little food can be embarrassing, while a lot of uneaten dishes can ruin the success of a party. Figure out quantities carefully in advance of the event.

When catering, remember that if you are providing a number of different dishes, people will only have a little of each.

Guests will eat less if it is a stand-up party, rather than a sit-down meal.

Serve

The appearance of the food you serve and eat is very important. I am not suggesting everything be served garnished with a tomato rose, but by simply ensuring the plates are clean, drops of sauce are wiped away from the rim, and adding a wedge of lemon or lime with certain dishes, or adding a scattering of fresh herbs on savoury recipes, will enhance a dish greatly. Bear the following tips in mind and your presentation will always be successful:

Serve hot food straight from the oven, therefore avoiding skin forming on the juices, which never looks attractive.

Try to choose textures and colours that complement each other – serve crisp green beans alongside mashed potatoes, puréed carrots with stir-fried broccoli, or peas with roasted parsnips.

Do not dress a salad too early, but rather just before serving, if possible, so that the leaves stay crisp.

Searing meat not only gives a better colour for presentation, but it also improves the flavour.

Avoid fussy garnishes on the plate that are not edible.

Desserts, cakes, and pastries served with a quick dusting of icing sugar will always look more appealing to the eye.

Useful Information

A Guide to Symbols

The recipes in this book are accompanied by symbols that alert you to important information.

🍴 Tells you how many people the recipe serves, or how much is produced.

🕐 Indicates how much time you will need to prepare and cook a dish. Next to this symbol you will also find out if additional time is required for such things as marinating, standing, proving, or cooling. You will have to read the recipe to find out exactly how much extra time is needed.

✓ Points out nutritional benefits, such as low fat or low GI.

❗ This is especially important, as it alerts you to what has to be done before you can begin to cook the recipe. For example, you may need to soak some beans overnight.

🍱 This denotes that special equipment is required, such as a deep-fat fryer or skewers. Where possible, alternatives are given.

❄ This symbol accompanies freezing information.

Roasting Meat

As all cuts of meat can vary, these times are intended as a general guide. When calculating timings, add an extra 450g (1lb) of weight to your joint if it weighs less than 1.35kg (3lb). Be sure to preheat the oven before cooking your meat, use a meat thermometer (inserted into the thickest part of the cut, away from any bones) for an accurate internal temperature, and always allow the meat to rest for 15–30 minutes before carving.

MEAT		OVEN TEMPERATURE	COOKING TIME	INTERNAL TEMPERATURE
Beef	Rare	180°C (350°F/Gas 4)	15 mins per 450g (1lb)	60°C (140°F)
	Medium	180°C (350°F/Gas 4)	20 mins per 450g (1lb)	70°C (160°F)
	Well-done	180°C (350°F/Gas 4)	25 mins per 450g (1lb)	80°C (175°F)
Veal	Well-done	180°C (350°F/Gas 4)	25 mins per 450g (1lb)	80°C (175°F)
Lamb	Medium	180°C (350°F/Gas 4)	20 mins per 450g (1lb)	70°C (160°F)
	Well-done	180°C (350°F/Gas 4)	25 mins per 450g (1lb)	85°C (175°F)

Roasting Poultry

Use these times as a guide, bearing in mind the size and weight of each bird vary. Be sure to preheat the oven before cooking your bird(s), and always check that the bird is fully cooked before serving.

MEAT		OVEN TEMPERATURE	COOKING TIME
Poussin		190°C (375°F/Gas 5)	12 mins per 450g (1lb) plus 12 mins
Chicken		200°C (400°F/Gas 6)	20 mins per 450g (1lb) plus 20 mins
Duck		180°C (350°F/Gas 4)	20 mins per 450g (1lb) plus 20 mins
Goose		180°C (350°F/Gas 4)	20 mins per 450g (1lb) plus 20 mins
Pheasant		200°C (400°F/Gas 6)	50 mins total cooking
Turkey	3.5–4.5kg (7–9lb)	190°C (375°F/Gas 5)	2½–3 hrs total cooking
	5–6kg (10–12lb)	190°C (375°F/Gas 5)	3½–4 hrs total cooking
	6.5–8.5kg (13–17lb)	190°C (375°F/Gas 5)	4½–5 hrs total cooking

Refrigerator and Freezer Storage Guide

FOOD	REFRIGERATOR	FREEZER
Raw poultry, fish, and meat (small pieces)	2–3 days	3–6 months
Raw minced beef and poultry	1–2 days	3 months
Cooked whole roasts or whole poultry	2–3 days	9 months
Cooked poultry pieces	1–2 days	1 month (6 months in stock or gravy)
Bread	-	3 months
Ice cream	-	1–2 months
Soups and stews	2–3 days	1–3 months
Casseroles	2–3 days	2–4 weeks
Biscuits	-	6–8 months

Oven Temperature Equivalents

CELSIUS	FAHRENHEIT	GAS	DESCRIPTION
110°C	225°F	¼	Cool
120°C	250°F	½	Cool
140°C	275°F	1	Very low
150°C	300°F	2	Very low
170°C	325°F	3	Low
180°C	350°F	4	Moderate
190°C	375°F	5	Moderately Hot
200°C	400°F	6	Hot
220°C	425°F	7	Hot
230°C	450°F	8	Very Hot

Volume Equivalents

METRIC	IMPERIAL	METRIC	IMPERIAL
25ml	1fl oz	200ml	7fl oz (⅓ pint)
50ml	2fl oz	225ml	8fl oz
75ml	2fl oz	250ml	9fl oz
100ml	3fl oz	300ml	10fl oz (½ pint)
125ml	4fl oz	350ml	12fl oz
150ml	5fl oz (¼ pint)	400ml	14fl oz
175ml	6fl oz	500ml	18fl oz

Basic Kitchen Equipment

There is no need to spend a fortune on gadgets to cook well, as good food comes from the ingredients and the cook, but certain tools of the trade will make the job more enjoyable:

Food processor	Colander
Citrus juicer – hand-held	Pastry brush
Knives – 1 large chopping,	Rolling pin
1 small serrated, 1 bread, and	Food weighing scales
1 carving knife	Wooden spoons
Vegetable peeler	Ladle
Cheese grater	Ice cream scoop
Fruit zester	Slotted spoon
Large chopping board	Spatula
Salad spinner	Fish slice
Roasting trays – for meat	Mixing bowls
Flat baking trays – for baking	Good non-stick frying pan
Electric hand whisk	Saucepans with lids in varying sizes
Hand-held balloon whisk	Kitchen scissors
Large fine sieve	Measuring jug
Garlic crusher	Oven gloves

Recipe Terms

Just as in any other activity, cooking has its own specialized vocabulary. Although in this book, recipes are written without unnecessary jargon, it can help to know exactly what is meant by specific terms.

FOOD PREPARATION

Drizzle refers to pouring a liquid, such as olive oil, slowly back and forth in a fine stream.

Fold refers to incorporating a light, airy mixture into a heavier mixture.

Marinate means to let a food soak in a liquid that will add flavour and/or tenderize it.

Pinch is an amount of a dry, powdery ingredient that you can hold between your thumb and forefinger.

Purée both an action and product, results in a smooth mixture when food is processed in a food processor, blender, or food mill.

Zest is both the action and product of removing the rind of a citrus fruit. Avoid zesting the bitter white pith.

Dice describes small, uniform cubes of approximately 5mm. To cut dice, first cut the food into matchsticks then, bundling the sticks together, cut crossways into uniform cubes.

Julienne are matchsticks that are thin and about 5cm long. To cut julienne, cut first to length, then stack the slices and cut lengthways into 3mm–wide sticks.

Chop means to cut food into small, irregular, pea-size pieces. The best way to do this is to roughly cut up the food first then place the pieces in a pile. Holding the tip and handle of a chef's knife and using a rocking motion, chop the pieces. "Finely chopped" indicates pieces, cut as described above, that are less than 3mm thick.

COOKING

Browning means cooking food quickly so it colours all over and the juices are sealed. It can be done in oil or butter on the stove top, under the grill, or in the oven.

Boiling occurs when a liquid reaches 100°C (212°F), and produces large bubbles that continuously rise and break the surface.

Simmering also produces bubbles but these rise in a steady stream, are much smaller and are just visible on the surface.

Reducing means to boil a liquid rapidly so that a proportion evaporates leaving a deeper, more concentrated sauce.

Seafood Starters

Smoked Eel Spread
Horseradish brings out the smokey flavour of the fish in this creamy spread

🕐 10 mins ❄ 1 month **page 29**

Salmon Rillettes
This piquant pâté from France has a coarse and buttery texture

🕐 15 mins ❄ 1 month **page 30**

Taramasalata
Made with smoked cod's roe, this is a perfect dip to serve as a snack or appetizer

🕐 15 mins **page 31**

Grilled Scallops with Prosciutto and Lime
Perfect for entertaining when served in the shell

🕐 15 mins **page 39**

Marinated Salmon
Allow 2 days for marinating, but the flavours that develop are worth the wait

🕐 20 mins **page 39**

Smoked Salmon Potato Cakes
This popular starter is easy to make at home

🕐 20 mins **page 40**

Prawns with Parmesan Cream
Prawns dressed in a creamy, rich sauce

🕐 25 mins **page 41**

Prawn Cocktail, Mexican-style
A Mexican twist to this perennial favourite

🕐 20–25 mins **page 41**

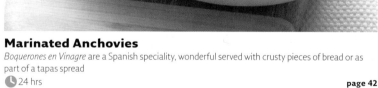

Marinated Anchovies
Boquerones en Vinagre are a Spanish speciality, wonderful served with crusty pieces of bread or as part of a tapas spread

🕐 24 hrs **page 42**

Fried Whitebait
Deep-frying is the best way to cook these tiny fish, which are eaten whole

🕐 35 mins **page 43**

Prawns with Mint, Chilli, and Ginger
Quick, easy, and ideal for a dinner party

🕐 10 mins **page 45**

Herbed Fish Goujons
Fish fingers for grown-ups

🕐 35 mins **page 46**

Seafood Ceviche
Lightly pickled, this dish is crisp and refreshing

🕐 35 mins **page 46**

Snacks on Toast

Smoked Salmon and Pancetta Crostini
The smokey flavour of the salmon is perfectly balanced by the cream and slightly salty pancetta

🕐 25 mins   page 48

Anchovies on Toast
Choose any canned anchovies to your taste

🕐 15 mins   page 42

Crostini with Green Olive Tapenade
A pâté of olives made into an attractive starter

🕐 10 mins   page 47

Scallop and Pesto Crostini
These stylish canapés can also be served as a simple first course

🕐 15–20 mins   page 49

Sesame Prawn Toasts
A combination of fresh Thai flavours on savoury fried toasts

🕐 30 mins   page 50

Broad Bean, Garlic, and Herb Crostini
Vibrant in colour, this looks and tastes great

🕐 30 mins   page 54

Aubergine and Goat's Cheese Crostini
Crisp crostini with a savoury grilled topping

🕐 30 mins   page 56

Croque Monsieur
In France, these toasted cheese and ham sandwiches are a popular snack or lunch dish

🕐 25 mins   page 88

Welsh Rarebit
This simple recipe can make a meal out of cheese on toast

🕐 15–20 mins   page 157

Anchovy and Olive Bruschette
These canapés are lovely passed around at a cocktail party

🕐 15 mins   page 49

Weekend Brunch

Savoury Onion Tart
Anchovies give a salty kick to this mild onion tart

🕐 1hr 30 mins ❄ 3 months   **page 57**

Seven-Grain Bread
A healthy bread with seven different grains

🕐 1 hr ❄ 3 months   **page 68**

Walnut Bread
In France, this savoury bread is a traditional accompaniment to the cheese course

🕐 1 hr 5 mins ❄ 3 months   **page 69**

Brioche
A sweet morning bread that is best served warm

🕐 55 mins – 1 hr   **page 70**

English Muffins
A soft traditional English bread, lovely with eggs

🕐 1 hr 20 mins   **page 76**

Croissants
Time-consuming to make, but the delicate and buttery texture makes them worth the wait

🕐 1 hr 25 mins   **page 79**

Buttermilk Biscuits
These are favourites from the American South and are best served straight from the oven

🕐 25–30 mins   **page 80**

Pizza Bianca
This tasty pizza is made without tomato sauce, but piled with fresh tomatoes and cured ham

🕐 55 mins   **page 99**

Scotch Pancakes
These thick little pancakes are delicious drizzled with sweet maple syrup

🕐 25 mins ❄ 1 month   **page 81**

Smoked Salmon and Cream Cheese Bagels
An American-style brunch sandwich

🕐 10 mins   **page 86**

Tarte Flambé
This thin-based, pizza-style tart from Alsace
has both sweet and savoury toppings

🕐 1 hr 10 mins   **page 101**

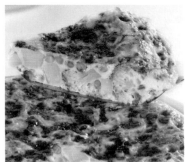

Tortilla
This variation of a traditional thick Spanish
omelette includes broccoli and peas

🕐 1 hr   **page 136**

Herb and Goat's Cheese Frittata
This popular Italian dish is lighter than a Tortilla

🕐 20 mins   **page 137**

Eggs Benedict
The smooth and rich Hollandaise sauce makes
this a truly indulgent breakfast or brunch

🕐 10–15 mins   **page 138**

Scrambled Eggs with Smoked Salmon
The ultimate feel-good weekend brunch recipe

🕐 20 mins   **page 139**

French Toast
Coated with a little egg, these are a hot, very
sweet treat

🕐 25 mins   **page 144**

Parsi Eggs
This Indian dish has its origins in ancient Persia

🕐 35 mins   **page 145**

Quiche Lorraine
A French classic, this egg and bacon flan is the
original and the best

🕐 1 hr 10 mins   **page 146**

Poached Eggs with Frisée
The egg makes the dish in this French favourite. Serve the salad as a starter or light lunch dish

🕐 35 mins   **page 147**

Baked Eggs in Cream
A simple way to prepare eggs with rich cream
and fresh chives

🕐 35 mins   **page 148**

Piperade
The filling makes this brunch dish savoury,
filling, and satisfying

🕐 25 mins   **page 150**

Omelette Arnold Bennett
A popular omelette, created in London

🕐 25 mins   **page 151**

Ricotta and Bacon Tart
A simple tart with a light cheese filling

🕐 1 hr 10 mins   ❄ 3 months   **page 163**

Healthy Snacks

Hummus
This chickpea and tahini dip is one of the most widely recognized of all Middle Eastern dishes

🕐 10 mins

page 32

Broad Bean Purée
This dip is savoury, but surprisingly fresh

🕐 1 hr 25 mins

page 32

Artichoke and Spring Onion Dip
A storecupboard recipe, made in a few minutes

🕐 5 mins

page 34

Stuffed Vine Leaves
Greek *dolmadakia* are filling, fresh snacks full of Mediterranean flavours

🕐 1 hr 10 mins

page 37

Herbed Cream and Prawn Wraps
A bite-sized twist on the classic prawn sandwich

🕐 15 mins

page 44

Melon and Nectarines with Parma Ham
Sweet and savoury, and simple to make

🕐 15 mins

page 67

Gazpacho
A savoury, chilled Spanish soup

🕐 1 hr 15 mins   ❄ 1 month

page 104

Warm Chicken Salad
This French *salade tiède*, or warm salad, is quick to cook and easy to assemble

🕐 10 mins

page 119

Tzatziki
This simple Greek dip is perfect to serve as a snack anytime with a selection of crudités

🕐 40 mins

page 28

Watercress and Roasted Walnut Salad
Try this dish served alongside savoury tarts

🕐 25 mins

page 123

Vietnamese Salad of Grilled Prawns with Papaya
Full of the fresh flavours of Vietnamese cuisine

🕐 18 mins

page 124

Prawn, Grapefruit, and Avocado Salad
Simple as an attractive and healthy lunch

🕐 15 mins

page 124

Tabbouleh
This Lebanese speciality, packed with parsley and mint, is bright and refreshing

🕐 35 mins

page 125

Oriental Cucumber Salad with Smoked Salmon
Freshly sliced cucumber is perfect with salmon

🕐 10 mins   **page 127**

Carrot and Orange Salad
This is a light and colourful salad, perfect as a snack or alongside a sandwich

🕐 20 mins   **page 128**

Roast Beetroot with Bresaeola
An unmistakeable deep pink colour, beetroot gives this dish an earthy flavour

🕐 25 mins   **page 126**

Shaved Fennel Salad
Thinly sliced fennel adds a crisp crunch to this healthy leafy salad

🕐 10 mins   **page 129**

Spinach, Pear, and Chicory Salad
Fresh pears are lovely with the spinach leaves

🕐 10 mins   **page 129**

Avocado, Tomato, and Mozzarella Salad
Only a light drizzle of oil and vinegar is needed

🕐 20 mins   **page 130**

Warm Green Bean Salad
This crunchy, nutty dish is great served cold as a light snack

🕐 25 mins   **page 131**

Greek Salad
A popular summer salad that is ideal for healthy meals outside

🕐 20 mins   **page 133**

Crab Salad
Crab works well with fruity flavours and is a lovely summer dish

🕐 15 mins   **page 129**

Red Pepper Salad
In this Spanish dish, sweet red peppers are gently stewed, then served cold

🕐 35 mins   **page 131**

Party Bites

Shrimp Spring Rolls
Savoury little bites that are delicious served with sweet chilli sauce
🕐 40 mins　　　　**page 40**

Smoked Salmon Blinis
Elegant party snacks that can be served on a platter with other little bites
🕐 40 mins　　　　**page 44**

Onion Bhajis
These crisp, onion snacks are made with chickpea flour
🕐 30 mins　　　　**page 50**

Vegetable Samosas
Serve these Indian pastries hot or cold
🕐 1 hr 35 mins　❄ 1 month　　**page 51**

Boreks
These cheese pastries from Turkey are traditionally made in cigar-shapes
🕐 35–40 mins　　　**page 53**

Cheese Straws
This classic, quick, and easy appetizer can be served with drinks on any occasion
🕐 35 mins　　　　**page 55**

Mushroom Vol-au-vents
Puff pastry cases enclosing a savoury mushroom filling
🕐 35 mins　　　　**page 55**

Smoked Trout Tartlets
Lovely tartlets to pass around at formal parties
🕐 1 hr　❄ 1 month　　**page 56**

Pizzette
Bite-sized pizzas with endless topping variations
🕐 35 mins　　　　**page 100**

Salted Roasted Almonds
Popular to serve with drinks at a cocktail party
🕐 30 mins　　　　**page 60**

Chicken Livers in Sherry
These livers, sweetened by the sherry, will entice more mature palates
🕐 10–15 mins　　　**page 60**

Buffalo Chicken Wings
Sticky charred chicken wings for picnics or watching a sports match
🕐 45 mins　　　　**page 61**

Chicken Satay
Ideal for parties, these can be eaten without a fork and plate
🕐 25 mins　　　　**page 62**

Devils on Horseback

These spicy savouries are often served as pre-dinner canapés

🕐 25–30 mins **page 63**

Chinese Dumplings

Healthy and easy to have ready in the freezer

🕐 30 mins ❄ 1 month **page 63**

Smoked Salmon Rolls

Simple to assemble, these can be served as a party appetizer with drinks

🕐 30 mins **page 64**

Oriental Meatballs with Peanut Sauce

Sweet peanut sauce is perfect for dipping

🕐 35 mins **page 65**

Crab Croustades

Lightly spiced crabmeat in a crispy case, versatile enough to be served before any meal

🕐 10 mins **page 59**

Pickled Figs Wrapped in Parma Ham

These one-bite party snacks contrast sweet and sour figs with rich Italian ham

🕐 10 mins **page 64**

Grissini

Italian-style breadsticks, perfect served alongside antipasti

🕐 35–40 mins ❄ 2 months **page 84**

Nachos

Quick and simple, these are always satisfying

🕐 15 mins **page 52**

Cheese Nuggets

Savoury cheese dippers everyone will enjoy

🕐 1hr 45 mins ❄ 3 months **page 155**

Feta Cheese Squares

Cheesy finger food for casual snacks

🕐 35 mins **page 159**

Lunch Box Ideas

Guacamole
Popular as a dip for tortilla chips, or served with tacos and sandwiches

🕐 25 mins **page 28**

Smoked Chicken and Spinach Filo Parcels
These parcels are delicious served hot or cold

🕐 45 mins ❄ 1 month **page 53**

Sausage Rolls
Bite-sized rolls, perfect to pack for picnics or take-away lunches

🕐 40–45 mins ❄ 3 months **page 66**

Ham Croissants
Easy croissants made with ready-made dough

🕐 20–25 mins **page 79**

Pan Bagnat
The traditional worker's sandwich in France

🕐 20 mins **page 87**

Coronation Chicken Rolls
These rolls are synonymous with British summer picnics and garden parties

🕐 20 mins **page 89**

Tomato and Pepper Focaccia
Filled with classic Italian flavours, this vegetarian sandwich is savoury and filling

🕐 40 mins **page 94**

Deluxe Peanut Butter Sandwiches
A "dressed-up" version of the popular sandwich

🕐 10 mins **page 97**

Reuben Sandwich
Popular in America, especially in New York City

🕐 20–25 mins **page 97**

Tarte Flambé
This thin-based, pizza-style tart from Alsace has both sweet and savoury toppings

🕐 1 hr 10 mins **page 101**

Potato Salad with Parma Ham
A dish that goes well with any lunchtime bite

🕐 35 mins **page 117**

Smoked Trout and Pancetta Salad
Smoked fish on light and crisp, bitter leaves

🕐 20 mins **page 123**

Crab Salad
Crab and avocado make a lovely summer lunch

🕐 15 mins **page 129**

Ensaladilla Rusa
A filling salad, widely enjoyed with tapas

🕐 40 mins **page 130**

Scotch Eggs
Great for picnics and packed lunches, serve with your favourite chutney or tomato ketchup

🕐 40 mins **page 139**

Pasta and Tuna Niçoise Salad
This easy summer dish is made with shell pasta

🕐 35 mins **page 117**

Hearty Soups

Watercress Soup
A velvety-smooth soup with Parmesan cheese

🕐 25 mins **page 104**

Porcini Mushroom Soup
This hearty Italian country soup is full of deep, rich flavours

🕐 1 hr 20 mins ❄ 3 months **page 108**

White Bean Soup
This thick soup from northern Italy is guaranteed to keep out the winter chills

🕐 2 hrs 30 mins **page 108**

Fish Soup with Saffron and Fennel
A rustic, Mediterranean-style fish soup

🕐 1 hr 10 mins **page 110**

Hungarian Goulash Soup
Warming flavours make this traditional soup a rich and satisfying meal

🕐 2 hrs 15 mins **page 111**

Tuscan Bean Soup
This soup, *Ribollita*, is thick, and filling

🕐 1 hr 35 mins **page 111**

French Onion Soup
This Parisian classic is given extra punch with a spoonful of brandy in each bowl

🕐 80 mins ❄ 1 month **page 112**

New England Clam Chowder
An American favourite, often served with crushed saltine crackers

🕐 50 mins **page 113**

Minestrone
This substantial soup makes a great lunch or supper dish, and you can add whatever vegetables are fresh in season

🕐 2 hrs 5 mins ❄ 1 month **page 112**

Bouillabaisse
Originally nothing more than a humble fisherman's soup

🕐 1 hr 25 mins **page 114**

Meat-free Starters

Baba Ganoush
No Middle Eastern meze table is complete without a bowl of this creamy dip
🕐 40 mins   **page 30**

Avocado Mousse with Lime
This smooth-textured mousse can be served as a starter light lunch
🕐 15 mins   **page 31**

Tapenade
A full-flavoured olive spread, popular in the Mediterranean
🕐 15 mins   **page 34**

Courgette Batons
These fritters make a lovely vegetarian party snack
🕐 30 mins   **page 35**

Grilled Mushrooms with Goat's Cheese
Warm cheese in savoury mushroom cups
🕐 35 mins   **page 36**

Artichoke Salad
The delicate and distinctive flavour of artichokes are balanced with peppery rocket
🕐 30 mins   **page 36**

Chargrilled Asparagus with Hollandaise
Asparagus made into something special
🕐 20 mins   **page 37**

Stuffed Vine Leaves
Greek *dolmadakia* are vine leaves stuffed with a vegetarian mix of rice, herbs, and tomatoes
🕐 1 hr 10 mins   **page 37**

Wild Mushroom and Chive Hollandaise Tartlets
These appetizers are a tasty meat-free option
🕐 1 hr 20 mins   **page 52**

Borscht
Thickly textured and satisfying, this classic Russian soup can be enjoyed on any occasion
🕐 1 hr 45 mins   **page 105**

Marinated Goat's Cheese Salad
A stylish dinner party starter
🕐 25 mins   **page 120**

White Bean Soup
This thick soup from northern Italy is guaranteed to keep out the winter chills
🕐 2 hrs 30 mins   **page 108**

Carrot and Orange Soup
A light, refreshing soup with a hint of spice, this is the perfect start to a summer meal
🕐 50 mins   **page 107**

Little Gem Salad
Make the Parmesan cheese shavings with a vegetable peeler for this bistro-style salad
🕐 30–35 mins   **page 120**

Roasted Tomato Salad with Lemon and Crème Fraîche
Sweet roasted tomatoes with a creamy dressing
🕐 2 hrs 15 mins   **page 121**

Waldorf Salad
A classic dish named after a prestigious hotel
🕐 20 mins   **page 121**

Grilled Courgette and Pepper Salad
A mix of vegetables topped with vinaigrette
🕐 40 mins   **page 122**

Steamed Aubergine Salad
This is a crunchy and zesty salad, best with sweet tomatoes
🕐 35 mins   **page 128**

Spinach Timbales
An individual vegetable-and-egg dish that is cooked in a mould
🕐 40 mins ❄ 3 months   **page 144**

Spinach and Mushroom Pancakes
Savoury pancakes, baked in a cheesy sauce
🕐 1 hr 40 mins ❄ 3 months   **page 148**

Egg Fu Yung
Light and tasty, these Chinese patties are made with prawns and vegetables
🕐 35 mins   **page 149**

Cheese Soufflé
The most popular savoury soufflé is this simple cheese one
🕐 55 mins   **page 150**

Twice-baked Cheese Soufflés
This foolproof recipe can be prepared several hours in advance
🕐 30–35 mins ❄ 3 months   **page 153**

Cheese Roulade
This makes a sumptuous first course or is perfect for a light lunch
🕐 45 mins   **page 161**

Feta Filo Pie
Crisp pastry encases a delicious blend of spinach, feta, and pine nuts
🕐 1 hr 50 mins   **page 158**

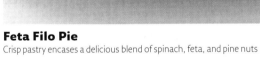

Warm Halloumi with Herbs
Halloumi is made from sheep and goat's milk
🕐 10 mins   **page 162**

Swiss Cheese Fondue
This is a wonderful dish for sharing
🕐 25 mins   **page 163**

Tandoori Paneer Kebabs
Paneer is a firm Indian cheese that takes up the flavour of other ingredients
🕐 30 mins   **page 165**

Gruyère Tart
This vegetarian tart, with crisp, thyme-flavoured pastry, is equally delicious served warm or cold
🕐 1 hr 10 mins   **page 165**

Tzatziki

This simple Greek dip makes a good start to a casual meal, served with a selection of crudités

 serves 4

 prep 10 mins, plus 30 mins standing

1 **cucumber**, peeled and coarsely grated

salt

350g (12oz) **Greek yogurt**

3 **garlic cloves**, crushed

2 tbsp chopped **mint** or **dill**

2 tbsp **extra virgin olive oil**

1 tbsp **red wine vinegar**

● **Prepare ahead** The dip can be made a day in advance and chilled; stir before serving.

1 Put the cucumber in a bowl, sprinkle with salt, and leave to stand for 30 minutes.

2 Rinse the cucumber well to remove the salt, then use your hands to squeeze out all the liquid.

3 Put the cucumber in a bowl, add the yogurt, and stir together. Add the garlic, herbs, the olive oil, and vinegar and stir together. Cover with cling film and chill until required.

● **Good with** warmed pitta bread and a variety of raw vegetables, such as carrot, celery, fennel, and pepper slices, for dipping. Tzatziki is also delicious served alongside grilled lamb or spicy sausages.

● **Leftovers** will keep covered in the refrigerator for 1 day.

Guacamole

This popular dip, which has its origins in Mexico, is perfect party food

 serves 6 as an appetizer, 12 as a condiment

 prep 25 mins

3 large, ripe **avocados**

juice of ½ **lime**

½ **onion**, finely chopped

1 ripe **tomato**, deseeded and chopped

1 **red chilli**, deseeded and finely chopped

10 sprigs of **coriander**, chopped, plus extra to garnish

salt

2 tbsp **soured cream** (optional)

● **Prepare ahead** Chop the onions, tomato, garlic, and chilli in advance but do not combine with the avocado until just before serving.

1 Prepare the avocados by removing and discarding the skins and stones. Place the avocados into a mixing bowl and mash with a fork to create a chunky mixture.

2 Add the lime juice, followed by the onion, tomato, and chillies. Mix well, stir in the chopped coriander, and salt to taste.

3 Fold in the cream, if using, then pile the guacamole into a serving bowl, garnish with coriander, and serve immediately.

● **Good with** tortilla chips.

● **Leftovers** can be used as a sandwich spread or as a topping for tacos and quesadillas.

Chicken Liver Pâté

The red wine adds flavour to this spread and cuts through the richness of the liver

🍴 serves 4

🕐 prep 10 mins, plus cooling and chilling • cook 15 mins

❄️ freeze the livers for up to 3 months before using

350g (12oz) **chicken livers**, thawed if frozen

115g (4oz) **butter**

¼ tsp **dried thyme**

150ml (5fl oz) **red wine**

10 **chives**, snipped, plus extra for garnishing

salt and freshly ground **black pepper**

⬤ **Prepare ahead** This is best made 1 day and a maximum of 3 days in advance so the flavours have time to develop. Keep covered and chilled in the refrigerator.

1 Rinse the chicken livers and pat them dry with kitchen paper. Trim away any white sinew or greenish portions from the livers with small scissors, then cut each in half.

2 Melt half the butter in a large frying pan over a medium heat until it foams. Add the livers and cook, stirring often, for 4 minutes, or until browned.

3 Add the thyme, wine, and chives to the pan. Bring to the boil then reduce the heat and cook, stirring occasionally for 4 minutes, or until the liquid is reduced and the livers are just cooked through when sliced open.

4 Remove the pan from the heat and leave to cool for 10 minutes. Add salt and pepper to taste, then tip the livers and sauce into a blender, and blend until smooth. Adjust the seasoning if necessary. Spoon the pâté into a serving bowl, pressing it down with the back of the spoon so it is firmly packed, then set aside.

5 Melt the remaining butter over a medium heat, then pour it over the top of the pâté. Chill, uncovered, for at least 2 hours. Serve garnished with snipped chives.

⬤ **Good with** toasted French bread slices or cornichons, which are the traditional French accompaniment.

Smoked Eel Spread

Horseradish can vary in spiciness from mild to fiery. Pick one to suit your taste

🍴 serves 4

🕐 prep 10 mins

⬚ food processor

❄️ freeze for up to 1 month without the paprika

250g (9oz) **smoked eel fillet**, skinned if necessary

100g (3½oz) **curd cheese** or **ricotta**

1–2 tsp creamed **horseradish**

juice of ½ **lemon**

freshly ground **black pepper**

pinch of **paprika**, for garnishing

⬤ **Prepare ahead** The spread can be made up to 24 hours in advance and stored in an airtight container in the refrigerator. Add the garnishes when ready to serve.

1 Cut the fillet into 2½cm (1in) pieces and place in a food processor with the curd cheese, horseradish, and lemon juice. Season with pepper and process until the mixture is smooth.

2 Transfer the spread to a bowl and sprinkle with paprika.

⬤ **Good with** melba toast, torn pieces of wholemeal bread, or toasted slices of baguette.

VARIATION

Smoked Salmon Spread

Use smoked salmon in place of eel. Trout, mackerel, or haddock would also be suitable for this spread.

Salmon Rillettes

This piquant pâté from France should have a fairly rough texture

 serves 4

 prep 15 mins

 freeze for up to 1 month

60g (2oz) **butter**, softened

250g (9oz) **hot-smoked salmon**, skinned

4 tbsp **Greek yogurt**

finely grated zest and juice of ½ **lemon**

2 tbsp snipped **chives**

50g jar **salmon caviar**

handful of **watercress**, to garnish

lemon wedges, to garnish

● **Prepare ahead** The rillettes can be prepared up to 24 hours in advance and stored in a covered container in the refrigerator.

1 **Put the butter** in a bowl and beat with a wooden spoon until smooth. Break up the salmon into small pieces, add to the bowl, and mash with a fork.

2 **Add the yogurt**, lemon zest and juice, and chives and stir until evenly combined.

3 **Spoon on to** serving plates and top with caviar. Garnish with watercress sprigs and lemon wedges to squeeze over.

● **Good with** small rounds of pumpernickel to make tasty and attractive canapés.

VARIATION

Poached Salmon Rillettes

Use the same quantity of poached fresh salmon fillet, removing the skin after the fish has been cooked.

Baba Ganoush

No Middle Eastern meze table is complete without a bowl of this creamy dip

 serves 6

 prep 10 mins, plus standing
• cook 25–30 mins

oil, for greasing

900g (2lb) **aubergines**, cut in half lengthways

2 large **garlic cloves**, crushed

2 tbsp **extra virgin olive oil**

2 tbsp **plain yogurt**

3–4 tbsp **tahini**

2–3 tbsp fresh **lemon** juice

salt and freshly ground **black pepper**

sprigs of **coriander**, to garnish

● **Prepare ahead** The dip can be made 1 day in advance. Cover and chill until 15 minutes before required, then return to room temperature to serve.

1 **Preheat the oven** to 220°C (425°F/Gas 7) and lightly grease a baking sheet. Score down the centre of each aubergine half without cutting through the skin, then place on the baking sheet, cut-sides down. Place in the oven and bake for 25–30 minutes, or until the flesh is thoroughly softened and collapsing.

2 **Transfer the aubergine** halves to a colander and set aside to stand for 15 minutes, or until they become cool enough to handle.

3 **Scoop the aubergine flesh** into a food processor or blender. Add the garlic, olive oil, yogurt, 3 tbsp tahini, and 2 tbsp lemon juice and process until smooth. Taste and adjust the tahini and lemon juice, if necessary, then season to taste with salt and pepper. Sprinkle with coriander, and serve.

● **Good with** warmed pitta bread, cut into strips.

● **Leftovers** can be kept in the refrigerator, covered, for 2 days.

PREPARE BY HAND

Preheat the grill to its highest setting, then grill the aubergine halves, cut-sides down, until thoroughly softened and collapsing. Alternatively, chargrill the aubergine halves in a very hot ridged cast-iron grill pan. Instead of using a food processor or a blender, the ingredients can be pounded to a paste using a pestle and mortar.

Avocado Mousse with Lime

This creamy textured mousse can be served as a starter but it will also make a perfect light meal

- serves 4
- prep 15 mins, plus chilling
- 4 x 100ml (3½ fl oz) ramekins

2 large ripe **avocados**

finely grated zest and juice of 1 **lime**

100g (3½oz) **low-fat cream cheese**

salt and freshly ground **black pepper**

2 tsp **powdered gelatine**

1 **egg white** (optional)

● **Prepare ahead** The mousse can be made up to 12 hours in advance. Place a layer of cling film over the top and press on to the surface, to prevent the mousse from turning brown. Chill until needed.

1 Halve the avocados and remove the stones. Scoop the flesh into a small bowl, add the lime zest and juice, and use a fork, hand blender, or food processor to mash until very smooth.

2 Beat in the cream cheese and season with salt and pepper.

3 Place 2 tbsp of water in a small heatproof bowl and sprinkle the gelatine over it. Leave it for 1 minute to go spongy, then place the bowl in a pan of hot water and stir the gelatine until it dissolves.

4 Whisk the egg white in a large bowl until standing in soft peaks. This will give the mousse a light texture. Drizzle the dissolved gelatine over the avocado mixture and stir until well combined. Add the egg white (if using), and carefully fold in, taking care not to knock out the air.

5 Spoon into ramekin dishes, cover closely with cling film, and chill for 2 hours, or until set.

Taramasalata

Tarama is Turkish for the salted and dried roe of grey mullet traditionally used in this recipe

- serves 4–6
- prep 15 mins, plus chilling
- soak the breadcrumbs for 15 mins before starting

250g (9oz) piece **smoked cod's roe**

juice of 1 **lemon**

60g (2oz) fresh **white breadcrumbs**, soaked in 3 tbsp cold water

75ml (2½ fl oz) **extra virgin olive oil**

1 small **onion**, grated, patted dry with kitchen paper

paprika, for sprinkling

● **Prepare ahead** You can make this dish up to 2 days in advance and store in the refrigerator, covered.

1 Split the roe down the centre using a sharp knife and carefully peel away the skin. Place in a blender with the lemon juice and soaked breadcrumbs; blend well.

2 With the motor running, very slowly add the oil in a thin steady stream until the mixture resembles smooth mayonnaise.

3 Spoon into a small serving dish and mix in the onion. Cover and chill for 30 minutes, then serve sprinkled with paprika.

● **Good with** olives, Greek or Turkish breads, and crunchy vegetable crudités.

VARIATION

Cheesy Taramasalata

Omit the breadcrumbs and oil and blend the roe with 150g (5½oz) soft cheese, along with the lemon juice.

Hummus

This chickpea and tahini dip is one of the most widely recognized of all Middle Eastern dishes

🍴 serves 4

🕐 prep 10 mins

400g can **chickpeas**

3 tbsp **tahini**

juice of 3 **lemons**

3 **garlic cloves**, chopped

½ tsp **salt**

paprika, for sprinkling

● **Prepare ahead** Make the dip up to 24 hours in advance, and chill, covered, until needed. Allow the hummus to stand at room temperature for 30 minutes before serving.

1 Drain and rinse the chickpeas, reserving 4–6 tbsp of the liquid from the can. Place the chickpeas in a blender or food processor with 3 tbsp of the reserved liquid.

2 Add the tahini, lemon juice, and garlic, then blend well for a few seconds until smooth and creamy. Add a little more of the liquid from the can, if required.

3 Season to taste with salt. Transfer the hummus to a small bowl, sprinkle with paprika, and serve at room temperature.

● **Good with** warm pitta bread and sticks of carrot, cucumber, celery, and sweet pepper. You can drizzle with olive oil for a traditional finish.

VARIATION

Red Pepper Hummus

Preheat the grill to its highest setting. Halve and deseed a small red pepper, then grill, skin-side up, for 4–5 minutes, or until the skin is lightly charred. Place in a plastic food bag until cool enough to handle, then peel away the skin. Roughly chop the pepper and add it to the blender along with the chickpeas, then make the recipe as above. Depending on the juiciness of the pepper, you may need less of the reserved liquid from the can. Add 1 tsp ground cumin for a spicier flavour.

Broad Bean Purée

Broad beans are among the oldest bean varieties and are best eaten when the pods are still young and tender

🍴 serves 6–8

🕐 prep 20 mins, plus soaking • cook 1¼ hrs

✓ low fat

❗ soak the beans overnight in cold water

250g (9oz) skinless **dried broad beans**, soaked overnight

3 **onions**

6 **garlic cloves**

bunch of **coriander**, chopped, plus extra to garnish

bunch of **flat-leaf parsley**, chopped, plus extra to garnish

2 tbsp chopped **mint**

1 tsp **ground cumin**

salt and freshly ground **black pepper**

1–3 tbsp **olive oil**

juice of 1 **lemon**

● **Prepare ahead** The purée can be prepared up to 2 hours in advance. Chill, covered with cling film, until needed.

1 Drain the beans, and place in a large pan. Pour in enough cold water to cover. Roughly chop 1 onion and 3 garlic cloves, add to the pan, then bring to the boil. Skim off any scum and lower the heat, then cover and simmer for 1 hour, or until the beans are soft.

2 Drain the beans, reserving the cooking liquid. Place the beans in a blender or food processor with the coriander, parsley, mint, cumin, and salt and pepper to taste, and blend to a smooth purée, adding enough of the reserved cooking liquid to ensure the mixture is not too dry. Transfer to a serving dish and keep warm.

3 Slice the remaining onions. Heat 1 tbsp oil in a frying pan, add the onions, and fry, stirring frequently, over a medium-high heat for 10–15 minutes, or until they are dark golden and slightly caramelized. Finely chop the remaining garlic, add it to the pan, and stir-fry for a further minute.

4 Spread the fried onions and garlic over the top of the purée, and drizzle with the lemon juice and remaining oil.

Duck Confit

This French speciality from the Gascony region takes a little time to make, but is worth the wait

- serves 4
- prep 15 mins, plus chilling and curing • cook 1½ hrs
- 4 medium Kilner jars
- freeze for up to 6 months

4 duck legs or 8 duck thighs

175g (6oz) coarse sea salt

30g (1oz) white peppercorns

1 tsp coriander seeds

5 juniper berries

4 garlic cloves, peeled and crushed

1 tbsp thyme leaves, chopped

1kg (2½lb) duck fat or goose fat, melted

● **Prepare ahead** You can make this dish up to 4 weeks in advance. Keep in the refrigerator until needed. To give you plenty of time, start the confit at least 1 day before you plan to serve it.

1 **Dry the duck legs** or thighs on kitchen paper. Pound the sea salt with the peppercorns, coriander seeds, juniper berries, garlic, and thyme until all are roughly crushed into a paste. Rub the mixture into the duck skin, and put duck, skin-side down, in a non-metallic dish. Cover with cling film and chill for 12 hours.

2 **Preheat the oven** to 140°C (275°F/Gas 1). Rinse the duck and pat dry, then put in a close-fitting ovenproof dish, and pour the melted fat over.

3 **Cook** for 1½ hours, or until cooked through and tender. It is cooked if a skewer slides in easily at the thickest part of the duck.

4 **Transfer the confit** to a plastic container. Ladle the fat over the duck through a fine sieve, being careful not to ladle in any of the juices from the bottom of the cooking dish. Cover the meat with at least 2.5cm (1in) of fat to keep the air from reaching it. Leave to cool in the fat, then transfer to sealed Kilner jars or freezer bags, and refrigerate until needed.

5 **When ready to serve,** remove from the fat and pan-fry until heated through.

● **Good with** salad leaves and some roasted beetroot.

Brandade de Morue

This dish of creamed salt cod is popular in Mediterranean countries, particularly in the south of France

- serves 4
- prep 20 mins, plus soaking and standing • cook 20 mins
- start soaking the cod at least 24 hrs in advance

450g (1lb) salt cod

2 garlic cloves, crushed

200ml (7fl oz) olive oil

100ml (3½fl oz) boiled milk

To serve

2 tbsp chopped flat-leaf parsley

olive oil, to drizzle

freshly ground black pepper

triangles of bread, fried in olive oil

black olives

1 **Soak the fish** in a bowl of cold water for 24 hours, changing the water 3–4 times.

2 **Drain the cod** and place in a large shallow pan, then cover it with cold water and bring to a gentle simmer. Cook for 10 minutes, then remove the pan from the heat, and leave the cod to sit in the water for a further 10 minutes before draining.

3 **Remove the skin** and bones from the fish, then flake the flesh into a bowl and pound to a paste with the garlic.

4 **Put the fish paste** in a pan over a gentle heat. Beat in sufficient olive oil and milk, a little at a time, to make a creamy white mixture that holds its shape.

5 **Serve hot,** with a drizzle of olive oil and some black pepper, alongside fried bread triangles and black olives.

> ### CAREFUL MIXING
> The oil and milk must be beaten very gradually into the cod or the mixture will separate. Should this happen, transfer the mixture to a bowl and whisk vigorously to bring it back together.

Coarse Meat Terrine

Full of rich flavour, this pâté is extremely versatile

🍴 serves 8

🕐 prep 30 mins, plus pressing • cook 1½ hrs

🍳 1.2 litre (2 pint) terrine dish

❄ freeze for up to 1 month

350g (12oz) rindless **streaky bacon rashers**

250g (9oz) **chicken livers**

300g (10oz) **minced pork**

450g (1lb) **minced veal**

1 **onion**, finely chopped

2 **garlic cloves**, crushed

1 tsp **dried oregano**

½ tsp **ground allspice**

115g (4oz) **butter**, melted

120ml (4fl oz) **dry sherry**

salt and freshly ground **black pepper**

● **Prepare ahead** You can start this recipe the day before, as the longer the cooked terrine is pressed with a heavy weight, such as unopened cans, the better the flavour and texture will be.

1 **Preheat the oven** to 180°C (350°F/Gas 4). Using the back of a knife, stretch the bacon rashers, and use them to line the terrine dish, or other ovenproof bowl or dish, leaving the ends hanging over the sides of the dish.

2 **Mince or chop** the chicken livers and mix with the minced pork, minced veal, onion, garlic, oregano, allspice, and melted butter. Stir in the sherry and season with salt and pepper.

3 **Spoon the mixture** into the dish and fold the ends of the bacon over the top. Cover tightly with foil or a lid, and stand the dish in a roasting tin, filled with enough hot water to reach halfway up the sides of the terrine dish.

4 **Cook in the oven** for 1½ hours, then remove and cover with fresh foil. Place a weight on top and leave for up to 24 hours, then turn out and cut into slices.

● **Good with** slices of warm crusty bread or toast, topped with a gherkin or cocktail onion.

Tapenade

A full-flavoured olive spread, popular in the Mediterranean

🍴 serves 4–6

🕐 prep 15 mins

2 large **garlic cloves**

250g (9oz) Mediterranean **black olives**, pitted

1½ tbsp **capers**, drained and rinsed

4 **anchovy fillets** in olive oil, drained

1 tsp **thyme** leaves

1 tsp chopped **rosemary**

2 tbsp fresh **lemon** juice

2 tbsp **extra virgin olive oil**

1 tsp **Dijon mustard**

freshly ground **black pepper**

12 slices **French bread**, toasted, to serve

1 **Place the garlic**, olives, capers, anchovies, thyme, and rosemary in a food processor or blender, and process until smooth.

2 **Add the lemon juice**, olive oil, mustard, and black pepper to taste, and blend until a thick paste forms. Transfer to a bowl and chill until ready to use.

3 **Serve in a small bowl** with slices of toasted French bread.

● **Good with** crudités and a spread of Mediterranean appetizers, such as olives and stuffed vine leaves.

Artichoke and Spring Onion Dip

A storecupboard recipe that takes just minutes to make

🍴 serves 6

🕐 prep 5 mins

390g can **artichoke hearts**, drained

1 **garlic clove**, halved

3 **spring onions**, coarsely chopped

2 tbsp **mayonnaise**

salt and freshly ground **black pepper**

● **Prepare ahead** The dip can be made up to 24 hours in advance, covered with cling film, and chilled until ready to serve.

1 **Place the artichokes**, garlic, spring onions, and mayonnaise in a food processor or blender and process to form a smooth purée.

2 **Season to taste** with salt and pepper, then spoon into a serving bowl, cover, and refrigerate until ready to use.

● **Good with** pitta bread, vegetable crudités, or breadsticks. Alternatively, spread on to chunks of French bread.

Courgette Batons

Crisp and moreish, these fritters make a lovely vegetarian party snack

🍴 serves 6

🕐 prep 15 mins • cook 15 mins

🍲 deep-fat fryer

3 large **courgettes**

100g (3½oz) fresh **breadcrumbs**

20g (¾oz) **parsley**

115g (4oz) **Parmesan cheese**, grated

salt and freshly ground **black pepper**

grated zest of ½ **lemon**

2 **eggs**

plain flour, to coat

sunflower oil, for frying

⬤ **Prepare ahead** You can slice and coat the courgettes 1 day in advance, then cover and chill.

1 **Wash and dry** the courgettes, then cut into batons.

2 **Put the breadcrumbs**, parsley, Parmesan, salt and pepper to taste, and lemon zest into a shallow bowl and mix thoroughly until well combined.

3 **Beat the eggs** with a fork in a separate bowl and place the flour in a third bowl.

4 **Dip the courgette batons** in the flour, then in the egg, and finally in the the breadcrumbs, ensuring they are evenly coated.

5 **Fry the batons**, in small batches, in hot sunflower oil in a deep-fat fryer or shallow frying pan until golden. Drain on a baking tray lined with kitchen paper, and keep warm until the last batch is finished.

Stuffed Mushrooms

Field mushrooms, or ones with open cups, make great bases for savoury fillings

🍴 serves 4

🕐 prep 15 mins • cook 20 mins

8 open-cup **mushrooms**

2 tbsp **olive oil**, extra for greasing

4 **shallots**, finely chopped

2 **garlic cloves**, crushed

120g (4oz) **pine nuts**, toasted

4 tbsp **basil**, roughly torn

4 tbsp **parsley**, finely chopped

salt and freshly ground **black pepper**

175g (6oz) firm **goat's cheese**

8 slices **pancetta**

1 **Preheat the oven** to 190°C (375°F/Gas 5). Place the mushrooms on an oiled baking tray.

2 **Heat the olive oil** in a large frying pan and fry the shallots over a medium heat for 2–3 minutes, or until softened, stirring frequently. Add the garlic, pine nuts, basil, and parsley, and season to taste with salt and pepper.

3 **Spoon the mixture** into the mushrooms and top with a slice of goat's cheese.

4 **Wrap a slice** of pancetta around each mushroom, tucking the ends underneath.

5 **Bake for** 15–20 minutes, or until the mushrooms are tender and the pancetta is crisp. Serve immediately.

⬤ **Good with** young salad leaves and a drizzle of balsamic vinegar.

Grilled Mushrooms with Goat's Cheese

Ideally, the grilled slices of bread or croûtes should be about the same size as the mushrooms, so choose an appropriately sized loaf

serves 6

prep 20 mins • cook 15 mins

baguette or crusty loaf

olive oil

6 large field mushrooms

150g (5½oz) log of goat's cheese

balsamic vinegar, for drizzling

salt and freshly ground black pepper

For the dressing

1 tbsp thyme leaves

2 tbsp balsamic vinegar

4 tbsp extra virgin olive oil

1 tsp Dijon mustard

1 garlic clove, chopped

12 black olives, pitted and chopped

● **Prepare ahead** The mushrooms and dressing can be prepared the day before, and chilled.

1 **Preheat the oven** to 180°C (350°F/Gas 4). To make the dressing, whisk together all the ingredients and set aside.

2 **Cut the bread** diagonally into 1cm (½in) slices. Brush both sides with olive oil and place on a baking tray. Bake for 10 minutes, or until crisp but not too browned.

3 **Remove the stems** from the mushrooms. Slice the goat's cheese into rounds. Place a slice in each mushroom cap. Preheat the grill on medium, then place the mushrooms on a grill pan. Drizzle with a little olive oil and balsamic vinegar, then season with salt and pepper. Place the mushrooms under

the grill for 5 minutes, or until the goat's cheese is bubbling and the mushrooms are tender.

4 **To serve**, place each croûte on a serving plate, top with a grilled mushroom, and drizzle with the dressing. Serve while still hot.

● **Good with** a side salad of peppery rocket leaves, sliced chicory, and radicchio.

VARIATION

Blue Cheese Mushrooms

Use a mild blue cheese, such as Roquefort or Gorgonzola, instead of goat's cheese.

Artichoke Salad

The delicate and distinctive flavour of artichokes goes well with rocket and Parmesan

serves 4

prep 25 mins, plus cooling • cook 10 mins

4 globe artichokes

3 lemons

salt

2 large handfuls of rocket

25g (scant 1oz) Parmesan cheese

2 tbsp extra virgin olive oil

1 tbsp balsamic vinegar

freshly ground black pepper

1 **Remove the hearts** of the artichokes and place them in a bowl. Juice 2 lemons over the hearts.

2 **Bring a saucepan** of water to the boil. Add 1 tsp salt and the juice of the remaining lemon. Place the artichokes into the pan and cook for 10 minutes, or until tender. Drain well and set aside to cool.

3 **When the hearts** are cool enough to handle, gently cut them into quarters.

4 **Divide the rocket** and artichokes between the serving plates. Using a vegetable peeler, shave pieces of Parmesan over each salad. Drizzle over olive oil and balsamic vinegar, and season to taste with salt and pepper to serve.

Stuffed Vine Leaves

Greek *dolmadakia* are vine leaves stuffed with a vegetarian mix of rice, herbs, and tomatoes

🍴 serves 6

🕐 prep 20 mins • cook 50 mins

❗ blanch fresh vine leaves for 5 mins; soak preserved vine leaves in hot water and then rinse several times to remove the brine

▣ heatproof plate

2 tbsp **olive oil**

2 **onions**, finely chopped

½ tsp **ground allspice**

200g (7oz) **long-grain rice**

600ml (1 pint) **vegetable stock**

3 **tomatoes**, skinned, deseeded, and chopped

1 tbsp chopped **dill**

1 tbsp chopped **mint**

salt and freshly ground **black pepper**

40 **vine leaves**

juice of 1 **lemon**

1 Heat the oil in a frying pan, add the onions, and fry gently until softened but not browned. Increase the heat, add the allspice and rice, stir, and cook for 2 minutes.

2 Pour in the stock and leave to simmer for 10 minutes, or until the rice is tender and has absorbed the liquid. Remove from the heat, stir in the tomatoes, dill, and mint, and season to taste with salt and pepper.

3 Place a vine leaf shiny-side down and spoon a little of the rice mixture in the centre. Fold in the sides and roll into a parcel. Repeat.

4 Pack the stuffed vine leaves tightly in a large saucepan, squeeze over the lemon juice, and add enough cold water to just cover. Put a heatproof plate with a weight on top so they don't unravel, and simmer gently for 30 minutes, topping up the water if necessary. Carefully drain the vine leaves and serve warm or cold.

Chargrilled Asparagus with Hollandaise

Classic hollandaise sauce, rich and tangy, is the perfect partner for new-season asparagus

🍴 serves 4

🕐 prep 10 mins • cook 10 mins

▣ ridged cast-iron grill pan

500g (1lb 2oz) fresh **asparagus spears**

1 tbsp **olive oil**

For the hollandaise

2 tbsp **white wine vinegar**

4 **egg yolks**

115g (4oz) **butter**, melted

salt and freshly ground **black pepper**

juice of ½ **lemon**

1 Trim or snap off the woody ends from the asparagus spears. Heat a ridged cast-iron grill pan and brush with the oil. When very hot, add the asparagus and grill for 5–6 minutes, depending on the thickness of the spears, turning once, until lightly charred and just tender.

2 Meanwhile, to make the sauce, heat the vinegar in a small pan and allow to bubble until it reduces by half. Remove from the heat, add 2 tbsp water, then whisk in the egg yolks one at a time.

3 Return the pan to a very low heat and whisk continuously until the mixture is thick and light. Remove from the heat and gradually whisk in the melted butter. Season to taste with salt and pepper and stir in the lemon juice.

4 Divide the asparagus between serving plates and serve with the sauce spooned over.

Stuffed Potato with Cheese and Bacon

Jacket potatoes make a filling starter or a meal on their own when served with a simple salad

 serves 4

 prep 30 mins • cook
1 hr 20 mins

4 small **baking potatoes**, scrubbed

200g (7oz) **bacon lardons**

2 **shallots**, finely chopped

25g (scant 1oz) **butter**, plus extra for greasing

100ml (3½fl oz) **milk**

75g (2½oz) **Cheddar cheese**, grated

2 tbsp chopped **flat-leaf parsley**

salt and freshly ground **black pepper**

1 Preheat the oven to 200°C (400°F/Gas 6). Prick the potatoes all over with a fork, then transfer to the oven and bake for 45 minutes, or until tender. Set aside and lower the oven temperature to 180°C (350°F/Gas 4).

2 Meanwhile, heat a frying pan and dry-fry the lardons for 2-3 minutes, or until golden. Then add the shallots, stir, and fry for a further 1-2 minutes.

3 Slice off the top third of each potato, horizontally. Use a spoon to scoop out the flesh into a large bowl. Reserve the hollowed-out skins and place into a lightly greased baking dish.

4 Mash the potato. Add the milk and butter and beat until smooth. Stir in the grated cheese, lardons, and shallots. Season to taste with salt and pepper.

5 Spoon the mixture back into the potato skins and bake for 20-25 minutes, or until the filling is heated through and golden on top. Serve hot with the chopped parsley sprinkled on top.

VARIATIONS

Potatoes with Crabmeat
Mix the potato with 170g can of white crabmeat, drained, 3 finely sliced spring onions, 1 finely diced red chilli, and 4 tbsp crème fraîche. Spoon into the skins, bake, and sprinkle with chopped coriander.

Potatoes with Chorizo
Mix the potato with 150g (5½oz) chopped chorizo sausage, 1 tomato, peeled, deseeded, and diced, and 150g (5½oz) diced mozzarella cheese. Spoon into the skins, bake, and sprinkle with chopped oregano.

Grilled Scallops with Prosciutto and Lime

A delicious, elegant starter

🍴 serves 6

🕐 prep 10 mins • cook 5 mins

📦 scallop shells, for serving

18 king **scallops**

30g (1oz) **butter**, melted

juice of 1 **lime**

2 **garlic cloves**, chopped

handful of **chopped herbs**, such as basil, parsley, chives, and coriander, plus extra to serve

salt and freshly ground **black pepper**

3 thin slices **prosciutto**, cut into strips

1 **lime**, cut into wedges, to serve

1 Trim the small white muscle off each scallop and place it in a scallop shell or ovenproof dish. Preheat the grill on its highest setting.

2 Combine the butter, garlic, lime juice, and herbs, and spoon it over the scallops.

3 Season with salt and pepper and scatter with the prosciutto. Place under the grill and cook for 5 minutes. Serve immediately with wedges of lime and a scattering of fresh herbs.

● **Good with** warm crusty bread.

Marinated Salmon

A Scandinavian favourite, and a refreshing change from plain smoked salmon

🍴 serves 6–8

🕐 prep 20 mins, plus chilling

❗ the salmon needs to be prepared at least 48 hours before required

2 **salmon fillets**, about 140g (5oz) each, skin on

3 tbsp **coarse sea salt**

3 tbsp **sugar**

1 tbsp coarsely crushed **black peppercorns**

3 tbsp **aquavit** or vodka

4 tbsp chopped **dill**, plus extra sprigs to serve

1 **lemon**, cut into wedges, to garnish

For the mustard sauce

4 tbsp **Dijon mustard**

4 tbsp **sunflower oil**

3 tbsp **sugar**

2 tbsp **white vinegar**

1 tsp **soured cream**

pinch of **salt**

1 Score each fillet on the skin side, making several diagonal cuts about 3mm (⅛in) deep.

2 Combine the salt, sugar, and pepper, and sprinkle a quarter of the mixture on the bottom of a shallow non-metallic dish. Place 1 fillet in the dish, skin-side down, and sprinkle with half the aquavit and another quarter of the mixture. Spread 2 tbsp of the dill in an even layer over the fillet.

3 Sprinkle the flesh side of the second fillet with another quarter of the dry mixture and place it, skin-side up, on top of the first fillet. Rub the remaining quarter of the mixture over the skin and sprinkle with the remaining aquavit.

4 Cover the salmon with a piece of cling film, then place a large flat plate or chopping board on top and weigh it down with weights or cans of food. Refrigerate for 24 hours, draining off any liquid that has accumulated in the dish after 5–6 hours, then again after a further 5–6 hours. Turn the salmon over and chill for another 24 hours, turning twice during this period.

5 To make the mustard sauce, place the ingredients into a blender and process for 1 minute, or until smooth and creamy. Alternatively, whisk together in a bowl for 1 minute. Chill for at least 1 hour, covered. Just before serving, add 2 tbsp chopped dill.

6 To serve, scrape the seasonings and dill from the salmon. Place the salmon, skin-side down, on a serving board. Slice the fish thinly on the slant, away from the skin. Serve with the mustard sauce, lemon wedges, and sprinkle with dill.

● **Good with** brown bread, or toasted sourdough bread.

● **Leftovers** can be layered on mini toasted bagels with cream cheese for bite-sized snacks.

Shrimp Spring Rolls

"Spring" rolls are so named because they were eaten to celebrate the Chinese New Year, or first day of spring

 makes 12

prep 25 mins • cook 15 mins

225g (8oz) raw **prawns**, peeled and chopped

½ **red pepper**, deseeded and finely chopped

115g (4oz) **mushrooms**, chopped

4 **spring onions**, thinly sliced

115g (4oz) **beansprouts**

2cm (¾in) fresh **root ginger**, grated

1 tbsp **rice wine vinegar**

1 tbsp **soy sauce**

vegetable oil, for shallow frying

225g (8oz) **cooked chicken**, chopped

6 **Chinese cabbage leaves**, halved

1 tbsp **cornflour**

12 **spring roll wrappers**

sweet chilli dipping sauce, to serve

● **Prepare ahead** Make the filling up to 3 hours in advance and fill the rolls just before frying.

1 **In a bowl**, mix together the prawns, red pepper, mushrooms, spring onions, beansprouts, ginger, vinegar, and soy sauce.

2 **Heat 2 tbsp oil** in a frying pan, add the prawn mixture, and stir-fry for 3 minutes. Set aside to cool, then stir in the chicken.

3 **In a small bowl**, mix the cornflour with 4 tbsp cold water.

4 **Lay a wrapper** on a work surface and top with half a cabbage leaf and 1 tbsp of the prawn mixture. Brush the edges of the wrapper with the cornflour mix and roll up, tucking in the sides and pressing the brushed edges together to seal. Repeat with the remaining wrappers and filling.

5 **Shallow-fry the rolls** in hot oil until golden brown on all sides. Drain on kitchen paper and serve at once with sweet chilli dipping sauce.

VARIATION

Meaty Spring Rolls
Use leftover cooked meats, such as chopped pork, beef, or ham, adding vegetables, such as peas or chopped green beans, to vary the filling.

Smoked Salmon Potato Cakes

This popular restaurant starter is easy to make at home

 serves 6

prep 10 mins • cook 10 mins

500g (1lb 2oz) **waxy potatoes**

250g (9oz) **smoked salmon**, finely chopped

handful of **chopped parsley**

3 **spring onions**, finely chopped

1 tsp grated **lemon** zest

1 **egg**, beaten

115g (4oz) **breadcrumbs**

1 tbsp chopped **dill**

1 tbsp chopped **parsley**

sunflower oil, for shallow-frying

watercress or rocket leaves, to garnish

1 **lemon**, cut into wedges

For the dill mayonnaise

1 tbsp Dijon **mustard**

2 **egg yolks**

1 tsp **caster sugar**

salt and freshly ground **black pepper**

juice of ½ **lemon**

200ml (7fl oz) **sunflower oil**

handful of chopped **dill**

● **Prepare ahead** The potato cakes can be made the day before and kept, covered, in the refrigerator until needed. The dill mayonnaise can be made 2 days in advance.

1 **To make the mayonnaise**, place the mustard, egg yolks, sugar, and lemon juice in a food processor and process until well combined. Add the oil slowly, with the motor running, until the dressing is thick and creamy. Stir in the dill and season to taste with salt and pepper. Keep in the fridge until needed.

2 **Boil the potatoes** in salted water for 5 minutes, then drain, cool, and grate into a large bowl.

3 **Combine the grated potato**, chopped salmon, parsley, spring onions, lemon zest, and egg. Season to taste with salt and pepper, and mix well. In a shallow dish, combine the breadcrumbs with the dill and parsley.

4 **Form the potato mixture** into 6 cakes and coat each in the breadcrumbs.

5 **Heat the oil** in a non-stick frying pan and fry the cakes until golden brown on both sides.

6 **Serve the fish cakes** warm, garnished with watercress or rocket and a wedge of lemon.

Prawn Cocktail, Mexican-style

Corn kernels and avocado give a south-of-the-border twist to this perennial favourite

 serves 4

prep 20 mins • cook 1–2 mins

devein the prawns through the back and remove the shells

250g (9oz) raw **tiger prawns**

1 tbsp **olive oil**

juice of 1 **lime**

1 tsp **Tabasco sauce**

1 tbsp **sun-dried tomato purée**

1 tbsp chopped **coriander**, plus extra sprigs to serve

4 tbsp **mayonnaise**

2 tbsp **soured cream**

¼ **iceberg lettuce**, washed and shredded

1 small **avocado**, stone removed, peeled, diced, and sprinkled with lime juice to prevent browning

2 tbsp canned **sweetcorn kernels**, drained

● **Prepare ahead** Step 1 can be completed several hours ahead.

1 **Heat the olive oil** in a frying pan and fry the prawns over a high heat for 1–2 minutes, or until they turn pink. Transfer to a bowl, sprinkle with the lime juice and Tabasco, stir well until the prawns are coated, and set aside to cool.

2 **Add the tomato purée** and chopped coriander to the mayonnaise and soured cream in a small bowl and stir until combined.

3 **Divide the lettuce** between 4 dessert glasses.

4 **Set aside 4 prawns** with their tails on, for a garnish, if you like, then peel the rest and return to the bowl. Stir in the diced avocado and sweetcorn, then spoon into the serving dishes on top of the lettuce.

5 **Top with the** mayonnaise sauce and garnish with the reserved prawns and coriander sprigs.

● **Good with** tortilla chips or wedges of lightly toasted flatbread.

Prawns with Parmesan Cream

King prawns are dressed in a flavourful, creamy sauce

 serves 6

prep 10 mins • cook 15 mins

24 raw **king prawns**, peeled and deveined

2 tbsp **olive oil**

115g (4oz) **pancetta** or streaky bacon rashers, diced

1 bunch of **spring onions**, sliced

2 **garlic cloves**, crushed

4 tbsp **crème fraîche**

juice of 1 **lemon**

salt and freshly ground **black pepper**

grated **Parmesan cheese**, to garnish

handful of **spinach leaves**, to garnish

1 **Heat the olive oil** in a large frying pan, add the pancetta, and fry for 5 minutes over a medium heat, stirring frequently. Add the spring onions and garlic and cook for a further 3 minutes, or until they are just beginning to soften.

2 **Add the prawns**, stir, and cook for several minutes until they turn pink; do not overcook.

3 **Add the crème fraîche** and bring to the boil. Pour in the lemon juice and season to taste with salt and pepper. Reduce the heat and simmer for 1–2 minutes.

4 **To serve**, transfer to a warm serving dish, sprinkle with Parmesan cheese, and garnish with spinach leaves.

VARIATION

Pasta with Prawns

Turn this into a main dish for 4 by serving it as a sauce over long, thin pasta. Add a touch of spice with a dash of chilli sauce.

Marinated Anchovies

Boquerones en Vinagre are a Spanish speciality,
ideal as tapas or as a lunchtime dish

 serves 4

prep 20 mins, plus
24–48 hrs marinating

500g (1lb 2oz) large fresh **anchovy fillets**

3 tsp **salt**

120ml (4fl oz) **sherry vinegar** or **wine vinegar**

75ml (2½fl oz) **extra virgin olive oil**

2 **garlic cloves**, sliced

3 tbsp chopped **parsley**

● **Prepare ahead** The anchovy fillets need to be left in the marinade for at least 24 hours, but can be marinated for up to 48 hours.

1 Wash the anchovies and remove any stray bones. Pat dry with kitchen paper.

2 Place half the anchovy fillets in a single layer in a shallow dish. Sprinkle with half the salt. Place the remaining anchovies in a single layer on top, laying the fillets at right angles to the previous layer. Sprinkle with the remaining salt and pour on the vinegar. Cover and refrigerate for at least 24 hours.

3 Before serving, pour off the vinegar, rinse the anchovies in cold water, and pat dry on kitchen paper. Arrange the anchovies in a shallow serving dish and pour the olive oil over them. Scatter the garlic slices on top and sprinkle with chopped parsley.

● **Good with** lightly toasted slices of crusty bread, rubbed with a cut garlic clove and drizzled with olive oil.

VARIATION

Lemon-marinated Anchovies

Cover the anchovies with the zest and juice of 2 lemons and marinate for 2 hours, then continue with the recipe from step 3.

USING CANNED ANCHOVIES

Preserved anchovies are great to have on hand, but can be too salty for some dishes. To mellow the sharp saltiness of the fish, remove the fillets from the brine, rinse, and soak in a bowl of milk for 20–30 minutes.

Anchovies on Toast

Choose any canned anchovies to your taste for this snack

 serves 4

prep 10 mins • cook 5 mins

2 small **baguettes**

4 large ripe **tomatoes**

100g (3½oz) **anchovy fillets** in oil, drained

2 tbsp **extra virgin olive oil**

freshly ground **black pepper**

1 **shallot**, finely chopped

2 tbsp chopped **flat-leaf parsley**

1 Preheat the grill on its highest setting. Cut each baguette in half lengthways and toast on both sides.

2 Cut 2 tomatoes in half and rub the tomato halves over the cut sides of the toasted baguettes, squeezing out the seeds and flesh. Discard the skins. Top with half the anchovy fillets.

3 Slice the remaining tomatoes thinly and arrange on the baguettes. Drizzle with oil, season with pepper, and scatter with the chopped shallot and parsley. Top with the remaining anchovies, and serve.

● **Good with** a green salad, as a starter or light lunch.

Smoked Haddock and Herb Fishcakes

Crisp fishcakes make a tasty starter, and are a good way to use up leftover mashed potato

 serves 6

 prep 10 mins, plus cooling • cook 30 mins

300g (10oz) **smoked haddock fillet**, skinned, bones removed

140g (5oz) **mashed potato**

½ tsp **Dijon mustard**

3 **spring onions**, finely chopped

grated zest and juice of ½ **lemon**

salt and freshly ground **black pepper**

30g (1oz) chopped **parsley**

45g (1½oz) **plain flour**

1 **egg**, beaten

85g (3oz) **dried breadcrumbs**

sunflower oil

● **Prepare ahead** You can prepare these up to the end of step 3 several hours in advance. Chill until required.

1 **Preheat the oven** to 190°C (375°F/Gas 5). Place the smoked haddock in an ovenproof dish with 2–3 tbsp water, cover with foil and bake for 15 minutes. Remove from the oven and leave to cool, then flake into pieces.

2 **Place the mashed potato**, mustard, spring onions, lemon juice and zest, and the parsley in a large bowl, add the flakes of smoked haddock and mix well. Season to taste with salt and pepper.

3 **Divide the mixture** into 12 equal portions and shape each portion into rounds. Place the flour in a small dish, the egg in another dish, and the breadcrumbs in another. Roll each fishcake in the flour, then dip into the egg, and finally coat with breadcrumbs.

4 **Shallow-fry** the fish cakes in a little vegetable oil, in batches for 5–7 minutes, turning once, or until crisp and golden all over. Drain on kitchen paper, and serve hot.

● **Good with** a simple salad of rocket and watercress, and tartare sauce or mayonnaise for dipping.

Fried Whitebait

Deep-frying is the perfect way to cook these tiny fish, which are eaten whole

 serves 4

 prep 15 mins • cook 20 mins

sunflower oil, for deep-frying

50g (1¾oz) **plain flour**

1 tsp **cayenne pepper**

1 tsp **salt**

450g (1lb) **whitebait**

1 **lemon**, cut into quarters, to serve

1 **Pour the oil** into a deep saucepan or wok and heat until a piece of day-old bread browns in less than 1 minute.

2 **Meanwhile, put the flour**, cayenne, and salt in a large bowl and mix together.

3 **Toss the whitebait** in the seasoned flour, making sure they are evenly coated. Tip them into a sieve and shake off the excess flour.

4 **Fry the whitebait** in batches, for 2–3 minutes each batch, or until they turn lightly golden. Use a slotted spoon to remove them from the oil and drain on kitchen paper.

5 **Serve immediately**, with lemon wedges to squeeze over.

● **Good with** thinly sliced brown bread and butter.

> **FRYING FISH**
> Frying the whitebait in small batches will prevent them from clumping together and turning soggy.

Smoked Salmon Blinis

Blinis are melt-in-the-mouth bases for bite-sized party canapés

makes 20

prep 20 mins, plus cooling • cook 20 mins

100g (3½oz) buckwheat flour

¼ tsp baking powder

¼ tsp salt

1 egg, separated

100ml (3½fl oz) milk

vegetable oil

120ml (4fl oz) crème fraîche

100g (3½oz) smoked salmon

freshly ground black pepper

small bunch of dill

1 lemon, cut into wedges

1 **Sift the flour**, baking powder, and salt into a mixing bowl. Make a hollow in the centre and add the egg yolk and half the milk. Beat the egg and milk together with a wooden spoon, gradually drawing in the flour from the sides.

2 **Add the remaining milk** and continue beating the mixture until the batter is smooth and free from lumps. Whisk the egg white until it holds soft peaks, then gently fold it into the batter.

3 **Brush a frying pan** with a little oil and place over a medium heat. Add a few teaspoons of the batter, well-spaced, and cook until bubbles appear, then turn over and cook for 2 minutes, or until golden. Remove from the pan, set aside, and cook the remaining blinis.

4 **Leave the blinis** to cool, then top each with a little crème fraîche, a piece of smoked salmon, pinch of black pepper, and a sprig of dill. Arrange on a serving plate with lemon wedges, for squeezing.

VARIATION

Smoked Salmon Corn Cakes

Cook 3 corn on the cobs in a large pan of boiling water for 5–7 minutes, or until tender. Drain and cool, then scrape off the corn kernels. Sift 45g (1½oz) polenta, 45g (1½oz) plain flour, ½ tsp baking powder, and a pinch of cayenne into a large bowl and season to taste with salt and pepper. In another bowl, whisk 150ml (5fl oz) double cream with 2 large egg yolks, then add to the flour mixture, along with the corn kernels, 2 tbsp melted butter, and 2 tbsp snipped chives. Mix well, cover, and set aside for 30 minutes. Cook as above for 3–4 minutes on each side, or until golden brown, and complete as above.

Herbed Cream and Prawn Wraps

A simple variation on the classic prawn sandwich

makes 18

prep 15 mins

175g (6oz) soft goat's cheese

small handful of soft herbs, such as chervil, dill, or chives, chopped

zest of 1 lemon

salt and freshly ground black pepper

3 large flour tortillas

200g (7oz) small peeled prawns

● **Prepare ahead** You can make these wraps 1–2 hours in advance and chill until needed.

1 **Mix the goat's cheese**, herbs, and lemon zest, and season to taste with salt and pepper.

2 **Spread the goat's cheese** over the tortillas. Top with prawns and roll each wrap tightly. Cover and chill until ready to serve.

3 **Before serving**, bring the wraps back to room temperature and cut on an angle to make 18 pieces.

Smoked Trout and Goat's Cheese Wraps

A delicious blend of smoked trout and herbed goat's cheese in a tortilla wrap

 makes 14

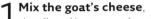 prep 15 mins

150g (5½oz) **soft goat's cheese**

15g (½oz) chopped **chervil** or dill

zest of 1 **lemon**

salt and freshly ground **black pepper**

2 large **flour tortillas**

2 **red peppers**, grilled, skinned, and sliced into thin strips

115g (4oz) **smoked trout**, cut into thin strips

1 **Mix the goat's cheese**, chervil, and lemon zest in a small bowl. Season to taste with salt and pepper.

2 **Place the tortillas** on a work surface and spread with the goat's cheese mixture. Spread the red peppers and trout evenly over the tortillas, then immediately roll each wrap tightly. Cover and chill until ready to serve.

3 **Before serving**, bring the wraps to room temperature. Cut on an angle to make a total of 14 pieces.

● **Prepare ahead** You can make the wraps up to 4 hours in advance and chill until needed.

Prawns with Mint, Chilli, and Ginger

Easy and quick to prepare, this is an ideal starter for an informal dinner party

 serves 6

prep 10 mins, plus marinating

36 cooked **king prawns**, peeled

18 small **chicory leaves**

bunch of **watercress**

1 **lime**, cut into wedges, to serve

For the marinade

juice of 1 **lime**

30g (1oz) **mint leaves**, torn

2 tbsp grated fresh **root ginger**

3 small **red chillies**, deseeded and finely chopped

1 **garlic clove**, chopped

4 tbsp **olive oil**

salt and freshly ground **black pepper**

1 **Mix all the marinade** ingredients together in a large bowl. Add the prawns, stir, and leave to marinate for at least 15 minutes and up to 1 hour.

2 **To serve**, divide the chicory leaves between serving plates and spoon the prawn mixture on to the leaves. Garnish with watercress and serve with lime wedges.

● **Good with** sesame breadsticks and other party bites.

● **Leftovers** are delicious mixed with mayonnaise or crème fraîche and used as a sandwich filling.

Herbed Fish Goujons

Fish fingers for grown-ups

 serves 4–6

 prep 20 mins
• cook 10–15 mins

115g (4oz) fresh **breadcrumbs**

handful of **parsley**, chopped

½ tsp **smoked paprika**

salt and freshly ground **black pepper**

85g (3oz) **plain flour**

1 large **egg**

225g (8oz) **white fish fillet**, such as haddock, cod, or plaice, skinned and boned

sunflower oil, for frying

parsley to garnish

lemon wedges, to garnish

1 Place the breadcrumbs, parsley, and smoked paprika into a bowl, season to taste with salt and pepper, and mix thoroughly.

2 Place the flour into a bowl, whisk the egg with 1 tbsp water in another bowl, and put the breadcrumb mixture into a third.

3 Slice the fish into thin strips. Dust the strips with flour, then dip into the egg, then place in breadcrumbs, and turn until they are completely coated. Place them on a plate and chill until needed.

4 Heat 2.5cm (1in) sunflower oil in a frying pan. The oil must be hot enough to sizzle when the fish is added. Fry the fish for 1 minute on each side, or until crisp, then drain on kitchen paper. Serve garnished with parsley and a wedge of lemon.

● **Good with** a herb- or gherkin-flavoured mayonnaise.

Seafood Ceviche

Ceviche is a brief, light pickling of raw fish to conserve freshness and bring out its true flavour

 serves 4

 prep 20 mins, plus marinating

❄ wrap the fish in cling film or foil, and put it in the freezer for 1 hour to firm up the flesh so that it will slice easily

450g (1lb) very fresh, firm-fleshed **fish**, such as salmon, turbot, halibut, or monkfish

1 **red onion**, thinly sliced

juice of 2 **lemons** or limes

1 tbsp **olive oil**

½ tsp **pimentón picante**

1 **chilli**, finely chopped

salt and freshly ground **black pepper**

2 tbsp finely chopped **parsley**

1 With a sharp knife, slice the fish into very thin slivers.

2 Spread the onion slices evenly in the bottom of a shallow non-metallic dish. Pour the lemon juice over the onion, then sprinkle the pimentón and chilli over the top.

3 Place the fish slivers over the layer of onion slices, gently turning them so that they are all fully coated with the marinade.

4 Leave to marinate in the refrigerator for at least 20 minutes, preferably over 1 hour. Season to taste with salt and pepper, then sprinkle with parsley, and serve.

● **Good with** crusty bread.

Stuffed Filo Tartlets

A stylish appetizer

 serves 6

prep 45 mins • cook 20 mins

6 loose-bottomed tartlet tins

12 sheets **filo pastry**, 40 x 30cm (16 x 12in)

olive oil, for brushing

3 **red peppers** or orange peppers, deseeded, and cut into quarters

300g (10oz) **chorizo sausage**, sliced

½ **red onion**, peeled and finely sliced

150g (5½oz) **goat's cheese** or feta, crumbled

1 Preheat the oven to 180°C (350°F/Gas 4). Brush each filo sheet with oil and cut in half. Place 4 sheets on top of each other in the tin, giving each a quarter turn. Push the sides into the edge of the tin. Bake for 10 minutes, or until the pastry is crisp. Set aside.

2 Preheat the grill on its highest setting. Grill the peppers until blackened all over, and place in a plastic bag to cool. Slip off the skins and thickly slice the peppers.

3 Heat a frying pan with a tiny drizzle of olive oil and fry the chorizo until crisp. Drain.

4 Arrange the peppers, onion, and cheese on the tarts. Top with hot chorizo to serve.

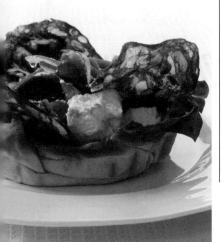

Empanadas

These savoury Spanish pastries make very versatile nibbles

 makes 24

prep 45 mins, plus chilling • cook 40–50 mins

 9cm (3½in) round pastry cutter

450g (1lb) **plain flour**, plus extra for dusting

salt and freshly ground **black pepper**

85g (3oz) **butter**, diced

2 **eggs**, beaten, plus extra to glaze

1 tbsp **olive oil**

1 **onion**, finely chopped

120g can **tomatoes**, drained

2 tsp **tomato purée**

140g can **tuna**, drained

2 tbsp finely chopped **parsley**

1 To make the pastry, sift the flour into a large mixing bowl with ½ tsp salt. Add the butter and rub in with your fingertips until it resembles fine breadcrumbs. Add the beaten eggs with 4–6 tbsp water and combine to form a dough. Cover with cling film and chill for 30 minutes.

2 Meanwhile, heat the oil in a frying pan, add the onion, and fry over a medium heat, stirring often, for 5–8 minutes, or until translucent. Add the tomatoes, tomato purée, tuna, and parsley, and season to taste with salt and pepper. Reduce the heat and simmer for 10–12 minutes, stirring occasionally.

3 Preheat the oven to 190°C (375°F/Gas 5). Roll out the pastry to a thickness of 3mm (⅛in). Cut out 24 rounds with a pastry cutter. Put 1 tsp of the filling on each, then brush the edges with water, fold over, and pinch together.

4 Place the empanadas on an oiled baking tray and brush with egg. Bake for 25–30 minutes, or until golden brown. Serve warm.

VARIATION

Empanaditas

Cut smaller circles of pastry to make bite-sized versions, which are ideal to serve as canapés. Replace the tuna with 140g (5oz) cooked chicken or chorizo. Bake for 15–20 minutes, or until brown.

Crostini with Green Olive Tapenade

This easy-to-make dish is great as an appetizer or snack

 makes 12

prep 10 mins

2 tsp **olive oil**

1 **garlic clove**

100g (3½oz) pitted **green olives**

grated zest of ½ **lemon**

few **basil leaves**

freshly ground **black pepper**

½ **baguette**, cut into 12 slices, toasted

6–8 **yellow cherry tomatoes** or red cherry tomatoes, roasted, to garnish (optional)

1 Place the oil, garlic, olives, lemon zest, and basil into a food processor or blender and process to a paste.

2 Divide the mixture between the 12 slices of toast and garnish each one with half a roasted cherry tomato (if using).

● **Good with** pre-dinner drinks.

Smoked Salmon and Pancetta Crostini

A popular hors d'oeuvre; crostini and bruschetta can be made in many variations.
The crème fraîche in this recipe is light and refreshing

🍴 makes 12

🕐 prep 10 mins • cook 15 mins

12 small slices of **bread**, cut from a baguette or ficelle

5 tbsp **olive oil**

6 slices of **pancetta**

200g (7oz) **smoked salmon**

200ml (7fl oz) **crème fraîche**

2 tbsp **wholegrain mustard**

3 tbsp **capers**, rinsed, drained, and finely chopped

1 tsp **lemon** zest

1 tsp **lemon** juice

freshly ground **black pepper**

12 **whole chives**, snipped into 2.5cm (1in) lengths, to garnish

● **Prepare ahead** The bread slices can be baked up to 2 hours ahead. The crème fraîche mixture can be made 24 hours in advance. Assemble the bruschetta just before serving.

1 **Preheat the oven** to 200°C (400°F/Gas 6) Preheat the grill on its highest setting. Brush each side of the bread slices with olive oil, place them on a baking sheet, and bake for 10 minutes or until crisp. Remove and leave to cool.

2 **Grill the pancetta** for a few minutes until crisp on both sides. Drain on kitchen paper.

3 **Meanwhile, cut the** smoked salmon into thin strips about 2cm (¾in) wide.

4 **Mix the crème fraîche** with the mustard, capers, and lemon zest and juice; season to taste with black pepper.

5 **Place the bread slices** on a serving plate, divide the crème fraîche mixture between the slices, and top with strips of smoked salmon, pieces of pancetta and chives to garnish.

VARIATION

Classic Italian Crostini

Remove the smoked salmon, replace the crème fraîche mixture with slices of fresh mozzarella, and use fresh basil instead of chives. Brush the bread slices with garlic and olive oil, then lightly pepper the mozzarella. Place a piece of basil on each piece of mozzarella, then wrap it in half a slice of prosciutto. Place the crostini under a hot grill for 3–5 minutes, or until the cheese melts.

Pancetta

Pancetta is widely available from delicatessens and supermarkets but if you cannot find any, use thinly sliced streaky bacon instead. A little grated horseradish can be used instead of mustard; the flavour goes well with the salmon and pancetta.

Anchovy and Olive Bruschetta

These salty canapés are ideal with pre-dinner drinks

🍴 makes 12

🕐 prep 10 mins • cook 5 mins

12 slices **Italian bread**, such as ciabatta, about 2cm (¾in) thick

½ **garlic clove**

extra virgin **olive oil**

3–4 tbsp bottled **tomato sauce**

salt and freshly ground **black pepper**

115g (4oz) **mozzarella cheese**, drained and cut into 12 thin slices

1 tsp dried **mixed herbs**

6 **black olives**, pitted and sliced

60g jar or can **anchovies in olive oil**, drained and cut in half lengthways

● **Prepare ahead** Steps 1 and 2 can be done 2 hours in advance and the bruschetta grilled before serving.

1 **Preheat the grill** on its highest setting and position the rack 10cm (4in) from the heat.

2 **To make the bruschetta** bases, toast the bread slices until golden on both sides. Rub 1 side with the cut side of the garlic clove. Brush the same side of each slice with a little olive oil.

3 **Spread each bruschetta** with about 2 tsp tomato sauce and season with salt and pepper to taste. Put 1 slice of mozzarella on each, sprinkle with herbs and top with olive slices and 2 pieces of anchovy in a criss-cross pattern.

4 **Grill the bruschetta** for 2–3 minutes until the mozzarella has melted and is bubbling. Serve hot.

● **Good with** a chilled glass of sparkling prosecco or a tall glass of cold beer.

Scallop and Pesto Crostini

These stylish canapés can also be served as a simple first course

🍴 makes 12

🕐 prep 10 mins • cook 7 mins

12 slices **Italian bread**, such as ciabatta, about 2cm (¾in) thick

½ **garlic clove**

3 tbsp **olive oil**

6 **scallops**, shucked

1 tbsp fresh **lemon** juice

salt and freshly ground **black pepper**

2 tbsp bottled **pesto**

2 tbsp **tomato purée**

12 **basil leaves**, to garnish

● **Prepare ahead** Step 1 can be done 1–2 hours in advance.

1 **Preheat the grill** on its highest setting. Toast the bread slices until golden on both sides. Rub one side with the cut side of the garlic clove. Lighty brush the same side of each slice with a little olive oil, then set aside.

2 **Heat the remaining oil** in a large frying pan over a medium heat. Add the scallops, sprinkle with lemon juice, and season to taste with salt and pepper. Fry for 2 minutes on each side, until cooked but still tender; keep warm.

3 **Spread one half** of each crostini with pesto and the other half with tomato purée.

4 **Cut each scallop** in half horizontally and put 1 scallop half on top of each crostini. Grind black pepper over the top and garnish each one with a single basil leaf. Serve at once.

Onion Bhajis

These crisp vegetable fritters are made with *besan*, also known as chickpea flour or gram flour, which can be found in Indian food shops

 serves 4

prep 15 mins • cook 15 mins

deep-fat fryer or large saucepan, half-filled with oil

225g (8oz) **onions**, chopped

115g (4oz) **besan** (gram flour)

2 tsp **cumin seeds**

½ tsp **turmeric**

1 tsp **ground coriander**

1 **green chilli** or red chilli, deseeded and very finely chopped

vegetable oil, for frying

● **Prepare ahead** The bhajis can be cooked up to the end of step 3 up to 4 hours in advance and then given their second frying just before serving.

1 In a large bowl, mix together the onions, besan, cumin seeds, turmeric, coriander, and chilli. Add enough cold water (about 8 tbsp) to bind the mixture together to make a thick batter.

2 Heat the oil in the deep-fat fryer to 190°C (375°F). When hot, carefully place spoonfuls of the mixture, roughly the size of golf balls, into the oil, turning occasionally, until all sides are golden.

3 Remove the bhajis from the oil using a slotted spoon, and drain on kitchen paper.

4 Return the bhajis to the pan and quickly fry a second time until crisp and golden brown all over.

5 Drain on kitchen paper and serve hot.

● **Good with** a simple raita made with chopped mint and a squeeze of lemon juice stirred into plain yogurt.

VARIATION

Vegetable Bhajis
Replace one-third of the onion with shredded spinach or grated carrot.

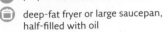

Sesame Prawn Toasts

A combination of flavours that work surprisingly well together

 serves 4

prep 15 mins • cook 15 mins

deep-fat fryer or large saucepan, half-filled with oil

250g (9oz) raw **tiger prawns**, peeled and roughly chopped

2 **spring onions**, roughly chopped

1cm (½in) piece of fresh **root ginger**, peeled and grated

1 tsp **light soy sauce**

½ tsp **sugar**

½ tsp **sesame oil**

1 small **egg white**, lightly beaten

freshly ground **black pepper**

3 large slices of **bread**, crusts removed

2 tbsp **sesame seeds**

vegetable oil, for deep-frying

coriander leaves, to garnish

● **Prepare ahead** Toasts can be prepared to the end of step 2 up to 4 hours in advance, ready to be fried just before serving.

1 Put the prawns and spring onions in a food processor and process for a few seconds to make a paste. Transfer the paste to a bowl and stir in the ginger, soy sauce, sugar, sesame oil, and enough egg white to bind the mixture together. Season with black pepper.

2 Cut each slice of bread into 4 triangles and spread each triangle thickly with the prawn paste. Sprinkle the sesame seeds evenly over the top.

3 Heat the oil in the deep-fat fryer to 180°C (350°F). Fry the toasts, in batches, prawn-side down, for 2 minutes. Carefully turn them over and fry for another 2 minutes, or until golden brown and crisp.

4 Lift the toasts out of the pan with a slotted spoon and drain on kitchen paper. Serve warm, garnished with coriander.

● **Good with** sweet chilli sauce and chilled sake (rice wine).

Vegetable Samosas

Serve these Indian pastries hot or cold. In India, they would be fried in ghee, a clarified butter that can be heated to a high temperature, but oil works equally well

 serves 4

 prep 45 mins, plus resting and cooling • cook 35–40 mins

 deep-fat fryer or large saucepan half-filled with oil

❄ freeze, uncooked, for up to 1 month, defrost, and pat dry with kitchen paper before frying

For the pastry

350g (12oz) **plain flour**, plus extra for dusting

salt and freshly ground **black pepper**

6 tbsp **vegetable oil** or ghee, plus extra for frying

For the filling

450g (1lb) **potatoes**

225g (8oz) **cauliflower**, chopped into small pieces

175g (6oz) **peas**, thawed if frozen

3 tbsp **vegetable oil** or ghee

2 **shallots**, sliced

2 tbsp **curry powder** or paste

2 tbsp chopped **coriander leaves**

1 tbsp **lemon juice**

● **Prepare ahead** The samosas can be prepared 1 day in advance, chilled, and fried just before serving.

1 To make the pastry, sift the flour into a bowl with ½ tsp salt. Stir in the oil or ghee and gradually add 120ml (4fl oz) warm water, mixing to make a dough.

2 Knead the dough on a floured surface until smooth. Wrap in cling film and leave to rest for at least 30 minutes.

3 To make the filling, cook the unpeeled potatoes in a saucepan of boiling water until tender. Drain and, when cool enough to handle, peel and chop into small pieces.

4 Blanch the cauliflower florets in a pan of boiling water for 2–3 minutes, or until just tender, then drain. If using fresh peas, blanch them with the cauliflower.

5 Heat the oil in a large frying pan and fry the shallots for 3–4 minutes, stirring frequently, until soft. Add the potatoes, cauliflower, peas, curry paste, coriander, and lemon juice and cook over a low heat for 2–3 minutes, stirring occasionally. Set aside to cool.

6 Divide the dough into 8 equal pieces. Roll them out so each forms an 18cm (7in) round. Cut each round in half and shape into a cone, dampening the edges to seal. Spoon a little of the filling into each cone, dampen the top edge of the dough, and press down over the filling to enclose it. Repeat with the rest of the dough and filling.

7 Heat oil in the deep-fat fryer to 180°C (350°F) and fry the samosas in batches for 3–4 minutes, or until golden brown on both sides. Drain on kitchen paper and serve hot or cold.

● **Good with** a bowl of chutney or raita. If serving these as a starter, arrange 2 on a serving plate with ribbons of cucumber and some raita.

VARIATION

Lamb Samosas

Replace half the quantity of potatoes with 225g (8oz) lean lamb mince. Fry the mince with the shallots until well browned before adding the potatoes and other ingredients to the frying pan and continuing with the recipe.

Wild Mushroom and Chive Hollandaise Tartlets

These substantial appetizers are a good meatless option

 serves 6

 prep 40 mins, plus chilling • cook 40 mins

 6 individual loose-bottomed tartlet tins, baking beans

For the pastry

175g (6oz) plain flour, plus extra for dusting

85g (3oz) butter, chilled, diced

1 small egg

For the filling

15g (½oz) dried wild mushrooms

30g (1oz) unsalted butter

1 small onion, peeled and chopped

400g (14oz) field mushrooms, sliced

juice of ½ lemon

salt and freshly ground black pepper

175g (6oz) cream cheese

For the hollandaise

225g (8oz) unsalted butter

4 egg yolks

freshly ground black pepper

1 tbsp white wine vinegar

bunch of chives

1 **To make the pastry**, place the flour and butter in a food processor and pulse until it resembles breadcrumbs. Add the egg and process until the pastry comes together into a ball. You may need 1–2 drops of cold water if the egg does not bring all the ingredients together. Place the pastry on a floured surface, divide into 6 pieces, and roll out to line 6 tartlet tins. Prick the pastry bases with a fork several times. Chill for at least 30 minutes.

2 **Preheat the oven** to 200°C (400°F/Gas 6) and blind bake the pastry cases, lined with greaseproof paper and baking beans, for 10 minutes. Then remove the paper and baking beans and continue to cook the pastry bases for another 5 minutes, or until the bases are crisp; remove from the oven and set aside. Do not turn off the oven.

3 **For the filling**, pour some boiling water over the dried mushrooms and leave for 10 minutes to soften. Meanwhile, melt the butter in a frying pan and cook the onion and field mushrooms over a medium heat. Drain the dried mushrooms, chop, and add to the mushroom mixture. Once all the mushrooms have wilted in the pan, increase the heat and boil until the liquid has evaporated. Add the lemon juice and seasoning. Remove from the heat to cool.

4 **Place the mushroom** mixture into the food processor with the cream cheese, and purée until fairly smooth. Taste to check the seasoning.

5 **To make the hollandaise**, melt 225g (8oz) butter in a small saucepan. Place the yolks, pepper and vinegar into a food processor. Purée for 1 minute, then gradually add the melted butter while the processor is running, until the sauce is thickened. Adjust the seasoning, if necessary, and set aside in a bowl until needed.

6 **Turn the oven** to 190°C (375°F/Gas 5). Spoon the mushroom mixture into the tartlets. Pour over the hollandaise and bake for 10 minutes. Remove the tartlets and push the pastry out of their tins. Top with snipped chives and serve hot.

> ## WILD MUSHROOMS
> Mushrooms grow wild throughout the year, but are most abundant from the summer to the first frost. Take care to learn the different mushroom varieties before going to gather them yourself, as many can be poisonous.

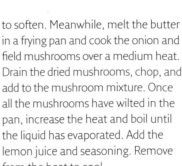

Nachos

Quick to make and great for sharing

 serves 4

prep 10 mins • cook 5 mins

200g tortilla chips

200g can chopped tomatoes

4 spring onions, finely chopped

75g sliced jalapeño peppers in brine, drained

1 avocado, diced

100g Monterey Jack or Cheddar cheese

2 tbsp chopped coriander

300g soured cream

1 **Preheat the grill** on its medium setting.

2 **Place the tortilla chips** in an even layer on a large heatproof platter and pour the chopped tomatoes over the top. Arrange the spring onions, peppers, and avocado over the dish, then scatter with the grated cheese.

3 **Grill for 4–5 minutes**, or until the cheese is melted.

4 **Serve immediately**, scattered with chopped coriander, and with soured cream on the side.

Boreks

These cheese pastries from Turkey are traditionally made in cigar-shapes and triangles

 makes 20

🕐 prep 25 mins • cook 10–12 mins

175g (6oz) **feta cheese**, finely crumbled

pinch of **ground nutmeg**

1 tsp **dried mint**

freshly ground **black pepper**

8 sheets of **filo pastry**, 40 x 30cm (16 x 12in), thawed if frozen

60g (2oz) **butter**, melted

flour, for dusting

● **Prepare ahead** The pastries can be prepared up to 24 hours in advance of baking.

1 Preheat the oven to 180°C (350°F/Gas 4). Place the feta cheese in a bowl, add the nutmeg and dried mint, then season to taste with black pepper.

2 Lay the filo sheets on top of each other and cut into 3 long strips, 10cm (4in) wide.

3 Taking one strip of pastry at a time, brush with butter and place 1 heaped tsp of the cheese mixture at one end. Roll up the pastry, like a cigar, folding the ends in about one third of the way down to encase the filling completely, then continue to roll. Make sure the ends are tightly sealed.

4 Lightly dust the work surface with flour and keep the rolled pastries in a pile, covered with a damp cloth, while preparing the remainder.

5 Place the pastries in a single layer on a large greased baking sheet. Brush with the remaining butter and bake for 10–12 minutes, or until crisp and golden. Best served hot or slightly warm.

● **Good with** Greek or Middle Eastern dishes as part of a meze.

> **VARIATION**

Spinach Boreks

In step 1, fry 2 chopped spring onions in 1 tbsp olive oil. Stir in 150g (5½oz) baby spinach leaves, fry until wilted. Drain, cool, then chop finely. Mix with 1 tbsp chopped dill and 75g (2½oz) crumbled feta cheese.

Smoked Chicken and Spinach Filo Parcels

These little parcels are delicious served hot or cold

 serves 6

🕐 prep 25 mins • cook 20 mins

❄ freeze, unbaked, for up to 1 month

225g (8oz) fresh **spinach**

olive oil

4 **spring onions**, finely chopped

115g (4oz) **smoked chicken**

85g (3oz) **crème fraîche**

1 tbsp chopped **tarragon**

60g (2oz) **pine nuts**, toasted

1 tsp **Dijon mustard**

grated zest of 1 **lemon**

freshly ground **black pepper**

200g packet **filo pastry**

60g (2oz) **butter**, melted

30g (1oz) **Parmesan cheese**, grated

● **Prepare ahead** The pastry parcels can be made the day before and chilled in the refrigerator until ready to cook.

1 Preheat the oven to 180°C (350°F/Gas 4). Wash the spinach, remove any tough stalks and wilt in a saucepan with a little olive oil. Drain well and cool. Place in a food processor with the spring onions, smoked chicken, crème fraîche, and tarragon, then process for a slightly chunky texture. The mixture should not be totally smooth. Add the pine nuts, mustard, and lemon zest. Season to taste with freshly ground black pepper.

2 Lay the filo pastry out on a clean surface. Cover with a clean, damp tea towel to stop the pastry drying out. Brush 1 strip of filo pastry with butter, then place another layer on top and brush with butter. Cut the pastry into 7.5cm (3in) strips, and place 1 rounded tsp of the spinach mixture near the top. Take the right corner and fold diagonally to the left to form a triangle over the filling. Fold along the crease of the triangle and repeat until you reach the end of the strip. Brush with butter once finished and scatter with Parmesan cheese. Place on a lined baking sheet.

3 Repeat with the rest of the pastry and filling to make 12 parcels. Bake for 20 minutes. Remove from the baking sheet and put on a wire rack to cool.

● **Good with** your choice of dipping sauce.

Cheesy Spinach Pie

This crisp spinach pastry or *Spanakopita* is popular in Greece,
and is often cut into diamonds or squares

makes 12 slices

prep 35 mins, plus
cooling • cook 1½ hrs

28 x 23 x 4cm (11 x 9 x 1½in)
cake tin or small roasting tin

4 tbsp **olive oil**

1 **onion**, peeled and chopped

1 bunch of **spring onions**, chopped

900g (2lb) **spinach**, shredded

small bunch of **dill**, chopped, or 4 tsp
dried dill

small bunch of **flat-leaf parsley**,
chopped

225g (8oz) **feta cheese**, finely
crumbled

4 **eggs**, beaten

freshly ground **black pepper**

150g (5½oz) **butter**, melted

250g (9oz) **filo pastry** or at least
14 sheets, about 40 x 30cm (16 x
12in), thawed if frozen

● **Prepare ahead** Rinse the
spinach well under cold water. Shake
well and pat dry using kitchen paper.

1 Heat the olive oil in a large
saucepan until hot and fry the
onion and spring onions for
5 minutes, or until softened but not
browned, stirring occasionally.

2 Add the spinach, mix well,
cover, reduce the heat, and cook
for 7–8 minutes, or until wilted,
stirring occasionally.

3 Stir in the chopped herbs,
increase the heat and cook,
uncovered, stirring, for 15 minutes,
or until the liquid evaporates and the
mixture starts to stick to the bottom
of the saucepan. Transfer to a bowl
lined with kitchen paper, and cool.

4 Remove the paper and stir in
the cheese and beaten eggs.
Season to taste with plenty of pepper.

5 Preheat the oven to 170°C
(325°F/Gas 3). Thickly brush the
tin with butter and line with a sheet
of filo pastry, carefully pressing it into
the sides and corners of the tin. Brush
with butter and lay another sheet on
top, pressing it down, as before.
Continue this layering process until
you have used half the pastry.

6 Spread the spinach mixture
into the pastry case. Place
another sheet of filo on top and brush
with butter. Continue this process
to use up the remaining sheets. Trim
the excess pastry away from the side
of the tin, using scissors. Brush the
top with any remaining butter and
bake in the centre of the oven for
1 hour, or until the pastry is crisp and
golden brown all over.

7 Cut into wedges and serve
hot or slightly warm.

● **Good with** other Greek or Middle
Eastern light dishes, such as hummus
and taramasalata, as a starter or part
of a buffet.

> ### VARIATION
>
> ## Spinach Pastries
> Divide the spinach into 2 equal
> portions, spread half into the pastry
> case, and top with 450ml (15fl oz)
> cold béchamel sauce and 2 chopped
> hard-boiled eggs. Carefully spread
> with the remaining spinach, and
> continue with the recipe.

> ### USING FILO
> Keep the sheets of filo pastry covered with
> a damp cloth while preparing the pie,
> to prevent them drying out. Take out each
> sheet as you need it and re-cover the rest.

Broad Bean, Garlic, and Herb Crostini

Ideal for parties or as an
appetizer with drinks

makes 12

prep 15 mins • cook 15 mins

½ **baguette**

3 tbsp **extra virgin olive oil**

salt and freshly ground **black pepper**

100g (3½oz) podded **broad beans**

1 small **shallot**

1 **garlic clove**

small bunch of **tarragon**

1 Preheat the oven to 150°C
(300°F/Gas 2). Slice the
baguette into 12 thin slices and
brush both sides with 2 tbsp olive oil.
Season with salt and pepper. Place
flat on a baking tray and bake for
15 minutes, or until crisp all the
way through.

2 Meanwhile, blanch the beans
in a pan of boiling water for
2 minutes, drain, and refresh in cold
water. Remove the tough outer skin
and discard. Remove a few beans for
garnish and place the remainder in
a food processor with the shallot,
garlic, 1 tbsp olive oil, and tarragon.
Process to form a thick paste. Season
to taste with salt and pepper.

3 Spread on to the prepared
crostini just before serving.
Garnish with the reserved beans and
a sprinkling of black pepper.

Cheese Straws

This classic, quick, and easy appetizer can be served with drinks at any occasion

🍴 makes 28

🕐 prep 20 mins • cook 15 mins

375g (13oz) puff pastry

plain flour, for dusting

2 tsp made English mustard

60g (2oz) mature Cheddar cheese, grated

30g (1oz) Parmesan cheese, grated

1 egg yolk

1 tbsp milk

● **Prepare ahead** The straws can be made 1 day in advance and kept chilled until ready to bake.

1 Preheat the oven to 190°C (375°F/Gas 5). Roll out the pastry on a lightly floured surface into a 25 x 35cm (10 x 14in) rectangle, trimming the edges to neaten.

2 Spread the English mustard over the top half of the pastry, leaving a 12mm (½in) gap all round, then top with the grated cheeses.

3 Mix together the egg yolk and milk, then brush this mixture around the edges of the pastry.

4 Fold over the pastry, then press together, sealing the edges. Lightly roll out to a 20 x 35cm (8 x 14in) rectangle.

5 Cut the pastry into strips 12mm (½in) wide, then, holding both ends of a strip, twist into a spiral and place, well spaced, on lightly greased baking trays.

6 Bake for 12–15 minutes, or until puffed and golden. Place on a wire rack and leave to cool slightly.

VARIATION

Blue Cheese Straws

Mix 75g (2½oz) crumbled Stilton with 50g (1¾oz) finely chopped walnuts; spread evenly over the pastry and follow the recipe above.

Mushroom Vol-au-vents

Vol-au-vents, or "puffs of wind", are little puff pastry cases enclosing a savoury filling, such as creamy mushrooms

🍴 makes 20

🕐 prep 20 mins • cook 15 mins

📦 6cm (2½in) and 4.5cm (1¾in) pastry cutters

20 button mushrooms

4 tbsp olive oil

2 tbsp lemon thyme leaves, chopped

salt and freshly ground black pepper

2 tbsp tapenade

1 tbsp crème fraîche

375g (13oz) puff pastry

plain flour, for dusting

1 egg, lightly beaten

1 Preheat the oven to 200°C (400°F/Gas 6). Put the mushrooms, oil, and lemon thyme leaves in a large bowl, season with salt and pepper, and mix together.

2 In another bowl stir together the tapenade and crème fraîche.

3 Roll out the pastry on a lightly floured surface. Stamp out 20 circles using the larger pastry cutter, then use the smaller cutter to make a shallow indent on each circle.

4 Transfer the pastry circles to a large baking tray and spoon a little of the tapenade mix on to the centre of each one, then sit a mushroom on top.

5 Brush the edges of the pastry circles with egg, then transfer them to the oven for 15 minutes, or until golden and puffed up.

VARIATIONS

Chicken and Pesto Vol-au-vents

Mix together 3 tbsp green pesto with 1 tbsp crème fraîche. Top with 125g (4½oz) diced, cooked chicken, then sprinkle with 2 tbsp pine nuts.

Smoked Salmon and Ricotta Vol-au-vents

Mix together 150g (5½oz) hot smoked salmon, flaked, with 4 tbsp ricotta cheese, and 2 tbsp chopped dill.

Aubergine and Goat's Cheese Crostini

Crisp crostini with a deliciously savoury topping

🍴 makes 12

🕐 prep 10 mins • cook 20 mins

12 slices French bread

2 tbsp olive oil

1 garlic clove, cut in half

1 firm aubergine

2 tbsp chopped mint

1 tbsp balsamic vinegar

salt and freshly ground black pepper

60g (2oz) soft goat's cheese

1 Preheat the oven to 180°C (350°F/Gas 4). Brush the bread on both sides with olive oil, then toast for 10 minutes, turning once, or until crisp. Cut the garlic in half and rub the cut side over each slice.

2 Preheat the grill. Slice the aubergine into 5mm (¼in) thick rounds, brush each side with olive oil, then grill on both sides until cooked.

3 Halve or quarter the aubergine slices, and place into a bowl. Add the remaining olive oil, mint, and balsamic vinegar, toss, and season to taste with salt and pepper.

4 Spread the crostini with goat's cheese, top with slices of aubergine, and serve.

Mushroom Bruschetta

A quick winter starter

🍴 makes 12

🕐 prep 10 mins • cook 20 mins

1 ciabatta, cut into 12 slices

olive oil, for brushing

60g (2oz) butter

4 shallots, finely chopped

2 garlic cloves, finely chopped

450g (1lb) field mushrooms, sliced

60ml (2fl oz) Marsala

100ml (3½fl oz) double cream

salt and freshly ground black pepper

3 tbsp grated Parmesan cheese

2 tbsp finely chopped parsley

1 Preheat the oven to 110°C (225°F/Gas 4). Brush the bread slices with olive oil, then bake for 10 minutes, turning, or until crisp.

2 Melt the butter in a pan, add the shallots and garlic, and fry gently for 5 minutes. Add the mushrooms, and fry until wilted. Add the Marsala, bring to the boil, then simmer until reduced to 1 tsp.

3 Reduce the heat, add the cream, and simmer gently for 5 minutes, stirring occasionally. Just before serving, adjust the seasoning, and stir in the parsley and Parmesan. Spoon the mixture over the top of the toasted bread and serve on a platter.

Smoked Trout Tartlets

These tartlets are perfect for a light supper or packed lunch

🍴 makes 6

🕐 prep 30 mins, plus chilling • cook 30 mins

🍽 6 x 10cm (4in) tartlet tins, baking beans

❄ freeze for up to 1 month

For the pastry

125g (4½oz) plain flour

75g (1½oz) butter, chilled and diced

1 small egg

For the filling

115ml (4fl oz) crème fraîche

1 tsp creamed horseradish

½ tsp lemon juice

zest of ½ lemon, grated

1 tsp capers, rinsed and chopped

salt and freshly ground black pepper

4 egg yolks, beaten

200g (7oz) smoked trout

bunch of dill, chopped

1 To make the pastry, place the flour and butter in a food processor with a pinch of salt, and process until the mixture resembles breadcrumbs. Add the egg and mix until incorporated.

2 Roll out the dough and line the tartlet tins. Line the pastry cases with baking parchment, fill with baking beans, and chill for 30 minutes.

3 Preheat the oven to 200°C (400°F/Gas 6). Bake blind the pastry cases for 10 minutes, then remove the beans and parchment, and bake for a further 5 minutes.

4 Mix the crème fraîche, horseradish, lemon juice and zest, and capers in a bowl, and season to taste with salt and pepper. Stir in the egg yolks, fish, and herbs.

5 Divide the mixture among the tart cases and return to the oven for 10–15 minutes, or until set. Allow to cool for 5 minutes before removing from the tins and serving.

● **Good with** a mixed leaf salad.

Enchiladas

This savoury, cheesy Mexican dish is an indulgent appetizer

 serves 4

prep 10 mins • cook 30 mins

2 tsp **olive oil**

1 small **red onion**, finely chopped

1 **red pepper**, chopped

4 **flour tortillas**

225g (8oz) **Cheddar cheese** or Monterey Jack, grated

For the sauce

2 tbsp **olive oil**

1 **onion**, chopped

1 **garlic clove**, crushed

1 tsp **chilli powder**

3 tbsp **tomato purée**

150ml (5fl oz) **chicken stock**

salt and freshly ground **black pepper**

1 tsp **ground cumin**

1 To make the sauce, heat the olive oil in a saucepan, add the onion, and fry for 10 minutes, or until golden. Add the garlic, chilli powder, tomato purée, and stock, and simmer for 5 minutes. Season with salt, pepper, and cumin.

2 Preheat the oven to 180°C (350°F/Gas 4). Heat the oil in a frying pan and fry the onion and red pepper for 5 minutes, or until soft.

3 Lay out the tortillas and spread a spoonful of sauce over each. Scatter the onion and red pepper over the sauce, and top with two-thirds of the cheese. Fold the sides of the tortillas in, roll up and enclose the fillings. Place in a greased ovenproof dish, fold-side down.

4 Pour the remaining sauce over the tortillas, and sprinkle with the remaining cheese. Bake for 15 minutes, or until the sauce bubbles and the cheese has melted.

VARIATION

Chicken Enchiladas

In step 3, add 115g (4oz) of shredded, seasoned chicken on top of the sauce. Add the cheese and bake.

Savoury Onion Tart

Anchovies give a salty kick to this mild onion tart

serves 4–6

prep 15 mins, plus chilling • cook 1 hr 15 mins

20cm (8in) loose-bottomed fluted tart tin, baking beans

freeze, without the anchovies, for up to 3 months

350g ready-made **shortcrust pastry**

2 tbsp **olive oil**

30g (1oz) **butter**

450g (1lb) **onions**, thinly sliced

750g (1lb 10oz) **curd cheese**

115ml (4fl oz) **milk**

2 large **eggs**

1 tsp **cumin seeds** or caraway seeds, crushed (optional)

salt and freshly ground **black pepper**

60g (2oz) **anchovy fillets**, halved lengthways

● **Prepare ahead** The tart can be cooked up to 1 day in advance, covered, and chilled. Reheat in a hot oven for 10 minutes, or until completely warmed through.

1 Roll out the pastry thinly on a lightly floured board, then use to line the tin. Chill for 30 minutes.

2 Heat the oil and butter in a pan, and add the onions. Cover and cook over a gentle heat, stirring occasionally, for 20 minutes, or until the onions are soft but not browned. Uncover and cook for a further 4–5 minutes, or until golden. Set aside to cool.

3 Preheat the oven to 200°C (400°F/Gas 6). Line the pastry case with greaseproof paper and baking beans, and bake blind for 15 minutes. Remove the beans and paper, and bake for a further 10 minutes.

4 Reduce the oven to 180°C (350°F/Gas 4). Spoon the onions into the pastry case, spreading them in an even layer. Beat together the curd cheese, milk, eggs, and cumin, if using. Season to taste with salt and pepper, then pour into the flan case. Lay the anchovy fillets in a lattice pattern on top, and bake for 25 minutes, or until the pastry is golden and the filling is set. Serve warm.

Goat's Cheese Croustades

Versatile, crisp croustade baskets can host a wide range of different fillings, such as this delicious combination of goat's cheese, mint, and roasted tomato

- 🍴 makes 12
- 🕐 prep 10 mins • cook 30 mins
- ⊜ 5cm (2in) pastry cutter, 12-hole mini-muffin tin

For the croustade baskets

4 slices of white bread or wholemeal bread

1 tbsp melted butter or olive oil

For the filling

6 cherry tomatoes

olive oil, for roasting

salt and freshly ground black pepper

85g (3oz) creamy goat's cheese

6–12 mint leaves

● **Prepare ahead** The croustade baskets will keep, in an airtight container, for up to 1 month. The roast tomatoes will keep for up to 3 days in the refrigerator.

1 Preheat the oven to 180°C (350°F/Gas 4). Remove crusts from the bread, flatten the slices with a rolling pin, and brush with the butter or oil.

2 Using the pastry cutter, stamp out 3 pieces from each slice of bread. Push the bread, butter- or oil-side down, firmly into the bases of the muffin tin and bake for 12–14 minutes, or until golden and crisp. Remove from the tin and leave to cool.

3 Halve the cherry tomatoes. Drizzle with oil and season to taste with salt and pepper, then roast on a baking tray for 25 minutes. Remove from the oven and leave to cool.

4 Spoon 1 tsp of goat's cheese into each pastry basket. Top with a tomato half, and garnish a few with mint leaves. Serve the croustades within 1 hour of filling.

Rich Smoked Salmon Croustades

Horseradish gives this smooth, creamy filling a little bite

- 🍴 makes 12
- 🕐 prep 10 mins, plus chilling • cook 30 mins

120ml (4fl oz) crème fraîche

1 tbsp creamed horseradish

freshly ground black pepper

12 croustade baskets (see Goat's Cheese Croustades, left)

60g (2oz) smoked salmon, sliced

25g (scant 1oz) red lumpfish caviar

25g (scant 1oz) black lumpfish caviar

a few chervil sprigs, to serve

1 Mix the crème fraîche and horseradish. Season to taste with pepper, and chill for 30 minutes.

2 Fill each croustade basket with 1 tsp of the crème fraîche mixture, add some smoked salmon, and top with a little caviar. Garnish with chervil, and serve within 1 hour.

VARIATION

Salmon and Tarragon Cream Croustades

Mix 120ml (4fl oz) crème fraîche, 150g (5½oz) finely chopped smoked salmon, 2 tbsp chopped tarragon, 1 tbsp lemon zest, and pepper to taste. Chill for 30 minutes, then spoon into croustade baskets and serve within 1 hour.

Soya Bean Croustades

When serving croustades, try using different-shaped pastry cutters to make the baskets

- 🍴 makes 12
- 🕐 prep 10 mins

100g (3½oz) frozen soya beans

1 small shallot

1 garlic clove

1 tbsp olive oil

small bunch of basil

salt and freshly ground black pepper

12 croustade baskets (see Goat's Cheese Croustades, far left)

● **Prepare ahead** The filling can be made several hours in advance. Fill the croustade baskets just before serving.

1 Cook the frozen beans for 2 minutes in lightly salted boiling water. Drain, rinse in cold water, and drain again.

2 Place the drained beans in a blender or food processor, add the shallot, garlic, olive oil, and basil, reserving a few leaves for a garnish, and process until smooth. Season to taste with salt and pepper.

3 Just before serving, spoon the mixture into the croustade baskets and top each with a basil leaf.

Chicken Croustades

Tarragon and chicken is a popular combination

🍴 makes 12
🕐 prep 15 mins

1 skinless boneless **chicken breast**, cooked

2 tbsp **mayonnaise**

1 tsp chopped **tarragon**, plus 12 leaves, to garnish

1 tsp **wholegrain mustard**

1 tsp **lemon** juice

salt and freshly ground **black pepper**

12 **croustade baskets** (see Goat's Cheese Croustades, far left)

● **Prepare ahead** The chicken filling can be prepared several hours in advance, and chilled until needed.

1 Shred the chicken into small pieces and set aside.

2 In a bowl, mix together the mayonnaise, tarragon, mustard, and lemon juice, and season to taste with salt and pepper. Add the chicken and stir until well combined.

3 Divide the mixture between the croustade baskets and garnish each one with a tarragon leaf. Serve within 1 hour of filling.

Roast Beef Croustades

Roast beef with a creamy mustard mayo combine in this popular party dish

🍴 makes 12
🕐 prep 15 mins

3 tbsp **olive oil**

225g (8oz) **beef fillet**

salt and freshly ground **black pepper**

12 **cherry plum tomatoes**

1 tsp **caster sugar**

12 **croustade baskets** (see Goat's Cheese Croustades, far left)

1 tbsp snipped **chives**, to garnish

For the mustard mayonnaise

1 **egg**

2 **egg yolks**

1 tbsp **white wine vinegar**

2 tsp **made English mustard**

3 tsp **caster sugar**

500ml (16floz) **sunflower oil**

1 Preheat the oven 200°C (400°F/Gas 6). Heat a roasting tin over high heat and add 2 tbsp olive oil. Season the beef with salt and pepper, and place in the pan. Cook for 2–3 minutes, turning to brown on all sides. Transfer the pan to the oven and roast the beef for 10 minutes. Remove from the oven and allow to cool, then slice into small strips.

2 Meanwhile, halve the cherry tomatoes and place, cut-side up, on a roasting tray. Sprinkle with salt, pepper and the caster sugar, and drizzle with the remaining olive oil, then roast for 30 minutes.

3 To make the mayonnaise, place the egg, egg yolks, vinegar, mustard, and caster sugar in a food processor and process briefly. With the motor running, slowly add the oil until the mixture is thick and creamy.

4 Place 2 strips of beef in each croustade basket, top with 1 tsp mayonnaise and top with 2 tomato halves and a few snipped chives. Serve within 1 hour of filling.

Crab Croustades

Lightly spiced crabmeat in a crispy case

🍴 makes 12
🕐 prep 10 mins

200g (7oz) **white crabmeat**

1.5cm (½in) piece of **ginger**, peeled and grated

grated zest and juice of 1 **lime**

3 tbsp **mayonnaise**

1 tbsp chopped **coriander leaves**

2 **spring onions**, finely chopped

salt and freshly ground **black pepper**

12 **croustade baskets** (see Goat's Cheese Croustades, far left)

1 **red chilli**, deseeded and finely chopped, to garnish

● **Prepare ahead** The filling can be made several hours in advance and kept, chilled, until needed.

1 In a bowl, mix together the crabmeat, ginger, lime zest and juice, mayonnaise, coriander, and spring onions, and season to taste with salt and pepper.

2 Divide the mixture between the croustade baskets and sprinkle each with the red chilli. Serve within 1 hour of filling.

Broad Beans with Ham

Spanish *Habas con jamón* is a popular tapas dish of soft beans and chewy, salty Serrano ham

🍴 serves 6 as a tapas dish, or 4 as a starter

🕐 prep 10 mins • cook 30 mins

2 tbsp **olive oil**

1 **onion**, finely chopped

200g (7oz) **Serrano ham**, diced

2 **garlic cloves**, finely crushed

500g (1lb 2oz) **broad beans**

120ml (4fl oz) **dry white wine**

200ml (7fl oz) light **chicken stock** or vegetable stock

1 tbsp chopped **flat-leaf parsley**, to garnish (optional)

1 Heat the oil in a saucepan and add the onion. Fry over a medium heat, stirring, until translucent and soft. Then increase the heat slightly and add the ham and garlic. Fry until the ham begins to brown.

2 Add the beans and the wine, and continue to cook for 8–10 minutes, stirring occasionally.

3 Reduce the heat and add the chicken stock. Stir thoroughly, and leave to simmer gently for 10 minutes. Transfer to a heated serving dish, and sprinkle with the chopped parsley, if using.

● **Good with** other Spanish-style tapas dishes, crusty bread, and chilled glasses of sherry.

● **Prepare ahead** The dish can be prepared up to 48 hours in advance. The flavours improve with reheating.

Salted Roasted Almonds

Almendras Tostadas are served with drinks in Spain

🍴 serves 8

🕐 prep 5 mins • cook 15–25 mins

500g (1lb 2oz) **blanched whole almonds**

2 tbsp **sea salt**

2 tsp **paprika**

1 Preheat the oven to 220°C (425°F/Gas 7).

2 Spread the almonds out on a baking tray, and sprinkle with a little water. This will dry out, and the salt and spices will cling to the nuts. Sprinkle the almonds with the salt and the paprika, tossing to ensure that they are all well coated. Spread them out evenly again.

3 Roast the almonds for 15–25 minutes, depending on how brown you wish them to be, but take care that they do not burn.

VARIATION

Spiced Nuts

Use a mix of nuts, such as cashews, hazelnuts, or brazils. Replace the paprika with ground cumin, coriander, or cayenne pepper.

Chicken Livers in Sherry

In *Higaditos al Jeréz*, the rich sweet sherry perfectly offsets the intensity of the meat

🍴 serves 4

🕐 prep 5 mins • cook 8 mins

200ml (7fl oz) **sweet sherry**

2 tsp **olive oil**

1 **garlic clove**, crushed

225g (8oz) **chicken livers**, trimmed

salt and freshly ground **black pepper**

2 tbsp chopped **parsley**, to garnish

1 Bring the sherry to the boil in a small saucepan over a high heat, and boil rapidly until it is reduced to a thin syrup.

2 Heat the oil in a frying pan over a medium heat. Cook the garlic for 1 minute, then increase the heat, add the chicken livers, and fry, stirring, for 3–4 minutes. The livers should be dark brown and crusty on the outside, but still slightly pink on the inside. Season to taste with salt and pepper.

3 Transfer to a serving plate, pour the sherry over, and garnish with chopped parsley.

● **Good with** small pieces of toast, or on skewers, as an appetizer.

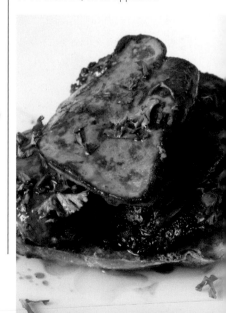

Peas with Ham

Guisantes con jamón is a classic tapas dish with delicious sweet and savoury flavours

serves 4

prep 5 mins • cook 15 mins

2 tbsp **olive oil**

1 **onion**, finely diced

200g (7oz) **Serrano ham**, diced

200ml carton **sieved tomatoes**

1 tsp **sweet paprika**

500g (1lb 2oz) **peas**

1 **garlic clove**, crushed

1 tbsp finely chopped **parsley**

salt and freshly ground **black pepper**

150ml (5fl oz) **dry white wine**

1 Heat the oil in a frying pan and add the onion. Fry for 5 minutes, stirring frequently, until soft.

2 Increase the heat, add the ham and fry until it begins to brown, then add the tomatoes and sweet paprika. Bring to boiling point, reduce the heat, and simmer for 3 minutes, stirring frequently. Stir in the peas.

3 Mix the garlic, chopped parsley, and 2 tsp salt together, then stir in the wine. Pour this mixture into the pan, and season to taste with pepper. Simmer for 5 minutes, then transfer to a heated serving dish and serve hot.

Buffalo Chicken Wings

Moreish, sticky charred chicken wings served with a rich blue cheesy dip

serves 4

prep 20 mins, plus marinating • cook 25 mins

large plastic food bag

2 tbsp **olive oil**, plus extra for oiling

1 **shallot**, finely chopped

1 **garlic clove**, crushed

2 tbsp **tomato purée**

1 tbsp **dried oregano**

few drops of **Tabasco sauce**

2 tsp **light soft brown sugar**

salt and freshly ground **black pepper**

12 **chicken wings**, tips removed

For the blue cheese dip

150ml (5fl oz) **soured cream**

75g (2½oz) **blue cheese**, such as Roquefort or Dolcelatte, crumbled

juice of ½ **lemon**

2 tbsp finely snipped **chives**

● **Prepare ahead** The chicken can be coated in the tomato mixture and left to marinate for a few hours until ready to cook.

1 Place the olive oil, shallot, garlic, tomato purée, oregano, Tabasco, and sugar in a blender, season with salt and pepper, and process until smooth. Spoon into a large food bag, and add the chicken wings. Shake the bag until the meat is well coated with marinade. Chill for at least 30 minutes to marinate.

2 Preheat the oven to 180°C (350°F/Gas 4). Remove the chicken wings from the bag and lay them, skin-side down, on 2 lightly oiled baking trays. Place in the oven and cook for 10 minutes. Turn the pieces over and cook for a further 15 minutes, or until cooked through.

3 Meanwhile, mix together all the ingredients for the blue cheese dip. Serve the chicken wings hot, with the dip on the side.

Chicken Satay

The authentic version is made with Indonesian soy sauce, kecap manis, but Chinese or Japanese soy can also be used

- serves 6
- prep 20 mins, plus marinating • cook 5 mins
- soak wooden skewers in cold water for at least 30 mins to prevent them burning under the grill
- wooden skewers

3 skinless boneless **chicken breasts**

½ tsp **salt**

2cm (¾in) piece of fresh **root ginger**, peeled and grated

2 **garlic cloves**, crushed

½ tsp **ground cumin**

2 tsp **ground coriander**

1 tsp **lemongrass purée**

4 tsp **brown sugar**

juice of ½ **lime**

2 tbsp **kecap manis** or soy sauce

vegetable oil

For the sauce

250g (9oz) **peanut butter**

2 **garlic cloves**, crushed

30g (1oz) **creamed coconut**, coarsely chopped

1 tbsp **dark soy sauce**

1 tbsp **dark brown sugar**

1cm (½in) piece of fresh **root ginger**, peeled and finely chopped

1 tbsp **lemon** juice

cayenne pepper

salt and freshly ground **black pepper**

lime wedges, to garnish

● **Prepare ahead** Complete steps 1 and 2 up to 24 hours in advance. The satay sauce can be made the day before and reheated.

1 Cut the chicken into thin strips across the grain of meat. Spread them out in a shallow, non-metallic dish.

2 In a small bowl, mix together the salt, ginger, garlic, cumin, coriander, lemongrass purée, sugar, lime juice, kecap manis, and 2 tsp of the vegetable oil. Spoon this mixture over the chicken, turning the strips until they are well coated. Cover the dish with cling film and place in the refrigerator to marinate overnight.

3 To make the satay sauce, put the peanut butter with half the garlic in a small saucepan and cook over a low heat for 2 minutes. Add 175ml (6fl oz) water, the creamed coconut, soy sauce, sugar, and ginger, and cook for 2 minutes, stirring until smooth.

4 Add the lemon juice and remaining garlic and season to taste with cayenne pepper, salt and

pepper. Let the sauce cool, cover with cling film, and chill.

5 When ready to cook, remove the chicken from the dish and thread the pieces on to the wooden skewers. In a pan over low heat, re-heat the satay sauce, stirring frequently to prevent lumps.

6 Brush the chicken with oil and grill or barbecue for 5 minutes, turning over once, or until the chicken is cooked through. Garnish with lime wedges and serve hot with the satay sauce.

VARIATION

Beef Satay

500g (1lb 20oz) beef, trimmed of any extra fat and cut into strips, then used in the recipe above, make a delicious alternative to chicken.

Falafel

Use dried chickpeas, soaked in advance, for the best flavour

- makes 12
- prep 25 mins, plus overnight soaking and standing • cook 15 mins

225g (8oz) **dried chickpeas**, soaked overnight in cold water

1 tbsp **tahini**

1 **garlic clove**, crushed

1 tsp **salt**

1 tsp **ground cumin**

1 tsp **turmeric**

1 tsp **ground coriander**

½ tsp **cayenne pepper**

2 tbsp finely chopped **parsley**

juice of 1 small **lemon**

vegetable oil, for frying

1 Drain the soaked chickpeas and place them in a food processor with the rest of the ingredients. Process until finely chopped but not puréed.

2 Transfer the mixture to a bowl and set it aside for at least 30 minutes (and up to 8 hours), covered in the refrigerator.

3 Wet your hands and shape the mixture into 12 balls. Press the tops down slightly to flatten.

4 Heat 5cm (2in) of oil in a deep pan or wok. Fry the balls in batches for 3–4 minutes, or until lightly golden. Drain on kitchen paper and serve immediately.

Chinese Dumplings

Wontons are healthy and great to have ready in the freezer

 makes 20

🕐 prep 20 mins • cook 10 mins

🍲 steamer, bamboo is preferred, and a wire rack

❄ freeze uncooked wontons for up to 1 month

175g (6oz) minced pork

2 spring onions, finely chopped

115g (4oz) shiitake mushrooms, finely chopped

1cm (½in) piece of fresh root ginger, peeled and grated

½ tsp sesame oil

1 tbsp chopped coriander leaves

1 tbsp light soy sauce

freshly ground black pepper

20 wonton wrappers

1 egg, beaten

lettuce or napa cabbage for steaming

● **Prepare ahead** Steps 1 and 2 can be completed several hours in advance, and the wontons covered with cling film and refrigerated.

1 In a bowl, mix together the pork, spring onions, mushrooms, ginger, sesame oil, coriander, and soy sauce. Season with black pepper.

2 Place each wonton wrapper on a clean surface and spoon a little of the pork mixture into the centre of each one. Brush the edges lightly with egg, fold the wrapper in half and crimp the edges to seal.

3 Fill a pan about one-quarter full of water and bring to the boil. Line the steamer with lettuce and add the wontons. Place the steamer on a rack so it sits above the water, cover and steam for 10 minutes, or until cooked. Serve at once.

● **Good with** soy sauce or your favourite dipping sauce.

VARIATION

Wonton Soup

The same filling may be used to make wonton soup. Instead of folding the wrappers in half, pinch them into a "money bag" shape. Simmer them in a well-flavoured broth and add vegetables, such as pak choi, baby corn, or Chinese broccoli.

Devils on Horseback

These spicy savouries are often served as pre-dinner canapés

 makes 16

🕐 prep 15 mins • cook 12 mins

🍲 cocktail sticks

1 tsp made English mustard

pinch of cayenne pepper

3 tbsp mango chutney

salt and freshly ground black pepper

16 prunes, pitted

8 rashers of streaky bacon

4 slices of white bread

butter for spreading

● **Prepare ahead** Steps 1 and 2 can be done ahead of time. Place the wrapped prunes on the baking tray and chill until ready to cook.

1 Preheat the oven to 220°C (425°F/Gas 7). Mix together the English mustard, cayenne, and mango chutney in a bowl, seasoning to taste with salt and pepper.

2 Make a small slit in each prune and fill with a little of the chutney mixture. Cut each bacon rasher in half across its width and wrap each strip around a prune, securing it with a cocktail stick.

3 Place the wrapped prunes on a greased baking tray and roast for 10–12 minutes, turning them over halfway through the cooking time. Cook until the bacon is crisp.

4 Place the bread under the grill or in a toaster and toast until golden. Remove the crusts and using a small biscuit cutter, cut each slice into 4 small rounds. Butter the toast rounds and top each one with a bacon-wrapped prune. Dust with a little sprinkle of cayenne pepper and serve immediately.

VARIATION

Angels on Horseback

Replace the prunes with oysters that have been removed from their shells. Lightly season with black pepper then wrap a strip of bacon around each oyster, securing it with a cocktail stick. Place on a baking tray and bake in the oven for 5–7 minutes, taking care not to overcook the oysters. These are delicious served with a squeeze of fresh lemon juice.

Smoked Salmon Rolls

Easy to make, these can be served as a party appetizer with drinks,
or as a first course with a salad garnish

- makes 16
- prep 30 mins
- low GI

350g (12oz) smoked salmon slices

1 cucumber

100g (3½oz) cream cheese

1 tsp chopped dill

2 tbsp lemon mayonnaise

1 tsp creamed horseradish

lemon wedges, to serve

sprigs of dill, to garnish

● **Prepare ahead** If making ahead, lay the rolls, on their ends, on a large plate and cover tightly with cling film to prevent them from drying out. Chill until ready to serve.

1 Cut the smoked salmon into 16 strips measuring 12 x 4cm (5 x 1½in). Cut the cucumber into batons measuring 4cm x 5mm (1½ x ¼in). Set both aside.

2 Put the cream cheese in a bowl and stir in the dill, mayonnaise, and horseradish until evenly combined.

3 Lay the smoked salmon strips on a board and spread with the cheese mixture, leaving 2.5cm (1in) clear at one short end. Lay a cucumber baton across each strip and roll up tightly from the short end where the cheese mixture comes to the edge.

4 Arrange the rolls on a serving platter, garnished with lemon wedges and sprigs of dill.

VARIATIONS

Smoked Salmon and Asparagus Rolls
Follow the recipe as above, but replace the cucumber with cooked asparagus spears that have been tossed in a little vinaigrette dressing while still warm, then left to cool.

Smoked Salmon and Prawn Rolls
Fill the salmon strips with prawns dressed with mayonnaise flavoured with a little tomato purée, lemon juice, and Tabasco. Garnish with sprigs of dill.

Smoked Salmon and Egg Rolls
Fill the salmon strips with 4 chopped hard-boiled eggs mixed with a mustard-flavoured mayonnaise, and garnish with mustard and cress.

Inside-out Smoked Salmon Rolls
Peel wide strips of cucumber using a vegetable peeler. Lay the strips out and spread the cream cheese mixture over each one. Scatter over finely chopped smoked salmon and roll up.

Pickled Figs Wrapped in Parma Ham

These one-bite party snacks contrast sweet and sour figs with rich Italian ham

- makes 24
- prep 10 mins
- cocktail sticks

12 baby pickled figs

6 large slices of Parma ham

24 rocket leaves, plus extra to garnish

freshly ground black pepper

Parmesan cheese, shaved, to serve

● **Prepare ahead** These bites can be made a few hours in advance, then stored, covered, and chilled.

1 Cut each fig in half and each slice of ham into 4 long strips. Thread the figs, ham, and rocket on to the cocktail sticks. Season to taste with black pepper.

2 Serve on a large plate, scattered with Parmesan shavings and extra rocket leaves.

VARIATION

Fresh Figs in Parma Ham
Instead of pickled figs, use 6 fresh figs, cut into quarters.

Kibbeh

Fragrant crisp-fried dumplings from the Middle East

 makes 12

 prep 30 mins, plus chilling • cook 25 mins

 soak the bulghur wheat for 20 mins in cold water, then drain, and squeeze out excess water before using

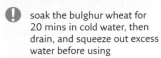 deep-fat fryer

For the filling

2 tbsp **olive oil**

1 small **onion**, peeled and finely chopped

85g (3oz) lean **minced beef** or lamb

1 tbsp **pine nuts**, lightly toasted

½ tsp ground **cinnamon**

salt and freshly ground **black pepper**

For the shells

1 small **onion**, peeled and roughly chopped

175g (6oz) **bulghur wheat**, soaked for 20 minutes in cold water

½ tsp ground **allspice**

250g (9oz) lean **minced beef** or lamb

vegetable oil or sunflower oil, for deep frying

1 **To make the filling**, heat the oil in a frying pan and fry the onion until softened. Add the meat and fry until lightly browned, stirring to break up clumps. Stir in the pine nuts and cinnamon; season to taste with salt and pepper. Set aside.

2 **To make the shells**, put the onion in a food processor and process to a paste. Add the bulghur wheat, allspice, and minced meat, season to taste with salt and pepper, and process thoroughly.

3 **Dampen your hands**, take a small egg-sized piece of the shell mixture, and press to a round 5mm (¼in) thick. Spoon a little of the filling on top and press the shell around it so it is enclosed. Shape each end of the kibbeh into a point. Repeat with the remaining filling and shell mixture to make 11 more kibbeh. Chill well for 1 hour or longer.

4 **Heat the oil** to 180°C (350°F) and deep-fry the kibbeh, 3 or 4 at a time, until golden brown. Drain on kitchen paper; serve hot.

● **Good with** a yogurt, cucumber, and mint sauce, and a tomato, red onion, and parsley salad.

Oriental Meatballs with Peanut Sauce

The sweet peanut sauce is a perfect accompaniment to these savoury bites

 serves 6–8

prep 15 mins • cook 20 mins

For the meatballs

450g (1lb) lean **minced beef** or pork, or a combination of both

1 **garlic clove**, finely chopped

1 tsp **lemongrass purée**

1 tbsp chopped **coriander**

1 tbsp **red curry paste**

1 tbsp **lemon** juice

1 tbsp **Thai fish sauce**

1 **egg**

salt and freshly ground **black pepper**

rice flour, for dusting

sunflower oil, for frying

lime wedges, to garnish

For the sauce

1 tbsp **vegetable oil**

1 tsp **red curry paste**

2 tbsp **crunchy peanut butter**

1 tbsp **brown sugar**

1 tbsp **lemon** juice

250ml (8fl oz) **coconut milk**

● **Prepare ahead** The meatballs can be made 1 day in advance, covered, and refrigerated. Dust with the rice flour just before frying.

1 **To make the peanut sauce**, heat the oil in a small saucepan, add the curry paste, and fry for 1 minute. Gradually stir in the rest of the ingredients, then bring to the boil. Reduce the heat and simmer for 5 minutes, or until thickened. If it is too thick, stir in a little water.

2 **For the meatballs**, combine the minced meat, garlic, lemongrass, coriander, curry paste, lemon juice, Thai fish sauce, and egg, and season to taste with salt and pepper. Roll the mixture into small walnut-sized balls and dust with the rice flour.

3 **Heat the oil** in a frying pan. Fry the meatballs in batches until browned and cooked through.

4 **Drain on kitchen paper**, then serve hot, with the warm peanut sauce and lime wedges.

Sausage Rolls

These bite-sized rolls are perfect for parties or take-away lunches

 makes 24

 prep 30 mins, plus chilling • cook 10–12 mins

 freeze, uncooked, for up to 3 months

400g (14oz) ready-made **puff pastry**, thawed if frozen

675g (1½lb) **sausage meat**

1 small **onion**, finely chopped

1 tbsp chopped fresh **thyme**

1 tbsp grated **lemon** zest

1 tsp **Dijon mustard**

1 **egg yolk**

salt and freshly ground **black pepper**

1 **egg**, beaten, to glaze

1 Preheat the oven to 200°C (400°F/Gas 6). Line a baking tray with greaseproof paper and chill.

2 Cut the puff pastry in half lengthways. Roll each piece out to form a 30 x 15cm (12 x 6in) rectangle, then chill, covered with cling film.

3 Meanwhile, combine the sausage meat with the onion, thyme, lemon zest, mustard, and egg yolk, and season with salt and pepper.

4 Lay the pastry on a floured surface. Form the sausage mixture into 2 thinly rolled tubes and place in the centre of each piece of pastry. Brush the inside of the pastry with the beaten egg, then roll the pastry over and press to seal. Cut each roll into 12 pieces.

5 Place the rolls on the chilled tray, make 2 snips in the top of each with scissors, then brush with beaten egg. Bake for 10–12 minutes, or until the pastry is golden and flaky. Serve warm, or transfer to a wire rack to cool completely before serving.

● **Good with** a spicy mustard dipping sauce.

Smoked Chicken and Tarragon Mousse

Quick, healthy, and impressive – chicory leaves are a great alternative to crackers or bread

 serves 10–12

prep 10 mins

225g (8oz) **smoked chicken breasts**

zest and juice of ½ **lemon**

1 tbsp chopped fresh **tarragon**

3 tbsp **mayonnaise**

2 tbsp **Dijon mustard**

sea salt and freshly ground **black pepper**

1 head of **red chicory**

1 head of **white chicory**

chives, to garnish (optional)

● **Prepare ahead** You can make the mousse 1 day in advance and chill. Once placed on the chicory leaves, serve within 1 hour.

1 Remove any skin and bone from the smoked chicken and discard. Cut the meat into small pieces. Place the chicken in a food processor with the lemon zest and juice, tarragon, mayonnaise, and mustard. Process until finely chopped. Season to taste with salt and pepper.

2 To serve, separate the chicory leaves and trim, if necessary. Place teaspoonfuls of the mousse on to the stalk ends of the chicory leaves. Garnish with chives, if using.

● **Leftovers** of the mousse are good spread on wholemeal toast or oatcakes.

Melon and Nectarines with Parma Ham

This is a great flavour combination, and is so simple to assemble

 serves 8–12

 prep 15 mins

 wooden cocktail sticks

1 small **honeydew melon**

4 **nectarines**, halved and stones removed

225g (8oz) thinly sliced **Parma ham**

freshly ground **black pepper** (optional)

● **Prepare ahead** These canapés can be made several hours in advance. Chill until required.

1 **Cut the honeydew melon** into 16 wedge-shaped slices and cut off the rind. Cut the nectarines into wedges.

2 **Cut the Parma ham** into thin strips. Thread a strip of ham and a piece of fruit on to cocktail sticks.

3 **Arrange the melon** on a serving platter and serve.

VARIATION

Melon, Fig, and Prosciutto Salad

Arrange rocket leaves on 4 small plates. Cut the melon as above, then divide between the plates. Cut 4 figs in quarters, but not through the base. Open out the figs and place 1 in the centre of each plate. Cut 8 slices of Parma ham in half lengthways and arrange between the melon slices. Sprinkle with pepper and drizzle with balsamic vinegar. Shave 75g (2½oz) pecorino cheese over the top.

Seven-Grain Bread

Full of healthy wheat, this chewy bread includes millet, rolled oats, polenta, quinoa, brown rice, rye flakes, and wheat

- makes 2 loaves
- prep 20 mins, plus rising • cook 35–40 mins
- 2 x 900g (2lb) loaf tins
- freeze for up to 3 months

85g (3oz) **bulgur wheat**

50g (1¾oz) **polenta**

50g (1¾oz) **millet**

50g (1¾oz) **quinoa**

450g (1lb) **strong white flour**

250g (9oz) **granary flour** or strong wholemeal flour

75g (2½oz) **rolled oats**

75g (2½oz) **rye flakes**

2 x 7g sachets **easy-blend dried yeast**

2 tsp **salt**

50g (1¾oz) cooked **long-grain brown rice**

4 tbsp **honey**, maple syrup or treacle, to taste

250ml (8fl oz) **milk**, warmed

2 tbsp **sunflower oil**, plus extra for brushing

600ml (1 pint) **water**, warmed

1 Put the first 4 ingredients into a heatproof bowl. Pour over 400ml (14fl oz) of water, stir, cover with a folded tea towel, and leave to stand for 15 minutes.

2 Put the next 6 ingredients into a separate bowl and combine well. Tip in the bulghur wheat mixture with any remaining water, add the brown rice, and stir.

3 Heat the honey and milk in a saucepan over a low heat until the honey dissolves. Add the milk mixture and the sunflower oil to the flour mixture and stir together. Gradually add up to 200ml (7fl oz) water, or until a soft, sticky dough forms. Dust a work surface with flour, turn out the dough, and knead for 10 minutes, or until elastic, adding extra flour as necessary.

4 Rub the inside of a dry bowl with sunflower oil. Shape the dough into a ball and lightly coat the ball with oil by turning it within the bowl. Cover the bowl with cling film and set aside in a warm, draught-free place until the dough doubles in size. Grease and flour the loaf tins.

5 Once risen, punch down the dough, turn out on to a floured surface and knead for 1 minute. (The dough will be sticky again.) Cut the dough into 2 equal-sized balls and use a floured rolling pin to roll each ball into a rectangle as wide as the tins and twice as long. Fold both ends to the centre and pinch the edges to seal. Place the dough in the tins, cover with tea towels, and set aside to rise until the dough reaches the tops of the tins. Meanwhile, preheat the oven to 220°C (425°F/Gas 7).

6 When the dough has risen, brush the tops with sunflower oil. Bake for 10 minutes, then reduce the heat to 190°C (375°F/Gas 5) for a further 25–30 minutes, or until the loaves sound hollow when tapped on the base. If not, return to the oven for 5–10 minutes.

VARIATION

Seven-Grain Rolls

Cut the risen dough into rolls and follow the rest of step 5. Bake for 20 minutes, or until they sound hollow when tapped on the base.

Walnut Bread

In France, this savoury bread is a traditional accompaniment to the cheese course

🍴 makes 2 loaves

🕐 prep 20 mins, plus rising
• cook 35–45 mins

❄ freeze for up to 3 months

350g (12oz) **strong wholemeal flour**

200g (7oz) **strong white flour**, plus extra for dusting

7g sachet **easy-blend dried yeast**

1½ tsp **salt**

1 tsp **sugar**

1 tbsp **walnut oil**, plus extra for brushing

150g (5½oz) **walnuts**, coarsely chopped

1 Mix the first 5 ingredients in a large bowl, making a well in the centre. Stir 360ml (12fl oz) tepid water and the walnut oil into the well. Gradually add up to 100ml (3½fl oz) more water until the flour is incorporated and the dough is soft.

2 Turn out the dough on to a lightly floured surface and knead for 5–8 minutes, or until smooth and elastic. Shape into a ball.

3 Rub the inside of a dry bowl with oil. Put the dough in the bowl, cover with cling film, and leave in a warm place until doubled in size. Meanwhile, lightly dust a large baking sheet with flour.

4 Punch down the dough, turn it out onto a floured surface, and knead for 1 minute. Pat the dough into a rectangle and sprinkle with the walnuts. Knead for a few more minutes, or until the nuts are evenly distributed.

5 Cut the dough in half and form each into a ball. Transfer to the baking sheet and flatten. Cover with a tea towel and leave to rise for 15 minutes. Preheat the oven to 220°C (425°F/Gas 7).

6 Lightly dust the dough with flour, then cut a 5mm (¼in) deep square, in the top of each. Bake for 10 minutes, reduce the temperature to 190°C (375°F/Gas 5), and bake for a further 25–35 minutes, or until the bases sound hollow when tapped. Transfer to a wire rack and leave to cool.

Herb and Olive Bread

Bursting with Mediterranean flavours, this bread is delicious dipped in olive oil

🍴 makes 2 loaves

🕐 prep 15 mins, plus rising
• cook 25–30 mins

750g (1lb10oz) **strong white flour**

7g sachet **easy-blend dried yeast**

1½ tsp **salt**

2 tbsp **olive oil**, plus extra for brushing

150g (5½oz) **Kalamata black olives**, pitted and chopped

4 tbsp finely chopped **Mediterranean herbs**, such as marjoram, flat-leaf parsley, rosemary, or thyme

1 Stir the flour, yeast, and salt together in a large bowl and make a well in the centre. Add the olive oil, 360ml (12 fl oz) tepid water, and stir. Gradually add up to 100ml (3½fl oz) more water until all the flour is combined and a soft dough forms.

2 Turn out the dough on to a lightly floured surface and knead for 5–8 minutes, or until it becomes smooth and elastic. Pat the dough into a thin rectangle and sprinkle the olives and herbs over. Roll the dough into a tube, then knead for a few more minutes, or until the ingredients are evenly distributed. Shape the dough into a ball.

3 Rub the inside of a dry bowl with olive oil. Put the dough into the bowl, cover with cling film, and leave in a warm, draught-free place until it doubles in size. Meanwhile, dust a large baking sheet with flour.

4 Punch down the dough, turn it out on to a lightly floured surface, and knead for 1 minute. Cut the dough into 2 equal-sized pieces and form each into a 25cm (10in) long sausage. Transfer the dough to the baking sheet and press down lightly. Cover with a tea towel and leave to rise for 15 minutes, or until doubled in size. Meanwhile, preheat the oven to 220°C (425°F/Gas 7).

5 Lightly brush the loaves with the olive oil and score 5 lines on the top of each. Bake for 25 minutes, or until the tops are golden brown and the bottoms sound hollow when tapped. Leave the loaves to cool completely on a wire rack.

● **Good with** a bowl of olive oil for dipping into.

Plaited Loaf

This enriched fruit loaf makes a lovely teatime treat, and it's also great toasted

 makes 1 loaf

prep 35 mins, plus resting • cook 40 mins

250ml (8fl oz) **whipping cream**

500g (1lb 2oz) **plain flour**

7g sachet **fast-action dried yeast**

85g (3oz) **caster sugar**

few drops of **pure vanilla extract**

zest of 1 **lemon**

pinch of **salt**

3 **eggs**

oil, for greasing

flour, for dusting

200g (7oz) **raisins**

2 tsp **milk**

1 **To make the dough**, gently warm the cream in a small saucepan. Mix together the flour and dried yeast in a large bowl, then add the sugar, vanilla extract, lemon zest, and salt.

2 **Separate 1 of the eggs** and set aside the yolk. Add the egg white to the flour mixture, along with the remaining 2 eggs and the warmed cream. Using a wooden spoon or mixer with a kneading hook, start mixing gently to combine the ingredients, then mix and knead together for about 5 minutes, or until it forms a smooth dough. Cover with a tea towel and put in a warm place until doubled in size.

3 **Grease a large** baking sheet. Dust the dough with flour and add the raisins. Remove from the bowl and knead briefly on a lightly floured surface until everything is incorporated. Take two-thirds of the dough and make 3 x 40cm (16in) long sausage shapes. Plait them together and put onto the baking sheet. Using a rolling pin, make a depression lengthways along the whole plaited bun.

4 **Beat together** the reserved egg yolk and milk and brush the depression with a little of this mixture. Divide the remaining dough into 3 equal portions, roll into thin sausage shapes about 35cm (14in) long and plait. Place this plait into the depression on the larger plait and brush all over with the egg and milk.

5 **Return, uncovered**, to a warm place until it has doubled in size. Preheat the oven to 180°C (350°F/Gas 4) for 40 minutes, or until golden brown and well risen. Leave to cool on a wire rack before serving.

● **Good with** a little butter and good strawberry jam.

VARIATION

Cranberry and Currant Loaf

Add 100g (3½oz) each of dried cranberries and currants, instead of the raisins.

Brioche

A sweet morning bread that is ideally served warm

 makes 12 brioche

prep 35–45 mins, plus chilling and rising • cook 10–12 mins

12 x 7.5cm (3in) brioche tins

375g (13oz) **strong white flour**

50g (1¾oz) **caster sugar**

7g sachet **fast-action dried yeast**

2 tsp **salt**

100ml (3½fl oz) **milk**, warmed

4 **eggs**, 1 beaten for glazing

175g (6oz) **butter**, softened

oil, for greasing

1 **Mix together** the flour, sugar, yeast, and salt, then add the milk and 3 of the eggs. Mix to a dough and knead for 10 minutes. Add the butter and knead for another 10 minutes. Put the dough in a lightly oiled bowl and refrigerate overnight.

2 **Grease the tins**. Lightly knead the dough, then divide into 12 pieces. Cut a quarter off 1 piece, and form both pieces into balls. Place the large ball in the tin and the small ball of dough on top, securing it by pressing the floured handle of a wooden spoon through the centre. Repeat with the remaining dough.

3 **Cover loosely** and leave to rise for 30 minutes. Preheat the oven to 190°C (375°F/Gas 5). Glaze the risen brioche with the beaten egg, making sure it doesn't drip down the sides. Bake for 10–12 minutes, or until golden brown, and cool on a wire rack.

Focaccia

This version of a traditional Italian-style bread is easy to make

 makes 1 loaf

 prep 15 mins, plus rising
• cook 30–35 mins

 freeze for up to 2 months

500g (1lb 2oz) **strong white flour**

7g sachet **fast-action yeast**

1 tsp **salt**

4 tbsp **olive oil**, plus extra for oiling

3 tbsp **extra virgin olive oil**

½–1 tbsp **coarse sea salt**

1 Tip the flour into a bowl and stir in the yeast and salt. Stir the olive oil into 300ml (10fl oz) tepid water and add to the bowl. Mix to a soft dough, adding more water if necessary. Turn the dough out on to a lightly floured surface and knead for 8–10 minutes, or until it is smooth and elastic. Cover the dough loosely with a piece of oiled cling film and leave it in a warm place for 1½ hours, or until doubled in size.

2 Roll the dough out to a 25 x 40cm (10 x 16in) rectangle. Brush half of the extra virgin olive oil over half of the dough. Brush water around the edges of the other half and fold the dough in half, to give a 25 x 20cm (10 x 8in) rectangle. Place it on the baking tray and press your knuckles down into the dough to give it a dimpled surface. Cover the dough with a tea towel and leave it to rise in a warm place for another 30–40 minutes.

3 Preheat the oven to 200°C (400°F/Gas 6). Drizzle the remaining extra virgin olive oil over the dough, leaving it to pool slightly in the dimpled dough. Sprinkle over the sea salt and bake in the centre of the oven for 30–35 minutes, or until it is risen and golden in colour.

4 Remove the baking tray from the oven, slide the bread on to a wire rack, and leave it to cool. Serve the bread on the day of baking, either warm or cold, cut into chunks.

Crusty White Loaf

A basic white bread, which can be moulded into different shapes, or made into smaller rolls

 makes 1 large loaf

 prep 35 mins, plus rising
• cook 40 mins

 900g (2lb) loaf tin

 freeze for up to 1 month

450g (1lb) **strong plain flour**, plus extra for dusting

1½ tsp **fast-action dried yeast**

1 tsp **salt**

1 tsp **sugar**

1 tbsp **vegetable oil**, sunflower, or light olive oil, plus extra for oiling

1 Stir the flour and yeast together in a large bowl, then mix in the salt and sugar. Make a well in the middle and pour in the oil and 300ml (10fl oz) tepid water. Mix to form a soft dough, adding more water if required.

2 Turn out on to a lightly floured work surface and knead the dough for 5–10 minutes, or until smooth and elastic. Shape into a round by tucking all of the edges into the middle, then turn into a large oiled bowl, smooth-side up. Cover loosely with oiled cling film and leave in a warm place for 1 hour, or until doubled in size.

3 Oil and flour the inside of the loaf tin, tapping out the excess flour. When the dough has risen, lightly knead the dough and press it into a rough rectangle. Tuck the shorter ends in, followed by the longer edges, then lay it, seam-side down, in the loaf tin. Cover loosely with the oiled cling film and leave for 30 minutes, or until risen.

4 Preheat the oven to 220°C (425°F/Gas 7). Dust the top of the loaf with more flour, slash the top with a sharp knife, then bake for 20 minutes. Reduce the oven to 200°C (400°F/Gas 6) and bake for another 20 minutes, or until risen with golden crust. Turn out the loaf and check that it is cooked; it will sound hollow when tapped on the base. Transfer to a wire rack to cool.

● **Good with** butter and jam or marmalade for breakfast, or with a savoury filling to make a sandwich.

Sourdough Bread with Fennel Seeds

Despite the need for forward planning, this bread is easy to make and the leftover starter can be used to make more loaves

- makes 1 large loaf
- prep 40 mins, plus standing and rising • cook 35–40 mins
- freeze for up to 1 month

For the starter

225g (8oz) strong white flour

7g sachet fast-action dried yeast

For the bread dough

675g (1½lb) strong white flour

7g sachet fast-action dried yeast

1 tbsp caster sugar

1 tsp salt

1 tbsp fennel seeds

● **Prepare ahead** Make the starter dough at least 2 days in advance.

1 To make the starter, mix together the flour and dried yeast in a large bowl. Using a wooden spoon, gradually stir in 600ml (1 pint) tepid water to make a smooth batter. Cover with a damp cloth and leave for 2 days, stirring daily and dampening the cloth when necessary to keep it moist.

2 For the bread, mix the flour, yeast, sugar, salt, and fennel seeds together in a large bowl. Make a hollow in the middle. Stir the starter dough, which will have separated, and add 150ml (5fl oz) of the starter and 360ml (12fl oz) tepid water to the dry ingredients.

3 Mix to a soft pliable dough. Add a further 1–2 tbsp of water if the mixture is too dry. Knead on a lightly floured surface for 10 minutes, or until the dough is smooth and elastic. Shape into a ball and place in an oiled bowl. Cover loosely and leave in a warm place for 1 hour, or until doubled in size.

4 Grease a large baking tray. Remove the dough from the bowl and knead briefly. Shape into a flattish round and place on the baking tray. Cover with a damp cloth and leave to rise for 1 hour, or until doubled in size.

5 Preheat the oven to 220°C (425°F/Gas 7). Lightly dust the loaf with flour, then, using a sharp knife, slash the top in a diamond pattern. Bake for 15 minutes, then reduce the temperature to 190°C (375°F/Gas 5) and bake for a further 20–25 minutes, or until the bread is golden and sounds hollow when tapped on the base. Transfer to a wire rack and leave to cool.

● **Leftover** starter dough will keep indefinitely, if fed regularly. To feed the starter, every 1–2 days, discard 150ml (5fl oz) of the starter and replace with the same amount of flour and water. Store, covered, in the refrigerator. When ready to use, bring it back to room temperature and leave to develop for 4–6 hours.

> **VARIATION**

German Sourdough Bread (Bauernbrot)

Replace up to half the flour in the main bread dough with rye flour. If preferred, use fresh yeast instead of dried: 15g (½oz) for the starter and 15g (½oz) for the main dough. In each case, blend the yeast with a little of the warm water in the bowl, then stir in the remaining water, flour, and additional ingredients.

Morning Rolls

Easy-to-make soft white rolls that are ideal for breakfast

- makes 16
- prep 40 mins, plus rising • cook 20 mins
- freeze for up to 3 months

500g (1lb 2oz) strong white flour

2 tsp light soft brown sugar

7g sachet fast-action dried yeast

2 tsp salt

1 Place the flour, sugar, yeast, and salt into a large bowl. Add 275ml (9fl oz) tepid water, or enough to form a soft, pliable dough. Knead well for 10 minutes. Place in a lightly oiled bowl and loosely cover. Leave in a warm place to rise for 1 hour, or until doubled in size.

2 Turn the dough out on to a lightly floured surface and knead briefly. Divide it into 16 pieces and shape into balls. Smooth the tops and place on to 2 lightly oiled baking trays. Leave enough space for them to spread out without touching. Leave to rise in a warm place for 30 minutes, or until doubled in size.

3 Preheat the oven to 200°C (400°F/Gas 6). Bake the rolls for 20 minutes, or until they are brown on top and sound hollow when tapped on the base.

Crumpets

Eaten for breakfast or at teatime, toasted crumpets are great with both sweet and savoury toppings

- makes 8
- prep 10 mins, plus resting • cook 20–26 mins
- crumpet rings or 10cm (4in) metal cutters
- freeze for up to 1 month

125g (4½oz) **plain white flour**

125g (4½oz) **strong white flour**

½ tsp **fast-action dried yeast**

175ml (6fl oz) tepid **milk**

½ tsp **salt**

½ tsp **bicarbonate of soda**

1 Mix together the flours and yeast. Stir in the milk and 175ml (6fl oz) tepid water, and leave for 2 hours, or until the bubbles have risen and then started to fall again. Mix the salt and bicarbonate of soda into 2 tbsp lukewarm water and whisk in. Set aside for 5 minutes.

2 Oil 4 crumpet rings. Lightly oil a large, heavy frying pan and place the rings in the pan.

3 Pour the batter into a jug. Heat the pan over a medium heat and pour batter into each ring to a depth of 1–2cm (½–¾in). Cook the crumpets for 8–10 minutes, or until the batter has set all the way through and the top is covered in holes. If no bubbles appear, the mixture is too dry so stir a little water into the remaining batter.

4 Lift the rings off the crumpets, turn them over, and cook for another 2–3 minutes, or until just golden. Repeat with the remaining batter. Serve the freshly cooked crumpets warm and buttered, or toast to reheat if serving them later.

Stottie Cakes

Not really cakes at all, but rather breads originating from north-east England

- makes 8
- prep 20 mins, plus rising • cook 15–20 mins
- freeze for up to 3 months

500g (1lb 2oz) **strong white flour**

1½ tsp **fast-action dried yeast**

1 tsp **caster sugar**

1½ tsp **salt**

45g (1½oz) **butter**

150ml (5fl oz) **full-fat milk**

flour, for dusting

1 Mix together the flour and dried yeast in a large bowl, then add the sugar and salt. Rub in the butter until well blended. Make a well in the centre and pour in the milk and 150ml (5fl oz) tepid water. Mix to a soft, pliable dough. Knead for 10 minutes, or until you have a smooth and elastic dough. Place in a lightly oiled bowl and loosely cover. Leave in a warm place to rise for 1 hour, or until doubled in size.

2 Dust the work surface with flour and knead the dough briefly until smooth. Divide it into 8 equal pieces and roll each piece out into a flat round, 10cm (4in) in diameter. Lightly flour 2 large baking trays and place 4 dough rounds on each tray. Dust with a little flour.

3 Preheat the oven to 220°C (425°F/Gas 7). Meanwhile, push the handle of a wooden spoon into the centre of each round, wiggling it to make a small hole. Prick the dough lightly with a fork, cover with oiled cling film, and leave in a warm place for 20 minutes, or until slightly risen and puffy.

4 Bake for 12–15 minutes, or until risen and lightly golden. Transfer the stottie cakes to a wire rack to cool.

● **Good with** sweet or savoury fillings; split through the middle and spread with your favourite.

● **Leftovers** can be made into breadcrumbs for stuffings or toppings. They are also great for making bread and butter pudding.

Wholemeal Bread

This recipe uses a blend of white and wholemeal flour to make a lighter, moister loaf

- makes 1 loaf
- prep 35 mins, plus rising • cook 40 mins
- 900g (2lb) loaf tin

225g (8oz) **strong white flour**, plus extra for kneading

225g (8oz) **strong wholemeal flour**, plus extra for dusting

1½ tsp **fast-action dried yeast**

1 tsp **salt**

1 tbsp **vegetable oil**, sunflower oil or light olive oil, plus extra for oiling

1 tbsp **honey**

200ml (7fl oz) lukewarm **milk**

beaten **egg**, to glaze

1 Mix the flours, yeast, and salt in a large bowl, then make a well. Stir the oil, honey, milk, and 150ml (5fl oz) lukewarm water in a jug until the honey has dissolved. Pour into the well in the centre of the dry ingredients. Mix to form a slightly sticky dough. Stand for 10 minutes.

2 Dust the work surface with a little flour, then knead the dough for 5–10 minutes, or until it is smooth and springs back when pressed lightly. Shape into a ball and place in a large oiled bowl. Cover loosely with oiled cling film and leave in a warm place for 1 hour, or until doubled in size. Meanwhile, oil and flour the inside of the loaf tin, tapping out the excess flour.

3 When risen, turn out on to a lightly floured surface and knead briefly. Press the dough into a rough rectangle and tuck the shorter ends in, followed by the longer edges. Lay it, seam-side down, in the tin, cover loosely with oiled cling film, and leave for 30 minutes, or until doubled in size.

4 Preheat the oven to 220°C (425°F/Gas 7). Sieve a little wholemeal flour, leaving the bran in the sieve. Brush the egg over the loaf to glaze, scatter the bran over, then slash it with a sharp knife. Bake for 20 minutes, then reduce the heat to 200°C (400°F/Gas 6) and bake for another 20 minutes, or until risen with a dark golden crust. Tip the loaf out of the tin, then let it cool completely on a wire rack.

● **Good with** butter and jam.

Moroccan Spiced Flatbreads

Best eaten on the day they are made, these breads are good as they are, or lightly chargrilled

- makes 8
- prep 25 mins, plus rising • cook 15 mins

1½ tsp **cumin seeds**, plus more to decorate

1½ tsp **ground coriander**

450g (1lb) **strong white flour**, plus extra for kneading

1 tsp **fast-action dried yeast**

1 tsp **salt**

small bunch of **coriander**, roughly chopped

200g can **chickpeas**, drained and roughly crushed

150g (5½oz) **plain yogurt**

1 tbsp **olive oil**, plus extra for brushing

1 Toast the cumin and ground coriander in a dry pan for 1 minute until fragrant. Mix the flour, yeast, and salt in a large bowl. Stir in the spices, coriander, and chickpeas, then make a well in the middle. Pour in the yogurt, oil, and 300ml (10fl oz) warm water, and bring together quickly to form a sticky dough. Set aside in the bowl for 10 minutes.

2 Turn the dough on to a lightly floured surface. Knead for 5 minutes. Shape into a ball and place in a large oiled bowl. Cover loosely with oiled cling film and leave for 1 hour in a warm place, or until doubled in size.

3 Lightly dust 2 large baking trays with flour. Preheat the oven to 220°C (425°F/Gas 7). Turn the dough out on to a floured surface and cut into 8 even-sized pieces. Using a rolling pin, flatten out into ovals about 5mm (¼in) thick. Place on the baking trays, brush with a little oil, and scatter with a few cumin seeds. Bake for 15 minutes, or until the breads are golden and puffed up.

● **Good with** lamb koftas, hummus, black olive tapenade, and salads.

Fougasse

Fougasse is the French equivalent of the Italian focaccia. This version has crispy bacon and onion blended into the dough

 makes 3 small loaves

🕐 prep 30–35 mins, plus rising • cook 15 mins

1 tbsp **oil**, for frying

1 **onion**, finely chopped

2 **back bacon rashers**, finely chopped

400g (14oz) **strong white bread flour**

7g sachet **fast-action dried yeast**

1 tsp **salt**

4 tbsp **olive oil**, plus extra for brushing

sea salt flakes, for sprinkling

1 Heat the oil in a frying pan. Fry the onion and bacon until browned, remove from the pan, and set aside.

2 Mix 200g (7oz) of the flour with the contents of the yeast sachet in a bowl. Add about 150ml (5fl oz) water, then mix for 3–4 minutes. Cover and leave to rise and then fall again. This should take about 4 hours.

3 Add the remaining flour, the salt, 150ml (5fl oz) water, and the olive oil, and mix well. Turn out on to a lightly floured work surface and knead to a smooth dough. Return to the bowl to rise for 1 hour, or until doubled in size.

4 Line 3 baking sheets with baking parchment. Punch down the dough, then tip on the onion and bacon. Knead well, to incorporate, then divide the dough into 3 balls. Flatten each ball to about 2.5cm (1in) high with a rolling pin, then shape each into a rough circle.

5 Preheat the oven to 230°C (450°F/Gas 8). Put the dough circles on to the baking sheets. To create the traditional leaf shapes, cut each circle with a sharp knife, twice down the centre, then 3 times on either side on a slant. Cut all the way through the thickness of the dough, but not through the edges. Brush with olive oil, sprinkle with sea salt, and leave to rise for 1 hour, or until doubled in size.

6 Bake the loaves for 15 minutes, until golden. Remove from the oven and allow to cool before serving.

Ciabatta

This classic slipper-shaped, soft Italian bread is made by using a starter that is left to rise overnight

 makes 1 loaf

 prep 30 mins, plus rising • cook 40 mins

For the starter

175g (6oz) **Italian "00" flour**

¼ tsp **fast-action dried yeast**

For the dough

450g (1lb) **Italian "00" flour**

1½ tsp **fast-action dried yeast**

2 tsp **olive oil**, plus extra for brushing

1 tsp **salt**

● **Prepare ahead** Make the starter the day before you want to bake the bread.

1 Place the flour, yeast, and 100ml (3½fl oz) lukewarm water in a bowl. Mix well for a few minutes until the mixture forms a ball. Place inside a lightly oiled bowl, roll around the bowl to coat in the oil, cover, and leave overnight in a warm place.

2 The next day, make the dough by mixing the flour, yeast, oil, salt, and 360ml (12fl oz) tepid water. Once combined, add the starter and continue kneading until you have a wet, sticky dough.

3 Place the dough in a lightly oiled bowl. Roll it around the bowl to coat in the oil, then leave to rise in a warm place for 2 hours, or until doubled in size.

4 Preheat the oven to 220°C (425°F/Gas 7). Punch the dough back and knead for 10 minutes, or until smooth and elastic. Mould the dough into a slipper shape and place it on an oiled baking tray. Bake for 10 minutes, reduce the temperature to 190°C (375°F/Gas 5), and bake for a further 30 minutes, or until a crust forms and the loaf sounds hollow when tapped underneath. Cool on a wire rack.

● **Good with** soup, Italian cheeses, or simply dipped into oil with a meal..

Onion and Herb Loaf

A delicious savoury loaf with herb-flavoured dough and a rich, tangy, fried onion filling

🍴 makes 1 loaf

🕐 prep 35 mins, plus rising • cook 55 mins

550g (1 ¼lb) strong white flour

1 tsp fast-action dried yeast

1 heaped tsp salt

1 tbsp finely chopped rosemary, plus 2–3 extra sprigs, rubbed in oil

5 tbsp extra virgin olive oil

1 egg, beaten

For the filling

2 tbsp olive oil

½ tsp salt

½ tsp coarsely crushed black pepper

2 onions, sliced

1 tbsp balsamic vinegar

3 tbsp golden caster sugar

1 tbsp rosemary or thyme, finely chopped

1 **Place 225g (8oz)** of the flour in a bowl, add 300ml (10fl oz) tepid water and the yeast, mix well, and leave for 1 hour. Add the remaining flour, salt, rosemary, and oil, and mix to a soft pliable dough. Knead on a lightly floured surface for 10 minutes, or until elastic.

2 **Shape the dough** into a ball and place in a large oiled bowl. Cover loosely with oiled cling film, and leave in a warm place for 1 hour, or until doubled in size.

3 **For the filling**, heat the oil in a frying pan, add the salt and black pepper, then add the onions and fry on a medium heat for 10 minutes, or until golden. Stir in the remaining ingredients and fry for 2–4 minutes, or until dark and sticky.

4 **Turn the dough out** on to a floured surface and knead briefly. Press out to a large rectangle, then spread with the filling. Fold the shorter sides in, then fold the bottom third up, and the top third down, like an envelope. Press gently then turn over and lift on to a lightly floured baking tray, and shape the ends of the loaf into slight points. Cover loosely and leave for 30 minutes, or until doubled in size. Preheat the oven to 220°C (425°F/Gas 7).

5 **Brush the dough** with beaten egg, sprinkle with flour, then slash it with a sharp knife to reveal the filling inside. Sprinkle with the rosemary rubbed in oil, then bake for 20 minutes. Reduce the oven to 200°C (400°F/Gas 6) and bake for 20 minutes, or until the bread is risen and a deep golden brown.

Wholemeal Rolls

Ideal with lunch or dinner

🍴 makes 16

🕐 prep 20–25 mins, plus rising • cook 15–20 mins

225g (8oz) strong white flour

225g (8oz) strong wholemeal flour

7g sachet fast-action dried yeast

1 tsp salt

1 tbsp sunflower oil

1 tbsp honey

200ml (7fl oz) tepid milk

1 egg, beaten

oats, to sprinkle

1 **Mix the flours**, yeast, and salt in a large bowl. Add the oil, honey, milk, and 150ml (5fl oz) tepid water, and mix to form a slightly sticky dough.

2 **Knead the dough** for 10 minutes, or until no longer sticky. Shape into a ball, then place in an oiled bowl. Cover loosely with oiled cling film and leave in a warm place for 1 hour, or until doubled in size.

3 **Knead the dough** lightly. Divide into 16 pieces and roll each into a ball, place on an oiled baking tray. Cover loosely with oiled cling film and leave for 30 minutes, or until doubled in size. Preheat the oven to 200°C (400°F/Gas 6).

4 **Brush the rolls** with beaten egg, and scatter a few oats on the top. Bake for 15–20 minutes, or until they sound hollow when tapped on the base. Cool on a wire rack.

English Muffins

A soft traditional English bread, great for brunch

🍴 makes 10

🕐 prep 25–30 mins, plus rising • cook 50 mins

450g (1lb) strong white flour

1 tsp fast-action dried yeast

1 tsp salt

25g (scant 1oz) butter, melted

25g (scant 1oz) ground rice or semolina

1 **Mix the flour**, yeast, and salt in a large bowl. Add the melted butter and 300ml (10fl oz) tepid water and mix to a soft pliable dough.

2 **Knead the dough** for 5 minutes. Shape into a ball and place in a large oiled bowl. Cover loosely with oiled cling film and leave in a warm place for 1 hour, or until doubled in size. Lay a tea towel on a tray and scatter with most of the ground rice.

3 **Turn out the dough**, knead briefly, and divide into 10 balls. Place on the tea towel and press into flattish rounds. Sprinkle with the rest of the ground rice and cover with another tea towel. Leave for 20–30 minutes, or until risen.

4 **Heat a large** lidded frying pan and cook the muffins in batches. Cover with the lid and cook very gently for 10–12 minutes, or until they puff up and the undersides are golden and toasted. Turn over and cook for 3–4 minutes, or until golden underneath. Cool on a wire rack.

Spiced Fruit Buns

These delicious sweetened rolls make a perfect afternoon snack

 makes 12

prep 30 mins, plus rising
• cook 15 mins

500g (1lb 2oz) **strong white bread flour**

7g sachet **fast-action dried yeast**

1 tsp **mixed spice**

½ tsp **ground nutmeg**

1 tsp **salt**

6 tbsp **caster sugar**

60g (2oz) **butter**

240ml (8fl oz) tepid **milk**

150g (5½oz) **mixed dried fruit**

2 tbsp **icing sugar**

¼ tsp **pure vanilla extract**

1 **Place the flour**, yeast, spices, salt, and caster sugar in a large mixing bowl. Rub in the butter. Add enough milk to form a soft pliable dough. Knead well for 10 minutes. Shape into a ball, then place in a lightly oiled bowl and cover loosely. Leave in a warm place to rise for 1 hour.

2 **Tip the dough** on to a lightly floured work surface and knead gently. Knead in the dried fruit. Divide the dough into 12 pieces, roll into balls, and place, well spaced, on lightly greased baking trays. Cover loosely and place in a warm place for 30 minutes, or until doubled in size.

3 **Preheat the oven** to 200°C (400°F/Gas 6). Bake for 15 minutes, or until the buns sound hollow when tapped on the bottom. Transfer to a wire rack to cool. While the buns are still hot, combine the icing sugar, vanilla essence, and 1 tbsp cold water, and brush over the top of the buns to glaze.

VARIATION

Maple and Pecan Buns

Replace the sugar with 3 tbsp maple syrup, and the fruit with 115g (4oz) chopped pecan nuts.

Rye Bread

Breads made with rye flour are very popular in central and eastern Europe

makes 1 large loaf

prep 25 mins, plus rising
• cook 40-50 mins

For the starter

150g (5½oz) rye flour

150g (5½oz) pot **live natural yogurt**

1 tsp **fast-action dried yeast**

1 tbsp **black treacle**

1 tsp **caraway seeds**, lightly crushed

For the dough

150g (5½oz) **rye flour**

200g (7oz) **strong white flour**, plus extra for dusting

2 tsp **salt**

1 **egg**, beaten

1 tsp **caraway seeds**, to decorate

● **Prepare ahead** The starter must be made the day before you want to make the loaf.

1 **Mix all of the starter** ingredients together with 250ml (8fl oz) tepid water. Cover and leave overnight, until bubbling.

2 **The next day**, mix the flours together with the salt, then stir into the starter. Mix to make a dough, adding a little extra water if required.

3 **Turn out on to** a lightly floured surface and knead the dough for 5-10 minutes, or until smooth and springy. Shape into a ball, put into an oiled bowl and cover loosely with oiled cling film. Leave in a warm place for 1 hour, or until doubled in size.

4 **Flour a baking tray**. Lightly knead the dough again, then form it into a rugby-ball shape. Lift onto the tray, re-cover it loosely, and leave to rise again for another 30 minutes. Preheat the oven to 220°C (425°F/Gas 7).

5 **Brush the dough** with the egg, sprinkle with the caraway seeds, and slash the loaf along its length with a sharp knife. Bake for 20 minutes, then reduce the heat to 200°C (400°F/Gas 6) and bake for another 20-30 minutes, or until dark golden with a hard shiny crust. Cool on a wire rack.

● **Good with** smoked salmon and pickles.

Cheesy Garlic Roll

A fabulous savoury loaf to serve with salads or casual suppers

 makes 1 loaf

🕐 prep 30 mins, plus rising
• cook 40–45 mins

500g (1lb 2oz) **strong white flour**

1½ tsp **salt**

1 tbsp **sugar**

7g sachet **fast-action dried yeast**

2 tbsp **olive oil**

15g (½oz) **butter**, melted

For the filling

8 **spring onions**, sliced

4 **garlic cloves**, chopped

8 **basil leaves**, shredded

200g (7oz) **mozzarella cheese**, diced or grated

1 Place the flour, salt, sugar, yeast, and olive oil into a large mixing bowl. Add 240ml (8fl oz) tepid water and mix to form a soft pliable dough. Knead well for 10 minutes. Place in a lightly oiled bowl and loosely cover. Leave to rise in a warm place for 1 hour.

2 Turn the dough out on to a lightly floured surface and lightly knead. Roll out to form a 35 x 23cm (14 x 9in) rectangle.

3 Combine all the ingredients for the filling. Spread the mixture over the surface of the dough, leaving a 2.5cm (1in) border along both long edges, and a 5cm (2in) border along one of the short ends.

4 Roll up like a Swiss roll, starting from the other short end. Pinch the ends together to seal in the filling. Place the loaf, seam-side down, on a greased baking tray. Cover loosely with oiled cling film and leave in a warm place for 1 hour, or until doubled in size.

5 Preheat the oven to 200°C (400°F/Gas 6). Bake for 40–45 minutes, or until the loaf is golden and sounds hollow when tapped underneath. Transfer to a wire rack, brush the top with the melted butter while still hot, and allow to cool.

Sesame Seed Buns

These little bread rolls are easy to make and perfect for sandwiches

🍴 makes 8

🕐 prep 30 mins, plus rising
• cook 20 mins

450g (1lb) **strong white flour**

1 tsp **salt**

1 tsp **fast-action dried yeast**

1 tbsp **vegetable oil**, sunflower oil, or light olive oil

1 **egg**, beaten

4 tbsp **sesame seeds**

1 Stir the flour, salt, and yeast together in a large bowl, then make a well in the middle. Pour the oil into 360ml (12fl oz) tepid water, then tip this liquid into the well and quickly stir together. Leave to stand for 10 minutes.

2 Turn the dough out on to a lightly floured surface. Knead, folding it over itself repeatedly using gentle pressure, for 5 minutes, or until it is smooth and springs back when pressed lightly. Shape into a ball by bringing the edges into the middle, then turn into a large oiled bowl, smooth-side up. Cover loosely with oiled cling film and leave in a warm place for 1 hour, or until doubled in size. Meanwhile, lightly dust a large baking tray with flour.

3 When ready, scoop the dough on to a lightly floured surface, dust with a little flour, then knead briefly. Pull the dough into 8 even-sized pieces, then shape into rounds. Place on to the floured baking tray, well spaced apart, then leave for 30 minutes, or until increased in size and pillowy. Preheat the oven to 200°C (400°F/Gas 6).

4 Once risen, brush the buns lightly with beaten egg and sprinkle ½ tbsp sesame seeds over each bun. Bake for 20 minutes, or until golden, risen, and round. Lift off the sheet and cool on a wire rack.

● **Good with** beef burgers and salad for a packed lunch.

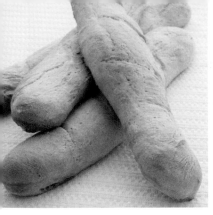

Ficelles

These are very thin baguettes with a light, crisp crust

🍴 makes 4

🕐 prep 15 mins, plus rising • cook 15-20 mins

500g (1lb 2oz) strong plain flour

4 tsp salt

7g sachet fast-action dried yeast

150ml (5fl oz) boiling water

1 Place the flour, 1 tsp of the salt, and the yeast in a bowl. Add 360ml (12fl oz) of tepid water and mix into a dough. Knead the dough on a lightly floured surface for 10 minutes.

2 Divide the dough into 4 and roll each into a 30cm (12in) long baguette shape. Slash diagonally with a sharp knife. Cover loosely and leave in a warm place for 1 hour, or until doubled in size.

3 Preheat the oven to 220°C (425°F/Gas 7). Dissolve the remaining salt in the boiling water. Brush over the loaves and bake for 15-20 minutes, or until they are a light golden colour.

4 Remove from the oven and slide on to a wire rack to cool. Serve warm, with lots of butter.

VARIATION

Seedy Ficelles
Scatter 1-2 tbsp poppy seeds or sesame seeds over the loaves after brushing them with salted water.

Croissants

These may take some time to make, but much of that is taken up chilling the dough and the final result is well worth the effort

🍴 makes 10

🕐 prep 1 hr, plus chilling and rising • cook 20-25 mins

300g (10oz) strong white flour

1 tsp salt

30g (1oz) sugar

7g sachet fast-action dried yeast

250g (9oz) butter, chilled

1 egg, beaten

⬤ **Prepare ahead** Start these the day before you want to eat them.

1 Place the flour, salt, sugar, and yeast in a large bowl. Using a table knife, slowly mix in enough water to form a soft dough. Knead on a lightly floured surface until the dough becomes more elastic. Place back in the bowl, cover with lightly oiled cling film, and chill for 1 hour.

2 Roll out a rectangle that measures 30 x 15cm (12 x 6in). Squash the butter, keeping the pat shape, until it is 1cm (½in) thick. The butter will make a smaller rectangle than the dough. If the butter has become too warm, chill it briefly. Place the butter in the centre of the dough. Fold the dough over so the butter is encased, and chill for 1 hour.

3 Roll out the dough on a lightly floured surface to a 30 x 15cm (12 x 6in) rectangle. Fold the right third over to the centre, then fold the left third over the top so you have 3 layers to your dough. Chill for 1 hour, until firm.

4 Repeat the folding and chilling process twice more, then wrap in cling film and chill overnight.

5 The next day, roll out the dough on a lightly floured surface to a 3mm (⅛in) thick square. Cut into 10 x 10cm (4 x 4in) squares, then cut diagonally to make triangles of dough. Holding the points at either end of the longer lengths, roll the dough towards you, pulling the points gently. The end points should not fold underneath the croissants; if they do, reshape them, rolling more loosely. Place on oiled baking trays, leaving plenty of space between each, and curve them into crescent shapes. Cover with lightly oiled cling film and leave for 1 hour, or until doubled in size but keeping their shape.

6 Preheat the oven to 240°C (475°F/Gas 9). Brush the croissants with the beaten egg and bake for 10 minutes, then reduce the oven temperature to 190°C (375°F/Gas 5) and bake for 10-15 minutes, or until golden brown. Cool on a wire rack.

Ham Croissants

Easy croissants made with ready-made dough

🍴 makes 6

🕐 prep 10 mins • cook 10-12 mins

250g can croissant dough, chilled

1 tsp clear honey

2 tbsp wholegrain mustard

salt and freshly ground black pepper

6 slices cooked ham

1 small egg, beaten

1 Preheat the oven to 200°C (400°F/Gas 6). Unroll the croissant dough and separate out the triangles.

2 In a small bowl, mix together the honey and mustard, and season to taste with salt and pepper. Spread over the croissant triangles.

3 Lay a slice of ham over each triangle. Don't worry too much if it doesn't fit the triangle, as the dough will expand during baking. Roll up each triangle, from its short side up towards the point.

4 Place on to a lightly greased baking tray, well spaced, and glaze the dough with the beaten egg.

5 Bake for 10-12 mins, or until the croissants are puffed up and golden. Serve immediately.

Buttermilk Biscuits

These are favourites from the American South and are best served straight from the oven

 makes 8–10

 prep 12 mins • cook 15 mins

 5.5cm (2⅓in) round biscuit cutter

500g (1lb 2oz) **strong white bread flour**, plus extra for dusting

1½ tsp **fast-action dried yeast**

1 tsp **caster sugar**

1½ tsp **salt**

45g (1½oz) **butter**

150ml (5fl oz) **full-fat milk**

1 Mix together the flour and dried yeast in a large bowl, then add the sugar and salt. Rub in the butter until well blended. Make a well in the centre and pour in the milk and 150ml (5fl oz) lukewarm water. Using a wooden spoon or mixer with a kneading hook, start mixing gently to combine. Knead for 5 minutes, or until it forms a smooth dough. Cover with a tea towel and put the dough in a warm place for 1 hour, or until it has doubled in size.

2 Dust the work surface with flour and knead the dough briefly until smooth. Divide it into 8 equal pieces and roll each piece out into a flat round shape 10cm (4in) in diameter. Lightly flour 2 large baking trays and place 4 dough rounds on each.

3 Preheat the oven to 220°C (425°F/Gas 7). Meanwhile, push the handle of a wooden spoon into the centre of each round, wiggling it to make a small hole. Prick the dough lightly with a fork, then cover with oiled cling film and leave in a warm place for about 20 minutes, or until slightly risen and puffy.

4 Bake for 12–15 minutes, or until risen and lightly golden. Carefully transfer the breads to a wire rack to cool.

● **Good with** sweet or savoury fillings when split through the middle.

● **Leftovers** can be made into breadcrumbs for stuffings or toppings. They are also great for making bread and butter pudding.

Irish Soda Bread

A traditional yeast-free bread. In baking, buttermilk produces a lighter texture than plain milk

 makes 1 loaf

prep 10 mins • cook 30–35 mins

450g (1lb) **strong white bread flour**, plus extra for dusting

2 tsp **bicarbonate of soda**

2 tsp **cream of tartar**

1 tsp **salt**

60g (2oz) **butter** or lard, diced

300ml (10fl oz) **buttermilk**

1 Preheat the oven to 220°C (425°F/Gas 7) and flour a baking tray. Sift the flour, bicarbonate of soda, cream of tartar, and salt into a mixing bowl and stir together. Add the butter and rub in with your fingertips to form fine crumbs.

2 Make a well in the centre of the dry ingredients. Pour in the buttermilk, then mix to form a soft dough. Tip the dough on to a lightly floured work surface and knead lightly, then shape into a ball and roll around to smooth the surface.

3 Place the ball on the prepared baking tray, flatten slightly, and very lightly dust with flour. Use a floured knife to cut into 6 sections without cutting all the way through the dough.

4 Bake for 30–35 minutes, or until the bread is well risen, golden brown, and sounds hollow when tapped on the bottom. Transfer to a wire rack and leave to cool.

● **Good with** a bowl of hot soup or with a wedge of good farmhouse cheese and cooked ham.

● **Leftovers** will become dry after a day, but make good toast and croutons for soup. Or, make breadcrumbs for using in other dishes, and freeze until needed.

VARIATION

Brown Irish Soda Bread
Replace all or half of the white flour with wholemeal flour.

BUTTERMILK
Look for buttermilk in the dairy cabinets, or make your own by stirring 1 tbsp lemon juice or distilled vinegar into 250ml (8fl oz) milk and leaving it to stand for 5 minutes.

Potato Scones

A cross between a pancake and a potato cake, these are popular in Scotland, where they are known as tattie scones

🍴 makes 8

🕐 prep 30 mins • cook 8–10 mins

❄ freeze layered between sheets of greaseproof paper for up to 6 months

450g (1lb) **floury potatoes**, peeled, diced, and boiled until tender

salt

50g (1¾oz) **self-raising flour**, plus extra for dusting

vegetable oil

1 Pat the potatoes dry and place in a pan or bowl. Mash well using a potato masher, or process them through a ricer, if you have one, for a finer texture.

2 While the mash is still warm, add a pinch of salt, sieve in the flour and gently work it into the potato using a wooden spoon. The mixture should form a pliable dough.

3 Turn on to a lightly floured work surface and knead gently until smooth. Roll the dough into a 20cm (8in) square. Cut this into quarters and then cut each on the diagonal to form 2 triangles.

4 Brush a griddle pan lightly with oil and heat until hot. Cook the scones in 2 batches for 2 minutes on each side, or until lightly golden. Keep warm while cooking the remaining scones. Best served warm.

⬤ **Good with** soft garlic-and-herb cheese and a chive garnish or butter and jam. Also good in place of rice or mashed potato, as part of a meal. Makes a hearty accompaniment to soups and stews.

VARIATION

Onion and Herb Potato Scones

Make the recipe as above but, before you roll out the dough, knead in 1 small onion, finely chopped, and a small handful of thyme leaves (removed from the stalks). Complete the recipe as above.

Scotch Pancakes

These thick little pancakes are also called drop scones because the batter is dropped on to a frying pan

🍴 makes 12

🕐 prep 10 mins • cook 15 mins

❄ freeze for up to 1 month

225g (8oz) **plain white flour**

4 tsp **baking powder**

1 large **egg**

2 tsp **golden syrup**

200ml (7fl oz) **milk**

vegetable oil

1 Place the griddle pan over a medium heat. Fold a tea towel in half and lay it on a baking tray.

2 Sift the flour and baking powder into a bowl; make a well in the centre and add the egg, golden syrup, and milk. Whisk well to make a smooth batter the consistency of thick cream. If the mixture is too thick, beat in a little more milk.

3 Test that the griddle pan is hot enough by sprinkling a little flour on to the hot surface; it should slowly brown. If it burns, the pan is too hot and needs to cool a little. When the temperature is right, carefully dust off the flour and rub a piece of kitchen towel dipped in cooking oil lightly over the surface. Use oven gloves to protect your hands.

4 Lift out 1 tbsp of batter, cleaning the back of the spoon on the edge of the bowl. Drop the batter from the tip of the spoon on to the hot pan to make a nice round shape. Repeat, leaving enough room between the rounds for the pancakes to rise and spread.

5 Bubbles will appear on the surface of the pancakes. When they begin to burst, ease a palette knife underneath the pancakes and gently flip to cook the other side. To ensure even browning, lightly press the flat blade on the cooked side after you have turned the pancake; place cooked pancakes inside the folded towel to keep them soft while you fry the rest of the batch.

6 Oil the hot pan after each batch and watch the heat. If the pancakes are pale and take a long time to cook, turn up the heat. If they brown too quickly on the outside and are still raw in the middle, reduce the heat. They are best eaten freshly baked and warm.

Chapatis

In India, these flat, unleavened breads would be cooked in a concave pan called a *tava* but a cast-iron frying pan works well

🍴 makes 8

🕐 prep 30 mins, plus resting • cook 10 mins

⊙ tava or heavy cast-iron frying pan

250g (9oz) **chapati flour** or wholemeal plain flour, plus extra for dusting

1 tsp **salt**

ghee or melted butter

1 Sift the flour into a bowl and discard any bran left in the sieve. Make a well in the centre, add 40ml (3tbsp) cold water and mix together. Work in the salt, then add another 60ml (2fl oz) cold water and mix until the dough starts to come together.

2 Gradually add another 60ml (2fl oz) cold water to make a sticky dough. Keep kneading the dough in the bowl until it is firm, elastic, and less sticky.

3 Cover with a tea towel and leave to rest for 15 minutes, or until the dough becomes firmer, and no longer sticky.

4 Dust your hands with flour and pull off egg-sized pieces of dough. Shape into balls, then roll out into rounds 18cm (7in) in diameter.

5 Heat the ungreased frying pan and cook the chapatis for 30 seconds on each side, or until golden and speckled. Remove from the pan, brush with ghee or melted butter, keeping them warm as you cook the rest.

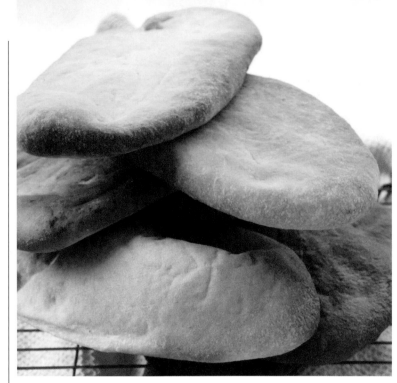

Pitta Bread

These Middle Eastern flat breads, best served warm, are essential for serving with salads and dips, such as hummus

🍴 makes 8

🕐 prep 20 mins, plus resting • cook 10 mins

❄ freeze, cooled and wrapped, for up to 3 months

500g (1lb 2oz) **strong white bread flour**, plus extra for dusting

1 tsp **fast-action dried yeast**

1 tsp **caster sugar**

1 tsp **salt**

4 tbsp **olive oil**, plus extra for greasing

1 Mix together the first 4 ingredients in a large bowl. Make a well in the centre and add 4 tbsp olive oil and 300ml (10fl oz) lukewarm water. Using a wooden spoon, start mixing gently to combine the ingredients and then mix and knead together for 5 minutes, or until it forms a smooth dough. Cover with a tea towel and put the dough in a warm place for 1 hour, or until it has doubled in size.

2 Dust the work surface with flour and knead the dough briefly until smooth. Divide into 8 equal pieces and roll each out into a thin oval shape, about 20cm (8in) long. Grease 2 large baking trays and place 4 dough ovals on each. Cover with oiled cling film and leave in a warm place for 20 minutes, or until the dough is slightly risen.

3 Preheat the oven to 220°C (425°F/Gas 7). Brush the tops with a little olive oil and bake for 10 minutes, or until puffed and golden brown.

4 Carefully transfer to a wire rack and serve while still warm.

⬤ **Good with** dips and salads or split and filled with shredded lettuce and your favourite sandwich filling.

VARIATION

Spiced Pittas

Before baking, sprinkle with lightly crushed coriander, cumin, or fennel seeds for a fragrant version, or add 2 tbsp toasted sesame seeds to the dough before rising.

Wholewheat Pooris

These deep-fried puffed Indian breads are ideal served with curries; chapati flour is available from Asian shops

🍴 makes 8

🕐 prep 15 mins, plus standing • cook 16 mins

250g (9oz) **wholewheat chapati flour** or plain wholemeal flour

1 tsp **salt**

½ tsp **caster sugar**

1 tsp **black onion seeds**

½ tsp **cumin seeds**

2 tsp **ghee**

vegetable oil, for deep-frying

● **Prepare ahead** The dough can be made up to 4 hours in advance, ready to be rolled out and deep-fried just before serving.

1 **Place the flour**, salt, sugar, onion seeds, and cumin seeds in a large mixing bowl and mix together, then add the ghee and rub in with your fingertips.

2 **Gradually add** 120ml (4fl oz) cold water and mix to make a stiff dough. Knead until smooth, then wrap in cling film and leave to rest for at least 30 minutes.

3 **Divide the dough** into 8 equal pieces and roll into balls. Heat the oil to 180°C (350°F).

4 **Roll each piece** of dough into a 12.5cm (5in) round and deep-fry each for 2 minutes or until puffed up, crisp, and golden on both sides. Drain on kitchen paper and serve hot.

● **Good with** all kinds of curries and spicy dishes.

Naan Bread

This familiar Indian flat bread is traditionally cooked in a tandoor oven but this recipe uses a conventional oven

🍴 makes 4

🕐 prep 20 mins, plus resting • cook 9 mins

❄ freeze, cooled and wrapped, for up to 3 months

500g (1lb 2oz) **strong white bread flour**, plus extra for dusting

1¼ tsp **fast-action dried yeast**

1 tsp **caster sugar**

1½ tsp **salt**

2 tsp **black onion seeds**

100ml (3½fl oz) **full-fat plain yogurt**

50g (2oz) **ghee** or butter, melted

1 **Mix together** the flour and the yeast in a large bowl, then add the sugar, salt, and onion seeds.

2 **Make a well** in the centre of the dry ingredients and add 200ml (7fl oz) lukewarm water, the yogurt, and the melted ghee. Using a wooden spoon, start mixing gently to combine the ingredients for 5 minutes, or until it forms a smooth dough. Cover with a tea towel and put it in a warm place for 1 hour, or until it has doubled in size.

3 **Preheat the oven** to its hottest setting and place 2 large baking trays in the oven. Dust the work surface with flour and knead the dough briefly until smooth. Divide into 4 equal pieces and roll each piece into an oval shape about 24cm (10in) long.

4 **Carefully transfer** the breads on to the preheated baking trays and cook in the oven for 6–7 minutes, or until well puffed.

5 **Meanwhile**, preheat the grill to its hottest setting. Transfer the breads to the grill pan and cook them for 30–40 seconds on each side, or until they brown and blister; take care not to put the breads too close to the heat source, otherwise they may catch and burn.

6 **Carefully transfer** to a wire rack and serve while still warm.

Grissini

Baked until dry, these Italian-style bread sticks are often served with antipasti

🍴 makes 20–24

⏱ prep 25 mins, plus rising • cook 10–12 mins

❄ freeze for up to 2 months

250g (9oz) **strong white bread flour**

1 tsp **salt**

1 tsp **sugar**

½ tsp **fast-action dried yeast**

1 tbsp **olive oil**

1 **egg**, beaten, to glaze

sesame seeds, to sprinkle

coarse sea salt, to sprinkle

● **Prepare ahead** The bread sticks will keep for several weeks if stored in an airtight container.

1 Mix the flour, salt, sugar, and yeast together in a large mixing bowl. Add 120ml (4½fl oz) water to mix to form a soft pliable dough. Knead well for 10 minutes. Place in a lightly oiled bowl and loosely cover with oiled cling film. Leave in a warm place to rise for 1 hour.

2 Lightly grease 2 baking trays. Preheat the oven to 220°C (425°F/Gas 7). Transfer the dough to a lightly floured work surface, punch down the dough, and lightly knead. Break off pieces of the dough the size of a walnut and roll each piece into a long stick about the thickness of a pencil. Place slightly spaced on the greased baking trays.

3 Brush the sticks of bread with the beaten egg and sprinkle half with sesame seeds and half with coarse sea salt. Do not leave the dough to rise after shaping. Bake for 12–15 minutes, or until golden and crisp. The sticks should snap easily and not be doughy in the middle.

4 Transfer to a wire rack and leave until completely cooled.

● **Good with** pre-dinner drinks or with dips, such as tomato salsa or soured cream and chive.

Cornbread

A golden quick bread, delicious straight from the oven

🍴 makes 1 loaf

⏱ prep 5 mins • cook 30 mins

🍲 21 x 16cm (8½ x 6½in) ovenproof dish

sunflower oil, for greasing

200g (7oz) **cornmeal** or medium-coarse polenta

75g (2½oz) **plain white flour**

1 tsp **baking powder**

1 tsp **salt**

1½ tbsp **caster sugar**

300ml (10fl oz) **milk**

25g (scant 1oz) **butter**, melted

1 **egg**

1 Preheat the oven to 190°C (375°F/Gas 5). Grease the ovenproof dish with the sunflower oil.

2 Place the cornmeal in a large bowl. Sift the white flour, baking powder, salt, and sugar into the cornmeal and stir together, making a well in the centre. Whisk together the milk, butter, and egg and pour it into the well, mixing to form a batter. Pour the batter into the dish, and smooth the surface.

3 Place the dish in the oven and bake for 25–30 minutes, or until the cornbread is browned around the edges and a skewer inserted into the centre comes out clean.

4 Cut the cornbread into squares and serve warm.

● **Good with** chilli butter.

Easy Flatbread

A simple yeast bread cooked in a frying pan

🍴 makes 8

⏱ prep 10 mins, plus rising • cook 40 mins

500g (1lb 2oz) **strong white flour**

2 tsp **salt**

7g sachet **fast-action dried yeast**

3 tbsp **olive oil**

1 Mix all the ingredients in a large bowl. Add 250–300ml (8–10fl oz) water, or enough to make a soft dough, and knead well. Place in a lightly oiled bowl, cover loosely with oiled cling film, and leave to rise for 45 minutes, or until doubled in size.

2 Turn the dough out on to a lightly floured surface and lightly knead. Divide into 8 equal pieces and flatten each piece to a 1cm (½in) thick circle. Use a rolling pin to flatten them a little more. Place on a lightly floured baking tray for 10 minutes to prove.

3 Heat a large frying pan on a medium heat, then add a flatbread. Fry until brown for 3 minutes, then turn over and fry for another 2 minutes. Set aside on a wire rack while you cook the rest of the batch, then serve.

● **Good with** curries and Moroccan dishes. Alternatively, use as a base for quick, deli-style pizzas, topped with sun-dried tomatoes, olives, and caramelized onions.

Waffles

These easy-to-make waffles are perfect for breakfast, a light snack, or dessert

 makes 6-8

🕐 prep 10 mins
  ● cook 20-25 mins

🗑 waffle maker or waffle iron

❄ freeze for up to 1 month

175g (6oz) **plain flour**

1 tsp **baking powder**

2 tbsp **caster sugar**

300ml (10fl oz) **milk**

75g (2½oz) **butter**, melted

1 tsp **pure vanilla extract**

2 large **eggs**, separated

● **Prepare ahead** Although best eaten as fresh as possible, you can make waffles up to 24 hours in advance and reheat in a toaster.

1 Place the flour, baking powder, and caster sugar in a food processor and process to mix. In a jug, combine the milk, melted butter, vanilla extract, and egg yolks. Pour in and process until just blended. If you do not have a food processor, place the dry ingredients in a bowl, make a well in the centre, and pour in the wet ingredients. Gradually whisk in the flour.

2 Preheat the waffle maker or iron. In a clean large bowl whisk the egg white until standing in soft peaks. Add to the processor or blender, and pulse for 1-2 seconds, or until just combined. Alternatively, fold into the batter with a metal spoon. Do not over-process or you will lose all the air and the waffles will be tough.

3 Preheat the oven to 130°C (250°F/Gas ½). Spoon a small ladleful of the batter on to the hot iron (or the amount recommended by the waffle maker manufacturer) and spread almost to the edge. Close the lid and bake until golden. Serve immediately, or keep warm in a single layer in the oven.

● **Good with** maple syrup, jam, fresh fruit, sweetened cream, or ice cream.

VARIATIONS

Buttermilk Waffles
Substitute buttermilk for the milk and add another 1 tsp baking powder.

Spiced Waffles
Add 2 tsp ground mixed spice to the dried ingredients.

Scones

There is nothing better for afternoon tea than freshly baked crumbly scones

🍴 makes 8

🕐 prep 25 mins
  ● cook 12-15 mins

🗑 7cm (2½in) round pastry cutter

225g (8oz) **self-raising flour**, plus extra for dusting

½ tsp **salt**

50g (1¾oz) **sultanas**

60g (2oz) **butter**, cubed

30g (1oz) **sugar**

150ml (5fl oz) **milk**

1 **egg**, beaten

1 Preheat the oven to 220°C (425°F/Gas 7). Sift the flour and the salt into a large mixing bowl, then add the sultanas and mix together. Rub in the butter with your fingertips, until the mixture resembles coarse breadcrumbs, then mix in the sugar. Make a well in the centre and pour in the milk, then stir together, bringing in the flour from the edges, with a knife or spoon.

2 Turn the soft, sticky dough on to a lightly floured work surface. Knead until smooth, then shape into a 2.5cm (1in) thick circle.

3 Dip the cutter in flour, then use to cut rounds from the dough. Re-form, if necessary, to cut sufficient scones.

4 Place the scones on a baking tray and brush the tops with a little beaten egg. Put the tray on to the top shelf of the oven and bake for 12-15 minutes, or until golden. Remove from the oven and cool on a wire rack. Serve while still warm.

● **Good with** strawberry or raspberry jam, and double cream.

> ### SHAPING SCONES
> Keep the cutter straight, without twisting it, as you pull it from the dough to ensure evenly baked scones.

Club Sandwich

This hearty sandwich of cooked chicken, bacon, tomatoes, and lettuce is layered between slices of toasted bread and is guaranteed to satisfy those hunger pangs

 serves 4

prep 15 mins, plus marinating • cook 15 mins

1 small **garlic clove**, crushed

1 tsp **dried mixed herbs**

2 tbsp **olive oil**

salt and freshly ground **black pepper**

3 boneless **chicken breasts**

16 **streaky bacon rashers**

12 slices of **white bread**

4 tbsp **mayonnaise**

1 tsp **wholegrain mustard**

butter, for spreading

4 ripe **tomatoes**, sliced

2 **Little Gem lettuces**, shredded

8 **cornichons**

● **Prepare ahead** Steps 1 and 5 can be made several hours in advance.

1 In a bowl mix together the garlic, herbs, and 1 tbsp of the olive oil. Season to taste with salt and pepper. Toss the chicken breasts in the mixture and set aside for at least 30 minutes.

2 Meanwhile, heat a large frying pan and pour in the remaining olive oil. Fry the bacon in batches for 2–3 minutes, or until crisp and golden. Drain on kitchen paper.

3 Using the same frying pan, add the chicken breasts, skin-side down, and cook for 4–5 minutes, or until the skin is nicely golden. Then turn over and cook for a further 4–5 minutes, or until cooked. Set aside on a plate to rest.

4 Meanwhile, toast the slices of bread and lay them out on a large chopping board, ready to start

assembling the sandwich. Remove the crusts, if desired.

5 In a bowl, mix together the mayonnaise and mustard, and season to taste with salt and pepper.

6 Spread the toast with the mustard mayonnaise. Slice the chicken breasts and arrange half of the pieces on 4 of the toast slices. Cut the bacon strips in half and evenly lay half on top of the chicken. Top with tomato slices followed by shredded lettuce. Top with a piece of toast and repeat the filling layer. Finish off by placing the remaining slices of toast on top.

7 Cut each sandwich in half, diagonally. Top with a cornichon

and push a cocktail stick down through the centre of each sandwich to hold it altogether.

● **Good with** gherkins and other pickles on the side.

▶ **VARIATION**

Fish Club Sandwich
Replace the chicken with pan-fried white fish fillets, such as cod or haddock. Use tartare sauce on the toast instead of the mayonnaise.

Smoked Salmon and Cream Cheese Bagels

A big breakfast or an American-style brunch dish for long, lazy Sundays

 serves 4

prep 10 mins

200g (7oz) **cream cheese**

1 tbsp finely chopped **dill**

1 tsp **creamed horseradish**

4 **bagels** (plain, poppy seed, or sesame seed), split in half and toasted

175g (6oz) **smoked salmon**

freshly ground **black pepper**

lemon wedges, to serve

1 In a bowl, mash the cream cheese with the dill and the creamed horseradish.

2 Spread the bottom halves of the bagels with the cream cheese mixture. Then top with the smoked salmon slices.

3 Season with freshly ground black pepper and replace the bagel tops. Serve with lemon wedges to squeeze over the salmon.

Fried Mozzarella Sandwich

Served hot, this is a truly indulgent snack

🍴 serves 4

🕐 prep 10 mins • cook 6 mins

8 slices of **sourdough bread**

olive oil, for drizzling

150g (5½oz) **mozzarella**, sliced

12 **mi-cuit tomatoes**, (roasted, semi-dried) roughly chopped

2 handfuls of **basil**, torn

salt and freshly ground **black pepper**

a handful of **rocket leaves**, to serve (optional)

1 tbsp **balsamic vinegar** (optional)

1 **Lay the slices** of bread on a board and drizzle both sides lightly with olive oil.

2 **Top 4 of the slices** with the mozzarella, tomatoes, and torn basil, and season to taste with salt and pepper.

3 **Top with the remaining** bread slices and squash down with your hands, making sure none of the filling is sticking out.

4 **Heat a large** frying pan and add 1 tbsp of olive oil. Carefully add 2 of the sandwiches and fry for 2–3 minutes, on each side, or until golden. Set aside and keep warm while frying the other 2 sandwiches.

5 **Slice each sandwich** in half and, if liked, serve with wild rocket drizzled with balsamic vinegar.

Pan Bagnat

Popular in the area around Nice in the south of France, this traditional worker's sandwich roughly translates as "wet bread"

🍴 serves 4

🕐 prep 20 mins, plus chilling

4 small, **crusty loaves**, such as half ciabattas or mini baguettes

2 **garlic cloves**, cut in half

2 tbsp **olive oil**

1 tsp **white wine vinegar**

salt and freshly ground **black pepper**

1 hard-boiled **egg**, sliced

2 large or 3 medium **tomatoes**, sliced

¼ **cucumber**, sliced

12 **anchovy fillets**

100g can **tuna**, flaked

½ **green pepper**, deseeded and sliced

2 **spring onions**, sliced

60g (2oz) cooked **green beans**

8 **black olives**, pitted

8 **basil leaves**

● **Prepare ahead** The pan bagnat is best made 1 hour before serving to give the flavours time to develop.

1 **Cut each loaf** in half and scoop out most of the soft crumbs. Rub the insides of the loaves with the cut sides of the garlic cloves, drizzle with the olive oil and vinegar, and season to taste with salt and pepper.

2 **Fill the loaves** with the egg, tomato, cucumber, anchovies, tuna, green pepper, spring onions, green beans, olives, and basil leaves, dividing the filling ingredients evenly between the loaves.

3 **Wrap the loaves** in cling film and chill in the refrigerator for at least 1 hour before serving.

Tuna Melt

An American diner classic, this sandwich appeals to adults and children alike. Serve it with your favourite pickles and relishes

 serves 4

 prep 15 mins • cook 10 mins

4 English muffins

1 tbsp olive oil

2 shallots, finely chopped

1 red pepper, deseeded and finely chopped

4 spring onions, thinly sliced

2 x 185g cans tuna chunks, drained

2 tbsp tomato ketchup or tomato relish

6 tbsp lemon mayonnaise

4 large, thin slices of mature Cheddar cheese or Edam cheese, halved diagonally

● **Prepare ahead** Though the shallots and peppers can be chopped and the spring onions sliced in advance, the tuna melts are best made and served straight away.

1 Heat the grill to high. Split each muffin in half and toast the cut sides.

2 Heat the oil in a frying pan and gently fry the shallot, red pepper and spring onions, stirring frequently, until softened but not browned. Add the tuna, breaking up the chunks with a fork. Cook for 1 minute, or until the tuna is heated through, then remove the pan from the heat and stir in the tomato ketchup or relish and 2 tbsp of the mayonnaise.

3 Spread the remaining mayonnaise over the cut sides of the muffins, spoon the tuna mixture on top, and arrange the cheese triangles over the tuna.

4 Pop under the grill until the cheese melts and top with the muffin "lids". Serve at once.

● **Good with** a selection of your favourite pickles such as pickled cucumbers and sweetcorn relish.

Croque Monsieur

In France, these toasted cheese and ham sandwiches are a popular snack

 serves 4

prep 15 mins • cook 10 mins

400g (14oz) Gruyère cheese, grated

60g (2oz) butter, plus extra for spreading

2 tbsp plain flour

2 tsp Dijon mustard

150ml (5fl oz) milk

8 slices of white sandwich bread

8 thin slices of ham

● **Prepare ahead** Steps 1 and 2 can be completed 1 day in advance but the assembled Croques Monsieur are toasted and eaten straight away.

1 Cut 115g (4oz) of the cheese into thin slices and grate the rest.

2 Melt the butter in a saucepan over a low heat. Remove from the heat and stir in the flour. Return to the hob and cook for 1 minute. Remove from the heat again and stir

in the grated cheese, mustard, and milk. When smooth, set aside until ready to use.

3 Toast 4 of the bread slices on 1 side only. Spread the untoasted sides lightly with butter and top with the ham and cheese slices. Press the remaining 4 slices of bread on top and spread with the cheese mixture.

4 Grill until the cheese is bubbling and golden brown. Serve at once.

● **Good with** a side salad and a portion of French fries for a quick but satisfying lunch.

Croque Madame

Top each toasted sandwich with a fried or poached egg.

Coronation Chicken Rolls

These rolls are synonymous with British summer picnics and garden parties

serves 4

prep 15 mins, plus cooling
• cook 5 mins

1 tbsp **sunflower oil**

1 **shallot**, finely chopped

1 tsp **curry paste** (either mild or hot, according to taste)

1 tbsp **tomato purée**

dash of **Worcestershire sauce**

115g (4oz) **mayonnaise**

6 **apricot halves** canned in fruit juice, drained

350g (12oz) **cooked chicken**, chopped or shredded into small bite-size pieces

8 **bridge rolls**, split and spread with butter or left plain as preferred

2 tbsp chopped **parsley**

● **Prepare ahead** The filling can be made 1 day in advance, then spooned on to the bridge rolls up to 1–2 hours before serving.

1 Heat the oil in a small pan and fry the shallot until softened but not browned. Add the curry paste, cook for 1 minute over a low heat, and then stir in the tomato purée and Worcestershire sauce. Remove from the heat and set aside to cool.

2 Place the onion mixture, mayonnaise, and apricot halves in a food processor or blender and process until smooth and creamy. Transfer to a bowl and stir in the chicken. Cover and chill until needed.

3 To serve, pile on to the bridge rolls and sprinkle with the chopped fresh parsley.

VARIATION

Egg Mayonnaise Rolls

Mix 4 chopped, hard-boiled eggs with the mayonnaise mixture or substitute a plain mayonnaise, if preferred. Make up the rolls, adding watercress leaves or mustard and cress.

Cucumber Sandwiches

These traditional dainty sandwiches are an essential part of an English tea party

serves 4

prep 15 mins, plus standing

1 **cucumber**, peeled

½ tsp **salt**

2 tsp **white wine vinegar**

8 thin slices of **white bread**

butter, softened for spreading

freshly ground **black pepper**

1 punnet of **mustard and cress**, snipped, for garnishing

● **Prepare ahead** Step 1 can be completed 1 hour in advance, and the cucumber slices kept covered in the refrigerator.

1 Using a sharp knife, carefully slice the cucumber into thin slices, no thicker than 3mm (⅛in) for each slice. Place the slices in a colander or sieve and sprinkle with the salt. Leave the colander to sit over a plate for 20–30 minutes to allow the excess water to drain out of the cucumber slices. When ready to use, sprinkle the slices with the vinegar.

2 Spread each slice of bread with the softened butter. Place the cucumber in an even layer over four of the bread slices. Grind with some black pepper then top with the remaining bread.

3 Cut off the crusts, then cut each sandwich into squares, triangles or fingers. Arrange the sandwiches on a serving plate and sprinkle with mustard and cress. Serve at once.

VARIATION

Cheese and Cucumber Sandwiches

Spread the bread with cream cheese instead of butter.

Sandwiches

When you are in a hurry for good food fast, make a sandwich. Be it for lunch, supper, a snack, or even breakfast, there are many types of sandwiches to choose from. Let your creativity run wild, and see what fantastic flavour combinations you can come up with.

Types of Sandwiches

The great thing about making sandwiches is that there are no rules. You can make them hot or cold, light and delicate, or hearty and filling. Place roasted vegetables inside a wholegrain pitta with fresh goat's cheese, or fill a crusty baguette with sliced duck breast and a sweet fruit preserve. When in need of inspiration, go back to the classics like a sliced bread sandwich (below).

Open-faced Sandwiches
Originally from Scandinavia, these are unique among sandwiches in that they are made with 1 slice of bread. Use a dense bread, such as pumpernickle, so you can pick it up easily.

Tips for Take-away

- Keep sandwiches fresh by wrapping them in paper, foil, or plastic bags as soon as they are assembled.
- Use crisp lettuce leaves to act as a barrier between the bread and watery ingredients, such as tomatoes.
- Never leave sandwiches with meat, poultry, or dairy fillings unrefrigerated for more than 2 hours.

Heros
Also called hogies, grinders, subs, and poor boys, these 2-handed sandwiches are small Italian or French loaves stuffed with a selection of thinly sliced meats, vegetables, and pickles.

TYPES OF BREAD

Great bread makes a great sandwich. Branch out from traditional sliced white bread, and try one of these:

Baguettes The versatile French favourite.

Sourdough Made popular in San Francisco, perfect with seafood, cheese, or pâtés.

Pitta Greek pockets, ideal for filling with a variety of salads.

Ciabatta Individual-sized Italian loaves make lovely paninis.

Mixed-grain Dense and chewy, ideal to balance cured meats, smoked fish, and richly flavoured spreads.

Paninis
Often made with ciabatta bread, paninis are toasted sandwiches from Italy. Add a quick-melting cheese for extra flavour.

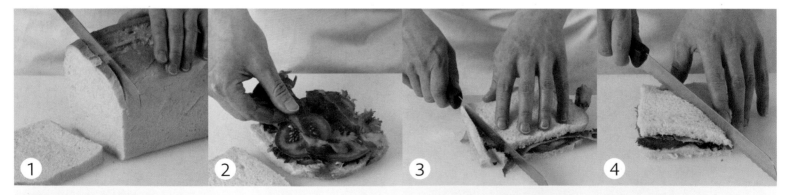

Sliced Bread Sandwich

1 **If you are using** an unsliced loaf, hold it firmly with one hand, while using a sawing motion with a serrated bread knife to cut 2 equal-sized slices. Spread one slice of bread with mayonnaise.

2 **Grill bacon rashers** until crisp, then leave on kitchen paper to drain. Place lettuce leaves on one slice of bread, then add tomato slices and bacon.

3 **Spread mayonnaise** on the second slice and place on top. Using the bread knife, carefully remove the crusts from the sandwich, while holding the stack firmly with your other hand.

4 **Cut the sandwich** diagonally into equal halves using the bread knife.

making & toasting sandwiches

Toasted Sandwich

1 **Butter both sides** of 2 slices of bread and add cheese, tomato slices, and basil leaves. Top with the second slice of bread.

2 **Heat a frying pan** over a medium-high heat. Add the sandwich and toast the first side for 2–3 minutes, or until the underside is toasted.

3 **Using a spatula**, turn the sandwich over to cook the second side for 2–3 minutes, or until the bread is toasted and the cheese is melted.

4 **Carefully remove** the toasted sandwich, place it on a cutting board, and use a bread knife to cut it in half.

Thin Layered Sandwich

1 **To cut thin slices** without tearing the bread, spread cream cheese over the end of an un-cut loaf, before slicing with a bread knife.

2 **Place a slice of bread** on the work surface and cover with smoked salmon. Sprinkle with snipped chives, then top with the second slice of bread, cream-cheese-side down. Repeat for the remaining sandwiches.

3 **Stack 2 sandwiches** on top of each other on a cutting board. Using the bread knife, cut the crusts off the sandwiches, holding the stack firmly with your other hand.

4 **Using the bread knife**, cut the stack of sandwiches in half diagonally, then cut in half again to make triangles.

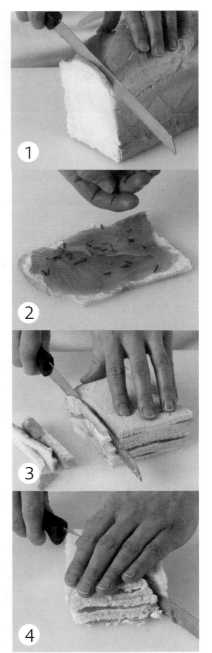

Alternatively...

You can also make tempting toasted cheese sandwiches by using the grill or a sandwich maker. Preheat the grill to its highest setting, then toast the sandwich on both sides until golden brown and the cheese has melted. Or, make your sandwich using an electric sandwich maker, following the manufacturer's instructions.

Alternatively...

To make party pinwheels, cover each bread slice with the smoked salmon and chives, then cut off and discard the crusts. Tightly roll each Swiss-roll style. Wrap each roll tightly in cling film, twisting the ends, and chill for up to a day. When ready to serve, unwrap each roll, and use a bread knife to cut into 5mm (¼in) slices.

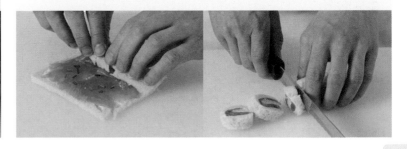

Sandwiches

Cheese and Chutney

Try these ingredients on toasted slices of crusty baguette.

Cheddar cheese, sliced

apple chutney

butter, softened

Avocado and Bacon

Use granary or mixed-grain bread. Spread both slices of bread with mayonnaise, then top one with the lettuce, avocado, and bacon. Place the second slice spread-side down, and press the sandwich together.

mayonnaise

cos lettuce leaves

avocado, peeled, stone removed, and sliced

streaky bacon rashers, cooked until crisp, and drained well

Hummus Special

Spread wholemeal slices of bread with hummus, then top with the vegetables, lettuce, and a second slice of bread.

hummus

red pepper, sliced

carrot, grated

tomatoes, sliced

mixed salad leaves

Toasted Fish

Split open a soft bun, spread with tartare sauce, and add the lettuce leaves. Top with the hot fish fingers, then slices of cheese. Add the top of the bun and press together.

tartare sauce

cos lettuce leaves, shredded

fish fingers, cooked

Cheddar cheese, sliced

Ham and Cheese

For a French classic, split open and butter a baguette, then add the ham and cheese.

Parma ham, sliced

Emmental cheese, sliced

butter, softened

Mediterranean Aubergine Panini

Slice a large piece of ciabatta bread in half. Spread with the pesto sauce, then add the aubergine, tomato, cheese, and rocket leaves. Top with the second half of ciabatta, and toast under a grill.

pesto sauce

grilled aubergine, sliced

tomatoes, sliced

provolone cheese, sliced

rocket leaves

Pâté Tartine

Spread a toasted slice of sourdough bread with pâté, then top with sliced gherkins.

chicken liver pâté

gherkins, sliced

Tuna-sweetcorn

Put the tuna in a bowl and stir in the mayonnaise. Add the sweetcorn and parsley, and season to taste with salt and freshly ground pepper. Spread onto wholemeal bread, then top with a second slice of bread.

canned tuna, drained and flaked

mayonnaise

canned sweetcorn, drained

chopped fresh parsley

salt and pepper

Mozzarella Panini

Cut open ciabatta bread and brush with oil. Add the remaining ingredients and toast.

olive oil

mozzarella cheese, sliced

sun-dried tomatoes

basil leaves

Greek Pockets

Toast wholemeal pitta bread, then split open, and add the fillings.

leftover cooked lamb

feta cheese, crumbled

red pepper, diced

cucumber, diced

All-day Breakfast

Toast a soft roll, then add the eggs, sausages, and tomato.

scrambled eggs

grilled sausages, sliced

tomato, sliced

Chicken Wrap

Mix the yogurt with the lime zest, and spread over a soft flour tortilla. Add the other ingredients and tightly roll the tortilla.

thick yogurt

zest of lime

roasted chicken, sliced

cucumber, sliced

rocket leaves

STACKS OF SANDWICHES
For a meal on the run it's hard to beat a simple but nutritious sandwich. With endless combinations of breads and fillings (see left), the choice is yours.

Tomato and Pepper Focaccia

Filled with classic Italian flavours, this vegetarian sandwich is savoury and filling

 serves 4

🕐 prep 20 mins, plus cooling
● cook 20 mins

2 orange peppers or yellow peppers

1 large or 2 medium garlic and rosemary focaccia

4 tbsp sun-dried tomato purée

8 plum tomatoes or cherry tomatoes, halved, plus extra to serve

2 tbsp extra virgin olive oil

freshly ground black pepper

225g (8oz) buffalo mozzarella, torn into small pieces

handful of basil leaves, plus extra to serve

1 **Preheat the grill** to its highest setting. Line the grill rack with a sheet of foil and place the peppers on it. Grill until their skins scorch and blacken, turning them regularly so they char evenly.

2 **Seal the peppers** in a plastic bag, allowing the steam to loosen the skins. When the peppers are cool enough to handle, remove the stalks from the peppers, peel away their skins, remove the seeds, and cut the flesh into thick strips.

3 **If using a large focaccia**, slice it in half through the centre, then across into 4 equal pieces. If using 2 medium focaccia, cut through the centre of each, then across in half. Toast the bread lightly on both sides and spread the cut sides with the sun-dried tomato purée.

4 **Line the grill rack** with foil, place the tomato halves on it, cut-sides up, and drizzle with the olive oil. Season to taste with black pepper and grill for 5 minutes, or until the tomatoes have softened but are not falling apart.

5 **Arrange the tomato halves** and pepper slices on the focaccia bases. Top with the mozzarella and a few basil leaves, whole or torn, and drizzle over any oil and juices from the grill rack. Place the remaining focaccia halves on top and serve with extra tomatoes and basil alongside.

TIME SAVER

If you are short of time, buy roasted peppers from the deli counter of your local supermarket rather than grilling your own.

BLT

The key to this classic sandwich is good-quality bacon and fresh bread

 serves 4

🕐 prep 10 mins ● cook 10 mins

12 smoked back bacon rashers

8 slices of bread, thickly sliced

butter, for spreading

mayonnaise, for spreading

¼ head of iceberg lettuce, shredded

2 ripe tomatoes, sliced

freshly ground black pepper

1 **Heat a large frying pan** over a high heat then add the bacon, reduce the heat to medium, and fry for 4–6 minutes, or until crisp, turning once. Drain on kitchen paper.

2 **Lightly toast the bread** on both sides.

3 **To assemble the sandwich**, spread each slice of bread with a little butter, then spread 4 slices with mayonnaise. Top with a little lettuce, followed by 3 rashers of bacon, a little more lettuce, and tomato slices. Season to taste with pepper, then place the remaining buttered bread slices on top and cut each sandwich in half. Secure with a cocktail stick, and serve at once.

Quesadillas with Salsa Mexicana

Traditionally, quesadillas are made with uncooked tortillas, stuffed with cheese, then folded, and deep-fried

 serves 8

prep 10 mins • cook 20 mins

8 flour tortillas

200g (7oz) mature Cheddar cheese, grated

guacamole, to serve

For the salsa

2 tomatoes, finely chopped

½ onion, finely chopped

1 green chilli, deseeded and finely chopped

handful of coriander leaves, chopped

1 tsp salt

juice of ½ lime

1 Heat a heavy frying pan over a medium heat. Make the salsa by combining all the ingredients in a bowl, then set aside.

2 Place 1 tortilla flat in the pan and heat for 30 seconds. Flip the tortilla over and sprinkle 25g (scant 1oz) of the cheese over the surface. Fold the tortilla in half over the cheese and press down lightly with a spatula.

3 Flip the quesadilla over, and cook until it is toasted on both sides and the cheese has melted. Repeat with the remaining tortillas.

4 Cut each quesadilla in half, to form triangles, and serve immediately with the Salsa Mexicana and guacamole on the side.

VARIATION

BBQ Chicken and Cheese Quesadillas

Mix 225g (8oz) cooked shredded chicken with 2 tbsp barbecue sauce, then add it with the cheese in step 2. Serve with soured cream instead of guacamole.

Deli Steak Sandwich

Great for lunch, this filling New York-style sandwich will keep you going through the day

 serves 4

 prep 15 mins • cook 10 mins

ridged cast-iron grill pan

4 crusty white rolls or small baguettes, split in half

4 rump steaks or sirloin steaks, 140g (5oz) each

2 tbsp oil

salt and freshly ground black pepper

2 tsp creamed horseradish

115g (4oz) cream cheese

115g (4oz) blue cheese, such as Stilton or Roquefort, crumbled

4 lettuce leaves

2 tomatoes, sliced

1 tbsp American mustard

1 onion, thinly sliced into rings

8 dill pickle slices

1 Heat a ridged cast-iron grill pan until very hot. Lay the cut sides of the bread on the pan and lightly toast them, in batches. Remove the bread from the pan and set aside. Brush the steaks with oil, season to taste with salt and pepper, and cook for 3–4 minutes on each side.

2 Meanwhile, mix together the creamed horseradish, cream cheese, and blue cheese. Spread the mixture on to the toasted sides of the bread, then lay the lettuce leaves and tomato slices on the bottom halves.

3 When the steaks are cooked, divide them between the bread rolls, add a little mustard to each, and pile onion rings and pickle slices on top. Replace the lids, secure with cocktail sticks, and serve.

Open Sandwiches

Reduce your bread intake with these clever single slice ideas

 serves 4

prep 10 mins

12 slices of **bread**, a mixture of white, wholemeal, and granary

2 tbsp **mayonnaise**

2 tsp **Dijon** mustard

To serve

mixed **salad leaves**

cooked peeled **prawns**

3 **ham** slices

1 **egg**, hard-boiled

chargrilled **aubergine**

mozzarella

lemon

tomato

salt and freshly ground **black pepper**

1 **Mix the mayonnaise** and mustard together in a bowl. Cut the egg, aubergine, mozzarella, lemon, and tomato into slices. Lay the bread slices on a board and spread with the mayonnaise.

2 **Top 3 slices of bread** with ham, sliced egg, and a few salad leaves. Divide the prawns between 3 slices with a lettuce leaf and a slice of lemon to squeeze over. Finally, layer the aubergine, mozzarella, and tomato slices and place each stack on the remaining bread slices.

3 **Top with leaves**, season to taste with salt and pepper, then transfer to a serving platter and let everyone help themselves.

Deluxe Peanut Butter Sandwiches

This "dressed-up" version of the popular peanut and jelly sandwich makes a nutritious, delicious snack

🍴 serves 4

🕐 prep 10 mins

115g (4oz) creamy or chunky **peanut butter**

2 tbsp orange **marmalade**

3 ripe **bananas**

8 slices **wholegrain bread**, toasted

1 **In a small bowl**, combine the peanut butter and marmalade until well mixed. Peel the bananas and cut them in half lengthways; then cut each half into 2 slices.

2 **Spread the peanut butter** equally over 4 slices of toast. Top with banana slices, then the second piece of toast.

3 **Cut each sandwich** in half diagonally, if you like.

● **Good with** slices of sweet apple or pear.

Reuben Sandwich

An all-time favourite of New York delicatessens, this sandwich is popular all over America and abroad

🍴 serves 4

🕐 prep 5 mins • cook 8–12 mins

225g (8oz) **sauerkraut**

8 slices **rye bread**

4 tbsp bottled **Russian Dressing** or Thousand Island salad dressing

8 slices **salt beef**, about 30g (1oz) each

8 slices of **Swiss cheese**, thinly sliced, or Emmental cheese, thickly sliced

4 tbsp **butter**

1 **Place the sauerkraut** in a sieve and rinse with cold water. Let it drain, pressing it down with a small plate.

2 **Lay out 4 slices of bread**. Top each with ½ tbsp dressing, 2 salt beef slices, a quarter of the sauerkraut, and 2 slices of cheese.

Spread ½ tbsp dressing on each of the remaining bread slices, then place them, dressing-side down, on top.

3 **Melt 1 tbsp of the butter** in a large frying pan, add the sandwiches, in 2 batches, and cook over a medium-low heat for 2–3 minutes, or until the bottom slices are toasted, pressing the sandwiches down with a plate.

4 **Carefully turn the** sandwiches over, add 1 tbsp butter, and cook for a further 2–3 minutes, or until the bottom slice is toasted and the cheese is melted. Cook the other sandwiches and serve while still warm.

● **Good with** sweet and sour pickles, sliced in half.

Tacos

Taco shells can be filled with all sorts of spicy fillings and make great party food

🍴 serves 4

🕐 prep 15 mins • cook 25 mins

2 tbsp **sunflower oil**

500g (1lb 2oz) **lean minced beef**

2–3 tbsp **taco seasoning**

12 **taco shells**

lettuce, shredded, to serve

Cheddar cheese, grated, to serve

1 **Heat the oil** in a large frying pan and cook the minced beef until evenly browned, stirring occasionally. Add the taco seasoning and stir in 120ml (4fl oz) water. Simmer over a low heat for 10 minutes, or until the meat mixture is thickened.

2 **Just before** the meat is ready, warm the taco shells in a low oven for 3–4 minutes.

3 **Spoon the meat** into the shells and top each with shredded lettuce and Cheddar cheese.

● **Good with** tomato salsa, jalapeno peppers, and soured cream.

Basic Pizza Dough

The starting point for countless great recipes

🍴 serves 4

🕐 prep 15 mins, plus rising
• cook 20-25 mins

500g (1lb 2oz) strong white plain flour, plus extra for dusting

2 x 7g sachets fast-action dried yeast

½ tsp salt

2 tbsp olive oil

● **Prepare ahead** The dough can be prepared the day before and stored in the refrigerator. The low temperature will retard the yeast, but if the dough rises to double its size, lightly knead and use as required.

1 Put the flour in a mixing bowl, stir in the yeast and salt. Add 2 tbsp of olive oil and 360ml (12fl oz) tepid water, then mix to a dough. Knead on a floured surface for 10 minutes, or until smooth.

2 Roll the dough into a ball, and place in a lightly oiled bowl. Cover loosely with oiled cling film. Leave in a warm place until the dough has doubled in size.

3 Preheat the oven to 200°C (400°F/Gas 6). Transfer the dough to a lightly floured surface, knead lightly, divide into 4 and roll out to 23cm (9in) rounds. Use with the topping of your choice.

Pissaladière

This version of the Italian pizza got its name from *pissala*, a paste made from anchovies

🍴 serves 4 as a main course, or 8 as canapés

🕐 prep 20 mins, plus rising
• cook 1 hr 25 mins

📷 32.5 x 23cm (13 x 9in) non-stick Swiss roll tin

❄ freeze for up to 3 months; thaw at room temperature and reheat in a warm oven

225g (8oz) **strong white flour**, plus extra for dusting

salt and freshly ground black pepper

1 tsp soft brown sugar

1 tsp easy-blend dried yeast

1 tbsp olive oil

For the topping

4 tbsp olive oil

900g (2lb) onions, finely sliced

3 garlic cloves

sprig of thyme

1 tsp herbes de Provence (dry mix of thyme, basil, rosemary, and oregano)

1 bay leaf

100g jar anchovies in oil

12 black pitted Niçoise olives, or Italian olives

freshly ground black pepper

1 For the base, combine the flour, 1 tsp salt, and black pepper to taste in a large bowl. Pour 150ml (5fl oz) tepid water into a separate bowl, and use a fork to whisk in the sugar, then the yeast. Set aside for 10 minutes to froth, then pour into the flour with the olive oil.

2 Mix to form a dough, adding a further 2 tbsp tepid water if the mixture looks too dry. Turn the dough out on to a floured board, and knead for 10 minutes, or until smooth and elastic. Shape the dough into a ball, return to the bowl, and cover with a tea towel. Leave in a warm place for 1 hour, or until doubled in size.

3 For the topping, put the oil in a saucepan over a very low heat. Add the onions, garlic, herbs, and bay leaf. Cover and simmer gently, stirring occasionally, for 1 hour, or until the onions look like a stringy purée. Be careful not to let the onions catch— if they begin to stick, add a little water. Drain well, and set aside, discarding the bay leaf.

4 Preheat the oven to 180°C (350°F/Gas 4). Knead the dough briefly on a floured surface. Roll it out so it is thin and large enough to fit the Swiss roll tin. Prick all over with a fork.

5 Spread the onions over the base. Drain the anchovies, reserving 3 tbsp oil, and slice the fillets in half lengthways. Embed the olives in rows in the dough, and drape the anchovies in a criss-cross pattern on top of the onions. Drizzle with the reserved anchovy oil, and sprinkle with pepper.

6 Bake for 25 minutes, or until the crust is brown. The onions should not brown or dry out. Remove and serve warm, cut into rectangles, squares, or wedges, or allow to cool before serving.

Pizza Bianca

This tasty pizza is made without tomato sauce and is packed with fresh Mediterranean flavours

🍴 serves 4

🕐 prep 25 mins
• cook 25–30 mins

🍽 2 large or 4 smaller baking trays

1 quantity of **Basic Pizza Dough** (see far left), rolled into 4 pizza bases

4 tbsp **extra virgin Italian olive oil**

140g (5oz) **Gorgonzola cheese**, rind removed, crumbled

12 slices of **Parma ham**, torn into strips

4 fresh **figs**, each cut into 8 wedges and peeled

2 **tomatoes**, deseeded and diced

115g (4oz) **wild rocket leaves**

freshly ground **black pepper**

1 **Preheat the oven** to 200°C (400°F/Gas 6). Place the pizza bases on greased baking trays. Brush with half the olive oil and scatter over the cheese.

2 **Bake in the oven** for 20 minutes, or until the bases are crisp and turning golden. Remove from the oven.

3 **Arrange the ham** strips, figs, and diced tomatoes on top, and return to the oven for 8 minutes, or until the toppings are just warmed and the bases are golden brown.

4 **Scatter over the rocket**, season with plenty of black pepper, and serve at once, drizzled with the rest of the olive oil.

VARIATION

Gruyère Pizza Bianca
Substitute 115g (4oz) Gruyère for the Gorgonzola and sprinkle with Fontina.

Four Seasons Pizza

These pizzas have different toppings, arranged separately, to represent the four seasons

🍴 serves 4

🕐 prep 15 mins • cook 20 mins

1 quantity of **Basic Pizza Dough** (see far left)

400ml (14fl oz) **passata** or thick tomato pasta sauce

175g (6oz) **mozzarella cheese**, thinly sliced

115g (4oz) **mushrooms**, thinly sliced

2 tbsp **extra virgin olive oil**

2 roasted **red peppers**, sliced into thin strips

8 **anchovy fillets**, halved lengthways

115g (4oz) **pepperoni**, thinly sliced

2 tbsp **capers**

8 canned or marinated **artichoke hearts**, drained and halved

12 **black olives**

1 **Make the pizza dough**, divide into 4, and roll or press out into 23cm (9in) rounds. Lift on to greased baking trays.

2 **Preheat the oven** to 200°C (400°F/Gas 6). Spread the passata over the pizza bases, leaving a 2cm (¾in) border around the edge of each. Top with mozzarella, dividing equally between the bases.

3 **Arrange the mushroom** slices on a quarter of each pizza and brush with the olive oil. Pile the roasted pepper slices on another quarter with the anchovy fillets on top. Cover a third quarter with the pepperoni and capers, and top the final quarter with the artichokes and black olives.

4 **Bake the pizzas** for 20 minutes, or until golden brown. Serve hot.

Pizzette

Mini party pizzas. Try the toppings below or create your own favourite combinations

 makes 24

prep 20 mins, plus rising • cook 12–15 mins

7.5cm (3in) round cutter

freeze the baked pizzettes for up to 1 month

1 quantity of **Basic Pizza Dough** (p98)

3 tbsp **green pesto**

3 tbsp **sun-dried tomato paste**

60g (2oz) sliced **salami** or pepperoni, cut into strips

6 pitted **black olives**, halved

60g (2oz) **mozzarella cheese**, sliced

30g (1oz) **wild rocket**, chopped

2 tbsp **pine nuts**

extra virgin olive oil, to drizzle

● **Prepare ahead** The pizzettes can be made up to 24 hours in advance. Reheat to serve.

1 **Knead the dough** on a lightly floured surface, and roll out to about 5mm (¼in) thick. With the plain cutter, stamp out 24 rounds, gathering up the dough trimmings and re-rolling as required. Lift on to greased baking trays.

2 **Spread half the rounds** with green pesto and half with sun-dried tomato paste. Top the pesto rounds with salami or pepperoni, black olives, and mozzarella. Top the sun-dried tomato rounds with wild rocket and pine nuts.

3 **Drizzle or brush** with the oil, and set aside for 20 minutes, or until puffed.

4 **Preheat the oven** to 220°C (425°F/Gas 7), and bake the pizzettes for 12–15 minutes, or until puffed and golden brown.

> ### Freezing Tip
> These little bites make a good snack to keep in the freezer. Batch freeze them in small quantities, then reheat in a hot oven before serving.

Pizza Florentina

An eye-catching pizza with spinach and a whole egg

serves 4

prep 15 mins • cook 20 mins

1 quantity of **Basic Pizza Dough** (p98)

350g (12oz) **tomato pasta sauce**

225g (8oz) **spinach**, cooked and chopped

¼ tsp freshly grated **nutmeg**

1 tsp **thyme leaves**

175g (6oz) **mozzarella cheese**, sliced

4 **eggs**

4 tbsp grated **Parmesan cheese**

freshly ground **black pepper**

1 **Preheat the oven** to 200°C (400°F/Gas 6). Divide the dough into 4 and roll out into 23cm (9in) rounds. Lift on to greased baking trays and spread with tomato sauce, leaving a 2.5cm (1in) border.

2 **Spread spinach** on top, in an even layer, and sprinkle with nutmeg and thyme. Lay on the cheese slices and crack an egg on each. Sprinkle with Parmesan. Bake for 20 minutes, or until the dough edges are crisp. Season to taste with pepper, and serve.

Tarte Flambé

This thin-based, pizza-style tart from Alsace has both sweet and savoury toppings

 serves 4

prep 20 mins, plus cooling • cook 50 mins

2 x Swiss roll tins, 32.5 x 23cm (13 x 9in)

1 quantity of **Basic Pizza Dough** (p98)

2 tbsp **vegetable oil**

30g (1oz) **butter**

4 large **sweet onions**, thinly sliced

200g (7oz) **fromage blanc**

2 tbsp **cornflour**

2 **eggs**

1 tbsp **crème fraîche**

115g (4oz) **smoked back bacon rashers**, chopped

1 **Preheat the oven** to 200°C (400°F/Gas 6). Halve the dough and roll or press out into 2 greased Swiss roll tins.

2 **Heat the oil** and butter in a large saucepan, add the onions, cover, and sweat over a low heat, until softened. Uncover, increase the heat to medium, and fry the onions until golden, stirring occasionally. Remove from the pan and leave to cool.

3 **In a bowl**, beat together the fromage blanc, cornflour, and eggs until smooth. Stir in sufficient crème fraîche to make the mixture soft enough to pour and spread.

4 **Pour the mixture** over the bases, and top with the onions and bacon. Bake for 30 minutes, or until the topping is golden and the base is crisp.

Calzone

These crescent-shaped folded pizzas can be filled with almost any pizza topping, but this is the most popular

serves 4

prep 20 mins, plus cooling • cook 25–30 mins

1 quantity of **Basic Pizza Dough** (p98)

3 tbsp **olive oil**

6 **back bacon rashers**, chopped

1 skinless boneless **chicken breast**, cut into small pieces

1 **green pepper**, deseeded and chopped

4 tbsp **sun-dried tomato paste**

200g (7oz) **mozzarella cheese**, sliced

4 tbsp chopped **flat-leaf parsley**

freshly ground **black pepper**

beaten **egg**, to seal

1 **Prepare the dough** and roll or press out into 4 rounds, each measuring 23cm (9in) in diameter. Lift on to greased baking trays.

2 **Preheat the oven** to 200°C (400°F/Gas 6). Heat 1 tbsp of the oil in a frying pan and fry the bacon, chicken, and green pepper for 5 minutes, or until the bacon and

chicken are lightly browned, stirring frequently. Remove from the pan and set aside to cool.

3 **Spread the tomato paste** over half of each dough round, keeping it away from the edges. Top with bacon, chicken, green pepper, mozzarella slices, and parsley and season with plenty of black pepper.

4 **Brush the edges** of the dough with beaten egg and fold over the plain half of each round to enclose the filling, pressing the edges together firmly with your fingers or a fork to seal.

5 **Brush with** the remaining olive oil and bake for 20–25 minutes, or until puffed, crisp, and golden brown. Serve hot.

● **Good with** a green salad.

VARIATION

Spicy Calzone
Fry 1–2 tsp of dried chilli flakes in the mix in step 2 for added heat.

Brown Meat Stock

Use either beef or lamb bones for this rich stock, not a mixture of the two

- 🍴 makes 2½ litres (4 pints)
- 🕐 prep 10 mins
  • cook 3½–4½ hrs
- ❄ freeze for up to 6 months

1.35kg (3lb) **beef** or lamb bones, raw or cooked

2–3 **onions**, unpeeled and cut in half

2–3 **carrots**, cut in half

vegetable trimmings, such as mushrooms peelings, celery tops, or tomato skins

bacon rinds

bouquet garni, made with 1 celery stick, 1 bay leaf, and a few sprigs of thyme and parsley

1 tbsp **black peppercorns**

● **Prepare ahead** The stock can be made up to 2 days before required. Chill until required, then bring to the boil before using.

1 **If the bones are raw**, put them in a roasting tin with the onions and carrots, roast at 200°C (400°F/Gas 6) oven for 30 minutes, or until browned, turning often. If you are using bones from cooked meat, omit this step.

2 **Transfer the bones**, onions, and carrots to a large saucepan, adding any vegetable trimmings, the bacon rinds, and the bouquet garni.

3 **Pour in enough** cold water to cover, and bring to the boil. Use a slotted spoon to remove any foam that rises to the surface. Lower the heat, add the peppercorns, and simmer for 3–4 hours.

4 **Allow the stock** to cool, then strain into a bowl or jug, discarding the flavourings. Chill overnight in the refrigerator so any fat solidifies on top and can be lifted off.

Vegetable Stock

If you make more of this than you need, freeze the leftovers to use in soups and casseroles

- 🍴 makes 1.2 litres (2 pints)
- 🕐 prep 10 mins • cook 1 hr
- ❄ freeze for up to 6 months

3 large **carrots**, scrubbed and coarsely chopped

3 large **onions**, coarsely chopped

3 large **celery sticks**, with leaves, coarsely chopped

2 **leeks**, chopped and rinsed

10 **black peppercorns**, lightly crushed

bunch of **flat-leaf parsley**, rinsed

2 **bay leaves**

½ tsp **salt**

● **Prepare ahead** The stock will keep, chilled, for up to 2 days; bring to the boil before using.

1 **Put the carrots**, onions, celery, and leeks in a large pan with 1.7 litres (3 pints) water. Bring to the boil. Use a slotted spoon to remove any foam that rises to the surface. Reduce the heat to low, then add the remaining ingredients, partially cover the pan, and simmer for 45 minutes, or until the stock is well flavoured.

2 **Strain the stock** into a large bowl, discarding the flavourings. The stock is now ready to use.

Fish Stock

A tasty, delicate stock that is quick and easy to make

- 🍴 makes 1.2 litres (2 pints)
- 🕐 prep 10 mins • cook 20 mins
- ❄ freeze for up to 6 months

3 **fish heads**, plus bones and/or trimmings, any blood rinsed off and the bones cracked

2 **onions**, coarsely chopped

1 **celery stick**, coarsely chopped

few sprigs of **thyme**

few sprigs of **flat-leaf parsley**

1 **bay leaf**

¼ tsp **salt**

● **Prepare ahead** The stock can be made and stored in the refrigerator for up to 2 days before it is needed. Bring to the boil before using.

1 **Put 1.7 litres** (3 pints) water, the fish trimmings, and onions into a large pan over a high heat and slowly bring to just below the boil. Use a slotted spoon to remove any foam as it rises to the surface.

2 **Add the remaining** ingredients, then partially cover the pan and leave to simmer for 20 minutes.

3 **Strain the stock** into a large bowl, discarding the flavourings. The stock is now ready to use.

OILY FISH

Avoid using oily fish, such as herring or mackerel, as the stock will turn cloudy and the flavour will be overpowering.

Chicken Stock

For a clear stock, make sure you remove any fat from the chicken before boiling, or it will turn cloudy. For a dark, golden stock, leave the onion unpeeled

- 🍴 makes 1 litre (1¾ pints)
- 🕐 prep 10 mins • cook 1 hr
- ❄ freeze for up to 6 months

1 **chicken carcass**, skin and fat removed

2 **celery sticks**, roughly chopped

1 **onion**, quartered

few sprigs of **flat-leaf parsley**

few sprigs of **thyme**

1 **bay leaf**

½ tsp **salt**

5 **black peppercorns**, lightly crushed

● **Prepare ahead** You can make the stock up to 2 days in advance. Leave to cool completely, then store in the refrigerator; lift off any fat that has risen to the surface. Bring to the boil before using.

1 **Put the chicken pieces**, celery, onion, herbs, and salt in a large pan with 2 litres (3½ pints) cold water and bring to boiling point over a high heat. Using a slotted spoon, skim off any foam as it rises to the surface. Reduce the heat to low, then add the peppercorns, partially cover the pan, and leave to simmer for about 1 hour.

2 **Strain the stock** into a large bowl, discarding the flavourings. It is now ready to use.

VARIATION

Turkey Stock

Instead of the chicken, use the turkey neck, wings and giblets.

Gazpacho

This chilled, no-cook Spanish soup is always popular
when temperatures are hot outside

 serves 4

prep 15 mins, plus at least 1 hr
for chilling

freeze, without the garnishes,
for up to 1 month

1 kg (2¼lb) **tomatoes**, plus extra to
serve

1 small **cucumber**, peeled and finely
chopped, plus extra to serve

1 small **red pepper**, deseeded and
chopped, plus extra to serve

2 **garlic cloves**, crushed

4 tbsp **sherry vinegar**

salt and freshly ground **black pepper**

120ml (4fl oz) **extra virgin olive oil**,
plus extra to serve

1 **hard-boiled egg**, white and yolk
separated and chopped, to serve

● **Prepare ahead** The soup can be
prepared 2 days in advance, kept
covered and chilled.

1 Bring a kettle of water
to the boil. Place the tomatoes
in a heatproof bowl, pour over
enough boiling water to cover, and
leave for 20 seconds, or until the
skins split. Drain and cool under cold
running water. Gently peel off the
skins, cut the tomatoes in half,
deseed, and chop the flesh.

2 Put the tomato flesh,
cucumber, red pepper, garlic,
sherry in a food processor or blender.
Season to taste with salt and pepper,
and process until smooth. Pour in the
olive oil and process again. Dilute
with a little water if too thick. Transfer
the soup to a serving bowl, cover with
cling film and chill for at least 1 hour.

3 When ready to serve, finely
chop the extra cucumber and red
pepper. Place the cucumber, pepper
and egg yolk and white in individual
bowls and arrange on the table, along
with a bottle of olive oil. Ladle the
soup into bowls and serve, letting
each diner add their own garnish.

Watercress Soup

Serve this velvety smooth soup hot, topped
with shavings of Parmesan cheese

 serves 4

prep 10 mins • cook 15 mins

freeze the soup, before the
cream is added, for up
to 3 months

25g (scant 1oz) **butter**

1 **onion**, peeled and finely chopped

175g (6oz) **watercress**

3 ripe **pears**, cored and roughly
chopped

1 litre (1¾ pints) **vegetable stock**

salt and freshly ground **black pepper**

200ml (7fl oz) **double cream**

juice of ½ **lemon**

Parmesan cheese, grated, to serve

olive oil, to drizzle

● **Prepare ahead** The soup can be
made up to 4 hours in advance and
refrigerated until ready to use.

1 Melt the butter in a saucepan
and cook the onion for
10 minutes, or until soft, stirring
occasionally to prevent burning.

2 Meanwhile, trim the
watercress and pick off the
leaves. Add the watercress stalks to
the onion with the pears and stock,
and season with salt and pepper.

3 Bring to the boil, cover and
simmer gently for 15 minutes.
Remove from the heat and pour into
a blender along with the watercress
leaves. Process until the soup is a
very smooth texture.

4 Stir in the cream and lemon
juice, adjust the seasoning and
serve sprinkled with Parmesan
shavings and drizzled with a little oil.

VARIATION

Spinach Soup

Use 175g (6oz) spinach instead of
the watercress and omit the pears.
Use 200ml (7fl oz) coconut milk
instead of the cream. Serve warm.

CHILLED SOUP

Allow to cool before chilling in the
refrigerator. To serve, pour the soup into
chilled bowls, top with crushed ice, and
drizzle with a little olive oil.

Curried Parsnip Soup

Gentle spices perk up this earthy-flavoured soup

🍴 serves 4

🕐 prep 10 mins • cook 50 mins

1 onion

300g (10oz) parsnips

1 carrot

1 potato

45g (1½oz) butter

2 tbsp plain flour

2 tbsp mild curry powder

1.2 litres (2 pints) vegetable stock

crème fraîche, to serve

parsley, chopped, to serve

1 Peel and roughly chop all the vegetables, keeping the onion separate.

2 Melt the butter in a large saucepan over a medium heat; add the onions, and cook, stirring frequently, until they are soft but not browned. Add the other vegetables, followed by the flour and curry powder and cook, stirring, for a further 2 minutes.

3 Gradually add the stock or water, stirring until well blended. Increase the heat and bring to the boil, then reduce the heat to a low simmer. Cover and leave to cook for 40 minutes, or until the vegetables are tender.

4 Turn the heat off, uncover, and allow the soup to cool slightly. Pour the soup into a blender or food processor and purée until completely smooth.

5 Reheat before serving, then pour into individual bowls. Add a swirl of crème fraîche and a scattering of chopped parsley.

● **Good with** crusty bread or cheese scones.

Borscht

Thickly textured and satisfying, this classic Russian soup can be enjoyed at any time of year and on any occasion

🍴 serves 4

🕐 prep 15 mins • cook 1½ hrs

▤ muslin

2 large beetroot

1 onion

1 carrot

1 celery stick

45g (1½oz) butter or goose fat

400g can chopped tomatoes

1 garlic clove, crushed (optional)

1.7 litres (3 pints) vegetable stock

2 bay leaves

4 cloves

2 tbsp lemon juice

salt and freshly ground black pepper

200ml (7fl oz) soured cream

1 Roughly grate the beetroot, onion, carrot, and celery stick.

2 Melt the butter in a large saucepan over a medium heat. Add the vegetables and cook, stirring, for 5 minutes, or until just softened.

3 Add the tomatoes and crushed garlic, if using, and cook for 2–3 minutes, stirring frequently, then stir in the stock.

4 Tie the bay leaves and cloves in a small piece of muslin and add to the pan. Bring the soup to the boil, then reduce the heat, cover, and simmer for 1 hour 20 minutes.

5 Discard the muslin bag. Stir in the lemon juice and season to taste with salt and pepper.

6 Ladle the soup into warm bowls and add a swirl of soured cream to each.

● **Good with** grated carrot piled on top and chunks of dark rye bread.

▬▬ VARIATION ▬▬

Lite Borscht

For a lighter soup, blend until smooth and add a little more stock or milk. Serve hot or chilled, garnished with a swirl of natural yogurt and a sprinkle of chopped parsley.

Vichyssoise

Despite its French name, this silky, smooth iced soup originates from America and may also be served hot

 serves 4

 prep 15 mins • cook 45 mins

 freeze the soup, before the cream is added, for up to 3 months; thaw at room temperature, then reheat, stir in the cream, and serve warm

30g (1oz) **butter**

3 large **leeks**, green ends discarded, finely sliced

2 **potatoes**, about 175g (6oz) in total, peeled and chopped

1 **celery** stick, roughly chopped

1.2 litres (2 pints) fresh **vegetable stock**

salt and freshly ground **black pepper**

150ml (5floz) **double cream**, extra for garnish

2 tbsp finely chopped **chives**, to serve

1 Heat the butter in a heavy saucepan over a medium heat and add the leeks. Press a piece of damp greaseproof paper on top, cover, and cook, shaking gently from time to time, for 15 minutes, or until the leeks are softened and golden.

2 Add the potatoes, celery, and stock, and season with salt and pepper. Bring to the boil, stirring, then cover and simmer for 30 minutes, or until the vegetables are tender.

3 Remove the pan from the heat and leave to cool slightly, then process in a blender until very smooth, in batches if necessary. Season to taste with salt and pepper and allow the soup to cool completely before stirring in the cream. Chill for at least 3 hours before serving.

4 To serve, pour into serving bowls, stir in a little cream, and sprinkle with chives and black pepper.

Tomato Soup

Easy to make, using canned tomatoes, this delicious soup can be enjoyed all year round

 serves 4

 prep 20 mins • cook 55 mins

 low fat

1 tbsp **olive oil**

1 **onion**, chopped

1 **garlic** clove, sliced

2 **celery** sticks, sliced

1 **carrot**, sliced

1 **potato**, chopped

2 x 400g cans **tomatoes**

750ml (1¼ pints) **vegetable stock** or chicken stock

1 **bay leaf**

1 tsp **sugar**

salt and freshly ground **black pepper**

● **Prepare ahead** Make the soup up to 48 hours in advance and reheat before serving.

1 Heat the oil in a large saucepan over a medium-low heat, add the onion, garlic, and celery, and fry, stirring frequently, until softened but not coloured.

2 Add the carrot and potato and stir for 1 minute, then add the tomatoes with their juice, stock, bay leaf, and sugar. Season to taste with salt and pepper, bring to the boil, then reduce the heat, cover, and simmer for 45 minutes, or until the vegetables are very soft.

3 Remove from the heat and allow to cool slightly, then process in a blender or food processor until smooth, working in batches if necessary. Taste and adjust the seasoning, then reheat and serve.

VARIATION

Roasted Red Pepper and Tomato Soup

Place 2 whole red peppers in a hot oven or under a hot grill and cook until the skin blackens. Place them in a plastic bag, leave until cool enough to handle, then peel off the blackened skin and remove the seeds and membranes. Omit the potato from the basic tomato soup recipe, then add the skinned and deseeded peppers when blending in step 3. Season with ½ tsp of smoked paprika.

Mushroom Soup

Using a selection of both wild and cultivated mushrooms will produce a soup that is bursting with flavour

- serves 4
- prep 10 mins • cook 45 mins
- freeze for up to 3 months

30g (1oz) butter

1 onion, finely chopped

2 celery sticks, finely chopped

1 garlic clove, crushed

450g (1lb) mixed mushrooms, roughly chopped

200g (7oz) potatoes, peeled and cubed

1 litre (1¾ pints) vegetable stock

2 tbsp finely chopped parsley

salt and freshly ground black pepper

● **Prepare ahead** The soup can be kept covered in the refrigerator for 2–3 days and reheated to serve.

1 Melt the butter in a large saucepan, add the onion, celery, and garlic, and fry for 3–4 minutes, or until softened.

2 Stir in the mushrooms and continue to fry for a further 5–6 minutes. Add the potatoes and stock and bring up to the boil. Reduce the heat and leave to simmer gently for 30 minutes.

3 Use a hand blender to process the soup until smooth, working in batches if necessary.

4 Sprinkle in the parsley and season to taste with salt and pepper. Serve immediately.

● **Good with** warm crusty rolls and a little horseradish cream in each bowl for added flavour and spice.

Carrot and Orange Soup

A light, refreshing soup with a hint of spice, this is the perfect start to a summer meal

- serves 4
- prep 10 mins • cook 40 mins
- low fat

2 tsp light olive oil or sunflower oil

1 leek, sliced

500g (1lb 2oz) carrots, sliced

1 potato, about 115g (4oz), chopped

½ tsp ground coriander

pinch of ground cumin

300ml (10fl oz) orange juice

500ml (16fl oz) vegetable stock or chicken stock

1 bay leaf

salt and freshly ground black pepper

2 tbsp chopped coriander, to garnish

● **Prepare ahead** The soup can be made up to 2 days in advance and reheated before serving.

1 Place the oil, leeks, and carrots in a large saucepan and cook over a low heat for 5 minutes, stirring frequently, or until the leeks have softened. Add the potato, coriander, and cumin, then pour in the orange juice and stock. Add the bay leaf and stir occasionally.

2 Increase the heat, bring the soup to the boil, then lower the heat, cover, and simmer for 40 minutes, or until the vegetables are very tender.

3 Allow the soup to cool slightly, then transfer to a blender or food processor and process, until smooth, working in batches if necessary.

4 Return to the saucepan and add a little extra stock or water if the soup is too thick. Bring back to a simmer, then transfer to heated serving bowls and sprinkle with chopped coriander.

● **Good with** a spoonful of low-fat plain yogurt, or a swirl of cream.

VARIATION

Sweet Potato Soup

Replace some or all of the carrots with orange sweet potatoes. Use apple juice instead of orange juice, and replace the ground coriander and cumin with 1 tsp paprika.

Porcini Mushroom Soup

This hearty Italian country soup is full of deep, earthy goodness

 serves 4

 prep 20 mins, plus standing • cook 1 hr

 low fat, low GI

❄ freeze, without the bread, for up to 3 months

30g (1oz) **dried porcini mushrooms**

3 tbsp **extra virgin olive oil**, plus extra to finish

2 **onions**, finely chopped

2 tsp chopped **rosemary leaves**

1 tsp **thyme leaves**

2 **garlic cloves**, finely sliced

115g (4oz) **chestnut mushrooms**, sliced

2 **celery sticks with leaves**, finely chopped

400g (14oz) can **chopped tomatoes**

750ml (1¼ pints) **vegetable stock**

salt and freshly ground **black pepper**

½ **stale ciabatta** or small crusty white loaf, torn into chunks

● **Prepare ahead** You can make the soup to the end of step 3 up to 2 days in advance; keep chilled until needed and reheat when ready to serve.

1 **Put the dried porcini** in a heatproof bowl, pour over 300ml (20fl oz) boiling water, and leave to stand for 30 minutes. Drain, reserving the soaking liquid, then chop any large pieces of mushroom.

2 **Heat the oil** in a saucepan, add the onions, cover, and leave to cook for 10 minutes, or until soft. Add the rosemary, thyme, garlic, chestnut mushrooms, and celery, and continue cooking, uncovered, until the celery has softened.

3 **Add the tomatoes**, porcini, and stock. Strain the soaking liquid through muslin or a fine sieve into the pan. Bring to the boil, then lower the heat and simmer gently for 45 minutes.

4 **Season to taste** with salt and pepper, and add the bread. Remove the pan from the heat. Cover and leave to stand for 10 minutes before serving. Spoon into deep bowls and drizzle each serving with a little olive oil.

● **Good with** bowls of spiced olives, and white crusty bread.

VARIATION

Fresh Porcini Mushroom Soup

Replace the dried porcini with 115g (4oz) fresh porcini. Do not soak them; instead, slice and add them to the soup along with the chestnut mushrooms. You will need an extra 250ml (8fl oz) vegetable stock.

White Bean Soup

This thick soup from northern Italy is guaranteed to keep out the winter chills

 serves 4

 prep 30 mins, plus soaking • cook 2 hrs

❗ soak the beans overnight to rehydrate them

3 tbsp **olive oil**

2 **onions**, finely chopped

2 **garlic cloves**, crushed

225g (8oz) **dried cannellini beans**, soaked overnight

1 **celery stick**, chopped

1 **bay leaf**

3 or 4 **parsley stalks**, without leaves

1 tbsp **lemon** juice

1.2 litres (2 pints) **vegetable stock**

salt and freshly ground **black pepper**

3 **shallots**, thinly sliced

60g (2oz) **pancetta**, chopped (optional)

80g **fontina cheese** or Taleggio cheese, chopped into small pieces

1 **Heat 2 tbsp** of the olive oil in a saucepan, add the onions, and fry over a low heat for 10 minutes, or until softened, stirring occasionally. Add the garlic and cook, stirring, for 1 minute.

2 **Drain the soaked beans** and add to the pan with the celery, bay leaf, parsley stalks, lemon juice, and stock. Bring to the boil, cover, and simmer for 1½ hours, or until the beans are soft, stirring occasionally.

3 **Remove the bay leaf** and liquidize the soup in batches in a blender, or through a hand mill. Rinse out the pan. Return the soup to the pan and season to taste with salt and pepper.

4 **Heat the remaining** olive oil in a small frying pan, and fry the shallots and pancetta until golden and crisp, stirring frequently to stop them sticking to the pan.

5 **Reheat the soup**, adding a little stock or water if it is too thick. Stir the fontina into the soup. Ladle into individual bowls, and sprinkle each serving with the shallots and pancetta.

Lobster Bisque

The name "bisque" refers to a shellfish soup with cream and is thought to have come from the Spanish Biscay region

 serves 4

 prep 45 mins
• cook 1 hr 10 mins

 freeze for up to 3 months; thaw at room temperature and reheat

1 lobster, cooked, about 1kg (2¼lb) in weight

50g (1¾oz) butter

olive oil

1 onion, finely chopped

1 carrot, finely chopped

2 celery sticks, finely chopped

1 leek, finely chopped

½ fennel bulb, finely chopped

1 bay leaf

1 sprig of tarragon

2 garlic cloves, crushed

75g (2½oz) tomato purée

4 tomatoes, roughly chopped

120ml (4fl oz) Cognac or brandy

100ml (3½fl oz) dry white wine or vermouth

1.7 litres (3 pints) fish stock

120ml (4fl oz) cream

salt and freshly ground black pepper

pinch of cayenne pepper

juice of ½ lemon

chives, to garnish

● **Prepare ahead** Steps 1–5 can be completed several hours in advance; keep the lobster meat refrigerated until ready to use.

1 Split the lobster in half, remove the meat from the body, and chop the meat into small pieces. Twist off the claws and legs, break the claws at the joints, and crack the shells with the back of a knife. Chop the shell into rough pieces.

2 Melt the butter in a large saucepan over a medium heat, add the vegetables, herbs, and garlic, and cook for 10 minutes, or until softened, stirring occasionally.

3 Add the chopped lobster shells. Stir in the tomato purée, chopped tomatoes, Cognac, white wine, and fish stock. Bring to the boil and simmer for 1 hour.

4 Leave to cool slightly, then ladle into a food processor. Process the soup in short bursts until the shell breaks into very small pieces.

5 Strain the soup through a coarse sieve, pushing as much liquid through as you can. Then pass the soup again through a fine mesh sieve before returning to the heat.

6 Bring to the boil, add the cream, then season to taste with salt and pepper and add cayenne pepper and lemon juice to taste. Serve in warm bowls, garnished with chives.

VARIATION

Crab Bisque

Follow the recipe above but use a cooked crab, about 1kg (2¼lb) in weight instead of the lobster. It is best to use a spider crab or velvet crab. Add a 2.5cm (1in) piece of fresh ginger, peeled and finely chopped, to the vegetables in step 2.

Salmorejo

A fresh soup from southern Spain, similar to Gazpacho

 serves 4

 prep 15 mins, plus soaking and chilling

115g (4oz) stale white bread, crusts removed, torn into bite-sized pieces

3 tbsp olive oil, plus extra to garnish

2 tbsp red wine vinegar

1 onion, roughly chopped

3 garlic cloves

1 red pepper, deseeded and chopped

5 tomatoes, skinned and deseeded

1 cucumber, peeled, deseeded, and chopped

salt and freshly ground black pepper

2 hard-boiled eggs, chopped

2 slices serrano ham, cut into strips

1 Place the bread into a bowl. Add the oil and vinegar, mix well, and set aside to soak for 10 minutes.

2 Place the onion, garlic, red pepper, tomatoes, and most of the cucumber in a blender or food processor with 90ml (3fl oz) water, and blend to a purée. Add the bread mixture, blend again, then season to taste with salt and pepper.

3 Chill for at least 30 minutes, pour into serving bowls, and top with hard-boiled eggs, strips of ham, and the remaining cucumber. Serve, drizzled with a little olive oil.

Fish Soup with Saffron and Fennel

This rustic, Mediterranean-style fish soup – robustly flavoured with brandy, orange, and fennel – is simple to prepare and sure to please

🍴 serves 4–6

🕐 prep 10 mins • cook 1 hr

30g (1oz) butter

3 tbsp olive oil

1 large fennel bulb, finely chopped

2 garlic cloves, crushed

1 small leek, sliced

4 ripe plum tomatoes, chopped

3 tbsp brandy

¼ tsp saffron threads, infused in a little hot water

zest of ½ orange

1 bay leaf

1.7 litres (3 pints) fish stock

300g (10oz) potatoes, diced and

parboiled for 5 minutes

4 tbsp dry white wine

500g (1lb 2oz) fresh black mussels, scrubbed and debearded

salt and freshly ground black pepper

500g (1lb 2oz) monkfish or firm white fish, cut into bite-sized pieces

6 raw whole tiger prawns

parsley, chopped, to garnish

1 Heat the butter with 2 tbsp of the oil in a large, deep pan. Stir in the fennel, garlic, and leek, and fry over a moderate heat, stirring occasionally, for 5 minutes, or until softened and lightly browned.

2 Stir in the tomatoes, add the brandy, and boil rapidly for 2 minutes, or until the juices are reduced slightly. Stir in the saffron, orange zest, bay leaf, fish stock, and potatoes. Bring to the boil, then reduce the heat and skim any scum from the surface. Cover and simmer for 20 minutes, or until the potatoes are tender. Remove the bay leaf.

3 Meanwhile, heat the remaining oil with the wine in a large deep pan until boiling. Add the mussels, cover, and continue on high heat for 2–3 minutes, shaking the pan often. Discard any mussels that do not open. Strain, reserving the liquid, and set the mussels aside.

4 Add the liquid to the soup and season to taste with salt and pepper. Bring to the boil, add the monkfish pieces and prawns, then reduce the heat, cover, and simmer gently for 5 minutes, or until the fish is just cooked and the prawns are pink. Add the mussels to the pan and bring almost to the boil.

5 Serve the soup sprinkled with chopped parsley.

Stracciatella with Pasta

A flavoursome light soup makes a perfect light lunch

🍴 serves 4–6

🕐 prep 10 mins • cook 20 mins

1.5 litres (2¾ pints) chicken stock

100g (3½oz) soup pasta

4 eggs

salt and freshly ground black pepper

½ tsp freshly grated nutmeg

2 tbsp grated Parmesan cheese

1 tbsp chopped parsley

1 tbsp olive oil

1 Place the stock in a large pan and bring to the boil. Add the pasta and cook according to packet directions, or until *al dente*.

2 Break the eggs into a small bowl, add the nutmeg, season to taste with salt and pepper, and whisk lightly with a fork to break up the egg. Add the Parmesan and parsley.

3 Add the olive oil to the simmering stock, reduce the heat to low, then stir the stock lightly to create a gentle "whirlpool". Gradually pour in the eggs and cook for 1 minute, without boiling, so they set into fine strands. Leave to stand for 1 minute before serving.

Tuscan Bean Soup

This classic dish, *Ribollita*, is named after the traditional method of re-boiling soup from the day before

🍴 serves 4

🕐 prep 15 mins
• cook 1 hr 20 mins

4 tbsp **extra virgin olive oil**, plus extra for drizzling

1 **onion**, chopped

2 **carrots**, sliced

1 **leek**, sliced

2 **garlic cloves**, chopped

400g can **chopped tomatoes**

1 tbsp **tomato purée**

900ml (1½ pints) **chicken stock**

salt and freshly ground **black pepper**

400g can **borlotti beans**, flageolet beans, or cannellini beans, drained and rinsed

250g (9oz) baby **spinach leaves** or spring greens, shredded

8 slices **ciabatta bread**

grated **Parmesan cheese**, for sprinkling

● **Prepare ahead** This soup improves with reheating, so it benefits from being made 1 day in advance. Reheat gently over a low heat.

1 **Heat the oil** in a large saucepan and fry the onion, carrot, and leek over a low heat for 10 minutes, or until softened but not coloured. Add the garlic and fry for 1 minute. Add the tomatoes, tomato purée, and stock. Season to taste with salt and pepper.

2 **Mash half the beans** with a fork and add to the pan. Bring to the boil, then lower the heat and simmer for 30 minutes.

3 **Add the remaining beans** and spinach to the pan. Simmer for a further 30 minutes.

4 **Toast the bread** until golden, place 2 pieces in each soup bowl, and drizzle with olive oil.

5 **To serve**, spoon the soup into the bowls, top with a sprinkling of Parmesan, and drizzle with a little more olive oil.

Hungarian Goulash Soup

The warming flavours of beef, onions, tomato, and paprika make this traditional soup a rich and satisfying meal

🍴 serves 6-8

🕐 prep 15 mins
• cook 2 hrs

120ml (4fl oz) **olive oil**

675g (1½lb) **onions**, peeled and sliced

2 **garlic cloves**, crushed

675g (1½lb) **chuck steak**, cut into 5cm (2in) cubes

salt and freshly ground **black pepper**

2 tbsp **paprika**

1 tsp **caraway seeds**

1 tsp **cayenne pepper**, plus extra, for sprinkling

4 tbsp **tomato paste**

1 litre (1¾ pints) **beef stock**

soured cream, to serve

1 **Heat a large** casserole over medium heat with 3 tbsp of the olive oil and cook the onions for 10 minutes, or until golden brown. Add the garlic for the final 2 minutes, stirring occasionally.

2 **Meanwhile, in a separate** pan, heat the remaining oil and brown the meat on all sides.

3 **Season the meat** with salt and add it to the onions, along with the spices and tomato paste. Cook for 5 minutes stirring all the time, before adding the stock.

4 **Simmer gently** for 1¾ hours, or until the meat is very tender. Season to taste with salt and pepper, serve with soured cream, a sprinkling of cayenne, and black pepper.

VARIATION

Goulash Soup with Dumplings

To make dumplings, a traditional accompaniment, mix 125g (4½oz) self-raising flour with 50g (1¾oz) shredded suet and enough cold water to bring the mixture together to form a smooth, elastic dough. Divide into 12 portions and, with floured hands, roll into balls. Place the dumplings in the soup for the last 25–30 minutes of cooking.

French Onion Soup

This Parisian classic is given extra punch with a spoonful of brandy in each bowl

serves 4

prep 10 mins • cook 1 hr

flameproof soup bowls

freeze the soup, without the bread or cheese, for up to 1 month

30g (1oz) **butter**

1 tbsp **sunflower oil**

675g (1½lb) **onions**, thinly sliced

1 tsp **sugar**

salt and freshly ground **black pepper**

120ml (4fl oz) **dry red wine**

2 tbsp **plain white flour**

1.5 litres (2¾ pints) **beef stock**

4 tbsp **brandy**

1 **garlic clove**, cut in half

4 slices of **baguette**, about 2cm (¾in) thick, toasted

115g (4oz) **Gruyère cheese** or **Emmental cheese**, grated

● **Prepare ahead** Steps 1 and 2 can be completed up to 1 day in advance, covered and chilled.

1 **Melt the butter** with the oil in a large, heavy pan over a low heat. Stir together the onions and sugar and season to taste with salt and pepper. Press a piece of wet, greaseproof paper over the surface and cook, stirring occasionally, uncovered, for 40 minutes, or until the onions are rich and dark golden brown. Take care that they do not stick and burn on the bottom.

2 **Remove the paper** and stir in the wine. Increase the heat to medium and stir for 5 minutes, or until the onions are glazed. Sprinkle with the flour and stir for 2 minutes. Stir in the stock and bring to the boil. Reduce the heat to low, cover, and leave the soup to simmer for 30 minutes. Taste and adjust the seasoning, if necessary.

3 **Meanwhile**, preheat the grill on its highest setting. Divide the soup between 4 flameproof bowls and stir 1 tbsp brandy into each. Rub the garlic clove over the toast and place 1 slice in each bowl. Sprinkle with the cheese and grill for 2–3 minutes, or until the cheese is bubbling and golden. Serve at once.

Minestrone

This substantial soup makes a great lunch or supper dish, and you can add whatever vegetables are in season

serves 4–6

prep 20 mins, plus soaking • cook 1¾ hrs

soak the beans before starting the recipe

freeze up to 1 month before the pasta is added in step 4

100g (3½oz) **dried white cannellini beans**

2 tbsp **olive oil**

2 **celery** sticks, finely chopped

2 **carrots**, finely chopped

1 **onion**, finely chopped

400g can **chopped tomatoes**

750ml (1¼ pints) **chicken stock** or **vegetable stock**

salt and freshly ground **black pepper**

60g (2oz) small **short-cut pasta**

4 tbsp chopped **flat-leaf parsley**

40g (1½oz) **Parmesan cheese**, finely grated

● **Prepare ahead** Steps 1 and 2 can be done 1 day before.

1 **Put the cannellini beans** in a large bowl, cover with cold water and leave to soak for at least 6 hours or overnight.

2 **Drain the beans**, place in a large saucepan, cover with cold water, and bring to the boil over a high heat, skimming the surface as necessary. Boil for 10 minutes, then reduce the heat to low, partially cover the pan, and leave the beans to simmer for 1 hour, or until just tender. Drain well and set aside.

3 **Heat the oil** in the rinsed-out pan over a medium heat. Add the celery, carrots, and onion and fry, stirring occasionally, for 5 minutes, or until tender. Stir in the beans, the tomatoes with their juice, the stock, and season to taste with salt and pepper. Bring to the boil, stirring, then cover and leave to simmer for 20 minutes.

4 **Add the pasta** and simmer for a further 10–15 minutes, or until cooked but still tender to the bite. Stir in the parsley and half the Parmesan, then adjust the seasoning. Serve hot, sprinkled with the remaining Parmesan.

New England Clam Chowder

Americans often serve this traditional, creamy soup with small oyster-shaped saltine crackers

 serves 4

 prep 15 mins • cook 35 mins

cook clams on day of purchase

36 live clams

1 tbsp oil

115g (4oz) thick-cut rindless streaky bacon rashers, diced

1 onion, finely chopped

2 floury potatoes, such as King Edward, peeled and cut into 1cm (½in) cubes

2 tbsp plain white flour

600ml (1 pint) whole milk

salt and freshly ground black pepper

125ml (4½fl oz) single cream

2 tbsp finely chopped flat-leaf parsley

1 **Discard any open clams**. Shuck the clams and reserve the juice, adding enough water to make 600ml (1 pint). Chop the clams.

2 **Heat the oil** in a large, heavy saucepan. Fry the bacon over a medium heat, stirring frequently, for 5 minutes, or until crisp. Remove the bacon from the pan with a slotted spoon, drain on kitchen paper and set aside.

3 **Add the onion** and potatoes to the pan and fry for 5 minutes, or until the onion has softened. Add the flour and stir for 2 minutes.

4 **Stir in the clam juice** and milk and season to taste with salt and pepper. Cover the pan, reduce the heat and leave to simmer for 20 minutes or until the potatoes are tender. Add the clams and simmer gently, uncovered, for 5 minutes.

5 **Stir in the cream** and heat through without boiling. Serve hot, sprinkled with bacon and parsley.

● **Good with** crumbled saltines or cream crackers.

VARIATION

Manhattan Clam Chowder

Unlike the New England version, this chowder recipe contains tomatoes. Follow the recipe above but replace the milk and cream with 2 x 400g cans of chopped tomatoes with their juice, and garnish with a sprinkling of thyme.

Cock-a-Leekie Soup

The traditional method involves the slow simmering of a whole chicken, but today it can be prepared with less time and effort

 serves 4

prep 10 mins • cook 1½ hrs

low fat

freeze for up to 3 months

450g (1lb) chicken breasts and thighs, skinned

1 litre (1¾ pints) chicken stock or vegetable stock

2 bay leaves

60g (2oz) long-grain rice

2 leeks, thinly sliced

2 carrots, grated

pinch of ground cloves

1 tbsp chopped parsley

1 tsp sea salt

1 **Place the chicken** in a pan with the bay leaves and pour in the stock. Bring to the boil then reduce the heat, cover, and simmer for 30 minutes.

2 **Skim the surface** of the soup and discard any scum that has formed. Add the vegetables, rice, cloves, and salt, bring back to the boil,

reduce the heat, cover, and simmer for a further 30 minutes.

3 **Remove the bay leaves** and discard. If you wish, you can lift out the chicken, remove the meat from the bones, then return the meat to the soup.

4 **Ladle the soup** into a warm tureen or divide between individual serving bowls and serve while still hot.

● **Good with** plenty of warm crusty bread. To make an even more substantial meal, add a few boiled potatoes to each serving.

VARIATION

Traditional Cock-a-Leekie Soup

Traditionally, prunes were included in this soup, as they add a delicious sweetness. Add a few with the vegetables in step 2. You can also make the soup with turkey instead of chicken, and add other vegetables such as peas, beans, or grated turnip.

Bouillabaisse

Originally nothing more than a humble fisherman's soup using the remains of the day's catch, bouillabaisse has evolved into one of the great Provençal dishes

serves 4

prep 20 mins • cook 45 mins

4 tbsp olive oil

1 onion, thinly sliced

2 leeks, thinly sliced

1 small fennel bulb, thinly sliced

2–3 garlic cloves, finely chopped

4 tomatoes, skinned, deseeded, and chopped

1 tbsp tomato purée

250ml (8fl oz) dry white wine

1.5 litres (2¾ pints) fish stock or chicken stock

pinch of saffron threads

strip of orange zest

1 bouquet garni

salt and freshly ground black pepper

1.35kg (3lb) mixed white and oily fish and shellfish, such as gurnard, John Dory, monkfish, red mullet, prawns, and mussels, heads and bones removed

2 tbsp Pernod

8 thin slices day-old French bread, toasted, to serve

For the rouille

125g (4½oz) mayonnaise

1 bird's-eye chilli, deseeded and roughly chopped

4 garlic cloves, roughly chopped

1 tbsp tomato purée

½ tsp salt

● **Prepare ahead** The rouille can be made up to 2 days in advance, covered, and chilled until needed.

1 **Heat the oil** in a large saucepan over a medium heat. Add the onion, leeks, fennel, and garlic and fry, stirring frequently, for 5–8 minutes, or until the vegetables are softened but not coloured. Add the tomatoes, tomato purée, and wine and stir until blended.

2 **Add the stock**, saffron, orange zest and bouquet garni. Season to taste with salt and pepper, and bring to the boil. Reduce the heat, partially cover the pan, and simmer for 30 minutes, or until the soup is reduced slightly, stirring occasionally.

3 **To make the rouille**, place all ingredients into a blender or food processor and process until smooth. Transfer to a bowl, cover with cling film, and chill until required.

4 **Just before** the liquid finishes simmering, cut the fish into chunks. Remove the orange zest and bouquet garni from the soup and add the firm fish. Reduce the heat to low and let the soup simmer for 5 minutes, then add the delicate fish and simmer for a further 2–3 minutes, or until all the fish is cooked through and flakes easily.

Stir in the Pernod, and season to taste with salt and pepper.

5 **To serve**, spread each piece of toast with rouille and put 2 slices in the bottom of each bowl. Ladle the soup on top and serve.

● **Good with** thick slices of lightly toasted crunchy French bread.

Winter Vegetable Soup

Some people call this "Penny Soup", not just because it is inexpensive to make but because the vegetables resemble coins

🍴 serves 4

🕐 prep 15 mins • cook 25 mins

1 leek

300g (10oz) new potatoes

250g (9oz) large carrots

175g (6oz) small sweet potatoes

15g (½oz) butter

1 tbsp olive oil

salt and freshly ground black pepper

600ml (1 pint) vegetable stock

1 tbsp chopped parsley

● **Prepare ahead** Cook the day before, cool, cover, and refrigerate. Reheat before serving.

1 Slice all the vegetables across into rounds about 2–3mm (⅛in) thick. The potatoes can be left peeled or unpeeled.

2 Melt the butter with the oil in a large saucepan or flameproof casserole and add the leeks. Cook over a medium heat for 3–4 minutes, or until soft, stirring frequently. Add the remaining vegetables and cook, stirring, for 1 minute.

3 Pour in the stock, bring to the boil, cover, and simmer for 18–20 minutes, or until the vegetables are tender but not soft.

4 Transfer about one-third of the vegetables into a blender or food processor with a little of the liquid. Blend to a smooth purée and return to the pan. Stir in the parsley, season to taste with salt and pepper, and serve, with the vegetables in a little mound in the centre.

Sopa de Tortilla

Fresh lime juice, coriander, and dried poblano chillies give a Mexican flavour to this tomato soup

🍴 serves 4

🕐 prep 15 mins • cook 50 mins

5 tbsp sunflower oil

½ onion, finely chopped

2 large garlic cloves, finely chopped

450g (1lb) tomatoes, skinned

1.5 litres (2¾ pints) chicken stock or vegetable stock

2 soft corn tortillas, cut into strips

1 or 2 dried poblano chillies, deseeded

3 tbsp chopped coriander

2 tbsp fresh lime juice

85g (3 oz) Gruyére cheese, grated

2 limes, cut into wedges, to serve

salt and freshly ground black pepper

● **Prepare ahead** Steps 1–4 can be prepared up to 1 day in advance and the tortilla strips stored in an airtight container.

1 Heat 1 tbsp of the oil in a large saucepan over a medium heat. Add the onion and fry, stirring, for 5 minutes, or until softened. Add the garlic and stir for 30 seconds.

Transfer to a food processor or blender with the tomatoes and process until smooth.

2 Tip the purée into the pan and simmer for 8–10 minutes, stirring constantly. Stir in the stock and bring to the boil. Reduce the heat, partially cover the pan, and simmer for 15 minutes, or until the soup has thickened.

3 Place a non-stick frying pan over a medium heat. Add the chillies and press them flat against the pan with a spatula until they blister, then repeat for the other side. Remove from the pan, cut into small pieces, and set aside.

4 Heat the remaining oil in the frying pan until sizzling hot. Add the tortilla strips in batches and fry just until crisp. Remove with a slotted spoon and drain on kitchen paper.

5 When ready to serve, add the chillies to the soup, bring to the boil and simmer for 3 minutes, or until the chillies are soft. Stir in the coriander and lime juice and salt and pepper to taste. Divide the toasted tortilla strips between 4 soup bowls. Ladle in the soup and top with a sprinkling of cheese.

Chicken Noodle Soup

This spicy Mexican soup, *Sopa Seca de Fideos*, is made with thin fideo noodles, which are similar to angel hair pasta

- serves 4
- prep 20 mins • cook 15 mins
- soak the dried chillies in water for 30 mins
- low fat

2 large ripe **tomatoes**, skinned and deseeded

2 **garlic** cloves

1 small **onion**, roughly chopped

2 dried **chipotle chillies**, soaked

900ml (1½ pints) **chicken stock**

3 tbsp **vegetable oil**

2 skinless boneless **chicken breasts**, diced

225g (8oz) **Mexican fideo** or dried angel hair pasta

4 tbsp **soured cream**, to serve

1 **avocado**, stone removed and chopped, to serve

● **Prepare ahead** The tomato sauce base for the soup can be prepared 1 day in advance. Chill until needed.

1 Put the tomatoes, garlic, onion, chillies, and 2 tbsp stock into a food processor or blender, and process to a purée. Set aside.

2 Heat 2 tbsp oil in a large pan and stir-fry the chicken for 2–3 minutes, or until just cooked. Remove from the pan, drain on kitchen paper, and set aside.

3 Add the remaining oil to the pan, add the noodles, and cook over a low heat until the noodles are golden, stirring constantly.

4 Pour in the tomato mixture, stir until the noodles are coated, then add the stock, and return the chicken to the pan. Cook the noodles for 2–3 minutes, or until just tender.

5 To serve, ladle into soup bowls, and top each with soured cream and chopped avocado.

VARIATION

Chinese Chicken Noodle Soup

Soak 40g (1½oz) dried Chinese mushrooms in 300ml (10fl oz) boiling water for 30 minutes. Strain the soaking water into a large saucepan and add 600ml (1pint) chicken stock. Slice the mushrooms and cut 2 skinless boneless chicken breasts into bite-sized pieces or thin strips. Break up 175g (6oz) dried rice vermicelli into short lengths, stir into the stock, and bring to a simmer. Cook for 2 minutes, then add the mushrooms, chicken, and 100g (3½oz) sweetcorn kernels. Simmer for a further 2 minutes. Spoon into bowls and serve at once.

Lentil Soup

This hearty vegetarian soup has just a touch of spice and is quick and easy to prepare

- serves 4
- prep 20 mins • cook 35 mins
- low fat

1 tbsp **olive oil**

2 **onions**, finely chopped

2 **celery sticks**, finely chopped

2 **carrots**, finely chopped

2 **garlic cloves**, crushed

1–2 tsp **curry powder**

150g (5½oz) **red lentils**

1.4 litres (2½ pints) **vegetable stock**

120ml (4fl oz) **tomato juice** or vegetable juice

salt and freshly ground **black pepper**

1 Heat the oil in a large pan over a medium heat, then add the onions, celery, and carrots. Cook, stirring, for 5 minutes, or until the onions are soft and translucent.

2 Add the garlic and curry powder and cook, stirring, for a further 1 minute, then add the lentils, stock, and tomato juice.

3 Bring to the boil, then lower the heat, cover, and simmer for 25 minutes, or until the vegetables are tender. Season to taste with salt and pepper, and serve hot.

● **Good with** a spoonful of natural yogurt and crusty bread.

Potato Salad with Parma Ham

A full-flavoured, hearty salad that can easily be doubled to serve a crowd

 serves 6

🕐 prep 10 mins • cook 25 mins

675g (1½lb) small **new potatoes**

1 tbsp **caraway seeds**

6 slices **Parma ham**, cut into thin strips

3–4 tbsp finely chopped **parsley** or chives

For the dressing

2 **shallots** or spring onions, finely chopped

150ml (5fl oz) **soured cream**

1 tsp **Dijon mustard**

1 tbsp **red wine vinegar**

1 **garlic clove**, crushed

salt and freshly ground **black pepper**

3 tbsp **olive oil**

1 **Place the potatoes** in a large pan, cover with cold water, add ½ tsp salt, and bring to the boil over a high heat. Reduce the heat, cover, and simmer for 12–15 minutes, or until tender. Drain well, then set aside to cool.

2 **Meanwhile,** heat a small frying pan over a medium-high heat. Add the caraway seeds and cook, stirring frequently, for 2 minutes, or until lightly toasted. Set aside.

3 **To make the dressing**, place the shallots, soured cream, mustard, vinegar, and garlic in a small bowl, season to taste with salt and pepper, then whisk in the olive oil.

4 **Cut each potato** in half and place in a large bowl. Add the caraway seeds and Parma ham, then pour the dressing over. Add all but 1 tbsp of the chopped parsley and toss gently to combine.

5 **Transfer to** a serving platter and scatter with the remaining chopped parsley.

Pasta and Tuna Niçoise Salad

This easy summer dish, made with shell pasta instead of potatoes, is great for summer lunches and outdoor eating

 serves 4

🕐 prep 20 mins • cook 15 mins

350g (12oz) dried **conchiglie pasta**

salt and freshly ground **black pepper**

140g (5oz) **French beans**

4 **tuna steaks**, 400g (14oz) in total

olive oil, for brushing

2 hard-boiled **eggs**, peeled

2 **Little Gem lettuce**

200g (7oz) **cherry tomatoes**, halved

45g (1½oz) **anchovy fillets**, rinsed

100g (3½oz) **black olives**, pitted

For the dressing

4 tbsp **extra virgin olive oil**

1 tbsp **lemon** juice

1 tbsp **balsamic vinegar**

1 tsp **wholegrain mustard**

● **Prepare ahead** You can complete steps 1–4 earlier in the day, then cover the bowl with cling film and refrigerate until needed.

1 **Cook the pasta** in a large pan of lightly salted boiling water for 8–10 minutes, or until *al dente*. Drain and rinse quickly under cold water.

2 **Meanwhile,** cook the beans in a pan of lightly salted boiling water for 4–5 minutes, or until almost tender but still firm to the bite. Drain and rinse in cold water.

3 **Preheat a frying pan** or griddle pan to hot. Brush the tuna lightly with olive oil, season, and cook for 2–3 minutes on each side, depending on thickness. The tuna should still be slightly pink inside.

4 **Roughly flake** the tuna and mix with the pasta and beans in a large bowl. Cut the eggs into quarters, roughly break up the lettuce leaves, and add to the bowl. Stir in the tomatoes, anchovies, and olives.

5 **Place all the dressing** ingredients in a screw-top jar and shake well. Season to taste with salt and pepper, then pour over the salad. Toss well, and serve.

● **Good with** chunks of French country bread.

Caesar Salad

Anchovies and Parmesan cheese combine to give this classic salad its traditional salty flavour

🍴 serves 6

🕐 prep 10 mins • cook 2 mins

2 small heads of **Cos lettuce**, torn into small pieces

2 large **eggs**

100g (3½oz) shop-bought **croutons**

60g (2oz) **Parmesan cheese**, shaved or grated

For the dressing

2 **garlic** cloves, crushed to a purée

2 **anchovy fillets** in olive oil, drained and finely chopped

1 tbsp fresh **lemon** juice

1 tsp **Worcestershire sauce**

120ml (4fl oz) **extra virgin olive oil**

freshly ground **black pepper**

● **Prepare ahead** The dressing can be made in advance, and chilled in an airtight container for up to 1 week.

1 **To make the dressing**, mash the garlic and anchovies together to make a thick paste. Transfer to a screw-top jar, add the olive oil, lemon juice, and Worcestershire sauce, then season to taste with pepper. Shake the dressing until well blended. Set aside.

2 **To assemble the salad**, toss the lettuce leaves with the croutons in a salad bowl. Bring a small saucepan of water to the boil over a high heat. Reduce the heat to medium, add the eggs, and boil gently for no more than 2 minutes. Drain and rinse with cold water.

3 **Crack open the eggs**, scoop on to the lettuce, and toss. Shake the dressing again, then add to the salad, and toss again. Sprinkle with the Parmesan and serve at once.

● **Good with** all barbecued meats. It is especially good served as a first course or a lunch dish with chunks of French bread.

VARIATION

Chicken Caesar Salad

Add 300g (10oz) of cooked shredded or sliced chicken for a delicious main course salad.

Rocket Salad with Parmesan

Quick to prepare, this makes an excellent first course or side salad

🍴 serves 4

🕐 prep 10 mins

100ml (3½fl oz) **extra virgin olive oil**

4 tbsp fresh **lemon** juice

2 tsp **sea salt**

large bunch of **rocket**

freshly ground **black pepper**

45g (1½oz) **Parmesan cheese**

● **Prepare ahead** Wash the rocket and refrigerate, wrapped in kitchen paper; shave the Parmesan.

1 **Whisk together** the olive oil, lemon juice, and sea salt in a large non-metallic bowl. Add the rocket leaves and toss together.

2 **Arrange the dressed** leaves on a serving platter.

3 **Use a potato peeler** to shave the Parmesan. Scatter these shavings over the rocket, add a generous amount of freshly ground pepper and serve.

● **Good with** barbecued meat, fish, seafood, vegetarian main courses, or as a first course with bread and olives.

VARIATION

Watercress Salad

Use the same amount of watercress, with a little radicchio for added colour if you like. Add shavings of smoked Gouda cheese to balance the slight bitterness of the watercress.

Layered Marinated Herring Salad

For convenience, and to save time, buy ready-marinated herring fillets at the supermarket or deli

 serves 6–10

prep 15 mins, plus soaking and chilling

1 sweet onion, thinly sliced

250ml (8fl oz) soured cream

120ml (4fl oz) plain yogurt

1 tbsp fresh lemon juice

¼ tsp caster sugar

2 tart dessert apples, peeled, cored, and thinly sliced

2 pickled dill cucumbers, sliced or chopped

salt and freshly ground black pepper

300g (10oz) marinated herring fillets, drained

2 cooked potatoes, diced (optional)

1 cooked beetroot, sliced (optional)

1 tbsp chopped dill, to garnish

● **Prepare ahead** The salad benefits from being assembled up to 2 days in advance and chilled.

1 Put the onion in a bowl, cover with cold water, and leave to soak for 15 minutes. Drain well, then toss with the soured cream, yogurt, lemon juice, and sugar. Stir in the apple and pickles, and season to taste with salt and pepper.

2 Place half the herring in a serving dish and top with the potatoes and the beetroot, if using. Cover with half the soured cream sauce. Layer the remaining herring, potatoes, and beetroot over the sauce, then add the remaining sauce.

3 Cover the dish tightly with cling film and refrigerate for at least 5 hours. Sprinkle with dill just before serving.

● **Good with** slices of sourdough bread or pumpernickel.

Warm Chicken Salad

Quick to cook and easy to assemble, this is an example of a French *salade tiède*, or warm salad

 serves 4

 prep 10 mins • cook 8 mins

4 tbsp extra virgin olive oil

4 chicken breasts, about 150g (5½oz) each, cut into thin strips

1 garlic clove, finely chopped

salt and freshly ground black pepper

60g (2oz) sun-dried tomatoes, thinly sliced

1 small head of radicchio, torn into small pieces

250g (9oz) asparagus spears, each trimmed and cut into 3 pieces

2 tbsp raspberry vinegar

½ tsp sugar

1 Heat 2 tbsp of the oil in a large non-stick frying pan over a medium-high heat. Add the chicken and garlic and fry, stirring, for 5–7 minutes, or until the chicken is tender and cooked through. Stir in the sun-dried tomatoes, and season to taste with salt and pepper.

2 Meanwhile, put the radicchio leaves in a large serving bowl. Remove the chicken from the pan, using a slotted spoon, and place in the bowl with the radicchio.

3 Add the asparagus to the fat remaining in the pan and fry, stirring constantly, for 1–2 minutes, or until just tender. Transfer to the bowl with the chicken.

4 Whisk together the remaining 2 tbsp oil, the vinegar and sugar, then pour into the pan and stir over a high heat until well combined. Pour this dressing over the salad and toss quickly so that all the ingredients are well mixed and coated with the dressing. Serve straight away.

Little Gem Salad

Make the Parmesan cheese shavings with a vegetable peeler for a bistro-style salad

🍴 serves 6

🕐 prep 20 mins • cook 10–15 mins

115g (4oz) piece of **baguette**

3 tbsp **olive oil**

salt and freshly ground **black pepper**

3 heads of **Little Gem lettuce**

Parmesan cheese shaved, to serve

For the dressing

2 **egg yolks**

1 **egg**

1 tsp **caster sugar**

1 tsp **Dijon mustard**

1 **garlic clove**, peeled

juice of ½ **lemon**

1 tsp **Worcestershire sauce**

2 **anchovies**, rinsed and drained

150ml (5floz) **sunflower oil**

60g (2oz) **Parmesan cheese**, grated

● **Prepare ahead** Baked croutons keep in an airtight container for at least a week, and the dressing in the refrigerator for 3 days.

1 Preheat the oven to 180°C (350°F/Gas 4). To make croutons, slice the bread thinly, then into quarters. Toss in olive oil, season with salt and pepper, then bake on a baking tray for 10–15 minutes, or until crisp. Set aside.

2 Place all the dressing ingredients, except the oil and cheese, into a food processor and process until smooth, then gradually drizzle in the oil until the mixture thickens to a slightly runny mayonnaise. Season to taste with salt and pepper and mix in the grated Parmesan cheese. Add a little cold water if it is too thick. Cover and chill.

3 Wash, dry, and tear the gem leaves into a large bowl and pour over the dressing, mixing lightly with 2 spoons. To serve, pile on to a large platter or individual plates and scatter over croutons and Parmesan cheese.

Marinated Goat's Cheese Salad

This simple, yet stylish, recipe makes a great dinner-party starter

🍴 serves 6

🕐 prep 15 mins, plus marinating • cook 5 mins

2 **garlic cloves**, chopped

small bunch of **basil**, shredded

1 tbsp grated **lemon** zest

2 **red chillies**, deseeded and finely chopped

sea salt and freshly ground **black pepper**

150ml (5fl oz) **olive oil**, plus extra for brushing

6 **goat's cheese crottins**

1 **baguette**

2 **white chicory heads**, leaves separated

1 bunch of **watercress**, washed

50g (1¾oz) **olives**, halved

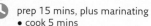

● **Prepare ahead** The marinade can be made and the goat's cheese marinated up to 24 hours in advance.

1 To make the marinade, mix the garlic, basil, lemon zest, and chilli. Season to taste with salt and pepper, then mix with the olive oil.

2 Place the goat's cheeses in a shallow non-metallic dish, and pour over the marinade, making sure they are coated evenly. Cover and chill for 24 hours.

3 The next day, preheat the oven to 180°C (350°F/Gas 4). Cut the baguette into 12 thick slices, brush with the olive oil, and bake until crisp and golden.

4 Preheat the grill on its highest setting, cut the goat's cheeses in half crossways, place on a baking tray, and grill for 5 minutes, or until golden. To serve, divide the chicory, watercress, and olives between 6 plates, place 2 pieces of toast on each plate, and top with the grilled goat's cheese. Spoon over any remaining marinade.

● **Good with** more salad leaves and extra olives to turn this starter into a main course lunch.

Roasted Tomato Salad with Lemon and Crème Fraîche

Slow-roasting tomatoes intensifies their sweet flavour, which is well matched with a creamy dresssing

 serves 4

prep 15 mins • cook 2 hrs

6 large **plum tomatoes**

2 tbsp **olive oil**

sea salt and freshly ground **black pepper**

2 bunches of **spring onions**

150g (5oz) **crème fraîche**

lemon-infused olive oil or a good extra virgin olive oil

● **Prepare ahead** The tomatoes can be roasted well ahead of time and the spring onions can be wilted 1 hour before.

1 Preheat the oven to 140°C (275°F/Gas 1). Halve and core the tomatoes and place, cut-side up, on a baking tray; drizzle with 1 tbsp olive oil, season with the sea salt and black pepper, and roast for 2 hours. Trim the spring onions, cut in half, then slice in half lengthways.

2 Preheat a heavy frying pan. Toss the onions in the remaining olive oil, and fry in the pan for 1–2 minutes, or until just wilted. Add salt to taste and set aside.

3 Once cool, arrange 3 tomato halves on each plate and add a dollop of crème fraîche and spring onions. Drizzle with lemon oil. Season to taste with the pepper, and serve.

● **Good with** herby ciabatta bread, olives, and roasted peppers.

VARIATION

Balsamic Tomatoes on Toast

Roast the tomatoes as above, drizzle with balsamic vinegar while still warm, and serve on wholegrain toast.

Waldorf Salad

A classic dish named after the prestigious Waldorf–Astoria hotel in New York

 serves 4

prep 20 mins, plus chilling

500g (1 2lb 2oz) crisp, **red-skinned apples**, cored and diced

juice of ½ **lemon**

4 **celery sticks**, thickly sliced crossways

150ml (5fl oz) **mayonnaise**

salt and freshly ground **black pepper**

85g (3oz) **walnuts**, coarsely chopped

snipped **chives**, to garnish

1 Place the diced apples into a mixing bowl and pour the lemon juice on top. Coat the apple well, as this will prevent discolouring.

2 Add the celery, mayonnaise, and season to taste with salt and pepper. Mix well, then cover and chill.

3 Remove the salad from the refrigerator, stir in the walnuts, sprinkle with the chives, and serve.

Grilled Courgette and Pepper Salad with Coriander and Cumin

A tasty mix of vegetables topped with a versatile vinaigrette

🍴 serves 6

🕐 prep 30 mins • cook 10 mins

🍲 ridged cast-iron grill pan

6 courgettes

olive oil, for brushing

3 red peppers or yellow peppers, quartered and deseeded

4 spring onions, thinly sliced

4 plum tomatoes (optional)

For the vinaigrette

15g (½oz) coriander, chopped

2 tbsp cumin seeds, roasted

juice and zest of 1 lemon

1 tbsp clear honey

2 garlic cloves, chopped

150ml (5fl oz) olive oil

salt and freshly ground black pepper

● **Prepare ahead** The vinaigrette can be made 3 days ahead.

1 Whisk together the vinaigrette ingredients and season to taste with salt and pepper. Set aside until needed.

2 Preheat a ridged cast-iron grill pan and preheat the grill. Slice the courgettes into thin strips, lightly brush with olive oil, and lay on the grill pan, in batches, until scored well on each side. Drain on kitchen paper. Place the peppers under the grill, skin-side up, and grill until well charred, then place in a plastic bag to cool slightly before peeling off their skins and cutting into strips.

3 Mix the peppers, courgettes, and spring onions together, add wedges of plum tomatoes (if using), and toss with the vinaigrette to serve.

Tuscan Bread Salad

This popular Italian dish, also known as *Panzanella*, is a great way to use up leftover ciabatta

🍴 serves 4

🕐 prep 25 mins, plus marinating

½ loaf ciabatta, about 300g (10oz), cut into bite-sized pieces

400g (14oz) small, ripe plum tomatoes, quartered or cut into chunks

½ red onion, thinly sliced

½ cucumber, peeled and cut into chunks

1 tbsp red wine vinegar

3 tbsp extra virgin olive oil

coarse sea salt and freshly ground black pepper

small bunch of flat-leaf parsley, coarsely chopped

8 basil leaves, torn into small pieces

● **Prepare ahead** If you make this dish 30–40 minutes in advance, the dressing and the juices from the tomatoes and cucumber have time to soak into the bread; add the herbs just before serving.

1 Place the bread, tomatoes, onion, and cucumber in a serving bowl. Sprinkle with the vinegar and oil and season to taste with salt and pepper, then mix well. Set aside for 30–40 minutes, mixing thoroughly once or twice to ensure the bread pieces soak up all the juices.

2 Just before serving, scatter the herbs over the salad.

● **Good with** cold meats or a cheese platter.

> **BREAD PIECES**
> If you do not have ciabatta, any good-quality, country-style bread will do.

Smoked Trout and Pancetta Salad

The bitter leaves and radishes combine well with the smoky fish in this light lunch or starter

 serves 6

prep 10 mins • cook 10 mins

350g (12oz) **hot smoked trout fillet**

12 thin slices of **pancetta**

2 bunches of **watercress**, washed

2 **white chicory**, leaves divided

140g (5oz) **feta cheese**, cubed

5 small **radishes**, finely sliced

2 **shallots**, peeled and finely sliced

For the dressing

1 tbsp good quality **red wine vinegar**

90ml (3fl oz) **extra virgin olive oil**

1 tsp **caster sugar**

juice of ½ **lemon**

1 tsp **Dijon mustard**

salt and freshly ground **black pepper**

1 Skin the trout and carefully remove the bones, keeping the flesh as intact as possible. Heat a frying pan and fry the pancetta for 5 minutes, or until crisp.

2 Whisk the dressing ingredients together and season to taste with salt and pepper. Place the watercress and chicory on to a serving plate, scatter over large flakes of the trout, then add the feta, bacon, radishes, and shallots. Drizzle the salad with a little of the dressing and serve.

VARIATION

Smoked Mackerel Salad

Replace the trout with flaked fillets of peppered smoked mackerel, and remove the radishes.

Watercress and Roasted Walnut Salad

Try this dish served alongside savoury tarts

 serves 6

prep 15 mins • cook 10 mins

100g (3½oz) **walnut pieces**

2 bunches **watercress**, washed and dried

2 **shallots**, finely chopped

For the dressing

1 tsp **Dijon mustard**

1 tbsp **red wine vinegar**

1 tsp **soft brown sugar**

salt and freshly ground **black pepper**

4 tbsp **walnut oil**

1 Preheat the oven to 180°C (350°F/Gas 4). Place the walnuts in a single layer on a baking tray and roast for 10 minutes, or until nicely browned, watching closely that they do not burn. Remove from the oven, let cool, slightly crush with your hands, then set aside.

2 To make the dressing, place the mustard, vinegar, and sugar in a bowl, season with salt and pepper, and slowly whisk in the walnut oil.

3 Place the watercress, shallots, and walnuts in a serving bowl. Toss with the dressing to serve.

Vietnamese Salad of Grilled Prawns with Papaya

Vietnamese cuisine has fresh, clean flavours with lime, mint, chillies, and fish sauce all ingredients that are widely used

 serves 4

 prep 15 mins • cook 2–3 mins

 low fat

12 large **raw prawns**

2 tbsp **vegetable oil**

1 tsp **rice wine vinegar**

1 tsp **sugar**

1 **red chilli**, deseeded and very finely chopped

2 **garlic cloves**, crushed

2 tbsp **Vietnamese fish sauce** or Thai fish sauce

1 tbsp **lime** juice

1 tbsp chopped *rau ram* (Vietnamese mint) or mint leaves

1 **green papaya**, deseeded, quartered lengthways, and thinly sliced

½ **cucumber**, deseeded and cut julienne

● **Prepare ahead** Steps 1 and 2 can be completed up to several hours in advance. Store, covered, in the refrigerator, until ready to serve.

1 **Peel and devein** the prawns, removing and discarding the heads and tails. Spread them out on a foil-lined grill rack, brush with the oil and grill for 2–3 minutes, or until they turn pink.

2 **Meanwhile**, whisk the rice wine vinegar, sugar, chilli, garlic, fish sauce, lime juice, and 75ml (3fl oz) cold water together in a bowl until the sugar dissolves. Add the cooked prawns to the bowl and stir well until they are coated in the dressing. Leave to cool completely.

3 **Add the chopped mint**, papaya, and cucumber and toss together. Transfer the salad to a serving platter, with the prawns on the top, and garnish with mint sprigs.

> ### Green Papaya
> Green papaya is crunchy and less sweet than the ripe, orange-fleshed fruit.

Prawn, Grapefruit, and Avocado Salad

A tangy salad to satisfy lovers of seafood, this is simple enough for brunch but special enough to serve to dinner guests

 serves 6

prep 15 mins

30 **king prawns**, cooked and peeled

2 large **pink grapefruit**, divided into segments

handful of **mint** leaves, torn

3 **red radishes**, finely sliced

3 **spring onions**, finely sliced

2 **avocados**, peeled and cut into chunks or slices

bunch of **watercress**

salad leaves

For the dressing

3 tbsp **Thai fish sauce**

3 tbsp **lime** juice

2 tbsp **caster sugar**

2 tbsp **olive oil**

● **Prepare ahead** The dressing can be made several days in advance and kept refrigerated.

1 **Make the dressing** by placing all the ingredients together in a jar and shaking vigorously.

2 **Pat the prawns** dry using kitchen paper, then toss them in a little of the dressing.

3 **Place the remaining** salad ingredients in a large bowl and toss well. Divide between 6 individual plates. Arrange 5 prawns on top of each plate and drizzle with some of the remaining dressing to serve.

VARIATION

Lobster and Crab Salad
Replace the prawns in the recipe with the same quantity of bite-sized pieces of lobster and crab claw meat.

Coleslaw

Home-made coleslaw is a great standby to have in the refrigerator. It is simple to make and much nicer than any shop-bought alternatives

 serves 4

 prep 15 mins

 grater, mandolin, or food processor with grater attachment

250g (9oz) **white cabbage**

2 large **carrots**, coarsely grated

2 **celery stalks**, finely sliced

2 **spring onions**, finely sliced

120ml (4fl oz) **mayonnaise**

4 tsp **milk**

juice of 1 small **lemon**

2 tbsp chopped **flat-leaf parsley**

1 tbsp snipped **chives**

salt and freshly ground **black pepper**

● **Prepare ahead** The coleslaw can be prepared as much as 2 days ahead, and kept in an airtight container in the refrigerator.

1 Slice the cabbage as finely as possible, discarding the stalk, and place the shreds in a large bowl. Add the prepared carrots, celery, and spring onions, and mix together.

2 In a small bowl, mix together the mayonnaise and milk, then the lemon juice, parsley, and chives, and season to taste with salt and pepper. Add this dressing to the vegetables and stir until well mixed. Cover and set aside for a couple of hours to allow the flavours to develop.

● **Good with** a jacket potato, or as part of a sandwich filling.

 VARIATION

Fruit and Nut Coleslaw

For extra sweetness and crunch, add 50g (1¾oz) chopped toasted walnuts or pecans and 50g (1¾oz) juicy sultanas or raisins before serving.

Tabbouleh

This Lebanese speciality of parsley, mint, tomatoes, and bulgur is refreshing all year round

 serves 4

🕐 prep 20 mins, plus standing

115g (4oz) **bulgur wheat**

juice of 2 **lemons**

75ml (2½fl oz) **extra virgin olive oil**

freshly ground **black pepper**

225g (8oz) **flat-leaf parsley**, coarse stalks removed

75g (2½oz) **mint** leaves, coarse stalks removed

4 **spring onions**, finely chopped

2 large **tomatoes**, deseeded and diced

1 head of **Little Gem lettuce**

1 Put the bulgur wheat in a large bowl, pour over cold water to cover, and leave to stand for 15 minutes, or until the wheat has absorbed all the water and the grains have swollen.

2 Add the lemon juice and olive oil to the wheat, season to taste with pepper, and stir to mix.

3 Just before serving, finely chop the parsley and mint. Mix the parsley, mint, and spring onions into the wheat.

4 Arrange the lettuce leaves on a serving plate and spoon the salad into the leaves.

VARIATION

Fruit Tabbouleh

Replace the chopped tomatoes with 2-3 tbsp pomegranate seeds or plump, juicy raisins, and the same quantity of toasted pine nuts.

Salad Niçoise

This well-known classic French salad is substantial enough to be served as a main dish

 serves 4

prep 25 mins • cook 10 mins

150g (5½oz) **green beans**, trimmed

4 x 150g (5½oz) **tuna steaks**

150 ml (5fl oz) **extra virgin olive oil**, plus extra for brushing

salt and freshly ground **black pepper**

2 tsp **Dijon mustard**

1 **garlic clove**, finely chopped

3 tbsp **white wine vinegar**

juice of ½ **lemon**

8 **anchovy fillets** in olive oil, drained

1 **red onion**, finely sliced

250g (9oz) **plum tomatoes**, quartered lengthways

12 **black olives**

2 **romaine lettuce hearts**, trimmed and torn into bite-sized pieces

8–10 **basil leaves**

4 **eggs**, hard-boiled

1 Cook the green beans in a saucepan of gently boiling water, for 3–4 minutes, or until just tender. Drain the beans and quickly place them into a bowl of ice water.

2 Preheat a ridged grill pan over a medium-high heat. Brush the tuna steaks with 1–2 tbsp olive oil and season to taste with salt and pepper. Sear the tuna steaks for 2 minutes on each side. The centres will still be slightly pink. Set the tuna aside. Drain the green beans.

3 Meanwhile, to make the vinaigrette, whisk together the Dijon mustard, garlic, vinegar, olive oil, and lemon juice. Season to taste with salt and pepper.

4 Place the green beans, anchovies, onion, tomatoes, olives, lettuce and basil in a large bowl. Drizzle with the vinaigrette and gently toss.

5 Divide the salad between 4 plates. Peel and quarter each egg and add them to the plates. Cut each tuna steak in half and arrange both halves on top of the salad.

VARIATION

Grilled Chicken Salad

Grill 4 chicken breasts instead of tuna. Both versions are good with the addition of capers and boiled new potatoes that have been chilled and sliced.

Roast Beetroot with Bresaeola

Freshly roasted beetroot gives this salad vibrant colour and a delicious earthy flavour

 serves 6

prep 10 mins • cook 15 mins

18 **baby beetroot**

2 sprigs of **thyme**

3 tbsp **extra virgin olive oil**

salt and freshly ground **black pepper**

2 tbsp **red wine vinegar**

handful of **rocket** leaves

12 slices **bresaeola**

chives, to garnish

For the dressing

1 tbsp **grated horseradish**

5 tbsp **crème fraîche** or soured cream

1 tsp **white wine** or rice vinegar

juice and zest of 1 **lemon**

● **Prepare ahead** The dressing can be made 2 days in advance and the beetroot cooked the day before.

1 Preheat the oven to 200°C (400°F/Gas 6). Place the beetroot on a large piece of heavy foil with the thyme and olive oil, and season with salt and pepper. Fold the foil into a packet, seal the edges, and bake for 45 minutes, or until the beetroot is easily pierced with a knife.

2 Unwrap the foil and trim off the excess beetroot stems. Rub the skins off the beetroot and cut each beetroot into slices. Place in a bowl and sprinkle with the vinegar.

3 Grate the zest and squeeze the juice from the lemon, and combine with the other dressing ingredients in a small bowl.

4 To serve, pile a handful of rocket on to each serving plate and drizzle the dressing over. Top with slices of beetroot and two slices of bresaeola. Garnish with chives.

> **TIP**
> When you rub the skins from the beetroot, wear rubber gloves to prevent staining your hands pink.

Oriental Cucumber Salad with Smoked Salmon

Cucumber slices combine well with the flavour of smoked salmon

 serves 6

 prep 10 mins

2 large **cucumbers**

salt and freshly ground **black pepper**

400g (14oz) **smoked salmon**, cut into long strips

1 **lime**, cut into 12 wedges, to garnish (optional)

For the dressing

1 **garlic clove**, finely chopped

1 tbsp **fish sauce**

2 tbsp **groundnut oil**

60ml (2fl oz) **white wine vinegar**

1 tbsp **Thai sweet chilli dipping sauce**

2 tbsp chopped **coriander**

1 **With a vegetable peeler**, slice the cucumber lengthways into ribbons, discarding the central core and seeds.

2 **Place the pieces** in a bowl and set aside. Put the dressing ingredients into a large, screw-top jar and shake well. Alternatively, whisk the ingredients together in a bowl.

3 **10 minutes before serving**, pour the dressing over the cucumber and season to taste with salt and pepper.

4 **To serve**, pile the cucumber on to individual plates, and arrange the smoked salmon strips on top. Sprinkle with black pepper and garnish with lime wedges (if using).

Carrot and Orange Salad

This light, colourful salad is good as an accompaniment to hot or cold meats, or served with a sandwich

🍴 serves 4

🕐 prep 20 mins

2 large **carrots**

2 large **navel oranges**

1 **fennel bulb**

85g (3oz) **watercress**

For the dressing

3 tbsp **light olive oil**

3 tbsp **grapeseed oil** or sunflower oil

1 tbsp **lemon** juice

3 tbsp **orange** juice

1 tsp **clear honey**

salt and freshly ground **black pepper**

2 tsp **sesame seeds**, lightly toasted

● **Prepare ahead** The salad can be prepared 3–6 hours in advance and kept in a covered bowl in the refrigerator, then dressed before serving. Toss the fennel in a little lemon juice to prevent discolouration.

1 Trim and peel the carrots using a vegetable peeler to make thin strips.

2 Cut away the peel and pith from the oranges and divide into segments. Do this over a bowl to catch any juice and use it for the dressing. Trim the fennel and thinly slice. Remove any yellow leaves or tough stalks from the watercress.

3 Put the carrot, orange, fennel, and watercress into a serving bowl. Whisk together the dressing ingredients and pour over. Toss lightly so all the ingredients are coated in the dressing, and serve.

Steamed Aubergine Salad

This crunchy, creamy, and zesty salad can be served alone or alongside roast lamb

🍴 serves 6

🕐 prep 15 mins • cook 20 mins

2 medium **aubergines**, peeled

60g (2oz) **soft goat's cheese**, crumbled

2 ripe **tomatoes**, deseeded and diced

1 small **red onion**, finely diced

handful of **flat-leaf parsley**, finely chopped

60g (2oz) **walnuts**, lightly toasted and roughly chopped

1 tbsp **sesame seeds**, lightly toasted

salt and freshly ground **black pepper**

For the dressing

1 **garlic clove**, crushed

salt and freshly ground **black pepper**

4 tbsp **walnut oil**

juice of 1 **lemon**

● **Prepare ahead** Make the dressing the day before and chop the ingredients. Refrigerate until needed.

1 Cut the aubergines into 2cm (¾in) cubes and steam, covered, for 10 minutes. As they cool, squeeze them gently to extract as much water as possible.

2 Combine all the ingredients in a mixing bowl and toss gently. Whisk together the dressing ingredients and toss it with the salad. Season to taste with salt and pepper.

VARIATION

Aubergine Salad with Feta and Pine Nuts

Replace the cheese and sesame seeds with feta and pine nuts.

Crab Salad

Crab works really well with fruity flavours and is a lovely summer lunch dish

🍴 serves 4

🕐 prep 15 mins

❗ purchase the crab on the day you intend to make the salad

few **mint leaves**, roughly chopped

handful of **coriander leaves**, roughly chopped

handful of **mixed salad leaves**, such as rocket, spinach, and watercress

1 **shallot**, finely chopped

350g (12oz) fresh **crab**, white and brown meat separated

1 ripe **avocado**, sliced lengthways

For the dressing

1 ripe **mango**, roughly chopped

zest and juice of ½ **lime**

3 tbsp **olive oil**

1 To make the dressing, put the mango, lime zest and juice, and olive oil in a food processor and process until smooth. Add a little water if too thick.

2 To make the salad, mix together the herbs with the salad leaves. Add the shallot and toss the salad leaves in a little of the dressing. Divide the salad between 4 plates and arrange a spoonful each of the white and brown crabmeat. Serve with the avocado slices and the remaining dressing on the side.

⚪ **Good with** slices of warm soda bread, or brown bread and butter.

⚪ **Leftovers** are perfect for piling on top of mixed salad leaves or used as a filling for vol-au-vents.

Shaved Fennel Salad

This is a fantastic salad to serve as a starter or side dish, or with cheese

🍴 serves 6

🕐 prep 10 mins, plus marinating

1 **fennel bulb**, sliced finely

½ tbsp aged **balsamic vinegar**

3 tbsp **extra virgin olive oil**

salt and freshly ground **black pepper**

1 **garlic clove**, crushed

150g (5½oz) **mixed salad leaves**, such as watercress, baby spinach, rocket or mache (lamb's lettuce)

1 Peel and discard the tough outer leaves and stalk of the fennel, then use a serrated knife to slice it as thinly as possible. Toss the fennel with a few drops of balsamic vinegar, 1 tbsp of the oil, and the garlic, then season with salt and pepper. Set aside to marinate for at least 1 hour before serving.

2 To serve, mix the leaves, fennel, remaining oil, and vinegar, then season to taste with salt and pepper. Divide the salad leaves between individual plates and serve.

⚪ **Good with** shavings of Parmesan cheese and good-quality pitted black olives scattered over the salad.

Spinach, Pear, and Chicory Salad

An ideal salad to serve alongside duck or red meat dishes

🍴 serves 6

🕐 prep 10 mins

200g (7oz) **baby spinach leaves**

2 heads of **white chicory**

2 firm, but ripe **pears**, peeled and sliced

3 **shallots**, finely sliced

For the vinaigrette

1 tbsp **clear honey**

½ tbsp **Dijon mustard**

6 tbsp **extra virgin olive oil**

2 tbsp **red wine vinegar**

salt and freshly ground **black pepper**

1 Place the honey, mustard, oil, and vinegar in a screw-top jar and shake well. Season to taste with salt and pepper. Alternatively, whisk the ingredients together in a bowl.

2 Place the spinach, chicory, sliced pears, and shallots in a salad bowl. Drizzle the vinaigrette over the salad, gently toss, and serve.

Avocado, Tomato, and Mozzarella Salad

Red, white, and green are the colours of the Italian flag and are echoed in this Italian dish

🍴 serves 4

🕐 prep 15 mins • cook 5 mins

200g (7oz) small **plum tomatoes**

salt and freshly ground **black pepper**

2 **garlic cloves**, peeled and thinly sliced

2 **spring onions**, trimmed and finely chopped

60ml (2fl oz) **extra virgin olive oil**

2 tbsp **balsamic vinegar**, plus extra for drizzling

2 tbsp small **capers**, drained and rinsed

150g (5½oz) small **buffalo mozzarella balls**, torn in half

handful of **basil leaves**, roughly chopped

2 ripe **Hass avocados**

1 Preheat the grill on its highest setting. Place the tomatoes in a single layer on a baking tray, season to taste with salt and pepper, and sprinkle the garlic and spring onions over the top. Drizzle with the olive oil.

2 Place the baking tray under the grill for 4–5 minutes, or until the tomatoes just begin to soften and the garlic turns golden brown.

3 Place the hot tomatoes, garlic, spring onions, and cooking juices in a bowl, and add the vinegar, capers, mozzarella, and basil. Toss gently and set aside.

4 Peel, stone, and quarter the avocados. Place 2 avocado quarters on each plate.

5 Spoon the tomato mixture over the avocado quarters and drizzle with balsamic vinegar. Serve immediately.

Ensaladilla Rusa

The name for potato salad in Spain is *Ensaladilla rusa*, or Russian Salad, and it is popular as tapas or a side dish

🍴 serves 4

🕐 prep 15 mins • cook 25 mins

400g (14oz) waxy **potatoes**, scrubbed

salt and freshly ground **black pepper**

1 **carrot**, finely diced

115g (4oz) **frozen peas**

90ml (3fl oz) **mayonnaise**

2 **roasted red peppers**, drained and cut into small strips

200g can **tuna** in oil, drained (optional)

2 hard-boiled **eggs**, cut into quarters

2 tbsp chopped **flat-leaf parsley**, to garnish

1 Boil the potatoes in salted water in a large saucepan for 15–18 minutes, or until tender. Drain and leave to cool slightly, then peel and cut into cubes.

2 Meanwhile, cook the diced carrot in a small saucepan for 5–6 minutes, or until almost tender. Add the peas, and cook for a further 2 minutes. Drain and cool under cold running water.

3 Put the mayonnaise in a bowl and add the potatoes, carrots, peas, and most of the roasted pepper strips. Add the tuna (if using), and mix gently. Season to taste with salt and pepper.

4 Spoon the salad into a serving dish and arrange the eggs and reserved pepper strips on top. Sprinkle with parsley and serve.

● **Prepare ahead** Steps 1 and 2 can be completed up to 4 hours in advance, and the vegetables chilled until ready to use. Bring to room temperature before mixing with the mayonnaise.

Warm Green Bean Salad

This crunchy, nutty recipe is also a great vegetable side dish

 serves 6

 prep 15 mins • cook 10 mins

3 tbsp **sesame seeds**

450g (1lb) fine **French beans**, trimmed

250g (9oz) **mangetout**

3 **shallots** or spring onions, finely chopped

1 **garlic clove**, chopped

1 tbsp **soy sauce**

½ tbsp **sesame oil**

½ tbsp **clear honey**

2.5cm (1 in) piece of fresh **root ginger**, grated

salt and freshly ground **black pepper**

● **Prepare ahead** The beans can be cooked and the dressing made up to 4 hours in advance. Reheat to serve.

1 Preheat the oven to 180°C (350°F/Gas 4). Place the sesame seeds on a roasting tray and roast for 8 minutes, or until the seeds are nicely browned; watch closely, as they burn easily.

2 Bring a large saucepan of salted water to the boil. Blanch the French beans for 3 minutes, then add the mangetout and blanch for another minute.

3 Drain the beans and mangetout in a colander, and shake off any excess water. Combine all the remaining ingredients in a large serving bowl. Add the beans and mangetout, and toss to coat well. Sprinkle with the seeds, and serve.

BLANCHING

To ensure the beans and mangetout keep their bright-green colour, place them directly into a bowl of iced water after blanching to stop the cooking.

Red Pepper Salad

In this Spanish dish, *Ensaladilla de pimientos*, sweet red peppers are gently stewed, then served cold

 serves 4

 prep 10 mins • cook 25 mins

3 tbsp **olive oil**

6 **red peppers**, deseeded and cut into large strips

2 **garlic cloves**, finely chopped

250g (9oz) ripe **tomatoes**, skinned, deseeded, and chopped

2 tbsp chopped **parsley**

salt and freshly ground **black pepper**

1 tbsp **sherry vinegar**

● **Prepare ahead** The dish can be made up to 2 days in advance and chilled until ready to use.

1 Heat the oil in a large frying pan, add the peppers and garlic, and fry over a low heat for 5 minutes, stirring, then add the tomatoes. Increase the heat, bring to simmering point, then reduce the heat to low, cover, and cook for 12–15 minutes.

2 Stir in the parsley, season well with salt and pepper, and cook for a further 2 minutes.

3 Using a slotted spoon, remove the peppers and arrange in a serving dish.

4 Add the vinegar to the pan, increase the heat, and simmer the sauce for 5–7 minutes, or until it has reduced and thickened.

5 Pour the sauce over the peppers and allow to cool.

● **Leftovers** are lovely served with grilled meats, chicken, or fish.

VARIATION

Red Pepper Dressing

Process the salad in a food processor until smooth. Whisk in enough olive oil to make a dressing and use to coat a mix of green leaves.

Lobster Salad with Watercress

A very special summer salad, ideal for outdoor dining

 serves 4

🕐 prep 20 mins

½ red onion, finely sliced

1 tsp red wine vinegar

4 cooked lobster tails, halved

1 large bunch of watercress, tough stalks removed

½ fennel bulb, very finely sliced

8 sun-blush tomatoes, chopped

fresh herbs, such as chervil, dill, or chives, to garnish

For the dressing

1 egg

1 egg yolk

2 tsp Dijon mustard

zest and juice of 1 lemon

400ml (14 fl oz) sunflower oil

10g (¼ oz) chervil or chives

salt and freshly ground black pepper

1 **To make the dressing**, place the egg, egg yolk, mustard, and lemon zest and juice into a blender. Blend on a low speed and slowly add the oil. Add the chervil. Season to taste with salt and pepper. Set aside.

2 **Place the sliced** red onion in a bowl with the vinegar, and leave to stand for 10 minutes.

3 **Remove all the meat** from the lobster tails, keeping the pieces of meat as whole as possible.

4 **Arrange the watercress** on plates, scatter over the fennel, the drained onion slices, and the tomatoes. Place the lobster meat on top, and drizzle over the dressing.

Spinach and Bacon Salad with Blue Cheese Dressing

Serve at room temperature to allow the flavours to develop

 serves 4

prep 15 mins
• cook 10–12 mins

8 streaky bacon rashers

225g (8oz) **fresh baby spinach leaves**

225g (8oz) **mushrooms**, sliced

2 **spring onions**, sliced

For the dressing

3 tbsp **olive oil**

2 tbsp **red wine vinegar**

60g (2oz) **blue cheese**, crumbled

2 tsp **Dijon mustard**

2 tsp finely chopped **shallots**

salt and freshly ground **black pepper**

pinch of **sugar**

● **Prepare ahead** The dressing can be made up to 48 hours in advance, and chilled.

1 Heat a frying pan and fry the bacon until crisp, turning occasionally. Drain on paper towels, cool, and crumble, then set aside.

2 In a large salad bowl, combine the spinach, mushrooms, and onions. Add the bacon and toss to mix.

3 To make the dressing, place all the ingredients in a lidded jar and shake well to combine. Drizzle over the salad and toss to combine.

VARIATION

Chicken Salad with Blue Cheese Dressing
Replace the bacon with 2 cooked chicken breasts, sliced, and continue with the recipe, as above.

Greek Salad

A popular summer salad that is ideal for a buffet or served alongside barbecued meats

 serves 4–6

 prep 20 mins

600g (1lb 5oz) ripe **plum tomatoes**

½ **cucumber**

200g (7oz) **feta cheese**

100g (3½ oz) **black olives**

juice of ½ **lemon**

handful of **Greek basil** or basil

3–4 tbsp **extra virgin olive oil**

salt and freshly ground **black pepper**

● **Prepare ahead** The salad can be made and dressed 1–2 hours in advance; add the basil, to serve.

1 Cut the tomatoes into chunks. Peel away some of the cucumber skin, quarter the cucumber lengthways, and remove the seeds, then cut into chunks. Arrange them both on a serving platter.

2 Drain the feta and cut into small cubes, then scatter the cheese and olives over the tomatoes and cucumber.

3 Sprinkle the lemon juice over the salad and scatter with the basil, drizzle with the oil, then season with salt and pepper to taste.

> **BUYING BASIL**
> Greek basil has a much smaller leaf than other varieties and a strong flavour, ideal for this summer salad. If it is not available, use the more readily available basil, torn into small pieces.

Blue Cheese Dressing

This creamy, flavoursome dressing is delicious over baby salad leaves

 makes 250ml (8fl oz)

🕐 prep 10 mins

200ml (7fl oz) soured cream

100g (3½ oz) Roquefort cheese, crumbled

1 garlic clove, crushed

1 tsp Dijon mustard

2 tbsp white wine vinegar

1 tbsp finely snipped chives

salt and freshly ground black pepper

● **Prepare ahead** This dressing can be made 3 days in advance and kept in the refrigerator.

1 **Place the soured cream**, cheese, garlic, mustard, white wine vinegar, and 3 tbsp of water in a food processor, and blend until smooth. Transfer the mixture to a bowl, and stir in the chives. Season to taste with salt and pepper.

2 **Pour into a serving bowl**, and chill until ready to serve.

● **Good with** green salads, or as a dressing for steamed new potatoes.

VARIATION

Cheese Dressing
The same quantity of crumbled Caerphilly or Cheddar cheese will make an equally creamy dressing.

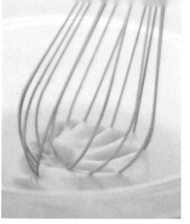

Vinaigrette Dressing

This versatile dressing is suitable for almost any salad

🍴 makes 200ml (7fl oz)

🕐 prep 5 mins

1 tbsp Dijon mustard

3 tbsp white wine vinegar

150ml (5fl oz) extra virgin olive oil

salt and freshly ground black pepper

1 **Place the mustard** and vinegar in a medium bowl, and whisk together.

2 **Gradually add the oil**, whisking to form a thick, smooth emulsion. Season to taste with salt and pepper, and serve over salad or as a light sauce with grilled vegetables.

VARIATION

Garlic Vinaigrette Dressing
Add 1 garlic clove, crushed to a paste with a little salt, in step 1.

> **PERFECT VINAIGRETTE**
> If you follow the recipe exactly, mixing the mustard and vinegar first, then adding the oil and whisking with a balloon whisk, you will achieve a thick emulsion that will not separate, even when stored.

Thousand Island Dressing

There is no need to limit this dressing to salads – it goes particularly well with seafood

🍴 makes 250ml (8fl oz)

🕐 prep 15 mins

150ml (5fl oz) mayonnaise

2 tbsp tomato ketchup

few drops of Tabasco

1 tsp Worcestershire sauce

1 small red pepper, deseeded and finely chopped

1 shallot, finely chopped

2 small gherkins, finely chopped

1 tbsp finely chopped parsley

salt and freshly ground black pepper

● **Prepare ahead** This dressing can be made 2 days in advance and kept chilled until ready to use.

1 **Mix together** the mayonnaise, tomato ketchup, Tabasco, Worcestershire sauce, red pepper, shallot, gherkins, and parsley in a bowl. Season to taste with salt and pepper.

2 **Pour into a bowl**, and chill until ready to serve.

● **Good with** salads containing prawns, crabmeat, or avocado.

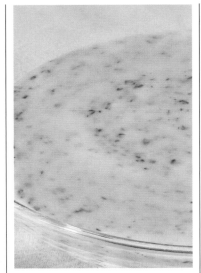

Yogurt Dressing

If made with fat-free yogurt, this is a healthy alternative to mayonnaise

🍴 makes 150ml-200ml (5-7fl oz)

🕐 prep 10 mins

150ml (5fl oz) natural yogurt

1 piece of preserved stem ginger, finely chopped

1 tsp ginger syrup, from the jar

1 tbsp finely chopped flat-leaf parsley

1 tbsp finely chopped dill

zest and juice of 1 small lemon

salt and freshly ground black pepper

● **Prepare ahead** Can be made up to 4 days ahead and kept in the refrigerator until ready to use.

1 **Place the yogurt**, ginger, syrup, herbs, lemon zest and juice in a bowl, and mix thoroughly. Season to taste with salt and pepper.

2 **Pour into a bowl** and chill until ready to serve.

● **Good with** falafel, grilled lamb, or any salad.

Mayonnaise

Making your own mayonnaise is easier than you might think, and allows you to choose your own flavourings

🍴 makes 360ml (12fl oz)

🕐 prep 10 mins

❗ make sure all the ingredients are at room temperature before starting to make the mayonnaise to help prevent curdling

2 egg yolks

2 tbsp white wine vinegar

1 tsp Dijon mustard

300ml (10fl oz) light olive oil

juice of ½ lemon

salt and freshly ground black pepper

● **Prepare ahead** Can be made a day in advance and kept chilled.

1 **Place the egg yolks**, white wine vinegar, and mustard in a food processor, and blend for 1–2 minutes, or until pale and creamy. Alternatively, whisk by hand in a large bowl, using a balloon whisk.

2 **With the motor** still running, or still whisking by hand, slowly pour in the olive oil in a steady stream through the feeder tube. Blend until thick, creamy, and smooth.

3 **Spoon into a bowl** and stir in the lemon juice. Season to taste with salt and pepper.

VARIATION

Basil and Lemon Mayonnaise

Replace 2 tbsp of the oil with walnut-flavoured olive oil. Stir in a handful of freshly chopped basil with the lemon juice in step 3.

Tortilla

This variation of a traditional thick Spanish omelette includes broccoli and peas, along with the more usual potatoes

- serves 4
- prep 15 mins • cook 45 mins
- 23cm (9in) non-stick frying pan

115g (4oz) **fresh** or **frozen peas**

115g (4oz) **broccoli florets**

6 tbsp **olive oil**

350g (12oz) **floury potatoes**, such as King Edward, peeled and cut into 2cm (¾in) cubes

2 small **red onions**, finely chopped

6 **eggs**, beaten

salt and freshly ground **black pepper**

● **Prepare ahead** The omelette can be made a day in advance.

1 Bring a large saucepan of lightly salted water to the boil over high heat. Add the peas and boil for 5 minutes, or until just tender. Use a slotted spoon to transfer the peas to a bowl of cold water. Return the pan to the boil, add the broccoli and boil for 4 minutes or until just tender. Remove the florets and add to the peas to cool, then drain both vegetables well, and set aside.

2 Heat 4 tbsp of the oil in the non-stick frying pan over a medium heat. Add the potatoes and onions, and cook for 10–15 minutes, stirring often, or until the potatoes are tender.

3 Beat the eggs in a large bowl, and season with salt and pepper.

4 Use a slotted spoon to transfer the potatoes and onions to the eggs. Add the peas and broccoli and gently stir. Discard the excess oil from the pan and remove any crispy bits stuck on the bottom.

5 Heat the remaining oil in the pan over a high heat. Add the egg mixture, instantly reduce the heat to low, and smooth the surface. Leave to cook for 20–25 minutes, or until the top of the omelette begins to set and the base is golden brown.

6 Carefully slide the tortilla on to a plate, place a second plate on top and invert so that the cooked side is on top. Slide the tortilla back into the pan and cook for 5 minutes, until both sides are golden brown and set.

7 Leave the omelette to set for at least 5 minutes. Serve warm or cooled, cut in wedges.

● **Good with** a dressed salad of mixed greens.

VARIATION

Quick Tortilla

For simple tortilla, omit the peas and broccoli. Use waxy potatoes, instead of floury ones, cut into matchsticks to speed up the cooking process.

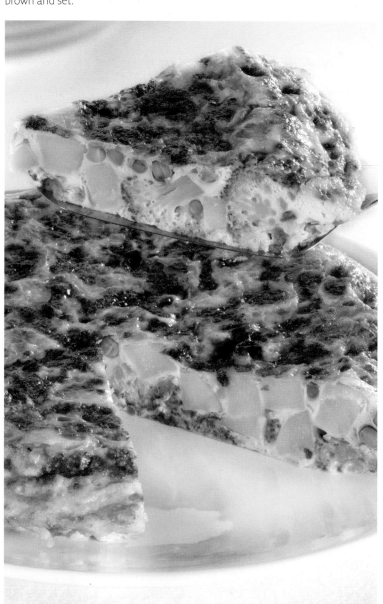

Egg Mayonnaise

This makes a delicious appetizer, or filling, for soft white rolls for a packed lunch or picnic

- serves 4
- prep 10 mins • cook 7 mins

4 tbsp **mayonnaise**

2 **spring onions**, finely sliced

1 tbsp chopped **chives**

salt and freshly ground **black pepper**

4 large **eggs**, hard-boiled

1 Mix the mayonnaise, the spring onions, and the chives in a small bowl. Season to taste with salt and pepper.

2 Remove the shells from the boiled eggs. Add the eggs to the mayonnaise and, using a fork, mash.

● **Good with** Little Gem leaves and buttered bread fingers.

> **PEELING EGGS**
>
> Cool the eggs rapidly after cooking, or a dark ring will form around the yolk. Peel the eggs in the cold water and the shells will slip off easily.

Devilled Eggs

Perfect party or picnic food, these halved boiled eggs have their yolks spiced with mustard and paprika

🍴 serves 4

🕐 prep 10 mins • cook 8 mins

6 eggs

3 tbsp mayonnaise

1 tsp mustard

1 tsp hot paprika, plus extra for dusting

salt and freshly ground black pepper

3 cherry tomatoes, cut in quarters

1 tbsp chopped chives

1 **Boil the eggs** for 8 minutes, then plunge into cold water and allow to cool. Peel off the shells, then cut each egg in half lengthways.

2 **Scoop out the** yolks and mash them with the mayonnaise, mustard, and paprika, and season to taste with salt and pepper.

3 **Divide the mixture** between the egg white halves and top each one with a cherry tomato quarter, a sprinkle of chives, and a dusting of paprika.

● **Good with** rounds of buttered toast and a few salad leaves.

● **Prepare ahead** The eggs can be made up to 24 hours in advance and chilled until needed.

Herb and Goat's Cheese Frittata

Thinner than a Spanish tortilla, this popular Italian dish is ideal for lunch or a light supper

🍴 serves 4

🕐 prep 10 mins • cook 20 mins

🍲 23cm (9in) non-stick frying pan with a lid and flameproof handle

6 eggs

4 sage leaves, finely chopped

salt and freshly ground black pepper

3 tbsp olive oil, plus extra for brushing

1 shallot, chopped

10 cherry tomatoes, halved

115g (4oz) goat's cheese, rind removed if necessary, and crumbled

1 **Preheat the grill** on its highest setting and position the rack 10cm (4in) from the heat. Beat the eggs in a bowl with the herbs, season to taste with salt and pepper, and set aside.

2 **Heat the oil** in the frying pan over a medium heat. Add the shallot and fry, stirring constantly, for 3 minutes, or until just softened but not browned.

3 **Add the eggs** to the pan and stir gently to combine. Reduce the heat, then cover and leave to cook gently for 10–15 minutes before removing the lid; the frittata should still be runny on top.

4 **Arrange the tomatoes** and goat's cheese over the surface and lightly brush with olive oil. Transfer the pan to the grill for 5 minutes or until the frittata is set and lightly browned. Leave to stand for 5 minutes before cutting into wedges. Serve warm or cooled.

● **Good with** plenty of Italian bread and a tomato salad.

VARIATION

Red Pepper and Salami Frittata

In step 2 add 1 red pepper, deseeded and cut into strips, and 75g (2½oz) thinly sliced salami, rinds removed, cut into strips. Replace the goat's cheese and tomatoes with 125g (4½oz) grated Cheddar cheese and grill for 5 minutes as before.

Curried Quails' Eggs

This quick recipe uses dainty quails' eggs, and the mild curry sauce tops the whole dish off perfectly

serves 4

prep 15 mins • cook 3 mins

4 quails' eggs

2 slices of brown bread

2 tbsp mayonnaise

4 tbsp low-fat plain yogurt

1 tsp mild curry paste

2 tbsp chopped coriander

salt and freshly ground black pepper

To serve

1 tsp lemon juice

1 tsp sunflower oil

bunch of coriander, stalks removed

bunch of flat-leaf parsley, stalks removed

● **Prepare ahead** The eggs and the sauce can be prepared several hours in advance and chilled, separately, until ready to use.

1 **Bring a small saucepan** of water to the boil. Have a bowl of cold water ready. Cook the eggs in the boiling water for 2½ minutes, then remove from the pan with a slotted spoon, and plunge into the cold water. Peel the eggs and set aside.

2 **Preheat the grill** on its highest setting. Lightly toast the bread, and cut 2 circles or ovals from each slice. Place on individual plates.

3 **Combine the mayonnaise,** yogurt, curry paste, and chopped coriander in a bowl to make a smooth sauce. Season to taste with salt and pepper, then set aside.

4 **Whisk the lemon** juice and oil together in a medium bowl, then add the leaves and toss to coat with the dressing.

5 **Cut each egg** in half and arrange on the toast. Spoon the curry sauce over the top. Serve immediately, garnished with the dressed herb leaves.

● **Leftovers** of both the eggs and curry sauce can be gently reheated and used to top cooked spinach for a quick and spicy variation of the classic Eggs Florentine (p147).

HENS' EGGS
This recipe works equally well with 2 hard-boiled hens' eggs. Boil for 6 minutes, peel, then cut into quarters.

Eggs Benedict

The smooth buttery sauce makes a truly indulgent breakfast or brunch

serves 4

prep 10 mins • cook 11 mins

8 large eggs

4 English muffins

butter, for spreading

1 quantity Hollandaise (p282), warmed

1 **Fill 2 large saucepans** with boiling water to a depth of 5cm (2in). When tiny bubbles appear at the bottom of the pan, carefully crack 4 eggs into each pan.

2 **Leave the pans** on the heat for 1 minute, then remove and let the eggs sit in the hot water for exactly 6 minutes. Remove the eggs, using a slotted spoon, and drain on kitchen paper.

3 **Meanwhile,** preheat the grill on its highest setting, split each muffin in half, and toast both sides.

4 **Butter each muffin half** and place 2 on each serving plate. Top each half with a poached egg and spoon the Hollandaise over the top.

● **Good with** ham or crisp grilled bacon rashers on the side.

Scrambled Eggs with Smoked Salmon

This is the ultimate feel-good Sunday brunch recipe

 serves 4

prep 10 mins • cook 10 mins

6 large **eggs**

2 tbsp **milk**

salt and freshly ground **black pepper**

45g (1½oz) **unsalted butter**

225g (8oz) **smoked salmon**, cut into thin strips, or hot smoked salmon, flaked

2 tbsp snipped **chives**

4 **English muffins**, split and toasted, to serve

1 Beat the eggs with the milk, and season to taste with salt and pepper.

2 Melt the butter in a medium non-stick saucepan and, when foaming, pour in the eggs. Stir with a wooden spoon over medium heat until almost set, then stir in the smoked salmon.

3 Cook until the eggs have just set, sprinkle with chives, season with pepper, and serve at once on toasted muffin halves.

VARIATIONS

Scrambled Eggs with Mushrooms

Replace the salmon with 225g (8oz) mixed wild mushrooms, whole or sliced, fried in butter.

Scrambled Eggs with Green Peppers and Tomatoes

Replace the salmon with 1 chopped green pepper fried in olive oil and 3 tomatoes, skinned, deseeded, and finely chopped.

Scotch Eggs

Great for picnics and packed lunches, serve these with a spoonful of your favourite chutney

 serves 4

prep 25 mins • cook 15 mins

3 **spring onions**, finely chopped

300g (10oz) **pork sausagemeat**

pinch of **crushed chilli flakes**

2 tsp **dried mixed herbs**

salt and freshly ground **black pepper**

4 **hard-boiled eggs**, shelled

25g (scant 1oz) **plain flour**

vegetable oil, for deep frying

1 **egg**, beaten

100g (3½oz) **dried golden breadcrumbs**

1 In a large bowl, mix together the spring onions, sausagemeat, chilli flakes, and herbs, and season with salt and pepper.

2 Coat the eggs in flour, then quarter the sausagemeat mixture, flatten it out and place an egg in the centre of each piece. Using your hands, gather up the mixture to totally encase the egg.

3 Pour the oil into a large saucepan and heat until a cube of bread dropped in sizzles and turns golden within 1 minute. Place the beaten egg and the breadcrumbs on separate plates. Dip each Scotch egg into the beaten egg, then into the breadcrumbs.

4 Carefully place in the hot oil and fry for 3–4 minutes, or until golden. Drain on kitchen paper and leave to cool on a wire rack.

VARIATION

Vegetarian Scotch Eggs

Instead of the sausagemeat, place a drained and rinsed 400g can of haricot beans in a food processor with 60g (2oz) soft goat's cheese and process until smooth. Transfer to a large bowl, add spring onions, chilli flakes, mixed herbs, and 3 tbsp of dried breadcrumbs. Coat and shape the mixture around the egg, then continue with the recipe as above.

Omelettes

Although cooks around the world make different omelettes, they are all similar in that they make quick meals at any time of the day – you can even enjoy omelettes for dessert!

Quail Egg
Tiny and speckled, these are best hard-boiled.

Bantam Chicken Egg
Bantams are small chickens, so these eggs are smaller than average.

Brown Leghorn Chicken Egg
This breed lays both white and brown eggs.

Welsummer Chicken Egg
Originally from Holland, these large eggs are dark reddish-brown.

Burford Browns Chicken Egg
These large eggs are recognized by their thick, dark brown shells.

Old Cotswold Legbar Chicken Egg
This breed lays eggs in pretty pastel colours.

Duck Egg
Larger than most chicken eggs, these have a richer flavour.

Goose Egg
These large eggs taste stronger than chicken eggs.

Choosing Eggs

The essential ingredient of any great-tasting omelette is fresh eggs. Many types of egg can be used in omelettes, and farmers' markets and supermarkets offer a large choice of chicken and other eggs.

When you are buying eggs, the box gives you information about the quality and types of eggs inside. The Lion Quality mark, stamped on the box and in red on the shells, means that the eggs come from hens vaccinated against salmonella. Look for a best-before date stamped on the shells, as well as on the box. Eggs sold as "free-range" come from birds with continuous daylight access to runs and a variety of vegetation.

- "Organic" eggs are from free-range hens fed an organic diet on farms approved by one of the several organic certification bodies.
- UK eggs sold for domestic use are graded as Class A.
- Check the condition of the eggs inside the box before you buy to ensure none are cracked.

Storing

- Store eggs in the refrigerator, not at room temperature.
- Egg shells are porous so, ideally, keep eggs in their box or in a closed compartment in the refrigerator door, which prevents them from absorbing other smells.
- When transferring eggs to a rack in the refrigerator, be sure to put them pointed-end down.
- Observe the best-before date.

HOW DO I KNOW IT'S FRESH?

Always check the best-before date on the box. Or you can use this simple test if you have thrown it away and have eggs without a best-before date: immerse the egg in water and see if it rises. A stale egg contains much more air and less liquid than a fresh one, so it will float. Do not use a stale egg.

Fresh

Borderline

Stale

Folded Omelette

1 **To make a 3-egg** omelette, melt 15–30g (½–1oz) butter in a 20cm (8in) non-stick frying pan over a high heat until foaming but not browning. Pour in the beaten eggs and shake the pan to distribute evenly. Stir with a table fork, keeping the rounded side of the fork flat. Stop stirring after 20–30 seconds, or when the eggs are set but still soft.

2 **Using the fork**, fold the of the omelette nearest you halfway over itself, as if folding a letter. Grasp the handle of the pan from underneath, and lift the pan to a 45 degree angle. Sharply tap the top of the handle closest to the pan, to encourage the omelette to curl over the folded portion. Use the fork to fully "close the letter".

3 **Bring a warmed** serving plate to the omelette, then tilt the pan so the omelette falls on to the plate. Serve immediately.

Flat Omelette

1 **Cook the filling ingredients** in a 20–25cm (8–10in) frying pan with a flameproof handle until they are all tender. Pour over the seasoned beaten eggs and stir to combine all the ingredients. Leave the omelette to cook, undisturbed, or until most of the egg is set and the base is golden brown. Meanwhile, preheat the grill on its highest setting.

2 **Test that the omelette** is set underneath by lifting the edge with a palette knife. Put the omelette under the grill for 2–3 minutes, or until the top is set.

3 **Remove the pan** from the heat and sprinkle cheese or any other ingredients over the top. Place under the grill until the cheese is melted and lightly browned and any other ingredients are cooked as required. If serving hot, transfer to a warmed serving plate; otherwise set aside and leave to cool completely to serve cold.

Soufflé Omelette

1 **Separate 2 eggs**. Beat the yolks with 1 tbsp caster sugar, 1 tbsp water, and ½ tsp pure vanilla extract. Beat the whites until stiff peaks form, then fold into the yolks. Preheat the grill on its highest setting. Melt 15–30g (½–1oz) clarified butter in a 18–20cm (7–8in) non-stick frying pan over a high heat until foaming.

2 **Reduce the heat** to medium, add the egg mixture, spread out, and cook for 30–45 seconds, or until the eggs are set underneath. Place under the grill and cook for 1 minute, or until the top is set. Quickly spread any filling, such as Cherry and Almond (p142), over half the omelette, then use a palette knife to fold the other half over.

3 **Slide the omelette** onto a warmed serving plate and dust with icing sugar. The omelette is now ready to serve, or you can decorate the top by using a red-hot skewer to scorch the sugar. Serve at once.

Simple Omelette Flavourings

Be inventive. Almost anything you have in the kitchen will add extra flavour and variety to folded and flat omelettes. Add any of these ingredients to the beaten eggs, with seasoning to taste, just before starting to cook.

Cheese Grated mature Cheddar, Lancashire, Parmesan, Gruyère, and Emmental, or crumbled feta, make flat omelettes more filling.

Spices Stir in a pinch of cayenne pepper, paprika, mustard powder, or mild curry powder for heat, or turmeric for a rich golden colour.

Bottled Sauces Add a splash of soy, Worcestershire, or chilli-hot Tabasco sauce.

Vegetable Flavourings For flat omelettes, add several crushed garlic cloves lightly sautéed with a finely chopped onion; several finely chopped spring onions; 1 tbsp deseeded and chopped green chilli; 1 thinly sliced skinned red pepper bottled in olive oil.

Herbs For a garden-fresh taste, add 1 tbsp chopped chervil, chives, parsley, or tarragon – or a mixture of 2 or more herbs. When fresh herbs are not available, stir in 1 tsp dried mixed herbs.

Beat the eggs *with salt and pepper and other flavourings, before cooking.*

Omelettes

Folded Omelette Fillings

Spinach, Cheddar, and Bacon
Cook the omelette, then spoon over the spinach. Sprinkle over the bacon and cheese, and season to taste with salt and pepper just before folding and sliding out of the pan.

60g (2oz) cooked, chopped **spinach**, kept hot

2 **streaky bacon rashers**, cooked until crisp, drained, crumbled, and kept hot

30g (1oz) **Cheddar cheese**, grated

salt and **black pepper**

Smoked Ham and Mustard
Beat the mustard into the eggs in the omelette recipe before adding to the pan. Cook the omelette, then sprinkle over the ham just before folding and sliding out of the pan.

1 tbsp **wholegrain mustard**

30g (1oz) wafer-thin **smoked ham**, thinly sliced

Soufflé Omelette Fillings

Cherry and Almond
Melt the jam and stir in the kirsch. Spread over half the cooked soufflé omelette and sprinkle with the almonds just before folding.

4 tbsp **cherry jam**

½ tbsp **kirsch**

30g (1oz) **blanched almonds**, coarsely ground

Apricot and Vanilla
Melt the jam and stir in the vanilla extract. Spread over half the cooked soufflé omelette just before folding, then dust with icing sugar.

4 tbsp **apricot jam**

2–3 drops of **pure vanilla extract**

1 tbsp **icing sugar**

Flat Omelette Fillings

Courgette and Feta

Fry the the onion and red pepper in the olive oil for 3 minutes. Add the courgettes with salt and pepper to taste and continue cooking for 3–5 minutes, or until all the vegetables are tender. Pour over the eggs from the omelette recipe and cook the omelette until is set underneath. Place under a preheated grill until the eggs are set. Sprinkle with the cheese and return to the grill until the cheese is soft and lightly browned.

1 **onion**, diced

1 **red pepper**, diced

1 tbsp **olive oil**

2 **courgettes**, diced

salt and **black pepper**

60g (2oz) **feta cheese**, drained and crumbled

Tomato and Asparagus

Fry the asparagus and onion in the oil until tender. Pour over the eggs from your omelette recipe and cook until the omelette is set. Sprinkle with the cheese, tomato, and salt and pepper to taste, then grill.

115g (4oz) **asparagus tips**

1 **onion**, sliced

1 tbsp **olive oil**

60g (2oz) **Emmental cheese**, grated

1 **tomato**, cut into wedges

salt and **black pepper**

PERFECT OMELETTES

- It is easiest to make 1 omelette per person, rather than trying to make a larger omelette to serve 2 people. Use 3 eggs for an omelette to serve 1. A 2-egg soufflé omelette serves 1 or 2 people.

- Use a non-stick or well-seasoned omelette or frying pan.

- An 18–20cm (7–8in) pan (measured across the base) is the best size to use for a 3-egg omelette. A sloping side enables the omelette to slide out more easily.

- Using clarified butter for soufflé omelettes is recommended so the bottom does not brown before the top is set.

- Beat the eggs in a bowl using a fork until the yolks and whites are well blended. Season to taste with salt and pepper and add any flavourings, such as herbs. Take a look at the suggestions on p141 (or above) for more inspiration.

- Have a warmed serving plate ready before you start cooking.

World Omelettes

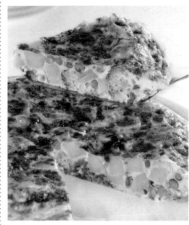

Tortilla

This variation of a traditional, thick Spanish omelette includes broccoli and peas along with the more usual potatoes and onion

🕐 1 hr **page 136**

Herb and Goat's Cheese Frittata

Thinner than a Spanish tortilla, this popular Italian flat omelette makes a great hot or cold lunch or light supper

🕐 30 mins **page 137**

Omelette Arnold Bennett

Originally created at London's Savoy Hotel, this traditional breakfast omelette is flavoured with chunky flakes of smoked haddock

🕐 25 mins **page 151**

Spinach Timbales

A *timbale* (the name is French) is an individual vegetable and egg dish that is cooked in a mould and turned out on to a plate for serving

serves 4

prep 10 mins • cook 30 mins

4 tin timbale moulds or ramekins

freeze for up to 3 months; reheat in a low oven to serve

50g (1¾oz) **butter**, plus extra for greasing

1 **onion**, finely chopped

1 **garlic clove**, crushed

300ml (10fl oz) **single cream**

salt and freshly ground **black pepper**

½ tsp **ground nutmeg**

125g (4½oz) **hard goat's cheese**, crumbled

125g (4½oz) **spinach**

5 **eggs**

25g (scant 1oz) **breadcrumbs**

For the salad

60g (2oz) **frisée**

½ **cucumber**, cut into batons

2 tbsp **extra virgin olive oil**

1 tbsp **balsamic vinegar**

1 **garlic clove**, crushed

salt and freshly ground **black pepper**

1 Preheat the oven to 180°C (350°F/Gas 4) and lightly grease 4 timbale moulds. Melt half the butter in a saucepan, add the onion and garlic, and cover and cook over a low heat for about 10 minutes, or until just cooked but not brown.

2 Add the cream, season with salt, pepper, and nutmeg, then bring to the boil. Take off the heat, add the goat's cheese, and stir until the cheese is melted.

3 In another saucepan, melt the remaining butter and cook the spinach until it begins to wilt and soften down. Add the cooked spinach to the cream mixture, and beat in the eggs and breadcrumbs.

4 Put the mixture into a blender and process until smooth, then pour it into the timbale moulds. Place the timbales in a roasting tin. Pour boiling water into the bottom of the tray, until it comes halfway up the timbales, and bake for 15–20 minutes, or until they have risen and are just firm to touch.

5 Meanwhile, prepare the salad. Arrange the salad leaves and cucumber on 4 serving plates. Whisk the olive oil, balsamic vinegar, and garlic, season to taste with salt and pepper, and drizzle over the salad. Turn out the timbales and serve.

French Toast

This makes a hot, satisfying breakfast or brunch

serves 4

prep 5 mins • cook 20 mins

3 large **eggs**

300ml (10fl oz) **milk**

300ml (10fl oz) **single cream**

1 tsp **pure vanilla extract**

2 tsp **caster sugar**

8 slices of **white bread**

75g (2½oz) **butter**

maple syrup, to serve

1 In a shallow dish, beat together the eggs, milk, cream, vanilla extract, and sugar until combined. Dip the bread slices into the mixture, so they are covered.

2 Melt a little of the butter in a large frying pan and fry the bread slices, in batches, for 2 minutes on each side, or until golden, adding more butter for each batch. Keep the cooked slices warm while you cook the other batches.

3 Cut the toasts in half diagonally, and arrange 4 pieces on each serving plate. Drizzle with maple syrup and serve.

● **Good with** a few summer berries or a spoonful of yogurt.

Buckwheat Galettes

Popular in Brittany, in northwest France, where the local cuisine is defined by rich, rustic flavours

 serves 4

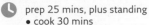 prep 25 mins, plus standing • cook 30 mins

20–23cm (8–9in) crêpe pan

freeze the unfilled pancakes for up to 3 months

75g (2½oz) **buckwheat flour**

75g (2½oz) **plain flour**

2 **eggs**, beaten

250ml (8fl oz) **milk**

sunflower oil, for frying

For the filling

2 tbsp **sunflower oil**

2 **red onions**, peeled and thinly sliced

200g (7oz) **smoked ham**, chopped

1 tsp **thyme** leaves

115g (4oz) **Brie**, cut into small pieces

100ml (3½fl oz) **crème fraîche**

● **Prepare ahead** Make the batter up to a few hours in advance and leave to stand until ready to cook. If it thickens too much, stir in a little water before using.

1 Sift the flours into a large mixing bowl, make a well in the centre and add the eggs. Gradually beat the eggs into the flour using a wooden spoon, then add the milk and 100ml (3½fl oz) water to make a smooth batter. Cover and leave to stand for 2 hours.

2 Heat the oil in a small frying pan, add the onions, and fry gently until softened. Add the ham and thyme, then remove from the heat and set aside.

3 Preheat the oven to 150°C (300°F/Gas 2). Heat the crêpe pan and grease lightly. Spoon in 2 tbsp of the batter and swirl so it coats the base of the pan. Cook for about 1 minute, or until lightly browned underneath, then flip over and cook for a further 1 minute, or until browned on the other side. Make 7 more crêpes, re-greasing the pan as necessary.

4 Stir the Brie and crème fraîche into the filling and divide between the pancakes. Roll or fold up the filled pancakes and place on a baking tray. Heat through in the oven for 10 minutes before serving.

Parsi Eggs

This Indian dish has its origins in ancient Persia

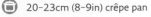 serves 4

prep 10 mins • cook 30 mins

60g (2oz) **unsalted butter**

4 **spring onions**, thinly sliced

1 tsp grated fresh **root ginger**

1 large **red** or green **chilli**, deseeded and finely chopped

2 tsp **mild curry powder**

4 **tomatoes**, deseeded and chopped

8 large **eggs**

2 tbsp **milk**

salt and freshly ground **black pepper**

2 tbsp chopped **coriander**

● **Prepare ahead** The vegetables can be prepared ahead, but the dish should be cooked just before serving.

1 Melt 30g (1oz) of the butter in a large non-stick frying pan and fry the onions, ginger, and chilli over a low heat for 2 minutes, or until softened, stirring often.

2 Add the curry powder and tomatoes and cook for 1 minute. Remove from the pan and set aside.

3 Add the rest of the butter to the pan. Beat the eggs and milk, and season with salt and pepper. Pour into the pan and stir until scrambled and almost set. Add the curried vegetables, stir well, and cook until just set. Scatter the chopped coriander over, and serve at once.

● **Good with** salad leaves, lightly toasted naan bread, or chapatis.

Parsi Bacon and Eggs

Add 115g (4oz) cooked, diced bacon to the pan in step 1.

Quiche Lorraine

A French classic, this egg and bacon flan is the original and the best

 serves 4-6

 prep 35 mins, plus chilling • cook 35 mins

 23cm (9in) x 4cm (1½in) deep pie dish

For the pastry

225g (8oz) plain flour, plus extra for dusting

115g (4oz) butter, cubed

1 egg yolk

For the filling

200g (7oz) bacon lardons

1 onion, finely chopped

75g (2½oz) Gruyère cheese, grated

4 large eggs, lightly beaten

150ml (5fl oz) double cream

150ml (5fl oz) milk

freshly ground black pepper

● **Prepare ahead** Cook up to 48 hours in advance, let cool, then refrigerate. Reheat at 160°C (325°F/Gas 3) for 15-20 mins.

1 To make the pastry, place the flour and butter in a food processor and blend until the mixture resembles fine crumbs. Add the egg yolk, and 3-4 tablespoons chilled water, enough to make a smooth dough. Turn out on a floured surface and knead briefly. Alternatively, rub the butter into the flour with your fingers until crumbly, then add the egg yolk and water. Cover and chill for at least 30 minutes. Preheat the oven to 190°C (375°F/Gas 5).

2 On a lightly floured surface, roll out the pastry and line the tin, pressing the dough to the sides. Prick the base of the pastry and line with greaseproof paper and baking beans. Bake blind for 12 minutes, then remove the paper and beans, and bake for a further 10 minutes, or until lightly golden.

3 Meanwhile, heat a large frying pan and dry-fry the bacon lardons for 3-4 minutes. Add the onion, fry for a further 2-3 minutes, then spread the onions and bacon over the pastry case. Add the cheese.

4 Whisk together the eggs, cream, milk, and black pepper, and pour into the pastry case. Place the tin on a baking tray and bake for 25-30 minutes, or until golden and just set. Allow to set, then slice and serve while still hot.

VARIATION

Mushroom Quiche

Instead of the onion, bacon and Gruyère, heat 2 tbsp of olive oil in a large pan and add 1 finely chopped red onion. Fry until softened, then add 300g (10oz) of sliced mixed mushrooms and 1 crushed garlic clove. Fry for a further 3-4 minutes, spoon into the pastry case and sprinkle with grated Parmesan and chopped parsley. Resume with step 4.

Poached Egg Muffins

A simple, satisfying breakfast that anyone can make

 serves 4

 cook 4-6 mins

4 large, very fresh eggs

splash of vinegar or lemon juice

4 English muffins, split and toasted

1 Bring a large, shallow pan of water to a gentle simmer, so small bubbles are just breaking at the surface. Add a splash of vinegar or lemon juice.

2 Crack an egg on to a saucer. Stir the water with a large, slotted spoon, then slip the egg into the water, letting the edge of the saucer touch the water so it does not splash. Repeat with the other eggs.

3 Using a slotted spoon, gently lift the white over the yolk until it is just set. Allow the eggs to simmer gently for 3-5 minutes, or until the whites are completely set.

4 Lift out each egg carefully and drain briefly on kitchen paper. Pull off any loose strands of egg white and serve immediately on the toasted muffins.

Poached Eggs with Frisée

This is a favourite starter or light lunch dish in France

 serves 4

 prep 15 mins • cook 20 mins

 low GI

For the salad

175g (6oz) **lardons** or thick-cut streaky bacon, chopped into small pieces

1 frisée lettuce

8 cherry tomatoes, cut in half

¼ cucumber, sliced

85g (3oz) walnut pieces

4 eggs, poached

For the dressing

2 tbsp cider vinegar

1 tsp wholegrain mustard

1 tbsp roughly chopped tarragon

6 tbsp extra virgin olive oil

salt and freshly ground black pepper

● **Prepare ahead** The dressing can be prepared several days in advance and stored in a screw-top jar. Shake well before using.

1 To make the dressing, whisk all the ingredients together.

2 Heat a non-stick frying pan over medium-high heat and dry-fry the lardons, until brown.

3 Meanwhile, break up the frisée into small sprigs and arrange on four serving plates with the cherry tomatoes, cucumber slices, and walnut pieces.

4 Place a poached egg in the centre of each and scatter the hot lardons over the top. Spoon over the dressing and serve immediately.

Eggs Florentine

This classic brunch dish, also good for lunch or supper, consists of spinach topped with a poached egg and cheese sauce

 serves 4

 prep 15 mins • cook 10 mins

 4 ramekins or small gratin dishes

60g (2oz) butter

30g (1oz) plain flour

300ml (10fl oz) milk

salt and freshly ground black pepper

2 egg yolks

2 tbsp double cream or single cream

115g (4oz) Gruyère cheese, grated

2 shallots, chopped

450g (1lb) fresh spinach

4 eggs

splash of vinegar or lemon juice

4 slices of toast, buttered, to serve

1 Melt half the butter in a small saucepan, stir in the flour, and cook for 1 minute. Remove the pan from the heat and gradually beat in the milk. Return the pan to the heat and cook, stirring, until the sauce thickens. Season to taste with salt and pepper. Whisk in the egg yolks and cream, then add most of the grated cheese, and stir until melted. Keep warm.

2 Bring a large, shallow pan of water to a gentle simmer, add a little vinegar, and place over a high heat. Crack an egg on to a saucer. Stir the water with a large, slotted spoon, then slip the egg into the water, letting the edge of the saucer touch the water so it does not splash. Repeat with the remaining eggs. Using a slotted spoon, lift the whites over the yolks until they are just set. Simmer gently for 3–5 minutes, or until the whites are completely set. Lift each egg out and drain briefly on kitchen paper.

3 Meanwhile, melt the remaining butter in a large saucepan and fry the shallots over a medium heat for 2–3 minutes, or until softened. Add the spinach, cover, and cook for a few minutes, or until the spinach has wilted, then drain well. Preheat the grill to High.

4 Divide the spinach between 4 individual flameproof ramekins or gratin dishes. Arrange 1 poached egg on top of each, then pour the sauce over the eggs until completely covered, and sprinkle with the remaining cheese. Place under a hot grill until the surface is golden and the sauce bubbles. Serve hot, with buttered toast.

Spinach and Mushroom Pancakes

These savoury filled pancakes, baked in a cheesy and creamy sauce, make a perfect mid-week meal and can be assembled in advance

- serves 4
- prep 30 mins
  - cook 1 hr 10 mins
- freeze the assembled unbaked dish for up to 3 months

For the pancakes

115g (4oz) plain flour

1 egg

1 egg yolk

300ml (10fl oz) milk

1 tbsp light olive oil or melted butter, plus extra for frying

For the filling

2 tbsp light olive oil or melted butter

200g (7oz) mushrooms, chopped

pinch of grated nutmeg

250g (9oz) cooked spinach, chopped

1½ quantity of white sauce (p518)

85g (3oz) grated Cheddar cheese

½ tsp dry mustard

salt and freshly ground black pepper

2 tomatoes, sliced

3 tbsp grated Parmesan cheese

● **Prepare ahead** The dish can be assembled and chilled ready for baking up to 12 hours in advance.

1 **To make the pancakes**, sift the flour into a bowl and make a well in the centre. Add the egg and egg yolk, plus a little of the milk, and whisk until smooth. Whisk in the rest of the milk and 1 tbsp oil or melted butter. Pour into a jug.

2 **Lightly grease** a 15–18cm (6–7in) heavy frying pan, add a little of the batter mix, and swirl so it coats the base of the pan in a thin layer. Cook until set and golden underneath, then flip the pancake over to cook the other side. Slide out of the pan on to a plate, then repeat with the remaining mixture to make 11 more pancakes, re-greasing the pan as necessary.

3 **To make the filling**, heat 2 tbsp oil or melted butter in a frying pan and fry the mushrooms until tender. Drain well. Transfer to a bowl and add the nutmeg, spinach, and 4 tbsp of white sauce.

4 **Preheat the oven** to 190°C (375°F/Gas 5). Divide the filling between the pancakes, roll up, and arrange in a shallow ovenproof dish.

5 **Stir the cheese** and mustard into the rest of the white sauce, season with salt and pepper, and spoon over the pancakes in an even layer. Arrange the tomato slices on top and scatter with the grated Parmesan. Bake for 30 minutes. Serve hot.

VARIATION

Spinach and Ricotta Pancakes

Replace the mushrooms with 300g (10oz) ricotta cheese. Add to the cooked spinach and fill the pancakes.

Baked Eggs in Cream

A simple but satisfying dish

- serves 4
- prep 10 mins, plus cooling
  - cook 25 mins
- 4 x 150ml (5fl oz) ramekins

2 tbsp olive oil

4 shallots, finely chopped

2 garlic cloves, crushed

1 tbsp chopped tarragon

175ml (6fl oz) double cream

4 large eggs

3 tbsp Gruyère cheese, grated

1 tbsp day-old breadcrumbs

1 tbsp chives, snipped

freshly ground black pepper

1 **Preheat the oven** to 160°C (325°F/Gas 3). Heat the oil in a pan. Fry the shallots and garlic over a low heat until softened, then increase the heat a little, and cook until the shallots are golden. Stir in the tarragon, and 2 tbsp of cream.

2 **Divide the shallot mixture** between 4 ramekins, spreading it over the base of each and hollowing the centres a little. Crack an egg into each dish. Divide the remaining cream between the ramekins.

3 **Mix the cheese**, breadcrumbs, and chives, and season with plenty of pepper. Pile this mixture on the eggs, and bake for 15 minutes, or until the eggs are cooked, and serve at once.

Spinach Soufflés

These soufflés are deliciously golden and puffy once cooked, and taste every bit as good as they look

- serves 4
- prep 20 mins • cook 20 mins
- 4 x 200ml (7fl oz) ramekins

225g (8oz) **spinach**

45g (1½ oz) **butter**, plus extra for greasing

45g (1½ oz) **plain flour**

360ml (12fl oz) **milk**

75g (2½ oz) **Parmesan cheese**, grated

pinch of grated **nutmeg**

salt and freshly ground **black pepper**

4 large **eggs**, separated

1 Place the spinach with the water that clings to its leaves after washing in a large pan. Place over a medium heat, cover, and leave for 2–3 minutes, or until wilted. Drain, squeezing out any excess water.

2 Preheat the oven to 200°C (400°F/Gas 6). Butter the ramekins and place on a baking tray.

3 Melt the butter in a pan and add the flour. Cook gently for a minute then gradually add the milk, bring to the boil, and leave to simmer for 3–4 minutes. Reserve 2 tbsp of the Parmesan and add the rest to the pan, along with the nutmeg, and season to taste with salt and pepper. Transfer the sauce to a large bowl.

4 Roughly chop the spinach and stir it into the mixture. Leave it to cool to room temperature, then stir in the egg yolks.

5 Whisk the egg whites until stiff. Stir in 2 tbsp of the egg whites into the sauce, then carefully fold the remainder into the mixture.

6 Carefully spoon the mixture into the preheated ramekins. Run a knife around the edge of the mixture to help them rise neatly. Sprinkle with the reserved Parmesan and bake for 20–25 minutes, or until well risen and golden. Serve at once.

● **Good with** warm, crusty bread and butter.

Egg Fu Yung

Light and tasty, these Chinese patties are made with prawns and stir-fried vegetables

- serves 4
- prep 15 mins • cook 20 mins
- wok

200ml (7fl oz) **vegetable stock**

1 tbsp **oyster sauce**

1 tbsp **light soy sauce**

1 tbsp **Chinese rice wine**

vegetable oil, for frying

3 **shallots**, thinly sliced

2 **garlic cloves**, crushed

1 **green pepper**, deseeded and chopped

1 **celery stick**, chopped

85g (3oz) **beansprouts**

115g (4oz) **prawns**, peeled

5 **eggs**, beaten

2 tsp **cornflour**

boiled rice, to serve

1 In a small saucepan, add the stock, oyster sauce, soy sauce, and rice wine. Set aside.

2 Heat 2 tbsp of oil in a wok and stir-fry the shallots, garlic, green pepper, and celery for 3 minutes. Add the beansprouts and stir-fry for 2 minutes. Then add the prawns, and stir-fry for 1 minute more. Transfer to a large bowl and set aside.

3 When the mixture is cool, stir in the beaten eggs. Wipe the pan with kitchen paper.

4 Return the wok to the heat and pour in 5cm (2in) oil. When hot, ladle one-quarter of the mixture into the oil and fry for 2 minutes, or until lightly browned, spooning over the oil so the top starts to set as well.

5 Carefully turn over and cook the other side. Drain and keep warm. Cook the rest of the mixture.

6 Mix the cornflour with a little water until smooth and stir into the stock mixture in the saucepan. Bring to the boil, stirring constantly until thickened and smooth, and simmer for 1 minute. Spoon over the egg fu yung patties and serve at once with boiled rice.

Cheese Soufflé

The most popular savoury soufflé is a simple cheese one. Any hard cheese can be used but pick one with a fairly strong flavour, such as mature Cheddar, or a mixture of Gruyère and Parmesan

serves 4

prep 20 mins
• cook 30–35 mins

1.2 litre (2 pint) soufflé dish

45g (1½oz) butter

45g (1½oz) plain flour

225ml (8fl oz) milk

salt and freshly ground pepper

125g (4½oz) mature Cheddar cheese, grated

½ tsp French mustard

5 large eggs, separated

1 tbsp grated Parmesan cheese

● **Prepare ahead** The recipe can be prepared to the end of step 1, up to 1 day in advance. Keep covered and chilled until needed.

1 Melt the butter in a small saucepan, stir in the flour until smooth, and cook over a medium heat for 1 minute. Whisk in the milk until blended, then bring to the boil, stirring constantly, until thickened and smooth. Remove the pan from the heat, season to taste with salt and pepper, and stir in the cheese and mustard.

2 Gradually stir in 4 of the egg yolks into the cheese. Save the remaining egg yolk for another recipe.

3 Preheat the oven to 190°C (375°F/Gas 5), and put a baking tray in the oven. In a large, clean bowl, whisk all the egg whites, until stiff peaks form. Stir 1 tbsp of the egg whites into the cheese mixture, to "loosen" it, then fold in the rest, using a large metal spoon.

4 Pour the mixture into the soufflé dish and sprinkle the Parmesan over the top. Place the dish on the baking tray, and bake for 25–30 minutes, or until the soufflé is puffed and golden brown. Serve at once in the soufflé dish.

● **Good with** a green salad and plenty of crusty bread.

VARIATIONS

Mushroom Soufflé
Replace the grated hard cheese and mustard with 175g (6oz) very finely chopped mushrooms, fried until tender with 1 finely chopped shallot. Drain the mushrooms thoroughly after frying, and stir in 2 tbsp chopped parsley, before adding to the soufflé mixture. Make the recipe as above.

Watercress Soufflé
Omit the grated hard cheese and mustard. Remove any coarse stalks from 2 bunches of watercress and discard any yellow leaves. Chop the leaves very finely and stir into the white sauce with 5 finely snipped chives. Make the recipe as above.

Carrot Soufflé
Replace the grated hard cheese and mustard with 175g (6oz) boiled carrots, mashed to a purée, and the finely grated zest of 1 small orange. Make the recipe as above.

Piperade
This savoury scrambled egg dish is from the Basque region of southwest France

serves 4

prep 5 mins • cook 20 mins

2 tbsp olive oil

1 large onion, finely sliced or chopped

2 garlic cloves, crushed

1 red pepper, deseeded and chopped

1 green pepper, deseeded and chopped

85g (3oz) serrano ham or Bayonne ham, chopped

4 tomatoes, chopped

8 eggs, beaten

salt and freshly ground black pepper

2 tbsp chopped parsley, to garnish

1 Heat the oil in a large frying pan and fry the onion over a gentle heat until softened. Add the garlic and peppers, and fry for 5 minutes, stirring occasionally.

2 Add the ham and cook for 2 minutes, then add the tomatoes and simmer for 2–3 minutes, or until any liquid has evaporated.

3 Pour the eggs into the pan and scramble, stirring frequently. Season to taste with salt and pepper, sprinkle with parsley, and serve.

Soufflé Omelette

This puffy omelette takes a little extra effort, but its lightness at the end makes it well worth making

- 🍴 serves 1
- 🕐 prep 10 mins • cook 5 mins
- ▦ palette knife

2 **eggs**, separated

salt and freshly ground **black pepper**

15g (½oz) **butter**

30g (1oz) **mature Cheddar cheese**, grated

30g (1oz) **Gruyère cheese**, grated

30g (1oz) sliced **ham**, cut into strips

2–3 chopped **chives**

1 Preheat the grill on its highest setting. Place the egg yolks in a small bowl and whisk until creamy. Season to taste with salt and pepper, add 2 tbsp water, and whisk again. Wash the whisk in hot soapy water and dry, then use to whisk the whites in a large, clean bowl, until they form soft peaks.

2 Heat the butter in a non-stick frying pan over a medium heat. Meanwhile, using a large metal spoon, quickly fold the egg yolks into the egg whites with half the cheese, taking care not to over-mix.

3 When the butter is foaming, pour the mixture into the pan, shaking the pan to make sure the mixture is evenly distributed. Cook the omelette for 1 minute, then slide a palette knife around the edge to loosen it from the pan. Scatter the omelette with the remaining cheese, and the ham, and place under the hot grill for 1 minute to allow the surface to cook.

4 Sprinkle the omelette with chives. To serve, slide the palette knife around the edge again, carefully fold the omelette in half, and slide on to a warmed plate.

● **Good with** a rocket and watercress salad.

Omelette Arnold Bennett

This famous dish was specially created for the Victorian novelist by the chefs at the Savoy Grill, London

- 🍴 serves 4
- 🕐 prep 5 mins • cook 20 mins

8 large **eggs**, separated

150ml (5fl oz) **single cream**

350g (12oz) **smoked haddock fillet**, cooked, skinned, and flaked

4 tbsp freshly grated **Parmesan cheese**

freshly ground **black pepper**

60g (2oz) **butter**

1 Beat the egg yolks in a bowl with 2 tbsp cream, until smooth and creamy. In a separate, clean bowl, whisk the egg whites until they form soft peaks. Add 1 tbsp of the whites to the egg yolk mixture, to "loosen" it, then fold in the rest, with the haddock and half the grated cheese, using a metal spoon. Season with plenty of black pepper.

2 Preheat the grill on its highest setting. Melt the butter in

a large non-stick frying pan and, when foaming, add the egg mixture. Cook until the eggs have set on the bottom, using a spatula to draw the edges of the omelette into the middle of the pan as they start to set, so the uncooked mixture can run out to the sides of the pan.

3 Once set on the bottom, scatter the remaining cheese over the top, and pour over the rest of the cream. Place the pan under the grill until the the omelette is lightly browned and set. Serve at once.

> ### SHOPPING FOR FISH
> Smoked haddock's yellow colour was once a product of the wood-smoking process, but today, the familiar tint is achieved with a natural food colouring. Most large supermarkets now sell both dyed and undyed haddock and there is no difference in taste.

Ranch-style Eggs with Refried Beans

This traditional breakfast dish, *Huevos Rancheros*, is eaten all over Mexico; here it is served with refried beans, *Frijoles Refritos*

🍴 serves 4

🕐 prep 25 mins • cook 35 mins

2 tbsp **sunflower oil**

4 corn **tortillas**

4 **eggs**

1 tbsp chopped **coriander**, to serve

1 **avocado**, sliced and peeled, to serve

For the refried beans

2 x 400g cans **pinto beans** or borlotti beans

3 tbsp **lard** or sunflower oil

1 **onion**, chopped

3 **garlic cloves**, chopped

1 **vegetable stock cube**, or salt to taste

For the sauce

750g (1lb 10oz) ripe **tomatoes**, peeled

4 small dried **hot red *pequín* chillies**, crumbled into 4 tbsp boiling water

2 **garlic cloves**, chopped

1 **onion**, chopped

1 tbsp **sunflower oil**

2 tbsp **tomato purée**

1 tsp **ground cumin**

1 tsp **dried oregano**

2 tbsp **white wine vinegar**

½ tsp **sugar**

1 **To make the refried beans**, drain the beans, reserving some of the liquid from the can. Rinse the beans and set aside. Heat the lard or oil in a frying pan and fry the onion and garlic over a medium heat for 5–10 minutes, or until golden. Increase the heat and add the beans in spoonfuls. Take care as they will spit as you stir them round quickly.

2 **Mash with** a potato masher, adding some of the reserved liquid, if necessary, to make a coarse purée. Add the stock cube or salt, and continue cooking over a low heat, stirring frequently, until thick.

3 **To make the sauce**, place the tomatoes, chillies, garlic, and onion in a blender or food processor and process to a paste. Heat the oil and fry the paste for 5 minutes, stirring frequently. Add the tomato purée, cumin, oregano, wine vinegar, and sugar, and allow to simmer for 10 minutes, adding water if the sauce becomes too thick.

4 **Heat 1 tbsp of the oil** in a frying pan until very hot. Fry each tortilla for approximately 30 seconds on each side, or until hot but not crisp. Keep warm. Add the remaining oil to the pan and fry the eggs.

5 **To serve**, place each tortilla on a warmed serving plate and place an egg on top. Spoon a generous amount of the heated sauce over each egg. Serve with the refried beans, a sprinkling of chopped coriander, and slices of avocado. Spoon any remaining sauce into a bowl to serve separately.

Yorkshire Puddings

Traditionally eaten with roast beef and gravy, these Sunday lunch classics also go well with hearty meat casseroles

🍴 serves 4

🕐 prep 10 mins, plus resting • cook 20–25 mins

▣ 12-hole bun tin

115g (4oz) **plain flour**

pinch of **salt**

1 **egg**

300ml (10fl oz) **milk**

60g (2oz) **butter** or lard, for greasing

1 **Sift the flour** and salt into a large mixing bowl. Make a hollow in the centre, then crack the egg into the middle, and add 100ml (3½fl oz) of the milk. Beat the egg and milk together with a wooden spoon, gradually drawing in the flour from the sides of the bowl.

2 **Add half** the remaining milk and continue beating the mixture until all the flour has been incorporated and the batter is smooth, then whisk in the remaining milk. Leave the batter to rest for 30 minutes.

3 **Preheat the oven** to 220°C (425°F/Gas 7). Generously grease the tin with the butter and place in the oven for 3–5 minutes, or until the fat is melted and really hot. Pour the batter into the tin and return to the oven immediately. Cook for 20–25 minutes, or until the puddings are well-risen, golden brown, and crisp. Serve immediately.

Cheese Puffs

These choux pastry balls are filled with a light and tangy blend of cheese, herbs, and spices

🍴 makes 16

🕐 prep 10 mins • cook 50 mins

❄️ freeze empty choux puffs for up to 1 month

60g (2oz) **butter** or margarine

75g (2½oz) **plain flour**, sifted

pinch of **salt**

2 large **eggs**, beaten

30g (1oz) grated **Parmesan cheese**

For the filling

150g (5½oz) **low-fat cream cheese** with garlic and herbs

2 tbsp **milk**

1 tsp fresh **lemon** juice

mild **chilli powder**, to taste

freshly ground **black pepper**, to taste

Parmesan cheese, Stilton, Gorgonzola, or mature Cheddar cheese, grated or crumbled, to taste

1 Heat the oven to 200°C (400°F/Gas 6). Bring the butter and 120ml (4fl oz) of water to the boil. Remove from the heat and add the sifted flour and salt, beating vigorously with a wooden spoon. Replace on to a very low heat and stir until the dough is smooth and comes away from the edge of the pan. Gradually stir in the beaten egg until the dough is glossy and thick. Remove from the heat.

2 When cool enough to handle, form the dough into 16 balls using 2 dessertspoons and place them, well spaced, on to a lightly greased non-stick baking tray. Bake for 20–25 minutes, or until puffed and golden.

3 Remove from the oven and use a sharp knife to make a slit in the side of each puff to allow the hot steam to escape. Using a spatula, lift the puffs on to a wire rack to cool.

4 Mix the filling ingredients. When the choux puffs are cool, open and spoon in the mixture.

VARIATION

Salmon Scramble Puffs

Melt grated Edam or Gouda cheese into hot scrambled egg and mix in some chopped smoked salmon. Use to fill the warm choux puffs.

Twice-baked Cheese Soufflés

This foolproof recipe can be prepared several hours in advance, so is ideal for serving at a dinner party

🍴 serves 4

🕐 prep 20 mins • cook 45 mins

🍴 4 x 150ml (5floz) ramekins or dariole moulds

❄️ freeze the soufflés at the end of step 4 for up to 3 months; thaw at room temperature, then complete the recipe

30g (1oz) **butter**, plus extra for greasing

30g (1oz) **plain flour**

240ml (8fl oz) **milk**

2 **eggs**, separated

125g (4½oz) **soft goat's cheese**

200ml (7fl oz) **double cream**

freshly ground **black pepper**

1 tbsp **Dijon mustard**

50g (1½oz) **Parmesan shavings**

rocket leaves, to serve

red onion chutney, to serve

● **Prepare ahead** The soufflés can be prepared up to the end of step 4 several hours ahead of time.

1 Preheat the oven to 180°C (350°F/Gas 4). Lightly butter the ramekins and line the bottoms with circles of greaseproof paper.

2 Melt the butter in a pan, stir in the flour, and mix to a smooth paste. Gradually add the milk, and stir continuously until the sauce thickens and is smooth.

3 Leave to cool slightly, then beat in the egg yolks and goat's cheese. Season well. Using an electric whisk, beat the egg whites in a bowl to soft peaks. Mix 1 tbsp egg white into the sauce, then gently pour the sauce over the remaining egg whites and carefully fold the ingredients together, using a metal spoon; do not over-mix. Spoon into the ramekins.

4 Place the ramekins in a roasting tin and add enough hot water to come halfway up the sides of the dishes. Cook in the oven for 15 minutes, or until firm. Remove from the tin and allow to cool. Run a round-bladed knife around the edge of each soufflé and carefully turn out on to a baking tray.

5 Increase the oven temperature to 200°C (400°F/Gas 6). Pour the cream, mustard, and pepper into a saucepan and bring to the boil, then allow to bubble until thickened. Top each soufflé with 2 tbsp of the mixture and the Parmesan. Bake for 20–25 minutes, or until golden. Serve with rocket leaves and red onion chutney.

Cheese and Pepper Jalousie

This puff pastry treat makes the most of ready-prepared ingredients, such as bottled mixed peppers in oil

🍴 serves 4

🕐 prep 20 mins • cook 25 mins

500g (1lb 2oz) puff pastry

flour, for dusting

3 tbsp sun-dried tomato purée

115g (4oz) mature Cheddar cheese, grated

280g jar sliced mixed peppers in oil, drained

115g (4oz) mozzarella cheese, cut into 1cm (½in) dice, or grated

freshly ground black pepper

beaten egg or milk, to glaze

1 Preheat the oven to 220°C (425°F/Gas 7). Roll out just less than half the pastry on a lightly floured surface to make a 30 x 15cm (12 x 6in) rectangle. Lay the pastry on a large dampened baking tray. Roll out the remaining pastry to a 30 x 18cm (12 x 7in) rectangle, lightly dust with flour, then fold in half lengthways. Make cuts 1cm (½in) apart along the folded edge to within 2.5cm (1in) of the outer edge.

2 Spread the tomato purée over the pastry on the baking tray

to within 2.5cm (1in) of the edges, and top with the Cheddar. Pat the peppers with kitchen paper to remove excess oil, and arrange on top of the cheese. Scatter with the mozzarella and season to taste with pepper.

3 Dampen the edges of the pastry with water. Carefully place the second piece of pastry on top and press the edges together to seal; trim off the excess. Brush the top with beaten egg and bake for 25 minutes, or until golden brown and crisp. Leave to cool for a few minutes before slicing and serving.

● **Good with** a green salad.

Red Onion and Goat's Cheese Jalousie

Fry 350g (12oz) thinly sliced red onions in 15g (½oz) unsalted butter and 1 tbsp olive oil over low heat, stirring frequently, for 10 minutes, or until soft. Stir in 1 tbsp balsamic vinegar, a pinch each of caster sugar and dried mixed herbs, and cook for a further minute, stirring all the time. Tip into a bowl and leave to cool, then mix in 115g (4oz) crumbled goat's cheese. Use instead of the cheese and pepper mixture.

Stilton Rarebit with Pear and Walnuts

This sophisticated cheese-on-toast recipe is a version of Welsh Rarebit, or *Caws Pobi*, which loosely translates as a "light bite"

🍴 serves 4

🕐 prep 10 mins • cook 20 mins

4–8 slices walnut bread

1 shallot, finely chopped

75ml (2½oz) dry cider

30g (1oz) butter

30g (1oz) plain flour

150ml (5fl oz) milk

100g (3½oz) Stilton cheese, crumbled

50g (1¾oz) Cheddar cheese, grated

1 tsp made English mustard

2 egg yolks

2 ripe pears, cored and sliced

small bunch of watercress

60g (2oz) walnuts, broken into pieces

1 tbsp balsamic vinegar

2 tbsp extra virgin olive oil

freshly ground black pepper

● **Prepare ahead** The sauce can be prepared several hours in advance, but do not spread it on the toast until ready to grill.

1 Lightly toast the bread; allow 1 or 2 slices per person, depending on the size of the slices.

2 Place the shallots and cider in a small saucepan and simmer over a low heat until the cider has almost completely evaporated. Remove from the pan and set aside.

3 Wash the pan and add the butter. Place over a medium-low heat until melted, then stir in the flour. Cook, stirring, for 1 minute, then remove the pan from the heat and gradually stir in the milk. Return to the heat and cook for 2–3 minutes, or until thickened, stirring constantly. Add the cheeses and stir until melted. Remove from the heat and stir in the mustard, egg yolks, and cooled shallots. Spread the mixture thickly on to each toasted bread slice.

4 Preheat the grill on its highest setting, then grill the toasts for 2 minutes, or until golden and bubbling.

5 Arrange the pears, watercress and walnuts on 4 serving plates, drizzle with a little balsamic vinegar and olive oil, and season with pepper. Place the toasts on the side and serve at once.

Labna

This fresh cheese is served as a meze dish in the Middle East

- serves 4
- prep 10 mins, plus draining
- muslin

600ml (1 pint) **plain Greek yogurt**

½ tsp **salt**

1 **Stir the yogurt** and salt together until evenly combined. Spoon on to a large square of muslin, then gather together the 4 corners and tie the top of the bundle with string, to make a bag.

2 **Suspend the bag** over a bowl and leave for at least 12 hours for the whey to drip through.

3 **Remove the strained** yogurt from the muslin and shape into a ball.

● **Good with** herbs or spices, such as finely chopped mint and parsley, sprinkled over, and served with toasted flat breads. Alternatively, for a sweet version, drizzle with clear honey, dust with cinnamon, and scatter with chopped pistachios.

Cheese Nuggets

These bite-sized nuggets have the great contrasting flavours of a creamy cheese filling and a fiery chilli dipping sauce

- serves 4
- prep 45 mins, plus chilling • cook 1 hr
- freeze the nuggets, cooked or uncooked, for up to 3 months

75g (2½oz) **butter**

75g (2½oz) **plain flour**, plus extra for coating

600ml (1 pint) **milk**

3 **egg yolks**

salt and freshly ground **black pepper**

pinch of grated **nutmeg**

250g (9oz) **Emmental cheese**, grated

2 **eggs**, beaten

140g (5oz) fresh **breadcrumbs**

sunflower oil, for shallow frying

For the spicy chilli dip

1 tbsp **olive oil**

1 **garlic clove**, crushed

1 **red pepper**, deseeded and chopped

1 large **red chilli**, deseeded and chopped

400g can **chopped tomatoes**

1 tsp **sugar**

100ml (3½fl oz) **single cream**

● **Prepare ahead** You can make both the dip and the nugget mixture the day before it is needed.

1 **To make the dip**, heat the oil in a frying pan and fry the garlic, pepper, and chilli over medium heat, stirring frequently, until softened. Add the tomatoes and sugar, cover the pan, and simmer for 30 minutes. Blend to a purée, then stir in the cream.

2 **To prepare** the nuggets, melt the butter in a saucepan, stir in the flour, and cook for 1 minute. Remove the pan from the heat and gradually stir in the milk, then return to the heat and cook until thickened and smooth, stirring constantly to prevent lumps forming.

3 **Cook gently** for 5 minutes, then remove the pan from the heat and beat in the egg yolks, one at a time. Season with salt, pepper, and nutmeg, and stir in the cheese. Spread out the mixture in a shallow rectangular dish in a layer about 2cm (¾in) deep, smoothing the top; leave in the refrigerator overnight.

4 **Cut the mixture** into blocks measuring roughly 2 x 5cm (¾ x 2in) and shape into nuggets. Roll in flour, brush all over with beaten egg, and roll in the breadcrumbs until coated. Chill for 1 hour.

5 **Shallow fry** in hot oil, turning frequently until the nuggets are golden brown all over. Drain on kitchen paper and serve hot with the dip, either cold or warmed through.

● **Good with** pre-dinner drinks or as part of a buffet.

VARIATION

Herbed Cheese Nuggets

Stir 2 tbsp chopped herbs, such as parsley, chives, and thyme, into the mixture with the cheese. You can substitute Gruyère instead of Emmental, or another cheese, such as Lancashire or Cheddar, for a different taste.

Cheese and Corn Pudding

This savoury baked dish is a wonderful way of celebrating fresh corn when it is in season

🍴 serves 8

🕐 prep 10 mins • cook 45 mins

🍽 1.4 litre (2½ pints) ovenproof serving dish

5 ears of **fresh corn**, kernels removed or 2 x 400g cans sweetcorn kernels, drained

280g (10g) **mature Cheddar cheese** or Monterey Jack, grated

25g (1oz) **butter**, melted, plus a little extra for greasing

2 large **eggs**

4 tbsp **plain white flour**

2 tbsp **sugar**

¼ tsp **salt**

pinch of **cayenne pepper**

⬤ **Prepare ahead** The kernels can be removed the night before, placed in a bowl, covered and chilled. Or, the entire dish can be assembled several hours in advance for last-minute cooking, topping with the remaining cheese just before baking.

1 Preheat the oven to 160°C (325°F/Gas 3) and lightly grease the serving dish. Put three-quarters of the corn kernels in a blender and blend to a purée. Add three-quarters of the cheese, the butter, eggs, flour, sugar, and salt and process with the corn kernels.

2 Pour the corn mixture into the prepared dish, stir in the remaining kernels and smooth the surface. Sprinkle the remaining cheese and cayenne pepper on top.

3 Bake for 45 minutes, or until set and golden. Leave the pudding to stand for 5 minutes, then serve hot from the dish.

⬤ **Good with** roast chicken, turkey, or ham. Leftovers can be covered, chilled, and reheated.

Paneer and Peas

This Indian restaurant favourite – called *matar paneer* on menus – is very easy to make at home

🍴 serves 4

🕐 prep 15 mins • cook 15 mins

groundnut oil or sunflower oil for frying

1 large **onion**, thinly sliced

2 large **garlic cloves**, coarsely chopped

1 **green chilli**, deseeded (optional) and chopped

1cm (½in) fresh **root ginger**, peeled and coarsely chopped

2 tsp **garam masala**

salt and freshly ground **black pepper**

400g can **chopped tomatoes**

225g (8oz) **paneer**, cut into bite-sized cubes

450g (1lb) **frozen peas**

1 Heat a large, heavy frying pan over a medium heat. Add 3 tbsp of the oil. When the oil is hot, fry the onion, stirring frequently, for 8–10 minutes, or until dark golden brown. Do not let it burn.

2 Meanwhile, put the garlic, chilli, and ginger into a blender and blend until a thick paste forms. Add the garam masala and season to taste with salt and pepper.

3 Add the spice mixture to the fried onions and stir for a couple of minutes. Pour into a large, heavy saucepan, add the tomatoes and 150ml (5fl oz) water and bring to the boil, stirring. Reduce the heat to low and leave to simmer and thicken while preparing the paneer, stirring.

4 Wash and dry the frying pan and place over a high heat. When the pan is hot, pour a thin layer of oil over the surface. Once hot, add as many pieces of paneer that will fit in a single layer and fry for 5 minutes, or until golden on all sides, using long-handled tongs to turn them. As the pieces are fried, transfer them into the simmering tomato mixture.

5 When all the paneer has been transferred, add the frozen peas to the saucepan, increase the heat and leave to cook for 5 minutes, or until the peas are cooked. Stir carefully to avoid breaking up the paneer. Taste and adjust the seasoning, if necessary.

Welsh Rarebit

Often pronounced as Welsh "rabbit", this simple recipe makes a meal out of cheese on toast

🍴 serves 4

🕐 prep 10 mins • cook 6 mins

❗ line the baking tray with kitchen foil before baking, as the cheese sauce will be runny

4 slices **white bread** or wholemeal bread

25g (1oz) **butter**

225g (8oz) **strong Cheddar cheese** or Lancashire cheese, grated

1 tbsp **English mustard powder**

3 tbsp **brown ale** or lager

Worcestershire sauce, to taste

1 Preheat the grill to high and position the rack 10cm (4in) from the heat. Toast the bread until golden brown, then turn over and toast the other side. Leaving the grill on, remove the toast from the heat and place on to a baking tray.

2 Meanwhile, melt the butter in a pan over a low heat. Add the cheese, mustard powder, and ale, and heat until creamy, stirring often.

3 Spread the sauce over the toast and splash a few drops of Worcestershire sauce on each. Return the cheese-covered toast to the grill for just a few minutes, or until the cheese is bubbling and golden. Cut each slice in half and serve.

⬤ **Good with** salad. You could also put cooked ham under the cheese sauce before grilling.

⬤ **Leftovers** can be cut into cubes and added to soups and salads in place of croûtons, or used as a topping for simple pasta dishes.

VARIATION

Golden Bucks

Prepare the recipe as above, using Lancashire cheese instead of Cheddar. Add a poached or fried egg to the top of each toast, and serve.

Gorgonzola with Figs and Honey

Grilling figs enhances their natural sweetness and the addition of blue cheese makes a great flavour contrast

🍴 serves 4

🕐 prep 10 mins • cook 10 mins

12 **ripe figs**, halved

175g (6oz) **Gorgonzola cheese**, crumbled

clear honey, to serve

1 Heat a ridged grill pan over medium-high heat. Add the figs, placing them cut-side down, and grill for 5 minutes, or until browned.

2 When the figs have nice grill marks, gently turn them over and cook on the other side for a further couple of minutes.

3 Remove the figs from the pan and place them in a shallow serving dish. Sprinkle with the Gorgonzola, drizzle with honey, and serve immediately.

⬤ **Good with** pre-dinner drinks, or served after a meal.

VARIATION

Savoury Fig Salad

For a sweet and savoury salad, replace honey with prosciutto and serve with a milder cheese such as provolone.

Feta Filo Pie

Crisp pastry encases a delicious blend of spinach, feta, and pine nuts in this classic Middle Eastern dish

🍴 serves 6

🕐 prep 30 mins, plus cooling and standing • cook 1 hr

🍲 20cm (8in) springform tin

900g (2lb) fresh **spinach leaves**

100g (3½oz) **butter**

1 tsp **ground cumin**

1 tsp **ground coriander**

1 tsp **ground cinnamon**

2 **red onions**, finely chopped

60g (2oz) **dried apricots**, chopped

60g (2oz) **pine nuts**, toasted

6 sheets **filo pastry**, 40 x 30cm (16 x 12in), thawed if frozen

salt and freshly ground **black pepper**

300g (10oz) **feta cheese**, crumbled

flat-leaf **parsley**, to garnish

lemon zest, to garnish

1 **Rinse the spinach leaves**, shake off the excess water, and pack into a large saucepan. Cover and cook over a medium heat for 8–10 minutes, turning occasionally, until just wilted. Drain well through a sieve or colander, pressing the spinach against the sides to extract as much water as possible. Set aside, still draining, to cool.

2 **Meanwhile**, melt 25g (1oz) butter until bubbling and gently fry the spices with the onion over a low heat, stirring occasionally, for 7–8 minutes, or until softened but not browned. Stir in the apricots and pine nuts, then set aside. Preheat the oven to 200°C (400°F/Gas 6). Grease and line the springform tin.

3 **To assemble the pie**, melt the remaining butter. Brush the prepared tin with melted butter and cover the base with a sheet of pastry, leaving the edges overhanging, and brush with butter. Continue with 5 more sheets, brushing each with butter. Leave the edges overhanging.

4 **Blot the cooled spinach** with kitchen paper, then chop finely. Stir into the cooked onion mixture, and season to taste with salt and pepper. Pile half into the pastry case and spread evenly.

5 **Sprinkle the cheese** over the spinach, then cover with the remaining spinach mixture. Fold the overhanging pastry over the spinach, piece by piece, brushing with butter. Brush the top with any remaining butter and place the tin on a baking tray. Bake for 35–40 minutes, or until crisp and golden. Let it stand for 10 minutes before carefully releasing from the tin.

6 **Serve hot or warm**, cut into wedges, and garnish with parsley and strips of lemon zest.

● **Good with** a crisp salad or seasonal vegetables.

● **VARIATION**

Blue Cheese Filo Pie

A crumbled blue cheese, such as Stilton, can be used instead of feta. For a non-vegetarian version, replace the cheese with the same quantity of chopped cooked chicken or cooked minced lamb.

Herbed Goat's Cheese Spread

Delicious on toast, this spread is also a great sandwich filling

🍴 serves 4

🕐 prep 10 mins, plus chilling

125g (4½oz) **soft goat's cheese**

2–3 tbsp low-fat **crème fraîche**

1 tsp chopped **thyme**

1 tsp snipped **chives**

1 tbsp chopped **parsley**

1 **sun-dried tomato** in oil, finely chopped

1 **garlic clove**, crushed

pinch of grated **nutmeg**

freshly ground **black pepper**

chives, to garnish

● **Prepare ahead** The spread can be made a day ahead, covered, and stored in the refrigerator.

1 **Beat the goat's cheese** and crème fraîche together in a medium bowl until smooth.

2 **Add the herbs**, tomato, and garlic, and season with nutmeg and pepper. Beat until well combined.

3 **Spoon into** a serving bowl and chill until required. Serve garnished with freshly snipped chives.

Feta Cheese Squares

These crunchy little biscuits are packed with the rich and salty flavours of the Greek feta cheese

🍴 makes 72 squares

🕐 prep 10 mins • cook 25 mins

❄ freeze for up to 1 month

125g (4½oz) unsalted butter, softened, plus extra for greasing

120ml (4fl oz) extra virgin olive oil

120ml (4 fl oz) milk

1½ tsp baking powder

250g (9oz) feta cheese, crumbled

400g (14oz) plain flour

1 tbsp poppy seeds

1 tsp cayenne pepper

● **Prepare ahead** The biscuits can be stored in an airtight container for up to a week. Heat through in a warm oven to refresh before serving.

1 Preheat the oven to 180°C (350°F/Gas 4). Grease 2 large baking trays. In a food processor, process the butter until soft and smooth. Slowly add the olive oil through the feeder with the machine running. Add the milk, baking powder, and cheese, and pulse 2 or 3 times until it comes together.

2 Add half the flour and pulse until evenly blended. Add the remaining flour and turn the mixture on to a clean surface and bring together to form a soft dough. Knead for 2 minutes. Stir in the cheese, then sprinkle the flour over the top and work in with your hands.

3 Divide the mixture in half. Press each dough out to create 2 squares, each about 15 x 15cm (6 x 6in) and 3mm (⅛in) thick. Sprinkle with poppy seeds and cayenne pepper. Using a sharp knife, cut through the dough to create 2.5cm (1in) squares.

4 Bake for 20-25 minutes, or until the tops are lightly brown. Remove from the oven and cut and trim the squares while still warm. Allow to cool on wire racks before storing in an airtight container.

Baked Ricotta with Roasted Tomatoes

With ripe tomatoes and good quality olive oil, this simple dish captures the flavours of the Mediterranean

🍴 serves 4 as a starter

🕐 prep 15 mins • cook 25 mins

2 tbsp extra virgin olive oil, plus extra for greasing

7 ripe cherry tomatoes, cut in half

salt and freshly ground black pepper

1 large red pepper

250g (9oz) ricotta cheese, drained

15g (½oz) Parmesan cheese, grated

● **Prepare ahead** The dish is best served hot, but it can also be baked up to 4 hours in advance and served at room temperature.

1 Preheat the oven to 220°C (425°F/Gas 7) and lightly grease a small roasting tin or dish. Reserve 2 tomato halves and place the rest in the tin, cut-sides up, then drizzle with 2 tbsp olive oil and sprinkle with salt and pepper. Bake the tomatoes for 7-10 minutes. or until they soften and start to collapse. Remove from the oven and set aside, but do not turn off the oven.

2 Meanwhile, place the pepper under a hot grill turning frequently for 4-5 minutes, or until blackened. Place the pepper in a plastic bag and set aside until cool enough to handle, then peel off the skin. Cut the pepper in half, discard the core and seeds, and cut into thin strips; set aside.

3 Cut the ricotta cheese in half horizontally. Remove the tomatoes from the tin. Place the bottom half of the ricotta, cut-side up, in the tin and season lightly with salt and pepper. Arrange the pepper strips on top, then the tomatoes, pressing down lightly. Drizzle with olive oil and top with the remaining ricotta, cut-side down.

4 Sprinkle with the Parmesan and drizzle with a little extra oil. Return to the oven and bake for 15 minutes, or until the cheese is hot and the top is golden. Top with the reserved tomato halves and a dash more pepper and serve.

● **Good with** focaccia, French bread, or a mixed salad.

Goat's Cheese Mousse with Grilled Peppers

A delicious cold dish for a summer's lunch or brunch

 serves 4

 prep 20 mins, plus marinating • cook 45–55 mins

4 ramekins

2 tbsp **olive oil**, plus extra for greasing

3 **peppers**, mixed colours, deseeded and quartered

dash of **balsamic vinegar**

1 **garlic clove**, finely chopped

2 tbsp **chopped basil**

salt and freshly ground **black pepper**

3 **eggs**

250ml (8fl oz) **double cream**

100g (3½oz) **creamy goat's cheese**

30g (1oz) **Parmesan cheese**, grated

grated **nutmeg**, to taste

● **Prepare ahead** These mousses can be made up to 2 days in advance, then covered and chilled.

1 Preheat the grill on its highest setting and lightly oil the ramekins.

2 Place the peppers on a grill rack and grill for 4–5 minutes, or until the skins are blackened, turning once or twice. Place in a plastic bag and leave until cool enough to handle, then remove from them from bag and peel off the skins. Slice the peppers into strips, place in a bowl, and add the olive oil, vinegar, garlic, and basil. Season to taste with salt and pepper and leave to marinate for 1 hour.

3 Meanwhile, preheat the oven to 180°C (350°F/Gas 4). Place the eggs, cream, goat's cheese, Parmesan, and nutmeg in a food processor, season to taste with salt and pepper, and process until well combined. Pour into the ramekins.

4 Place the ramekins in a roasting tin and pour in boiling water to come halfway up the sides of the ramekins. Bake, uncovered, for 30–40 minutes, or until set, then remove from the tin. Leave to cool, then chill for several hours.

5 To serve, run a blunt knife around each ramekin and turn the mousses out on to individual serving plates. Divide the peppers between the plates and drizzle with the dressing.

● **Good with** warm crusty bread.

Fonduta

This nourishing meatless dish is a variation of the Italian classic from northern Italy, where polenta is favoured over pasta

 serves 4

prep 5 mins • cook 25 mins

175g (6oz) **polenta**

2 tbsp **butter**

175g (6 oz) **fontina cheese**, coarsely grated

125ml (4½fl oz) **milk**

3 large **egg yolks**

pinch **ground white pepper**

sliced mushrooms, to serve

baby carrots, to serve

1 To prepare the polenta, bring 1 litre (1¾ pints) water to a boil in a medium saucepan. In a small bowl, combine the polenta with 240ml (8fl oz) water. Stir the polenta mixture into the boiling water and cook, stirring constantly, for 5 minutes, or until thickened. Reduce the heat to a low heat, cover, and cook for 5 minutes, then remove from the heat.

2 Meanwhile, place the butter in a heatproof bowl over a pan of gently simmering water. When it has melted, add the cheese and milk. Cook, stirring constantly, until the cheese melts, then add the egg yolks and continue cooking and stirring until the mixture is smooth. Season to taste with pepper.

3 Spoon a quarter of the polenta on to each of 4 serving plates and form a mound. Using the back of a spoon, make an indentation in each mound. Pour the cheese sauce into each indentation and serve the vegetables alongside.

COOKING OVER HOT WATER

When cooking with a bowl over a pan of simmering water, make sure the bottom of the bowl does not touch the water. This ensures very gentle cooking without direct heat, which is ideal for melting chocolate, cooking egg sauces, and (as in this case) melting cheese without over-cooking it. Over-cooking the cheese would toughen it and prevent it combining with the other ingredients to form a smooth sauce.

Cheese Roulade

This makes a sumptuous first course or light lunch, served warm or at room temperature

 serves 4–6

 prep 20 mins • cook 25 mins

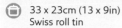 33 x 23cm (13 x 9in)
Swiss roll tin

50g (1¾oz) **butter**, plus extra for greasing

50g (1¾oz) **plain flour**

300ml (10fl oz) **milk**

75g (2½oz) **Parmesan cheese**, finely grated

2 tsp **Dijon mustard**

salt and freshly ground **black pepper**

4 **eggs**, separated

225g (8oz) **ricotta cheese**

115g (4oz) **watercress**, tough stalks removed

● **Prepare ahead** The roulade can be completed several hours in advance up to the end of step 4. The cooked roulade can be stored in the refrigerator for up to 24 hours.

1 **Preheat the oven** to 190°C (375°F/Gas 5). Grease and line the Swiss roll tin with greaseproof paper.

2 **Melt the butter** in a large saucepan, add the flour, and stir until evenly blended. Remove the pan from the heat and gradually beat in the milk, return to the heat and bring to the boil, stirring constantly, until the sauce is thick and smooth. Remove from the heat again and stir in half the Parmesan, the mustard, and seasoning. Allow to cool slightly, then add the egg yolks and beat until well incorporated.

3 **Using a hand whisk**, beat the egg whites in a large bowl until they stand in soft peaks. Mix a large spoonful of the egg whites into the sauce, then gently pour the sauce over the remaining egg whites, and carefully fold together. Take care not

to over-mix. Spread the mixture evenly into the prepared tin.

4 **Bake for 15–20 minutes**, or until golden brown and the top springs back when touched lightly. Turn out on to a large piece of greaseproof paper dusted with the remaining Parmesan.

5 **Peel away the paper** and trim off the crispy edges of the roulade. Spread the surface with the ricotta, leaving a 2.5cm (1in) gap at one short end, then cover with the watercress. Roll up the roulade, using the paper to help. Cut the roulade into slices to serve.

VARIATION

Sun-blushed Tomato and Spinach Cheese Roulade
Mix a pinch of nutmeg into the ricotta before spreading over the roulade. Replace the watercress with spinach and add 85g (3oz) roughly chopped sun-blush tomatoes before rolling in step 5.

Feta and Pumpkin Pastries

Popular Middle Eastern snacks, these tasty crisp filo pastries are filled with a sweetly spiced mixture

 makes 24

 prep 20 mins, plus cooling • cook 30 mins

100g (3½oz) **pumpkin** or squash, peeled and deseeded

25g (scant 1oz) **raisins**, chopped

100g (3oz) **feta cheese**, finely crumbled

freshly ground **black pepper**

½ tsp ground **cinnamon**

6 sheets **filo pastry**, 40 x 30cm (16 x 12in), thawed if frozen

50g (1¾oz) **butter**, melted, plus extra for greasing

flour, for dusting

● **Prepare ahead** The pastries can be prepared up to 24 hours in advance of baking and chilled.

1 Finely dice the pumpkin flesh and place it in a small saucepan. Pour in enough water to just cover the pumpkin, bring to the boil, cover, and simmer gently for 5 minutes, or until tender. Drain well and allow to cool.

2 Preheat the oven to 180°C (350°F/Gas 4). Mix the pumpkin with the raisins and feta cheese. Season with pepper and add the cinnamon. Set aside.

3 Lay the filo sheets on top of each other and cut into 4 long strips, about 7.5cm (3in) wide. Stack the strips on top of each other and cover with dampened kitchen paper.

4 Taking 1 strip of pastry at a time, brush with butter, and place a heaped tsp of the pumpkin mixture 2.5cm (1in) at one end. Fold over the end of the strip of pastry to cover the filling.

5 Fold a corner of the pastry over diagonally to form a triangular pocket of filled pastry. Working upwards, keep folding diagonally, from one side to the other, to retain the triangular shape, until all the pastry is folded, making sure any gaps in the pastry are pressed closed.

6 Lightly dust the work surface with flour, and keep the triangles in a pile, covered with a damp cloth to stop them drying out, while preparing the other pastries.

7 Transfer the triangles to a greased baking tray. Brush with the remaining butter and bake for 20–25 minutes, or until crisp and golden. Serve while still warm.

● **Good with** other Greek or Middle Eastern dishes as part of a meze meal, or as a light snack or canapé.

VARIATION

Cheese and Potato Pastries

Replace the pumpkin with finely diced potato or sweet potato.

Warm Halloumi with Herbs

Halloumi is made from sheep and goat's milk

 serves 4-6

 prep 5 mins • cook 3–5 mins

 rinse the halloumi cheese before using to rid it of excess salt; dry well on kitchen paper

2 x 250g packets **halloumi cheese**

flour, for dusting

120ml (4fl oz) **olive oil**, plus extra for drizzling

2 handfuls of **thyme** or oregano leaves

juice of 2 **lemons**

1 **lemon**, cut into wedges, to serve

1 Cut the halloumi cheese into 1cm (½ in) thick slices and lightly dust with flour. Heat the oil in a non-stick frying pan over a high heat and fry the cheese for 2–3 minutes on each side, or until golden brown.

2 Remove from the pan and sprinkle with the thyme and lemon juice. Serve immediately with a little extra oil drizzled over the cheese and lemon wedges.

● **Good with** crusty bread, and a spinach and red onion salad.

Ricotta and Bacon Tart

A simple, stylish tart with a light cheese filling

 serves 4

 prep 35 mins, plus chilling
• cook 1 hr 10 mins

23cm (9in) flan tin, baking beans

can be frozen for up to 3 months, wrapped in cling film

For the pastry

175g (6oz) **plain flour**, plus extra for dusting

85g (3oz) **butter**, cut into small pieces

For the filling

15g (½oz) **butter**

1 medium **onion**, chopped

115g (4oz) **lean bacon**, chopped into small pieces

250g (9oz) **ricotta cheese**

2 **eggs**

90ml (3fl oz) **milk**

3 tbsp freshly grated **Parmesan cheese**

1 tbsp **chives**, snipped

1 tbsp **thyme**, chopped

salt and freshly ground **black pepper**

1 Sift the flour into a large bowl. Add the butter and rub into the flour, using your fingertips, until the mixture resembles coarse breadcrumbs. Add about 3 tbsp cold water and mix in with a knife to make a firm dough. Roll out the pastry on a floured surface and use it to line the tin. Chill for at least 20 minutes.

2 Heat the oven to 200°C (400°F/Gas 6). Put the tin on a baking tray, line with greaseproof paper and baking beans, and bake blind for 10 minutes. Remove the paper and beans and bake for a further 5 minutes. Remove from the oven and allow to cool. Reduce the oven temperature to 180°C (350°F/Gas 4).

3 Meanwhile, melt the butter in a saucepan and add the onion. Cook over a low heat, covered, for 10–15 minutes, stirring occasionally, until soft and translucent. Remove the lid and add the bacon. Cook over a medium heat, stirring occasionally until the bacon is cooked through and colours slightly.

4 Mix the ricotta cheese with the eggs and milk. Add the Parmesan and herbs, and season to taste with salt and pepper. Stir in the bacon and onion and pour the mixture into the pastry case. Bake for 35 minutes, or until the filling has set. Leave to cool slightly in the tin, then transfer to a serving plate.

Swiss Cheese Fondue

This is a dish designed to be shared; the term "fondue" refers to the vessel in which the cheese is melted

 serves 4

prep 15 mins • cook 10 mins

fondue set

1 large **garlic clove**, cut in half

360ml (12fl oz) **dry white wine**

200g (7oz) **Gruyère cheese**, grated

200g (7oz) **Emmental cheese**, grated

2 tsp **cornflour**

3 tbsp **kirsch** or brandy

1 tbsp **lemon** juice

freshly ground **black pepper**

1 large day-old **baguette**, cut into bite-sized pieces

1 Rub the cut side of the garlic clove around the inside of your fondue pot. Discard the garlic.

2 Add the wine to the pot and bring it to the boil over a medium heat. Turn the heat down and add the cheeses in handfuls, stirring until completely melted.

3 Mix the cornflour with the kirsch and lemon juice, and stir into the cheese. Cook on a low heat for 2–3 minutes, stirring, until the cheese is thick and creamy, then remove from the heat. Season to taste with pepper.

4 If the mixture is too thin, add more cheese or stir in a little more cornflour, blended with wine. If it's too thick, stir in a little warmed white wine.

5 To serve, transfer the pot to a burner on the table. Stirring often, to keep the fondue smooth, spear the bread on fondue forks and dunk into the cheese.

Goat's Cheese Tartlets

Individual oat pastry cases are the perfect container for a light tangy goat's cheese and yogurt filling, for a starter or light lunch

 serves 4

prep 25 mins, plus chilling
• cook 35–40 mins

4 loose-bottomed tartlet tins
12.5cm (5in) in diameter and
2.5cm (1in) deep, baking beans

For the pastry

85g (3oz) plain flour, plus extra
for dusting

pinch of salt

25g (scant 1oz) rolled oats

60g (2oz) cold butter, diced

2 tbsp chilled water

For the filling

2 large eggs

90ml (3fl oz) Greek yogurt

150ml (5fl oz) milk

2 tbsp snipped chives

salt and freshly ground black pepper

85g (3oz) goat's cheese, crumbled

● **Prepare ahead** Make the pastry and line the tartlet tins up to 1 day in advance. If serving cold, the tartlets can be refrigerated, and covered with cling film, for up to 48 hours.

1 **To make the pastry**, sift the flour and salt into a large mixing bowl and stir in the oats. Add the butter and rub in until the mixture resembles breadcrumbs. Sprinkle with 2 tbsp chilled water and mix in, using a round-bladed knife. Gather the dough together and lightly knead on a floured surface for a few seconds, or until smooth. Wrap in cling film and chill for 30 minutes.

2 **Preheat the oven** to 200°C (400°F/Gas 6) and place a baking tray inside. Divide the pastry dough into 4 pieces. Roll out each one thinly on a lightly floured surface and use to line the tartlet tins. Prick the pastry bases several times with a fork, and line each with a piece of foil and baking beans. Bake for 10 minutes, then remove the foil and beans and return to the oven for

5 minutes. Remove from the oven and reduce the oven temperature to 180°C (350°F/Gas 4).

3 **Whisk the eggs**, yogurt, milk, chives, and salt and pepper in a jug. Divide the cheese between the pastry cases, then carefully pour over the egg mixture. Bake for 20–25 minutes, or until the filling is lightly set and beginning to brown.

4 **Leave to cool slightly**, then remove from the tins and serve warm, or at room temperature.

● **Good with** salad leaves and scattered with toasted nuts.

VARIATION

Sun-dried Tomato and Goat's Cheese Tartlets
Use kitchen scissors to snip a couple of sun-dried tomatoes into the base of each tartlet with the goat's cheese, or spread 1 tbsp good-quality tomato chutney over each pastry base before adding the egg mixture.

Goat's Cheese in Herb Oil

Use individual cheeses or a whole cheese for this recipe

 serves 4

prep 10 mins

screw-top 500ml (16fl oz) glass jar

225g (8oz) goat's cheese, cut into
4 slices if large

2 garlic cloves, halved

1 tbsp mixed peppercorns

2–3 sprigs of rosemary

4–5 sprigs of thyme

2–4 dried red chillies (optional)

360ml (12fl oz) extra virgin olive oil

● **Prepare ahead** Marinate the goat's cheese at least 3–4 days before serving; they will keep for up to 3 months.

1 **Carefully place** the individual cheese slices in a clean glass jar. Arrange the garlic cloves, peppercorns, herbs, and chillies (if using) around the goat's cheeses.

2 **Pour in enough** olive oil to completely cover the ingredients. Seal the jar.

3 **Store at room temperature** for a few hours, then refrigerate. Remove and bring to room temperature before serving.

● **Good with** bread or crackers, or chopped and placed on pieces of toast as a canapé. Alternatively, grill and serve on a bed of chicory leaves as a starter.

Tandoori Paneer Kebabs

Paneer is a firm Indian cheese that takes up the flavour of other ingredients

🍴 serves 4

🕐 prep 20 mins, plus marinating • cook 10 mins

❗ soak the wooden skewers in cold water for 30 mins before using to prevent them burning

🗔 wooden skewers

150g (5½oz) thick **natural yogurt**

1 tbsp **tandoori curry paste**

1 tbsp **lemon** juice

250g (9oz) **paneer**, cut into 2.5cm (1in) cubes

1 **red pepper**, deseeded and cut into 2.5cm (1in) chunks

12 **button mushrooms**

1 large **courgette**, cut into 1cm (½in) slices

2 tbsp **vegetable oil**

⬤ **Prepare ahead** The recipe must be started a day ahead.

1 In a bowl, mix the yogurt, curry paste, and lemon juice. Add the paneer, and stir well. Cover, chill, and marinate for up to 24 hours.

2 Thread the paneer cubes on to skewers, alternating with the pepper, mushrooms, and courgette. Brush with oil and grill or barbecue for 10 minutes, or until the vegetables are cooked.

Gruyère Tart

This vegetarian tart, with crisp, thyme-flavoured pastry, is equally delicious warm or cold

🍴 serves 6

🕐 prep 25 mins, plus chilling • cook 45 mins

🗔 35 x 12cm (14 x 5in) tranche tin, baking beans

For the pastry

140g (5oz) **plain flour**, plus extra for dusting

60g (2oz) **wholemeal flour**

125g (4½oz) **cold butter**, diced

1 tsp chopped **thyme**

For the filling

15g (½oz) **butter**

1 tbsp **olive oil**

1 large **onion**, thinly sliced

pinch of freshly grated **nutmeg**

1 tsp **caster sugar**

115g (4oz) **Gruyère cheese**, grated

3 **eggs**

100ml (3½fl oz) **double cream**

60ml (2fl oz) **milk**

1 tsp **Dijon mustard**

salt and freshly ground **black pepper**

⬤ **Prepare ahead** Make the pastry and onion mixture up to 24 hours in advance, cover with cling film, and chill. Bring to room temperature before using.

1 To make the pastry, mix the flours together in a large bowl. Using your fingertips, rub in the butter until the mixture resembles fine breadcrumbs. Stir in the thyme and sprinkle with 3–4 tbsp chilled water. Mix with a round-bladed knife to make a firm dough. Knead on a lightly floured surface for a few seconds, until smooth. Shape into a slightly flattened ball and wrap in lightly oiled cling film. Chill for 30 minutes.

2 Meanwhile, heat the butter and oil in a large frying pan, add the onion, and fry over a low heat for 15 minutes, or until soft, stirring frequently. Stir in the nutmeg and sugar, then cook for a further 2–3 minutes, or until beginning to colour. Remove from the pan, and leave to cool.

3 Roll out the pastry on a lightly floured surface, and use it to line the tin. Chill for 15 minutes.

4 Place a baking tray in the oven and preheat to 200°C (400°F/Gas 6). Prick the pastry base all over with a fork, then line with greaseproof paper and baking beans. Bake for 15 minutes, then remove the paper and beans. Return to the oven for a further 5–10 minutes, or until crisp. Lower the oven to 190°C (375°F/Gas 5).

5 Stir half the cheese into the cooled onion mixture, then spoon into the pastry case. Sprinkle with the remaining cheese. Beat together the eggs, cream, milk, and mustard in a jug, and season to taste with salt and pepper. Pour over the cheese and onions, and bake for 30 minutes, or until lightly set.

6 Leave to cool for 10 minutes, then carefully remove from the tin. Serve warm or cold.

⬤ **Good with** a rocket or watercress salad, with sliced plum tomatoes and black olives, tossed in a lemon-flavoured dressing.

VARIATION

Roquefort and Walnut Tart

Use 2 leeks, finely sliced, instead of the onion, and substitute crumbled Roquefort for the Gruyère. Add 50g (2oz) finely chopped, toasted walnuts to the pastry when making.

Fresh Mango Chutney

This "chutney" is not the usual simmered, sweetly spiced preserve but a fresh, appetizing relish

- serves 4-6
- prep 15 mins
- low fat, low GI

2 ripe **mangoes**

1 **red chilli**, deseeded, membrane removed, chopped

2 tsp **soft brown sugar**

2 tsp **white wine vinegar**

4 tsp **rapeseed oil** or light olive oil

salt and freshly ground **black pepper**

ground coriander

1 tbsp chopped **mint**

● **Prepare ahead** This chutney is best made at least 2 hours before serving, so the flavours develop.

1 Peel the mangoes and use a sharp knife to cut the flesh from the stones. Cut the flesh into small dice and put into a mixing bowl.

2 Add the chilli to the bowl with the sugar, vinegar, and oil, and mix well. Season to taste with salt,

pepper, and a generous sprinkling of ground coriander.

3 Put into an airtight container and chill in the fridge to allow the flavours to develop. Just before serving, stir in the chopped mint, adjust the seasoning if needed, and serve. Eat within 3 days.

● **Good with** hot and cold meats, and cheeses.

VARIATION

Smooth Mango Chutney
Prepare the chutney as above up to the end of step 2. Place in a food processor and add 1 tbsp desiccated coconut and 1 tbsp chopped coriander. Process until smooth, adding a little water if needed, to achieve the consistency of thick double cream. Serve at once, scattered with a few torn coriander leaves. This is good served as a sauce with seared salmon, or as an exotic dressing for a smoked fish starter.

Pickled Vegetables

This recipe is an exciting combination of crunchy seasonal vegetables, pickled in a herb and spice vinegar

- makes 5-6 jars
- prep 20 mins, plus standing
- 5-6 x 450g (1lb) jam or Kilner jars

900g-1kg (2-2¼lb) **mixed seasonal vegetables**, such as small cucumbers, small onions, cauliflower, green beans, and small green tomatoes

salt

For the vinegar

1 litre (1¾ pints) **malt vinegar** or white wine vinegar

4 **bay leaves**

8 **whole cloves**

small handful of **peppercorns**

small piece fresh **root ginger**, bruised

25g (scant 1oz) **allspice berries**

1 tsp **dried chilli flakes**

● **Prepare ahead** Make this preserve at least 1 month in advance to allow the flavours to develop. The vinegar can be made up to 2 months before pickling the vegetables.

1 Put the vinegar, herbs and spices into a bottle or jar, seal the lid, and leave to infuse for at least 2 weeks. If you want to use the vinegar immediately, you can speed up the infusion process by putting the mix into a bowl over boiling water and steaming it for 10 minutes to heat it. Cover and leave in a cool place to infuse and cool.

2 Prepare the vegetables of your choice, cutting into small bite-sized pieces. Place in a deep glass bowl, sprinkle liberally with salt, cover and leave in a cool place for 24 hours.

3 Drain the vegetables thoroughly and then pack into clean jars. Strain the vinegar and discard the herbs and spices. Cover the vegetables with the prepared vinegar, seal, and label. Keep in a cool, dark place for at least 1 month before using. Once opened, keep in the refrigerator and use within 1 week.

● **Good with** hot and cold meats, cheese, and salads, and in sandwiches and burgers.

Apple and Pear Chutney

Make this fruity, spicy chutney at harvest time and you will have a good supply to last for months

🍴 makes 4–5 jars

🕐 prep 1 hr • cook 45 mins

🍲 preserving pan or large stainless steel saucepan, 4–5 x 450g (1lb) jam or Kilner jars

1kg (2¼lb) **apples**, peeled, quartered, and cored

450g (1lb) **pears**, peeled, quartered, and cored

225g (8oz) **onions**, quartered

225g (8oz) **seedless raisins**

450g (1lb) **sultanas**

4 **garlic cloves**, peeled

60g (2oz) fresh **root ginger**, peeled and chopped

1 fresh **chilli**, deseeded and chopped, or 10g (¼oz) dried chilli flakes

1 **lemon**, quartered and pips removed

15g (½oz) **mustard seeds**

600ml (1 pint) **malt vinegar**

450g (1lb) **light soft brown sugar**

2 tsp **salt**

1 Put the apples, pears, onions, raisins, sultanas, garlic, ginger, chilli, and lemon in a food processor and process briefly to make a coarsely chopped mixture. Alternatively, chop by hand. Spoon into a preserving pan and add the remaining ingredients.

2 Heat to boiling point, stirring constantly, then leave to cook, uncovered, for 40 minutes, stirring occasionally to prevent sticking.

3 Preheat the oven to 180°C (350°F/Gas 4). While the chutney is cooking, heat the clean jars in the oven for 10 minutes.

4 Put the heated jars on a tray and divide the chutney between them. Screw the lids in place while hot, to seal, or leave the chutney to cool, then cover with wax discs and pot covers. Label and date the jars before storing. Once opened, store in the refrigerator and consume within 1 week.

● **Good with** bread and cheese, and cold meats, such as ham or roast pork, lamb, chicken, or duck.

Lime Pickle

These pungently spiced preserved limes will enhance curries or pilafs, and are wonderful with fish or chicken

🍴 makes 1–2 jars

🕐 prep 20 mins, plus standing • cook 5 mins

🍲 1–2 x 450g (1lb) jam or Kilner jars

600ml (1 pint) **light olive oil**

1 tbsp **dried cumin seeds**

1 tbsp **dried chillies**, chopped

1 tbsp **black peppercorns**

1 tbsp **dried coriander seeds**

10 **limes**, cut into wedges

3 tbsp **sea salt**

1 tsp **ground ginger**

pinch of **whole cloves**

3 **garlic cloves**, crushed

2 **bay leaves**

● **Prepare ahead** The pickle needs to be made at least 4 weeks before required.

1 Heat the oil in a saucepan until very hot but do not allow it to reach smoking point. Then turn off the heat and leave it to cool gently.

2 Crush the cumin seeds, chillies, peppercorns, and coriander seeds roughly in a blender or with a pestle and mortar.

3 Put the limes into a shallow bowl. Sprinkle them with the salt and ground spices, then add the remaining ingredients. Stir well and leave for 30 minutes.

4 Put the limes and spices in the jars and pour in enough cooled oil to cover them. Cover the jar with a muslin cloth and leave it in a warm place for 6 days, stirring it daily.

5 Seal the jar well and store it in a cool, dark cupboard for at least 3 weeks to allow the flavours to develop and the rinds to soften. The pickle will keep for up to 6 months. The colour may change slightly.

● **Good with** fish, chicken, curries, rice dishes, or in salads.

VARIATION

Lemon Pickle

Replace the limes with 6 lemons, and complete the recipe as above.

Green Tomato Chutney

Apple, ginger, and mild onion make this chutney especially sweet, rather than spicy

- 🍴 makes 5–6 jars
- 🕐 prep 30 mins
  - cook 2 hrs 10 mins
- 🔲 extra large stainless steel saucepan or preserving pan, 5–6 x 450g (1lb) jam or Kilner jars

1kg (2¼lb) **green tomatoes**, coarsely chopped

675g (1½lb) **Spanish onions**, chopped

1kg (2¼lb) **apples**, cored and chopped

450g (1lb) **light muscovado sugar**

1 tbsp **ground ginger**

1 tbsp **peppercorns**, black or mixed

600ml (1 pint) **malt vinegar**

● **Prepare ahead** Although this chutney is best when freshly prepared, you can mix the tomatoes and onions up to 24 hours in advance, then store, covered, in a cool place until needed.

1 **Mix the tomatoes**, onions, and apples in a preserving pan and stir in the rest of the ingredients.

2 **Bring to the boil**, stirring all the time to make sure the sugar dissolves evenly. Then simmer very slowly for 1¾ hours, or until thick and pulpy, stirring regularly with a large wooden spoon so the mixture does not stick to the pan.

3 **Meanwhile**, wash the jars well, then sterilize them by heating in the oven at 180°C (350°F/Gas 4) for 20 minutes.

4 **Put the jars** on to a baking tray and carefully fill them with the hot chutney. A safe way to do this is to ladle the chutney into a large heat-resistant jug with a wide pouring spout, and use it to fill the jars. Screw on the lids tightly, while still hot, wearing oven gloves. Leave to cool.

5 **When the chutney** has cooled, label with the name and date, and store in a cool dark place. Once opened, keep chilled and use within 1 week.

> **VARIATION**

Banana and Green Tomato Chutney

Replace the apples with bananas and the spices with 1 tbsp mild curry powder, 1 heaped tsp allspice and 1 tsp ground ginger. Cook as above. This chutney is great as a side dish with an Indian meal.

Corn Relish

A refreshing cross between a salsa and a true cooked relish

- 🍴 serves 4
- 🕐 prep 15 mins, plus standing
  - cook 10 mins, plus chilling

2 tsp **olive oil**

1 **red onion**, finely chopped

225g (8oz) **cherry tomatoes**

1 small **red chilli**, deseeded and chopped

1 tsp **cayenne pepper**

1 tsp **light soft brown sugar** or honey

1 tbsp **tomato ketchup**

2 tsp **white wine vinegar**

450g can **sweetcorn**, with no added salt or sugar, drained

salt and freshly ground **black pepper**

1 tbsp chopped **coriander**

1 **Heat the oil** in a saucepan and fry the onion for 2 minutes, or until softened, stirring all the time.

2 **Add the cherry tomatoes**, chilli, cayenne, and sugar, and stir together. Cook, covered, over a low heat for a few minutes, or until the tomatoes have softened.

3 **Remove from the heat** and leave to cool, then stir in the ketchup, vinegar, and sweetcorn, and season with salt and pepper. Chill for at least 12 hours. Stir in the chopped coriander just before serving. Once opened, keep chilled for up to 1 week.

● **Leftovers** can be used to top baked potatoes or mixed with chopped cooked chicken or flaked tuna to make a sandwich filling.

> **VARIATION**

Cool Corn Relish

For a refreshing, non-spicy version of this relish, remove the red chilli and cayenne pepper. With the sweetcorn, add a finely sliced red onion and half a cucumber, skin-on and diced.

Piccalilli

This is a modern version of a traditional Indian pickle called *peccalillo*

 makes 5–6 jars

 prep 20 mins, plus standing
• cook 10 mins

✔ low fat, low GI

❗ make the pickle at least 4 weeks before required to allow the flavours to develop

🍲 extra large stainless steel saucepan or preserving pan, 5–6 x 225g (8oz) jam or Kilner jars

900g (2lb) **mixed fresh seasonal vegetables**, such as cauliflower, shallots, cucumber, young kidney beans, carrots, and French beans

50g (1¾oz) **salt**

For the piccalilli sauce

15 small whole **chillies**, washed

600ml (1 pint) **malt vinegar**

175g (6oz) **granulated sugar**

50g (1¾oz) **ground mustard**

15g (½oz) **turmeric**

3 tbsp **cornflour**

1 Cut the vegetables of your choice into bite-sized pieces and place into a glass bowl. Sprinkle with the salt, cover, and leave overnight in a cool place.

2 The following day, drain the vegetables. Boil the chillies in the vinegar for 2 minutes, allow to stand for 30 minutes, strain the chillies from the vinegar and discard.

3 Mix together the sugar, mustard, turmeric, and cornflour, then form a smooth paste using a little of the cooled vinegar. Bring the remaining vinegar to the boil, then gradually pour it into the paste, stirring continuously.

4 Place the mixture back into the pan and boil gently over a medium–high heat, for 3 minutes, stirring continuously. Remove from the heat, and stir in the vegetables.

5 Pack into clean jars and seal tightly while still hot. Allow the chutney to cool, then label and store the jars in a cool dark place. Leave for at least 1 month before opening, to allow the flavours to develop, and the vegetables to soften. Once opened, keep chilled and eat within 1 week.

● **Good with** crusty bread and a robust farmhouse cheese, or with cold meats and pork pies.

Plum Chutney

The sweet fruit in this recipe is gently balanced with a combination of cinnamon, allspice, and ginger

 makes 5–6 jars

 prep 15 mins
• cook 1 hr 15 mins

🍲 extra large stainless steel saucepan or preserving pan, 5–6 x 450g (1lb) jam or Kilner jars

1.35kg (3lb) **plums**, stones removed and cut into quarters

2 **apples**, peeled, cored, and chopped

2 **onions**, chopped

1 tbsp **ground ginger**

1 tbsp **ground cinnamon**

1 tbsp **allspice**

2 tsp **salt**

450ml (15fl oz) **cider vinegar**

350g (12oz) **soft brown sugar**

● **Prepare ahead** The chutney benefits from being made several weeks in advance to allow the flavours to develop.

1 Place all the ingredients into a preserving pan, and bring to the boil, stirring continuously, to dissolve the sugar evenly.

2 Reduce the heat and simmer for 1 hour, or until the mixture is soft and thickened, stirring frequently with a large wooden spoon. Taste and adjust the seasoning if necessary.

3 Meanwhile, wash the jars thoroughly and sterilize them by placing them in an oven heated to 180°C (350°F/Gas 4) for 20 minutes.

4 Using oven gloves, place the jars on a baking tray and carefully fill with the hot chutney. A safe way to do this is to ladle the chutney into a large, heat-resistant jug with a wide pouring spout, and use it to fill the jars. Seal the jars tightly, wearing oven gloves, while the chutney is still hot.

5 Wipe the jars clean. When cool, label with the name and date, and store in a cool dark place, ideally for a few weeks for the flavour to develop. Once opened, keep chilled and use within 1 week.

Hot Mains Under 30 Minutes

Pasta alla Carbonara
An Italian classic with a unique combination of eggs and crispy pancetta

🕐 20 mins   **page 202**

Spaghetti, Roman-style
Widely popular, a staple that always pleases a hungry crowd

🕐 25 mins   **page 190**

Singapore Noodles
A quick combination of Chinese, Indian, and Malay flavours

🕐 25 mins   **page 191**

Orecchiette with Pancetta
A light pasta dish with bright colours

🕐 20 mins   **page 196**

Fettucine Alfredo
Simple pleasures of egg noodles and Parmesan cheese make this dish a much-loved classic

🕐 20 mins   **page 192**

Linguine Alle Vongole
A popular classic mix of thin linguine and clams in a tomato sauce

🕐 25 mins   **page 188**

Grilled Halibut with Green Sauce
A fresh-tasting dish that cooks in minutes

🕐 10-15 mins   **page 264**

Chinese-style Steamed Bass
An easy to prepare restaurant-style dish bursting with delicious flavours

🕐 25-30 mins   **page 270**

Leaf-wrapped Asian Sole
Gently steamed fish wrapped in pak choi makes a healthy, tasty supper

🕐 25 mins   **page 272**

Seared Tuna with Cucumber and Fennel
Enjoy the fresh, crisp flavours of this warm tuna salad, served rare so it takes hardly any time to prepare

🕐 20-25 mins   **page 270**

Seafood Curry
This quick curry is lightly flavoured with chillies, coconut, and lime

🕐 20-25 mins   **page 274**

Shrimp Diabolo
Quick and easy prawns in a spicy tomato sauce

🕐 25 mins   **page 275**

Moules Marinières
A classic French recipe for mussels cooked in wine, garlic, and herbs

🕐 25 mins   **page 275**

Thai Green Chicken Curry
By using a shop-bought jar of Thai curry paste, this flavoursome dish is very quick to prepare

🕐 20 mins   **page 288**

Devilled Turkey
Serve these spicy stir-fried turkey strips as a healthy lunch or supper

🕐 25 mins   **page 308**

Steak au Poivre
This restaurant classic can easily be made and enjoyed at home

🕐 20-25 mins   **page 320**

Veal Scaloppine
This popular Italian dish uses a quick, classic method to prepare veal

🕐 15-20 mins   **page 321**

Frikadeller
This is a Danish classic with the fresh flavours of thyme and lemon

🕐 25 mins   ❄ 3 months   **page 336**

Beef with Walnut Pesto
A great dish for autumn, when fresh walnuts are readily available. The bright green colour of the walnut pesto comes from fresh tarragon and parsley

🕐 25-30 mins   **page 334**

Pork Chops with Green Peppercorn Sauce
Mild peppercorns add gentle spice

🕐 25 mins   **page 337**

Pork Chops with Blue Cheese Stuffing
Pecans add a crunchy texture to the stuffing

🕐 25-30 mins   **page 337**

Lamb with Blueberries
Sweet blueberries and fresh mint offset the richness of the meat

🕐 20-25 mins   **page 340**

Sauté of Liver, Bacon, and Onions
A quick dish with a rich, savoury flavour

🕐 20 mins   **page 351**

Vegetarian Mains

Butternut Squash Penne
Sweet squash with a savoury cheese sauce makes for a filling main dish
🕐 55 mins
page 194

Ravioli with Ricotta and Spinach
Spinach and ricotta make a perfect-tasting pair
🕐 1 hr 15 mins
page 195

Spinach and Ricotta Cannelloni
A baked pasta dish with a rich tomato sauce
🕐 1 hr
page 195

Penne Primavera
This classic dish is a celebration of the best of spring flavours
🕐 45 mins
page 197

Mushroom Risotto
Creamy risotto with the earthy flavour of fresh mushrooms
🕐 50 mins
page 207

Mediterranean Lasagne
A simple baked pasta dish full of Italian flavours and plenty of vegetables
🕐 1 hr 30 mins
page 203

Quinoa Tabbouleh
A healthy salad, full of fresh flavours, and the crunchy texture of quinoa
🕐 30 mins
page 208

Kasha Pilaf
A tasty side dish to serve with Middle Eastern-style dishes
🕐 30 mins
page 211

Puy Lentils with Goat's Cheese
Goat's cheese brightens the earthy lentils
🕐 40 mins
page 209

Cabbage Rolls
Stuffed cabbage leaves in tomato sauce make a delicious and satisfying supper dish
🕐 2 hrs 10 mins
page 220

Chilli Tofu Stir-fry
This quick and easy dish shows tofu's ability to take on the flavour of other ingredients
🕐 25 mins
page 221

Chillies en Nogada
Traditionally, heart-shaped green poblano chillies from Mexico's Pueblo region are used
🕐 1 hr ❄ 1 month
page 222

Parmesan Cheese and Walnut Tart
A lovely tart for lunch or part of a light supper
🕐 1 hr 10 mins
page 223

Vegetable Curry
Cardamom, cloves, coriander, and cumin seeds add warming flavour to this Indian favourite

🕐 1 hr 5 mins   ❄ 3 months   **page 224**

Potato and Fennel Pancakes with Mushrooms
A delicious way to use leftover mash

🕐 1 hr 40 mins   **page 225**

Stuffed Aubergines
A popular Turkish meze of cold and spicy stuffed aubergines

🕐 20 mins   ❄ 1 month   **page 226**

Tofu and Mushroom Stroganoff
Traditional stroganoff with a vegetarian twist

🕐 35 mins   **page 225**

Olive, Thyme, and Onion Tart
Quick to make and full of savoury flavours

🕐 1 hr 10 mins   **page 226**

Aubergine Parmigiana
This is one of Italy's most popular dishes

🕐 1 hr 10 mins   ❄ 1 month   **page 228**

Vegetable Biryani
A curry that both vegetarians and meat eaters will enjoy

🕐 1 hr 15 mins   **page 227**

Vegetable Moussaka
Lentils replace the lamb, and yogurt is a light alternative to béchamel sauce

🕐 1 hr 50 mins   **page 227**

Leek and Cheese Flamiche
This puff pastry savoury tart comes from the Burgundy and Picardy regions of France

🕐 1 hr 15 mins   ❄ 1 month   **page 229**

Squash and Gorgonzola Tart
This works well with either a creamy or firm Gorgonzola cheese

🕐 1 hr 50 mins   ❄ 1 month   **page 229**

Vegetarian Sides

Kasha Pilaf
A tasty side dish to serve with Middle Eastern-style dishes
🕐 30 mins   **page 211**

Rice and Peas
A West Indian dish, the "peas" are known as gungo peas in Jamaica and pigeon peas in Trinidad
🕐 55 mins   **page 216**

Thai Coconut Rice
Coconut and kaffir lime leaves flavour this traditional rice dish
🕐 1 hr 5 mins   **page 215**

Rice Timbales
Lightly spiced rice pressed into moulds
🕐 40 mins   **page 218**

Risotto Balls
Crispy on the outside and soft and creamy on the inside
🕐 40 mins ❄ 2 months   **page 216**

Potato Gnocchi
Light-as-air potato dumplings, served with a simple sage and butter sauce
🕐 55 mins   **page 218**

Braised Red Cabbage with Apple
Cabbage cooked in a sweet-sour sauce
🕐 1 hr 50 mins   **page 234**

Courgettes in Batter
Crisp and delicious fritters
🕐 40 mins   **page 235**

Spiced Pilaf
Subtly spiced, this versatile rice dish can be served hot or cold
🕐 30 mins   **page 211**

Grilled Vegetables
A herby blend of peppers, courgettes, aubergine, and fennel
🕐 55 mins – 1 hr   **page 235**

Brussels Sprouts with Orange
Citrus flavours bring added sunshine
🕐 20–25 mins   **page 237**

Roasted Acorn Squash
Butter-and sugar-basted squash halves
🕐 45 mins   **page 237**

Ratatouille
This popular Mediterranean dish is delicious hot or cold
🕐 55 mins   **page 236**

Braised Chicory with Thyme
Slow-cooked chicory with herb topping

🕐 35 mins **page 238**

Glazed Shallots with Red Wine
A typical dish from France's wine regions

🕐 50 mins **page 240**

Pak Choi with Oyster Sauce
A lovely leafy accompaniment to any main dish

🕐 15 mins **page 239**

Mixed Root Vegetable Gratin
A creamy, warming cheese-topped dish

🕐 1 hr 10 mins **page 241**

Roast Artichokes with Tomato and Garlic
Colourful and tasty vegetable dish

🕐 1 hr 5 mins **page 242**

Potato Gratin
Gratin Dauphinoise is rich with cream and fragrant with garlic and nutmeg

🕐 1 hr 50 mins **page 242**

Roast Sweet Potato with Sesame Glaze
Honey and soy sauce-infused potato cubes

🕐 1 hr **page 243**

Potato and Parmesan Cakes
A rich cheese and potato mash in a mini cake form

🕐 40 mins **page 245**

Sweet Potato and Sage Gratin
This gratin is indulgent and warming: perfect comfort food

🕐 1 hr 20 mins **page 241**

Grilled Aubergines with Pomegranate Vinaigrette
Pomegranate seeds enliven this warm dish

🕐 20 mins **page 245**

Potato Pancakes
Traditional *latkes*, served with soured cream and apple sauce

🕐 50 mins **page 246**

Sweet Potato Purée with Horseradish
Intensely sweet and full of flavour

🕐 1 hr 20 mins ❄ 3 months **page 247**

Creamed Spinach with Pine Nuts
A rich and crunchy dish

🕐 10–15 mins **page 247**

Light Lunches

Singapore Noodles
This popular dish combines Chinese, Indian, and Malay flavours
🕐 25 mins   **page 191**

Lentil Salad with Lemon and Almonds
A mix of the fragrant and the crisp
🕐 30 mins   **page 205**

Egg Noodles with Lemon and Herbs
Fresh lemon and herb dressing on egg noodles
🕐 25 mins   **page 212**

Roast Beetroot and Feta Salad
A colourful and delicious dish
🕐 1 hr 25 mins   **page 221**

Baked Salmon with Cucumber Dill Sauce
Equally good using salmon steaks or fillets, this simple summery dish is quick to make, very healthy and tastes delicious
🕐 20 mins   **page 257**

Chilli Tofu Stir-fry
Vegetable and tofu chunks in a spicy sauce
🕐 25 mins   **page 221**

Vegetable Biryani
A filling meatless curry served over rice
🕐 1 hr 15 mins   **page 227**

Squash and Gorgonzola Tart
A rich vegetable and cheese quiche to serve with a green salad
🕐 1 hr 55 mins   ❄ 1 month   **page 229**

Salmon Fishcakes
Flavoured poached fillets with crispy breadcrumb coating
🕐 1 hr   ❄ 1 month   **page 255**

Mackerel with Cucumber Salad
A simple grilled fish and salad combo
🕐 40 mins   **page 265**

Seafood Salad
Suitable for lunch, a picnic, or a light supper in the garden, this is an ideal summer dish
🕐 45 mins   **page 268**

Leaf-wrapped Asian Sole
Gently steamed fish in pak choi
🕐 25 mins   **page 272**

Calamari Salad with Mint and Dill
A warm salad of fresh herbs and grilled seafood
🕐 25 mins   **page 274**

Low-fat Dishes

Chicken and Chickpea Pilaf
This one-pot rice dish is full of flavour and is easy to make

🕐 55 mins   **page 205**

Clams in White Wine
Almejas al vino blanco is a popular dish throughout the Mediterranean
🕐 25 mins   **page 276**

Chicken Cacciatore
This Italian dish translates as "hunter-style chicken", and is traditionally served with polenta
🕐 55 mins–1 hr   **page 298**

Chicken in Balsamic Vinegar
A cold chicken dish with a hint of sweetness
🕐 1 hr 10 mins   **page 299**

Chicken Jalfrezi
A hot and spicy chicken curry
🕐 45 mins ❄ 3 months   **page 310**

Roast Quail with Apple and Calvados
Wrapping in pancetta keeps the flesh moist
🕐 35–40 mins ❄ 3 months   **page 317**

Balsamic Beef Salad
Colourful and filling, this makes a substantial summer salad
🕐 1 hr 25 mins   **page 324**

Swordfish Baked with Herbs
Rosemary is not usually used with fish, but perfectly complements the strong flavours of this dish
🕐 40 mins   **page 272**

Beef Salad with Caramelized Walnuts
A hearty salad, good served warm or cold
🕐 20 mins   **page 333**

Lamb Kebabs
Melt-in-the-mouth marinated lamb cubes with baby vegetables
🕐 2 hrs 30 mins   **page 343**

Storecupboard Dishes

Tuna and Pasta Bake
This one-dish meal, using dried pasta and canned tuna, is ideal at the end of a busy day

🕐 50 mins   page 190

Potato Gnocchi
These light-as-air dumplings make a simple, but filling dish from potatoes, flour, and eggs

🕐 55 mins   page 218

Macaroni Cheese
Quick to make if you have dried macaroni and cheese on hand

🕐 55 mins   page 191

Fettucine Alfredo
A simple supper made with a few good quality ingredients

🕐 20 mins   page 192

Spaghetti Puttanesca
Canned anchovies, olives, and capers add fresh Mediterranean flavour to this spicy pasta dish

🕐 40 mins   page 201

Lentil Salad with Lemon and Almonds
Almonds and preserved lemon add crisp flavour

🕐 30 mins   page 205

Egg Fried Rice
This popular Chinese-style rice dish is an excellent way to use up leftover rice

🕐 15 mins   page 212

Rice and Peas
The ingredients are easy to keep on hand for this perfect last-minute side dish

🕐 55 mins   page 216

Linguine Alle Vongole
Versions of this popular classic combine thin dried linguine and canned clams

🕐 25 mins   page 188

Polenta
This easy cornmeal "porridge" is served in northern Italy as an accompaniment to meat dishes

🕐 20 mins   page 214

One-pot Meals

Tuna and Pasta Bake
This simple recipe uses mostly storecupboard ingredients to make a satisfying meal
🕐 50 mins   **page 190**

Chicken and Noodle Stir-fry
A variety of vegetables add colour and texture to the noodles in this easy Chinese-style dish
🕐 30 mins   **page 204**

Vegetable Biryani
A curry that both vegetarians and meat eaters will enjoy. Fresh vegetables and frozen peas are combined with basmati rice and flavoured with ground spices and mild curry paste
🕐 1 hr 15 mins   **page 227**

Paella
Cooked on the hob, this version of the classic Spanish rice dish contains a mixure of seafood
🕐 40 mins   **page 206**

Hoppin' John
In the American South this dish of ham hock, rice, and beans is served on New Year's Day
🕐 3 hrs 45 mins   **page 206**

Kedgeree
Salmon is added to this Anglo-Indian rice dish along with the traditional smoked haddock
🕐 40 mins   **page 209**

Jambalaya
This spicy meal captures the authentic flavours of cooking along the Louisiana bayous
🕐 1 hr 15 mins   **page 210**

Chicken in a Pot
Cooking the chicken and vegetables in dry cider and stock creates a no-effort sauce
🕐 2 hrs ❄ 3 months   **page 289**

Arroz con Pollo
This colourful chicken and rice dish from Latin America is cooked and served in the same pot
🕐 1 hr 5 mins   **page 294**

Chicken Chow Mein
This Chinese favourite contains noodles with a colourful mix of chicken and vegetables
🕐 30 mins ❄ 3 months   **page 296**

Chicken Casserole with Herb Dumplings
Hearty and filling, this is a good winter warmer
🕐 1 hr 5 mins   **page 302**

Chicken Biryani
Often served for special occasions, this mildly spiced dish combines chicken and basmati rice
🕐 50 mins   **page 305**

Roast Lamb with Flageolets
Perfect to cook for Sunday lunch, the beans mean there's no need to prepare potatoes
🕐 55 mins   **page 343**

Family Favourites

Baked Ziti with Sausage and Tomatoes
A rich, meaty sauce makes this a filling dish
🕐 1 hr 10 mins **page 189**

Macaroni Cheese
This easy dish makes a family meal that can be assembled in advance for last-minute cooking
🕐 55 mins **page 191**

Aubergine Parmigiana
This is one of Italy's most popular dishes and a great choice for vegetarians
🕐 1 hr 10 mins ❄ 1 month **page 228**

Irish Stew
Lamb, potatoes, and carrots are cooked slowly for maximum flavour and tenderness
🕐 1 hr **page 3 42**

Battered Cod and Chips
Adding yeast to the batter produces a particularly crisp, golden coating after frying
🕐 50 mins **page 252**

Cod in Tomato Sauce
Fresh plum tomatoes and onions add sweetness to this traditional Spanish dish
🕐 40 mins **page 263**

Grilled Halibut with Green Sauce
A fresh-tasting dish that is easy to prepare
🕐 10–15 mins **page 264**

Salmon en Papillote
Individual packets of moist, delicious salmon that everyone will enjoy
🕐 40 mins **page 268**

Tandoori Chicken
As tender and flavourful as the restaurant favourite, this version has a more natural colour
🕐 50 mins **page 294**

Southern Fried Chicken
From America's Deep South, this succulent dish is served with a smooth cream sauce
🕐 45 mins **page 295**

Chicken Korma
This popular restaurant curry, with its fragrant, mild, creamy sauce, is easy to make at home
🕐 1 hr 5 mins **page 297**

Lemon Chicken, Chinese-style
Delectable citrus flavour sealed in a crisp skin
🕐 50 mins **page 297**

Chicken Croquettes
These golden, savoury nuggets are crunchy outside and meltingly soft inside
🕐 50 mins ❄ 3 months **page 299**

Meat Loaf
This recipe is great served hot for a weekday meal, or cold in a packed lunch or sandwich
🕐 50 mins **page 322**

Sausages with Butter Beans
This satisfying supper dish is great at any time of year but particularly good in winter
🕐 40 mins ❄ 3 months **page 352**

Sausage, Bacon, and Egg Pie
A filling pie like this is good to have around on weekends to cater for irregular mealtimes
🕐 1 hr 5 mins **page 353**

Chicken Pinwheels with Pasta

Little rolls of flavourful stuffed chicken

🕐 1 hr   ❄ 1 month   **page 302**

Roast Turkey with Cranberry Pistachio Stuffing

Turkey and stuffing are perfectly for any occasion

🕐 4 hrs 15 mins   ❄ 3 months   **page 312**

Autumn Game Casserole

A mix of different game makes a wonderfully rich-flavoured dish

🕐 1 hr 50 mins   ❄ 3 months   **page 317**

Hungarian Goulash

This warming winter stew makes an easy and great main course for entertaining

🕐 2 hrs 55 mins   ❄ 3 months   **page 326**

Chicken in Garlic Sauce

A lot of garlic, but the flavour will mellow nicely in the cooking

🕐 50 mins   ❄ 3 months   **page 307**

Chicken Tikka Masala

An adored Indian restaurant dish made popular in Britain

🕐 45 mins   ❄ 3 months   **page 314**

Swedish Meatballs

Regarded as a Swedish national dish, but popular in every home

🕐 50 mins   ❄ 3 months   **page 321**

Roast Lamb with Flageolets

A perfect Sunday lunch; the beans make a tasty change to potatoes

🕐 1 hr 55 mins   **page 343**

Duck Breasts with Cherries

Pan-fried duck with fresh cherries, when in season, is a treat for a smart dinner party

🕐 35 mins   **page 311**

Thai Red Beef Curry

Bird's-eye chillies in the curry paste make this dish delicious and fiery

🕐 35 mins   **page 324**

Shepherd's Pie

Traditionally, a recipe to use up meat and potatoes from a Sunday roast

🕐 1 hr   **page 344**

Roast Beef

Sunday lunch doesn't come any better than this

🕐 1 hr 50 mins – 2 hrs 20 mins   **page 333**

Rabbit Provençale

A French bistro dish that makes the most of this healthy and easy-to-cook meat

🕐 1 hr 30 mins   **page 356**

Great on a Barbecue

Vegetable Kebabs
Colourful and nutritious, these kebabs are equally good barbecued or grilled
🕐 30 mins   **page 223**

Mediterranean Vegetable Duo
Grilled courgette and aubergine slices
🕐 45 mins   **page 244**

Swordfish Skewers with Rocket Salsa
Serve hot, straight from a barbecue or grill
🕐 20–25 mins   **page 262**

Honey Mustard Barbecued Chicken
Chicken legs in a delicious marinade
🕐 40 mins   **page 284**

Saffron Chicken Brochettes
These can be barbecued as well as grilled
🕐 20 mins   **page 286**

Lamb Brochettes
Tender pieces of lamb served hot with a fresh tomato vinaigrette
🕐 20 mins   **page 348**

Garlic Chicken
Based on the Indian classic *Murg Massalam*, this dish can be left to cool and taken on a picnic
🕐 1 hr 10 mins   ❄ 1 month   **page 298**

Grilled Quail with Ginger Glaze
Sour-sweet birds great for the barbecue
🕐 30 mins   ❄ 1 month   **page 316**

Chicken Piri-Piri
Flavoured with chillies and paprika, this chicken is suitable for barbecuing as well as roasting
🕐 1 hr 35 mins   **page 314**

Skewered Beef with Lime, Ginger, and Honey
Marinating ensures tender beef
🕐 25–30 mins   **page 335**

Barbecue Spare Ribs
Popular with adults and children alike, these sticky ribs are great for serving at parties
🕐 1 hr 35 mins   **page 339**

Turkey Kebabs
Chunks of turkey, peppers, and courgettes great for the grill, and served with a yogurt sauce
🕐 30–35 mins   **page 313**

Hamburgers
These are pan-fried, but can also be barbecued for an outdoor meal
🕐 25 mins   ❄ 3 months   **page 322**

Cooking for a Crowd

Macaroni Bake with Ham and Peppers
This makes a satisfying informal party dish
🕐 35 mins   **page 192**

Lasagne al Forno
A perfect dish for casual entertaining, this can be prepared in advance
🕐 2 hrs   **page 202**

Couscous Royale
This richly spiced dish makes an inexpensive, colourful Moroccan feast for a party
🕐 1 hr 30 mins ❄ 1 month **page 207**

Chicken Gumbo
The quantities in this recipe can easily be doubled or tripled
🕐 1 hr 10 mins   **page 301**

Turkey à la King
This is an excellent way of using leftover turkey when entertaining over the Christmas season
🕐 30 mins ❄ 3 months **page 304**

Autumn Game Casserole
Either game birds or venison can be used for this richly flavoured dish
🕐 1 hr 50 mins ❄ 3 months **page 317**

Hungarian Goulash
This stew makes a great main course for entertaining, as all the work is done in advance
🕐 2 hrs 55 mins ❄ 3 months **page 326**

Coq au Vin
Use a good-quality red wine for this stylish chicken casserole that tastes best when it is made in advance and reheated
🕐 2 hrs ❄ 3 months   **page 315**

Burgundy Beef
A cook-ahead French classic, this can easily be made to feed any number of guests
🕐 2 hrs 55 mins ❄ 3 months **page 326**

Daube of Beef with Wild Mushrooms
A stew with tender beef and plenty of rich sauce
🕐 2 hrs 30 mins ❄ 3 months **page 327**

Chilli con Carne
A Tex-Mex classic that is inexpensive and easy to make for large numbers
🕐 55 mins ❄ 3 months **page 332**

Cassoulet
This hearty bean and meat stew comes from southwest France
🕐 3 hrs 15 mins   **page 338**

Navarin of Lamb
This French one-pot meal is traditionally made with young spring vegetables
🕐 2 hrs ❄ 3 months **page 342**

Dinner Party

Paella
This Spanish rice dish will both impress and satisfy your guests

 40 mins   3 months   **page 206**

Vegetable Tempura
Battter-covered vegetables lightly fried

 30 mins   **page 228**

Chargrilled Tuna with Tomato Salsa
Spicy salsa tops tuna steak

 1 hr 20 mins   **page 253**

Baked Trout with Almonds
Delicate trout enhanced with citrus and nut flavours when baked

35 mins   **page 254**

Skate Wings with Brown Butter
The classic French dish

20 mins   **page 255**

Salmon in Puff Pastry
Baked salmon en croute is moist and succulent

55 mins   **page 262**

Halibut with Chunky Romesco
Fish with a Spanish tomato sauce

30 mins   **page 266**

Salmon en Papillote
Salmon baked in tightly sealed paper

40 mins   **page 268**

Seared Tuna with Cucumber and Fennel
It is essential that the tuna is as fresh as possible

20 mins   **page 270**

Lobster Thermidor
Grilled lobster topped with a creamy sauce

45 mins   **page 273**

Moules Marinières
This French recipe for mussels in wine, garlic, and herbs means "in the style of the fisherman"

25 mins   **page 275**

Creamy Tarragon Chicken
Fresh tarragon and cream is a classic pairing in French cuisine

45 mins   1 month   **page 288**

Chicken Schnitzels
Fillets rolled in breadcrumbs and quickly fried

50-55 mins   3 months   **page 289**

Duck with Shallot Confit
Spices and melted honey imbue duck with delicious winter flavours

30 mins   **page 304**

Chicken Wrapped in Pancetta and Sage
Delicious chicken parcels

1 hr 35 mins   **page 306**

Poached Guinea Fowl with Spiced Lentils
A healthy, satisfying winter main course

1 hr 35 mins   **page 308**

Chilli and Orange Duck
Citrus and spice balance the rich flavour of the duck in this elegantly coloured dish
🕐 50 mins   **page 310**

Roast Quail with Apple and Calvados
Petite game birds in an apple sauce
🕐 40 mins   ❄ 3 months   **page 317**

Pot-roast Pheasant
This game bird is made flavourful and moist by being cooked in red wine
🕐 2 hrs 20 mins   **page 318**

Beef Wellington
Beef fillet topped with mushrooms and encased in pastry
🕐 1 hr 30 mins   **page 325**

Beef Strogonoff
A classic Russian dish of beef and mushrooms in a sour cream sauce
🕐 40 mins   **page 323**

Blanquette de Veau
Veal cubes in a delicate creamy vegetable sauce
🕐 1 hr 45 mins   **page 325**

Ragout of Venison with Wild Mushrooms
A stew with rich, concentrated flavours
🕐 2 hrs 15 mins   ❄ 3 months   **page 357**

Roast Fillet of Beef with Redcurrant Jus
A rich sauce adds plenty of flavour to this dish
🕐 1 hr 40 mins   **page 335**

Osso Bucco
Milanese rich veal stew flavoured with garlic and salty anchovies
🕐 2 hrs   ❄ 1 month   **page 327**

Braised Lamb
This dish packs plenty of flavour with its tomato, olive, and herb sauce
🕐 1 hr 50 mins   ❄ 1 month   **page 341**

Honeyed Lamb with Carrot Salsa
Marinated lamb slices with fresh crisp salsa
🕐 35 mins   **page 345**

Rabbit Provençale
Healthy and easy-to-cook meat in a tomato and wine sauce
🕐 1 hr 30 mins   **page 356**

Rabbit with Honey and Thyme
Chunks of meat in a creamy cider sauce
🕐 55 mins   **page 357**

Linguine Alle Vongole

Versions of this popular classic mix of thin linguine and clams are cooked all along the Italian Mediterranean and Adriatic coasts

 serves 4

prep 5 mins • cook 20 mins

2 tbsp olive oil

1 onion, finely chopped

2 garlic cloves, finely chopped

400g can chopped tomatoes

2 tbsp sun-dried tomato purée

120ml (4fl oz) dry white wine

2 x 140g jars clams in natural juice, strained, with the juice reserved

salt and freshly ground black pepper

350g (12oz) dried linguine

4 tbsp finely chopped flat-leaf parsley, plus extra to garnish

● **Prepare ahead** The tomato sauce in step 1 can be made a day in advance and reheated before adding the clams and parsley.

1 **Heat the oil** in a large saucepan over medium heat. Add the onion and garlic and fry, stirring frequently, for 5 minutes or until softened. Add the tomatoes with the juices, tomato paste, wine and reserved clam juice, and season to taste with salt and pepper then bring to the boil, stirring. Reduce the heat to low, partially cover the pan and leave to simmer for 10–15 minutes, stirring occasionally.

2 **Meanwhile**, bring a large pan of salted water to the boil over a high heat. Add the linguine, stir and boil for 10 minutes, or according to the packet instructions, until the pasta is tender to the bite. Drain the pasta into a large colander and shake to remove any excess water.

3 **Add the clams** and chopped parsley to the sauce and continue to simmer for 1–2 minutes to heat through. Season with salt and pepper to taste.

4 **Add the linguine** to the sauce and use 2 forks to toss and combine all the ingredients so the pasta is well coated and the clams evenly distributed. Sprinkle with extra parsley and serve at once.

● **Good with** crusty Italian bread, as a substantial starter or lunch dish, accompanied by a green salad.

> **CANNED CLAMS**
>
> These are a great storecupboard ingredient but you could use fresh clams, if available, and garnish the finished dish with a few clams still in their shells.

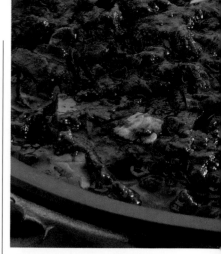

Tomato Sauce

Easy to make, this sauce is wonderfully versatile

 makes 600ml (1 pint)

prep 5 mins • cook 30 mins

❄ freeze for up to 1 month

4 tbsp sunflower oil

1 onion, chopped

1 garlic clove, chopped

4 tbsp tomato purée

2 x 400g cans chopped tomatoes

8 basil leaves, torn

salt and freshly ground black pepper

1 **Heat the oil** in a large saucepan over medium heat. Add the onion and garlic and fry, stirring occasionally, for 5–8 minutes, or until soft and golden.

2 **Stir in the tomato purée**, the tomatoes with their juice, half the basil leaves, and salt and pepper to taste. Lower the heat and simmer, uncovered, for 20 minutes, or until the sauce has thickened.

3 **Stir in the** remaining basil leaves just before serving.

Chilli Tomato Sauce

Add 1 chopped fresh red chilli to the sauce with the tomatoes, including the seeds if you want a very hot sauce, or omitting them if you don't.

Baked Ziti with Sausage and Tomatoes

Ziti are small, dried pasta tubes, like straight macaroni but slightly larger in size. Here they are baked in a rich, meaty sauce

🍴 serves 4

🕐 prep 20 mins • cook 50 mins

🍲 large deep skillet, 4 individual heatproof dishes or 1 large 33 x 23cm (13 x 9in) casserole dish

500g (1lb) Italian sausages, pricked with a fork

2 large onions, coarsely chopped

2 garlic cloves, finely chopped

2 x 400g cans chopped tomatoes

2 tbsp chopped basil

500g (1lb) ziti

125g (4½oz) mozzarella cheese, shredded

salt and freshly ground black pepper

basil leaves, to garnish

1 Fill a deep saucepan with water and bring to the boil. Put the sausages in the pan and simmer for 2 minutes, or until the casings become pale. Drain the sausages and allow them to cool. Once cool enough to be handled, remove the casings and break up the meat.

2 Drain the skillet, return to the heat, add the sausagemeat, and cook for 5 minutes. Add the onions and garlic and cook for another 3 minutes, or until softened.

3 Stir in the tomatoes and the basil, and season to taste with salt and pepper. Allow the sauce to simmer for 10 minutes, or until it has thickened, stirring occasionally.

4 Meanwhile, preheat the oven to 180°C (350°F/Gas 4). Bring a large pan of salted water to the boil and add the ziti. Remove and drain the ziti 3 minutes before the time recommended on the packet, then return them to the pot.

5 Mix most of the sausage and tomato sauce with the ziti. Divide between 4 serving dishes, or place in 1 large dish, then spoon the reserved sauce on top. Sprinkle with the shredded cheese.

6 Bake for 20 minutes, or until the sauce bubbles and the cheese is melted and golden. Serve hot, garnished with basil leaves.

Linguine with Scallops

Succulent scallops with a hint of chilli and lime make this a perfect pasta dish for lunch, supper, or entertaining

🍴 serves 4

🕐 prep 10 mins • cook 8 mins

🍲 large ridged griddle pan

400g (14oz) linguine

salt and freshly ground black pepper

5 tbsp olive oil, plus extra for brushing

1 lime

1 fresh red chilli, finely chopped

12 king scallops

2 tbsp chopped coriander

● **Prepare ahead** The dressing in step 2 can be made 1 hour ahead.

1 Cook the linguine in boiling, salted water for 8 minutes or according to packet instructions. Drain and keep warm.

2 While the pasta is cooking, make the dressing: squeeze the juice from 1 of the limes and whisk with 5 tbsp oil. Stir in the chopped chilli and half the chopped coriander. Season with salt and pepper to taste. Toss the dressing with the drained linguine, set aside, and keep warm.

3 Heat a large griddle pan or large, heavy frying pan over high heat. Brush the scallops with olive oil, place in the pan and sear for 3 minutes, turning once. Do not overcook or the scallops will be tough.

4 Divide the linguine between 4 serving plates and arrange the scallops on top. Serve immediately, with the remaining coriander sprinkled on top.

● **Good with** chunks of crusty bread and a side salad of peppery rocket or watercress leaves dressed with olive oil and scattered with Parmesan shavings.

Tuna and Pasta Bake

This is a quick, one-dish storecupboard meal that is ideal at the end of a busy day

🍴 serves 6

🕐 prep 10 mins • cook 40 mins

200g (7oz) pasta shells

300g can condensed cream of mushroom soup

120ml (4fl oz) milk

200g can tuna in brine, drained and flaked

200g can sweetcorn, drained and rinsed

1 onion, finely chopped

1 red pepper, cored and finely chopped

4 tbsp chopped flat-leaf parsley

pinch of chilli powder (optional)

115g (4oz) Cheddar cheese or Cheshire cheese, grated

salt and freshly ground black pepper

● **Prepare ahead** The whole dish can be assembled, covered, and chilled several hours in advance. Remove the dish from the refrigerator at least 10 minutes before cooking.

1 **Bring a large** saucepan of salted water to the boil over a high heat. Add the pasta, stir, and cook for 2 minutes less than the time specified on the packet.

2 **Meanwhile**, preheat the oven to 220°C (425°F/Gas 7) and grease a 1.5 litre (2¾ pint) ovenproof serving dish.

3 **Drain the pasta** and set it aside. Heat the mushroom soup and milk over a low heat in the same saucepan. Add the tuna, sweetcorn, onion, pepper, parsley, chilli powder, if using, and half of the cheese, and stir. Once the soup is heated, stir in the cooked pasta. Season to taste with salt and pepper.

4 **Tip the mixture** into the prepared dish and smooth the top. Sprinkle with the remaining cheese. Place the dish in the oven and bake for 30–35 minutes, or until the top is golden brown. Serve hot, straight from the dish.

● **Good with** hot garlic bread and a tossed green salad on the side.

VARIATION

Chicken and Pasta Bake

Replace the tuna with 200g (7oz) cooked chicken breasts, chopped and mixed in before the cooked pasta.

Spaghetti, Roman-style

Quick to prepare and cook, this is a great meal when time is short

🍴 serves 4

🕐 prep 10 mins • cook 15 mins

4 tbsp olive oil

2 small onions, thinly sliced

175g (6oz) pancetta or unsmoked back bacon, rind removed, and cut into thin strips

150ml (5fl oz) dry white wine

2 x 400g cans chopped tomatoes

salt and freshly ground black pepper

450g (1lb) dried spaghetti

150g (5½oz) mature pecorino cheese, grated

● **Prepare ahead** Steps 1 and 2 can be done a day in advance and reheated before adding to the pasta.

1 **Heat the oil** in a large saucepan over a medium heat. Add the onions and fry, stirring, for 5 minutes, or until softened but not browned. Add the pancetta and continue frying, stirring, for 5 minutes, or until cooked through.

2 **Add the wine** and cook until it evaporates by half. Stir in the tomatoes, reduce the heat to low and leave to bubble for 15 minutes, or until blended and thickened. Season to taste with salt and pepper.

3 **Meanwhile**, bring a large pan of salted water to the boil over a high heat. Add the spaghetti, stir and boil for 10 minutes, or according to the packet instructions, or until the pasta is tender to the bite. Drain the spaghetti well, then stir it into the sauce, making sure all the strands are coated. Stir in the cheese, adjust the seasoning if necessary, and serve.

Singapore Noodles

This popular dish combines the delicacy of Chinese cooking, the heat of Indian spices, and the fragrance of Malay herbs

 serves 4

 prep 15 mins • cook 10 mins

 low fat

 cook the prawns on the day of purchase

wok

2 tbsp **vegetable oil**

140g (5oz) skinless boneless **chicken breasts**, cut into thin strips

140g (5oz) raw **prawns**, peeled and deveined

1 **onion**, thinly sliced

½ **red pepper**, deseeded and cut into strips

1 head of **pak choi**, thinly sliced

2 **garlic cloves**, finely chopped

1 fresh **red chilli**, deseeded and finely chopped

115g (4oz) **beansprouts**

1 tbsp **curry paste**

2 tbsp **light soy sauce**

150g (5½oz) **vermicelli egg noodles**, cooked according to the packet instructions

2 large **eggs**, beaten

coriander, to garnish

● **Prepare ahead** On the day, slice the chicken, chop the vegetables, and prepare the prawns. Chill in separate bowls covered with cling film until ready to cook.

1 **Heat half the oil** in a wok, add the chicken and stir-fry for 1 minute. Add the prawns and stir-fry for another 2 minutes. Remove them from the wok and set aside.

2 **Add the rest** of the oil to the wok and stir-fry the onion for 2 minutes, then add the pepper, pak choi, garlic, and chilli and cook for a further 2 minutes.

3 **Tip in the beansprouts**, stir-fry for 30 seconds, then stir in the curry paste, soy sauce, and stir-fry for 1 minute. Add the noodles, pour in the eggs, and toss everything together over the heat for 1 minute, or until the egg starts to set.

4 **Return the chicken** and prawns to the wok and stir-fry for 1 minute. Serve with the coriander scattered over.

> ### FRESH EGG NOODLES
>
> These can be added straight to the wok. Increase the quantity to 250g (9oz).

Macaroni Cheese

This simple dish makes a nourishing family meal

serves 6

prep 20 mins • cook 35 mins

400g (14oz) **dried macaroni**

85g (3oz) **butter**

100g (3½oz) fresh **breadcrumbs**

4 tbsp **plain flour**

1 tsp **mustard powder**

pinch of **ground nutmeg**

400ml (14fl oz) **milk**, warmed

175g (6oz) **Cheddar cheese**, coarsely grated

100g (3½oz) **mozzarella cheese**, drained and finely diced

60g (2oz) **Parmesan cheese**, coarsely grated

● **Prepare ahead** The whole dish can be assembled up to a day in advance and refrigerated for last-minute cooking. Add the fresh breadcrumbs and cheese topping just before baking.

1 **Bring a large pan** of lightly salted water to the boil over a high heat. Add the macaroni and boil for 2 minutes less than specified on the packet. Drain well and set aside, shaking off any excess water.

2 **Meanwhile**, preheat the oven to 200°C (400°F/Gas 6) and grease an ovenproof serving dish. Melt 25g (scant 1oz) of the butter in a small pan. Add the breadcrumbs, stir, then remove the pan from the heat and set aside.

3 **Melt the remaining butter** in a large saucepan over a medium heat. Sprinkle over the flour, then stir for 30 seconds. Stir in the mustard powder and nutmeg, then remove the pan from the heat and slowly whisk in the milk. Return the pan to the heat and bring the mixture to the boil, whisking, for 2–3 minutes, or until the sauce thickens. Remove from the heat. Stir in the Cheddar cheese, until melted and smooth, then add the macaroni and mozzarella and stir together.

4 **Transfer the mixture** to the prepared dish and smooth the surface. Toss the breadcrumbs with the Parmesan cheese and sprinkle over the top. Place the dish on a baking tray and bake for 25 minutes, or until heated through and golden brown on top. Leave to stand for 2 minutes, then serve straight from the dish.

● **Good with** a green salad or garlic bread.

Macaroni Bake with Ham and Peppers

Quick to make and full of rich flavours, this pasta bake makes a satisfying mid-week meal or an informal dinner party dish

 serves 4

 prep 10 mins
• cook 20–25 mins

400g (14oz) dried macaroni

salt and freshly ground black pepper

1 tbsp olive oil

1 red onion, thinly sliced

1 garlic clove, crushed

1 red pepper, thinly sliced

400g can chopped tomatoes

250g (9oz) piece smoked ham, diced

3 tbsp dry white wine or stock

2 tsp dried oregano

75g (2½oz) fresh white breadcrumbs

3 tbsp freshly grated Parmesan cheese

2 tbsp melted butter

Prepare ahead Prepare up to the end of step 3, then tip the mixture into the dish and top with the breadcrumb mixture. Cool, cover with foil, and chill for up to 8 hours. To serve, bake for 15 minutes, then remove the foil and bake for a further 10–15 minutes, or until thoroughly heated through and golden.

1 Preheat the oven to 200°C (400°F/Gas 6). Bring a large saucepan of lightly salted water to the boil, then add the macaroni. Simmer for 8–10 minutes, or according to packet instructions, until cooked but still firm to the bite. Drain well.

2 Meanwhile, heat the oil in a saucepan and fry the onion, garlic, and red pepper over a medium heat, stirring often, for 5 minutes, or until softened but not browned.

3 Add the tomatoes, ham, wine, and oregano and bring to the boil. Simmer uncovered for a further 2–3 minutes to reduce slightly. Remove from the heat, stir in the macaroni, and season to taste with salt and pepper.

4 Tip the mixture into an ovenproof dish and spread evenly. Mix the breadcrumbs with the Parmesan and butter, then spread over the top. Place the dish on a baking tray and bake for 15–20 minutes, or until golden and bubbling, then serve at the table in the dish.

Good with a rocket or spinach side salad.

Fettucine Alfredo

A simple supper made with a few good quality ingredients

 serves 4

 prep 5 mins • cook 15 mins

600g (1lb 5oz) fresh fettucine, or 450g (1lb) dried fettucine

115g (4oz) unsalted butter, cubed

250ml (8fl oz) double cream

75g (2½oz) freshly grated Parmesan cheese, plus extra shavings to serve

salt and freshly ground black pepper

1 Bring a large saucepan of lightly salted water to the boil, then add the pasta. Simmer for 1–2 minutes, if using fresh fettucine, or 10–12 minutes, if using dried, or until the pasta is cooked, but still firm to the bite. Drain well, return to the pan, and cover to keep warm.

2 In a separate large pan, melt the butter, then add the cream, and heat until hot but not boiling. Reduce the heat to low, add the cooked pasta and the grated Parmesan, and season to taste with pepper. Gently toss the pasta to coat and serve immediately, scattered with Parmesan shavings.

VARIATION

Alfredo Light

For a lighter version of this dish, omit the butter and cream, and toss the hot pasta in 4 tbsp extra virgin olive oil and 115g (4oz) freshly grated Parmesan cheese.

Pappardelle Ragù

The rich, meaty, slow-simmered sauce goes well with spaghetti or tagliatelle, or used in a lasagne

🍴 serves 4

🕐 prep 15 mins • cook 2 hrs

❄ freeze the sauce for up to 3 months

30g (1oz) **butter**

2 tbsp **olive oil**

100g (3½oz) **pancetta**, diced

1 small **onion**, finely chopped

1 **celery stick**, finely chopped

1 **carrot**, finely chopped

2 **garlic cloves**, crushed

400g (14oz) lean **beef steak**, minced

100ml (3½fl oz) **beef stock**

2 tbsp **tomato purée**

400g can **chopped tomatoes**

salt and freshly ground **black pepper**

75ml (2½fl oz) **milk**, warmed

450g (1lb) dried **pappardelle pasta**

Parmesan cheese, grated, to serve

1 Melt the butter with the oil in a deep, heavy saucepan and fry the pancetta for 1–2 minutes. Add the onion, celery, carrot, and garlic, and continue to fry, stirring occasionally, for 10 minutes, or until softened but not browned.

2 Stir in the meat, breaking up any lumps, then cook for a further 10 minutes, or until it is evenly coloured, stirring frequently. Stir in the stock, tomato purée, and tomatoes, season to taste with salt and pepper, then bring to the boil.

3 Reduce the heat to very low, cover the pan, and simmer very gently for 1½ hours. Stir occasionally to prevent sticking, adding more stock, if necessary. Stir the milk into the ragù, cover, and simmer for a further 30 minutes.

4 Bring a large pan of boiling, lightly salted water to the boil. Add the pappardelle and simmer for 8–10 minutes, or until cooked but still firm to the bite. Drain well, spoon the ragù over, and serve with freshly grated Parmesan.

VARIATION

Pappardelle alla Bolognese

For a richer sauce, cook the vegetables and pancetta in step 1. Replace half the minced steak with 200g (7oz) lean pork mince, plus 100g (3½oz) dried macaroni, and continue with the recipe as above.

Kasspatzle

When tossed with cheese and eggs, *spatzle*, a popular noodle dish in Switzerland, makes a delicious one-pot meal

🍴 serves 4

🕐 prep 20 mins • cook 10 mins

400g (14oz) **plain flour**

1½ tbsp **semolina** or ground rice

6 **eggs**

100ml (3½fl oz) **milk**

½ tsp freshly grated **nutmeg**

60g (2oz) **butter**

115g (4oz) **Gruyère cheese**, grated

freshly ground **black pepper**

2 **spring onions**, finely chopped

1 Sift the flour into a bowl and stir in the semolina. Lightly beat 4 eggs with the milk, nutmeg, and 100ml (3½fl oz) cold water. Add to the flour, mixing to make a slightly sticky elastic dough, adding more flour, if necessary.

2 Bring a large saucepan of water to the boil. Press the mixture through the holes of a colander (the holes should be medium sized) over the saucepan, letting the noodles drop into the water. Take care to protect your hands from the steam.

3 Cook for 2–3 minutes, or until the noodles float to the top. Drain and run cold water over to stop them cooking any further.

4 Heat the butter in a large frying pan, add the noodles, and toss over a low heat until coated and starting to turn golden. Sprinkle in the cheese; beat the remaining 2 eggs and pour over the *spatzle*. Season to taste with black pepper and cook for 1–2 minutes, or until the cheese melts and the eggs set. Serve with the spring onions scattered over.

Spaghetti Frutti di Mare

A traditional spaghetti dish with a hint of spice and the season's freshest seafood

 serves 4

 prep 25 mins • cook 20 mins

tap the mussels and discard any that do not close

3 tbsp **olive oil**

1 small **onion**, finely chopped

2 **garlic cloves**, finely chopped

500ml (16fl oz) chunky **passata**

¼ tsp **chilli flakes**

450g (1lb) **mussels**, cleaned

450g (1lb) **baby squid**, cleaned and tubes sliced into rings

4 tbsp **dry white wine**

½ **lemon**, sliced

450g (1lb) **dried spaghetti**

salt and freshly ground **black pepper**

12 large raw **tiger prawns**, peeled and deveined

3 tbsp chopped **flat-leaf parsley**

1 Heat the oil in a large saucepan and fry the onion and garlic over a low heat, stirring, for 3–4 minutes, or until softened but not brown. Add the passata and chilli flakes, then simmer for 1 minute.

2 Meanwhile, place the mussels and squid in a large pan with the wine and lemon slices, cover tightly, and bring to the boil. Cook for 3–4 minutes, or until the shells have opened, shaking the pan occasionally. Remove from the heat, strain the liquid through a fine sieve and reserve. Discard the lemon slices and any unopened shells. Reserve a few mussels in their shells for garnishing and remove the rest from their shells.

3 Cook the spaghetti in a large pan of lightly salted boiling water according to packet instructions, or until *al dente*.

4 Meanwhile, add the reserved shellfish liquid to the sauce and simmer, uncovered, for 2–3 minutes, or until slightly reduced. Add the prawns to the sauce and simmer, stirring, for 2 minutes, or until just pink. Add the shellfish to the sauce, stir in the parsley, and season to taste with salt and pepper.

5 Drain the pasta thoroughly, return to the pan, and toss in the seafood and sauce. Tip into a large serving bowl, place the reserved mussels in their shells to the side of the pasta, and serve.

Butternut Squash Penne

The cheese complements the sweet roasted squash

 serves 6

 prep 15 mins • cook 40 mins

1kg (2¼lb) **butternut squash**, peeled, deseeded, and cubed

2 **red onions**, roughly chopped

2 **garlic cloves**, crushed

olive oil, for drizzling

2 tbsp **balsamic vinegar**

salt and freshly ground **black pepper**

600g (1lb 5oz) **dried penne**

140g (5oz) **Gruyère cheese**, grated

6 tbsp **crème fraîche**

10 **sage leaves**, roughly chopped

Parmesan cheese, grated, to serve

1 Preheat the oven to 190°C (375°F/Gas 5). Place the squash, onion, and garlic into a large roasting tin, drizzle well with olive oil and balsamic vinegar, and season to taste with salt and pepper. Roast for 40 minutes, or until cooked through and slightly caramelized, tossing from time to time.

2 Meanwhile, cook the pasta in a pan of salted boiling water according to the packet instructions, or until *al dente*, and drain. Stir the Gruyère and crème fraîche into the vegetables to make a thick sauce. Add the sage leaves.

3 Pour the sauce over the pasta with a drizzle of olive oil. Serve sprinkled with grated Parmesan.

Spinach and Ricotta Cannelloni

The classic pairing of spinach and ricotta is topped with rich béchamel and tangy Napoli sauce

🍴 serves 4

🕐 prep 25 mins • cook 35 mins

450g (1 lb) cooked **spinach**

250g (9oz) **ricotta cheese**

1 **egg**, beaten

60g (2oz) **Parmesan cheese**, grated

pinch of freshly grated **nutmeg**

salt and freshly ground **black pepper**

16 **cannelloni tubes**

1 quantity **béchamel sauce** (p518)

For the Napoli sauce

1 tbsp **extra virgin olive oil**

1 small **red onion**, finely chopped

1 **celery stick**, finely chopped

2 **garlic cloves**, crushed

400g can **chopped tomatoes**

75ml (2½ fl oz) **vegetable stock**

handful of **basil leaves**, torn

1 Drain the spinach well, press out any extra water, then chop roughly. Put the ricotta in a bowl and mix in the beaten egg and half the Parmesan. Add the spinach, mix, then season to taste with nutmeg, salt, and pepper. Spoon the filling into the cannelloni tubes and place them in a lightly oiled baking dish.

2 To make the Napoli sauce, heat the oil in a saucepan, and gently cook the onion for 5–6 minutes, or until beginning to soften. Add the celery and garlic, cook for 2 minutes, then stir in the tomatoes and stock and simmer for 15 minutes, or until the vegetables are soft and the sauce has reduced a little. Stir in the basil.

3 Preheat the oven to 190°C (375°F/Gas 5). Pour the béchamel sauce over the cannelloni tubes, then spoon the Napoli sauce on top. Sprinkle over the remaining Parmesan. Bake for 35 minutes, or until the top is golden and bubbling, and the cannelloni is cooked. Serve with a baby leaf salad.

VARIATION

Spinach and Mushroom Cannelloni

Replace the ricotta in the filling with 200g (7oz) mushrooms, chopped and fried, and 60g (2oz) diced ham.

Ravioli with Ricotta and Spinach

In Italy, these little cheese and spinach-filled ravioli are often served on Christmas Eve

🍴 serves 4

🕐 prep 30 mins, plus standing • cook 10–15 mins

200g (7oz) **Italian "00" flour**

pinch of **salt**

2 **eggs**, beaten

1 tbsp **olive oil**

For the filling

350g (12oz) young **spinach leaves**

200g (7oz) **ricotta cheese**

45g (1½ oz) **Parmesan cheese**, grated

1 **egg**, beaten

¼ tsp freshly grated **nutmeg**

salt and freshly ground **black pepper**

melted butter or olive oil, to serve

● **Prepare ahead** The ravioli can be assembled several hours in advance, and refrigerated on baking trays, covered with cling film.

1 Sift the flour and salt on to a work surface, make a well in the centre, and pour the eggs and oil into it. Using your fingertips, draw the flour into the centre, gradually incorporating all the liquid to form a sticky dough. Knead for 10 minutes, or until completely smooth and elastic. Wrap in oiled cling film and leave to rest for 30 minutes.

2 Meanwhile, to make the filling, place the spinach in a heavy pan. Cover and cook for 2–3 minutes, or until the leaves are wilted, shaking occasionally. Drain, pressing out as much water as possible, then chop finely. Stir together the spinach, ricotta, Parmesan, egg, and nutmeg, and season to taste.

3 Divide the pasta in half and roll out each piece to a rectangle about 3mm (⅛ in) thick. Keep half-covered with a tea towel while working with the other half. Place teaspoonfuls of the filling in rows of small mounds on 1 sheet of pasta, keeping the mounds 4cm (1½ in) apart. Brush a little beaten egg between the mounds, then place the second sheet of pasta on top. Press the pasta down between the mounds with your fingertips to seal, pushing the air out as you go.

4 Cut between the mounds with a pasta wheel or sharp knife, dividing the ravioli into squares. Place on a floured tea towel and leave to dry for 1 hour. Bring a large pan of salted water to the boil and cook the ravioli in batches for 4–5 minutes, or until the ravioli float to the surface. Remove with a slotted spoon and serve with melted butter or olive oil, and season to taste with black pepper.

Soba Noodles with Prawns and Avocado

Soba noodles, usually made from buckwheat flour, originate from Japan and are served with hot or cold broth, a light sauce, or dressing

 serves 4

 prep 15 mins, plus standing • cook 15 mins

250g (9oz) **soba noodles**

45g (1½oz) **dried wakame seaweed**

2 tbsp **vegetable oil** or groundnut oil

16 raw **tiger prawns**, peeled, deveined, with tails left on

6 **shiitake mushrooms**, sliced

4 **cherry tomatoes**, halved

2 tbsp **pickled ginger**, rinsed and finely chopped

4 tbsp **mirin**

2 tbsp **rice vinegar**

2 tbsp **Japanese soy sauce**

1 **avocado**, peeled and sliced

2 tbsp **sesame seeds**

2 tbsp roughly chopped **coriander** leaves

● **Prepare ahead** As the dish is served cold, all the ingredients can be prepared and cooked a few hours in advance, except for the avocado, which should be peeled and sliced just before serving.

1 Cook the noodles in a pan of boiling water as directed on the packet, or until they are just tender. Drain and rinse under cold running water until cool. Drain again, and set aside in a bowl.

2 Soak the wakame seaweed in cold water until soft, then drain, and cut into strips. Set aside.

3 Heat the oil in a frying pan or wok, add the prawns and mushrooms, and stir-fry for 1 minute. Add the cherry tomatoes and stir-fry for a further 1 minute, or until the prawns turn pink and the mushrooms and tomatoes have softened. Set aside to cool, then add to the noodles.

4 Make a dressing by mixing together the pickled ginger, mirin, vinegar, and soy sauce. Add the dressing, wakame, and avocado to the noodles and vegetables, tossing everything together gently.

5 Divide among 4 serving plates, and sprinkle with sesame seeds and chopped coriander to serve.

▬▬ **VARIATION**

Soba Noodles with Tofu
Cut 250g (9oz) of firm tofu into 8 cubes and place them on to a hot grill pan, turning the pieces to brown evenly on each side. Add the cooked tofu pieces in place of the prawns in step 3, then continue with the recipe.

> ### JAPANESE INGREDIENTS
> You should be able to find soba, wakame seaweed, pickled ginger, and mirin in most Asian food stores.

Orecchiette with Pancetta

A quick and light pasta dish

 serves 4

🕐 prep 10 mins • cook 10 mins

450g (1lb) **dried orecchiette**

2 tbsp light **olive oil**, plus extra to drizzle

175g (6oz) **pancetta**, chopped

2 **courgettes**, chopped

3 **garlic cloves**, crushed

½–1 tsp **chilli flakes**

175g (6oz) **frozen peas**

salt and freshly ground **black pepper**

6 tbsp grated **pecorino cheese** or Parmesan cheese

3 tbsp chopped **flat-leaf parsley**

1 Cook the orecchiette in plenty of lightly salted boiling water for 7–8 minutes, or as directed on the packet.

2 Meanwhile, heat the oil in a large frying pan, add the pancetta, and fry until lightly golden. Add the courgettes, garlic, chilli flakes, and frozen peas, and fry for 2–3 minutes, or until the peas are heated through.

3 Drain the cooked orecchiette and add to the frying pan. Season to taste with salt and pepper, and stir well. Scatter over the cheese and parsley. Drizzle with olive oil to serve.

Penne Primavera

Depending on availability, almost any spring vegetable can be used, such as green peas, courgette, and cauliflower

🍴 serves 4-6

🕐 prep 20 mins • cook 25 mins

450g (1lb) **dried penne**

350g (12oz) **broccoli** florets

175g (6oz) **asparagus** tips

115g (4oz) **mangetout**, tips and strings removed

2 large **carrots**, cut julienne

2 tbsp chopped **basil** or oregano

For the vinaigrette

175ml (6fl oz) **olive oil**

6 tbsp **wine vinegar**

1 tbsp **Dijon mustard**

1 **garlic clove**, finely chopped

salt and freshly ground **black pepper**

1 Cook the penne in plenty of lightly salted boiling water for 10-12 minutes, or as directed on the packet.

2 Meanwhile, steam the vegetables for 5-6 minutes, or until tender but still crisp. Drain the vegetables thoroughly, place in a large bowl, and add the basil.

3 To make the vinaigrette, put all the ingredients in a small bowl and beat with a fork. Pour the vinaigrette over the vegetables and herbs. Drain the penne thoroughly. Add the pasta to the vegetables and toss gently to combine.

⬤ **Good with** hot crusty garlic rolls.

VARIATION

Creamy Pasta Primavera

In place of the vinaigrette, add 200g (7oz) crème fraîche and 1 tsp wholegrain mustard to the vegetables and pasta. Vary the vegetables used according to what is available; peas, courgettes, baby carrots, or sugar snap peas are all ideal. You can also change the pasta shape used; try rigatoni or fusilli.

Spaghetti Mare e Monti

The ingredients, as the name of this well-known pasta dish suggests, come from the sea and the mountains

🍴 serves 4

🕐 prep 15 mins, plus soaking • cook 15 mins

✓ low fat

15g (½oz) **dried porcini mushrooms**, rinsed

300ml (10fl oz) **boiling water**

6 ripe plum **tomatoes**

2 tbsp **extra virgin olive oil**

150g (5½oz) **baby button mushrooms**

2 **garlic cloves**, finely chopped

1 **bay leaf**

150ml (5fl oz) **white wine**

225g (8oz) cooked **tiger prawns**, defrosted if frozen

salt and freshly ground **black pepper**

400g (14oz) **dried spaghetti**

1 Place the porcini in a bowl and pour half of the boiling water over. Leave to soak for 30 minutes. Remove the mushrooms with a slotted spoon and chop, then strain the soaking liquid through a fine sieve and reserve.

2 Meanwhile, put the tomatoes in a heatproof bowl. Make a small nick in the skin of each with the point of a sharp knife, then pour over enough boiling water to cover. Leave for 30 seconds, then drain, peel, deseed, and roughly chop.

3 Heat the oil in a large frying pan. Add the porcini and button mushrooms and fry, stirring, until golden. Add the garlic and cook for 30 seconds. Pour in the reserved porcini soaking liquid, add the bay leaf, and simmer briskly until the liquid is reduced to a glaze. Reduce the heat to low.

4 Pour in the wine and tomatoes and simmer for 7-8 minutes, or until the liquid is slightly reduced and the tomatoes break down. Remove the bay leaf, add the prawns, and cook for 1 minute, or until heated through. Season to taste with salt and pepper.

5 Meanwhile, cook the spaghetti in plenty of lightly salted boiling water for 10 minutes, or as directed on the packet. Drain thoroughly, then return to the pan. Add the sauce, toss to combine, and serve immediately.

Pasta and Noodles   197

Crispy Rice Noodles with Beef

A combination of crunchy textures and Asian flavours

 serves 4

prep 20 mins • cook 15 mins

groundnut oil, for frying

140g (5oz) dried rice vermicelli

2 tbsp oyster sauce

3 tbsp dark soy sauce

1 tbsp soft brown sugar

350g (12oz) sirloin steak, sliced

2 garlic cloves, thinly sliced

1 tsp grated ginger

12 thin asparagus spears, cut into 2.5cm (1in) lengths

6 spring onions, cut into 2.5cm (1in) lengths

toasted sesame oil

2 tbsp roasted cashews, chopped

1 **Heat 5cm (2in) oil** in a large pan to 190°C (375°F) or until a piece of stale bread browns in less than 1 minute. Snip the vermicelli into short lengths and deep-fry in batches for a few seconds, or until white and crisp. Remove and drain well on kitchen paper. Keep warm.

2 **Mix the oyster sauce**, soy sauce, sugar, and 1 tbsp water. Set aside. Heat 2 tbsp oil in a wok over a high heat and stir-fry the beef for 2 minutes, or until browned. Remove.

3 **Add a little more oil**, and stir-fry the garlic and ginger for 30 seconds. Add the asparagus and spring onions, stir-fry for 2 minutes, then add the sauce, and return the beef to the pan. Cook for 1 minute, then drizzle with sesame oil.

4 **Pile the stir-fry** on top of the vermicelli, scatter with the cashews, and serve immediately.

Fideua

This Spanish pasta dish, with a tasty mixture of seafood, is hearty and filling

 serves 4

prep 15 mins • cook 25 mins

low fat

pinch of **saffron threads**

750ml (1¼ pints) hot **fish stock**

2–3 tbsp **olive oil**

1 **onion**, finely chopped

2 **garlic cloves**, crushed

3 ripe **tomatoes**, skinned, deseeded, and chopped

1 tsp **sweet paprika** or smoked paprika

300g (10oz) **spaghetti** or linguine, broken into 5cm (2in) lengths

225g (8oz) raw **prawns**, peeled and deveined

8 small **scallops**, cut in half

12 **clams** or mussels

225g (8oz) firm **white fish**, such as cod, haddock, or monkfish, cut into 2cm (¾in) pieces

140g (5oz) **frozen peas**

salt and freshly ground **black pepper**

2 tbsp chopped fresh **parsley**

1 **Put the saffron threads** in a small bowl and add 2 tbsp of the hot fish stock. Set aside.

2 **Heat the oil** in a large frying pan or paella pan over a medium heat. Add the onion and garlic and fry for 5–8 minutes, or until soft and translucent, stirring frequently. Add the tomatoes and paprika and cook for a further 5 minutes. Add the saffron with its soaking liquid and half the remaining stock, increase the heat, and bring to the boil.

3 **Add the spaghetti**, reduce the heat, and simmer, uncovered, stirring occasionally for 5 minutes. Add the prawns, scallops, clams, white fish, and the peas, and cook for a further 5 minutes, or until the pasta and fish are cooked through. If the mixture begins to dry out too much, add a little more stock. Season to taste with salt and pepper, sprinkle with the parsley, and serve hot, straight from the pan.

● **Good with** aioli and chunks of crusty bread to mop up the juices.

Tagliatelle all'Amatriciana

This fresh tomato pasta sauce, flavoured with tiny cubes of pancetta, gets its spicy kick from a finely chopped hot red chilli

serves 4

prep 20 mins • cook 25 mins

900g (2lb) ripe, full-flavoured **tomatoes**

2 tbsp **extra virgin olive oil**

115g (4oz) **pancetta**, cubed

1 **onion**, finely chopped

1 **celery stick**, finely chopped

2 **garlic cloves**, crushed

1 hot **red chilli**, deseeded and finely chopped

salt and freshly ground **black pepper**

600g (1lb 5oz) fresh **tagliatelle** or 450g (1lb) dried

1 **Put the tomatoes** in a heatproof bowl. Nick each with the point of a sharp knife, then pour over enough boiling water to cover. Leave for 30 seconds, or until the skins start to split. Drain, leave to cool a little, then peel and roughly chop.

2 **Heat the oil** in a heavy-based non-stick saucepan and cook the pancetta over a moderately high heat for 2–3 minutes, or until beginning to brown. Remove from the pan with a slotted spoon, leaving the fat behind, and transfer to a small plate. Reduce the heat.

3 **Add the onion** and celery to the pan, and cook for 5–6 minutes, or until softened. Stir in the garlic and chilli and cook for 1 minute, then add the chopped tomatoes, and season to taste with salt and pepper. Simmer gently, stirring occasionally, for 15 minutes, or until the sauce is well reduced and thick.

4 **Meanwhile**, cook the pasta in plenty of lightly salted boiling water, for 1–2 minutes if using fresh tagliatelle, or 10–12 minutes if using dried, or until the pasta is *al dente*. Drain well.

5 **Tip the pasta** back into the pan, add the pancetta, and pour in the sauce. Gently toss together, season to taste with salt and freshly ground black pepper, and serve.

TOMATOES

If you can't find ripe, full-flavoured tomatoes, use two 400g cans of plum tomatoes with their juice instead. Taste the sauce after making, and if it needs a little more flavour, stir in 1 tbsp sun-dried tomato paste.

Thai Noodle Stir-fry

A fragrant and colourful stir-fry with the flavours of Thailand

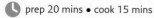 serves 4

prep 20 mins • cook 15 mins

✓ low fat

175g (6oz) thin rice noodles

1 stalk lemongrass

3 tbsp groundnut oil or vegetable oil

3 skinless boneless chicken breasts, cut into thin strips

1 onion, sliced

1 tsp finely grated root ginger

1 fresh red chilli, deseeded and finely chopped

1 orange pepper, deseeded and sliced

115g (4oz) shiitake mushrooms, sliced

2 heads of pak choi, shredded

2 tbsp light soy sauce

1 tbsp Thai fish sauce

1 tsp sweet chilli sauce

1 **Soak the noodles** in a bowl of boiling water until softened, or as directed on the packet. Drain and set aside. Meanwhile, remove and discard the outer leaves of the lemongrass and trim away the tough woody end. Finely chop.

2 **Heat 2 tbsp** of the oil in a wok and stir-fry the chicken over a high heat for 2–3 minutes, or until lightly browned. Remove from the pan and set aside.

3 **Reduce the heat** to medium, add the remaining oil, and stir-fry the onion for 2 minutes. Add the lemongrass, ginger, chilli, orange pepper, and mushrooms, and stir-fry for 2 minutes.

4 **Add the pak choi** and stir-fry for a further 2 minutes, then return the chicken to the pan and add the noodles. Pour in the soy sauce, fish sauce, and sweet chilli sauce, and toss everything together over the heat for 2–3 minutes, or until piping hot and the chicken is cooked through. Serve at once.

Hokkien Noodles with Char-sui Pork

Char-sui is pork fillet marinated in hoisin, oyster sauce, and red pepper, then barbecued to give it a shiny scarlet glaze

 serves 4

prep 20 mins, plus soaking • cook 10 mins

45g (1½oz) dried Chinese mushrooms, such as Cloud Ear

2 tbsp oyster sauce

2 tbsp light soy sauce

1 tsp clear honey

2 tbsp groundnut oil or vegetable oil

2 garlic cloves, crushed

2 tsp finely grated fresh root ginger

1 red pepper, deseeded and finely sliced

140g (5oz) mangetout, halved lengthways

500g (1lb 2oz) fresh Hokkien noodles (thick egg noodles)

350g (12oz) char-sui pork, thinly sliced

1 **Put the mushrooms** in a heatproof bowl, cover with boiling water, and set aside for 30 minutes to soak. Strain and cut the mushrooms into thin strips.

2 **Simmer a large pan** of water ready to cook the noodles. In a cup or small bowl, mix together the oyster sauce, soy sauce, and honey.

3 **Heat the oil** in a wok or large frying pan. Stir-fry the garlic and ginger for 30 seconds. Add the red pepper, stir-fry for 3 minutes, then add the mangetout and mushrooms, and stir-fry for 1 minute.

4 **Drop the noodles** into the pan of simmering water and cook for 1 minute, or until tender. Meanwhile, add the pork to the wok, pour in the oyster sauce mixture and toss over the heat for 1 minute, until everything is combined and piping hot. Drain the noodles, mix with the stir-fried pork and vegetables, and serve at once.

MUSHROOM WATER

Don't discard the mushroom-soaking water; strain it to remove any grit and use to flavour a sauce, soup, or gravy.

Spaghetti Puttanesca

This spicy pasta dish is popular in Italy

🍴 serves 4

🕐 prep 15 mins • cook 25 mins

4 tbsp **extra virgin olive oil**

2 **garlic cloves**, finely chopped

½ fresh **red chilli**, deseeded and finely chopped

6 canned **anchovies**, drained and finely chopped

115g (4oz) **black olives**, pitted and chopped

1–2 tbsp **capers**, rinsed and drained

450g (1lb) **tomatoes**, skinned, deseeded, and chopped

450g (1lb) **spaghetti**

chopped **parsley**, to serve

Parmesan cheese, to serve

1 Heat the oil in a saucepan, add the garlic and chilli, and cook gently for 2 minutes, or until the garlic is slightly coloured. Add all the other sauce ingredients and stir, breaking down the anchovies to a paste.

2 Reduce the heat and let the sauce simmer, uncovered, for 10–15 minutes, or until the sauce has thickened, stirring frequently.

3 Cook the spaghetti in plenty of lightly salted boiling water for 10 minutes, or as directed on the packet. Drain.

4 Toss the spaghetti with the sauce, and serve sprinkled with parsley and Parmesan cheese.

⬤ **Good with** a simple spinach salad and crusty bread.

VARIATION

Spaghetti all'Arrabiata

Make as above, but omit the olives, capers and anchovies. Use 1 whole fresh red chilli instead of ½, and replace the parsley with the same quantity of basil leaves.

Vietnamese Beef and Noodle Salad

Green papayas are under-ripe fruit that make a refreshing addition to many south-east Asian salads

🍴 serves 4

🕐 prep 20 mins, plus standing • cook 8 mins

350g (12oz) **fillet steak**, or thick rump steak

200g (7oz) **rice vermicelli** or mung bean noodles

250g (9oz) **green papaya**, peeled, deseeded, and cut into matchsticks or coarsely grated

4 tbsp **roasted unsalted peanuts**, coarsely chopped

For the dressing

1 tsp **lemongrass purée**

1 tsp finely grated fresh **root ginger**

2 tbsp chopped **coriander**

2 tbsp **Vietnamese nuoc mam** or Thai fish sauce

2 tbsp chopped **mint**

juice of 2 **limes**

1 tsp **brown sugar**

2 fresh **red chillies**, deseeded and finely chopped

⬤ **Prepare ahead** Grill the steak several hours in advance, and slice it just before adding to the salad.

1 Preheat the grill to high. Trim any fat from the steak and grill for 3–4 minutes on each side, or until browned but still pink in the centre. Set aside for at least 15 minutes before slicing into thin strips.

2 Soak the vermicelli in boiling water until softened, or as directed on the packet. Drain, rinse in cold water, then cut into manageable lengths with kitchen scissors. Set aside.

3 To make the dressing, mix together the lemongrass, ginger, coriander, fish sauce, mint, lime juice, sugar, and chillies.

4 Pile the noodles, papaya, and steak into a serving dish and add the dressing. Toss lightly together and scatter with peanuts before serving.

Lasagne al Forno

The perfect dish for family meals or casual entertaining

serves 4

prep 25 mins
• cook 1 hr 35 mins

20 x 30cm (8 x 12in) shallow ovenproof dish

1 tbsp **olive oil**

1 large **onion**, chopped

2 **celery sticks**, chopped

2 small **carrots**, chopped

50g (2oz) **pancetta**, diced

500g (1lb 2oz) **minced beef**

400g can **chopped tomatoes**

1 tsp **dried oregano**

50g (1¾oz) **butter**

50g (1¾oz) **plain flour**

600ml (1 pint) **milk**

salt and freshly ground **black pepper**

150g (5½oz) **ricotta cheese**

12 pre-cooked **lasagne sheets**

50g (1¾oz) **Parmesan cheese**, grated

● **Prepare ahead** Assemble the lasagne up to 24 hours in advance and chill. Add an extra 10–15 minutes to the cooking time.

1 To make the ragù sauce, heat the oil in a saucepan and sauté the onion, celery, carrots, and pancetta for 5 minutes, or until beginning to brown. Add the beef and cook until browned, breaking up with the side of a spoon. Add the tomatoes, oregano, and 150ml (5fl oz) water. Bring to the boil, then reduce the heat and simmer for 40 minutes.

2 Meanwhile, to make the béchamel sauce, melt the butter in a small saucepan and stir in the flour. Cook over a low heat, stirring, for 1 minute. Remove the pan from the heat and gradually beat in the milk. Return to the heat and cook, stirring constantly, until the sauce thickens. Season to taste with salt and pepper, then stir in the ricotta.

3 Preheat the oven to 190°C (375°F/Gas 5). Spread a little béchamel sauce over the base of the ovenproof dish. Arrange a layer of

lasagne sheets on top, then add a third of the ragù sauce in an even layer. Drizzle 1 or 2 spoonfuls of the béchamel over the meat sauce and top with another layer of lasagne.

4 Repeat until all the lasagne and sauce has been used, finishing with a thick layer of béchamel sauce. Sprinkle Parmesan on top and bake for 45 minutes, or until piping hot and the sauce bubbles around the edge.

VARIATION

Vegetarian Lasagne

Replace the ragù with a vegetable sauce: sauté 1 chopped onion and 2 chopped celery stalks in 2 tbsp olive oil. Add 2 sliced courgettes, 1 red pepper, deseeded and chopped, and 1 small aubergine, cut into small cubes, and sauté for 20 minutes, or until softened and beginning to brown. Add 2 tbsp sun-dried tomato purée, a 400g can chopped tomatoes, 1 vegetable stock cube, and 200ml (7fl oz) water. Bring to the boil, then lower the heat and simmer, covered, for 20 minutes.

Pasta alla Carbonara

A popular Italian classic

serves 4–6

prep 10 mins • cook 10 mins

450g (1lb) **dried pasta**, such as tagliatelle, spaghetti, or linguine

4 tbsp **olive oil**

175g (6oz) **pancetta** or cured unsmoked bacon rashers, rind removed, and finely chopped

2 **garlic cloves**, crushed

5 large **eggs**

75g (2½oz) **Parmesan cheese**, grated, plus extra to serve

75g (2½oz) **pecorino cheese**, grated, plus extra to serve

freshly ground **black pepper**

sprigs of **thyme**, to garnish

1 Bring a large saucepan of salted water to the boil. Add the pasta, and bring to the boil for 10 minutes, or according to the packet instructions, until the pasta is *al dente*.

2 Meanwhile, heat half the oil in a large frying pan over a medium heat. Add the pancetta and garlic and fry, stirring, for 5–8 minutes, or until the pancetta is crispy.

3 Beat the eggs and cheeses together and add pepper to taste. Drain the pasta well and return to the pan. Add the eggs, pancetta, and the remaining oil, and stir until the pasta is coated. Serve while still hot, sprinkled with the extra cheese and garnished with sprigs of thyme.

Pad Thai

This is one of Thailand's national dishes, where it is often served rolled up in a thin omelette

 serves 4

🕐 prep 20 mins • cook 10 mins

2 tbsp chopped **coriander**

1 red Thai **chilli**, deseeded and finely chopped

4 tbsp **vegetable oil**

250g (9oz) raw **tiger prawns**, peeled

4 **shallots**, finely chopped

1 tbsp **sugar**

4 large **eggs**, beaten

2 tbsp **oyster sauce**

1 tbsp Thai **fish sauce**

juice of 1 **lime**

350g (12oz) **flat rice noodles**, cooked according to packet instructions

250g (9oz) **beansprouts**

4 **spring onions**, sliced

115g (4oz) **unsalted roasted peanuts**, coarsely chopped

1 **lime**, cut into 4 wedges, to serve

1 Mix together the coriander, chilli, and vegetable oil. Heat half the mixture in a wok, add the prawns, and stir-fry for 1 minute. Remove and set aside.

2 Add the remaining herb oil to the wok and stir-fry the shallots for 1 minute. Add the sugar and the eggs, and cook for 1 minute, stirring frequently to scramble the eggs as they begin to set.

3 Stir in the oyster sauce, fish sauce, lime juice, noodles, and beansprouts, and return the prawns to the wok. Stir-fry for 2 minutes, then add the spring onions and half the peanuts. Toss everything together for 1–2 minutes, or until piping hot.

4 To serve, divide between 4 individual bowls, scatter the remaining peanuts on top, and add a lime wedge.

⬤ **Good with** a fresh salad of beansprouts and shredded carrot, tossed with lime juice.

Mediterranean Lasagne

A simple baked vegetarian pasta dish full of Italian flavours

🍴 serves 4

🕐 prep 20 mins • cook 1 hr 10 mins

🍲 20 x 15cm (8 x 6in) shallow ovenproof dish

6 baby **aubergines**, halved lengthways

1 large **red pepper**, deseeded and sliced

2 large **flat mushrooms**, cut into chunks

salt and freshly ground **black pepper**

375g pack **fresh lasagne sheets**

500ml (16fl oz) **tomato sauce** (p188)

350g (12oz) **mozzarella cheese**, thinly sliced

225g (8oz) **ricotta cheese**

4 tbsp grated **Parmesan cheese**

⬤ **Prepare ahead** Assemble the lasagne up to 24 hours in advance and keep chilled. Add an extra 10–15 minutes to the cooking time.

1 Preheat the oven to 190°C (375°F/Gas 5) and heat the grill to High. Grill the aubergine, red peppers, and mushrooms for 5–10 minutes, or until they are softened but still hold their shape. Season to taste with salt and pepper.

2 Briefly drop each pasta sheet in a bowl of lukewarm water, then drain. Lightly oil the ovenproof dish and spoon in a ladleful of the tomato sauce. Top with a layer of pasta, some vegetables, another ladleful of sauce, then some of the mozzarella and ricotta. Repeat the layers, finishing with tomato sauce, topped with some vegetables. Sprinkle with the Parmesan cheese.

3 Cover the dish with oiled aluminium foil. It's important that the dish is tightly sealed so the pasta continues cooking without drying out. Bake for 30–40 minutes.

4 Remove the foil, return the dish to the oven, and bake for 15 minutes, or until the top is golden and the sauce bubbles around the edge of the dish. Allow to stand for 10 minutes before serving.

⬤ **Good with** garlic bread and a green salad.

Chicken and Noodle Stir-fry

A colourful Chinese favourite, packed with contrasting flavours and textures

 serves 4

 prep 20 mins • cook 10 mins

wok

vegetable oil, for frying

2 skinless boneless **chicken breasts**, cut into bite-sized pieces

½ red pepper, deseeded and chopped

½ green pepper, deseeded and chopped

½ yellow pepper or orange pepper, deseeded and chopped

2.5cm (1 in) piece of fresh **root ginger**, peeled and grated

115g (4oz) shiitake mushrooms, quartered

120ml (4fl oz) chicken stock

2 tbsp tomato ketchup

2 tbsp light soy sauce

1 tsp cornflour

350g (12oz) fresh medium egg noodles

few drops of toasted sesame oil

2 tbsp sesame seeds, for garnish

1 **Heat 1 tbsp** of the vegetable oil in a wok until hot. Add the chicken and stir-fry for 3 minutes. Remove and set aside.

2 **Add the peppers**, ginger, and mushrooms to the wok and stir-fry for 3 minutes.

3 **Mix together the chicken** stock, ketchup, soy sauce, and cornflour until smooth. Return the chicken to the wok, add the noodles, and pour in the stock mixture. Toss everything together over the heat for 3 minutes, or until piping hot.

4 **Just before serving**, drizzle with sesame oil, sprinkle the sesame seeds on top, and serve.

VARIATION

Vegetable and Noodle Stir-fry

Add 115g (4oz) tender-stem broccoli, 1 sliced yellow courgette, and 4 halved cherry tomatoes. Cook the broccoli and yellow courgette with the ginger but add the tomatoes with the noodles so they don't overcook and fall apart. Sliced onion is also good.

Spaghetti with Clams

This simple seafood spaghetti brings out the best of the fresh, briny flavour of the clams

 serves 4

prep 20 mins • cook 15 mins

1.1kg (2¼lb) live clams

15g (½oz) butter

5 tbsp olive oil

2 garlic cloves, coarsely chopped

115g (4oz) fresh breadcrumbs

salt and freshly ground black pepper

350g (12oz) spaghetti

½ tsp crushed red chillies

75ml (2½fl oz) dry white wine

1 tbsp extra virgin olive oil

2 tbsp grated Parmesan cheese

4 tbsp freshly chopped parsley

1 **Wash the clams** under cold running water, scrubbing the shells with a stiff brush. Discard any that do not close when tapped.

2 **Heat the butter** with 2 tbsp of the olive oil in a large, heavy frying pan and stir in half the garlic.

Add the breadcrumbs and fry gently, stirring, for 2 minutes, or until the crumbs are golden. Remove from the heat and season with salt and pepper.

3 **Cook the spaghetti** in a large pan of lightly salted boiling water according to packet directions. Drain.

4 **Meanwhile**, heat the remaining olive oil in a large, deep pan, add the remaining garlic and the crushed chilli, and stir over a moderate heat for 1 minute. Add the wine, season to taste with salt and pepper, bring to the boil, then add the clams. Cover with a lid and cook over a high heat for 4–5 minutes, shaking the pan often, until all the clams have opened.

5 **Remove the clams** with a slotted spoon, then boil the juices rapidly, uncovered, until reduced by about half.

6 **Return the clams** to the pan with the spaghetti; toss lightly. Serve drizzled with oil, sprinkled with the garlic breadcrumbs, grated Parmesan, and chopped parsley.

Chicken and Chickpea Pilaf

This one-pot rice dish is full of flavour and is easy to make

 serves 4

prep 20 mins • cook 35 mins

low fat

pinch of **saffron threads**

2 tsp **vegetable oil**

6 skinless boneless **chicken thighs**, cut into small pieces

2 tsp **ground coriander**

1 tsp **ground cumin**

1 **onion**, sliced

1 **red pepper**, deseeded and chopped

2 **garlic cloves**, peeled and crushed

225g (8oz) **long-grain rice**

750ml (1¼ pint) hot **chicken stock**

2 **bay leaves**

400g can **chickpeas**, drained and rinsed

60g (2oz) **sultanas**

60g (2oz) **flaked almonds** or pine nuts, toasted

3 tbsp chopped **flat-leaf parsley**

1 **Crumble the saffron** threads into a small bowl, add 2 tbsp boiling water, and set aside for at least 10 minutes.

2 **Meanwhile**, heat half the oil in a large saucepan, add the chicken, coriander, and cumin, and fry over a medium heat for 3 minutes, stirring frequently. Remove from the pan and set aside. Lower the heat, add the rest of the oil, the onion, red pepper, and garlic, and fry for 5 minutes, or until softened.

3 **Stir in the rice**, return the chicken to the pan and pour in about three-quarters of the stock. Add the bay leaves and saffron with its soaking water and bring to the boil. Simmer for 15 minutes, or until the rice is almost cooked, adding more stock as needed. Stir in the chickpeas and sultanas, and continue cooking until the rice is tender. Transfer to a warm serving platter and serve hot, sprinkled with the toasted nuts and chopped parsley.

Lentil Salad with Lemon and Almonds

Puy lentils have a crisp taste when combined with the refreshing flavours of fragrant coriander and preserved lemon

 serves 4

prep 10 mins, plus standing • cook 15–20 mins

400g (14oz) **Puy (French) green lentils**

2 **preserved lemons**, rinsed and cut into small dice

2 tbsp chopped **coriander**

2 **spring onions**, thinly sliced

3 tbsp **red wine vinegar**

100ml (3½fl oz) **extra virgin olive oil**

salt and freshly ground **black pepper**

4 tbsp **flaked almonds**, toasted

coriander leaves, to garnish

● **Prepare ahead** The salad can be prepared several hours in advance. Cover and refrigerate until required.

1 **Bring a large pan** of water to the boil and add the lentils. Return to the boil, reduce the heat, cover, and simmer for 15–20 minutes, or until the lentils are just tender. Drain, then rinse quickly in cold water and drain well.

2 **Place the lentils** into a large bowl and stir in the diced lemons, chopped coriander, and half the spring onions. Whisk together the wine vinegar and oil, season to taste with salt and pepper, and stir into the lentils.

3 **Cover the salad** and leave to stand for 20 minutes to allow the flavours to develop.

4 **Mix the almonds** with the remaining spring onion and the coriander leaves, then scatter over the salad and toss lightly to serve.

● **Good with** grilled chicken or lamb chops, or with roasted white fish, such as cod or monkfish.

● **Leftovers** can be mixed with cooked leftover wild rice to make a tasty accompaniment to Middle Eastern dishes.

Paella

This Spanish rice dish has many regional variations. This version, *Paella Marinera*, contains a delicious mix of seafood

- serves 4
- prep 10 mins • cook 30 mins
- tap the mussels and discard any that do not close

1.2 litres (2 pints) hot **fish stock**

large pinch of **saffron threads**

2 tbsp **olive oil**

1 **onion**, finely chopped

2 **garlic cloves**, crushed

2 large **tomatoes**, skinned and diced

12 **king prawns**, peeled

225g (8oz) **squid**, sliced into rings

400g (14oz) **paella rice**

85g (3oz) **petit pois**

4 **langoustines** or Dublin Bay prawns

12–16 **mussels**, cleaned

1 tbsp chopped **parsley**, to garnish

1 **Pour a little** of the hot fish stock into a cup or jug, add the saffron threads, and set aside to infuse. Heat the oil in a paella pan or large frying pan, and fry the onion and garlic until softened. Add the tomatoes and cook for 2 minutes, then add prawns and squid and fry for 1–2 minutes, or until the prawns turn pink.

2 **Stir in the rice**, then stir in the saffron liquid, peas, and 900ml (1½ pints) of stock. Simmer, uncovered, without stirring, over a low heat for 12–14 minutes, or until the stock has evaporated and the rice is just tender, adding a little extra stock if necessary.

3 **Meanwhile**, cook the langoustines in 150ml (5fl oz) simmering stock for 3–4 minutes, or until cooked through. Transfer to a warm plate with a slotted spoon. Add the mussels to the stock, cover, and cook over a high heat for 2–3 minutes, or until open. Remove from the pan with a slotted spoon, discarding any that have not opened.

4 **Reserve** 8 mussels for garnish. Remove the rest from their shells and stir into the paella. Arrange the reserved mussels and langoustines on top, and garnish with parsley.

Hoppin' John

This is a traditional dish from the American South

- serves 4
- prep 12 mins • cook 3–3½ hrs
- flameproof casserole with fitted lid

1 smoked **ham hock**, 1.1kg (2¼lb)

1 fresh **bouquet garni** of celery, thyme sprigs, and 1 bay leaf

2 large **onions**, chopped

1 dried **red chilli**, chopped (optional)

1 tbsp **groundnut oil** or sunflower oil

200g (7oz) **long-grain rice**

2 x 400g cans **black-eyed beans**, drained and rinsed

salt and freshly ground **black pepper**

hot pepper sauce, to serve

● **Prepare ahead** Step 1 can be prepared 1 day in advance. Chill the meat until ready to use.

1 **Put the ham hock** with cold water to cover in a saucepan and set over a high heat. Slowly bring to the boil, skimming the surface as necessary. Reduce the heat to low, add the bouquet garni, half the onions, and the chilli, then re-cover the pan and leave to simmer for 2½–3 hours, or until the meat is very tender when pierced with a knife.

2 **Place a colander** over a large heatproof bowl and strain the cooking liquid. Reserve the liquid and set the ham hock aside to cool.

3 **Heat the oil** in the flameproof casserole over a medium heat. Add the remaining onion and fry for 5 minutes, or until softened but not coloured, stirring occasionally. Add the rice and stir.

4 **Stir in 450ml** (15fl oz) of the reserved cooking liquid and the black-eyed beans. Season to taste with salt and pepper. Bring to the boil, then reduce the heat to low, cover tightly, and simmer for 20 minutes, without lifting the lid.

5 **Meanwhile**, remove the meat from the bone and cut into large chunks.

6 **Remove the casserole** from the heat and leave to stand for 5 minutes without lifting the lid. Using a fork, stir in the ham. Serve with a bottle of hot pepper sauce on the side.

VARIATION

Spicy Hoppin' John

For extra spice, add a good pinch of Cajun or Creole seasoning in step 4. Add a 400g can of chopped tomatoes at the same time to make the dish go further.

Couscous Royale

This richly-spiced dish makes a colourful Moroccan feast

- serves 6
- prep 10 mins
  - cook 1 hr 20 mins
- large flameproof casserole
- freeze for up to 1 month

2 tbsp **olive oil**

600g (1lb 5oz) **lean lamb leg**, cut into chunks

6 **chicken drumsticks** and **thighs**

1 large **red onion**, sliced

2 **garlic cloves**, finely chopped

1 **red pepper**, deseeded and diced

1 **aubergine**, diced

4 tsp **harissa paste**

1 tbsp **paprika**

1 tsp **ground turmeric**

2 **courgettes**, sliced

200ml (7fl oz) **chicken stock**

400g can **chickpeas**, drained

400g can **chopped tomatoes**

175g (6oz) **chorizo** or cooked Merguez sausage, thickly sliced

salt and freshly ground **black pepper**

large sprig of fresh **thyme**

1 **bay leaf**

450g (1lb) **couscous**, cooked according to packet instructions

chopped **coriander**, to garnish

● **Prepare ahead** You can prepare steps 1–4, then cool, and refrigerate. To serve, reheat with the cooking liquid until piping hot.

1 Heat the oil in the casserole and brown the lamb and chicken in batches, turning occasionally. Remove from the pan and set aside to drain on kitchen paper.

2 Add the onion, garlic, pepper, and aubergine and fry, stirring, for 3–4 minutes. Stir in the harissa, paprika, and turmeric, and cook for a further 1 minute.

3 Add the lamb and chicken, courgettes, chicken stock, chickpeas, tomatoes, and chorizo, and season to taste with salt and pepper. Bring to the boil, then add the thyme and bay leaf, reduce the heat, cover tightly, and simmer gently over a low heat for 1 hour, or until the meats are tender.

4 Strain off the liquid, pour it into a wide pan, and bring to the boil, until slightly reduced.

5 Stir the meats and vegetables into the cooked couscous. Pour the reserved liquid over, and sprinkle with chopped coriander to serve.

Mushroom Risotto

Choose an authentic Italian short-grain rice, such as arborio or carnaroli, to ensure the risotto has a creamy consistency

- serves 6
- prep 10 mins • cook 40 mins

4 tbsp **sunflower oil**

1 **onion**, chopped

400g (14oz) **arborio rice** or carnaroli rice

1.5 litres (2¾ pints) **vegetable stock** or water, simmering

60g (2oz) **butter**, diced

450g (1lb) **chestnut mushrooms**, sliced

45g (1½oz) **Parmesan cheese**, grated, plus extra shavings to serve

1 Heat the oil in a large heavy saucepan over a medium heat. Add the onion and fry, stirring, for 5 minutes, or until golden. Add the rice and stir for 2 minutes. Then add 120ml (4fl oz) stock and continue stirring until the liquid is absorbed. Slowly add the stock, 1 ladleful at a time, and stirring constantly until it is absorbed before adding more, for 20 minutes, or until the rice is cooked, but not too soft.

2 Meanwhile, melt the butter in a pan over a medium heat. Add the mushrooms and fry, stirring frequently, for 10 minutes, or until the mushrooms have browned and their liquid evaporates.

3 Stir the mushrooms into the rice and turn off the heat. Stir in the cheese, then leave to rest, covered, for 5 minutes. Place into warmed serving bowls with the Parmesan shavings on top.

● **Leftovers** can be shaped into patties, coated with fine breadcrumbs, and pan-fried.

VARIATION

Porcini Mushroom Risotto

Soak 20g (¾oz) dried porcini mushrooms in boiling water for 20 minutes, then strain, reserving the soaking liquid. Use these in place of the chestnut mushrooms, and stir the liquid into the risotto for the last addition of stock.

Quinoa Tabbouleh

In this healthy salad, the quinoa has a creamy, nutty taste with a slight crunch once it is cooked

🍴 serves 4

🕐 prep 10 mins • cook 20 mins

200g (7oz) quinoa

½ tsp salt

juice of 1 large lemon

250ml (9fl oz) olive oil

1 large cucumber, peeled, deseeded and chopped

1 large red onion, chopped

45g (1½oz) chopped parsley

45g (1½oz) chopped mint

115g (4oz) feta cheese, crumbled

100g (3½oz) Kalamata olives, pitted

salt and freshly ground black pepper

1 **Rinse the quinoa** thoroughly in a fine mesh strainer. Drain and place it in a heavy pan. Heat, stirring constantly until the grains separate and begin to brown.

2 **Add 600ml (1 pint) water** and the salt and bring to the boil, stirring. Reduce the heat and cook for 15 minutes, or until the liquid is absorbed. Transfer to a bowl and set aside to cool.

3 **Whisk together** the lemon juice and 1 tbsp of the oil in a small bowl. Set aside.

4 **Place the remaining oil**, cucumber, onion, parsley, and mint in a separate, larger bowl. Add the quinoa and the lemon and oil dressing and toss. Sprinkle with the feta cheese and olives. Season to taste with salt and pepper.

Kasha with Vegetables

Kasha is a healthy and delicious wholegrain cereal that is prepared similarly to risotto. This makes a hearty vegetarian main course

🍴 serves 4

🕐 prep 10 mins • cook 40 mins

2 tbsp olive oil

1 onion, finely chopped

1 carrot, finely chopped

1 garlic clove, finely chopped

2 flat mushrooms, sliced

1 celery stick, finely chopped

550g (1¼lb) kasha

120ml (4fl oz) dry white wine

1.2 litres (2 pints) hot vegetable stock or water

1 beetroot, steamed or roasted until tender, chopped

2 tbsp chopped parsley

60g (2oz) goat's cheese, crumbled

1 **Heat the oil** in a large saucepan. Add the onion, carrot, garlic, mushrooms and celery and sauté for 8–10 minutes, stirring frequently, until brown. Add the kasha and cook, stirring for another 2–3 minutes. Add the wine and continue stirring until all the liquid has been absorbed.

2 **Gradually add the** hot vegetable stock, 120ml (4fl oz) at a time, and stirring until it has been absorbed before adding more. Cook for about 20 minutes, or until the kasha is soft and chewy.

3 **Toss in the** chopped beetroot and remove from the heat. Serve with parsley and goat's cheese.

● **Good with** crusty bread, as a main meal.

Puy Lentils with Goat's Cheese, Olives, and Fresh Thyme

Small, grey-green Puy lentils are valued because of the way they hold their shape during cooking

 serves 4

prep 10 mins • cook 30 mins

350g (12oz) **Puy lentils**, rinsed

1 **carrot**, peeled and diced

1 **shallot** or small onion, finely chopped

2 sprigs of **thyme**

1 **bay leaf**

175g (6oz) **black olives**, pitted and chopped

85g (3oz) **goat's cheese**, rind removed, crumbled

2 tbsp **extra virgin olive oil**

salt and freshly ground **black pepper**

salad leaves, to serve (optional)

● **Prepare ahead** The lentils can be cooked ahead in step 1 and gently reheated, or the whole dish can be assembled in advance and served chilled as a salad.

1 Place the lentils, carrot, shallot, thyme, and bay leaf in a saucepan with 1.2 litres (2 pints) of water. Simmer gently for 15–20 minutes or until the lentils are tender.

2 Drain the lentils well, transfer to a serving bowl and remove the bay leaf and thyme sprigs. Add the olives, goat's cheese, and olive oil and stir together. Season to taste with salt and pepper and serve warm.

● **Good with** grilled spicy sausages, lamb chops, or pork chops. For a vegetarian meal, serve with a salad of mixed green leaves.

VARIATION

Dressed Lentils

For a simple warm side dish, cook the lentils as in step 1. Drain, dress with 2 tbsp balsamic vinegar, olive oil, and season to taste with salt and pepper. Stir in chopped parsley before serving.

Kedgeree

This Anglo-Indian brunch dish is traditionally made with just smoked haddock, but this version also includes salmon for added colour, texture, and flavour

 serves 4

 prep 20 mins • cook 20 mins

300g (10oz) **undyed smoked haddock**

300g (10oz) **salmon fillets**

200g (7oz) **basmati rice**

pinch of **saffron threads**

60g (2oz) **butter**

4 **eggs**, hard boiled

salt and freshly ground **black pepper**

2 tbsp chopped **parsley**, plus extra to garnish

1 **lemon**, cut into wedges

1 Place the fish in a single layer in a large frying pan. Pour over enough water to cover and heat gently to simmering point. Simmer for 5 minutes, then drain.

2 Meanwhile, cook the rice in boiling, salted water with a few saffron threads for 10-12 minutes, or according to packet instructions. When the rice is cooked, drain and stir in the butter.

3 Flake the fish into large chunks and add them to the rice. Discard the skin and bones.

4 Remove the yolks from the hard boiled eggs and reserve. Chop the egg whites and stir into the rice. Add the chopped parsley, and season to taste with salt and pepper.

5 Divide the mixture between heated plates and crumble the reserved egg yolks across the top with more chopped parsley. Serve garnished with lemon wedges.

● **Good with** triangles of buttered wholemeal toast.

Jambalaya

This one-pot meal captures authentic Creole and cajun flavours of Louisiana

🍴 serves 4–6

🕐 prep 30 mins • cook 45 mins

🍲 large flameproof casserole

60g (2oz) **dripping** or 4 tbsp sunflower oil

4 skinless boneless **chicken thighs**, cut into bite-sized pieces

225g (8oz) mix of **garlic and spicy sausages** (and smoked if liked), cut into thick slices

1 **onion**, finely chopped

2 **garlic cloves**, finely chopped

1 **red pepper**, deseeded and finely chopped

1 **green pepper**, deseeded and finely chopped

1 **celery stick**, thinly sliced

1 **Scotch bonnet chilli**, deseeded and chopped (leave the seeds in if you like your dish very hot)

350g (12oz) **long-grain rice**

1 tsp **chilli powder**

1 tsp **Worcestershire sauce**

2 tbsp **tomato purée**

2 **bay leaves**

2 tsp **dried thyme**

1 tsp **salt**

½ tsp **smoked paprika**

pinch of **sugar**

freshly ground **black pepper**

400g can **chopped tomatoes**

600ml (1 pint) **chicken stock**, vegetable stock or water

12 large raw **prawns**, heads and tails removed and deveined

hot pepper sauce, to serve

1 Melt half the dripping in the casserole over a high heat. Add the chicken pieces and fry, stirring occasionally, for 10 minutes, or until browned and the juices run clear. Remove with a slotted spoon and set aside on to kitchen paper.

2 Add the remaining dripping to the pan and heat. Add the sausages but not smoked sausages (if using), and fry, stirring occasionally, for 5 minutes, or until browned. Remove with a slotted spoon and set aside with the chicken.

3 Add the onion, garlic, peppers, celery, and chilli to the pan and fry for 5 minutes, or until softened, stirring frequently. Add the rice, and chilli powder, and cook, stirring for 1–2 minutes. Add the Worcestershire sauce and tomato purée, and cook, stirring for a further minute.

4 Return the chicken to the casserole, along with all the sausages, including smoked (if using), bay leaves, thyme, salt, paprika, and sugar, and season to taste with pepper. Pour in the tomatoes with their juice and the stock, and bring to the boil, stirring. Reduce the heat to a low heat, cover, and simmer for 12–15 minutes, or until the peppers are tender.

5 Add the prawns, and simmer covered, for 3–5 minutes, or until the prawns are pink. The rice should be tender and the mixture a little soupy. Transfer to a serving bowl. Serve with the hot pepper sauce alongside.

● **Good with** rustic bread to mop up the juices.

German Bread Dumplings

This recipe is traditionally served with soups and stews

🍴 serves 4

🕐 prep 20 mins • cook 50 mins

2 white bread rolls

1 tbsp sunflower oil

2 streaky bacon rashers, finely chopped

1 small onion, finely chopped

1 tbsp finely chopped parsley

1 tsp dried marjoram

1 large egg

100ml (3½fl oz) milk

1 **Preheat the oven** to 130°C (250°F/Gas ½). Cut the rolls including the crusts, into small cubes. Spread out on a baking tray and bake for 30–40 minutes, or until dry.

2 **Heat the oil** in a pan and fry the bacon and onion until lightly browned. Stir in the herbs and leave to cool. Beat the egg and milk together. Stir the bread and bacon mixture into the beaten egg and milk, and mix well. The dough should be firm enough to shape into dumplings.

3 **With damp hands**, form the dough into 8 small dumplings. Cook, covered in a pan of boiling water for 10 minutes, or until cooked through. Drain and serve.

● **Good with** the spicy pot-roasted German beef dish Sauerbraten (p334), or soups and stews.

Spiced Pilaf

Subtly spiced, this versatile rice dish can be served hot or cold

🍴 serves 4

🕐 prep 5 mins • cook 25 mins

2 tsp sunflower oil

1 tsp black mustard seeds

15g (½oz) unsalted butter

1 small onion, finely chopped

1 tsp cardamom pods

1 tsp ground coriander

225g (8oz) basmati rice

600ml (1 pint) vegetable stock, or chicken stock, or water

1 tbsp chopped coriander leaves

1 **Heat the oil** in a large pan over a medium heat. Add the mustard seeds and fry for 1 minute, shaking the pan, until they begin to pop.

2 **Add the butter** and onion, and fry, stirring frequently, for 5 minutes, or until the onion is golden. Add the cardamom pods, ground coriander, and rice, and cook, stirring, for 1 minute.

3 **Pour in the stock**, bring to the boil, cover, and simmer for 10–12 minutes, or until the rice is tender and has absorbed the liquid.

4 **Transfer to a warmed** serving bowl, and serve hot, with the coriander sprinkled on top.

● **Good with** grilled meats, curries, and stews.

VARIATION

Persian-style Rice
Cook as above, replacing the onion and spices with ½ tsp salt. Tip the rice out of the pan and keep warm. Wipe out the pan, then, while still hot, brush 2 tsp oil and dot with 15g (½oz) butter. Line with a layer of thinly sliced raw potato. Return the rice to the pan and dot the surface with a further 15g (½oz) butter. Place a tea towel on top of the pan, replace the lid, and cook on the lowest heat for 45 minutes, or until the potato is cooked and slightly crisp. Turn off the heat but do not remove the lid. Stand for up to 2 hours before serving.

Kasha Pilaf

A tasty accompaniment to Middle Eastern-style dishes

🍴 serves 4–6

🕐 prep 5 mins • cook 25 mins

2 tbsp butter

1 large onion, chopped

2 celery sticks, sliced

1 large egg

200g (7oz) coarse kasha (buckwheat groats) or whole kasha

1 tsp ground sage

1 tsp ground thyme

115g (4oz) raisins

115g (4oz) walnut pieces, coarsely chopped

salt

1 **In a large frying pan**, melt the butter and gently fry the onion and celery for 3 minutes, or until the vegetables begin to soften.

2 **In a small bowl**, mix the egg with the kasha, then add the mixture to the pan. Cook, stirring constantly, for 1 minute, or until the grains are dry and separated. Add 500ml (16fl oz) water, the sage, and thyme to the kasha. Bring to the boil, then reduce the heat, cover, and simmer for 10–12 minutes.

3 **Stir the raisins** and walnuts into the kasha. Cook for a further 4–5 minutes, or until the kasha is tender and all the liquid has been absorbed. Season to taste with salt.

Egg Fried Rice

This popular Chinese-style rice dish is an excellent way to use up leftover rice

- serves 4–6
- prep 5 mins • cook 10 mins
- cook the rice and chill rapidly, or freeze until ready to use
- wok

1 tbsp **groundnut oil** or sunflower oil

1 **onion**, diced

1 **green pepper** or red pepper, deseeded and diced

500–675g (1lb 2oz–1½lb) **cold cooked rice**

2 **eggs**, whisked

2 tbsp **soy sauce**

1 **Heat a wok** or large frying pan over a high heat until very hot. Add the oil and swirl around. Add the onion and pepper and stir-fry for 3–5 minutes, or until softened but not coloured.

2 **Add the rice** to the pan and stir around until it is mixed with the vegetables and heated through. Push the rice away from the centre of the pan, pour in the eggs, and stir until scrambled and set.

3 **Once the eggs** are scrambled, toss all the ingredients together, add the soy sauce, and serve at once.

● **Good with** all stir-fried dishes, such as beef with peppers, or chicken with cashew nuts.

VARIATION

Special Fried Rice

Add chopped celery, peas, sweetcorn, sliced cabbage, deseeded and sliced mild jalapeño peppers, or any other leftover vegetables, along with cubes or strips of cooked meat or chicken. Add beansprouts at the last minute or they will lose their crunchiness.

Egg Noodles with Lemon and Herbs

These fresh Asian noodles, made of eggs and flour, absorb the flavours they are cooked in

- serves 4
- prep 10 mins • cook 5 mins
- low fat
- wok

2 tbsp **vegetable oil**

4 **spring onions**, finely sliced

1 stalk **lemongrass**, very finely sliced

2.5cm (1in) piece of fresh **root ginger**, peeled and grated

350g (12oz) fresh **egg noodles** or 175g (6oz) dried egg noodles, cooked

2 tbsp **light soy sauce**

juice of 1 **lemon**

pinch of **sugar**

2 tbsp snipped **chives**

2 tbsp chopped **parsley**

lemon zest, cut into fine strips, to garnish

1 **spring onion**, finely shredded, to garnish

1 **Heat the oil** in a wok or large, deep frying pan, add the spring onions, sliced lemongrass, and ginger, and stir-fry for 1 minute.

2 **Add the noodles** and toss over the heat for 2 minutes. Mix together the soy sauce, lemon juice, and sugar, and pour over the noodles. Stir-fry for a further 2 minutes, or until the noodles are heated through.

3 **Sprinkle the chives** and parsley over the top, then toss with the noodles and transfer to a serving bowl. Serve at once, garnished with the lemon zest and spring onion.

● **Leftovers** are lovely chopped and mixed with shredded carrot and finely sliced cucumber to make a delicious cold salad.

LEMON AND ONION CURLS

Before squeezing the juice from lemon, pare off the zest using a vegetable peeler and cut into fine strips. Trim a spring onion, cut into 5cm (2in) lengths and cut into fine shreds. Leave the zest and spring onion shreds in a bowl of cold water in the refrigerator for 1 hour so they curl attractively. Drain just before using.

Lemon Rice

This is a wonderful side dish from south India

 serves 4

🕐 prep 10 mins • cook 15 mins

3 tbsp vegetable oil

1 tsp yellow mustard seeds

6 green cardamom pods, split

10 fresh or dried curry leaves

2 red chillies, split lengthways

½ tsp turmeric

1cm (½ in) piece fresh root ginger, peeled and finely chopped

1 garlic clove, crushed

3 tbsp lemon juice, or to taste

300g (10oz) basmati rice, cooked according to packet instructions

60g (2oz) cashews, lightly toasted

2 tbsp chopped coriander leaves

1 **Heat the oil** in a large frying pan, add the next 7 ingredients and fry over a moderate heat for 2 minutes, or until aromatic, stirring all the time.

2 **Add the lemon juice** and cook for 1 minute, then stir in the rice. Cook until the rice is heated through and coated in the spices.

3 **Transfer to a serving** dish, scatter with the cashews and chopped coriander, and serve at once.

Porcini Polenta

Using dried mushrooms guarantees a rich, earthy flavour, which is ideal for serving alongside the subtle-tasting polenta

🍴 serves 4

🕐 prep 5 mins, plus soaking • cook 20 mins

½ tsp salt

175g (6oz) quick-cook polenta

For the mushrooms

15g (½oz) dried porcini mushrooms

4 tbsp olive oil

1 garlic clove, chopped

450g (1lb) chestnut mushrooms, wiped, trimmed, and sliced

salt and freshly ground black pepper

few sprigs of thyme

● **Prepare ahead** The mushrooms can be prepared and cooked up to 4 hours in advance and reheated.

1 **Put the dried mushrooms** in a heatproof bowl and pour over enough boiling water to cover, then leave to stand for 20 minutes. Line a fine sieve with muslin or kitchen paper, place over a jug, and strain the mushrooms through it. Rinse the mushrooms and set aside with the soaking liquid.

2 **Meanwhile,** heat the oil in a large saucepan over a medium heat. Add the garlic and fry, stirring, for 2–3 minutes, or until golden. Stir in the chestnut mushrooms and season to taste with salt and pepper. Add the porcini mushrooms and their soaking liquid, and stir for 3 minutes, or until the mushrooms are lightly browned and the liquid has almost completely evaporated.

3 **Bring 1.75 litres (3 pints)** lightly salted water to a rolling boil in a large heavy saucepan over a high heat. Drizzle in the polenta,

while stirring all the time. Continue stirring until the polenta is tender and all the liquid absorbed. Season to taste with salt and pepper.

4 **Divide the polenta** between 4 serving bowls and make an indentation in the centre of each mound. Spoon the mushrooms over the tops and serve at once, garnished with the thyme.

● **Good with** a mixed green salad as a main course, or starter.

VARIATION

Parmesan Polenta

Omit the mushrooms. When the polenta is tender, stir in 85g (3oz) diced butter and 85g (3oz) grated Parmesan cheese. Serve as an accompaniment to grilled meat.

Spanish Lentils

This classic Spanish dish of brown lentils, *Cocida de Lentejas*, relies on salty bacon, spicy chorizo, and paprika for its flavour

 serves 4

prep 15 mins • cook 1 hr

500g (1lb 2oz) **brown lentils**, washed and drained

2 **bay leaves**

85g (3oz) **chorizo**, cut into slices 3cm (1¼in) in diameter

2 tbsp **olive oil**

2 **garlic cloves**, sliced

1 small **slice of bread**

salt

1 **onion**, finely chopped

75g (2½oz) thickly sliced **tocino** or streaky bacon, cut into strips

1 tbsp **flour**

1 tsp **pimenton dulce** (sweet paprika)

90ml (3½fl oz) **vegetable stock**

● **Prepare ahead** The whole dish can be made 1 day in advance. Cover, chill, and reheat before serving.

1 Place the lentils in a large saucepan with 1 litre (1¾ pints) water, the bay leaves, and chorizo. Bring to the boil, then simmer for 35–40 minutes, or until the lentils are tender.

2 Meanwhile, heat 1 tbsp oil in a frying pan over a medium-low heat and fry the garlic, stirring, for 30 seconds, or until softened but not browned. Remove from the pan.

3 Add the bread to the pan and fry over a medium heat until lightly browned on both sides. Remove, place in a food processor along with the garlic, and season to taste with salt. Process to produce coarse crumbs.

4 When the lentils are cooked, drain, then return to the pan. Stir in the crumb mixture until combined.

5 Add the remaining oil to the frying pan along with the onion and tocino. Fry for 3–4 minutes, or until the onion is soft and the bacon is cooked. Stir in the flour and pimenton dulce and cook, stirring, for 1 minute, then stir in the stock. Bring to the boil and simmer for 2 minutes, then stir into the lentils.

6 If necessary, add a little more stock or water, to moisten the lentils and heat through. Transfer to a heated serving dish.

● **Good with** crusty bread.

● **Leftovers** of the lentils can be used as a topping for baked potatoes, or more stock can be added to serve them as a hearty soup.

Polenta

This cornmeal "porridge" is served in northern Italy as an accompaniment to meat dishes

 serves 4

prep 10 mins • cook 10 mins

1.4 litres (2½ pints) **chicken stock** or vegetable stock

350g (12oz) **quick-cook polenta**

30g (1oz) **butter**

75g (2½oz) grated **Parmesan cheese**, plus extra to serve

freshly ground **black pepper**

1 In a large saucepan, heat the stock until almost boiling.

2 Gradually whisk in the polenta, then continue to stir until the mixture is thick, but soft, adding a little more stock or water, if necessary.

3 Stir the butter and Parmesan into the mixture, and season to taste with black pepper. Scatter with a little more Parmesan, and serve immediately.

● **Leftovers** can be spooned into a shallow dish, spread in an even layer, and set aside to cool and become firm. To serve, cut into slices or wedges, and fry in a little oil until golden on both sides.

Rice Porridge

Known in Asia as Rice Congee or *Jook*, this dish is eaten for breakfast in China when the weather is cold

 serves 4

 prep 20 mins, plus standing • cook 1 hr

✔ low fat

6 dried Chinese mushrooms

2 tbsp vegetable oil

1cm (½in) piece fresh root ginger, peeled and grated

1 garlic clove, finely chopped

1 carrot, cut julienne

½ tsp dried chilli flakes

200g (7oz) long-grain rice

900ml (1½ pints) chicken stock

2 skinless boneless chicken breasts, cut into small pieces

4 spring onions, chopped

2 tbsp light soy sauce

freshly ground black pepper

2 tbsp chopped coriander

● **Prepare ahead** Although best fresh, the porridge can be prepared in advance and reheated, adding stock or water if it has become too thick.

1 Put the mushrooms in a bowl and pour over enough boiling water to cover. Set aside for 20 minutes to soak. Drain, reserving the soaking water, then snip the mushrooms into small pieces using kitchen scissors.

2 Heat the oil in a wok or large frying pan, add the ginger, garlic, carrot, and chilli, and fry gently for 5 minutes. Stir in the rice and add the stock. Measure 150ml (5fl oz) of the soaking water from the mushrooms and strain this into the pan.

3 Bring to a simmer and cook for 20 minutes, then add the chicken and cook for a further 30 minutes, or until the rice has broken down to a porridge-like consistency. Stir in the spring onions and soy sauce. Season to taste with black pepper. Serve hot, sprinkled with chopped coriander.

Thai Coconut Rice

Traditional flavourings of coconut and kaffir lime leaves are mixed with plain rice to create this popular Asian accompaniment

 serves 4-6

prep 25 mins • cook 40 mins

10g (¼oz) coriander

2 tbsp olive oil

25g (scant 1oz) butter

1 red chilli, chopped

2 shallots, finely chopped

75g (2½oz) Thai red curry paste

grated zest of 1 lime

400g (14oz) Thai jasmine rice

1½ tsp salt

400ml can coconut milk

large pinch of shredded kaffir lime leaves

2 spring onions, thinly sliced

1 Pick the coriander leaves off the stalks; finely chop the stalks and reserve the leaves.

2 Heat the oil and butter in a large frying pan with a lid over a low heat. Add the chilli and shallots, and fry, stirring, for 5 minutes, or until they start to turn golden. Stir in the curry paste and cook for 30 seconds.

3 Add the lime zest, coriander stalks, rice, and 1 tsp salt and mix everything together until the grains of rice are coated in the curry paste. Pour in the coconut milk and 400ml (14fl oz) water and stir well. Bring to simmering point over a medium heat, stirring occasionally so the rice doesn't stick. Scatter in the lime leaves and simmer, uncovered, for 5 minutes.

4 Give the rice a thorough stir, then cover and leave over a very low heat for 15 minutes, or until the rice is tender. If the liquid has been absorbed but the rice is still not ready, add a little extra water. When ready to serve, stir in the spring onions and sprinkle over the reserved coriander leaves, to taste.

● **Good with** a Thai red or green curry, soy-marinated roast fish, or stir-fried chicken.

> ### COCONUT MILK
> Coconut milk is readily available in supermarkets. For a healthier dish, try the half-fat versions.

Rice and Peas

In this West Indian dish, the "peas" are known as gungo peas in Jamaica and pigeon peas in Trinidad

 serves 4

prep 10 mins • cook 45 mins

400g can **gungo peas** or black-eyed peas, drained and rinsed

400ml can **coconut milk**

1 large **onion**, finely chopped

1 **green pepper**, deseeded and chopped

salt and freshly ground **black pepper**

125g (4½oz) **long-grain rice**

chilli powder, to garnish

● **Prepare ahead** The dish can be prepared in advance and reheated until piping hot at 180°C (350°F/ Gas 4) in a shallow dish tightly covered with foil.

1 **Put the peas**, coconut milk, onion, and green pepper in a saucepan. Season to taste with salt and pepper and simmer over a low heat for 5 minutes.

2 **Stir in the rice**, cover, and cook gently for 35 minutes, or until the rice is tender, stirring. Serve sprinkled with chilli powder.

● **Good with** grilled or roasted meat and poultry, and fried fish.

Risotto Balls

Crispy on the outside and soft and creamy on the inside, these tasty rice balls make an unusual side dish, or can be eaten hot or cold as a party nibble with a tomato or sweet chilli dipping sauce

 serves 4–6

 prep 15 mins
• cook 20–25 mins

 freeze the uncooked rice balls for up to 2 months

175g (6oz) **risotto rice**

1 **vegetable stock cube**

60g (2oz) **Gruyère cheese**, grated

2 tbsp **pesto**

60g (2oz) dried **breadcrumbs**

oil, for frying

basil leaves, to garnish (optional)

● **Prepare ahead** The balls can be made up to 24 hours in advance and stored in an airtight container in the refrigerator until required.

1 **Place the rice** and stock cube in a saucepan and pour in 900ml (1½ pints) water. Place over a high heat, and bring to the boil. Cover, and simmer for 15 minutes, or until the rice is just tender.

2 **Drain the rice** thoroughly, then stir in the cheese and pesto and allow to cool.

3 **Using dampened hands**, divide the rice and roll into walnut-sized balls. Roll in the breadcrumbs to coat well.

4 **Heat about 1cm** (½in) oil in a frying pan. Fry the balls for 5–10 minutes, or until crisp and golden on the outside. Drain on kitchen paper and serve with basil leaves (if desired). Alternatively, the balls can be deep-fried for 2–3 minutes, or until golden.

● **Good with** roast chicken, ham, or pork.

● **Leftovers** can be added to salads or eaten as a snack.

Couscous with Pine Nuts and Almonds

A tasty alternative to rice; serve hot as a side dish or cold as a salad

 serves 4

🕐 prep 15 mins, plus standing

175g (6oz) couscous

boiling water, to cover

1 red pepper, deseeded and chopped

100g (3½oz) raisins

100g (3½oz) dried apricots, chopped

½ cucumber, seeded and diced

12 black olives, pitted

60g (2oz) blanched almonds, lightly toasted

60g (2oz) pine nuts, lightly toasted

4 tbsp light olive oil

juice of ½ lemon

1 tbsp chopped mint

salt and freshly ground black pepper

● **Prepare ahead** The couscous can be prepared several hours in advance, if serving cold.

1 **Put the couscous** in a bowl and pour over enough boiling water to cover it by about 2.5cm (1in). Set aside for 15 minutes, or until the couscous has absorbed all the water, then fluff the grains up lightly with a fork.

2 **Stir in the pepper**, raisins, apricots, cucumber, olives, almonds, and pine nuts.

3 **Whisk together** the olive oil, lemon juice, and mint. Season to taste with salt and pepper and stir into the couscous. Serve at once while warm, or leave to cool.

● **Good with** grilled meats, chicken, or fish.

German Potato Dumplings

These light, but sustaining dumplings, *kartoffelkloesse*, are often served in a hearty meat stew or spicy goulash

 serves 4

🕐 prep 15 mins, plus cooling
● cook 35 mins

350g (12oz) floury potatoes

1 egg, beaten

30g (1oz) plain flour, plus extra for dusting

45g (1½oz) semolina

½ tsp caraway seeds

salt and freshly ground black pepper

● **Prepare ahead** You can prepare the dumplings 1 hour in advance, and chill until ready to cook.

1 **Peel the potatoes**, cut into even-sized pieces, and boil in a large pan of water until tender. Drain, return the potatoes to the pan, and stir over a low heat for 1 minute to dry, then mash. Leave to cool.

2 **Place the cold mashed** potatoes in a large bowl. Add the egg, flour, semolina and caraway seeds, and season to taste with salt and pepper. Stir until well combined. The mixture should hold its shape; if it doesn't, add a little more flour.

3 **With floured hands**, shape the mixture into 12 balls, then roll into sausage shapes. Place in a single layer on a plate, and chill until ready to cook.

4 **Bring a large pan** of water to the boil, add the dumplings, reduce the heat, and simmer for 15 minutes, or until they puff up and float to the top. Drain and serve.

● **Good with** Sauerbraten (p334) with braised red cabbage for a traditional German meal.

● **Leftovers** can be sliced, fried in butter, and served as a tasty snack.

Potato Gnocchi

These light-as-air potato dumplings, served with a simple sage and butter sauce, make a good supper side dish

🍴 serves 4

🕐 prep 30 mins • cook 25 mins

750g (1lb 10oz) **floury potatoes**

2 **eggs**, beaten

200g (7oz) **plain flour**

For the sauce

150g (5½oz) **unsalted butter**

20 **sage leaves**, chopped, plus extra to garnish

juice of ½ **lemon**

freshly ground **black pepper**

● **Prepare ahead** Make the gnocchi 2 hours in advance up to the end of step 3. Keep covered with a damp cloth until required.

1 Cook the whole, unpeeled potatoes in a pan of boiling water until just tender. Drain and, when just cool enough to handle, peel them and push through a potato ricer or metal sieve so they are finely mashed with no lumps.

2 Put the warm mash on a board. Make a well in the centre and add the beaten eggs and a quarter of the flour. Mix everything together with your hands, adding more flour as necessary but be careful not to add too much. The dough should be just firm enough to shape, but not sticky.

3 Divide the dough into quarters. With your hands, roll each piece on a lightly floured surface to form a 2cm (¾in) thick sausage. Cut into pieces 3cm (1¼in) long. Press each piece lightly with the back of a fork.

4 Bring a large pan of water to a gentle boil, add the gnocchi, and cook for 2 minutes, or until the pieces float to the surface.

5 Meanwhile, make the sauce by heating the butter in a pan with the sage leaves until the butter has melted. Add the lemon juice and season to taste with plenty of pepper.

6 Drain the gnocchi and toss in the sauce. Serve immediately, garnished with sage leaves.

Rice Timbales

Lightly spiced rice can be pressed into moulds to make an eye-catching and stylish accompaniment

🍴 serves 4

🕐 prep 20 mins • cook 20 mins

🗄 4 ramekins

2 tbsp **olive oil**

½ **red pepper**, deseeded and finely chopped

2 **shallots**, finely chopped

2 tsp **ground coriander**

1 tsp **ground cumin**

1 tsp **sesame seeds**

½ tsp dried **oregano**

300g (10oz) **long-grain rice**

600ml (1 pint) hot **chicken stock**

4 tbsp **olive oil**, to serve

zest and juice of 1 **lemon**, to serve

2 tbsp chopped **parsley**, to serve

1 Heat the oil in a pan, add the red pepper and shallots, and fry gently for 5 minutes. Add the coriander, cumin, sesame seeds, and oregano, and fry for a further 2 minutes. Stir in the rice, pour in the stock, and bring to the boil. Cook for 10–12 minutes, or until the rice is tender and has absorbed the stock.

2 Meanwhile, heat the olive oil and lemon zest and juice in a pan until boiling, then add the parsley, and keep warm.

3 Lightly grease the ramekins. When the rice is cooked, spoon into the moulds, pressing it down quite firmly with the spoon. Turn out the rice on to serving plates and drizzle the hot lemon oil over the top. Serve at once.

● **Good with** meat, poultry, and fish dishes.

▭ VARIATION

Vegetarian Timbales

To make the timbales suitable for vegetarians, replace the chicken stock with the same quantity of vegetable stock. Follow the recipe above, and serve with roasted Mediterranean-style vegetables.

Semolina Dumplings

These little dumplings are a popular garnish for soups in Bavaria, southern Germany

- serves 4
- prep 20 mins • cook 25 mins

15g (½oz) butter

150ml (5fl oz) milk

pinch of grated nutmeg

60g (2oz) semolina

1 egg

salt and freshly ground black pepper

chicken soup, or meat soup, to serve

● **Prepare ahead** You can make the dumplings several hours in advance, and keep them tightly covered with cling film to prevent them drying out.

1 Put the butter, milk, and nutmeg in a pan and bring to a simmer. Remove from the heat and stir in the semolina. Continue stirring until the mixture forms a soft, smooth dough.

2 Beat in the egg and season to serve with salt and pepper. If necessary, add a little extra semolina or milk to keep the dough at the correct consistency: it should be soft but firm enough to shape.

3 Shape the mixture into small dumplings using 2 spoons, and drop into a large pan of hot soup. Simmer for 10 minutes, or until cooked. Serve the soup in shallow bowls with the dumplings divided among them.

Spiced Orzo with Spinach

Orzo is a tiny soup pasta which looks similar to rice. It makes an ideal side dish for Mediterranean-style dishes

- serves 4–6
- prep 5 mins • cook 25 mins
- low fat

200g (7oz) orzo

1½ tbsp olive oil

1 onion, finely chopped

2 garlic cloves, finely chopped

1 tsp ground coriander

½ tsp ground cumin

pinch of cayenne pepper

150g (5½oz) baby spinach leaves

4 tbsp chopped coriander or flat-leaf parsley

salt and freshly ground black pepper

● **Prepare ahead** The whole dish can be made up to 1 day in advance, refrigerated, and served cold. Add extra olive oil and toss, if needed.

1 Bring a large saucepan of salted water to the boil. Add the orzo and cook for 15 minutes, or according to the packet instructions.

2 Meanwhile, heat the olive oil in a large saucepan. Add the onion and fry over a medium heat for 3 minutes, or until just soft but not coloured. Stir in the garlic, coriander, cumin, and cayenne, and continue frying for a further minute.

3 Add the spinach to the pan with the water clinging to its leaves from washing. Cook, stirring, for 3 minutes, or until it is just wilted.

4 Drain the orzo well, shaking off any excess water. Tip the orzo into the pan with spinach and mix the ingredients together, using 2 spoons or forks. Stir in the coriander and season to taste with salt and pepper. Transfer to a serving bowl and serve.

VARIATION

Spiced Orzo and Spinach Salad

Follow the recipe as above, then leave to cool. Stir well, squeeze over lemon juice to taste, add extra virgin olive oil, and toss. Sprinkle with crumbled feta cheese. Serve with warm pitta bread.

Cabbage Rolls

Stuffed cabbage leaves in tomato sauce make a delicious and satisfying supper dish

 serves 4

 prep 45–50 mins
• cook 1 hr 20 mins

 low GI

1 tbsp **oil**, plus extra for greasing

1 **leek**, white part only, finely chopped

115g (4oz) **chanterelle mushrooms**, finely chopped

1 **celery stick**, finely chopped

115g (4oz) fresh **brown breadcrumbs**

1 **egg**

2 tbsp chopped fresh **parsley**

pinch of **ground coriander**

1 tbsp **lemon** juice

sea salt and freshly ground **black pepper**

8 large **savoy cabbage** leaves or winter cabbage leaves, stalks removed

For the sauce

1 tbsp **olive oil**

1 **onion**, finely chopped

2 **garlic cloves**, crushed

400g carton **passata**

150ml (5fl oz) **vegetable stock**

1 Heat the oil in a frying pan and fry the leek, mushroom, and celery over a low heat for 5 minutes, or until soft but not coloured.

2 Remove from the heat. Stir in the breadcrumbs, egg, parsley, coriander, and lemon juice, and season to taste with salt and pepper. Set aside until needed.

3 Preheat the oven to 160°C (325°F/Gas 3). Blanch the cabbage leaves in boiling salted water for 2 minutes, then rinse in cold water, and drain well.

4 Lay the leaves flat and divide the stuffing among them. Roll up each leaf, folding in the sides to make a neat parcel. Pack the rolls tightly in an oiled ovenproof dish, pour in the vegetable stock, and bake for 45–55 minutes, or until tender.

5 Meanwhile, to make the tomato sauce, heat the oil in the frying pan over a medium heat, and fry the onion and garlic, stirring frequently, for 4–5 minutes, or until soft but not coloured. Add the passata, stir well, and simmer on a low heat, stirring occasionally, for 10 minutes. Season to taste with salt and pepper.

6 Lift the rolls out of the dish using a slotted spoon and discard the stock. Spoon some of the tomato sauce on to serving plates and place the cabbage rolls on top. Serve immediately, with the remaining sauce served separately.

● **Good with** crusty bread, sautéed potatoes, or brown rice.

VARIATION

German Cabbage Rolls (*Kohlrollen*)

For the stuffing, mix together 250g (9oz) minced pork or beef, 60g (2oz) fresh brown breadcrumbs, and 1 egg, and season to taste with salt and pepper. Make the tomato sauce and stuff the cabbage leaves as above, securing each leaf with string. Place in a single layer in a saucepan, add 115g (4oz) chopped smoked bacon, lightly fried and pour in enough tomato sauce to cover. Simmer, covered, over a low heat for 40 minutes, or until tender and cooked through.

Celeriac Timbales

A stylish vegetable main dish

 serves 4

 prep 10 mins • cook 35 mins

 4 x 200ml (7fl oz) ramekins

400g (14oz) **celeriac**, peeled and diced

200g (7oz) **potatoes**, diced

3 **eggs**

1 **egg yolk**

150ml (5fl oz) **double cream**

1 **garlic clove**

pinch of grated **nutmeg**

salt and freshly ground **black pepper**

1 Preheat the oven to 190°C (375°F/Gas 5). Place the celeriac and potatoes in a large pan of cold water. Bring to the boil, then cover and simmer for 8–10 minutes, or until tender. Drain well.

2 Place the celeriac and potato in a food processor or blender with the eggs, egg yolk, cream, garlic, and nutmeg; season to taste with salt and pepper. Process until smooth.

3 Butter the ramekins and place in a roasting tin. Divide the mixture among the dishes and pour enough boiling water into the tin to come halfway up the sides of the ramekins. Cover the tin with foil and bake for 25 minutes, or until just firm. Turn out on to plates, and serve.

● **Good with** roasted seasonal vegetables, or dressed spinach.

Chilli Tofu Stir-fry

This quick and easy dish plays on tofu's ability to take on the flavour of other ingredients

- serves 4
- prep 10 mins • cook 15 mins
- wok

2 tbsp **sunflower oil**

90g (3oz) unsalted **cashew nuts**

300g (10oz) firm **tofu**, cubed

1 **red onion**, thinly sliced

2 **carrots**, peeled and thinly sliced

1 **red pepper**, deseeded and chopped

1 **celery stick**, chopped

4 **chestnut mushrooms**, sliced

175g (6oz) **beansprouts**

2 tsp **chilli sauce**

2 tbsp **light soy sauce**

1 tsp **cornflour**

175ml (6fl oz) **vegetable stock**

1 Heat the oil in a wok and add the cashews; stir-fry for 30 seconds, or until lightly browned. Drain and set aside.

2 Add the tofu and stir-fry until golden. Drain and set aside. Stir-fry the onion and carrots for 5 minutes, then add the red pepper, celery, and mushrooms and stir-fry for 3–4 minutes. Finally, add the beansprouts and stir-fry for 2 minutes. Keep the heat under the wok high, so the vegetables fry quickly, without overcooking.

3 Return the cashews and tofu to the pan and drizzle in the chilli sauce. In a small bowl, mix the soy sauce with the cornflour and pour into the pan, along with the stock. Toss over the heat for 2–3 minutes, or until the sauce is bubbling.

● **Good with** boiled rice or Chinese-style egg noodles.

Roast Beetroot and Feta Salad

A colourful and delicious salad to serve for lunch or a light summer supper

- serves 4
- prep 10 mins • cook 1–1¼ hrs

6 small raw **beetroot**, unpeeled

olive oil

salt and freshly ground **black pepper**

1 **red onion**, very finely sliced

50g (1¾oz) **rocket**

100g (3½oz) **feta cheese**, cubed

handful of **mint leaves**, torn, to garnish

For the dressing

3 tbsp **olive oil**

1 tbsp **balsamic vinegar**

1 tbsp **Dijon mustard**

1 tsp clear **honey**

1 Preheat the oven to 200°C (400°F/Gas 6). Place the beetroot in a roasting tin. Pour a little water around them, drizzle with olive oil, and season with salt and pepper, then cover tightly with foil and roast for 1–1¼ hours, or until tender.

2 Remove the beetroot from the oven and allow to cool. Peel and cut into large cubes.

3 Whisk together the dressing ingredients. Put the beetroot and onion in a bowl and toss them in the dressing, then scatter the rocket over them. Top with feta cubes, garnish with mint, and serve.

● **Prepare ahead** You can cook the beetroot and make the dressing up to 3 days in advance. Cover and refrigerate until needed.

VARIATION

Roast Beetroot and Goat's Cheese Salad

Replace the feta cheese with 100g (3½oz) hard, crumbly goat's cheese. Scatter the dressed salad with a small handful of pomegranate seeds or toasted pine nuts, if you like.

Chillies en Nogada

Heart-shaped green poblano chillies from Mexico's Pueblo region are traditionally used for this recipe but you can substitute ordinary green peppers

 serves 4

 prep 30 mins, plus cooling • cook 30 mins

❄ freeze the stuffed peppers, without the sauce and garnishes, for up to 3 months

250g (9oz) smoked tofu, chopped

juice of ½ lime

salt and freshly ground black pepper

1 tbsp vegetable oil

1 onion or 2 shallots, finely chopped

1 garlic clove, crushed

2 large green chillies or red chillies, deseeded and chopped

1 red pepper, deseeded and chopped

8 green olives, pitted and chopped

2 tbsp raisins

4 tbsp tomato purée

250ml (8fl oz) vegetable stock

4 poblano chillies or green peppers

¼ iceberg lettuce, shredded

4 tbsp pomegranate seeds

1 tbsp chopped coriander

For the sauce

60g (2oz) ground green walnuts or ground almonds

150ml (5fl oz) soured cream

60g (2oz) cream cheese

● **Prepare ahead** The peppers can be prepared up to 24 hours before needed, adding the sauce and garnishes just before serving.

1 **To make the filling**, mix together the smoked tofu and lime juice, and season with salt and pepper. Heat the oil in a frying pan and fry the onion, garlic, chillies, and red pepper over a low heat for 5 minutes, stirring frequently.

2 **Stir in the smoked tofu,** breaking up the pieces of tofu with a spoon, then increase the heat and fry briefly, stirring frequently, until heated through. Set aside. Add the olives, raisins, tomato purée, and stock to the pan, and simmer gently for 10 minutes, or until the liquid has evaporated and the mixture is thick, stirring occasionally. Add the tofu, and set aside to cool.

3 **Preheat the grill** on its highest setting and line the grill pan with foil. Grill the green peppers until the skins are scorched on all sides. Wrap the foil around the peppers to make a tightly sealed parcel and leave until cool enough to handle. Strip the skin off the peppers, without removing the stalks.

4 **Cut open each pepper,** without dividing them completely in half, and remove the core and seeds. Spoon in the filling and reshape the peppers.

5 **To make the sauce**, whisk together the ground walnuts, soured cream, and cream cheese.

6 **Line a serving dish** with the shredded lettuce and arrange the peppers on top. Scatter the pomegranate seeds and spoon the sauce on to the side. Garnish with a little chopped coriander.

> **GREEN WALNUTS**
> Soft green walnuts should be used to make the sauce, but, as their season is short, ground almonds make a good year-round alternative.

Baked Stuffed Tomatoes

Beef tomatoes are perfect for filling

 serves 4

🕐 prep 40 mins, plus standing • cook 15–20 mins

4 large ripe beef tomatoes

salt and freshly ground black pepper

1 tbsp olive oil

2 anchovies, finely chopped

1 garlic clove, crushed

4 tbsp fresh breadcrumbs

4 tbsp mascarpone cheese

125g (4½oz) ricotta cheese

2 tbsp basil leaves, finely chopped

1 **Cut each tomato** in half horizontally. Scoop out the insides, and discard. Sprinkle the tomato halves with salt, and drain upside down for 30 minutes.

2 **Preheat the oven** to 220°C (425°F/Gas 7). Heat the olive oil in a pan, add the anchovies and garlic, and cook for 30 seconds. Stir in the breadcrumbs and cook for 2 minutes.

3 **Mix together** the mascarpone, ricotta, and basil. Season with black pepper. Fill each tomato with the cheeses and top with the breadcrumb mixture.

4 **Transfer the tomatoes** to a baking tray or shallow baking sheet and bake for 15–20 minutes, or until they are slightly blistered and the tops are golden.

Vegetable Kebabs

Cook these under the grill, or on a barbecue

 serves 4

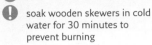 prep 15 mins • cook 15 mins

soak wooden skewers in cold water for 30 minutes to prevent burning

wooden skewers

1 courgette

1 red pepper, deseeded

1 green pepper, deseeded

1 red onion

8 cherry tomatoes

8 button mushrooms

5 tbsp olive oil

1 garlic clove, crushed

½ tsp dried oregano

pinch of chilli flakes

● **Prepare ahead** Steps 1 and 2 can be completed several hours in advance.

1 **Trim the courgette** and cut into 8 chunks. Cut the peppers into 2.5cm (1in) pieces. Peel the onion, and cut into wedges, leaving the root end intact so that the wedges do not fall apart.

2 **Thread the vegetables** on to 4 large or 8 small skewers. Whisk the remaining ingredients together in a small bowl with a fork.

3 **Preheat the grill** on a medium-high setting. Place the kebabs on the grill rack and brush generously with the flavoured oil. Cook for 10–15 minutes, or until the vegetables are just tender, turning frequently and brushing with more of the oil as you do so. Drizzle any remaining oil over the cooked kebabs.

● **Good with** a leafy salad, for a light vegetarian lunch, or alongside hamburgers, grilled meat, or fish.

● **Leftovers** can be eaten cold, drizzled with a little balsamic vinegar.

VARIATION

Mushroom Kebabs

Try making skewers of button mushrooms or mixed wild mushrooms and onion wedges.

Parmesan Cheese and Walnut Tart

This nutty pastry works brilliantly with the creamy cheese and potato filling and makes a delicate starter or main course

 serves 6–8

prep 25 mins, plus chilling • cook 45 mins

23 x 23cm (9 x 9in) or 35 x 11cm (14 x 4½in) loose-bottomed flan tin

freeze for up to 3 months

50g (1¾oz) walnut halves

225g (8oz) plain flour, plus extra for dusting

125g (4½oz) salted butter, chilled and diced

300ml (10fl oz) double cream

115g (4oz) mashed potato

2 large eggs

2 large egg yolks

150g (5½oz) Parmesan cheese, grated

freshly ground black pepper

pinch of nutmeg

● **Prepare ahead** The tart can be made up to 2 days in advance.

1 **Preheat the oven** to 200°C (400°F/Gas 6). Pulse the walnuts in a food processor until finely ground, add the flour and butter until it resembles fine breadcrumbs, pour in 2–3 tbsp of cold water and pulse to a firm dough.

2 **Roll the pastry** on a floured surface and use to line the tart tin. Prick the base and chill for 30 minutes.

3 **Place greaseproof paper** and baking beans into the tart tin. Bake blind for 10 minutes, then remove the paper and beans and cook for another 10 minutes to crisp the base. Lower the temperature to 180°C (350°F/Gas 4).

4 **Beat the cream**, mashed potato, whole eggs and egg yolks together well. Stir in the cheese and some black pepper and nutmeg. Pour into the pastry case and bake for 25 minutes, or until set. Allow it to stand for 10 minutes, then carefully remove the tart from the tin. Cut into slices and serve warm.

● **Good with** mixed leaves and a mild chutney or tomato salad.

Vegetable Curry

In Indian cooking, cardamom, cloves, coriander, and cumin seeds are all considered "warming spices" that heat the body from within, making this an excellent winter dish

 serves 4–6

 prep 20 mins
• cook 35–45 mins

 freeze for up to 3 months

4 tbsp **ghee** or sunflower oil

300g (10oz) waxy **potatoes**, diced

5 green **cardamom** pods, cracked

3 **cloves**

1 **cinnamon** stick, broken in half

2 tsp **cumin** seeds

1 **onion**, finely chopped

2 tsp fresh **root ginger**, peeled and grated

2 large **garlic** cloves, crushed

1½ tsp **turmeric**

1 tsp **ground coriander**

salt and freshly ground **black pepper**

400g can **chopped tomatoes**

pinch of **sugar**

2 **carrots**, peeled and diced

2 green **chillies**, deseeded (optional) and sliced

150g (5½oz) **Savoy cabbage** or green cabbage, sliced

150g (5½oz) **cauliflower** florets

150g (5½oz) **peas**

2 tbsp chopped **coriander leaves**

almond flakes, toasted, to garnish

● **Prepare ahead** The whole dish can be cooked 1 day in advance and reheated; if it is too thick, stir in a little extra water.

1 **Melt the ghee** or heat the oil in a large deep-sided frying pan over a high heat. Add the potatoes and stir-fry for 5 minutes, or until golden brown. Remove from the pan with a slotted spoon and set aside to drain on kitchen paper.

2 **Reduce the heat** to medium, add the cardamom pods, cloves, cinnamon, and cumin seeds, stirring just until the seeds begin to crackle. Add the onion and continue stir-frying for 5–8 minutes, or until softened. Add the ginger, garlic, turmeric, and ground coriander, then season to taste with salt and pepper and stir for 1 minute.

3 **Stir in the tomatoes** and sugar. Return the potatoes to the pan, add the carrots, chillies, and 250ml (8fl oz) water, and bring to the boil, stirring often. Reduce the heat to low and simmer for 15 minutes, or until the carrots are just tender, stirring occasionally. Add a little water, if needed.

4 **Stir in the cabbage**, cauliflower, and peas, and increase the heat to medium. Let the liquid gently bubble for a further 5–10 minutes, or until all the vegetables are tender. Stir in the coriander and adjust the seasoning, if necessary. Remove and discard the cardamom pods and cloves. Transfer to a serving bowl and sprinkle with almond flakes.

● **Good with** lots of freshly boiled basmati rice, or naan bread.

VARIATION

Paneer and Vegetable Curry

Cut 300g (10oz) paneer into bite-sized cubes. Heat a thin layer of sunflower oil in large frying pan over a high heat and fry the paneer until golden brown on all sides. Drain on kitchen paper and stir into the curry in step 4. Take care not to break up the paneer.

Stuffed Red Peppers

A fun way to serve peppers as a main course

 serves 4

prep 15 mins • cook 1 hr 15 mins

4 red **peppers**

115g (4oz) **basmati rice**

1 tbsp chopped **parsley**

1 tbsp chopped **chives**

1 tsp chopped **lovage**

1 tbsp **lemon** juice

salt and freshly ground **black pepper**

150ml (5fl oz) **vegetable stock**

olive oil, for drizzling

100g (3½oz) grated **cheese**, to serve

1 **Cut the top** off each pepper and scoop out the seeds and membranes. Cook the rice according to packet instructions. Drain well, and stir in the parsley, chives, lovage, and lemon juice. Season to taste with salt and pepper, and set aside.

2 **Preheat the oven** to 160°C (325°F/Gas 3). Place a large pan of salted water on the boil. Add the peppers, blanch for 2–3 minutes, drain, and place in an ovenproof dish.

3 **Divide the rice** between the peppers, replace the lids, drizzle with a little oil, and pour the stock into the dish. Cover with foil, and bake for 1 hour, or until tender. Serve with the grated cheese alongside.

Potato and Fennel Pancakes with Mushrooms

Goes well with a mix of cultivated and wild mushrooms

 serves 4

prep 15 mins • cook 1 hr 30 mins

3 baking potatoes

1 onion, peeled and finely chopped

1 fennel bulb, trimmed and finely chopped

2 tbsp plain flour

2 eggs

pinch of nutmeg

salt and freshly ground black pepper

1 garlic clove, chopped

225g (8oz) mixed mushrooms

dash of lemon juice

2 tbsp thyme leaves

2 tbsp chopped parsley

Parmesan cheese shavings, to garnish

4 tbsp crème fraîche, to serve

1 **Place the potatoes** in large pan of cold salted water and cover. Bring to boil, then simmer for 3 minutes. Drain, cool, and peel off the skins. Grate the potato and put into a bowl. Set aside.

2 **Heat a little oil** and butter in a frying pan and fry the onion for 5 minutes. Add the fennel and cook gently for 5 minutes to soften. Allow to cool, then add the potatoes along with the flour, eggs, and nutmeg, and season to taste with salt and pepper. Mix together well.

3 **In a non-stick frying pan**, melt a knob of butter and some olive oil; when sizzling hot, add a heaped tbsp of the mixture, pressing down to flatten into a round disc. Cook for 5 minutes on each side, turning once. Keep warm in a low oven until needed. Repeat this process until 12 pancakes are made.

4 **Heat a little olive oil** and butter in the non-stick frying pan. Add the garlic and cook over a low heat until softened, then add the mushrooms and cook for 5 minutes, or until wilted and sizzling hot. Season to taste with salt and pepper, and add the lemon juice, then the thyme and parsley.

5 **Divide the pancakes** between 4 plates. Spoon over the mushrooms and top with Parmesan shavings and crème fraîche.

● **Good with** a green salad.

Tofu and Mushroom Stroganoff

This recipe gives the traditional stroganoff a tasty vegetarian twist by substituting tofu chunks for the meat

 serves 4

 prep 15 mins • cook 20 mins

2 tbsp sunflower oil

350g (12oz) firm tofu, cut into strips or bite-sized cubes

1 red onion, thinly sliced

2 garlic cloves, crushed

1 red pepper, deseeded and sliced

1 orange pepper, deseeded and sliced

250g (9oz) mixed mushrooms, quartered

2 tbsp tomato purée

2 tbsp smooth peanut butter

150ml (5fl oz) vegetable stock

2 tsp cornflour

200g (7oz) crème fraîche or Greek-style natural yogurt

salt and freshly ground black pepper

chives, to serve

200g (7oz) long-grain rice, boiled to serve

1 **Heat 1 tbsp of the oil** in a large frying pan or wok and stir-fry the tofu over a fairly brisk heat until golden. Remove from the pan and set aside.

2 **Add the rest of the oil** to the pan, reduce the heat, and add the onion and garlic. Fry until softened, add the peppers and mushrooms, and fry for 5 minutes, stirring frequently.

3 **Add the tomato purée** and peanut butter and return the tofu to the pan. Stir in the stock.

4 **Mix the cornflour** to a paste with a little water and stir in to the pan. Simmer for 2–3 minutes.

5 **Stir in the crème fraîche** or yogurt, season to taste with salt and pepper, and simmer for 2 minutes. Sprinkle with chives and serve with rice.

> **USING YOGURT**
>
> If you use yogurt instead of crème fraîche, stir it in gradually and don't let the sauce boil or it will curdle.

Olive, Thyme, and Onion Tart

A great tart recipe to have to hand, especially as there no need to blind bake the pastry case

- serves 4-6
- prep 40 mins • cook 30 mins
- 20cm (8in) loose-bottomed tart tin

For the pastry

115g (4oz) butter

3 tbsp milk

150g (5½oz) self-raising flour

For the filling

3 tbsp olive oil

3 onions, peeled and finely sliced

1 tsp caster sugar

2 tbsp chopped thyme leaves

1 tsp salt

240ml (8fl oz) double cream

3 eggs, beaten

freshly ground black pepper

30g (1oz) Parmesan cheese, grated

2 tbsp black olive tapenade

1 To make the pastry, heat the butter and milk together in a saucepan until the butter is melted. Stir in the flour and mix until a ball forms. When cool enough to handle, press the pastry into the tart tin, and chill for 30 minutes.

2 Preheat the oven to 190°C (375°F/Gas 5). Heat the olive oil in a heavy frying pan, and add the onion, stirring, over a high heat for 5 minutes. Add the sugar, thyme, and salt, then reduce the heat, and cook slowly, stirring occasionally, for 30 minutes, or until the onions are very soft and slightly caramelized. Meanwhile, whisk together the cream, eggs, black pepper, and Parmesan cheese.

3 Place the tart tin on a baking tray, and spread the tapenade over the base of the pastry. Spread the onions on top and carefully pour over the cream filling. Bake the tart for 30 minutes, or until set. Serve while still warm, or leave to cool completely and serve cold.

● **Prepare ahead** The pastry case can be made 1 day in advance, and chilled until ready to serve.

● **Good with** a rocket salad dressed with a nutty vinaigrette.

Stuffed Aubergines

A popular Turkish meze, *Imam Bayildi* are cold and spicy stuffed aubergines

- serves 4
- prep 20 mins, plus chilling • cook 1 hr 10 mins
- ✓ low GI
- ❄ freeze for up to 1 month

4 aubergines

6 tbsp olive oil

2 large onions, finely sliced

3 garlic cloves, crushed

1 tbsp ground coriander

1 tbsp ground cumin

1 tsp ground turmeric

½ tsp ground cardamom

2 x 400g cans chopped tomatoes

85g (3oz) sultanas

2 tbsp chopped coriander

1 tbsp chopped mint

1 tbsp chopped parsley

● **Prepare ahead** This dish benefits from being made 24 hours in advance and chilled, covered, to allow the flavours to develop.

1 Preheat the oven to 180°C (350°F/Gas 4). Cut the aubergines in half lengthways, and score the flesh in a criss-cross pattern using a sharp knife.

2 Brush the aubergine flesh with 4 tbsp oil, and place the halves, cut-sides up, in a roasting tin. Bake for 30–35 minutes, or until the flesh is tender.

3 Leave the aubergine halves to cool, then scoop out and chop the flesh. Take care not to split the skins, and leave a thin layer of flesh in place to support them.

4 Heat the rest of the oil in a large, heavy pan, and cook the onion and garlic over a medium-low heat until softened. Add the spices and fry until they smell fragrant, stirring occasionally.

5 Stir in the tomatoes, bring to the boil, then reduce the heat and simmer for 30 minutes, or until the mixture is reduced, stirring occasionally. Add the sultanas and aubergine flesh and cook, stirring, for a further 10 minutes, or until heated though. Leave to cool, then stir in the coriander, mint, and parsley.

6 Spoon the mixture into the aubergine shells and chill for at least 3 hours, or overnight if possible.

● **Good with** a herb salad and Greek yogurt.

Vegetable Biryani

A curry that both vegetarians and meat eaters will enjoy

 serves 4

 prep 30 mins • cook 45 mins

low fat

350g (12oz) **basmati rice**

1 large **carrot**, sliced

2 **potatoes**, peeled and cut into small pieces

½ **cauliflower**, cut into small florets

3 tbsp **vegetable oil**

1 **red onion**, chopped

1 **red pepper**, deseeded and chopped

1 **green pepper**, deseeded and chopped

1 **courgette**, chopped

85g (3oz) **frozen peas**

1 tsp **turmeric**

1 tsp mild **chilli powder**

2 tsp **ground coriander**

2 tsp mild **curry paste**

1 tsp **cumin seeds**

150ml (5fl oz) **vegetable stock**

60g (2oz) **cashew nuts**, lightly toasted

1 **In a pan** of simmering water, cook the rice for 10 minutes, or until just tender. Drain and set aside.

2 **Cook the carrot** and potatoes in a pan of boiling water for 5 minutes, or until almost tender. Add the cauliflower and cook until the vegetables are tender. Drain.

3 **Heat the oil** in a large frying pan, add the onion, and fry over a medium-low heat until softened. Add the red and green pepper and the courgette, and fry for 5 minutes, stirring occasionally.

4 **Add the boiled vegetables** and frozen peas, then stir in the turmeric, chilli powder, coriander, curry paste, and cumin seeds. Fry for a further 5 minutes, then add the stock, stirring. Preheat the oven to 180°C (350°F/Gas 4).

5 **Spoon half the rice** into an ovenproof dish and spread the vegetable mixture on top. Cover with the rest of the rice, cover with foil, and bake for 30 minutes, or until hot. Scatter over the cashews, and serve.

● **Good with** naan bread, mango chutney, lime pickle, or raita.

Vegetable Moussaka

Lentils replace the lamb, and yogurt is a light alternative to béchamel sauce, in this vegetarian version of a Greek favourite

 serves 4–6

 prep 20 mins • cook 1 hr 30 mins

2 **aubergines**, about 600g (1lb 5oz) in total, cut into 1cm (½in) slices

2 **courgettes**, thickly sliced

2 **onions**, thickly sliced

2 **red peppers**, cored, deseeded, and thickly sliced

4 tbsp **olive oil**

salt and freshly ground **black pepper**

2 **garlic cloves**, coarsely chopped

1 tbsp chopped **thyme leaves**

400g can **chopped tomatoes**

300g can **green lentils**, drained and rinsed

2 tbsp chopped **flat-leaf parsley**

2 **eggs**, lightly beaten

300g (10oz) **Greek-style yogurt**

pinch of **paprika**

85g (3oz) **feta cheese**, crumbled

2 tbsp **white sesame seeds**

1 **Preheat the oven** to 220°C (425°F/Gas 7). Place the aubergine, courgettes, onions, and red peppers into a roasting tin. Drizzle over the olive oil, toss together to coat the vegetables evenly, then season to taste with salt and pepper.

2 **Roast for 10 minutes**, toss, add the garlic and thyme, and roast for a further 30–35 minutes, or until the vegetables are tender. Reduce the temperature to 180°C (350°F/Gas 4).

3 **Stir the tomatoes** with their juices, the lentils, and the parsley into the roast vegetables. Taste and adjust the seasoning, if necessary. Transfer the vegetables to a 23cm (9in) square ovenproof serving dish.

4 **Beat the eggs** and yogurt with the paprika, and season to taste with salt and pepper. Spread the mixture over the vegetables, and sprinkle the feta cheese on top. Put the dish on a baking tray and bake for 40 minutes. Sprinkle with the sesame seeds and bake for 10 minutes, or until the top is golden. Leave to stand for at least 2 minutes, then serve while still warm.

● **Good with** a mixed green salad on the side, and crusty country-style bread for mopping up the juices.

Vegetable Tempura

Making the batter with plain flour and iced water helps to guarantee a delicate, light finish

- serves 4
- prep 10–20 mins
  - cook 10 mins
- deep-fat fryer or large deep saucepan half filled with oil

750–900ml (1¼–1½ pints) **sunflower oil**, for deep-frying

200g (7oz) **plain flour**

450ml (16fl oz) **iced water**

1 **egg yolk**

selection of **crisp vegetables**, such as broccoli, carrots, French beans, and spring onions, trimmed and thinly sliced, or chopped as required

For the dipping sauce

2 tbsp **sake**

2 tbsp **soy sauce**

2 tbsp **caster sugar**

strips of **spring onion**, to garnish

● **Prepare ahead** The dipping sauce can be made up to 2 days in advance and stored in the refrigerator, covered, until required.

1 **To make the dipping sauce**, put the sake, soy sauce, sugar, and 2 tbsp water in a small bowl, mix together, then set aside.

2 **Pour in oil** to a depth of 7.5cm (3in) in a heavy saucepan and place over a medium-high heat to 190°C (375°F), or until a cube of day-old bread browns in less than 1 minute. Meanwhile, lightly whisk together the flour, iced water, and egg yolk in a bowl. The batter should remain lumpy, which is what makes the tempura light.

3 **Dip the vegetable** pieces into the batter in batches, letting any excess batter drip back into the bowl. Drop the battered vegetables into the hot oil and deep-fry for 1–2 minutes on each side, or until golden brown. Use a slotted spoon to remove them from the pan and drain well on kitchen paper. Keep warm while frying the remaining vegetables.

4 **Serve immediately** with small individual bowls of the dipping sauce.

Aubergine Parmigiana

This is one of Italy's most popular dishes and a great choice for vegetarians

- serves 4
- prep 40 mins • cook 30 mins
- shallow, ovenproof serving dish
- freeze, assembled in an ovenproof dish for up to 1 month; bake as in step 4

2 large **eggs**

salt and freshly ground **black pepper**

45g (1½oz) **plain white flour**

2 **aubergines**, thinly sliced lengthways

4 tbsp **sunflower oil**

600ml (1 pint) **tomato sauce**

60g (2oz) **Parmesan cheese**, grated

bunch of **basil** (reserve a few leaves, to garnish)

300g (10oz) **mozzarella cheese**, sliced

● **Prepare ahead** Steps 1 and 2 can be done a day in advance. Or, the entire dish can be assembled a day in advance and baked just before ready to serve.

1 **Preheat the oven** to 160°C (325°F/Gas 3). Beat the eggs in a shallow bowl and season with salt and pepper. Put the flour on a plate. Coat an aubergine slice in the flour, shaking off the excess, then tip it into the egg and let the excess drip back into the bowl. Repeat with the remaining slices.

2 **Heat the oil** in a large frying pan over a medium heat. Working in batches if necessary, fry the aubergine slices for 5 minutes on each side, or until golden. Drain well on kitchen paper, then continue until all the slices are fried.

3 **Layer the tomato sauce**, aubergine slices, Parmesan, basil leaves, and mozzarella in a shallow ovenproof serving dish. Continue layering until all the ingredients are used, finishing with a layer of tomato sauce and the cheese on top. Season to taste with salt and pepper.

4 **Place the dish** on a baking tray and bake for 30 minutes, or until the sauce is bubbling and the cheese has melted. Top with extra basil leaves and serve hot.

● **Good with** a simple salad as a main meal, or as a side dish for grilled meats.

VARIATION

Courgette Parmigiana

Substitute the same weight of aubergines with courgettes thickly sliced lengthways.

Leek and Cheese Flamiche

This puff pastry savoury tart comes from the Burgundy and Picardy regions of France

serves 6

prep 30 mins • cook 45 mins

freeze for up to 1 month

400g (14oz) puff pastry

45g (1½oz) butter

500g (1lb 2oz) leeks, sliced

150g (5½oz) cream cheese

4 tbsp double cream

2 tbsp chopped chives

60g (2oz) Parmesan cheese, grated

pinch of nutmeg

freshly ground black pepper

1 egg yolk, beaten

● **Prepare ahead** This can be made up to 2 days in advance, covered in cling film and chilled.

1 Preheat the oven to 200°C (400°F/Gas 6). Line a large baking tray with greaseproof paper. Cut the pastry in half and roll each piece into a 30 x 20cm (12 x 8in) rectangle. Place 1 piece on the baking tray and chill. Wrap the remaining piece in cling film and chill.

2 Melt the butter in a frying pan, add the leeks, and cook gently, stirring occasionally, for 15 minutes. Remove the pan from the heat and leave to cool.

3 Mix the cream cheese, cream, chives, Parmesan, nutmeg, and a pinch of pepper together and stir into the leeks. Remove the pastry from the fridge, spread the leek mixture across the base, leaving a 2cm (¾in) border of pastry all around the edge. Brush the border with egg yolk.

4 Place the pastry lid on top and pinch the edges together to seal. Brush the top with egg yolk. Make a few small cuts in the centre of the pie to allow steam to escape, and decorate the top with the point of a knife in a criss-cross pattern. Bake for 30 minutes, or until golden. Allow the flamiche to cool for 10 minutes before serving.

● **Good with** a leafy green salad, or a tomato and onion salad.

Squash and Gorgonzola Tart

This works well with either type of Gorgonzola cheese. Dolce is creamy and piccante is firm with a fuller flavour

serves 6

prep 25 mins, plus chilling • cook 1 hr 30 mins

20cm (8in) loose-bottomed flan tin, baking beans

freeze the unbaked pastry case for up to 1 month

225g (8oz) plain flour

115g (4oz) butter, chilled

iced water

450g (1lb) squash, peeled and seeds removed

olive oil

400g (14oz) spinach

2 large eggs

1 egg yolk

300ml (10fl oz) double cream

50g (1¾oz) Parmesan cheese, grated

nutmeg, grated

salt and freshly ground black pepper

115g (4oz) Gorgonzola, crumbled

1 For the pastry, put the flour and butter into a food processor and pulse until it resembles breadcrumbs. Add just enough iced water to bind the pastry, roll it out, and line the tin. Chill for 30 minutes.

2 Preheat the oven to 180°C (350°F/Gas 4). Prick the bottom of the tart case, line it with a circle of greaseproof paper, and add baking beans. Bake blind for 10 minutes, remove the paper and beans, and let it bake for another 10 minutes to crisp.

3 Slice the squash into thick slices, put on a roasting tray and brush lightly with olive oil. Bake for 30 minutes, or until tender. Meanwhile, place the spinach and a little olive oil in a saucepan and cook over a medium heat for 4 minutes. Drain and leave to cool. Whisk the eggs, egg yolk, cream, Parmesan, and nutmeg together and season to taste with salt and pepper.

4 Squeeze the spinach dry and spread it across the bottom of the tart case, then add slices of squash and crumble over the Gorgonzola. Pour in the egg mixture and bake for 30–40 minutes, or until the filling is set. Remove from the oven and leave it to sit for 10 minutes before serving.

Potatoes

Potatoes are one of the most versatile ingredients in the kitchen. They are cheap to buy, can be cooked in a variety of ways, and are always popular. The selection of main-crop and new potatoes provides plenty of variety throughout the year.

Choosing Potatoes

Potatoes come in many shapes, sizes, and colours, but they are all, to varying degrees, either floury or waxy, both of which are best suited to different cooking techniques. Waxy potatoes hold their shape when cooked, making them ideal for boiling for salads or serving hot with butter and salt and pepper. Floury potatoes become soft and fluffy, so they are great for baking, frying, and mashing. Always buy firm potatoes with smooth skins without green patches, mould, or sprouts.

Storing

Potatoes should be stored in a cool, dark place, ideally not the refrigerator, because if they are exposed to light they develop green patches, which can be poisonous. Remove potatoes from plastic bags that can cause mould to develop.

ALL-ROUNDER POTATOES

Vivaldi
With a creamy texture and buttery flavour, this potato makes excellent gratins. It is also popular with dieters because it contains less carbohydrate than most potatoes.

Sweet Potato
These come with white or orange flesh and have a rich, sweet flavour. Sweet potatoes are not a true potato, but can be cooked like any other all-round potato.

Desirée
An easily identified red-skinned potato, this has a texture that falls between floury and waxy. It can be baked, boiled, fried, and mashed.

Mayan Gold
The buttery yellow flesh is as intense as the flavour of this quick-cooking potato. Especially good roasted and fried.

FLOURY POTATOES

King Edward
This popular main-crop potato makes great mash, chips, and roast potatoes. It is also good for serving boiled.

Maris Piper
A favourite with a soft, creamy flesh that makes great chips, mash, and jacket potatoes.

Arran Victory
Named to celebrate the end of WW1, this potato has a distinctive purple-blue skin and a delicious white flesh. It is best mashed and roasted.

WAXY POTATOES

Anya
A relatively recent hybrid of new potatoes, Anya is recognized by its long, knobbly thumb shape. It has a rich flavour and smooth texture.

Charlotte
This small, oblong waxy potato is favoured for its fine flavour. Best boiled or sliced and pan-fried, it also makes excellent salads.

Jersey Royal
A new potato, with a short season from April to June, this is especially valued for its flavour. Good for boiling and serving in salads.

Nicola
This small waxy potato is oval with a smooth, creamy skin and pale yellow flesh. It is best simply boiled.

Vales Emerald
A cross between Maris Piper and Charlotte, it is a flavourful, small, round potato. Serve it scrubbed and boiled with plenty of butter, or chopped in salads.

Scrub

Many recipes call for unpeeled potatoes, in which case they need to be scrubbed first. Wash them in water, lightly rubbing with a small vegetable brush to remove any dirt. Be very careful not to tear the skin.

Peel

Potatoes can be peeled before or after cooking; if cooked first, leave them until cool enough to handle before peeling. Hold the potato firmly in 1 hand and use a vegetable peeler or paring knife to cut off the skin in long strips.

Slice

Firmly hold the potato on a cutting board with one hand and hold a chef's knife in your other hand. Cut downwards into slices as thick or thin as required. Cut slices to the same thickness so they cook evenly.

Chip

The first step to good, chunky chips is cutting large, floury potatoes into slices 1cm (½in) thick. Stack several slices on top of each other and then cut into chips about 7.5cm (3in) long.

Dice

Dices are equal-sized cubes. Stack slices (see above) on top of each other and cut lengthways to the desired thickness. Turn the stack 45 degrees and cut crossways into equal-sized cubes.

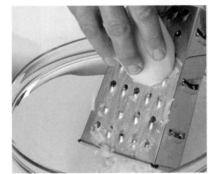

Grate

Both cooked and uncooked potatoes can be grated, most frequently for pan-frying as potato pancakes. Rub the potatoes downwards over the coarse holes on a grater into a bowl.

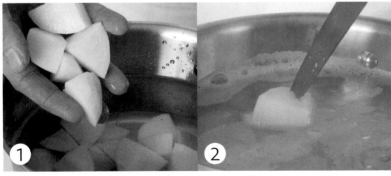

Boil

1 **Potatoes can be boiled** peeled or unpeeled. Cut the potatoes into equal-sized pieces and put them into a pan with lightly salted cold water to cover. Cover the pan tightly, place over a high heat, and bring the water to the boil.

2 **As soon as the water** boils, reduce the heat slightly, uncover the pan, and leave the potatoes to gently boil until they offer no resistance when tested with the tip of a knife and easily slide off the knife.

Mash

1 **Boil the potatoes** (see above) until they are tender. Drain them in a colander, shaking off any excess water. Return the potatoes to the pan. Add butter, cream, and salt, pepper, and nutmeg to taste. Re-cover the pan and leave for 5 minutes.

2 **Using a potato masher**, mash the potatoes until they are smooth and fluffy. Adjust the seasoning and add extra butter and cream, if desired. Keep hot until ready to serve.

Potatoes

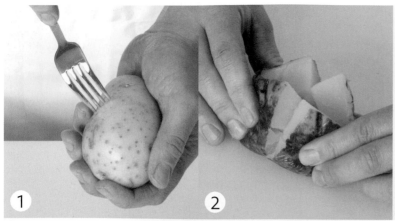

Bake

1 Preheat the oven to 220°C (425°F/Gas 7). Scrub unpeeled, large floury potatoes, such as King Edward, and pat dry completely. Prick all over with a fork to speed up the cooking time, then rub with olive or sunflower oil.

2 Place the potatoes directly on the oven shelf and roast for 1 hour, or until they feel soft when squeezed or pierced with a knife. Remove the potatoes from the oven, cut a large, deep "X" in the top, and squeeze open. Add the topping of your choice and serve hot.

Deep-fry

1 For twice-fried golden potatoes, heat enough oil for deep-frying in a deep-fat fryer to 160°C (325°F). Add the chips and fry for 5–6 minutes, or until lightly coloured. Remove the potatoes from the hot fat, drain well, and leave to cool.

2 Reheat the oil to 180°C (350°F). Deep-fry the potatoes again for 1–2 minutes, or until crisp and golden brown all over. Remove from the oil and drain well on folded kitchen paper. Sprinkle with salt and serve hot.

Roast

1 Peel and cut the potatoes into equal-sized pieces. Put in a pan with lightly salted cold water to cover and boil (p231) for 10 minutes. Drain the potatoes well and set aside until cool enough to handle. Using a fork, score the potatoes all over.

2 Meanwhile, preheat the oven to 200°C (400°F/Gas 6) with a roasting pan with a thin layer of vegetable oil or duck fat inside. Turn the potatoes in the hot fat to coat, then roast for 1 hour, or until crisp. Use tongs or a large fork to remove the potatoes from the pan and drain on kitchen paper. Sprinkle with salt and serve hot.

Pan-fry

1 Heat a thin layer of sunflower or olive oil in a frying pan over a medium-high heat until hot. Reduce the heat to medium, add as many potato slices that will fit in a single layer, and fry for 8–10 minutes, or until the bottoms are golden.

2 Using a fish slice or spatula and a knife, turn the potato slices over and fry for 5 minutes, or until both sides are golden and tender when tested with the tip of a knife. Drain the potatoes on kitchen paper, season to taste with salt, and serve hot.

PAN-FRIED POTATOES

Leftover potatoes are perfect sliced and pan-fried in olive oil with garlic and herbs.

Stuffed Potatoes with Cheese and Bacon

Significantly reduce the cooking time of this filling dish by using leftover jacket potatoes

🕑 1 hr 50 mins   **page 38**

Potato Salad with Parma Ham

Any variety of cooked new potato can be used in this chunky Italian-style salad

🕑 35 mins   **page 117**

Potato and Parmesan Cakes

The sharp taste of Parmesan cheese enlivens the flavour of leftover mashed potatoes

🕑 40 mins   **page 245**

Shepherd's Pie

The topping is leek-flavoured mash, but any mashed potatoes can be used

🕑 1 hr   **page 344**

Carrot and Parsnip Purée with Tarragon

This rich, creamy pureé can be made lighter by using vegetable stock instead of milk or double cream

 serves 4

🕐 prep 10 mins • cook 10-15 mins

📦 blender or food processor

5 large **carrots**, peeled and chopped

2 large **parsnips**, peeled and chopped

1 large **baking potato**, such as King Edward, chopped

1 tbsp **olive oil**

100ml (3½fl oz) **full-fat milk** or double cream

2 tsp chopped **tarragon**

salt and freshly ground **white pepper**

⬤ **Prepare ahead** The purée can be made a day in advance and gently reheated; stir in a little extra milk or cream if the consistency is too thick.

1 **Bring a large saucepan** of lightly salted water to the boil over a high heat. Add the carrots and boil for 5 minutes, then add the parsnips and potatoes, bring back to the boil, then reduce the heat and simmer for 5 minutes longer, or until the vegetables are very tender.

2 **Drain well**, shaking off any excess water.

3 **Put the vegetables** and olive oil in a blender or food processor and blend to a purée. With the motor running, add the milk or cream.

4 **Transfer to a heated bowl**, stir in the tarragon and season to taste with salt and pepper. Serve hot.

⬤ **Good with** roasted or grilled meats, poultry, and game.

Braised Red Cabbage with Apple

Most cabbage varieties are best cooked quickly but red cabbage is an exception, benefiting from long, slow cooking

🍴 serves 4

🕐 prep 10 mins • cook 1hr 25 mins-1 hr 40 mins

2 **streaky bacon rashers**, diced

1 **onion**, finely chopped

1 tbsp **sugar**

1 large **tart apple**, peeled, cored, and chopped

900g (2lb) **red cabbage**, quartered, cored, and shredded crossways

60ml (2fl oz) **red wine vinegar**

salt

1 **In a large frying pan** or flameproof casserole, over low heat, fry the bacon until it renders its fat. Add the onion and cook for about 5 minutes, or until softened. Add the sugar and cook for 5 minutes, until the mixture is golden, then add the apple. Cover and cook, stirring from time to time, for 3-4 minutes.

2 **Add the cabbage** to the pan. Toss to coat thoroughly with the bacon fat, then stir in the vinegar and toss together. Cover the pan and cook over a low heat for 10 minutes, or until the cabbage changes colour.

3 **Add salt to taste** and 150ml (5fl oz) water. Cover and simmer over a medium-low heat, stirring occasionally, for 1-1¼ hours, or until the cabbage is very tender. Add a little more water, if necessary, to prevent the cabbage from drying out. Just before serving, season to taste with salt. Serve hot.

⬤ **Good with** all roast meats, particularly pork, duck, and venison.

Courgettes in Batter

Crisp and delicious, you could make a double batch of these fritters for a party platter

serves 4

prep 15 mins • cook 15 mins

2 **courgettes**, sliced diagonally

1 sachet (¼oz) **active dried yeast**

60g (2oz) **plain flour**

150ml (5fl oz) **sunflower oil**

salt and freshly ground **black pepper**

1 **Stir the yeast** into 250ml (8fl oz) warm water in a small bowl and set aside for 10 minutes, or until foamy.

2 **Combine the flour** with salt and pepper to taste in a large bowl and make a well in the centre. Pour the yeast liquid into the well and gradually incorporate the flour to form a batter.

3 **Heat the oil** in a large frying pan or wok over a medium heat. Working in batches to avoid overcrowding the pan, dip the courgette slices in the batter and fry them for 5 minutes on each side, or until golden.

4 **Drain the fried courgette** slices on kitchen paper and sprinkle with salt. Transfer to a heated serving dish and serve immediately.

● **Good with** a little dish of your favourite dipping sauce, such as a sweet chilli sauce, tomato ketchup, barbecue sauce or a mixture of soy sauce and vinegar. These bite-sized fritters are delicious as an appetizer and also make a good side dish to grilled or fried white fish or chicken.

Grilled Vegetables

Perfect for summer, these vegetables are easy to prepare and go well with any main dish

serves 4

prep 20 mins, plus marinating • cook 4–6 mins

large, non-metallic dish, heat-resistant pastry brush

2 **courgettes**, halved lengthways

1 large **red pepper**, quartered lengthways and deseeded

1 large **yellow pepper**, quartered lengthways and deseeded

1 large **aubergine**, sliced

1 **fennel bulb**, quartered lengthways

120ml (4fl oz) **olive oil**, plus extra for brushing

3 tbsp **balsamic vinegar**

2 **garlic cloves**, chopped

4 tbsp coarsely chopped, **flat-leaf parsley**, plus extra to serve

salt and freshly ground **black pepper**

● **Prepare ahead** The vegetables can marinate for up to 4 hours. Or, cook the vegetables a day in advance and serve at room temperature.

1 **Arrange the vegetables**, cut-side up, in a large non-metallic dish. Whisk together the oil, vinegar, garlic and parsley, and season to taste with salt and pepper. Spoon over the vegetables and leave to marinate for at least 30 minutes.

2 **Light the barbecue** or preheat the grill on its highest setting. Grease the grill rack.

3 **Lift the vegetables** out of the marinade and place them on the barbecue or under the grill for 3–5 minutes on each side, or until tender and lightly charred, brushing with any extra marinade. Serve sprinkled with parsley, with any remaining marinade spooned over.

Corn on the Cob

A herb and garlic butter makes a flavourful coating for this popular vegetable

🍴 serves 8

🕐 prep 10 mins • cook 15 mins

8 corn cobs

salt and freshly ground black pepper

For the herb butter

125g (4½oz) butter, softened

1 tsp Dijon mustard

juice of ½ small lemon

1 garlic clove, finely chopped

1 shallot, finely chopped

1 tbsp snipped chives

1 tbsp chopped parsley

1 tbsp chopped basil

1 tbsp chopped mint

1 Make the herb butter. In a medium bowl, combine all the ingredients together until well mixed. Transfer the butter to a sheet of greaseproof paper and mould it into a roll. Wrap the roll with the paper and twist the ends to seal. Chill in the refrigerator until the butter becomes firm enough to slice.

2 Just before cooking the corn, bring a large pan of water to the boil. Remove the husks and the silky threads from the corn and discard. Add the corn to the boiling water and cover the pan.

3 Once the water has returned to the boil, turn off the heat and let the corn stand, covered, for 5 minutes to continue cooking.

4 Carefully remove the corn with kitchen tongs and place on a serving platter. Cut the butter into 8 slices and place 1 slice on each cob.

Ratatouille

This popular Mediterranean dish is delicious hot or cold

🍴 serves 4

🕐 prep 15 mins • cook 40 mins

4 tbsp olive oil

1 onion, chopped

1 garlic clove, chopped

1 courgette, sliced

1 small aubergine, about 225g (8oz), cut into 2.5cm (1in) cubes

1 red pepper, cored, seeded and cut into 2.5cm (1in) pieces

150ml (5½fl oz) vegetable stock

400g (14oz) can chopped tomatoes

2 tsp chopped oregano, plus 2–3 sprigs to serve

salt and freshly ground black pepper

1 Heat the oil in a large casserole over moderate heat. Add the onion and cook for 5 minutes, until soft and transparent. Stir in the garlic, courgette, aubergine, and red pepper, and fry for 5 minutes, stirring.

2 Add the stock, tomatoes with their juice, and the chopped oregano to the casserole and bring the mixture to the boil. Reduce the heat to low and partially cover the pan. Cook until the vegetables are tender, stirring occasionally.

3 Season to taste with salt and black pepper. Spoon the ratatouille into a serving bowl and serve immediately, garnished with oregano sprigs, or cover and refrigerate then serve cold.

● **Good with** a bowl of grated cheese for sprinkling, if served hot, or a bottle of fruity olive oil for drizzling, if served cold.

Roasted Acorn Squash

This winter squash has sweet, slightly fibrous flesh

 serves 4

prep 10 mins
•cook 35 mins

2 acorn squashes, halved and deseeded

25g (scant 1oz) butter, softened

4 tsp light soft brown sugar

● **Prepare ahead** Steps 1 and 2 can be done several hours ahead.

1 Preheat the oven to 190°C (375°F/Gas 5). Brush the inside of each squash half with a quarter of the butter and sprinkle with 1 tsp of the brown sugar.

2 Place the halves, cut sides up, in an ovenproof dish large enough to hold them upright, and add water to a depth of 2.5cm (1in).

3 Place the dish in the oven and roast for 35 minutes. About midway through cooking, spoon the butter and sugar mixture over the flesh. Continue cooking until the squash are browned on top and tender when pricked with a knife.

● **Good with** roast meat, especially roast loin of pork or baked ham.

● **Leftovers** can be made into a soup or reheated.

Baked Courgettes

A tasty but easy-to-prepare accompaniment

serves 4

prep 5 mins • cook 15 mins

4 small courgettes, washed and halved lengthways

1 tbsp olive oil

2 garlic cloves, very finely chopped

50g (1¾oz) Parmesan cheese, grated

salt and freshly ground black pepper

● **Prepare ahead** Step 1 can be prepared several hours in advance and the courgettes cooked when ready to serve.

1 Preheat the oven to 200°C (400°F/Gas 6). Arrange the courgettes, cut-sides up, in an ovenproof dish large enough to hold them in a single layer. Lightly brush with the olive oil, then sprinkle with the garlic, Parmesan cheese, and salt and pepper to taste.

2 Place the dish in the oven and bake for 15 minutes, or until the courgettes are tender and the cheese is browned.

● **Good with** roast leg of lamb.

Brussels Sprouts with Orange

Fresh orange zest along with orange and lime juice adds a burst of sunshine to this winter vegetable

serves 4

prep 15 mins, plus blanching • cook 7–8 mins

450g (1lb) Brussels sprouts

salt and freshly ground black pepper

25g (scant 1oz) butter

1 shallot, finely chopped

finely grated zest and juice of 1 orange

1 tbsp fresh lime juice

● **Prepare ahead** Steps 1 and 2 can be done several hours in advance. In which case, drain the sprouts, then immediately tip them into a bowl of iced water to stop the cooking process and preserve the fresh green colour.

1 Using a small knife, remove the outer leaves from the Brussels sprouts and cut an "x" into the bottom of each, as this helps the sprouts to cook evenly and quickly.

2 Bring a large saucepan of lightly salted water to the boil. Add the sprouts, return the water to the boil and boil for 8 minutes. Drain the sprouts well and set aside until cool enough to handle, then cut each in half and set aside.

3 Melt the butter in a large frying pan over a medium high heat. Add the shallot and fry, stirring, for 3–5 minutes until golden brown. Add the sprouts and continue to cook, stirring, until tender.

4 Add the orange zest and juice and stir for 2 minutes or until the liquid is reduced by half. Remove from the heat and season with salt and pepper to taste, then add the lime juice. Serve hot.

● **Good with** roasts, such as turkey, ham, or pork.

● **Leftovers** can be cut into thin slices and added to salad leaves for a green salad with a twist.

Cauliflower Cheese

A great comfort food side dish that works equally well as a vegetarian main course

serves 4–6

prep 15 mins • cook 15 mins

1 head of **cauliflower**, outer leaves removed, separated into large florets

salt and freshly ground **black pepper**

100g (3½ oz) fresh **breadcrumbs**

For the cheese sauce

30g (1oz) **butter**, diced

3 tbsp **plain white** or wholemeal **flour**

1½ tsp **mustard powder**

450ml (15fl oz) **milk**

125g (4½oz) **mature Cheddar cheese**, grated

1 Bring a large saucepan of salted water to the boil. Add the cauliflower florets and boil for 7 minutes, or until just tender. Drain well and rinse with cold water to stop the cooking. Arrange the florets in an ovenproof serving dish.

2 Preheat the grill on its highest setting. To make the cheese sauce, melt the butter in a pan over a low heat, add the flour and mustard powder, and stir to combine. Cook for 2 minutes, stirring all the time. Remove from the heat, add the milk, and stir constantly until smooth. Return to the heat and bring slowly to the boil, then reduce the heat and simmer to thicken for 1–2 minutes. Remove the pan from the heat and stir in three-quarters of the cheese until melted. Season to taste with salt and pepper, then pour the sauce over the florets.

3 Toss the remaining cheese with the breadcrumbs and sprinkle over the florets. Place the dish under the grill for 10 minutes, or until the sauce bubbles and the top is golden. Serve hot from the dish.

● **Good with** any roast meat, grilled bacon or sausages.

● **Leftovers** can be refrigerated for up to 1 day and reheated in an oven preheated to 180°C (350°F/Gas 4), covered with foil, shiny-side down.

VARIATION

Herb Cauliflower Cheese

For a crispy, herby topping, fry the breadcrumbs in a little oil until crisp and golden. Add a handful of chopped herbs, such as flat-leaf parsley, chives, and thyme, stir well with the remaining cheese, and sprinkle over the cauliflower just before baking.

Braised Chicory with Thyme

Slow cooking chicory reduces its natural bitterness

serves 4

prep 5 mins • cook 30 mins

2 tbsp **olive oil**

4 heads of **chicory**

1 **shallot**, chopped

2 sprigs of **thyme**

1 **bay leaf**

salt and freshly ground **black pepper**

1 Heat the oil in a large deep frying pan over a medium heat. Add the chicory heads, shallot, and bay leaf and fry for 2 minutes, or until they are golden on both sides, turning the chicory heads.

2 Add 2 tbsp water, then reduce the heat to low, cover the pan, and leave to simmer for 20–25 minutes, or until the chicory heads are tender when pierced with a knife. Season to taste with salt and pepper, then serve with the pan juices spooned over, and garnished with the fresh sprigs of thyme.

● **Good with** grilled lamb chops, or sliced and tossed with orange segments and vinaigrette dressing to make a salad.

Chickpeas with Spinach

Chickpeas are widely used in Spain as a basis for a variety of stews such as this one

serves 4

prep 15 mins • cook 10 mins

3 tbsp olive oil

1 thick slice of crusty white bread, torn into breadcrumbs

750g (1lb 10oz) spinach leaves

240g can chickpeas, rinsed and drained

2 garlic cloves, finely chopped

salt and freshly ground black pepper

1 tsp paprika

1 tsp ground cumin

1 tbsp sherry vinegar

1 **Heat 1 tbsp** of oil in a frying pan and fry the bread, stirring, until crisp. Remove from the pan, drain on kitchen paper, and reserve.

2 **Rinse the spinach** and shake off any excess water. Place it in a large saucepan and cook over a low heat, tossing constantly so it does not stick to the pan. When it has wilted, transfer the spinach to a colander and squeeze out as much water as possible by pressing it with a wooden spoon, then place on a chopping board and chop coarsely.

3 **Heat the remaining** oil in the frying pan, add the spinach and allow it to warm through before stirring in the chickpeas. Season to taste with salt and pepper. Add the paprika and cumin, then crumble the reserved fried bread into the mixture.

4 **Add the vinegar** and 2 tbsp water and allow to heat through for several minutes. Divide between 4 small serving dishes or ramekins and serve immediately.

Pak Choi with Oyster Sauce

Baby pak choi look more attractive but regular pak choi can be used if cut into thick slices before cooking

serves 4

prep 10 mins • cook 5 mins

wok

500g (1lb 2oz) baby pak choi, halved

1 tbsp vegetable oil

2.5cm (1in) piece of fresh root ginger, peeled and grated

2 garlic cloves, chopped

3 tbsp oyster sauce

1 tbsp light soy sauce

1 tbsp rice wine or dry sherry

pinch of sugar

120ml (4fl oz) chicken stock

2 tsp cornflour

1 **Bring a large** saucepan of water to the boil, add the pak choi and blanch for 1 minute. Drain and cool in cold water to preserve their colour.

2 **Heat the oil** in a wok, add the ginger and garlic and stir-fry for 30 seconds. Add the pak choi and stir-fry for 1 minute.

3 **Mix together the** oyster sauce, soy sauce, rice wine, sugar, chicken stock, and cornflour until smooth. Pour into the wok and stir until the sauce has thickened and coats the pak choi. Transfer to a serving plate and serve at once.

● **Good with** a variety of Chinese dishes, this also makes a good side dish alongside grilled meat or fish.

● **Prepare ahead** Step 1 can be completed several hours in advance.

Peas with Lettuce

This traditional French dish is often made with tinned petit pois when fresh tender baby peas are not available

🍴 serves 4–6

🕐 prep 10 mins • cook 10 mins

250g (9oz) **button onions**

75g (2½oz) **butter**, softened

500g (1lb 2oz) **shelled peas** or frozen petit pois

120ml (4fl oz) **ham stock** or water

1 tsp **sugar**

salt and freshly ground **black pepper**

1 tbsp **plain flour**

2 tbsp finely chopped **mint** or parsley

2 **lettuce hearts**, such as Little Gem, trimmed and finely shredded

⬤ **Prepare ahead** Step 1 can be completed several hours ahead. Refrigerate until ready to use.

1 Put the onions in a bowl and cover with boiling water. Drain, and remove the skins, keeping the root of the onion intact.

2 Melt 50g (1¾oz) of the butter in a large saucepan and add the onions. Cook over a medium heat for 2 minutes.

3 Add the peas and stock and bring to the boil. Skim off any sediment, then add the sugar and season to taste with salt and pepper. Lower the heat and simmer for a further 5–8 minutes.

4 Mix the remaining butter to a smooth paste with the flour. Gradually add this mixture to the peas, stirring to thicken the sauce. Stir continuously until it has been completely incorporated and there are no lumps.

5 Stir in the mint and shredded lettuce, transfer to a serving dish, and serve immediately.

⬤ **Good with** hot or cold boiled ham dishes; this recipe is a good way to use up ham stock. It also makes a lovely accompaniment for roast or grilled lamb.

Glazed Shallots with Red Wine

Shallots are particularly associated with the cooking of Burgundy and Normandy in France

🍴 serves 4

🕐 prep 10 mins • cook 40 mins

❄️ freeze for up to 3 months

60g (2oz) **butter**

450g (1lb) small **shallots**, trimmed

360ml (12fl oz) **Burgundy red wine**

2 tbsp **red wine vinegar**

1 tsp **caster sugar**

salt

1 sprig of **thyme**

1 **bay leaf**

⬤ **Prepare ahead** The shallots can be prepared a few hours in advance, and gently reheated before serving.

1 Heat a wide, shallow saucepan and add 30g (1oz) butter and the shallots. Cook over medium heat until golden, turning occasionally.

2 Add the wine, vinegar, sugar, salt, thyme, and bay leaf. Simmer over a low heat for 30 minutes, or until tender.

3 Transfer the shallots to a serving bowl, using a slotted spoon. Allow the liquid in the pan to bubble over a high heat until syrupy, then whisk in the remaining butter.

4 Discard the thyme sprig and bay leaf, and pour the sauce over the shallots. Serve immediately.

⬤ **Good with** steaks, beef fillet, or grilled duck breasts.

Mixed Root Vegetable Gratin

A creamy, warming cheese-topped dish

🍴 serves 4–6

🕐 prep 10 mins • cook 1 hr

🍲 25cm (10in) ovenproof gratin dish

butter, for greasing

200g (7oz) parsnips, peeled and thinly sliced

200g (7oz) potatoes, peeled and thinly sliced

200g (7oz) celeriac, peeled and thinly sliced

150ml (5fl oz) milk

450ml (15fl oz) double cream

1 garlic clove, crushed

salt and freshly ground black pepper

pinch of nutmeg

60g (2oz) Gruyère cheese, grated

1 **Preheat the oven** to 180°C (350°F/Gas 4). Butter the gratin dish; arrange parsnips in it, overlapping with a neat layer of potato, followed by the celeriac.

2 **Mix the milk**, cream, and garlic together, season with salt, pepper, and nutmeg, and pour over the vegetables. Scatter the cheese and bake for 1 hour, or until the vegetables are tender and golden.

Sweet Potato and Sage Gratin

This gratin is indulgent and warming: perfect comfort food

🍴 serves 6

🕐 prep 20 mins • cook 1 hr

🍲 24 x18 cm (9½ x 6¾in) ovenproof gratin dish

300ml (10fl oz) double cream or soured cream

2 pinches of nutmeg

2 tbsp chopped sage

salt and freshly ground black pepper

60g (2oz) butter, plus extra for greasing

1kg (2¼lb) sweet potatoes, peeled and thinly sliced

● **Prepare ahead** Make up to 2 days in advance, refrigerate, then reheat until piping hot before serving.

1 **Preheat the oven** to 200°C (400°F/Gas 6). Whisk the cream with the nutmeg and sage. Season with salt and pepper. Butter the gratin dish and put a layer of sweet potato slices on the bottom. Cover with a layer of the cream mixture. Repeat until all the potato and cream are used up, ending with a layer of cream, then dot with butter.

2 **Cover with foil** and bake for 1 hour, or until completely soft when tested with a sharp knife.

● **Good with** roast lamb, chicken, beef, or cold, cooked ham.

VARIATION

Gruyère Gratin

Scatter Gruyère cheese over the top and serve with a crisp salad for a vegetarian main course.

Potato-Herb Galette

A good accompaniment for roasted and grilled meats

🍴 serves 6

🕐 prep 20 mins • cook 25 mins

450g (1lb) potatoes, peeled, boiled, drained, and cooled

1 small onion, finely chopped

good handful of herbs, such as parsley, thyme, and chives

pinch of nutmeg

1 egg

2 tbsp flour

salt and freshly ground black pepper

olive oil or sunflower oil, for frying

● **Prepare ahead** This can be made up to 4 hours in advance.

1 **Preheat the oven** to 180°C (350°F/Gas 4). Grate the potatoes and combine with all the remaining ingredients except the oil.

2 **Put a little oil** in the frying pan and, once hot, add the potato mixture, pressing it to make 1 thick potato pancake. Cook over a medium heat for 5 minutes, or until well browned. Place a baking tray on top of the pan, flip the galette over, then slide it back into the pan to brown the other side for 5 minutes. Place in the oven for 15 minutes, or until cooked through. Serve immediately.

Ultimate Mashed Potatoes

Mash with a twist

🍴 serves 6

🕐 prep 10 mins • cook 45 mins

1.35kg (3 lbs) floury **potatoes**, such as King Edward or Maris Piper, peeled

2 tbsp **double cream**

2 tbsp **milk**

85g (3oz) **butter**

125g (4½oz) **Cheddar cheese**, grated

1 tbsp **horseradish**

4 **spring onions**, chopped

2 tbsp chopped **parsley**

2 tbsp chopped **chives**

salt and freshly ground **black pepper**

1 Cut the potatoes into even-sized pieces. Place in a large pan and cover with water. Bring to the boil, add a little salt, then cover and simmer for 25 minutes, or until the potatoes can be pierced easily with a skewer or knife.

2 Remove from the heat and drain well.

3 Place the hot potatoes back into the pan with the cream, milk, and butter. Mash with a potato masher. Add the remaining ingredients, mix well, and serve.

Potato Gratin

This regional French dish, *Gratin Dauphinoise*, is rich with cream and fragrant with garlic and nutmeg

🍴 serves 4–6

🕐 prep 15–20 mins • cook 1½ hrs

🍲 mandolin or food processor fitted with fine slicing blade, 21cm (8½ in) ovenproof gratin dish

45g (1½ oz) **butter**, at room temperature, plus extra for greasing

900g (2lb) even-sized **waxy potatoes**

salt and freshly ground **black pepper**

600ml (1 pint) **double cream**

1 **garlic clove**, cut in half

pinch of freshly **ground nutmeg**

⬤ **Prepare ahead** The potatoes can be peeled and sliced several hours in advance and left in water.

1 Preheat the oven to 180°C (350°F/Gas 4). Butter the ovenproof gratin dish.

2 Peel the potatoes and slice them into even rounds, 3mm (⅛in) thick. Use a mandolin or a food processor fitted with a fine slicing blade, if you have one. Rinse the potato slices in cold water, drain,

and pat dry with kitchen paper or a tea towel.

3 Arrange the potatoes in layers in the prepared ovenproof dish. Season with salt and pepper.

4 Bring the cream to the boil in a saucepan with the garlic and nutmeg, then pour the cream over the potatoes. Dot the top with a few knobs of butter.

5 Cover and place in the oven for about 1–1½ hours, or until the potatoes are tender. During the last 10 minutes of cooking, remove the cover and increase the heat to get a fine golden crust on the top. Serve hot, straight from the oven.

⬤ **Good with** salad for supper, or as a side dish with smoked fish, or grilled or roast meats.

VARIATION

Potato and Cheese Gratin

Add 2 finely chopped anchovies to the cream in step 4. Sprinkle 125g (4½oz) grated Gruyère cheese between the potato layers, saving a little for sprinkling on the top.

Roast Artichokes with Tomato and Garlic

This is such a simple accompaniment, but very colourful and tasty

🍴 serves 4

🕐 prep 5 mins • cook 1 hr

400g can **artichoke hearts**, drained and halved

8 small **plum tomatoes** on the vine

12 **garlic cloves**, unpeeled

2 tbsp **olive oil**

2 tsp **balsamic vinegar**

few sprigs of **thyme**

sea salt and freshly ground **black pepper**

1 Preheat the oven to 140°C (275°F/Gas 1).

2 Place the artichoke hearts in a roasting tray with the tomatoes, keeping them on the vine, and scatter the garlic cloves in the tray. Drizzle with the oil and balsamic vinegar, add the thyme, and season to taste with salt and pepper.

3 Roast for 1 hour, or until the vegetables are cooked, and serve.

⬤ **Good with** roast or grilled meats, fresh breads, and savoury tarts.

Roast Sweet Potato with Sesame Glaze

Roasting sweet potato brings out its natural sweetness

🍴 serves 6

🕐 prep 10 mins • cook 50 mins

5 orange **sweet potatoes**, peeled

2 tbsp **olive oil**

sea salt and freshly ground **black pepper**

1 tbsp **clear honey**

1 tbsp **light soy sauce**

2 tbsp **sesame seeds**

1 Preheat oven to 200°C (400°F/Gas 6). Cut the potatoes into large chunks and place on a roasting tray, drizzle with olive oil, and season with salt and pepper. Roast the potatoes for 30 minutes, turning halfway through, or until just tender.

2 Mix together the honey, soy sauce and sesame seeds, then add the potato chunks, toss until coated, and roast for a further 20 minutes, or until well coloured.

● **Good with** roast chicken or pork.

Carrot and Tarragon Timbales

The aromatic flavour of tarragon permeates these soft carrot-and-cheese custards

🍴 serves 4

🕐 prep 10 mins • cook 25 mins

🍲 ramekins

❄ freeze, in the ramekins, for up to 3 months

butter, for greasing

350g (12oz) **carrots**, peeled and coarsely grated

2 **eggs**, lightly beaten

175g (6oz) **Gruyère cheese**, grated

½ tsp made **English mustard**

2 tbsp **crème fraîche**

2 tbsp **tarragon**, finely chopped

freshly ground **black pepper**

● **Prepare ahead** The timbales can be assembled several hours in advance, and stored covered in the refrigerator until ready to bake.

1 Preheat the oven to 200°C (400°F/Gas 6). Butter the ramekins and line the bottoms with buttered greaseproof paper discs.

2 Put a medium saucepan half full of water on a high heat. When the water has come to a rolling boil, add the grated carrot for 30 seconds, then drain and rinse under cold running water. Use your hands to squeeze the carrot dry, then put it into a mixing bowl.

3 Stir the eggs, cheese, mustard, crème fraîche, and tarragon into the carrots and mix well. Season to taste with pepper and spoon the mixture into the prepared ramekins. Cover each ramekin with a circle of buttered greaseproof paper or wax paper.

4 Put the ramekins into a deep-sided roasting tin and add enough hot water to come halfway up the sides of the ramekins. Bake for 25 minutes, or until they are just set and firm on top.

5 Remove from the roasting tin and run a blunt knife around the sides of the timbales to loosen them. After removing the top sheet of paper from each timbale, put a small plate over the top of the ramekin and invert it. Remove the ramekin and the paper before serving.

● **Good with** a tomato salad as a starter, or as an accompaniment to roast chicken or roast beef.

VARIATION

Sweet Potato and Herb Timbale

Replace the carrot with sweet potatoes and use a milder cheese, such as Cheddar. Instead of using tarragon, try parsley, sage, or chives.

Mediterranean Vegetable Duo

This dish is best served at room temperature so the dressing can infuse the vegetables

🍴 serves 6

🕐 prep 15 mins, plus standing • cook 30 mins

▭ ridged cast-iron grill pan

2 **aubergines**, thinly sliced lengthways

salt and freshly ground **black pepper**

2 **garlic cloves**, peeled and chopped

1 tbsp **balsamic vinegar**

2 tbsp **extra virgin olive oil**, plus extra for brushing

4 **courgettes**, trimmed and sliced

mint leaves, to garnish

1 Sprinkle the aubergine slices with a little salt and set aside for 30 minutes.

2 Make the dressing by whisking together the garlic, vinegar, and oil, and season to taste with salt and pepper. Set aside.

3 Preheat the ridged grill pan until smoking hot. Brush the courgettes with a little oil, and season with salt and pepper. Grill the courgettes on both sides until tender. Transfer to a large serving bowl.

4 Rinse the aubergines and pat dry with kitchen paper. Brush both sides of the aubergines with oil and grill for several minutes on both sides. Add the aubergines to the courgettes and pour over the dressing. Toss in the mint leaves and leave for 15 minutes for the flavours to blend before serving.

● **Good with** barbecued, grilled, or roast meats.

Glazed Carrots with Thyme

These carrots are a good accompaniment to roast beef, pork, lamb, or poultry

🍴 serves 4

🕐 prep 10 mins • cook 15 mins

450g (1lb) **carrots**, cut across into thin slices

thinly pared zest and juice of 1 **orange**

25g (1oz) **butter**

1 tbsp **soft brown sugar**

1 **garlic clove**, crushed

salt and freshly ground **black pepper**

½ tsp **thyme leaves**

● **Prepare ahead** Complete to the end of step 2 several hours in advance, then finish cooking just before serving.

1 Place the carrots in a small saucepan with the orange zest and juice, butter, sugar, and garlic, and season to taste with salt and pepper. Add enough cold water to just cover the carrots.

2 Bring to the boil, then cover and cook over a moderate to high heat for about 8–10 minutes, or until the carrots are just tender.

3 Remove the lid and allow to bubble until all the liquid has evaporated and the carrots are glazed and golden at the edges, shaking the pan occasionally to prevent sticking. Just before serving, sprinkle over the thyme leaves.

● **Leftovers** can be finely chopped with fresh parsley and added to mashed potatoes.

Potato and Parmesan Cakes

These little cakes make a nice change from the usual mash

🍴 serves 4

🕐 prep 20 mins • cook 20 mins

750g (1lb 10oz) **floury potatoes**, such as Maris Piper, peeled and cut into chunks

1 large **egg yolk**

50g (1¾oz) **Parmesan cheese**, finely grated

salt and freshly ground **black pepper**

30g (1oz) **plain flour**

sunflower oil or vegetable oil, for frying

1 tbsp **capers**

1 **lemon**, cut into wedges

● **Prepare ahead** The cakes can be made 2–3 days in advance, then covered, and chilled in the refrigerator before cooking.

1 **Place the potatoes** in a pan of cold salted water, bring to the boil, and simmer for 15 minutes, or until tender. Drain well, then pass through a potato ricer or sieve set over a bowl. Alternatively, mash well.

2 **Add the egg yolk** and cheese to the potato, season to taste with salt and pepper, and mix. Divide into 8 equal balls and flatten into little cakes, each 5cm (2in) in diameter. Tip the flour on to a plate, season with salt and pepper, then coat the potato cakes in the flour and chill until needed.

3 **Pour enough oil** into a frying pan to cover the bottom of the pan and set it over a medium heat. Fry the potato cakes in batches for 2 minutes on each side, or until golden and hot. Remove from the pan and drain on kitchen paper.

4 **Increase the heat** and fry the capers for 45 seconds, or until crisp. Drain on kitchen paper. Lift the cakes on to warm plates, scatter the capers, and serve with lemon wedges.

Grilled Aubergines with Pomegranate Vinaigrette

Fresh pomegranate seeds enliven this warm salad

🍴 serves 6

🕐 prep 10 mins • cook 10 mins

🍳 ridged cast-iron grill pan

6 tbsp **olive oil**, plus extra for brushing

3 tbsp **pomegranate syrup**

3 tbsp chopped **coriander**

salt and freshly ground **black pepper**

3 large **aubergines**, cut into 1cm (½in) thick slices

2 **shallots**, very finely sliced

fresh **pomegranate seeds**, to garnish

1 **To make the vinaigrette**, whisk together the oil, pomegranate syrup, and chopped coriander, and season to taste with salt and pepper. Set aside until ready to serve.

2 **Preheat the grill** pan over a high heat. Brush both sides of the aubergine slices with olive oil, season to taste with salt and pepper, then grill on both sides until tender.

3 **Layer the aubergines** and shallots in a serving dish and pour over the vinaigrette. Scatter with fresh pomegranate seeds and serve.

VARIATION

Grilled Aubergines with Cheese and Pomegranate Vinaigrette

Use finely sliced red onion instead of the shallots and scatter with 60g (2oz) crumbled feta cheese to serve.

Potato Pancakes

What could be simpler than *latkes*, traditionally served with soured cream, apple sauce, or both

 serves 4

 prep 20 mins, plus standing • cook 30 mins

 low GI

4 large **potatoes**, grated

2 **onions**, grated or finely chopped

2 **eggs**, beaten

1–2 tbsp **matzo meal** or flour

salt and freshly ground **black pepper**

vegetable oil, for frying

apple sauce, to serve (optional)

soured cream, to serve (optional)

1 Place the grated potatoes in a sieve, rinse with cold water, and leave to drain for 10 minutes. Tip on to a clean tea towel or piece of muslin, and squeeze out as much liquid as possible.

2 Transfer the potatoes to a large bowl, add the onion and egg, and mix well. Stir in matzo meal and season with plenty of salt and pepper.

3 Heat 5mm (¼in) oil in a large frying pan and drop in tablespoonfuls of the mixture. Flatten each slightly with a spatula and fry over a medium heat for 3–4 minutes, or until browned on both sides and cooked through. Drain well on kitchen paper; keep warm. Repeat until all the mixture has been used.

4 Serve hot, with small bowls of apple sauce and soured cream on the side, if liked.

VARIATIONS

German Potato Pancakes
Reibeplatzchen or *Kartoffel Puffer* are made in a similar way. Save the water from draining the potatoes, carefully pour away the liquid, and add the starchy residue to the potato mixture, then add 1–2 tbsp flour or oats to bind. Serve with herb butters and smoked salmon for a starter, or with a generous sprinkling of sugar as a dessert.

Swedish Potato Pancakes
Raggmunk are similar pancakes but are fried in butter and usually served with fried salt pork and lingonberries. Use starchy potatoes for the best result. Whisk together 90g (3¼oz) plain flour and 360ml (12fl oz) milk, then stir in 800g (1¾lb) grated potatoes, and plenty of seasoning, but no onion. Melt 60g (2oz) butter in a frying pan and fry the pancakes, in batches if necessary, pressing them down flat, so they are thin and crisp.

Corn and Peppers

Colourful and popular with children, this is a good side dish for everyday meals

 serves 4

 prep 15 mins • cook 8 mins

4 **corn on the cob**

2 tbsp **butter**

2 **spring onions**, sliced

½ small **green pepper**, deseeded and diced

½ small **red pepper**, deseeded and diced

salt and freshly ground **black pepper**

1 Remove the husks and silks from the corn. Using a sharp knife, cut the corn kernels from the cobs. Break up any kernels that are stuck together.

2 In a large saucepan, melt the butter over medium heat. Add the corn, onions, green and red pepper, and 60ml (2fl oz) water. Bring the mixture to the boil and cook, stirring occasionally, for 5 minutes, or until the water has evaporated and the corn is tender. Season to taste with salt and pepper, and serve.

> ### USING CANNED OR FROZEN CORN
> If you are in a hurry, this recipe also works well with 225g (8oz) frozen corn or canned corn.

Sweet Potato Purée with Horseradish

Baking sweet potatoes makes them intensely sweet and full of flavour

🍴 serves 4–6

🕐 prep 10 mins
• cook 45 mins – 1 hr

❄️ freeze for up to 3 months

1.1kg (2½lb) whole **sweet potatoes**, pricked with a fork

salt and freshly ground **black pepper**

4 tbsp **olive oil**

150ml (5fl oz) **double cream**, plus extra for drizzling

1 tbsp **horseradish cream**

● **Prepare ahead** Complete the recipe up to 1 day in advance. Cool, cover, and chill until needed.

1 Preheat the oven to 220°C (425°F/Gas 7). Place the potatoes on a foil-lined baking tray and bake for 45 minutes to 1 hour, or until tender. Cool, then peel off the skins.

2 Put the cooked flesh into a food processor, season to taste with salt and pepper, and process to a purée. With the motor running, gradually add the oil and cream.

3 To serve, stir in the horseradish and drizzle extra cream on top.

Fennel Remoulade

This fresh-tasting Italian bulb works well with the creaminess of the sauce

🍴 serves 6

🕐 prep 15 mins

1 large **fennel bulb**

2 **shallots**, peeled and finely chopped

2 tbsp **flat-leaf parsley**, finely chopped

2 tbsp **tarragon**, finely chopped

2 tbsp **Dijon mustard**

1 tsp **capers**, rinsed

½ tbsp chopped **gherkins**

3 tbsp **mayonnaise**

juice of 1 **lemon**

salt and freshly ground **black pepper**

● **Prepare ahead** Combine the first 7 ingredients up to 1 day in advance. Chill until needed, then add the mayonnaise, lemon juice, and seasoning 1 hour before serving.

1 Remove the base and the tough outer leaves from the fennel. Shred the bulb very finely in a food processor or with a sharp knife.

2 Place the shredded fennel into a large bowl, mix well with the other ingredients, and season to taste with salt and pepper.

● **Good with** crab cakes, smoked fish, or cold meats.

VARIATION

Celeriac Remoulade

Blanch a celeriac in salted boiling water for 2 minutes. Drain, pat dry, and cut into fine strips. Use instead of the fennel.

Creamed Spinach with Pine Nuts

Make the most of fresh spinach when it's available for this versatile side dish

🍴 serves 4

🕐 prep 10 mins • cook 3–4 mins

675g (1½lb) fresh **spinach**

3 tbsp **crème fraîche**

½ tsp grated **nutmeg**

salt and freshly ground **black pepper**

60g (2oz) **pine nuts**, toasted

1 Pick over the spinach leaves, discarding any yellowing ones, and cut away any tough stalks. Rinse well in cold water and shake dry.

2 Place the spinach in a large saucepan, cover, and cook over a low heat for 3–4 minutes, until just wilted.

3 Stir in the crème fraîche and nutmeg, and season to taste with salt and black pepper.

4 Spoon into a serving dish, scatter the pine nuts on top, and serve at once.

● **Good with** roast meats, poultry, and full-flavoured fish, such as salmon, tuna, or smoked haddock.

Creamed Swede

This delicious and versatile vegetable purée can be served in place of mashed potatoes

🍴 serves 4–6

🕐 prep 10 mins • cook 25 mins

1.1kg (2½lb) **swede**, peeled and cut into chunks

salt and freshly ground **black pepper**

60g (2oz) **butter**

2–3 tbsp **double cream**

pinch of grated **nutmeg**

● **Prepare ahead** To save time when planning a big meal, this purée can be made up to 2 days in advance. Chill until required and reheat just before serving.

1 **Place the swede** in a large saucepan. Add enough cold water to cover, and a pinch of salt. Bring to the boil, cover, reduce the heat, and simmer for 20 minutes, or until tender. Drain well.

2 **Return the drained swede** to the saucepan and place over a very low heat. Add the butter, mash well, then add the cream and grated nutmeg. Season to taste with salt and pepper, and mash again until the swede is smooth.

● **Good with** roast and grilled meats, and vegetarian dishes.

Pisto Manchego

This Spanish dish, similar to the French ratatouille, goes particularly well with spicy chorizo sausage

🍴 serves 4–6

🕐 prep 10 mins • cook 30 mins

2 tbsp **olive oil**

1 **garlic clove**, chopped

2 **onions**, finely chopped

2 **green peppers**, deseeded and sliced

1 **red pepper**, deseeded and sliced

3 **courgettes**, cut into chunks

250g (9oz) ripe **tomatoes**, skinned and quartered

½ tsp **sugar**

1 tbsp **red wine vinegar**

salt and freshly ground **black pepper**

2 tbsp chopped **parsley**

● **Prepare ahead** This can be made up to 2 days in advance and chilled until required. Reheat gently or serve at room temperature.

1 **Heat the oil** in a pan over a medium heat. Add the garlic and onions and fry, stirring frequently, for 5 minutes, or until the onions are soft and translucent.

2 **Add the peppers** and continue to cook, stirring, for 5 minutes. Add the courgettes, cook for a further 5 minutes, then add the tomatoes, sugar, and vinegar and continue to cook for 15 minutes, stirring occasionally.

3 **Season to taste** with salt and pepper, transfer to a warm serving dish, and scatter with parsley.

● **Good with** grilled meats and fish. It can also be served as a starter; top with slices of fried chorizo and chopped hard-boiled eggs.

Onion Confit

A sweet and tangy accompaniment that complements most roasted or grilled dishes

🍴 makes 750g (1lb 10oz)

🕐 prep 5 mins • cook 35–45 mins

30g (1oz) **butter**

900g (2lb) **onions**, peeled and finely sliced

100g (3½oz) **demerara sugar**

3 tbsp **sherry vinegar**

1½ tbsp **crème de cassis** (optional)

2 tsp **salt**

● **Prepare ahead** The dish can be made up to 1 week ahead and stored in the refrigerator until ready to serve.

1 **Melt the butter** in a heavy saucepan and add the onions; stir and cook for 5 minutes.

2 **Add the remaining** ingredients, stir well, and simmer uncovered for 30–40 minutes, stirring occasionally so the confit does not stick too much.

● **Good with** grilled or roasted meat and poultry.

● **Leftovers** are wonderful spread thinly on toasted bread and piled with slices of cooked ham or chicken with a handful of rocket leaves for a delicious sandwich.

Cajun-spiced Potato Wedges

This peppery dish was developed by the French settlers of Louisiana

 serves 6

 prep 10 mins
● cook 35–45 mins

4 potatoes, unpeeled

1 lemon, cut into 6 wedges

12 garlic cloves

3 red onions, cut into 8 wedges

4 bay leaves

3 tbsp lemon juice

1 tbsp tomato purée

salt and freshly ground black pepper

1 tsp paprika

½ tsp cayenne pepper

1 tsp dried oregano

1 tsp dried thyme

½ tsp ground cumin

6 tbsp olive oil

● **Prepare ahead** The potatoes can be prepared, up to the end of step 2, several hours in advance.

1 Preheat the oven to 200°C (400°F/Gas 6). Cut the potatoes into thick wedges. Cook in a large pan of salted boiling water for 3 minutes, then drain well and place in a large roasting tin with the lemon, garlic, onions, and bay leaves.

2 Whisk together the remaining ingredients with 6 tbsp water and pour evenly over the potatoes; toss well to coat.

3 Roast for 30–40 minutes, or until the potatoes are tender and the liquid has been absorbed. Gently turn the potatoes frequently during cooking using a fish slice. Serve hot.

Mushrooms in Cream Sauce

Make the most of seasonal mushrooms with this filling side dish

 serves 4

prep 10 mins • cook 25 mins

125g (4½oz) **streaky bacon rashers**, chopped

60g (2oz) **butter**

1 **onion**, finely chopped

2 **garlic cloves**, crushed

450g (1lb) mixed **mushrooms**, such as field, shiitake, brown cap, and button

120ml (4fl oz) **dry white wine**

pinch of finely grated **nutmeg**

300ml (10fl oz) **crème fraîche**

1 tbsp **cornflour**

salt and freshly ground **black pepper**

1 tbsp chopped **tarragon**

toasted **ciabatta bread**, to serve

cherry tomatoes, to serve

1 In a large shallow pan, fry the bacon until lightly browned. Remove from the pan and set aside; keep warm.

2 Melt the butter in the pan and cook the onion and garlic for a few minutes, or until they are lightly browned and softened.

3 Halve any large mushrooms, then add all of the mushrooms to the pan and cook gently for 10 minutes, or until tender, stirring often. Add the wine and nutmeg, and bring to the boil. Cover and simmer for 5 minutes.

4 Stir in the crème fraîche and the cooked bacon. Mix the cornflour with 1 tbsp water and stir into the sauce. Season to taste with salt and pepper. Cook, stirring, until the sauce thickens. Just before serving, stir in the chopped tarragon. Serve on toasted ciabatta with cherry tomatoes on the side.

Asparagus with Mustard Sauce

Briefly cooked, this bright green vegetable is ideal as a side dish or a stylish, simple starter

 serves 4

prep 15 mins • cook 3-4 mins

675g (1½lb) **asparagus**

2 tbsp chopped **red onion**

For the mustard sauce

60ml (2oz) **olive oil**

1 tbsp **white wine vinegar**

1 tbsp **Dijon mustard**

2 tbsp **Greek yogurt**

salt and freshly ground **black pepper**

⬤ **Prepare ahead** The asparagus and sauce can be made several hours in advance. Chill until required.

1 Snap off the tough ends of the asparagus and peel the lower half of each stem with a vegetable peeler. Fill a large frying pan with 1.5cm (½in) of water. Bring to the boil over a high heat and add the asparagus. Reduce the heat to low, cover, and cook for 3-4 minutes, or until just tender. Drain and rinse with cold water; pat dry with kitchen paper. Chill while preparing the sauce.

2 In a small bowl, whisk together the oil, vinegar, and mustard. Beat in the yogurt and season to taste with salt and pepper.

3 Divide the asparagus between 4 plates. Spoon some of the mustard sauce over and sprinkle with the onion. Serve the remaining sauce separately.

VARIATION

Asparagus with Creamy Garlic Sauce

Combine 15ml (4fl oz) plain yogurt, 1 tbsp snipped chives, 1 garlic clove, ½ tsp finely grated lemon zest, and a pinch of cayenne pepper in a bowl. Chill, covered, for at least 2 hours. Remove the garlic before serving.

Roast Squash with Ginger

Spicy vegetables make a punchy side dish

 serves 3–4

prep 20 mins • cook 40 mins

1 butternut squash, peeled

5 tbsp olive oil

1 tsp salt

2 red chillies, deseeded and finely chopped

60g (2oz) fresh root ginger, peeled and grated or finely sliced

1 tbsp clear honey

freshly ground black pepper

handful of mint leaves, torn

2 limes, cut into wedges

1 Preheat the oven to 180°C (350°F/Gas 4). Slice the squash into long thick strips and place in a roasting tin. Mix together 2 tbsp warm water, the olive oil, salt, chillies, ginger, honey, and pepper to taste. Drizzle the sauce over the squash, mixing to coat well.

2 Bake the squash for 40 minutes, or until tender, shaking occasionally during cooking to avoid sticking. If the squash dries out, add a little more olive oil.

3 Transfer the warm squash to a large serving dish, and scatter with torn mint. Serve with lime wedges to squeeze over.

Tomato and Aubergine Confit

An ancient method of preserving meat, confit infuses flavour into vegetables

 serves 6

prep 5 mins, plus standing • cook 10 mins

2 tbsp olive oil

5 tbsp vegetable oil or sunflower oil

300g (10oz) aubergines, cut into 7.5cm (3in) batons

4 tbsp garlic-infused oil

125g (4½oz) cherry tomatoes, halved

salt and freshly ground black pepper

10 basil leaves, torn into pieces, plus whole leaves to garnish

1 Heat the olive and vegetable oils in a large frying pan over a medium-high heat until they begin to smoke. Add the aubergine batons and fry, stirring often, for 3 minutes, or until golden brown. Drain on kitchen paper.

2 Add the garlic oil to the pan, then add the cherry tomatoes. Cook for 2 minutes, or until softened.

3 Place the aubergine batons in a large bowl. Add the basil and the tomatoes, and mix gently. Cover and leave to infuse for up to 1 hour in a warm place.

4 Season to taste with salt and pepper and serve warm.

Stir-fried Broccoli with Sesame Seeds

The added flavourings make broccoli into something special

serves 4

prep 5 mins • cook 6 mins

1 tbsp sesame seeds

1 tbsp vegetable oil

1 tbsp light soy sauce

pinch of dried chilli flakes

675g (1½lb) broccoli florets and stems

60ml (2fl oz) vegetable stock or water

salt and freshly ground black pepper

1 Heat a large non-stick frying pan or wok. Add the sesame seeds and toast them, shaking the pan constantly for 1–2 minutes, or until the seeds turn golden. Transfer to a plate.

2 Add the oil, soy sauce, and dried chilli flakes to the pan; stir to combine. Add the broccoli and stir-fry for 2 minutes.

3 Pour in the stock and cover the pan. Cook for 1–2 minutes, or until the broccoli is tender but still crisp. Stir in the sesame seeds and season to taste with salt and pepper.

● **Good with** grilled meats, poultry, and fish.

Battered Cod and Chips

Yeast batter is particularly good for fish, as it is easy to make and remains crisp through frying

 serves 4

 prep 20 mins, plus standing • cook 30 mins

deep-fat fryer or large saucepan

85g (3oz) **plain flour**, plus extra for dusting

pinch of **sugar**

7g sachet **easy-blend dried yeast**

60ml (2fl oz) **milk**, warmed

900g (2lb) **floury potatoes**

vegetable oil, for deep-frying

675g (1½lb) **cod fillet**, skinned and cut into 4 pieces

salt and freshly ground **black pepper**

● **Prepare ahead** Steps 1 and 2 can be completed up to 1 hour before serving.

1 To make the batter, sift the flour into a bowl and stir in the sugar and yeast. Pour in the warmed milk and 120ml (4fl oz) warm water, and whisk to make a smooth batter. Cover and leave to stand for 1 hour, or until frothy.

2 Peel the potatoes and cut them into 1 x 6cm (½ x 2½in) pieces. Rinse, drain, and pat dry with kitchen paper.

3 Heat the oil for deep-frying to 160°C (325°F) or half-fill a large saucepan with oil and heat until a piece of day-old bread browns in under 1 minute. Place half the chips in a frying basket and lower carefully into the hot oil. Fry for 5 minutes, or until the chips are tender but still pale. Drain, then fry the remaining chips in the same way. Preheat the oven to 130°C (250°F/Gas ½).

4 Season the pieces of cod with salt and pepper and dust with flour. Increase the frying temperature to 190°C (375°F). Stir the batter and coat the cod in it evenly. Fry the fish, 2 pieces at a time, for about 5 minutes each, or until golden and crisp. Drain on kitchen paper and keep warm, uncovered, in the oven.

5 Return all the chips to the basket and fry for 3–4 minutes, or until they are golden and crisp, shaking the basket occasionally. Drain, salt, and serve with the fish.

DEEP-FRIED PARSLEY

Tie several sprigs together with string, lower into the hot oil and fry for about 5 seconds, or until the sprigs darken and become crisp. Snip off the string and serve as a bunch on the side of the plate, or crumble over the fish. Alternatively, use uncooked parsley sprigs as a garnish along with lemon wedges.

Seafood and Tomato Stew

This rustic stew is delicious served for lunch or dinner

 serves 4

 prep 10 mins • cook 30 mins

2 tbsp **olive oil**

2 **shallots**, finely chopped

1 **celery stick**, finely chopped

2 **garlic cloves**, chopped

2 **anchovies**, rinsed

pinch of **crushed chilli**

salt and freshly ground **black pepper**

300ml can **chopped tomatoes**

250ml (8fl oz) **white wine**

200ml (7fl oz) **fish stock** or vegetable stock

400g (14oz) **mix raw prawns, scallops**, and **monkfish**

zest and **juice** of 1 **lemon**

1 tsp **small capers**, drained and rinsed

1 Heat the oil in a saucepan. Add the shallots, celery, garlic, anchovies, and chilli. Season to taste with salt and pepper, and cook gently for 5 minutes, stirring.

2 Add the tomatoes, wine, and stock. Cook over a medium heat for 15–25 minutes, or until the sauce reduces slightly. Add the prawns, scallops, lemon zest and juice, and capers. Cook the shellfish for 5 minutes, or until the prawns are just pink.

Chargrilled Tuna with Tomato Salsa

These should be served straight from the pan while still sizzling hot

serves 4

prep 10 mins, plus marinating • cook 10 mins

ridged cast-iron grill pan

2 **tuna steaks**, each weighing 450–600g (1–1lb 5oz)

6 tbsp **olive oil**

2 **garlic cloves**, finely chopped

juice of 1 **lime** or 1 **lemon**

sprig of **rosemary**, finely chopped

salt and freshly ground **black pepper**

280g (10oz) **tomatoes**, halved, deseeded and chopped

4 **spring onions**, finely chopped

pinch of **dried chilli flakes** (optional)

handful of **rocket**, chopped

lime or lemon wedges, to garnish

1 **Put the tuna** in a non-metallic bowl. Whisk 4 tbsp oil with half the garlic, half the lime juice, the rosemary, and season to taste with pepper. Pour the mixture over the tuna, coating the steaks evenly, then cover the bowl with cling film and leave to marinate in a refrigerator for 1 hour.

2 **Meanwhile**, to make the salsa, put the tomatoes, spring onions, and chilli flakes (if using) in another non-metallic bowl. Add 2 tbsp olive oil, the rest of the garlic and the lime juice, and season to taste with salt and pepper. Stir together, then cover and chill until ready to serve.

3 **Remove the tuna** and salsa from the refrigerator 10 minutes before cooking. Heat the grill pan over a high heat, and brush the ridges with a little of the marinade.

4 **Place the tuna** on the pan and grill for 3 minutes, brushing with the reserved marinade. Carefully turn over the tuna and grill for a further 2–4 minutes, or until the outside is browned and the centre slightly pink.

5 **Leave the tuna** to stand for 2 minutes, then cut each one in half and transfer to separate plates. Combine the rocket leaves with the salsa and serve alongside the tuna pieces. Garnish with the lime wedges and serve immediately.

Haddock Mornay

With a layer of freshly-cooked spinach under the poached haddock, this classic dish is a colourful one-pot meal

serves 4

prep 25 mins • cook 25 mins

freeze for up to 1 month

675g (1½lb) **haddock fillet**, skinned and cut into 4 equal pieces

150ml (5fl oz) **fish stock** or water

300ml (10fl oz) **milk**

45g (1½oz) **butter**, plus extra for greasing

45g (1½oz) **plain flour**

115g (4oz) **Cheddar cheese**, grated

salt and freshly ground **black pepper**

250g (9oz) **spinach**, chopped

pinch of grated **nutmeg**

60g (2oz) fresh **wholemeal breadcrumbs**

2 tbsp chopped **parsley**

60g (2oz) **Parmesan cheese**, grated

● **Prepare ahead** The dish can be made a day in advance, reheated in a 180°C (350°F/Gas 4) oven for 25–30 minutes, before being browned under a hot grill.

1 **Place the haddock** in a deep frying pan and pour over the stock and milk. Slowly bring to the boil, then lower the heat, cover, and simmer for 6–8 minutes, or until the fish is cooked. Lift the fish from the pan and keep warm, reserving the poaching liquid.

2 **Melt the butter** in a saucepan and stir in the flour until smooth. Cook for 1 minute, then gradually whisk or stir in the poaching liquid until evenly combined. Stir over the heat until the sauce is thickened and smooth. Stir in the Cheddar until melted, then season to taste with salt and pepper. Remove from the heat.

3 **Put the spinach** in a saucepan, cover, and cook over a low heat for 1 minute, or until the leaves have wilted. Season with the nutmeg, transfer to a greased, shallow, ovenproof dish, and spread it out in an even layer. Preheat the grill.

4 **Place the poached haddock** on the spinach and pour the cheese sauce over the fish. Mix together the breadcrumbs, parsley, and Parmesan, and sprinkle over the sauce. Place the dish under the grill until golden.

VARIATION

Smoked Haddock Mornay

The dish can be made using smoked haddock instead, but season carefully as the fish is already salted.

Fish   253

Fish Coconut Stew

This popular Brazilian stew is called *Moqueca de Peixe*. The palm oil (*dendê*) lends a distinctive flavour as well as an orange colour, but you can use a lighter oil or leave it out altogether

 serves 4

prep 15 mins • cook 35 mins

4 tbsp **olive oil**

1 **onion**, thinly sliced

3 ripe **tomatoes**, skinned, deseeded, and chopped

1 **red pepper**, deseeded and thinly sliced

1 **green pepper**, deseeded and thinly sliced

salt and freshly ground **black pepper**

300ml (10fl oz) **coconut milk**

3 tsp **tomato purée**

800g (1¾lb) **white fish**, cut into large chunks or strips

3 tbsp **palm oil** (optional)

1 tbsp chopped **coriander leaves**

For the chilli salsa

1 ripe **tomato**, skinned, deseeded, and chopped

1 small **red onion**, finely chopped

1 **garlic clove**, finely chopped

1 tbsp **red wine vinegar**

1 tbsp **lime** juice

1 tbsp **sunflower oil**

1 tbsp chopped **flat-leaf parsley**

1 tsp **chilli sauce**

● **Prepare ahead** Make the stew up to the end of step 1 the day before and chill. The salsa also can be made up to 24 hours in advance, stirring in the parsley at the last minute.

1 Heat the oil in a deep frying pan over medium heat. Add the onion and fry, stirring frequently, for 5 minutes, or until soft but not coloured. Add the tomatoes and the red and green peppers, lower the heat, and simmer, stirring from time to time, for 20 minutes, or until the vegetables have softened. Season to taste with salt and pepper, stir in the coconut milk and tomato purée, and bring back to the boil.

2 Meanwhile, make the chilli salsa. Mix all the ingredients together and place in a serving bowl. Set aside.

3 Add the fish to the vegetables in the pan and cook, stirring occasionally, for 5–10 minutes, according to the size of the pieces, until just cooked through. Do not overcook. Stir in the palm oil, if using.

4 Transfer the stew to a serving dish and scatter with coriander. Serve with the salsa alongside.

● **Good with** boiled white rice and *farofa de dendê*.

VARIATION

Farofa de Dendê

To make this traditional side dish, heat 30g (1oz) of palm oil in a frying pan. Fry 1 large chopped onion, until soft. Add 60g (2oz) manioc flour, 15 rehydrated and finely chopped dried shrimps, and continue frying for 5 minutes. Carefully salt to taste as the shrimp is salty.

Baked Trout with Almonds

Delicate trout enhanced with citrus and nutty texture

 serves 4

prep 10 mins • cook 25 mins

4 fresh **trout**, gutted and rinsed

2 **lemons**, cut into thin slices and halved

125g (4½oz) **butter**, melted

60g (2oz) **flaked almonds**

90ml (3fl oz) **dry white wine**

salt and freshly ground **black pepper**

3 tbsp finely chopped **flat-leaf parsley**

1 Preheat the oven to 200°C (400°F/Gas 6). Make 3 or 4 diagonal slashes about 5mm (¼in) deep on either side of each fish. Place the fish side by side in a shallow ovenproof dish. Tuck the halved lemon slices into the slashes.

2 Spoon over half the melted butter. Bake uncovered for 20 minutes, or until the fish flakes easily with a fork.

3 Heat the remaining butter in a small saucepan. Add the almonds and fry until lightly browned. Add the wine and season to taste with salt and pepper. Bring to the boil and bubble for 1–2 minutes. Mix in the parsley and spoon the sauce over the trout. Serve immediately.

Skate Wings with Brown Butter

This classic French dish, *raie au beurre noisette*, requires care to ensure the butter doesn't burn, but gently browns instead

🍴 serves 4

🕐 prep 10 mins • cook 25 mins

4 small **skate wings**, skinned

175g (6oz) **unsalted butter**

4 tsp **lemon** juice

3 tbsp finely chopped **flat-leaf parsley**

2 tbsp **capers** in brine, rinsed, dried, and chopped

For the court bouillon

5 tbsp **dry white wine**

1 **garlic clove**, crushed

½ **lemon**, sliced

½ **onion**, thickly sliced

5 **black peppercorns**, crushed

2 sprigs of **flat-leaf parsley**

2 sprigs of **thyme**

1 **bay leaf**

1 tsp **salt**

● **Prepare ahead** The court bouillon can be made up to 3 days in advance, strained, and refrigerated, or frozen for up to 3 months.

1 **Put 1 litre** (1¾ pints) water and all the ingredients for the court bouillon in a large saucepan and slowly bring to the boil. Reduce the heat and simmer for 10 minutes. Leave the stock to cool until just warm before using.

2 **Put the fish wings** in a large frying pan, or 2 medium-sized pans, with court bouillon to cover. Bring the liquid to just below boiling, cover, and poach for 7–10 minutes, or until the thick part of the flesh at the top of the wing easily lifts away from the large bone. Remove the skate from the pan and drain well. Put on plates and keep warm.

3 **Place the butter** in a large saucepan over a medium-high heat, swirling the pan so it melts evenly. Cook until the butter turns a hazelnut colour; it will splutter as its water content evaporates, then foam. Remove from the heat once the butter has browned and add the lemon juice.

4 **Scatter the parsley** and capers over the skate wings, then pour over the butter. Serve at once.

Salmon Fishcakes

Ideal as a main course or as a bite-sized canapé

🍴 serves 6

🕐 prep 30 mins, plus cooling and chilling • cook 30 mins

❄ once cooked can be frozen for up to 1 month

450g (1lb) **potatoes**, cubed

900g (2lb) **salmon fillets**, skinned and boned

1 **onion**, halved

2–3 **bay leaves**

1 tsp **black peppercorns**

4 **spring onions**, finely chopped

2 tbsp **horseradish cream**

salt and freshly ground **black pepper**

juice and zest of 1 **lemon**

large handful of **dill**, chopped

pinch of **cayenne pepper**

For the coating

225g (8oz) fresh **breadcrumbs**

2 tbsp chopped **chives** (optional)

2 tbsp chopped **parsley** (optional)

plain flour, for coating

2 **eggs**, whisked

sunflower oil, for frying

1 **Place the potatoes** in a saucepan of cold water and boil for 20 minutes, or until very tender. Drain and mash. Set aside.

2 **Place the salmon** in cold water with the onion, bay leaves, and peppercorns. Bring to the boil, simmer for 2 minutes, then turn off the heat and leave to cool for 20 minutes. Drain well, discarding the cooking liquids, and cool.

3 **Flake the salmon** into a large bowl. Fold in the cooled mashed potato and all the other fishcake ingredients. Mix well and shape into 12 round cakes. Chill for 1 hour, ideally, before coating.

4 **Thoroughly mix** the breadcrumbs with the herbs (if using). Put the flour, eggs, and breadcrumbs on separate plates and roll the salmon cakes in flour, then egg, then breadcrumbs.

5 **Heat the sunflower oil** in a frying pan and fry the fishcakes for 3–4 minutes on each side, or until crisp and hot in the middle. Drain on kitchen paper and serve while hot.

● **Good with** hot chunky chips, garden peas, and wedges of lemon.

Fisherman's Pie

A British favourite, with its creamy filling and mashed-potato topping. It can be as luxurious or as homely as you like, depending on the seafood used

 serves 4

 prep 25 mins • cook 50 mins –1 hr

 oval pie dish or ovenproof serving dish

500g (1lb 2oz) floury potatoes, such as King Edward or Maris Piper, peeled and cut into chunks

450ml (15fl oz) milk

100g (3½oz) butter, plus extra for topping

salt and freshly ground black pepper

300g (10oz) raw prawns, shells on

400g (14oz) fresh haddock fillets

200g (7oz) un-dyed smoked haddock fillets

4 black peppercorns, lightly crushed

1 bay leaf

several sprigs of flat-leaf parsley

4 tbsp plain flour

squeeze of lemon juice

2 tbsp double cream

4 tbsp chopped flat-leaf parsley

pinch of cayenne pepper

● **Prepare ahead** Step 1 can be completed up to a day in advance. The fish can also be poached 1 day in advance; cover and chill the fish and reserve the milk until needed. The prawns can be shelled and deveined several hours in advance, and chilled until needed.

1 **Place the potatoes** in a large saucepan with cold salted water. Boil for 10–15 minutes, or until the potatoes are tender when pierced with a knife; drain well. Mash until smooth, then beat in 150ml (5fl oz) milk and 60g (2oz) butter. Season to taste with salt and pepper. Set aside.

2 **Meanwhile,** remove the prawn heads and shells and reserve the shells. Then devein the prawns and set aside.

3 **Put the fresh** and smoked fish in a frying pan with the remaining milk. Bring to a gentle simmer, and simmer for 10 minutes, or until the flesh flakes easily. Use a slotted spoon to remove the fish from the pan and set aside. Add the prawn shells, peppercorns, bay leaf, and parsley sprigs to the milk and simmer over a very low heat for 10 minutes.

4 **Meanwhile,** preheat the oven to 220°C (425°F/Gas 7). Melt the remaining butter in a saucepan over a medium heat. Sprinkle in the flour and cook for 1 minute. Remove from the heat. Strain the milk and gradually stir into the butter mixture. Return to the heat and simmer until the sauce thickens. Stir in the lemon juice and cream, and season to taste with salt and pepper. Stir in the chopped parsley, cayenne, and prawns, and flake in the fish.

5 **Spoon the fish mixture** into the pie dish, top with the mashed potatoes, and dot with a little extra butter. Place the dish on a baking tray and bake for 20–25 minutes, or until the topping is golden and the filling is hot when you test the centre with a knife. Remove the pie from the oven and serve immediately.

● **Good with** a bowl of minted peas on the side.

> ### Choosing Fish
> This recipe includes both fresh and smoked haddock, but cod, hake, halibut, salmon, and monkfish are all suitable. A large scallop per diner adds a real touch of luxury.

Tuna Carpaccio

The original dish was made with beef instead of tuna at Harry's Bar in Venice, in 1950

 serves 4

prep 10–15 mins • cook 20 mins

1 sprig of thyme, leaves chopped

2 tsp finely grated lemon zest

5 tbsp extra virgin olive oil

5 Charlotte potatoes, unpeeled

salt

4 tbsp mayonnaise

1 heaped tbsp small capers, rinsed

2 tbsp olive oil, for frying

400g (14oz) sashimi-grade tuna loin fillet, cut into 8 equal pieces

1 **Mix the thyme leaves,** lemon zest, and extra virgin olive oil together, then set aside.

2 **Boil the potatoes**. Drain and peel once cool enough to handle. Cut into thick slices and place in a bowl. Season to taste with salt, add a little of the flavoured olive oil, and mix with the mayonnaise; set aside.

3 **Pat the capers** dry with kitchen paper. Fry them in the olive oil for 2 minutes, or until crisp, then drain off the oil.

4 **Pound each piece of tuna** between 2 pieces of cling film until uniformly very thin, then peel off the film. Scatter with capers, season to taste, and drizzle over the remaining flavoured olive oil. Serve with the potatoes.

Baked Plaice with Bacon

This is a tasty and unusual way of cooking and serving plaice, or similar flat fish

🍴 serves 4

🕐 prep 10 mins • cook 20 mins

✓ low GI

2 tbsp olive oil

4 back bacon rashers, chopped

3 spring onions, chopped

4 plaice fillets, 175g (6oz) each

freshly ground black pepper

60g (2oz) butter

juice of ½ large lemon

1 tbsp chopped parsley

1 Preheat the oven to 200°C (400°F/Gas 6). Heat the oil in a roasting tin over medium heat, add the bacon and spring onions, and fry for 2 minutes, stirring frequently.

2 Add the plaice, skin-side down, baste with the oil, and season to taste with pepper.

3 Place the tin in the oven and bake the fish for 15 minutes, basting once or twice.

4 Transfer the cooked plaice to warmed serving plates. Drain the bacon and spring onions from the tin and set aside.

5 Heat the butter in a small saucepan until golden brown, add the lemon juice, bacon, and onions, and stir in the parsley. Spoon over the plaice and serve at once.

⬤ **Good with** stir-fried or steamed vegetables, such as spinach, green beans, or carrots.

Baked Salmon with Cucumber Dill Sauce

Equally good with salmon steaks or fillets, this simple summery dish is quick to make and very healthy

🍴 serves 4

🕐 prep 10 mins, plus standing • cook 10 mins

½ cucumber

salt and freshly ground black pepper

250g (9oz) plain yogurt

2 tsp Dijon mustard

1 spring onion, finely chopped

1 tbsp chopped dill

4 salmon steaks or fillets, skinned

2 tsp olive oil

juice of ½ lemon

⬤ **Prepare ahead** The sauce can be prepared up to 2 days in advance, covered, and chilled. The salmon can be cooked up to 24 hours in advance if served cold. Chill until required.

1 Finely dice the cucumber and place in a sieve over a bowl. Sprinkle with salt and leave to drain for 1 hour. Rinse with cold water and pat dry with kitchen paper. Stir the drained cucumber into the yogurt and add the mustard, spring onion, and dill. Season to taste with salt and pepper. Set aside.

2 Preheat the oven to 200°C (400°F/Gas 6). Arrange the salmon fillets in a shallow baking dish, brush with oil, and season to taste with salt and pepper.

3 Sprinkle the salmon with lemon juice and roast for 8–10 minutes, depending on the thickness, until just cooked through but still moist inside. Remove from the oven and stir the juices from the dish into the cucumber sauce.

4 Serve the salmon hot or cold, with the sauce spooned over it.

VARIATION

Salmon Pasta

Flake the salmon and toss with cooked, drained, and cooled pasta. Stir the sauce through to make a quick pasta salad.

Fish

There are many ways to cook fresh fish, and straightforward, uncomplicated cooking techniques produce the best results. As an added bonus, fishmongers do all the gutting, filleting, and scaling. So, when you want a healthy meal in a hurry, think fish – we've even got inspirational ideas for using the leftovers.

Choosing Fish

Freshness is the most important consideration when buying fish. If the fish smells "fishy" or there is any hint of ammonia, don't buy it. All fish come from one of three basic groups:

Oily round fish have plump, rounded bodies. The dense, rich flesh can be barbecued, grilled, or pan-fried.

White round fish have similiar bodies, but the flesh is more tender and flaky, and responds well to stuffing, frying, grilling, and steaming.

Flat fish are almost 2-dimensional with delicate flesh. They are sold whole or filleted.

OILY ROUND FISH

Mackerel
Often served with gooseberries to cut the richness. This versatile fish can be fried or grilled. Great for quick pâtés, too.

Salmon
Available farmed and wild, and smoked and plain, salmon is a very versatile oily fish.

Tuna
Whole tuna is very large, so it is usually sold cut into steaks. The meaty flesh can be barbecued, grilled, pan-fried, or roasted.

Sardine
An oily fish that is cooked whole or in fillets. It is especially good barbecued.

WHITE ROUND FISH

Haddock
With its flavourful white flesh, this fish is excellent for making fish and chips.

Seabass
Popular in Chinese cookery, this white-fleshed fish can be barbecued, grilled, or pan-fried.

FLAT FISH

Lemon Sole
A delicate flat fish that requires quick, gentle cooking to avoid over-cooking.

Turbot
The most expensive flat fish, this has delicate flesh that is excellent pan-fried.

WHAT TO LOOK FOR

If possible, press the flesh gently to test that it is firm and stiff, not limp or floppy.

The eyes should be bright with black pupils and transparent corneas, not sunken or cloudy.

The tail should look fresh and moist, not dry or curled.

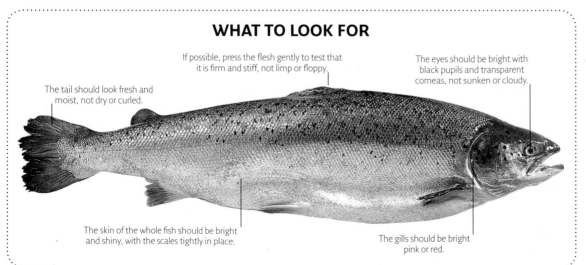

The skin of the whole fish should be bright and shiny, with the scales tightly in place.

The gills should be bright pink or red.

Storing

After buying, take fish home immediately, ideally in a cool bag. Loose fish should be rinsed with cold water, patted dry, and then put on a plate with a lip. Cover with cling film and place in the bottom of the refrigerator to prevent any raw juices dripping on other food. Cook within a day. Packaged fish from the supermarket should be left in the packaging and refrigerated immediately. Cook according to the use-by date on the label. Keep all fish refrigerated until just before cooking – never leave at room temperature.

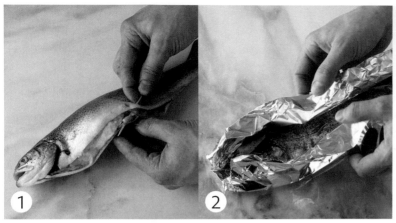

Bake in Foil

1 **Use this technique** for baking a whole fish. If the recipe includes a stuffing, spoon it into the cavity, then secure in place with 1 or 2 wooden cocktail sticks.

2 **Wrap the fish** in lightly greased or buttered foil to make a well-sealed parcel. Bake in a preheated oven at 180°C (350°F/Gas 4) for 25 minutes for small fish, or 35–40 minutes for large fish, or until the flesh along the backbone is opaque.

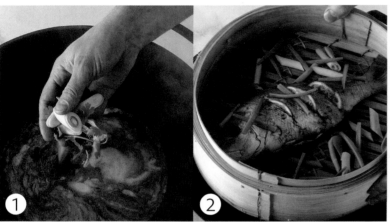

Steam

1 **To use a bamboo steamer**, pour water into a wok to just below where the steamer fits. Add any flavourings, such as lemons and herbs, then bring the water to a simmer. Put the basket in the wok, making sure the base does not touch the water.

2 **Put the fish in the** steamer and sprinkle over any extra flavourings. Cover tightly and steam fillets for 3–4 minutes, whole fish up to 350g (12oz) for 6–8 minutes, and whole fish up to 900g (2lb) for 12–15 minutes, or until the flesh is opaque and flakes easily.

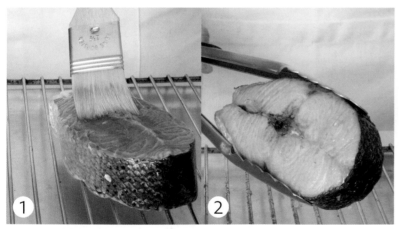

Grill

1 **Brush a grill rack** with vegetable oil. Add the fish, brush the surface with a little oil, and season to taste with salt and pepper. Position the grill rack 10cm (4in) from the heat and grill for half the time specified in the recipe.

2 **Using tongs**, carefully turn the fish over and continue grilling for the remaining time, or until the flesh flakes easily.

Pan-fry

1 **Heat equal** amounts of oil and butter in a heavy frying pan over a medium-high heat until foaming. Season the fish, then add it to the pan, skin-side down, and fry for half the time specified in the recipe. Use a spatula or fish slice to turn the pieces over.

2 **Continue frying** the fish for the remaining cooking time, or until it is golden brown and the flesh flakes easily when tested with a fork.

Fish

Marinades

Teriyaki Marinade
Mix all the ingredients together, then use to marinate the fish for up to 2 hours. Use any leftover marinade to baste the fish while grilling or barbecuing.

- 3 tbsp **soy sauce**
- 1 tbsp **sesame oil**
- 1 tbsp **sweet sherry**
- 1 tbsp **sunflower oil**
- 1 tbsp chopped **spring onion**
- 2 tsp grated **orange** zest
- 1 **garlic clove**, crushed
- pinch of **ground ginger**

Yogurt-mint Marinade
Mix the ingredients and marinate the fish for up to 2 hours. Remove from the marinade and scrape off the excess before grilling or barbecuing.

- 150g (5½oz) **plain yogurt**
- 2 tbsp **olive oil**
- 2 tbsp chopped **mint**
- 1 tbsp grated **lemon** zest
- ¼ tsp **ground coriander**
- ¼ tsp **ground cumin**
- **salt** and **pepper**, to taste

Sauces

Balsamic Sauce
Bring all the ingredients to the boil. Reduce the heat and simmer, stirring, until thickened.

- 1 tbsp **brown sugar**
- 2 tbsp **balsamic vinegar**
- 1 tsp **cornflour**
- 1 **vegetable stock cube**, crumbled
- 150ml (5fl oz) **water**

Tarragon Sauce
Combine all the ingredients, cover, and chill until required. Serve with fried fish.

- 150ml (5fl oz) **soured cream**
- 4 tbsp chopped **tarragon**
- 1 tsp **Dijon mustard**
- squeeze of **lemon** juice
- **salt** and **pepper**, to taste

Flavoured Butters

Anchovy Butter
Beat all the ingredients together, then roll in greaseproof paper and chill until required.

- 60g (2oz) **butter**, softened
- 2 **anchovy fillets**, drained and finely chopped
- ½ tbsp grated **lemon** zest
- pinch of **cayenne pepper**
- **black pepper**, to taste

Herbed Green Butter
Beat all the ingredients together, then roll in greaseproof paper and chill until required.

- 60g (2oz) **butter**, softened
- 6 **spinach leaves**, blanched, dried, and very finely chopped
- 1 **shallot**, finely chopped
- 1 tsp each finely chopped **chervil**, **parsley**, and **tarragon**
- **salt** and **pepper**, to taste

NO-FUSS FLAVOURINGS

- **Add a Little Citrus** Drape fillets with thin lemon, lime, or orange slices just before baking. You can also perk up poached and fried fish with a squeeze of lemon when serving.

- **Think Asian** Add grated fresh root ginger, shredded spring onions, thinly sliced deseeded chillies, and a splash of soy sauce when baking or poaching fish, especially oily fish like mackerel and salmon.

- **Add Mexican Flair** Serve grilled fish with a spicy tomato salsa, chopped fresh coriander, and lime juice.

- **Go for Herbs** If you use herb leaves in a poaching recipe, add the flavour-packed stems to the liquid.

- **Add a Taste of the Med** Serve grilled or fried fish with Rouille (p114), Salsa Verde (p281), or Quick Aioli (p280) for a taste of the Mediterranean.

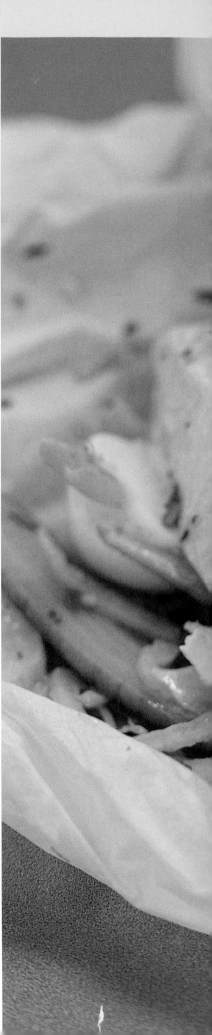

flavourings & leftovers

BAKING EN PAPILLOTE

Cooking fish en papillote, or wrapped in greaseproof paper (p506) with herbs and vegetables, and a splash of stock, white wine, or water, guarantees tender, moist results.

Ideas for Using Leftovers

Salmon Rillettes
Leftover cooked salmon can be combined with the smoked salmon in this rich pâté-like spread

🕑 15 mins   **page 30**

Smoked Haddock and Herb Fishcakes
Use any leftover white fish in place of haddock

🕑 40 mins   **page 43**

Fish Stock
Most leftover fish bones and heads make good stock, but do not use those from oily fish

🕑 30 mins   **page 103**

Pasta and Tuna Niçoise Salad
Swordfish or salmon can be used instead of tuna

🕑 35 mins   **page 117**

Kedgeree
Flaked, cooked cod, monkfish, or trout can be incorporated into this traditional breakfast dish

🕑 40 mins   **page 209**

Salmon Fishcakes
Leftover salmon, or any cooked oily fish, can be used in these easy-to-make fishcakes

🕑 1 hr   **page 255**

Fisherman's Pie
Use large chunks of leftover fish in this dish so they don't fall apart

🕑 1 hr 15 mins – 1 hr 25 mins   **page 256**

Seafood Salad
Add flakes of any cooked white fish to this colourful salad with its spicy dressing

🕑 40 mins   **page 268**

Fish   261

Swordfish Skewers with Rocket Salsa

Tender and flavoursome, these can be cooked on the barbecue or under a hot grill

 serves 4

 prep 15 mins, plus marinating • cook 5–8 mins

8 long metal skewers

6 tbsp **olive oil**, plus extra for greasing

juice of 1 **lemon**

4 tbsp finely chopped **flat-leaf parsley**

½–1 tsp **chilli powder**, to taste

4 **swordfish steaks**, about 225g (8oz) each, deboned and skinned, and cut into 2.5cm (1in) cubes

2 **orange**, **yellow** or **red peppers**, cored, deseeded, and cut into 2.5cm (1in) pieces

For the rocket salsa

1 bunch **rocket**, finely chopped

2 **garlic cloves**, finely chopped

120ml (4fl oz) **extra virgin olive oil**

4 tbsp **balsamic vinegar**

salt and freshly ground **black pepper**

1 **Whisk together** the olive oil, lemon juice, parsley, and chilli powder to taste in a large non-metallic bowl. Add the swordfish pieces and gently stir around. Cover and leave to marinate in the fridge for 30 minutes–1 hour, turning the fish cubes over once.

2 **Meanwhile**, make the rocket salsa by whisking together the rocket leaves, garlic, olive oil, and vinegar, and season to taste with salt and pepper; set aside.

3 **When ready to cook**, preheat the grill on its highest setting, position the rack 10cm (4in) from the heat, and grease 8 long metal skewers. Thread the fish and peppers on to the skewers. Grill for 5–8 minutes, or until the fish is cooked through and flakes easily, brushing with the marinade and turning once or twice.

4 **Put the remaining** marinade in a small pan and boil rapidly for 1 minute. Serve the fish with the marinade spooned over it, accompanied by the rocket salsa.

Salmon in Puff Pastry

Baking salmon en croûte keeps it moist and succulent

 serves 4

prep 25 mins • cook 30 mins

85g (3oz) **watercress**, coarse stems removed

115g (4oz) **cream cheese**

salt and freshly ground **black pepper**

600g (1lb 5oz) skinless **salmon fillet**

400g (14oz) **puff pastry**

flour, for dusting

beaten **egg** or milk, to glaze

● **Prepare ahead** The whole dish can be made up to 12 hours before baking. Cover with cling film and chill until ready to cook.

1 **Preheat the oven** to 200°C (400°F/Gas 6). Chop the watercress very finely, place in a bowl, add the cream cheese, season generously with salt and pepper, and mix well.

2 **Cut the salmon fillet** into 2 pieces. Roll out the pastry on a lightly floured surface to a thickness of 3mm (⅛in). It should be roughly 7.5cm (3in) longer than the salmon pieces and just over twice as wide. Trim the edges straight. Transfer to a lightly greased baking tray.

3 **Place 1 piece** of salmon in the middle of the pastry. Spread the top with the watercress cream and place the other piece of salmon on top. Lightly brush the pastry edges with water, then fold the 2 ends over the salmon. Fold in the sides so they overlap slightly and press together to seal. Re-roll the trimmings and use to decorate the top of the pastry, if liked. Brush with beaten egg, and make 2 or 3 holes with a skewer to allow steam to escape.

4 **Bake for 30 minutes**, or until the pastry is well risen and golden brown. Test if the salmon is cooked by pushing a skewer halfway through the thickest part and leaving for 4–5 seconds; when removed, it should feel hot.

5 **Remove from the oven** and allow to stand for a few minutes, then slice and serve.

Herrings in Oatmeal with Gooseberry Sauce

Gooseberry sauce is a traditional accompaniment to oily fish, such as herrings, mackerel, tuna, and swordfish

 serves 4

prep 10 mins • cook 25 mins

freeze the gooseberry sauce for up to 6 months

4 **herrings**, gutted and fins trimmed

125g (4½oz) fine **oatmeal**

For the gooseberry sauce

350g (12oz) fresh or frozen **gooseberries**

30g (1oz) **butter**

30g (1oz) **sugar**

¼ tsp **nutmeg**, freshly grated

salt and freshly ground **black pepper**

● **Prepare ahead** The sauce can be made several hours in advance.

1 Put the gooseberries in a saucepan with 1–2 tbsp water and cook for 4–5 minutes, or until tender. Purée in a food processor, then add the butter, sugar, and nutmeg, and season with salt and pepper. Set aside while you prepare the herrings.

2 Cut the heads off the herrings and slit them open along the belly right down to the tail. Open the fish out flat and place, skin-side up, on a chopping board. Bone each fish into a "butterfly" by pressing firmly all along the backbone with the heel of your palm until it is completely flat, then turning it over and pulling away the backbone, snipping it off at the tail end with scissors. Remove any small bones left behind in the fish with a pair of tweezers. Alternatively you can cut them into 2 fillets.

3 Preheat the grill on its highest setting. Spread the oatmeal on to a large plate and season well. Coat the herrings in the oatmeal, pressing it well on to the fish. Arrange the herrings in a grill pan and grill for 6–8 minutes, or until tender and flaky, turning once.

4 Gently warm the gooseberry sauce; serve with the herrings.

Cod in Tomato Sauce

The tomatoes and wine add sweetness to this Spanish dish

 serves 4

prep 10 mins • cook 30 mins

2 tbsp **olive oil**

1kg (2¼lb) skinless **cod fillet**, cut into 4 pieces

1 large **onion**, finely sliced

1 **garlic clove**, finely chopped

4 large **plum tomatoes**, skinned, deseeded, and chopped

2 tsp **tomato purée**

1 tsp **sugar**

300ml (10fl oz) **fish stock**

120ml (4fl oz) **dry white wine**

2 tbsp chopped **parsley**

salt and freshly ground **black pepper**

1 Preheat the oven to 200°C (400°F/Gas 6). Heat the oil in a flameproof casserole large enough to accommodate the cod in 1 layer. Fry the fish, skin-side down, over a medium-high heat, for 1 minute, or until the skin is crisp. Turn over and cook for 1 further minute. Remove with a slotted spoon and set aside.

2 Add the onions and garlic to the casserole and fry over a medium heat for 4–5 minutes, or until softened, stirring frequently. Add the tomatoes, tomato purée, sugar, stock, and wine, bring to a simmer, and cook, stirring, for 10–12 minutes.

3 Place the fish on top of the sauce and bake for 5 minutes. Remove from the oven, lift out the cod, and keep warm.

4 Place the casserole over a medium-high heat and allow the sauce to bubble for 3–4 minutes, until reduced and thickened. Stir in half the parsley and season to taste with salt and pepper. Divide the sauce between 4 warm plates and place a piece of fish on top. Serve at once, sprinkled with the remaining parsley.

VARIATION

Halibut in Tomato Sauce
Replace the cod with the same quantity of halibut and sprinkle the finished dish with basil and dried chilli flakes, instead of the parsley.

Stuffed Sardines in Vine Leaves

Fresh sardines are full of flavour, and this easy rice and herb stuffing soaks up the tasty juices from the fish

serves 4

prep 10 mins • cook 25 mins

For the stuffing

50g (1¾oz) short-grain rice

50g (1¾oz) pine nuts, toasted

45g (1½oz) currants

3 tbsp chopped parsley

1 tbsp chopped mint

1 tbsp chopped dill

juice of ½ lemon

salt

pinch of cayenne pepper

For the fish

12 whole sardines, cleaned

12 large preserved vine leaves, rinsed in cold water

2 tbsp olive oil

lemon wedges, to serve

1 Bring a large saucepan of lightly salted water to the boil and cook the rice for 20 minutes, or until just tender. Drain, rinse in cold water to cool, and drain again.

2 Place the rice in a bowl and stir in the pine nuts, currants, parsley, mint, dill, and lemon juice. Season to taste with salt and a pinch of cayenne pepper.

3 Divide the stuffing among the sardines, packing it into each cavity. Wrap each with a vine leaf to hold it together and brush lightly with oil.

4 Preheat the grill on its highest setting or a barbecue to hot, then cook the sardines for 4–5 minutes, turning once. Serve on a plate with lemon wedges to squeeze over.

● **Good with** new potatoes and a crisp, refreshing salad.

Grilled Halibut with Green Sauce

A fresh-tasting dish that is easy to prepare and cooks in minutes

serves 6

prep 10 mins • cook 4 mins

For the sauce

45g (1½oz) mixed herbs, such as parsley, chives, mint, tarragon, and chervil

2 garlic cloves

8 tbsp olive oil

1 tbsp tarragon vinegar

salt and freshly ground black pepper

pinch of caster sugar

For the fish

6 x chunky halibut fillets, 140g (5oz) each

1 tbsp olive oil

lemon wedges, to serve

1 Place all the ingredients for the sauce in a food processor, process until smooth, and season to taste with salt and pepper, and the pinch of caster sugar. Chill until needed.

2 Preheat the grill on its highest setting or a barbecue to hot. Lightly brush the halibut with oil, and season to taste with salt and pepper. Cook the fish for 2 minutes on each side, and serve with the green sauce and lemon wedges to squeeze over.

VARIATION

Seared Salmon with Green Sauce

Replace the halibut with 6 salmon fillets, omit the oil for brushing, and grill, as above. Serve with the sauce.

Mixed Fried Fish

This works best with firm white fish, but you can also use squid, sliced into rings

 serves 4

prep 20 mins • cook 10 mins

For the sauce

60g (2oz) **rocket**, plus extra to serve

1 **garlic clove**, crushed

100ml (4fl oz) **mayonnaise**

1 tsp **lemon** juice

salt and freshly ground **black pepper**

For the fish

4 tbsp **plain flour**

2 **eggs**, lightly beaten

85g (3oz) dried white **breadcrumbs**, or Panko breadcrumbs

115g (4oz) **cod fillet**, skinned

115g (4oz) **salmon fillet**, skinned

115g (4oz) **snapper fillets**, skinned

12 raw **king prawns**, shelled, heads removed

oil, for deep frying

1 **Place all the ingredients** for the sauce in a food processor, season to taste with salt and pepper, and process until smooth. Set aside.

2 **Season the flour** with salt and pepper. Place the flour, beaten eggs, and breadcrumbs in separate dishes. Cut each fish fillet into 4 pieces. Toss the fish and prawns in the flour, then dip in the egg, and coat in breadcrumbs.

3 **Heat the oil** to 180°C (350°F) in a large pan or deep-fat fryer. Fry the fish in batches for 2–3 minutes, or until crisp and golden. Drain on kitchen paper.

4 **Place a few rocket leaves** on each serving plate with the fish on top. Serve immediately, with the sauce served alongside.

> ### BREADCRUMBS
> Japanese Panko breadcrumbs have a light crisp texture and are perfect for deep frying. They are available from large supermarkets or Asian stores.

Mackerel with Cucumber Salad

Perfect for a summer lunch, the mackerel can be grilled or cooked on the barbecue

 serves 4

prep 30 mins • cook 10 mins

1 **cucumber**

1 **shallot**, finely chopped

1 tbsp **chopped dill**, plus extra to garnish

½ **green pepper**, deseeded and chopped

juice of ½ **lemon**

½ tsp **Dijon mustard**

4 tbsp **light olive oil**, plus extra to serve

salt and freshly ground **black pepper**

4 whole **mackerel**, boned

boiled **new potatoes**, to serve

1 **To make the salad**, top and tail the cucumber, then run a vegetable peeler down its length to shave it into long, thin strips. Put the strips in a bowl and add the shallot, dill, and green pepper.

2 **Whisk the lemon** juice, mustard, and olive oil, and season to taste with salt and pepper. Pour the dressing over the cucumber mixture. Toss lightly to coat, then set aside.

3 **Preheat the grill** on its medium-high setting. Cut 2 or 3 slashes into the skin of each side of the fish. Grill for 5 minutes, then turn them and grill for a further 3–4 minutes, or until cooked.

4 **Serve hot with** the cucumber salad and new potatoes tossed in olive oil, garnished with a little dill.

● **Leftovers** can be flaked and used as a tasty omelette filling, or added to a salad.

Halibut with Chunky Romesco

Romesco is a classic sauce from Catalonia, Spain, made from tomatoes, garlic, onion, peppers, almonds, and olive oil

🍴 serves 6

🕐 prep 10 mins • cook 30 mins

3 tbsp **extra virgin olive oil**, plus extra for greasing

1 kg (2¼lb) **halibut fillets**, 2cm (¾in) thick

salt and freshly ground **black pepper**

2 **garlic cloves**, finely chopped

75g (2½oz) **almonds**, coarsely chopped

125g (4½oz) **breadcrumbs**

3 tbsp chopped **flat-leaf parsley**

For the sauce

350g (12oz) jar **roasted red peppers**, rinsed, patted dry, and coarsely chopped

1 tbsp **sherry vinegar**

¼ tsp **cayenne pepper**

pinch of **smoked paprika**

1 Preheat the oven to 230°C (450°F/Gas 8). Brush the bottom of an ovenproof dish with olive oil, and add the fish, skin-side down. Season to taste with salt and pepper.

2 Heat 2 tbsp oil in a heavy frying pan. Add the garlic, almonds, and breadcrumbs, and fry over a medium heat, stirring, for 6–8 minutes, or until just golden. Do not let the nuts burn. Stir in the parsley, then spoon the mixture over the fish.

3 Bake the fish uncovered for 5 minutes, then loosely cover with foil, and bake for 15 minutes, or until just cooked through. The fish will flake easily when it is ready. Remove from the oven and sprinkle 1 tbsp of the olive oil over the fish.

4 Meanwhile, to make the romesco, combine all the ingredients for the sauce. Serve the fish topped with the sauce, or serve the sauce separately in a bowl.

Monkfish with Mussels and Pancetta

The firm, slightly sweet flavour of monkfish is delicious with salty pancetta and fresh tomatoes

🍴 serves 4

🕐 prep 20 mins • cook 30 mins

❗ tap the mussels and discard any that do not close

1 tbsp **olive oil**

15g (½ oz) **butter**

1 **onion**, chopped

pinch of **salt**

3 **garlic cloves**, chopped

400g (14oz) **tomatoes**, chopped

450g (1lb) **monkfish**, cut into chunks

120ml (4fl oz) **dry white wine**

100g (3½ oz) **pancetta**, sliced

1 kg (2.2lb) **mussels**, cleaned

100 ml (3½fl oz) **double cream**

juice of ½ **lemon**

handful of **parsley**, chopped

1 Heat the oil and butter in a large pan, and fry the onion and garlic with the salt over a low heat for 5 minutes. Add the tomatoes, simmer for 5 minutes, then add the monkfish and wine and simmer for a further 10 minutes.

2 Meanwhile, in a separate pan, grill the pancetta until crisp, then chop coarsely when cool enough to handle.

3 Add the mussels to the tomatoes and fish, and cover. Shake the pan after 2 minutes, then cook for a further 4 minutes, or until the mussels have opened. Discard any that remain closed.

4 Remove the mussels and monkfish with a slotted spoon into a large, warm serving bowl, then cover to keep warm. Simmer the pan juices, then add the pancetta, cream, lemon juice, and half of the parsley. Return to a simmer, then pour over the mussels. Scatter over the remaining parsley and serve.

● **Good with** a crisp green salad, and warm crusty bread.

Baked Bream

This classic Iberian dish, *Besugo al Horno*, combines fish and potatoes

 serves 4

 prep 10 mins, plus marinating • cook 1 hr

2 **sea bream**, 600g (1 lb 5oz) each

1 tbsp **tapenade**

2 **lemon** slices, thickly sliced

juice of 1 **lemon**

3 tbsp **olive oil**

700g (1½lb) **potatoes**, very thinly sliced

1 **onion**, thinly sliced

2 **peppers**, deseeded and sliced into thin rings

4 **garlic** cloves, chopped

2 tbsp chopped **parsley**

1 tsp **hot paprika** (pimentón picante)

120ml (4fl oz) **dry white wine**

salt and freshly ground **black pepper**

● **Prepare ahead** The fish can be prepared to the end of step 1 and marinated up to 6 hours in advance, then covered and chilled.

1 Make 2 diagonal cuts on each side of the thickest part of both fish. Place in a non-metallic dish and spread the tapenade over the inside and outside of each fish. Tuck a lemon slice into the gills of each fish, drizzle with the lemon juice, and place in the refrigerator to marinate for 1 hour.

2 Preheat the oven to 190°C (375°F/Gas 5). Grease an ovenproof dish with 1 tbsp of the olive oil. Layer half the potatoes in the dish, then the onions and peppers on top. Scatter with the garlic and parsley, and sprinkle with the paprika, before layering the remaining potatoes on top. Drizzle over the remaining olive oil, and sprinkle with 2–3 tbsp of water. Cover with foil and bake for 40 minutes, or until the potatoes are cooked and golden.

3 Increase the temperature to 220°C (425°F/Gas 7). Place the fish on top of the potatoes, pour over the wine, season with salt and pepper, and return to the oven, uncovered, for 20 minutes, or until the fish is cooked. Serve immediately.

Salt Cod Braised with Vegetables

In this dish, known in Spain as *Bacalao a la cazuela*, salt cod is tender and fragrant with the classic Spanish aromas of garlic, bay leaves, and saffron

 serves 4

 prep 20 mins, plus soaking • cook 40 mins

 soak the fish for at least 24 hrs in enough water to cover it, changing the water 2–3 times to remove saltiness of the brine

3 tbsp **olive oil**

1 **onion**, finely diced

white parts of 2 **leeks**, finely sliced

3 **garlic** cloves, minced

3 **tomatoes**, peeled, deseeded, and chopped

500g (1 lb 2oz) **potatoes**, diced

salt and freshly ground **black pepper**

2 **bay leaves**

large pinch of **saffron threads**

800g (1¾lb) thick-cut **bacalao** (salt cod), soaked and cut into 4 pieces

120ml (4fl oz) **dry white wine**

2 tbsp chopped **parsley**

1 Heat the oil in a large, shallow, heatproof casserole. Add the onion and leek, and fry gently, stirring constantly for 5 minutes, or until soft.

2 Add the garlic and tomatoes, and cook for a further 2 minutes, stirring continuously. Add the potatoes, season to taste with salt and pepper, and add the bay leaves and saffron.

3 Add the bacalao, skin-side up, on top of the vegetables. Pour in the wine, plus 250ml (8fl oz) water, then bring gently to a simmer and cook for 25–30 minutes. Shake the casserole once or twice every 5 minutes to help release gelatine from the fish to thicken the sauce.

4 Sprinkle over the chopped parsley, and serve straight from the casserole.

Salmon en Papillote

Cooking in a tightly sealed parchment packet or *papillote* ensures that the cooking juices are retained and keeps the fish moist

🍴 serves 4

🕐 prep 25 mins • cook 15 mins

4 **salmon steaks** or fillets, 175g (6oz) each

olive oil, for greasing

4 **tomatoes**, sliced

2 **lemons**, sliced

8 sprigs of **tarragon**

freshly ground **black pepper**

● **Prepare ahead** The salmon parcels can be prepared several hours in advance and chilled until needed.

1 **Cut 8 circles** of baking parchment large enough for the salmon steaks to fit on half of a circle. Place 2 circles on top of each other to create a double thickness of parchment. Lightly grease the top circle's surface with olive oil. Repeat with the other circles.

2 **Preheat the oven** to 160°C (325°F/Gas 3). Divide the tomato slices among the circles, placing them on one half. Place the salmon on the tomatoes, then top with the lemon slices and tarragon; season to taste with pepper. Fold up the parchment to enclose the fish. Crimp the edges to create a tight seal. Place the parcels on a baking tray and bake for 15 minutes.

3 **Place the salmon** on warm plates, and serve immediately.

● **Good with** *Beurre Blanc* (a classic butter sauce) poured over the fish or served alongside.

Seafood Salad

Suitable for lunch, a picnic, or a light supper in the garden, this is an ideal summer dish

🍴 serves 4

🕐 prep 20 mins • cook 25 mins

3 tbsp **olive oil**

8 small **scallops**

8 raw **tiger prawns**, peeled with tail intact

400g (14 oz) **salmon fillet**, cut into strips

85g (3oz) **watercress**

½ **cucumber**, cut in half lengthways, seeded, and thinly sliced

For the dressing

1 **red chilli**, deseeded and finely sliced

1 tbsp clear **honey**

finely grated zest and juice of 1 **lemon**

juice of 1 **lime**

salt and freshly ground **black pepper**

2 tbsp chopped **coriander**

1 **Make the dressing** by mixing all of the ingredients with 2 tbsp olive oil, then set aside.

2 **Heat 1 tbsp** of the olive oil in a heavy frying pan. Fry the scallops for 1–2 minutes each side, or until just cooked. Transfer to a bowl. Add the prawns to the pan and fry for 2–3 minutes, or until pink and cooked through, and add to the scallops. Finally, fry the salmon for 2–3 minutes, or until cooked, taking care not to break up the fish too much as it cooks; add extra oil if required. Add to the bowl with the shellfish, toss in half the dressing, and set aside.

3 **To serve**, spread the watercress and cucumber over a large serving platter and drizzle with the remaining salad dressing. Arrange the seafood on top.

Mediterranean-style Grilled Sardines

Popular in coastal regions all over southern Europe, this is the way to enjoy these oily fish at their very best

serves 4

prep 15 mins, plus marinating • cook 5 mins

8 large whole **sardines**, cleaned

8 sprigs of **thyme** or lemon thyme, plus extra to garnish

4 **lemons**

3 tbsp **olive oil**

2 **garlic cloves**, crushed

1 tsp **ground cumin**

● **Prepare ahead** The flavours of this dish benefit from marinating for at least 2 hours before cooking. Chill until ready to use.

1 **Rinse the sardines** inside and out, and pat dry. Put a sprig of thyme inside each fish, and place them in a shallow non-metallic dish. Grate the zest and squeeze the juice from 3 of the lemons and place in a small bowl. Add the oil, garlic, and cumin, and whisk together. Pour this mixture over the sardines, cover, and refrigerate for at least 2 hours.

2 **Preheat the grill** on its highest setting. Transfer the sardines to a grill pan and grill for 2–3 minutes on each side, basting with the marinade.

3 **Cut the remaining lemon** into 8 wedges. Transfer the sardines to a heated serving plate and serve immediately, garnished with lemon wedges and sprigs of thyme.

Fisherman's Tuna Stew

This fish stew, which Basque fisherman call *marmitako de bonito*, was originally made at sea to provide for a hungry crew

serves 4

prep 10 mins • cook 35 mins

900g (2lb) **potatoes**

750g (1lb 10oz) fresh **tuna**

350g (12oz) jar **roasted red peppers**

3 tbsp **olive oil**

1 large **onion**, finely sliced

2 **garlic cloves**, crushed

1 **bay leaf**

salt and freshly ground **pepper**

400g (14oz) can **chopped tomatoes**

300g (10oz) frozen **petits pois**

2 tbsp chopped **parsley**

1 **Peel the potatoes** and cut into thick rounds. Cut the tuna into pieces roughly the same size as the potatoes, and slice the red peppers into strips.

2 **Heat the oil** in a casserole, stir in the onion, garlic, and bay leaf, and cook , stirring, until the onions are translucent. Add the potatoes, stir well, season to taste with salt and pepper, then cover with water. Boil for 10 minutes, or until the potatoes are almost cooked, then add the tomatoes, and continue to cook for a further 5 minutes.

3 **Reduce the heat** to low, add the tuna, and cook for a further 5 minutes, then add the petits pois and the red peppers, and cook very gently for 10 minutes. Sprinkle with parsley to serve.

VARIATION

Fisherman's Stew
Make the recipe above, but use 750g (1lb 10oz) mixed fish and shellfish, such as cod, haddock, and large peeled prawns, instead of tuna.

Chinese-style Steamed Bass

An impressive restaurant-style dish that brings out the clean, delicate flavours of the fish and is easy to prepare

 serves 4

 prep 15 mins • cook 10–12 mins

 steamer, or a wok with steaming rack and lid

8 tbsp **soy sauce**

8 tbsp **Chinese rice wine** or dry sherry

6 tbsp thinly sliced fresh **root ginger**

4 small **sea bass**, gutted and rinsed

2 tbsp **sesame oil**

1 tsp **salt**

4 **spring onions**, trimmed and thinly sliced

8 tbsp **sunflower oil**

4 **garlic cloves**, chopped

2 small **red chillies**, deseeded and thinly sliced

thinly sliced zest of 2 **limes**

1 Prepare a steamer, or position a steaming rack in a wok with water so it doesn't touch the water. Bring to the boil.

2 Stir together the soy sauce, rice wine, and 4 tbsp ginger, and set aside. Using a sharp knife, make slashes in the fish, 2.5cm (1in) apart and not quite as deep as the bone, on both sides. Rub the fish inside and out with the sesame oil and salt.

3 Scatter one-quarter of the spring onions over a heatproof serving dish that will hold 2 fish and fit in the steamer or on the steaming rack. Place 2 fish on the dish and pour over half the sauce.

4 Place the dish in the steamer or on the rack, cover, and steam for 10–12 minutes, or until the fish is cooked through and flakes easily when tested with a knife. Remove the fish, cover, and keep warm. Repeat with the remaining fish.

5 Meanwhile, heat the sunflower oil in a small saucepan over a medium-high heat until shimmering. Scatter the fish with remaining spring onions and ginger, and the garlic, chilli, and lime zest. Drizzle the hot oil over the fish and serve.

Seared Tuna with Cucumber and Fennel

This tuna is served very rare, so it is essential that it is bought as fresh as possible

 serves 4

 prep 15 mins, plus cooling • cook 6 mins

6 tbsp **olive oil**, plus extra for brushing

4 x 150g (5½oz) **tuna steaks**

salt and freshly ground **black pepper**

1 **fennel bulb**, sliced

2 **shallots**, finely chopped

1 **cucumber**, deseeded, skinned and finely chopped

30g (1oz) **mint**, **parsley** and **chervil** leaves, torn and mixed

8 **anchovy fillets**

juice of 1 **lemon**

lemon wedges, to serve

1 Rub 2 tbsp of oil over the tuna steaks and sprinkle with plenty of black pepper. Set aside.

2 Heat 2 tbsp olive oil and sauté the fennel for 4–5 minutes, or until just tender. Season with salt and pepper. Tip the fennel into a large bowl and set aside to cool a little.

3 Add the shallots, cucumber and herbs to the fennel. Stir in the lemon juice and remaining oil.

4 Heat a heavy frying pan or grill pan until smoking. Lightly brush the tuna steaks with oil, then pan-fry for 30 seconds. Brush the top with a little more oil, turn over, and cook for a further 30 seconds.

5 Place a tuna steak on each serving plate, with the salad piled on top, and 2 anchovies draped over. Drizzle with the remaining lemon and oil from the bowl, and serve with a wedge of lemon.

● **Good with** a salad of warm parsley-buttered new potatoes.

Spiced Fish and Prawns

A fine example of the Nonya cuisine of Singapore

 serves 4

 prep 30 mins • cook 20 mins

1 small **onion**, roughly chopped

2 **garlic cloves**, crushed

2 **red chillies**, deseeded and roughly chopped

30g (1oz) **dried shrimp**

1 tsp **shrimp paste**

150ml (5fl oz) **groundnut oil**

1 **red onion**, thinly sliced

1 **red pepper**, deseeded and chopped

1 **green pepper**, deseeded and chopped

115g (4oz) **baby corn**, halved lengthways

350g (12oz) firm **white fish** fillets, such as monkfish, skinned and cut into bite-size pieces

16 raw **tiger prawns**, peeled

1 **Put the onion**, garlic, chillies, dried shrimp, and shrimp paste in a blender. Pour in 75ml (2½fl oz) of the oil and process until smooth.

2 **Heat 2 tbsp oil** in a wok, add the blended mixture, and fry over a fairly low heat for 10 minutes, stirring frequently. Scoop the paste out of the wok and set aside.

3 **Wipe out the wok**, add 2 tbsp oil and stir-fry the sliced onion for 2 minutes. Add the red and green peppers and stir-fry for 3 minutes. Add the baby corn and stir-fry for a further 2 minutes, then transfer the vegetables to a plate and set aside.

4 **Add 1 tbsp** of oil to the wok, add the fish and prawns and stir-fry for 1–2 minutes, until the fish turns opaque and the prawns pink. Return the paste and vegetables to the wok and toss everything together for 1 minute over the heat. Serve at once.

● **Good with** rice or noodles and a stir-fried vegetable dish.

● **Leftovers** can be finely chopped and used to stuff vol-au-vents or rolled in filo pastry as cocktail snacks.

Smoked Haddock with Spinach and Pancetta

This deliciously satisfying dish is great for a quick supper

 serves 6

 prep 10 mins • cook 15–20 mins

15g (½oz) **butter**, plus extra for greasing

1 tbsp **olive oil**

1 **onion**, finely chopped

100g (3½oz) **pancetta** or bacon, chopped

450g (1lb) **spinach**

100g (3½oz) **crème fraîche**

salt and freshly ground **black pepper**

75g (2½oz) **Parmesan cheese**, grated

800g (1¾lb) **smoked fillets of haddock** or cod, skinned

juice of ½ **lemon**

30g (1oz) fresh **breadcrumbs**

● **Prepare ahead** Prepare up to 1 day in advance, and refrigerate until ready to cook.

1 **Preheat the oven** to 190°C (375°F/Gas 5) and butter an ovenproof serving dish. Melt the oil and butter together in a frying pan and fry the onion and pancetta for 5 minutes.

2 **Add the spinach** and stir until wilted, then stir in the crème fraîche, seasoning, and three-quarters of the Parmesan. Simmer until slightly thickened.

3 **Spoon the spinach** mixture into the ovenproof dish and place the fish on top. Sprinkle with lemon juice. Scatter with breadcrumbs and the remaining Parmesan, and bake for 15–20 minutes, or until the fish is cooked through and flakes easily.

Leaf-wrapped Asian Sole

Gently steamed fish makes a healthy, tasty supper

🍴 serves 4

🕐 prep 15 mins • cook 10 mins

✓ low fat

4 **sole fillets**, 175g (6oz) each

4 tsp **lemon** juice

4 tsp **soy sauce**

2 tsp fresh **root ginger**, grated

sesame oil, to drizzle

¼ tsp **ground white pepper**

16–20 large **pak choi leaves**, tough stalks removed

1 Drizzle each sole fillet with 1 tsp lemon juice, 1 tsp soy sauce, ½ tsp ginger, and a light, even drizzle of sesame oil. Gently roll the fillets lengthways and arrange them on a heatproof plate.

2 Fill a large saucepan fitted with a steamer with 2.5cm (1in) water; bring to the boil, then reduce the heat to a simmer.

3 Blanch the pak choi leaves for several seconds in simmering water, or until soft, then place them briefly into a bowl of iced water.

4 Wrap each fillet in 4–5 leaves, securing with cocktail sticks if necessary. Set the plate with the fish on the steamer rack, place the lid on the steamer, and steam for 8–10 minutes, or until the fish becomes opaque.

● **Good with** a mix of stir-fried vegetables, or with boiled white rice.

VARIATION

Spinach-wrapped Sole

Use spinach instead of pak choi without blanching it. Replace the soy sauce, ginger, and sesame oil with a little butter over the fillets, and sprinkle with dried mixed herbs.

Steaming Fish

Steaming fish ensures that none of the flavours are lost during cooking.

Swordfish Baked with Herbs

Rosemary is not often used with fish, but it perfectly complements the strong flavours of this dish

🍴 serves 4

🕐 prep 20 mins • cook 15–20 mins

✓ low fat

4 **swordfish steaks**, about 175g (6oz) each, skinned

freshly ground **black pepper**

2 tbsp **extra virgin olive oil**, plus extra for greasing

1 **fennel bulb**, thinly sliced

4 **tomatoes**, sliced

1 **lemon**, sliced

4 tbsp chopped **flat-leaf parsley**

1 tbsp chopped **mint**

4 sprigs of **thyme**

2 tsp chopped **rosemary leaves**

100ml (3½fl oz) **dry white wine**

1 Preheat the oven to 180°C (350°F/Gas 4). Season the swordfish steaks with plenty of pepper. Lightly grease an ovenproof

dish with the oil and place the sliced fennel in an even layer in the dish.

2 Lay the fish in the dish in a single layer and top with the tomato and the lemon slices. Sprinkle with the parsley, mint, thyme, and rosemary, and pour the wine over the fish. Drizzle with the olive oil and cover the dish tightly with foil.

3 Bake for 15–20 minutes, or until the swordfish steaks are just cooked. Serve immediately, spooning the juices in the dish over the fish.

● **Good with** steamed new potatoes and green vegetables, such as broccoli or French beans.

VARIATION

Tuna Baked with Herbs

Replace the swordfish with 4 fresh tuna steaks of the same weight. Throw in a handful of pitted black olives and complete as above.

Tiger Prawns with Chilli and Cheese

A quick-to-prepare supper to serve for friends

 serves 6

🕐 prep 10 mins, plus marinating
• cook 15–16 mins

🍽 large flameproof serving dish

600g (1lb 5oz) raw **tiger prawns**, peeled

juice of 2 **limes**

few drops of **Tabasco sauce**

2 tbsp **olive oil**

2 **red onions**, finely sliced

3 **red chillies**, deseeded and finely chopped

3 **garlic cloves**, crushed

salt and freshly ground **black pepper**

250ml (8fl oz) **double cream**

85g (3oz) **Gruyère cheese** or **Parmesan cheese**, grated

1 Put the prawns in a large bowl, toss in the lime juice and Tabasco sauce, cover, and leave to marinate in the refrigerator for 30 minutes.

2 Preheat the grill on its highest setting. Heat the oil in frying pan and lightly fry the onions for 5 minutes before adding the chillies and garlic. Continue to cook for another 5 minutes.

3 Put the onion mixture into the serving dish. Drain the prawns, spread over the onions, then season to taste with salt and pepper. Pour the cream over the prawns and sprinkle with the grated cheese.

4 Place under the grill and cook for 5–6 minutes, or until the prawns turn pink and the cheese is golden brown and bubbling. Serve at once.

⬤ **Good with** fresh bread and a crisp green salad.

> ### OVEN COOKING
> As an alternative, you can bake the prawns at 200°C (400°F/Gas 6) for 20 minutes.

Lobster Thermidor

This irresistibly indulgent seafood dish is thought to be named in honour of a play called *Thermidor* that opened in 1894 in Paris

🍽 serves 4

🕐 prep 25 mins • cook 20 mins

2 cooked **lobsters**, about 675g (1½lb) each

paprika, to sprinkle

lemon wedges, to serve

For the sauce

30g (1oz) **butter**

2 **shallots**, finely chopped

120ml (4fl oz) **white wine**

120ml (4fl oz) **fish stock**

150ml (5fl oz) **double cream**

½ tsp made **English mustard**

1 tbsp **lemon** juice

2 tbsp **parsley**, chopped

2 tsp **tarragon**, chopped

salt and freshly ground **black pepper**

75g (2½oz) **Gruyère cheese**, grated

1 Cut the lobsters in half lengthways. Remove the meat from the claws and tail, along with any coral or meat from the head. Cut the meat into bite-sized pieces. Clean out the shells and reserve.

2 To prepare the sauce, melt the butter in a small saucepan, add the shallots, and fry gently until softened but not browned. Add the wine and boil for 2–3 minutes, or until the liquid is reduced by half.

3 Add the stock and cream and boil rapidly, stirring, until reduced and slightly thickened. Stir in the mustard, lemon juice, and herbs, then season to taste with salt and pepper. Stir in half the cheese.

4 Preheat the grill on its highest setting. Add the lobster meat to the sauce, then divide between the lobster shells. Top with the remaining cheese.

5 Place the lobsters on a foil-lined grill pan and grill for 2–3 minutes, or until bubbling and golden. Sprinkle with a little paprika and serve hot, with lemon wedges.

Calamari Salad with Mint and Dill

Fresh herbs and grilled seafood make a delicious warm salad

 serves 4

prep 20 mins, plus marinating
● cook 5 mins

1kg (2¼lb) small **calamari**, cleaned

For the marinade

2 tbsp chopped **flat-leaf parsley**

1 tbsp chopped **mint**

1 **garlic clove**, crushed

2 tsp **ground coriander**

1 tsp **ground cumin**

2 tsp **paprika**

4 tbsp **olive oil**

For the salad

85g (3oz) **lamb's lettuce** or watercress

12 **mint sprigs**

1 small **red onion**, thinly sliced

juice of 1 **lime**

2 tbsp chopped **dill**

4 tbsp **extra virgin olive oil**

salt and freshly ground **black pepper**

1 Cut off the calamari tentacles and remove the beak-like mouth from the centre. Cut the body in half lengthways and score the flesh in diagonal cuts to form a diamond pattern. Cut the tentacles into bite-sized pieces. Place in a bowl.

2 Combine the marinade ingredients, adding the oil gradually to make a paste. Coat the calamari in the mixture. Cover, chill, and marinate for at least 30 minutes.

3 Combine the lamb's lettuce with the mint sprigs and onion. Set aside.

4 Preheat the grill on its highest setting. Arrange the calamari on a foil-lined grill pan and grill for 4–5 minutes, or until just cooked, turning once. Season to taste with salt and pepper and sprinkle with a little of the lime juice.

5 Place the remaining lime juice, dill, and olive oil in a small jug, season with salt and pepper, then whisk well. Spoon the dressing over the salad leaves and top with the grilled calamari. Serve immediately.

Seafood Curry

This quick curry is flavoured with chillies, coconut, and lime

 serves 4

prep 15 mins ● cook 12 mins

600g (1lb 5oz) skinless boneless **white fish**, such as cod or haddock, cut into bite-sized pieces, rinsed and patted dry

½ tsp **salt**

½ tsp **turmeric**

½ **onion**, chopped

1cm (½in) piece fresh **root ginger**, peeled and coarsely chopped

1 **garlic clove**, crushed

2 tbsp **sunflower oil**

1 tsp **black mustard seeds**

4 **green cardamom pods**, crushed

2–4 **dried red chillies**, crushed

100g (3½oz) **creamed coconut**, dissolved in 500ml (16fl oz) boiling water

12 **king prawns**, peeled and deveined

2 tbsp fresh **lime** juice

freshly ground **black pepper**

coriander leaves, to garnish

lemon wedges, to garnish

1 Put the fish in a non-metallic bowl, sprinkle over the salt and turmeric, and turn over so both sides are lightly covered. Set aside.

2 Put the onion, ginger, and garlic in a food processor or blender and process until it makes a paste. Heat a deep frying pan over a high heat until hot. Add the oil and swirl around, then reduce the heat to medium, add the onion paste, and fry, stirring, for 3–5 minutes, or until it just begins to colour. Stir in the mustard seeds, cardamom, and chillies and stir for 30 seconds.

3 Stir in the coconut mixture. Leave to bubble for 2 minutes, then reduce the heat to medium-low, add the fish pieces and any juices in the bowl, and spoon the sauce over the fish. Simmer for 2 minutes, spooning the sauce over the fish once or twice as it cooks, taking care not to break up the pieces.

4 Add the prawns to the pan and simmer for 2 minutes, or until they turn pink and the fish flakes easily. Add lime juice and season to taste with salt and pepper. Serve garnished with coriander leaves and lemon wedges.

Shrimp Diabolo

Quick and easy prawns in a spicy tomato sauce

🍴 serves 4

🕐 prep 5 mins • cook 20 mins

2 tbsp **olive oil**

1 **onion**, chopped

1 **red pepper**, deseeded and sliced

3 **garlic cloves**, crushed

120ml (4fl oz) **dry white wine** or stock

250ml (8fl oz) **passata** (sieved tomatoes)

450g (1lb) cooked peeled **tiger prawns**, thawed if frozen

1–2 tbsp **chilli sauce**

2 tsp **Worcestershire sauce**

⬤ **Prepare ahead** The sauce can be prepared up to 2 hours in advance. Add the prawns just before serving.

1 **Heat the oil** in a large saucepan and fry the onion for 5 minutes, or until softened and beginning to turn golden. Add the pepper and fry for another 5 minutes, or until softened.

2 **Add the garlic** and fry for a few seconds. Stir in the wine and let it bubble away for 1–2 minutes.

3 **Stir in the passata** and bring to the boil, stirring, then reduce the heat and simmer for 5 minutes, or until reduced slightly.

4 **Add the prawns** and stir until piping hot. Do not overcook or the prawns will become tough. Stir in the chilli and Worcestershire sauces, and serve immediately.

⬤ **Good with** boiled rice.

VARIATION

Shrimp à la Basquaise
Dice the red pepper and add 1 diced green pepper. Cook as above, omitting the chilli and Worcestershire sauces.

Moules Marinières

The title of this classic French recipe for mussels cooked in wine, garlic, and herbs means "in the style of the fisherman"

🍴 serves 4

🕐 prep 15 mins • cook 10 mins

❗ tap the mussels and discard any that do not close

60g (2oz) **butter**

2 **onions**, finely chopped

3.6kg (8lb) fresh **mussels**, cleaned

2 **garlic cloves**, crushed

600ml (1 pint) **dry white wine**

4 **bay leaves**

2 sprigs of **thyme**

salt and freshly ground **black pepper**

2–4 tbsp chopped **parsley**

1 **Melt the butter** in a very large heavy saucepan, add the onion, and fry gently until lightly browned. Add the mussels, garlic, wine, bay leaves, and thyme, and season to taste with salt and pepper. Cover, bring to the boil, and cook for 5–6 minutes, or until the mussels have opened, shaking the pan frequently. If you do not have a large enough saucepan for all the mussels, cook them in 2 pans instead.

2 **Remove the open mussels** with a slotted spoon, discarding any that remain closed. Transfer the mussels to warmed bowls, cover, and keep warm.

3 **Strain the liquor** into a pan and bring to the boil. Season to taste with salt and pepper, add the parsley, pour it over the mussels, and serve at once.

⬤ **Good with** plenty of French bread for mopping up the juices.

⬤ **Leftovers** can be added cold to salads, or gently reheated with their juices to dress cooked pasta.

SERVING MUSSELS
Provide diners with additional plates for the empty shells and finger bowls with warm water and a slice of lemon.

Sweet and Sour Prawns

Prawns stir-fried in a fragrant sauce spiked with chilli, garlic, and ginger makes a deliciously different main course

- 🍴 serves 4
- 🕐 prep 20 mins • cook 10 mins
- 🔲 wok

3 tbsp **rice wine vinegar**

2 tbsp **clear honey**

1 tbsp **caster sugar**

2 tbsp **light soy sauce**

2 tbsp **tomato ketchup**

2 tbsp **vegetable oil**

3 **shallots**, peeled and sliced

2cm (¾in) piece of fresh **root ginger**, peeled and grated

1 **red chilli**, deseeded and finely chopped

1 **garlic clove**, crushed

1 small **carrot**, cut into matchsticks

1 **celery stick**, cut into matchsticks

1 **green pepper**, deseeded and cut into strips

500g (1lb 2oz) raw **tiger prawns**, peeled and deveined

2 **spring onions**, sliced lengthways, to garnish

● **Prepare ahead** Step 1 can be completed several hours in advance.

1 **Heat the first** 5 ingredients together in a small saucepan, until the honey and sugar melt. Remove from the heat and set aside.

2 **Heat the oil** in a wok, add the shallots, ginger, chilli, garlic, carrot, celery, and green pepper and stir-fry for 4 minutes.

3 **Add the prawns** and stir-fry for a further 2 minutes or until the prawns turn pink. Pour in the vinegar-and-sugar mixture and stir-fry for 1 minute, or until the prawns and vegetables are coated and everything is heated through.

4 **To serve**, transfer to a platter and garnish with spring onions.

● **Good with** boiled rice.

VARIATION

Sweet and Sour Fish

Cubes of firm white fish such as monkfish or strips of sole, plaice, or sea bass also work well in this recipe. Take care not to overcook them or they will disintegrate.

Clams in White Wine

Versions of this dish, *Almejas al vino blanco*, can be found throughout the Mediterranean

- 🍴 serves 4-6
- 🕐 prep 10 mins, plus soaking time • cook 15 mins
- ❗ soak the clams for 1 hr to clean them; discard any that are already open

2 tbsp **olive oil**

1 medium **onion**, finely diced

2 **garlic cloves**, finely chopped

1kg (2¼lb) small **clams**, thoroughly washed

2 **bay leaves**

1 tsp fresh **thyme** (or a pinch of dried thyme)

120ml (4fl oz) **dry white wine**

1 tbsp chopped **parsley**

1 **Heat the oil** in a large flameproof casserole. Add the onion and garlic and fry, stirring, for 4-5 minutes, or until translucent.

2 **Add the clams** with the bay leaves and thyme. Stir thoroughly, cover, and allow to steam for 3-4 minutes, or until the clams have opened.

3 **Add the white wine** and cook for a further 3-4 minutes, shaking the pot a few times to allow the sauce to thicken slightly.

4 **Sprinkle with parsley** and serve straight from the casserole.

● **Good with** crusty bread, to soak up the juices.

Thai Crab Cakes

These make a delicious lunch or light supper dish
served with rice noodles

🍴 makes 20

🕐 prep 30 mins, plus 1 hr chilling
• cook 20 mins

❄️ freeze for up to 1 month; do not
refreeze if the crabmeat has
previously been frozen

500g (1lb 2oz) **white crabmeat**

115g (4oz) **green beans**, trimmed
and finely chopped

1 **green chilli** or red chilli, deseeded
and very finely chopped

1 tsp **lemongrass purée**

finely grated zest of 1 **lime**

1 tbsp Thai **fish sauce**

1 tbsp finely chopped **Chinese
chives** or garlic chives

1 **egg white**, lightly beaten

plain flour, to dust

vegetable oil, for deep-frying

1 **Flake the crabmeat** into
a bowl, picking it over carefully
to remove any small, sharp pieces of
shell. Add the green beans, chilli,
lemongrass purée, lime zest, fish
sauce, and chives and mix.

2 **Add the egg white**, stirring
to bind the mixture together.
Dust your hands with flour and shape
the mixture into 20 small balls.
Flatten them slightly into round
cakes, place on a plate or board,
spaced slightly apart so they don't
stick together and chill for 1 hour,
or until firm.

3 **In a large, deep frying pan**,
heat the oil to 160°C (325°F).
Dust the crab cakes with flour and
deep-fry them in batches for
3 minutes, or until golden. Drain on
a plate lined with kitchen paper and
serve warm.

● **Good with** a spicy dipping sauce
and a Thai noodle salad. Or try them
broken over a leafy salad for a simple
lunch dish.

● **Prepare ahead** Steps 1 and
2 can be completed several hours
ahead. Keep crab cakes refrigerated
until ready to cook.

Squid in Olive Oil and Paprika

Calamares con pimentón picante is made here with hot paprika
(picante) but you could use a sweeter version

🍴 serves 4

🕐 prep 5 mins • cook 5 mins

❗ buy squid already cleaned

450g (1lb) **squid**, cleaned

2 tbsp **olive oil**

2 **garlic cloves**, finely chopped

salt

2 tsp **hot paprika**

1 tbsp fresh **lemon** juice

lemon wedges, to serve

1 **Slice the squid** "tube" into
rings then each tentacle in half.

2 **Heat the oil** in a frying pan on
a medium heat, add the garlic
and fry for 1 minute, stirring, then
increase the heat and add the squid.
Fry for 3 minutes on a high heat,
stirring frequently.

3 **Season to taste** with salt, then
add the paprika and lemon juice.

4 **Transfer to small** serving
plates and serve immediately,
with lemon wedges for squeezing.

● **Good with** other tapas, such as
chorizo and olives.

Coquilles St Jacques

This seafood classic makes an impressive and elegant main course

 serves 4

prep 20 mins • cook 50 mins

4 scallop shells or 4 ramekins, piping bag

freeze for up to 3 months

8 **scallops**, white muscle and orange roe removed

6 tbsp **medium white wine**

1 **bay leaf**

7.5cm (3in) piece of **celery**

4 **black peppercorns**

small sprig of **thyme**

salt and freshly ground **black pepper**

225g (8oz) **button mushrooms**

juice of ½ **lemon**

60g (2oz) **butter**

1 tbsp **plain flour**

6 tbsp **double cream** or **crème fraîche**

50g (1¾oz) **Gruyère cheese** or Emmental cheese, grated

For the piped potatoes

450g (1lb) **floury potatoes**, peeled and cut into 2–3 pieces

30g (1oz) **butter**

large pinch of grated **nutmeg**

salt and freshly ground **black pepper**

3 **egg yolks**

● **Prepare ahead** This can be prepared several hours in advance up to the end of step 5. Chill until ready to complete the recipe.

1 Boil the potatoes and mash them with the butter, nutmeg, and season to taste with salt and pepper, then beat over a low heat, or until fluffy. Remove from the heat, and beat in the egg yolks. Allow to cool slightly, then spoon into a piping bag with a plain nozzle. Pipe

a generous border of potato around the edges of each shell or ramekin.

2 Preheat the oven to 220°C (425°F/Gas 7). Place the scallops in a small saucepan, add 150ml (5fl oz) water, the wine, bay leaf, celery, peppercorns, thyme, and a good pinch of salt. Bring slowly to the boil, cover, and simmer gently for 1–2 minutes, or until the scallops just whiten. Transfer them to a bowl, strain the liquid, reserve to make the sauce, and discard the vegetables.

3 Gently cook the mushrooms with the lemon juice, 2 tbsp water, and salt and pepper to taste in a covered pan for 5–7 minutes, or until tender. If any liquid remains, simmer, uncovered, until it has evaporated. Add the mushrooms to the scallops.

4 Melt the butter in a pan. Stir in the flour, and cook gently for 1 minute, stirring constantly. Remove from the heat, and gradually stir in the reserved liquid. Slowly bring to the boil, and continue to cook, stirring constantly, until thickened. Season to taste with salt and pepper, and simmer gently for 4–5 minutes. Reduce the heat and stir in the cream, and half the cheese.

5 Cut each cooked scallop into 2 or 3 pieces, and stir into the sauce with the mushrooms.

6 Spoon the mixture into each shell or ramekin, and sprinkle the remaining cheese on top. Bake for about 15 minutes, or until the sauce and potatoes are golden, and serve.

Breaded Fried Prawns

Freshly cooked, these are tastier than shop-bought

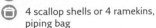 serves 4

prep 20 mins, plus chilling • cook 15 mins

deep-fat fryer or large deep saucepan half-filled with oil

12 tbsp dry **breadcrumbs**

6 tbsp **polenta**

2 tsp dried **marjoram** or oregano

2 tsp dried **thyme**

freshly ground **black pepper**

3–4 **eggs**, beaten

24 raw king **prawns**, peeled and deveined

flour, to dust

sunflower oil, for deep-frying

1 Mix the breadcrumbs, polenta, marjoram, thyme, and pepper, and spread out on a plate.

2 Pat the prawns dry with kitchen paper and dust with flour, leaving the tails clear. Brush with beaten egg, then press into the breadcrumb mixture and evenly coat. Chill for 30 minutes.

3 Heat the oil for deep-frying to 180°C (350°F). Deep-fry the prawns in batches for 2–3 minutes each, or until the tails turn pink and the coating is golden and crisp. Drain on kitchen paper and serve at once.

● **Good with** herb-flecked thin rice noodles.

Mussels with Tomatoes and Chilli

This dish allows the warm Mediterranean aroma of smoked paprika to add its own special flavour to mussels

 serves 4

 prep 15 mins • cook 10 mins

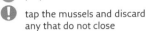 tap the mussels and discard any that do not close

2 tbsp **extra virgin olive oil**

30g (1oz) **unsalted butter**

2 **shallots**, finely chopped

½ tsp **smoked paprika**

1 **celery stick**, finely chopped

1 **garlic clove**, crushed

1 large **red chilli**, deseeded and finely chopped

1.8kg (4lb) **mussels**

2 **tomatoes**, chopped

90ml (3fl oz) **dry white wine**

2 tbsp chopped **flat-leaf parsley**

1 Heat the oil and butter in a large, deep saucepan with a tight-fitting lid. Add the shallots, smoked paprika, celery, garlic, and chilli, and fry over a low heat until the shallots have softened.

2 Add the mussels, tomatoes, and wine, stir well, and increase the heat to medium-high. Cover and cook for 2–3 minutes, or until the mussels have opened. Discard any that remain closed.

3 Transfer the mussels to deep serving bowls and sprinkle with parsley. Serve at once.

⬤ **Good with** thin-cut chips or pieces of warm crusty bread to mop up the rich juices.

COOKING MUSSELS

Stir the mussels once or twice while they cook. Those at the bottom will open more quickly because they are nearer the heat, so they need to be lifted up to allow those on top to drop down.

Oysters Rockefeller

A traditional brunch dish from New Orleans

 serves 4

 prep 15 mins • cook 30 mins

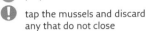 oyster knife, 4 large ovenproof serving dishes

100g (3½oz) **baby leaf spinach**

24 live **oysters** in their shells

75g (2½oz) **shallots**, chopped

1 **garlic clove**, chopped

4 tbsp chopped **flat-leaf parsley**

115g (4oz) **butter**

50g (1¾oz) **plain flour**

2 **anchovy fillets**, drained and finely chopped

pinch of **cayenne pepper**

salt and freshly ground **black pepper**

rock salt or dishwasher salt

3 tbsp **Pernod**

1 Put the spinach in a saucepan over a medium heat with the water clinging to its leaves from washing, and cook, stirring occasionally, for 5 minutes, or until wilted. Drain well, squeeze to remove any excess liquid, and set aside.

2 Meanwhile, discard any open oysters. Shell 1 oyster, reserving the liquid from the shell, then refrigerate the oyster in its shell and repeat until all the oysters are open. Chill the oyster liquid until needed.

3 Chop the spinach, shallots, garlic, and parsley very finely with a knife, or in a blender or food processor, then set aside.

4 Melt the butter in a small saucepan over a medium heat, add the flour, and stir for 2 minutes, without letting it brown. Slowly stir in the reserved oyster liquid so the mixture is smooth. Then stir in the spinach mixture, anchovies, cayenne, and salt and pepper to taste (keeping in mind that the anchovies are salty). Cover the pan and leave to simmer for 15 minutes.

5 Meanwhile, preheat the oven to 200°C (400°F/Gas 6). Arrange a thick layer of rock salt in the serving dishes, then put in the oven to warm briefly.

6 Uncover the pan and stir in the Pernod. Taste the sauce and adjust the seasoning, if necessary. Remove the dishes with the salt from the oven and arrange 6 oysters in their shells on each. (The salt keeps the oysters level during cooking.) Spoon the sauce over the oysters and bake for 5–10 minutes, or until the sauce looks set. Serve immediately.

Herbed Green Mayonnaise

Use a combination of your favourite herbs in this sauce, or use just one

🍴 makes 450ml (15fl oz)

🕐 prep 10 mins

2 tbsp white wine vinegar

1 egg

2 egg yolks

1 tbsp Dijon mustard

1 tbsp light soft brown sugar

1 garlic clove

salt and freshly ground black pepper

300ml (10fl oz) sunflower oil

30g (1oz) green herbs, such as basil, dill, coriander, or sorrel, finely chopped

● **Prepare ahead** This sauce can be made 2–3 days in advance, and chilled until ready to use.

1 Put the vinegar, egg, egg yolks, mustard, sugar, and garlic in a food processor and add ½ tsp each of salt and pepper. With the motor running, slowly pour in the oil in a steady stream until the sauce is thick and creamy.

2 Stir in the chopped herbs until thoroughly incorporated.

Quick Aioli

This rich, creamy, garlicky sauce is delicious with fish

🍴 makes 450ml (15fl oz)

🕐 prep 10 mins

2 tbsp white wine vinegar

1 egg

2 egg yolks

1 tbsp Dijon mustard

1 tbsp soft brown sugar

salt and freshly ground black pepper

300ml (10fl oz) sunflower oil

3 garlic cloves, crushed

2 tbsp lemon juice

1 Place the vinegar, egg, egg yolks, mustard, and sugar, in a food processor. Season to taste with salt and pepper, then blend until combined. With the motor running, pour in the oil in a steady stream.

2 When the sauce is thick and creamy, add the crushed garlic and lemon juice, and process until well combined and smooth.

VARIATION

Classic Aioli

To make this sauce by the traditional method, place the vinegar, egg, and egg yolks (all at room temperature), with the mustard, sugar, and salt and pepper in a small bowl set on a folded tea towel. Using a balloon whisk, beat until thick. Add the oil, drop by drop, whisking constantly. Whisk in the remaining oil, 1 tbsp at a time. Then whisk in the garlic and lemon juice.

Tartare Sauce

The classic, piquant mayonnaise-based sauce, traditionally served with fish

🍴 makes 360ml (12fl oz)

🕐 prep 10 mins, plus standing

300g (10oz) mayonnaise

2 tbsp capers, finely chopped

6 cornichons, finely chopped

1 shallot, finely chopped

2 tbsp finely chopped parsley

2 tbsp finely chopped tarragon

juice of ½ lemon

salt and freshly ground black pepper

● **Prepare ahead** The sauce can be prepared up to 4 days ahead, and chilled until ready to use.

1 Place all the ingredients in a bowl and stir together. Season to taste with salt and pepper.

2 Leave to stand for at least 20 minutes before serving to allow the flavours to develop.

● **Good with** fried or grilled fish, shellfish, and crab and fish cakes.

Beurre Blanc

This classic French sauce is simple to make

🍴 makes 275ml (9fl oz)

🕐 prep 5 mins • cook 10 mins

200ml (7fl oz) dry white wine

1 shallot, finely chopped

1 tbsp chopped flat-leaf parsley

1 bay leaf

4 black peppercorns

175g (6oz) unsalted butter, diced

salt and freshly ground black pepper

1 Put the wine, shallot, parsley, bay leaf, and peppercorns into a small saucepan. Bring to the boil, then simmer slowly for 4–5 minutes, or until reduced by half. Remove from the heat.

2 Strain the reduced liquid through a sieve into a heatproof bowl. Place the bowl over a pan of gently simmering water and, whisking constantly, add the cubes of butter, 1 at a time. When it becomes an emulsified sauce it is ready to use. Season to taste with salt and pepper.

● **Good with** pan-fried fish and steamed vegetables.

CHOOSING A DRY WHITE WINE FOR COOKING

Using wine in certain dishes adds a bright flavour without overpowering the ingredients. If a dish calls for a dry white wine, a neutral French wine is the most versatile. Sauvignon Blanc or Chablis are great in sauces, and Rieslings are delicious with fruit.

Salsa Verde

This strong-flavoured Italian green sauce is packed with herbs and is very versatile

 makes 360ml (12fl oz)

 prep 15 mins

6 **spring onions**, finely chopped

1 **garlic clove**, crushed

3 tbsp **capers**, chopped

4 **anchovies**, chopped

3 tbsp chopped **flat-leaf parsley**

2 tbsp chopped **basil**

2 tbsp chopped **mint**

2 tsp **Dijon mustard**

2 tbsp **sherry vinegar**

8 tbsp **extra virgin olive oil**

salt and freshly ground **black pepper**

● **Prepare ahead** The salsa can be made up to 24 hours in advance and stored in the refrigerator.

1 Place the spring onions, garlic, capers, and anchovies in a bowl, then stir in the parsley, basil and mint.

2 Using a fork, whisk in the mustard, then the vinegar. Gradually whisk in the olive oil.

3 Season to taste with salt and pepper and transfer to a serving bowl. Serve at room temperature.

● **Good with** grilled oily fish, grilled chicken or pork. It is also great as a dressing for salads.

● **Leftovers** can be stirred into hot, cooked pasta for a quick midweek supper. There is no need to heat the salsa, it will be warmed through by the hot pasta.

Chimichurri Sauce

A spicy sauce from Argentina that is great with grilled salmon

🍴 makes 250ml (8fl oz)

🕐 prep 5 mins

6 garlic cloves

175g (6oz) parsley, large stalks removed

6 tbsp extra virgin olive oil

2 tbsp white balsamic vinegar or white wine vinegar

1 tbsp chopped oregano

¼ tsp dried chilli flakes

salt and freshly ground black pepper

● **Prepare ahead** You can make the sauce in advance and store for 2–3 days, covered, in the refrigerator.

1 Place all the ingredients along with 2 tbsp cold water in a food processor or blender and process until smooth.

2 Season to taste with salt and pepper, and keep covered until needed. Before serving, whisk in a little more olive oil or water for a thinner consistency.

● **Good with** salmon, steaks, or chicken, or drizzled over roasted vegetables or steamed broccoli.

Chilli Butter

Use this flavouring wherever a touch of spice would be welcome

🍴 makes 250g (10oz)

🕐 prep 10 mins, plus chilling

250g (9oz) butter, softened

2 tbsp chilli powder

2 tsp ground cumin

2 garlic cloves, crushed

4 tbsp finely chopped coriander or parsley

salt and freshly ground black pepper

● **Prepare ahead** The chilli butter can be made up to 3 days in advance, and chilled until ready to use.

1 Place the butter, chilli powder, cumin, garlic, and herbs in a mixing bowl and beat together until well combined. Season to taste with salt and pepper and stir again. Transfer to a sheet of greaseproof paper and mould it into a roll.

2 Wrap the roll with the paper and twist the ends to seal. Chill in the refrigerator for 1 hour, or until firm enough to slice.

● **Good with** all kinds of grilled or barbecued fish, corn on the cob, and baked potatoes.

● **Leftovers** can be kept, wrapped in greaseproof paper, in the refrigerator, then sliced and melted for a quick butter sauce for pasta. Once melted, add a generous handful of cooked prawns. Heat through, and stir to coat everything in the sauce.

Hollandaise Sauce

A quick version of the classic sauce

🍴 makes 200ml (7fl oz)

🕐 prep 10 mins • cook 5 mins

1 tbsp white wine vinegar

juice of ½ lemon

3 large egg yolks

salt and ground white pepper

175g (6oz) butter

1 Put the vinegar and lemon juice in a small saucepan. Bring to the boil and remove from the heat.

2 Meanwhile, place the egg yolks in a food processor or blender, season with a little salt and pepper, and blend for 1 minute. With the motor running, slowly add the lemon juice and vinegar mixture.

3 Put the butter in the same pan and leave over a low heat until melted. When it begins to foam, remove from the heat. With the motor of the food processor or blender running, gradually add the butter to form a thick sauce. Serve the sauce immediately.

● **Good with** white fish, salmon, lightly poached eggs, or steamed vegetables, such as asparagus tips.

Béchamel Sauce

This white sauce uses a classic roux base; use for prawns, salmon, or a fish pie

- makes 300ml (10fl oz)
- prep 5 mins, plus standing • cook 5 mins
- freeze for up to 6 months

300ml (10fl oz) milk

1 onion, sliced

1 bay leaf

2–3 parsley stalks

6 black peppercorns

60g (2oz) butter

60g (2oz) flour

pinch of nutmeg

salt and ground white pepper

● **Prepare ahead** Step 1 can be made several hours in advance and chilled, until ready to use.

1 Pour the milk into a pan and add the onion, bay leaf, parsley, and peppercorns. Slowly bring to the boil, remove from the heat, and stand for 20 minutes to infuse. Strain the milk and discard the flavourings.

2 Melt the butter over a low heat in a clean pan, add the flour, and cook for 1–2 minutes to form a thick paste. Remove from the heat.

3 Gradually pour in the milk, stirring constantly. Return the pan to a low heat and cook, stirring constantly, until the sauce is smooth and thick. Simmer for a further 1–2 minutes, stirring constantly. Add a pinch of nutmeg and season to taste with salt and pepper.

VARIATIONS

Cheese Sauce
Follow the recipe and, off the heat, add 75g (3oz) grated mature Cheddar cheese and a large pinch of mustard powder.

Parsley Sauce
Stir in 2 tbsp finely chopped parsley at the end.

Mustard Sauce
Add 1 tbsp Dijon mustard at the end.

Rouille

A rich Provençale sauce, traditionally served with fish soup

- makes 450ml (15fl oz)
- prep 10 mins, plus standing

¼ tsp saffron threads

2 tbsp white wine vinegar

1 egg

2 egg yolks

1 tbsp Dijon mustard

1 tbsp light soft brown sugar

4 garlic cloves, crushed

pinch of cayenne pepper

salt and freshly ground black pepper

300ml (10fl oz) sunflower oil

● **Prepare ahead** The sauce can be made in advance and stored for up to 1 week, covered, and chilled.

1 Put the saffron threads in a small bowl, add 2 tbsp hot water and leave to soak for 5 minutes.

2 Put the saffron and water in a food processor with the vinegar, egg, egg yolks, mustard, sugar, garlic, cayenne, and ½ tsp each of salt and pepper. Process to combine, then, with the motor running, very slowly pour in the oil until the sauce is thick and creamy. Chill until needed.

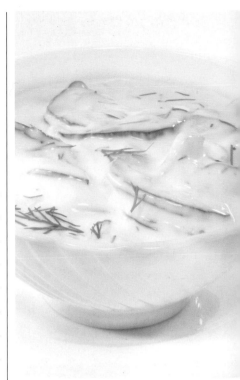

Cucumber and Dill Sauce

A fresh-tasting sauce, good with hot and cold fish dishes

- makes 300ml (10fl oz)
- prep 5 mins

150g (5½oz) soured cream

2 tbsp mayonnaise

grated zest of ½ lemon

few sprigs of fresh dill or ½ tsp dried

salt and ground white pepper

140g (5oz) cucumber, halved lengthways, seeded and finely sliced

2 tsp finely chopped Spanish onion

1 Combine the soured cream, mayonnaise, lemon zest, and dill in a bowl, mixing well. Season to taste with salt and pepper.

2 Stir in the cucumber and onion. Chill until required.

Baked Poussin with Lemon and Paprika

A meltingly succulent dish that gets its subtle flavours from a blend of Egyptian and Spanish influences

 serves 4

 prep 15 mins • cook 45 mins

 low fat

❄ freeze for up to 2 months

4 **lemons**, plus extra, cut into wedges, to serve

4 large ripe **tomatoes**, peeled and chopped, or 225g can chopped tomatoes

1 large **onion**, finely chopped

1 tbsp **paprika**

sea salt

clear honey, or soft brown sugar

hot chilli powder

4 **bay leaves**, plus extra to garnish

4 **poussins**, cavity rinsed

8 **garlic cloves**

1–2 tsp **balsamic vinegar**

1 Preheat the oven to 200°C (400°F /Gas 6). Cut 2 of the lemons in half, then into thick slices. Put the tomatoes, onion, and lemon slices into the base of the casserole, sprinkle with the paprika, and mix together. Season with salt and add a drizzle of honey, or a sprinkling of brown sugar. Add the chilli powder to taste, then the bay leaves.

2 Cut the 2 remaining lemons into quarters. Insert 2 quarters into the cavity of each poussin, along with 2 cloves of garlic. Lay poussins on top of the tomato mix in the casserole and season with sea salt.

3 Put the lid on the casserole and bake on the middle shelf for 20 minutes, then turn down the heat to 180°C (350°F/Gas 4) and cook, uncovered, for a further 25 minutes, or until cooked and browned. Remove the bird from the oven, place onto a serving plate, and keep warm.

4 Skim the fat from the juices in the pan and discard the lemon slices and bay leaves. Pour into a food processor or blender and process until smooth. Add the balsamic vinegar, then season to taste with salt and pepper. Serve the poussin with the sauce, garnished with bay leaves, and lemon wedges.

Honey Mustard Barbecued Chicken

The sweetness of honey and the tang of wholegrain mustard make a delicious glaze for barbecued chicken

 serves 4

🕐 prep 10 mins, plus marinating • cook 30 mins

8 **chicken drumsticks** or thighs

120ml (4fl oz) **tomato ketchup**

2 tbsp **olive oil**

120ml (4fl oz) **orange** juice

60ml (2fl oz) **balsamic vinegar**

1 tsp **dried oregano**

¼ tsp freshly ground **black pepper**

1 **garlic clove**, crushed

For the glaze

2 tbsp **clear honey**

2 tbsp **wholegrain mustard**

zest of 1 **lemon**

● **Prepare ahead** You can marinate the chicken for up to 24 hours.

1 Make 2 or 3 cuts into each chicken portion and place in a large bowl. Make the marinade by putting the tomato ketchup, olive oil, orange juice, vinegar, oregano, pepper, and garlic into the bowl and whisking together with a fork until well mixed. Pour the marinade over the chicken, and turn the pieces to coat evenly. Refrigerate for at least 6 hours, or overnight if possible, turning the chicken occasionally.

2 Preheat the barbecue or grill to medium. Remove the chicken from the marinade, reserving it for basting. Barbecue over a medium-low heat for 15 minutes, turning once, and basting frequently with the reserved marinade.

3 Combine the honey, mustard, and zest to make a glaze, and brush the chicken. Cook for a further 10–15 minutes, turning, or until browned and cooked through. To test if the chicken is cooked, the juices should run clear and the meat should no longer be pink in the centre when a knife or skewer is inserted.

VARIATION

Honey Mustard Barbecued Pork

Replace the chicken with the same quantity of pork. Cook until the juices run clear and the the skin is brown.

Seared Herbed Chicken with Green Herb Sauce

The herbed crust seals in the juices, keeping the meat succulent

serves 6

prep 20 mins
• cook 20–30 mins

freeze for up to 2 months

6 skinless boneless **chicken breasts**, about 175g (6oz) each

2 tbsp **plain flour**

350g (12oz) **breadcrumbs**

2 tbsp chopped **thyme**

2 tbsp chopped **parsley**

salt and freshly ground **black pepper**

175g (6oz) **Parmesan cheese**, finely grated

2 **eggs**, lightly beaten

4 tbsp **olive oil**

4 tbsp **sunflower oil**

For the green herb sauce

2 tbsp **white wine vinegar**

2 **egg yolks**

1 **egg**

1 tbsp **Dijon mustard**

1 tbsp **soft brown sugar** or caster sugar

salt and freshly ground **black pepper**

300ml (10fl oz) **sunflower oil**

20g (¾oz) **mixed herbs**, such as parsley, basil, dill, watercress, coriander, and chives, roughly chopped

1 For the sauce, place the vinegar, yolks, egg, mustard, and sugar into a food processor or blender, then gradually add the oil with the motor running to form a thick and creamy mayonnaise. Once all the oil has been added, blend in the herbs. Season to taste with salt and pepper and set aside.

2 Cut the chicken into halves and dust lightly with flour. Place the breadcrumbs in a bowl with thyme, parsley, and Parmesan, season to taste with salt and pepper, and mix well. Coat the chicken in the egg, then the breadcrumbs.

3 Heat the frying pan with some of each oil. Fry the chicken in 2–3 batches for 5 minutes on each side, or until crisp and golden, adding more oil with each batch. Drain, then serve with the green herb sauce.

Pot-roast Guinea Fowl with Cabbage and Walnuts

Guinea fowl cooked this way are moist and packed with flavour, as all the tasty juices are sealed within the pot

serves 4

prep 20 mins • cook 1 hr

2 **guinea fowls**, about 1.25kg (2¾lb) each

salt and freshly ground **black pepper**

30g (1oz) **butter**

2 tbsp **olive oil**

1 small **onion**, finely chopped

1 **leek**, thinly sliced

2 **celery sticks**, sliced

100g (3½oz) **smoked streaky bacon rashers**, diced

85g (3oz) **walnuts**, halved

1 small **Savoy cabbage**, about 400g (14oz)

100ml (3½fl oz) hot **chicken stock**

1 Preheat the oven to 200°C (400°F/Gas 6). Season the guinea fowl to taste with salt and pepper.

2 Heat the butter with half the oil in a large, deep, flameproof casserole, and fry the guinea fowls on a medium heat for 10 minutes, turning to brown on all sides. Remove from the heat and lift out the birds.

3 Add the remaining oil to the pan with the onion, leek, celery, and bacon, and fry, stirring, for 2–3 minutes, or until lightly coloured. Add the walnuts, then place the guinea fowl back on top of the fried vegetables.

4 Cut the cabbage into 8 wedges, leaving the leaves attached to the core. Tuck them loosely into the pot. Pour over the hot stock and season lightly. Bring to the boil, then cover and cook in the oven for 40–45 minutes, or until the vegetables are tender and the guinea fowl juices run clear when pierced.

5 Leave to stand for about 10 minutes before serving. To serve, remove the guinea fowls and cut each one in half. Arrange on plates and serve with vegetables and stock straight from the casserole.

● **Leftovers** can be coarsely chopped with the cabbage and walnuts, stirred into cooked rice, and shaped into timbales.

Chicken Pot Pie

This is a great recipe for transforming leftover roast chicken into a satisfying family meal

 serves 4

prep 15 mins • cook 20 mins

pie dish or ovenproof serving dish with flat rim

freeze the pie filling after step 3, once cooled completely, for up to 3 months; do not refreeze if the chicken has previously been frozen

2 carrots, sliced

2 parsnips, peeled and sliced

600ml (1 pint) hot chicken stock

30g (1oz) butter

1 onion, finely chopped

2 celery stalks, roughly chopped

20g (¾oz) plain flour

280g (10oz) frozen peas, thawed

¼–½ tsp mustard powder

salt and freshly ground black pepper

350g (12oz) skinless boneless cooked chicken, cubed

250ml (8fl oz) double cream

250g (9oz) frozen puff pastry, thawed

1 small egg, beaten, to glaze

● **Prepare ahead** The pie can be assembled a day in advance, refrigerated then baked.

1 **Preheat the oven** to 200°C (400°F/Gas 6). Put the carrots, parsnips, and stock in a large saucepan over a high heat and bring to the boil, then boil for 5 minutes or until the vegetables are just tender. Drain and reserve the stock.

2 **Melt the butter** in another pan over a medium heat. Add the onion and celery and fry, stirring frequently, for 5 minutes, or until softened. Add the flour and continue stirring for 2 minutes.

3 **Gradually stir in the stock** and bring to the boil, stirring. Reduce the heat and simmer for 2 minutes. Stir in the peas, the mustard and salt and pepper to taste. Leave the mixture to cool, then stir in the root vegetables, chicken, and cream. Pour into a 1.5 litre (2¼ pint) pie dish or ovenproof serving dish.

4 **Roll out the pastry** on a lightly floured surface until about ½cm (¼in) thick. Cut out a piece of pastry slightly larger than the dish. Brush the rim with water, then position the pastry over the filling and fold over the excess to make a stand-up edge. Crimp the edge, glaze the top with the beaten egg, and cut a small hole in the top to allow steam to escape.

5 **Place the pie** on a baking sheet and bake for 20 minutes, or until the pastry is puffed and golden and the filling is hot. Leave to stand for a few minutes, then serve.

● **Good with** steamed broccoli and, for heartier appetites, some boiled new potatoes.

VARIATION

Chicken and Leek Pie
Replace the onion with chopped leek for a subtle flavour change, and add or substitute other vegetables, such as broad beans or sweetcorn.

Saffron Chicken Brochettes

Ideal for a summer barbecue

serves 6

prep 10 mins, plus marinating • cook 10 mins

soak wooden skewers in cold water for 30 mins before use

12 wooden skewers

6 x 175g (6oz) skinless boneless chicken breasts, cubed

2 tbsp olive oil

zest and juice of 3 lemons

salt and freshly ground black pepper

4 pinches of saffron powder, dissolved in 1 tbsp boiling water

2 red onions, finely sliced

30g (1oz) butter

basil leaves, to garnish

1 **Put the chicken** in a large bowl. Whisk together the oil, lemon zest, the juice from 2 lemons and the saffron. Season to taste with salt and pepper. Add the sliced onions and pour over the chicken. Mix, cover, and chill for 2 hours or overnight.

2 **When ready to cook**, melt the butter in a small pan with the remaining lemon juice.

3 **Preheat the grill** to High. Remove the chicken from the marinade and thread on to skewers. Place under the grill with the onions. Turn and brush with lemon butter. Arrange on a heated plate and serve hot, scattered with herbs.

Chicken and Apricot Tagine

The dried fruit and warm spices in this dish are the unmistakable flavours of the Middle East

🍴 serves 4

🕐 prep 15 mins • cook 35–40 mins

🍲 large flameproof casserole

2 tbsp **sunflower oil**

1 **onion**, finely chopped

1 **garlic clove**, finely chopped

1 tsp **ground ginger**

1 tsp **ground cumin**

1 tsp **turmeric**

pinch of **ground cinnamon**

pinch of **dried chilli flakes** (optional)

1 tbsp **tomato purée**

600ml (1 pint) **chicken stock**

4 tbsp fresh **orange** juice

250g (9oz) mixed **dried fruit**, such as **apricots** and **raisins**

salt and freshly ground **black pepper**

675g (1½lb) skinless boneless **chicken breasts** and **thighs**, cut into large chunks

2 tbsp chopped **coriander**, to garnish

● **Prepare ahead** The tagine can be cooked in advance, left to cool, and refrigerated for up to 2 days; reheat gently but thoroughly.

1 Heat the oil in a large flameproof casserole over a medium heat. Add the onion, garlic, ground spices, and chilli flakes, if using, and fry, stirring, for 5 minutes, or until the onions have softened. Stir in the tomato purée and stock and bring to the boil, stirring.

2 Add the orange juice, dried fruits, and salt and pepper to taste. Reduce the heat, partially cover the pan, and simmer for 15 minutes, or until the fruits are soft and the juices have reduced slightly.

3 Add the chicken, re-cover the casserole, and continue simmering for 20 minutes, or until the chicken is tender and the juices run clear. Adjust the seasoning, if necessary, then garnish with coriander and serve hot.

● **Good with** couscous.

Chicken Paprikash

Spicy paprika adds both flavour and colour to this hearty stew from Hungary

🍴 serves 4

🕐 prep 10 mins • cook 40–45 mins

🍲 large flameproof casserole

❄ freeze, without the parsley or soured cream, for up to 1 month; thaw at room temperature

2 tbsp **sunflower oil**

2 small **red onions**, sliced

1 **garlic clove**, finely chopped

1 tbsp **sweet paprika**

¼ tsp **caraway seeds**

8 **chicken thighs**

250ml (8fl oz) hot **chicken stock**

1 tbsp **red wine vinegar**

1 tbsp **tomato purée**

1 tsp **sugar**

salt and freshly ground **black pepper**

250g (9oz) **cherry tomatoes**

chopped **flat-leaf parsley**, to garnish

soured cream, to serve

● **Prepare ahead** Steps 1 and 2 can be prepared up to 2 days in advance. Reheat until the chicken is piping hot.

1 Heat the oil in a large flameproof casserole over a medium heat. Add the onion, garlic, paprika, and caraway seeds and fry, stirring, for about 5 minutes, or until the onions are softened. Use a slotted spoon to remove the ingredients from the pan and set aside.

2 Add the chicken thighs, skin-side down, to any oil remaining in the pan and fry for 3 minutes, then turn over and continue frying for a further 2 minutes. Return the onions and spices to the pan.

3 Mix together the stock, vinegar, tomato purée, sugar, and salt and pepper to taste. Pour over the chicken and bring to the boil, then reduce the heat to low, cover, and leave to simmer for 25 minutes, or until the chicken is tender.

4 Add the cherry tomatoes and shake the casserole vigorously to mix them into the sauce. Cover and simmer for a further 5 minutes. Sprinkle with parsley and serve with soured cream on the side.

● **Good with** creamy mashed potatoes or buttered noodles.

Thai Green Chicken Curry

By using a shop-bought jar of Thai curry paste, this flavoursome dish is very quick to prepare

 serves 4

prep 10 mins • cook 10 mins

1 tbsp olive oil

4 tsp shop-bought Thai red curry paste or green curry paste (use more paste for a spicier sauce)

4 skinless boneless chicken breasts, about 140g (5oz) each, cut into bite-sized pieces

2 tbsp light soy sauce

400ml can coconut milk

175g (6oz) open-cap mushrooms, chopped

6 spring onions, trimmed, with the green part cut into 5mm (¼in) slices

salt and freshly ground black pepper

chopped coriander, to garnish

● **Prepare ahead** Complete up to 24 hours in advance and reheat.

1 Heat the oil in a large frying pan over a medium heat. Add the curry paste and stir. Add the chicken and stir-fry for 2 minutes, or until lightly browned.

2 Pour in the soy sauce and coconut milk and bring to the boil, stirring. Lower the heat, stir in the mushrooms and most of the spring onions, and season with salt and pepper to taste, then simmer for about 8 minutes, or until the chicken is tender and cooked through.

3 Serve hot, garnished with coriander, and the remaining sliced spring onions.

● **Good with** boiled or steamed long-grain rice or plain noodles, as a starter or part of a Thai buffet.

Creamy Tarragon Chicken

Fresh tarragon and cream is a classic pairing in French cuisine

serves 4

prep 10 mins • cook 35 mins

large flameproof casserole

freeze the dish after step 2, once cooled completely, for up to 1 month; thaw at room temperature, then complete the recipe

30g (1oz) butter

1 tbsp rapeseed oil

4 chicken breasts, on the bone

250g (9oz) shallots, sliced

1 tsp dried *herbes de Provence*

2 garlic cloves, finely chopped

salt and freshly ground black pepper

250ml (8fl oz) hot chicken stock

120ml (4fl oz) dry white wine

250g (9oz) crème fraîche

2 tbsp chopped tarragon, plus extra sprigs to garnish

● **Prepare ahead** Steps 1 and 2 can be prepared up to 2 days in advance and kept in a covered container in the fridge. Reheat, making sure the chicken is completely heated through before stirring in the crème fraîche.

1 Melt the butter with the oil in a large flameproof casserole over medium-high heat. Add the chicken breasts, skin-side down, and fry for 3 minutes, or until golden brown, then turn over and continue browning for a further 2 minutes.

2 Keep the chicken breasts skin-side up, then sprinkle with the shallots, dried herbs, garlic, and salt and pepper to taste. Add the stock and wine and bring to the boil. Reduce the heat to low, cover the casserole and leave to simmer for 25 minutes, or until the chicken is tender and the juices run clear when pierced with a knife. Lift out the chicken and set aside, then boil the sauce until it is reduced by about half.

3 Stir in the crème fraîche and chopped tarragon, and continue cooking until thickened. If the sauce becomes too thick, add more chicken stock; adjust the seasoning, if necessary. Serve the chicken sliced off the bone, coated with the sauce and garnished with tarragon sprigs.

● **Good with** boiled long-grain rice, or try it with mashed potatoes with olive oil, black pepper, and chopped pitted black olives.

Chicken in a Pot

A one-pot meal wonderfully flavoured with cider and root vegetables

 serves 4

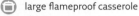 prep 10 minutes • cook 1¾ hrs

large flameproof casserole

freeze after step 3, once cooled completely, for up to 3 months; thaw at room temperature, then reheat

2 tbsp **sunflower oil**

1 **chicken**, about 1.5 kg (3lb 3oz), cleaned and trussed

1 tbsp **plain flour**

500ml (16fl oz) **dry cider**

250ml (8fl oz) **chicken stock**

1 **bouquet garni**

salt and freshly ground **black pepper**

350g (12oz) **baby carrots**, scraped

350g (12oz) **baby new potatoes**

2 **leeks**, thickly sliced

2 tbsp chopped **parsley**

● **Prepare ahead** Steps 1–3 can be prepared up to 2 days in advance. Slowly bring to the boil before completing step 4.

1 Preheat the oven to 170°C (325°F/Gas 3). Heat the oil in the casserole over a medium heat. Add the chicken and brown on all sides, then lift out and set aside. Sprinkle the flour into the casserole and cook, stirring, for 2 minutes. Stir in the cider and stock and bring to the boil.

2 Return the chicken to the casserole, breast-side up, and add the bouquet garni and salt and pepper to taste. Cover and put in the oven for 1¼ hours. Add the vegetables and baste the chicken.

3 Return the casserole to the oven for 30–45 minutes, or until the vegetables are tender and the chicken juices run clear when you pierce the thickest part of a leg.

4 Remove from the oven and leave the chicken to stand in the broth for 10 minutes, then taste and adjust the seasoning. Sprinkle with the parsley and serve hot.

Chicken Schnitzels

This quick dish is suitable for a family supper or a dinner party

 serves 4

prep 10 mins, plus chilling • cook 12 mins

freeze for up to 3 months; thaw at room temperature, then reheat

45g (1½oz) **plain flour**

1 **egg**, beaten

about 60g (2oz) **fine breadcrumbs**

4 skinless boneless **chicken breasts**

salt and freshly ground **black pepper**

6 tbsp **rapeseed oil**

2 **lemons**, cut in half, to serve

● **Prepare ahead** The chicken can be prepared up to step 3, then covered and chilled for up to 8 hours.

1 Put the flour in a shallow bowl, the egg in another bowl, and the breadcrumbs in a third bowl. Set aside.

2 Put the chicken breasts, and the thin, small fillets, if attached, between 2 sheets of greaseproof paper and pound with a rolling pin until they are very thin. Season to taste with salt and pepper.

3 Coat the chicken in the flour, then in the beaten egg, and then in the breadcrumbs, pressing them evenly on to both sides. Place on a baking tray or plate in one layer and chill in the refrigerator, uncovered, for at least 30 minutes.

4 Heat 3 tbsp of the oil in a non-stick frying pan over a medium-high heat. Add 2 of the schnitzels and fry for 3 minutes on each side, or until golden brown and cooked through. Drain on kitchen paper and keep hot.

5 Add the remaining oil to the pan, and fry the remaining schnitzels, as before.

6 Serve immediately, garnished with lemon halves, for squeezing over the schnitzels.

● **Good with** sautéed potatoes and green beans, or served cold, cut into slices, with potato salad.

VARIATION

Veal Schnitzels

Substitute 4 thinly sliced veal escalopes for the chicken. Prepare and cook as above.

Roast Chicken

Taking the same level of care and concentration with a simple process such as roasting chicken as with a complex culinary *tour de force* produces surprisingly fine results. As with all cooking, the enemy is dryness, and this can be avoided by paying attention to detail: the heat of the oven and the chicken's position in it, the amount of butter or oil, and the length of time allocated to cooking. Buy the biggest bird you can afford – and be inspired by our ideas for leftovers, overleaf.

 serves 6

 prep 15 mins • cook 15 mins per 450g (1lb), plus 15 mins resting

✓ low GI

1 oven-ready **chicken**, about 2.2kg (5lb)

30g (1oz) **butter** or 2 tbsp **olive oil**

salt and freshly ground **black pepper**

300g (10oz) **stuffing of your choice** (optional; see p360–61)

CHOOSING YOUR BIRD

Age, exercise, and a good diet all add flavour – and it must be said expense – to chickens. Supermarkets and butchers sell many varieties of birds that reflect all these conditions.

Supermarket birds, the most economical, are fed a special diet that puts weight on the breasts quickly. The birds will most likely have been raised indoors with little exercise, so, consequently, they have very little flavour.

Here are some common labels for chicken:

Free-range These birds cannot be stocked more than 13 per square metre, and should have access to daytime open-air runs for at least half their life.

Traditional Free-range The poultry houses for these chickens shouldn't contain more than 4000 birds. These cannot be stocked more than

12 per square metre, and must be one of the slow-growing breeds.

Free-range Total Freedom In addition to the traditional free-range specifications (above), these birds should have unlimited open-air runs.

Organic These birds must come from a farm with organic status as recognized by one of the certification bodies. As well as being fed a diet of organic grains and soybeans, organic chickens cannot be treated with drugs or antibiotics, and must have outdoor access.

When you get your chicken home from the shop, immediately put it in the bottom of the refrigerator in its wrapping on a plate with a rim, or put it in a covered container. Do not let any raw juices drip on any cooked food. Keep the chicken refrigerated and observe the use-by date.

COMMON CLASSIFICATIONS

Stewing Chicken   Chicken   Poussin

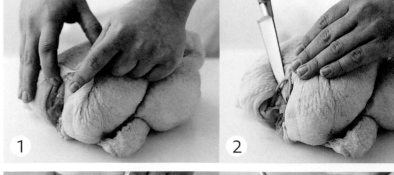

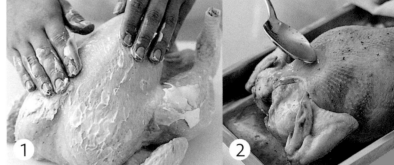

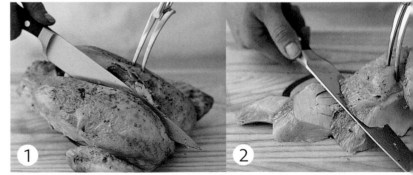

Add Stuffing

Stuffing can be pushed under the skin, rather than putting it in the central cavity, to help keep the breast meat moist as the bird roasts. Blend the stuffing ingredients together (see right), then carefully ease the skin away from the breast and gently push the stuffing under the skin from the neck end (see far right). This also ensures the stuffing cooks through.

Remove the Wishbone

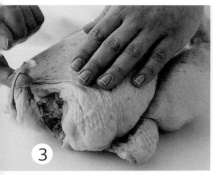

1 **Put the raw bird** on a large, clean cutting board and pull the skin back from around the neck cavity. Locate the wishbone with your finger and work it loose by gently moving your finger back and forth.

2 **Insert a small, sharp** knife behind the bone and gently work it down to the bottom of one of the wishbone's "arms", then cut it free from the flesh. In an older chicken the wishbone will be quite strong.

3 **Pull the wishbone out** by hooking your finger under the centre and gently tugging until it comes free. Removing the wishbone before roasting makes the bird much easier to carve when serving.

Prepare, Baste, & Roast

1 **Smear butter** or rub oil all over the outside of the bird, then season well with salt and pepper inside and out. (If you are stuffing the bird, push the stuffing under the breast skin.)

2 **Baste the chicken** at regular intervals while it roasts. Turn the bird breast-side down after the first 30 minutes of the cooking time so the juices help baste the breast meat.

3 **Turn the chicken** breast-side up for the last 20 minutes of the cooking time to crisp and brown the skin. The bird is cooked when the juices run clear when skewered in the thickest part of the leg.

Rest & Carve

1 **Transfer the bird** to a cutting board, breast-side up, cover with foil, and leave to rest for 15 minutes in a warm place. This allows the juices to flow throughout the bird and keep the meat moist.

2 **To carve the bird**, remove the legs by cutting the skin between the leg and the body and pushing the blade down to where the leg bone joins the body. It is easiest if you angle the blade into the body slightly.

3 **Work the blade** from side to side a little to loosen the joint, then, with a slight sawing motion, push the blade through the joint, cutting the leg free. Transfer the leg to a warmed serving plate and repeat with the other leg.

Portion

1 **Remove a breast** by cutting as if you are dividing the bird in half, just to one side of the breastbone. As the blade hits the bone, cut along the bone; remove all the meat; repeat on the other side.

2 **Place one breast** cut-side down on the cutting board. Using horizontal strokes, slice the breast into as many slices as possible, leaving the wing with a piece of breast meat attached.

3 **Carve each leg** by cutting it in half through the joint at the midway point. You shouldn't need to cut through any bone. As you reach the joint, work the blade into the joint to separate the pieces.

Make Gravy

Using a large spoon (see right), skim off most of the fat from the pan juices. Put the roasting pan over a low heat. Mix 1 tbsp plain white flour with 1 tbsp of the chicken fat and whisk it into the remaining pan juices. Add 300ml (10fl oz) stock or water and bring to the boil, whisking constantly (see far right). Strain the gravy and pour into a sauce boat to serve hot.

Roast Chicken

Serve with...

Roast potatoes (p231) and a green vegetable of your choice are traditional accompaniments for roast chicken, but there are plenty of other choices. Avoid getting in a rut and try these recipes for variety:

- Lemon Rice (p213)
- Brussels Sprouts with Orange (p237)
- Peas with Lettuce (p240)
- Ultimate Mashed Potatoes (p242)
- Potato Gratin (p242)
- Corn and Peppers (p246)
- Creamed Spinach with Pine Nuts (p247)
- Grilled Vegetables (p235)
- Cauliflower Cheese (p238)
- Bread Sauce (p358)

A Flavour Booster

Cranberry and Sage Sauce

This is a quick-and-easy sauce that really perks up a roast chicken meal. You can make it while the chicken is resting before it is carved.

6 tbsp **cranberry jelly**

3 tbsp **lemon** juice

2 tbsp chopped fresh **sage**

salt and freshly ground **black pepper**

Mix all the ingredients together in a small pan over a medium heat. Simmer, stirring, until the jelly dissolves. Stir in a couple of tablespoons of the roasting juices and season to taste with salt and pepper. Serve hot with the carved chicken.

ROASTING POUSSINS

Each roast poussin will serve 2 people. Calculate the cooking time at 12 minutes per 450g (1lb), plus 12 minutes extra. Since the flavour has less time to develop in these small birds, consider adding your own flavour booster (see above). The meat dries out quickly, so protect the breasts and add extra flavour by covering them with streaky bacon rashers before roasting.

SERVING ROAST CHICKEN

After carving your chicken, arrange it on a hot serving plate or platter, along with any stuffing, ready for serving at the table. Pour the hot gravy into a warmed sauce boat, or jug.

Chicken Croustades
Flavoured with tarragon, this recipe transforms leftover chicken into a stylish party bite

🕐 15 mins   **page 59**

Coronation Chicken Rolls
Perk up packed lunches and picnics with these dainty, lightly curried sandwiches

🕐 20 mins   **page 89**

Club Sandwich
You can cut the cooking time to less than half when you use leftover chicken in this traditional two-handed sandwich

🕐 30 mins   **page 86**

Chicken Stock
Leftover chicken bones make a flavoursome stock for using in soups, stews, and casseroles

🕐 1 hr 10 mins   **page 103**

Cock-a-Leekie Soup
Traditionally made with a whole chicken, this is just as hearty with pieces of cooked chicken

🕐 1 hr 40 mins   **page 113**

Chicken and Noodle Stir-fry
This quick one-pot meal becomes even quicker when made with cooked chicken

🕐 30 mins   **page 204**

Jambalaya
Cooked chicken, spicy sausages, and prawns are combined to make a filling one-pot dish

🕐 1 hr 15 mins   **page 210**

Thai Green Chicken Curry
Using a jar of green curry paste along with cooked chicken makes a speedy supper dish

🕐 20 mins   **page 288**

Chicken Croquettes
These can be served as a snack with drinks or as part of a simple family meal

🕐 50 mins   **page 299**

Tandoori Chicken

As tender and flavoursome as the classic restaurant dish, this recipe has a more natural colour

 serves 4

prep 10-15 mins, plus at least 3 hrs marinating • cook 25-35 mins

8 **chicken pieces**, such as breasts, thighs and legs, skin removed

groundnut oil or sunflower oil, for brushing

60g (2oz) **ghee** or butter, melted

1 **red onion**, thinly sliced to serve

lemon wedges, to serve

For the tandoori marinade

1 **onion**, coarsely chopped

2 large **garlic cloves**

1cm (½in) piece fresh **root ginger**, peeled and coarsely chopped

3 tbsp fresh **lemon** juice

¼ tsp **salt**

1¼-1½ tsp **chilli powder**, to taste

1 tsp **garam masala**

pinch of **turmeric**

pinch of **Kashmiri chilli powder**

pinch of **saffron powder**

● **Prepare ahead** The chicken can be marinated for up to 24 hours in the refrigerator.

1 Use a fork to prick the chicken pieces all over, then place them in a non-metallic bowl and set aside.

2 To make the marinade, put the onion, garlic, and ginger in a blender or food processor and blend until a paste forms, scraping down the side of the bowl. Add the lemon juice, salt, and the spices, and process again.

3 Pour the marinade over the chicken and rub in well. Cover the bowl with cling film, and leave to marinate in the refrigerator for at least 3 hours, occasionally turning the chicken pieces in the marinade.

4 Preheat the oven to 220°C (425°F/Gas 7) and remove the chicken from the fridge. Put a rack in a roasting pan lined with kitchen foil, shiny-side up, and grease the rack. Arrange the chicken on the rack, then brush with melted ghee. Roast for 20-25 minutes, or until the juices run clear.

5 Preheat the grill on its highest setting. Pour off the juices that have accumulated in the bottom of the pan. Brush the chicken with more ghee and place under the grill for 5-10 minutes, or until the edges are lightly charred. Serve with the onion slices and lemon wedges.

Arroz con Pollo

This colourful chicken and rice dish from Latin America is cooked and served in one pot

serves 4

prep 20 mins • cook 45 mins

low fat

2 tbsp **olive oil**

8 **chicken thighs**

1 **Spanish onion**, finely sliced

1 **green pepper**, deseeded and chopped

1 **red pepper**, deseeded and chopped

2 **garlic cloves**, finely chopped

1 tsp **smoked paprika**

1 **bay leaf**

230g can **chopped tomatoes**

1 tsp **thyme leaves**

1 tsp **dried oregano**

175g (6oz) **long-grain rice**

pinch of **saffron threads**

750ml (1¼pint) **chicken stock**

2 tbsp **tomato purée**

juice of ½ **lemon**

salt and freshly ground **black pepper**

100g (3½oz) **frozen peas**

1 Preheat the oven to 180°C (350°F/Gas 4). Heat half the oil in a large flameproof casserole and fry the chicken thighs over high heat, turning frequently, or until evenly browned. Remove from the casserole, drain, and set aside.

2 Add the remaining oil, reduce the heat and fry the onion until softened. Add the chopped peppers and garlic and fry for 5 minutes, or until they start to soften. Add the paprika, bay leaf, tomatoes, thyme, and oregano, and stir in the rice. Fry for 1-2 minutes, stirring constantly.

3 Crumble in the saffron, add the stock, tomato purée, and lemon juice, and season to taste with salt and pepper.

4 Return the chicken thighs to the casserole, pushing them down into the rice, cover, and cook in the oven for 15 minutes. Add the peas and return to the oven for a further 10 minutes, or until the rice is tender and has absorbed the cooking liquid. Serve hot, straight from the casserole.

Chicken Kiev

The classic garlic- and butter-stuffed chicken dish; the breadcrumbed coating prevents the butter leaking out

 serves 4

prep 25 mins, plus chilling • cook 8–10 mins

100g (3½oz) **butter**, softened

2 **garlic cloves**, crushed

finely grated zest of 1 **lemon**

2 tbsp chopped **parsley**

salt and freshly ground **black pepper**

4 skinless boneless **chicken breasts**

3 tbsp **plain flour**

1 **egg**, beaten

150g (5½oz) fresh **breadcrumbs**

sunflower oil, for deep-frying

● **Prepare ahead** The flavoured butter can be made up to 1 day in advance and chilled.

1 Place the butter in a bowl and stir in the garlic, lemon zest, and parsley. Season to taste with salt and pepper. Form into a block, wrap in cling film, then chill until firm.

2 Place each chicken breast between 2 sheets of cling film; pound them flat using a rolling pin.

3 Cut the butter into 4 sticks and place one on each of the breasts. Fold the other side of the chicken up and over the butter, enclosing it completely.

4 Season the flour with salt and pepper. Keeping the chicken closed, dip each piece in the seasoned flour, then in beaten egg, and finally into the breadcrumbs to coat evenly.

5 Heat the oil to 180°C (350°F). Fry the chicken for 6–8 minutes depending on size, or until golden brown.

6 Remove and drain on kitchen paper. Serve hot.

● **Good with** a fresh mixed salad and sautéed potatoes.

Southern Fried Chicken

This is succulent comfort food from America's Deep South, with the traditional accompaniment of a smooth cream sauce

serves 4

prep 20 mins, plus chilling • cook 25 mins

plastic food bag, deep-fat fryer or large deep saucepan half-filled with oil

225g (8oz) **plain flour**

salt and freshly ground **black pepper**

1 tsp **dried thyme**

1 tsp **Cajun seasoning**

1 tsp **sugar**

4 **chicken drumsticks**

4 **chicken thighs**

1 **egg**, beaten

vegetable oil, for deep-frying

For the cream sauce

1½ tbsp **plain flour**

250ml (9fl oz) **full-fat milk**

● **Prepare ahead** Steps 1 and 2 can be completed 1 hour or more before cooking.

1 Put the first 5 ingredients in a freezer bag, hold the top firmly together and shake well.

2 Add the chicken drumsticks and thighs to the bag one at a time and shake until coated.

3 Dip the pieces into the beaten egg, then repeat step 2. Lay the coated chicken on a plate in a single layer and chill for 30 minutes.

4 Heat the oil for deep-frying to 170°C (325°F) and fry the chicken for 15–20 minutes, or until golden brown and cooked through, then drain on kitchen paper.

5 To make the cream sauce, spoon 2 tbsp of the fryer oil into a saucepan and stir in the flour. Cook over a low heat for 1 minute, then gradually whisk in the milk and black pepper to taste. Stir over a low heat until thickened and smooth.

● **Good with** mashed potatoes and corn on the cob.

Chicken Chow Mein

This popular one-pot Chinese dish is a colourful, tasty medley of noodles, chicken, mushrooms, and vegetables

serves 4

prep 15 mins • cook 15 mins

low fat

4 tsp **vegetable oil**

4 **spring onions**, cut into 2.5cm (1in) lengths

2cm (¾in) piece of fresh **root ginger**, peeled and grated

140g (5oz) **shiitake mushrooms** or oyster mushrooms, sliced

1 **red pepper**, deseeded and chopped

6 skinless boneless **chicken thighs**, cut into bite-sized pieces

115g (4oz) **green beans**, cut into 2.5cm (1in) lengths

350g (12oz) fresh fine **egg noodles**

4 tbsp **light soy sauce**, plus extra for sprinkling

1 tbsp **rice wine** or dry sherry

120ml (4fl oz) **chicken stock**

1 tsp **cornflour**

● **Prepare ahead** The vegetables and chicken can be chopped several hours in advance and kept in covered bowls in the refrigerator.

1 **Heat half the oil** in a wok or large frying pan and stir-fry the spring onions, ginger, mushrooms, and red pepper over high heat for 5 minutes. Remove and set aside.

2 **Add the remaining oil** and stir-fry the chicken over a high heat for 3 minutes, in separate batches if necessary, then remove from the pan and set aside.

3 **Add the green beans** and stir-fry for 2 minutes. Add the noodles and return the chicken and vegetables to the pan.

4 **Mix together** the soy sauce, wine, stock, and cornflour until smooth and well blended, then pour into the pan. Toss everything together for 2 minutes, or until piping hot.

5 **Serve immediately**, with extra soy sauce to sprinkle over.

● **Good with** other Chinese dishes, as part of a themed meal.

VARIATION

Seafood Chow Mein

Instead of chicken, use 225g (8oz) raw prawns, shelled and deveined, or a mixture of prawns and other seafood, such as scallops. In step 2, reduce the cooking time to 1–2 minutes. In step 3, add 15g (4oz) of beansprouts along with the green beans.

STIR-FRY NOODLES

Always add fresh noodles towards the end of a stir-fry recipe. They will go soggy if overcooked. If using dried noodles, boil them first, then rinse and drain until ready to use.

Chicken with Pancetta

Olives and capers give this dish a Mediterranean flavour

serves 4

prep 15 mins • cook 45 mins

6 **chicken breasts**, about 175g (6oz) each

2 tbsp **flour**

salt and freshly ground **black pepper**

4 tbsp **olive oil**

4 tbsp **butter**

4 **garlic cloves**, chopped

225g (8oz) **pancetta**, diced

2 tbsp **white wine vinegar**

4 tbsp **capers**

12 pitted **black olives**, chopped

2 tbsp chopped **thyme**

120ml (4fl oz) **double cream**

1 **Toss the chicken** in seasoned flour and shake off the excess. Heat the oil and butter in a large frying pan and fry the garlic and pancetta over a medium-low heat for 3–4 minutes. Remove and set aside.

2 **Add the chicken** to the pan and brown on both sides. Return the pancetta and garlic to the pan and add the vinegar, capers, olives, and thyme. Lower the heat, cover, and cook for 35 minutes.

3 **Remove the chicken**; keep warm. Pour the cream into the pan and cook for 1–2 minutes to thicken. Serve the chicken with the sauce poured over.

Lemon Chicken, Chinese-style

This popular Cantonese dish from Hong Kong is something of a one-off, as lemons are rarely used in Chinese cooking

- serves 4
- prep 20 mins, plus standing • cook 30 mins
- deep-fat fryer or large saucepan

200g (7oz) self-raising flour

¼ tsp bicarbonate of soda

4 skinless boneless chicken breasts

vegetable oil, for deep-frying

For the lemon sauce

30g (1oz) cornflour

120ml (4fl oz) fresh lemon juice

360ml (12fl oz) chicken stock

2 tbsp clear honey

4 tbsp soft light brown sugar

1cm (½in) piece of fresh root ginger, peeled and grated

● **Prepare ahead** The batter can be made up to 2 hours in advance. Add a little water if it becomes too thick.

1 Sift the flour and bicarbonate of soda into a large bowl, add 300ml (10fl oz) of cold water, and whisk to make a smooth batter. Set aside for 30 minutes.

2 Heat the oil for deep-frying to 180°C (350°F). Coat the chicken in the batter, then deep-fry in batches for 5 minutes, or until golden. Drain on kitchen paper.

3 Meanwhile, make the sauce by whisking the cornflour with the lemon juice to make a smooth paste. Pour this into a small saucepan and add the stock, honey, sugar, and ginger. Stir over a low heat until the sauce comes to the boil. Simmer for 1 minute, or until it thickens and becomes translucent.

4 Arrange the chicken on a serving platter and spoon the hot sauce over the top.

● **Good with** boiled rice and pak choi or steamed greens as a tasty lunch or supper dish, or as part of a larger Chinese-themed menu.

● **Leftovers**, once the skin is removed, can be mixed with chopped coriander, crème fraîche, and diced cucumber, and served cold with salad leaves or in a sandwich.

Chicken Korma

A mild curry popular in Indian restaurants, this is a fragrant and aromatic dish with a creamy sauce

- serves 4
- prep 20 mins • cook 45 mins
- freeze for up to 1 month

4 tbsp vegetable oil or ghee

8 skinless boneless chicken thighs, cut into 2½cm (1in) pieces

2 large onions, thinly sliced

1 tbsp ground coriander

1 tbsp ground cumin

1 tsp ground turmeric

½ tsp ground ginger

1 tsp chilli powder

1 tsp ground cardamom

2 garlic cloves, crushed

150g (5½oz) thick plain yogurt

1 tbsp plain flour

300ml (10fl oz) chicken stock

150ml (5fl oz) double cream

1 tbsp lemon juice

1 Heat half of the oil in a large pan and fry the chicken in batches over a high heat until lightly browned on both sides. Remove from the pan and set aside.

2 Lower the heat, add the rest of the oil to the pan, and fry the onions until soft and golden. Add the spices and garlic and fry for 2 minutes, stirring occasionally.

3 Gradually stir in the yogurt. Put the flour in a small bowl, add a little stock and mix to a smooth paste. Pour the paste into the pan with the rest of the stock and bring to the boil, stirring constantly, then lower the heat. Return the chicken to the pan and simmer gently, for 15 minutes, or until cooked through, stirring occasionally.

4 Stir in the cream and lemon juice and simmer for a further 5 minutes before serving.

● **Good with** herb-flecked boiled rice, naan bread and a variety of chutneys.

Garlic Chicken

Based on a classic Indian dish called *Murg Massalam*, this recipe can be oven-cooked, grilled or barbecued

- serves 4
- prep 10 mins, plus marinating • cook 1 hr
- freeze up to 1 month

1 medium-sized **whole chicken**, cut into 8 portions, skin removed

For the marinade

1 tbsp **clear honey** or golden syrup

2 **garlic cloves**, peeled and crushed

1 tsp **ground ginger**

½ tsp **cardamom seeds**

½ tsp **ground coriander**

¼ tsp **ground cumin**

¼ tsp **ground turmeric**

2 tbsp fresh **lemon** juice

1 tsp **salt**

4 tbsp low-fat natural **yogurt**

1 With a sharp knife, make a few slashes in the chicken flesh to ensure even cooking.

2 Make the marinade by mixing together all the ingredients in a large bowl. Place the chicken pieces into the marinade and mix until well coated. Cover and refrigerate for at least 1 hour to allow the flavours to develop.

3 Preheat the oven to 200°C (400°F/Gas 6) and line a deep roasting tin with foil. Arrange the chicken in the tin and pour in about 150ml (5fl oz) of cold water. Spoon any remaining marinade over the chicken pieces and bake for 30–40 minutes, or until the chicken pieces are golden and crisp on the outside and soft and tender inside.

4 Transfer to a heated serving dish and serve hot, or allow to cool completely if serving cold.

● **Good with** basmati rice, flavoured with a cinnamon stick and a few cardamom pods.

VARIATION

Grilled Garlic Chicken

To barbecue, cook the chicken portions in the oven for 40 minutes, then place over hot coals to brown and crisp. To grill, place the marinated chicken on the grill rack and cook under a low heat, turning frequently, until tender and cooked through. Increase the heat and crisp the skin on each side.

Chicken Cacciatore

This Italian dish translates as "hunter-style chicken", and is traditionally served with polenta to soak up the delicious juices

- serves 4
- prep 20 mins • cook 35–40 mins
- low fat
- flameproof casserole

4 **chicken legs**, about 1.5kg (3lb 3 oz) total weight

salt and freshly ground **black pepper**

2 tbsp **olive oil**

2 **garlic cloves**, sliced

1 medium **onion**, chopped

200ml (7fl oz) **dry white wine**

1 **celery stalk**, chopped

200g (7oz) **button mushrooms**, sliced

400g can **chopped tomatoes**

150ml (5fl oz) **chicken stock**

1 tbsp **tomato purée**

2 tsp chopped **rosemary**

2 tsp chopped **sage**

8 pitted **black olives**, halved

1 Trim any excess fat from the chicken and season with salt and pepper. Heat half the oil in a large, heavy frying pan and fry the chicken in batches, until brown on all sides. Remove and keep hot. Pour the excess fat out of the pan.

2 Add the remaining oil, garlic and onion and fry gently for 3–4 minutes, to soften but not brown. Add the wine and boil for 1 minute. Stir in the celery, mushrooms, tomatoes, stock, purée, rosemary, and sage.

3 Return the chicken to the pan, cover and cook over a low heat for 30 minutes, or until the chicken is cooked through.

4 Remove the lid, add the olives, then cover and cook for a further 5–10 minutes. Serve hot.

● **Good with** soft polenta and a side salad of fresh mixed leaves.

Chicken Croquettes

These golden, savoury nuggets, crunchy outside and meltingly soft inside, are a popular Spanish first course

- serves 4
- prep 30 mins • cook 20 mins
- freeze for up to 3 months

100g (3½oz) **butter**

115g (4oz) **flour**

750ml (1¼ pints) **milk**

400g (14oz) **cooked chicken**, shredded

2 tsp **tomato purée**

salt and freshly ground **black pepper**

8–9 tbsp fine **breadcrumbs**

3 **eggs**, beaten

oil, for shallow frying

● **Prepare ahead** The béchamel sauce can be prepared ahead and allowed to cool. The croquettes can be made up to 24 hours in advance and fried before serving.

1 Melt the butter in a saucepan over a medium-low heat and add the flour, stirring continuously. Cook the mixture for 1–2 minutes, then stir in the milk to make a smooth, thick sauce.

2 Add the shredded chicken and the tomato purée and season to taste with salt and pepper. Continue to cook for 5 minutes, or until the mixture thickens. Remove the pan from the heat and leave to cool completely.

3 Use two spoons to form croquettes about 3–4cm (1½–2in) long. Roll them in the breadcrumbs, coat in the egg and roll in the breadcrumbs again.

4 Heat the oil in a heavy frying pan. When hot, fry the croquettes in batches for 5 minutes, turning frequently, until they are golden all over. Remove with a slotted spoon and drain on kitchen paper.

5 Transfer the croquettes to a heated serving plate and serve while still hot.

● **Good with** garlic mayonnaise or *Salsa Rosa*, made from 2 parts mayonnaise to 1 part tomato ketchup. The croquettes can also be served cold, making them excellent picnic food.

Chicken in Balsamic Vinegar

This cold chicken dish has a lovely hint of sweetness from the balsamic vinegar and raisins

- serves 6
- prep 50 mins, plus marinating • cook about 20 mins

4 skinless boneless **chicken breasts**

salt and freshly ground **black pepper**

200ml (7fl oz) **white wine**

4 tbsp **balsamic vinegar**

200ml (7fl oz) **fruity olive oil**

2 tbsp fresh chopped **basil** or tarragon

zest of 1 **lemon**

4 tbsp **raisins**, soaked in boiling water for 10 mins and drained

rocket, to serve

watercress, to serve

1 **lemon**, cut into wedges, to serve

60g (2oz) **pine nuts**, toasted, to serve

1 Preheat the oven to 190°C (375°F/Gas 5). Flatten the chicken breasts by placing them between two sheets of cling film and bashing gently with a rolling pin. Place the chicken in a lightly oiled, shallow roasting tin. Season with salt and pepper, then pour the wine over, cover with greaseproof paper and bake for 20 minutes, or until cooked through. Take the chicken out and set aside to cool in the tin. Reserve 2 tbsp of the cooking liquid.

2 Whisk together the balsamic vinegar and oil, then add the reserved cooking liquid. Add the basil, lemon zest, and raisins. Arrange the chicken in a dish, pour the dressing over, cover and chill for 12 hours or overnight, turning the chicken once.

3 To serve, bring back to room temperature, slice thinly and arrange on a serving plate. Pour the marinade over. Garnish with salad leaves and lemon wedges, then scatter with the pine nuts.

● **Good with** roasted cherry tomatoes on the vine, and hot, buttered new potatoes.

Chicken Pasties

A complete and filling lunch in a pastry packet

 serves 4

prep 30 mins, plus chilling • cook 35 mins

For the pastry

350g (12oz) **plain flour**

175g (6oz) **butter**, chilled and diced

2 **eggs**

For the filling

115g (4oz) **cream cheese**

6 **spring onions**, sliced

2 tbsp chopped **parsley**

salt and freshly ground **black pepper**

2–3 **chicken breasts**, about 350g (12oz), cut into 2cm (¾in) chunks

1 **potato**, about 150g (5½oz), cut into 1cm (½in) cubes

1 **sweet potato**, about 150g (5½oz), cut into 1cm (½in) cubes

1 **To make the pastry**, sift the flour into a bowl, then rub in the butter until the mixture resembles fine breadcrumbs. Beat the eggs and 3 tbsp of cold water together. Set aside 1 tbsp of the mixture for glazing, and pour the rest over the dry ingredients, and mix to a dough. Wrap in oiled cling film and chill for 20 minutes.

2 **Meanwhile**, mix the cream cheese, onions, and parsley in a bowl, and season to taste with salt and pepper. Stir in the chicken, potato, and sweet potato.

3 **Preheat the oven** to 200°C (400°F/Gas 6). Divide the pastry into 4 pieces. Roll out each piece on a lightly floured surface and, using a small plate as a guide, cut into a 20cm (8in) round.

4 **Spoon a quarter** of the filling into the centre of each round. Brush the edges with water and bring together to seal, then crimp.

5 **Place the pasties** on a baking tray and brush with the reserved egg mixture. Make a slit in the tops and bake for 10 minutes, then reduce the heat to 180°C (350°F/Gas 4) and cook for 25–30 minutes, or until a thin knife comes out clean when inserted into the centre.

6 **Remove from the oven** and serve the pasties hot or cold.

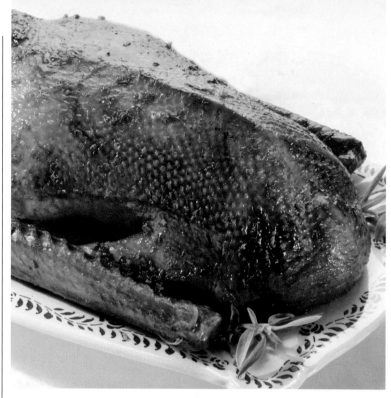

Roast Goose

Goose meat is rich in flavour, making it a perfect choice for a festive dinner party or special Sunday meal

 serves 4

 prep 20 mins • cook 3 hrs

freeze, cooked, for up to 3 months

1 large oven-ready **goose**, about 5kg (11lb)

salt and freshly ground **black pepper**

2 small **onions**, halved

1 tbsp **olive oil**

150ml (5fl oz) **red wine**

sprigs of **sage**, to garnish

1 **Preheat the oven** to 180°C (350°F/Gas 4). Weigh the goose and calculate the cooking time, allowing 30 minutes per 1kg (2¼lb), plus 20 minutes. Prick the skin all over with a fork, rub with salt, and sprinkle with pepper. Tuck half the onion in the neck cavity and the other half into the body cavity. Brush with the olive oil.

2 **Place the goose**, breast-side up, on a rack in a roasting tin, and roast for the calculated time.

3 **About 40 minutes** before the goose is finished cooking, remove from the oven and lift off the foil. Carefully pour out the excess fat from the tin and set aside. Brush the leftover juices evenly over the skin. Return to the oven and repeat the brushing every 15 minutes until the goose is a rich amber-brown colour.

4 **To test** whether the goose is cooked, pierce the thickest part of a leg with a metal skewer or thin knife to see if the juices run. If the juices are still pink, cook for a further 15 minutes, then check again.

5 **Remove the goose**, cover with foil, and leave to stand for 15–20 minutes before carving. Skim the excess fat from the juices and pour in the wine over a medium heat, stirring to loosen the sediment. Boil to reduce slightly, then add the remaining glaze, and serve alongside the goose. Garnish with the sage leaves to serve.

● **Leftovers** can be rolled into Chinese pancakes with slices of spring onion, cucumber, and Hoisin sauce.

Duck Breasts with Mushroom Sauce

Tender duck breasts are complemented by crisp white wine and tangy mushroom sauce

serves 4

prep 20 mins • cook 25 mins

ridged cast-iron grill pan

2 tbsp light **olive oil**

4 **spring onions**, chopped

175g (6oz) **button mushrooms**, halved or quartered

1 tbsp **lemon** juice

1 tbsp **sun-dried tomato purée**

1 tsp **cornflour**

300ml (10fl oz) **chicken stock**

2 tbsp chopped **parsley**, plus extra to garnish

salt and freshly ground **black pepper**

4 **duck breasts**

2–3 tbsp **white wine**

1 **Heat the oil** in a frying pan and fry the spring onions and mushrooms over a low heat for 3 minutes, or until softened. Stir in the lemon juice and sun-dried tomato purée.

2 **Mix the cornflour** with a little of the stock until smooth. Bring the stock to the boil, then gradually stir in the cornflour mixture, until thickened and smooth. Add the chopped parsley and season to taste with salt and pepper. Set aside and keep warm.

3 **Score the skin** of the duck breasts a few times with a sharp knife. Heat a ridged grill pan over a medium-high heat, add the duck and grill for 10 minutes, or until cooked to your liking, turning once.

4 **Remove the duck breasts** from the pan and keep warm. Pour off the excess fat, then add the wine to the pan. Cook for 2 minutes, scraping the pan to incorporate any cooking juices or sediment, then pour into the reserved sauce.

5 **Serve the duck** immediately, with the sauce spooned over, and sprinkled with chopped parsley.

Chicken Gumbo

Traditionally made with seafood in Louisiana, this version is made with chicken instead

serves 4

prep 20 mins • cook 50 mins

1 tbsp **sunflower oil**

1 **onion**, chopped

2 **celery sticks**, chopped

1 **green pepper**, deseeded and chopped

1 **garlic clove**, chopped

450g (1lb) skinless boneless **chicken breasts**, cubed

½ tsp dried **oregano**

2 tsp **hot paprika**

½ tsp **ground cumin**

1 tbsp **plain flour**

115g (4oz) **spicy sausage**, such as chorizo, sliced

400g can **chopped tomatoes**

450ml (15fl oz) **chicken stock**

225g (8oz) frozen sliced **okra**, or baby courgettes, sliced

1 **Heat the oil** in a large saucepan and fry the onion, celery, and pepper over a medium heat for 5 minutes, or until softened, stirring frequently. Add the garlic and fry for a further few seconds.

2 **Add the chicken** and fry, turning frequently, until evenly browned. Sprinkle with the oregano, paprika, cumin, and flour. Stir well and cook for 1 minute, then add the sausage, tomatoes, and stock.

3 **Bring to the boil**, stirring, frequently, then reduce the heat and simmer for 20 minutes. Add the okra, return to simmering point, and let cook for a further 20 minutes.

VARIATION

Seafood Gumbo

Replace the chicken with 450g (1lb) large raw prawns, shelled, and deveined, and add in step 3 with the okra.

Chicken Casserole with Herb Dumplings

This hearty winter casserole is a main meal in itself, but is especially good when served with freshly steamed greens

 serves 4

 prep 15 mins • cook 50 mins

large flameproof casserole

freeze, without dumplings, for up to 3 months

1 tbsp **plain flour**

salt and freshly ground **black pepper**

8 **chicken thighs** and **drumsticks**

2 tbsp **olive oil**

2 **carrots**, sliced

2 **leeks**, sliced

2 **celery sticks**, sliced

½ **swede**, diced

500ml (16fl oz) **chicken stock**

2 tbsp **Worcestershire sauce**

For the dumplings

125g (4½oz) **self-raising flour**

60g (2oz) **light suet**, shredded

1 tbsp **parsley**, chopped

1 tsp **dried mixed herbs**

salt and freshly ground **black pepper**

1 Season the flour with salt and pepper. Toss the chicken pieces in the flour to coat. Heat half the oil in the casserole and fry the chicken, turning often, for 6 minutes, or until brown all over. Remove and keep warm. Pour the fat from the pan.

2 Add the remaining oil, carrots, leeks, celery, and swede to the casserole, and stir over the heat for 3–4 minutes to colour lightly. Return the chicken to the casserole, and add the stock and Worcestershire sauce. Bring to the boil, then reduce the heat, cover, and simmer for 20 minutes.

3 Meanwhile, to make the dumplings, place the flour in a bowl and stir in the suet, parsley, and dried herbs, and season to taste with salt and pepper. Stir in 5–6 tbsp cold water, or just enough to make a soft, not sticky, dough. With lightly floured hands, divide into 12 balls.

4 Remove the casserole lid and arrange the dumplings over the top. Cover and simmer for a further 20 minutes, or until the dumplings are risen and fluffy. Serve in the casserole.

Chicken Pinwheels with Pasta

These light and healthy little rolls of chicken breast are very easy to make and packed with Mediterranean flavours

serves 4

prep 20 mins • cook 40 mins

low fat

freeze the pinwheels for up to 1 month

4 **chicken breasts**, skin removed

salt and freshly ground **black pepper**

1 **garlic clove**, crushed

25g (scant 1oz) **basil leaves**, plus extra to garnish

115g (4oz) **sun-dried tomatoes in oil**, drained

1 tbsp **olive oil**

200ml (7fl oz) **passata**

200ml (7fl oz) **dry white wine**

cooked pasta, to serve

● **Prepare ahead** Prepare to the end of step 3, then cover and refrigerate until ready to bake.

1 Preheat the oven to 200°C (400°F/Gas 6). Lay the chicken breasts on a board between 2 sheets of cling film and beat out flat with a rolling pin to 5mm (¼in) thick.

2 Season with salt and pepper then spread the breasts with the garlic. Arrange the basil leaves and sun-dried tomatoes evenly over the surface of the chicken.

3 Roll up the chicken from the shorter sides to enclose the filling, forming a firm roll. Secure with fine string or wooden cocktail sticks. Heat the oil in a frying pan and brown the chicken rolls on all sides. Transfer to a shallow ovenproof dish. Brush with oil and bake for 20–25 minutes.

4 Place the passata and wine in a saucepan and simmer gently for 10 minutes, or until thickened slightly. When the chicken is cooked, remove from the dish and pour any juices into the passata.

5 Cut the chicken into neat slices. Arrange the slices on individual serving plates and serve with the pasta and sauce on the side. Garnish with basil.

● **Good with** new potatoes, or boiled rice.

● **Leftovers** can be chopped, added to pasta with the sauce, and baked until heated through.

Sweet and Sour Chicken

This classic dish from Hong Kong is popular in Cantonese restaurants around the world

 serves 4

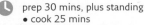 prep 30 mins, plus standing • cook 25 mins

deep-fat fryer or large deep saucepan half-filled with oil, wok

vegetable oil, for deep-frying and stir-frying

4 skinless boneless chicken breasts, cut into 2.5cm (1in) pieces

flour, to dust

2 tbsp unsalted cashew nuts or whole blanched almonds

½ red pepper, deseeded and chopped

8 spring onions, cut into 2.5cm (1in) pieces

1 pineapple ring, cut into chunks

For the batter

115g (4oz) self-raising flour

pinch of salt

½ tsp baking powder

240ml (8fl oz) lager

For the sauce

120ml (4fl oz) chicken stock

3 tbsp light soy sauce

1 tbsp clear honey

3 tbsp rice vinegar

2 tbsp tomato ketchup

2cm (¾in) piece of fresh root ginger, peeled and grated

1 tsp cornflour

● **Prepare ahead** Steps 1 and 2 can be completed several hours in advance.

1 To make the batter, sift the flour, the salt, and the baking powder into a large bowl. Make a well in the centre and add half the lager. Gradually combine, then whisk in the rest of the beer to make a smooth batter. Set aside for 30 minutes.

2 To make the sauce, put all the ingredients, except the cornflour, in a pan and stir over a low heat until the honey melts. Mix the cornflour with a little cold water until smooth, then add to the pan and stir until thickened and smooth. Simmer for 1 minute, then set aside. Preheat the oven to 130°C (250°F/Gas ½).

3 Heat the oil for deep-frying to 180°C (350°F). Dust the chicken pieces with flour, coat in the batter and deep-fry in batches for 3-4 minutes, or until golden brown and crisp. Drain and keep warm, uncovered, in the oven.

4 Heat 2 tbsp oil in a wok, add the nuts, and stir-fry for 30 seconds, or until golden. Remove and set aside to drain on kitchen paper. Add the red pepper and stir-fry for 3 minutes, then add the spring onions and pineapple, and stir-fry for 1 minute.

5 Pour the sauce into the wok, add the chicken, stir until coated, and simmer for 2 minutes. Serve immediately, scattered with the nuts.

CHECKING THE OIL TEMPERATURE

If you don't have a cooking thermometer, check the oil temperature by dropping in a piece of day-old bread; if it browns in under 1 minute, the oil is hot enough.

Chicken with Herb Sauce

A punchy sauce for chicken

 serves 4

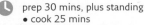 prep 10 mins • cook 30 mins

4 skinless boneless chicken breasts, about 175g (6oz) each

1 small onion, sliced

1 carrot, chopped

1 celery stick, chopped

few sprigs of parsley

For the sauce

60g (2oz) parsley

60g (2oz) basil

1 garlic clove

2 anchovies

1 tbsp capers, rinsed

1 tbsp red wine vinegar

salt and freshly ground black pepper

120ml (4fl oz) olive oil

1 Preheat the oven to 190°C (375°F/Gas 5). Place the chicken in a roasting tin, add the vegetables, parsley, and enough water to cover. Cover the tin with foil and bake for 30 minutes. Remove from the oven and leave to cool in the liquid.

2 Make the sauce by placing all the ingredients, except the olive oil, into a food processor, process briefly, then, with the motor running, slowly pour in the olive oil.

3 To serve, slice the chicken thinly and discard the liquid. Spoon the sauce over the sliced chicken breast.

Duck with Shallot Confit

The spices and melted honey lend comforting winter flavours to the duck

serves 6

prep 10 mins • cook 30 mins

6 duck breasts

1 tbsp honey

½ tsp five-spice powder

salt and freshly ground black pepper

For the shallot confit

30g (1oz) fresh root ginger, peeled and crushed or finely grated

225g (8oz) shallots, sliced

150ml (5fl oz) clear honey

150ml (5fl oz) red wine vinegar

● **Prepare ahead** The shallot confit can be made up to 3 days in advance, covered, and refrigerated.

1 **To make the confit**, place the ginger, shallots, and honey into a saucepan over a medium heat. Cook for 10 minutes, stirring often, or until the shallots are softened.

2 **Stir in the vinegar** and bring to the boil. Reduce the heat and simmer for 5–10 minutes, or until the confit is reduced and syrupy, stirring occasionally.

3 **Add 150ml (5fl oz) water** and cook for 5–10 minutes, or until the mixture is golden, and has thickened slightly.

4 **Meanwhile**, preheat the oven to 200°C (400°F/Gas 6). Trim any excess fat from the duck breasts and heat a heavy frying pan over a high heat. When the pan is hot, place the duck skin-side down and cook for 5 minutes, or until brown. Then turn and brown the other sides.

5 **Place the duck breasts** in a roasting tin and brush with honey. Add the five-spice powder, and season to taste with salt and pepper. Roast for 8–10 minutes, or until the middle is cooked through to your taste.

6 **Remove from the oven** and allow to rest for 5 minutes. Carve, and serve with the shallot confit.

● **Good with** a sweet potato purée, sautéed pak choi, or mixed and dressed green beans.

Turkey à la King

This is a great family supper, and an excellent way of using up leftover Christmas turkey

serves 4

prep 15 mins • cook 15 mins

freeze for up to 3 months; thaw completely before reheating

2 tbsp sunflower oil

60g (2oz) butter

1 onion, finely sliced

1 green pepper, deseeded and chopped

1 red pepper, deseeded and chopped

175g (6oz) mushrooms, sliced

30g (1oz) plain flour

1 tsp paprika

salt and freshly ground black pepper

450ml (15fl oz) milk

500g (1lb 2oz) cooked turkey, cut into bite-sized pieces

● **Prepare ahead** The dish can be prepared up to 24 hours in advance and reheated thoroughly when ready to serve.

1 **Heat the oil** and butter in a large pan and fry the onion gently until softened. Add the peppers and fry for 5 minutes.

2 **Stir in the mushrooms** and fry for 5 minutes, or until the peppers and mushrooms have softened slightly.

3 **Sprinkle in the flour** and paprika, season to taste with salt and pepper, and take the pan off the heat. Gradually blend in the milk, return the pan to a low heat, and stir until the sauce comes to the boil and is thickened and smooth.

4 **Stir in the turkey** and simmer, stirring occasionally, for 5 minutes, or until the turkey is heated through, and serve.

VARIATION

Chicken à la King

Substitute the turkey with the same quantity of chicken. Replace half the milk with chicken stock, and the mushrooms with sliced courgettes.

Chicken Jalousie

Although it looks impressive, this dish is quick to make with shop-bought puff pastry and cooked chicken

 serves 4

prep 25 mins • cook 25 mins

25g (scant 1oz) **butter**

2 **leeks**, thinly sliced

1 tsp chopped fresh **thyme** or ½ tsp dried thyme

1 tsp **plain flour**, plus extra for dusting

90ml (3fl oz) **chicken stock**

1 tsp **lemon** juice

500g packet **puff pastry**

300g (10oz) skinless boneless **cooked chicken**, chopped

salt and freshly ground **black pepper**

1 **egg**, beaten, to glaze

1 Melt the butter in a saucepan. Add the leeks and cook over a low heat, stirring frequently, for 5 minutes, or until fairly soft. Stir in the thyme, then sprinkle over the flour and stir in. Gradually blend in the stock and bring to the boil, stirring until thickened. Remove from the heat, stir in the lemon juice, and leave to cool.

2 Meanwhile, preheat the oven to 220°C (425°F/Gas 7). Roll out just under half of the pastry on a lightly floured work surface to a 25 x 15cm (10 x 6in) rectangle. Lay the pastry on a large dampened baking tray. Roll out the remaining pastry to a 25 x 18cm (10 x 7in) rectangle, lightly dust with flour, then fold in half lengthways. Make cuts 1cm (½in) apart along the folded edge to within 2.5cm (1 in) of the outer edge.

3 Stir the chopped chicken into the leek mixture and season generously with salt and pepper. Spoon evenly over the pastry base, leaving a 2.5cm (1in) border. Dampen the edges of the pastry with water. Place the second piece of pastry on top and press the edges together to seal; trim off the excess. Brush the top with beaten egg and bake for 25 minutes, or until golden brown and crisp. Leave to cool for a few minutes before serving.

● **Good with** roasted vegetables, such as shallots, courgettes, peppers, and aubergines.

Chicken Biryani

For special occasions, this subtly spiced, aromatic dish from India is traditionally decorated with pieces of edible silver leaf

 serves 4

 prep 20 mins • cook 30 mins

✔ low fat

2 tbsp **vegetable oil**

30g (1oz) **butter** or ghee

1 large **onion**, thinly sliced

2 **garlic cloves**, crushed

6 **curry leaves**

6 **cardamom pods**

1 **cinnamon stick**, broken into 2 or 3 pieces

1 tsp **ground turmeric**

½ tsp **ground cumin**

4 skinless boneless **chicken breasts**, cut into 2.5cm (1in) pieces

3 tbsp **mild curry paste**

300g (10oz) **basmati rice**

85g (3oz) **sultanas**

900ml (1½ pints) **chicken stock**

2 tbsp flaked **almonds**, toasted

● **Prepare ahead** Although the biryani is best cooked and eaten straight away, it can be made ahead, placed in a shallow ovenproof dish, with a little extra melted butter or ghee poured on top, covered tightly, and baked until thoroughly heated.

1 Heat the oil and butter in a large deep saucepan, and gently fry the onion and garlic until softened and starting to turn golden. Add the curry leaves, cardamom pods, and cinnamon stick, and fry for 5 minutes, stirring occasionally.

2 Add the turmeric and cumin, fry for 1 minute, then add the chicken, and stir in the curry paste.

3 Add the rice and sultanas, stir well, then pour in enough of the stock to cover the rice. Bring to the boil, lower the heat, and cook gently for 10–12 minutes, or until the rice is cooked, adding more stock if the mixture becomes dry.

4 Transfer to a serving dish, fluff up the rice with a fork, and serve with flaked almonds scattered over the top.

Chicken Wrapped in Pancetta and Sage

This is a light but elegant main course to which you can add grilled peppers and olives

 serves 6

 prep 20 mins
• cook 1 hr 15 mins

12 baby plum tomatoes, halved

3 tbsp olive oil, plus extra to drizzle

salt and freshly ground black pepper

3 large boneless skinless chicken breasts

12 sage leaves

12 slices of pancetta or Parma ham

baby salad leaves, watercress, or rocket

For the dressing

90ml (3fl oz) olive oil

2 tbsp cider vinegar

2 tsp chopped flat-leaf parsley

1 shallot, finely chopped

1 tsp brown sugar

salt and freshly ground black pepper

● **Prepare ahead** The chicken can be wrapped 1 day in advance, covered with cling film and chilled.

The dressing can be made up to 1 week in advance and stored in an airtight container in a refrigerator.

1 Preheat the oven to 150°C (300°F/Gas 2). Put the tomatoes into a roasting tin, drizzle with olive oil, and season to taste with salt and pepper. Roast in the oven for 1 hour, or until slightly dried and caramelized.

2 To make the dressing, place the ingredients in a small bowl and whisk together until thickened slightly. Season to taste with salt and pepper.

3 Cut each chicken breast into 4 pieces. Top each with a sage leaf, then wrap as tightly as possible with a piece of pancetta.

4 Heat the olive oil in a large frying pan and brown the chicken pieces on each side. Lower the heat and continue to cook the chicken, turning, for 10 minutes, or until cooked through.

5 Serve the chicken with salad leaves and the roasted tomatoes, and drizzle over a little dressing.

French Roast Chicken

This traditional method of roasting uses frequent basting, producing a really succulent roast

 serves 4

 prep 15 mins
• cook 1 hr 30 mins

4 tbsp chopped fresh herbs, such as tarragon and flat-leaf parsley

2 garlic cloves, finely chopped

115g (4oz) unsalted butter, softened

1 chicken, about 1.5kg (3lb 3oz)

1 lemon, pricked with a fork

120ml (4fl oz) dry white wine

500ml (16fl oz) chicken stock

salt and freshly ground black pepper

● **Prepare ahead** The herb butter can be made up to 1 day in advance and kept chilled.

1 Preheat the oven to 190°C (375°F/Gas 4). Add the herbs and garlic to the butter and combine. Ease your fingers between the breast skin and flesh of the chicken, being careful not to tear the skin, and spread the butter under the skin using your fingertips. Place the lemon inside the bird, then truss.

2 Put the chicken on a rack in a roasting pan. Pour all of the wine and three-quarters of the stock over the chicken, then season to taste with salt and pepper. Roast for 1 hour 25 minutes, or until the juices run clear when you pierce the thickest part of the leg. Using a large spoon, baste the bird with the pan juices during cooking. If the liquid evaporates from the bottom of the pan, add a little more wine.

3 Remove the chicken from the pan and allow to rest, covered with foil, for 10 minutes. Skim the fat from the pan, then add the remaining stock and bring to the boil, stirring, until slightly reduced, then strain into a jug and serve with the chicken.

Chicken Fricassée

This is a classic one-pot French dish in which chicken is simmered until the meat falls off the bone

 serves 4

🕐 prep 15 mins
● cook 1 hr 15 mins

✓ low fat

2 tbsp olive oil

salt and freshly ground black pepper

4 chicken legs, divided into drumstick and thigh joints, skin removed

2 tbsp plain flour

115g (4oz) button mushrooms

4 shallots, sliced

2 garlic cloves, crushed

4 waxy potatoes, peeled and cut into small pieces

2 tsp finely chopped rosemary leaves

150ml (5fl oz) dry white wine

300ml (10fl oz) chicken stock

1 bay leaf

1 Heat the oil in a large deep casserole. Season the flour to taste with salt and pepper. Dust the chicken pieces with the flour and fry over a medium-high heat until golden brown, turning often. Remove from the pan and set aside.

2 Slice the mushrooms. Add the shallots to the pan and fry for 2–3 minutes, stirring often. Add the garlic, mushrooms, potatoes, and rosemary, and fry for 2 minutes.

3 Pour in the wine and bring to the boil. Allow to bubble and reduce for 1 minute, then pour in the stock, and bring to the boil. Return the chicken to the pan, add the bay leaf, and cover tightly. Reduce the heat and cook gently for 45 minutes, or until the chicken is very tender. Discard the bay leaf and adjust the seasoning, if necessary. Serve hot.

VARIATION

Huhnerfrikasee

For a German-style fricassée, add a squeeze of lemon juice, a pinch of grated nutmeg, and a dash of Worcestershire sauce, then cook for 45–50 minutes. Towards the end of cooking, stir in a 200g can of drained peas. To serve, mix together 1 egg yolk and 75ml (2fl oz) whipping cream and stir into the sauce, off the heat. Serve with boiled rice.

Chicken in Garlic Sauce

Don't be put off by the large quantity of garlic, as the flavour will mellow in the cooking

 serves 4

 prep 10 mins ● cook 40 mins

🍲 shallow flameproof casserole

❄ freeze, without the cream and thyme, for up to 3 months

15 garlic cloves, unpeeled

salt and freshly ground black pepper

2 tbsp olive oil

30g (1oz) unsalted butter

4 chicken breasts, skin on

1 bay leaf

450ml (15fl oz) dry cider

200ml (7fl oz) apple juice

200ml (7fl oz) double cream

1 tbsp thyme leaves

1 Preheat the oven to 180°C (350°F/Gas 4). Cook the whole, unpeeled garlic cloves in a pan of boiling salted water for 4 minutes. Drain, cool slightly, then peel and set aside.

2 Heat the oil and butter in the casserole. When sizzling, add the chicken, skin-side down, and cook for 4–5 minutes, or until deep golden brown. Turn the chicken over and add the garlic cloves, bay leaf, cider, and apple juice. Cover and transfer to the oven for 20–25 minutes, or until the chicken is cooked through.

3 Lift the chicken out of the pan. Remove half the garlic cloves and discard. Bring the remaining juices up to the boil. Crush the garlic into the juices with a fork, then boil until reduced and thickened slightly.

4 Add the cream, season to taste with salt and pepper, and simmer for 1 minute. Return the chicken to the sauce and baste with the juices; add the thyme leaves and serve immediately.

● **Good with** boiled new potatoes and green beans.

Devilled Turkey

Serve these spicy stir-fried turkey strips as
a healthy lunch or supper

🍴 serves 4

🕐 prep 10 mins • cook 15 mins

2 tbsp **wholegrain mustard**

2 tbsp **mango chutney**

2 tbsp **Worcestershire sauce**

¼ tsp **ground paprika**

3 tbsp **orange juice**

1 **red chilli**, chopped (optional)

2 tbsp **olive oil**

450g (1lb) **turkey breast escalope**,
cut into strips

1 **onion**, peeled and finely chopped

1 **red pepper**, cored and cut into
strips

1 **orange pepper**, cored and cut into
strips

1 **garlic clove**, crushed

1 **Mix the mustard**, chutney,
Worcestershire sauce, paprika,
orange juice, and chilli, if using,
together until well combined.

2 **Heat the oil** in a frying pan or
wok, add the turkey, and cook
over a high heat until browned.
Remove the turkey from the pan and
set aside, covered to keep it warm.

3 **Add the onion** to the pan and
fry for 2–3 minutes, or until
beginning to colour. Add the
peppers and garlic and fry, stirring
constantly, for 3–4 minutes, or
until tender.

4 **Stir in the mustard mixture**
and return the turkey to the pan.
Cook for 5 minutes or until piping hot
and the turkey is cooked through.

⬤ **Good with** stir-fried spinach and
rice or noodles.

VARIATION

Devilled Chicken
This recipe also works well using the
same weight of chicken, cut into
strips, instead of the turkey.

Poached Guinea Fowl with Spiced Lentils

This simple dish makes a healthy, satisfying winter main course

🍴 serves 4

🕐 prep 20 mins
• cook 1 hr 15 mins

1.35kg (3lb) **guinea fowl**

2 **carrots**, cut into chunks

2 **celery sticks**, halved

2 **shallots**, halved

1 **bay leaf**

10 **black peppercorns**

2 tbsp **olive oil**

140g (5oz) **pancetta**, finely diced

1 **garlic clove**, crushed

1 small **red chilli**, deseeded and
finely chopped

300g (10oz) dried **Puy lentils**, rinsed
and well drained

4 tbsp chopped **flat-leaf parsley**

salt and freshly ground **black pepper**

1 **Put the guinea fowl** in a pan
with the carrots, celery, shallots,
bay leaf, and peppercorns. Cover with
cold water, bring to the boil, then
simmer for 45 minutes, covered.

2 **Lift the guinea fowl** on
to a plate; keep warm. Strain the
poaching liquid back into the pan and
boil for 10 minutes, or until reduced.

3 **Meanwhile, heat** the oil in
a pan and fry the pancetta. Add
the garlic and chilli, and fry gently for
2–3 minutes. Remove from the heat
and add the lentils.

4 **Pour** 400ml (14fl oz) of the
reduced stock into the lentils.
Bring to the boil, then simmer,
uncovered, for 15 minutes, stirring.
Add more stock as necessary. Add the
chopped parsley and season to taste
with salt and pepper.

5 **Meanwhile**, remove the
skin from the guinea fowl and
cut into pieces.

6 **Serve the lentils**, topped with
pieces of guinea fowl. Spoon over
the stock, if desired.

Lemon Honey Chicken with Mustard Mayonnaise

A simple but tasty dish that can be griddled, grilled, or barbecued

 serves 6

 prep 25 mins, plus marinating
● cook 15–20 mins

6 skinless boneless **chicken breasts**, about 175g (6oz) each

2 tbsp **clear honey**

2 **garlic cloves**, crushed

2 fresh **red chillies**, deseeded and finely chopped

juice of 1 **lemon**

3 tbsp **light soy sauce**

3 tbsp **olive oil**

4 tbsp **balsamic vinegar**

salt and freshly ground **black pepper**

For the mustard mayonnaise

2 **egg yolks**

½ tbsp **mild mustard**

2 tbsp **sherry vinegar**

200ml (7fl oz) **sunflower oil**

2 tbsp **lemon** juice

large bunch of **basil**

● **Prepare ahead** The mayonnaise can be made 1 day in advance and the chicken can marinate overnight.

1 **Score a criss-cross pattern** on one side of each chicken breast. Place in a shallow dish. Mix the honey, garlic, chilli, lemon juice, soy sauce, oil, and vinegar together, and season to taste with pepper. Pour the marinade over the chicken and turn the chicken to coat. Cover and chill for 2 hours.

2 **To make the mayonnaise,** place the egg yolks, mustard, and vinegar in a food processor, and season to taste with salt and pepper. With the motor running, slowly add the oil until it thickens. Continue to add the oil in a steady drizzle, then add lemon juice to taste and the basil. Chill for at least 1 hour.

3 **Preheat the grill to high**. Remove the chicken from the marinade and grill for 15–20 minutes, or until well coloured and cooked through, turning every 5 minutes, and basting well. Slice the chicken breasts and serve with the mayonnaise spooned over.

Roast Chicken with Thyme and Lemon

Lemon and thyme are traditional roasting ingredients and make a simple, yet delicious, glaze when added to the butter

 serves 4

 prep 15 mins, plus standing
● cook 1 hr

 low fat

1.8kg (4lb) **chicken**, jointed into 8 pieces

1 **lemon**

2 **garlic cloves**, peeled and crushed

15g (½oz) **butter**

1 tbsp **olive oil**

small bunch of **thyme**, leaves removed from stalks

salt and freshly ground **black pepper**

120ml (4fl oz) **dry white wine**

1 **Preheat the oven** to 200°C (400°F/Gas 6). Place the chicken pieces in the roasting tin, in one layer.

2 **Finely grate** 2 tsp zest from the lemon, reserving the lemon. Place the zest in a bowl with the garlic, butter, oil, and thyme, and

season to taste with salt and pepper. Beat with a wooden spoon to mix.

3 **Dot the lemon** and thyme butter evenly over the chicken pieces. Cut the reserved lemon into chunks and tuck around the chicken, then pour over the wine.

4 **Roast the chicken**, turning and basting the chicken pieces occasionally, for 50–60 minutes, or until the chicken is golden brown and cooked through and the juices run clear when the meat is pierced with a knife. Add a little more wine if the juices start to boil dry.

● **Good with** a mixed salad and oven-baked potato wedges.

● **Leftovers** are delicious shredded and served cold on top of mixed salad leaves, in a sandwich, on top of baked potatoes, or made into a pot pie.

Chicken Jalfrezi

A spicy dish, with chillies and mustard seeds,
for those who like their curries hot

🍴 serves 4

🕐 prep 20 mins • cook 25 mins

✓ low fat

❄ freeze for up to 3 months

2 tbsp **sunflower oil**

2 tsp **ground cumin**

2 tsp yellow **mustard seeds**

1 tsp **ground turmeric**

2 tbsp **masala curry paste**

2.5cm (1in) piece fresh **root ginger**, peeled and finely chopped

3 **garlic cloves**, crushed

1 **onion**, sliced

1 **red pepper**, deseeded and sliced

½ **green pepper**, deseeded and sliced

2 **green chillies**, deseeded and finely chopped

675g (1½lb) boneless **chicken thighs** or breasts, skinned and cut into 2.5cm (1in) pieces

225g can **chopped tomatoes**

3 tbsp chopped **coriander**

● **Prepare ahead** The curry can be made up to 2 days in advance, chilled, and reheated to serve.

1 Heat the oil in a large pan over a medium heat, add the cumin, mustard seeds, turmeric, and curry paste, and stir-fry for 1–2 minutes.

2 Add the ginger, garlic, and onion and fry, stirring frequently, until the onion starts to soften. Add the red and green peppers and the chillies and fry for 5 minutes.

3 Increase the heat to medium-high, add the chicken, and fry until starting to brown. Add the tomatoes and coriander, reduce the heat, and simmer for 10 minutes, or until the chicken is cooked through, stirring often. Serve hot.

● **Good with** basmati rice and poppadums.

Chilli and Orange Duck

The traditional flavour combination of rich duck and tangy
orange is given a modern twist in this recipe

🍴 serves 6

🕐 prep 15–20 mins • cook 25–30 mins

6 small **duck breasts**, about 200g (7oz) each

sea salt and freshly ground **black pepper**

2 tbsp **clear honey**

drizzle of **olive oil**

2 **spring onions**, trimmed

For the sauce

3 large **oranges**

100g (3½oz) **sugar**

1 tbsp grated fresh **root ginger**

1 **red chilli**, deseeded and finely sliced

2 **star anise**

1 **cinnamon stick**

1 tbsp **sweet chilli sauce**

1 tbsp **Thai fish sauce**

1 tbsp **rice vinegar**

4 tbsp **red wine**

● **Prepare ahead** Make the sauce the day before and chill. Sear the duck up to 2 hours in advance and keep chilled. Cook in a preheated oven at 220°C (425°F/Gas 7) for 6–10 minutes when required.

1 Preheat the oven to 220°C (425°F/Gas 7). To make the sauce, peel the zest from 1 orange using a potato peeler and cut the zest into thin strips. Juice the oranges to make 360ml (12fl oz) juice. Combine the orange zest and juice with the rest of the sauce ingredients in a saucepan and bring to the boil, stirring. Simmer, stirring occasionally, for 12 minutes, or until lightly syrupy.

2 Trim the duck breasts of excess fat. Season the breasts to taste with salt and pepper, and brush a little honey over the skin. Heat the oil in a frying pan, set over a medium-high heat, add the duck breasts, skin-side down, and fry for 3–4 minutes, or until crispy and golden. Turn over the breasts, then transfer them to the oven for 8–10 minutes, or until just cooked through and still pink in the middle. Rest for 5 minutes before serving.

3 Cut the spring onions into finger-length pieces, then slice into thin strips. Slice the duck breasts, arrange on warmed plates, and scatter with the shreds of spring onion. Spoon over the sauce.

● **Good with** sweet potato mash and crunchy steamed green beans.

Duck Breasts with Cherries

Pan-fried duck with fresh cherries, when in season, is a treat for a smart dinner party

 serves 4

 prep 15 mins • cook 20 mins

4 large **duck breasts**, about 350g (12oz) each

sea salt and freshly ground **black pepper**

For the sauce

15g (½oz) **butter**

1 **shallot**, finely chopped

1 tbsp **maple syrup**

1 sprig of **rosemary**

75ml (2½fl oz) **ruby port**

100ml (3½fl oz) **chicken stock**

400g (14oz) fresh dark red **cherries**, pitted

● **Prepare ahead** Make the sauce up to 2 days in advance, and chill until you are ready to cook the duck.

1 Score the skin of each duck breast with a sharp knife and rub salt and pepper into the cuts.

2 Heat a heavy frying pan. Add the breasts, skin-side down, and fry over a medium-high heat for 3–4 minutes. Turn the breasts over and cook for a further 2 minutes. Reduce the heat and cook for 6–8 minutes, or until cooked through. Remove from the heat and allow to rest for 5 minutes.

3 To make the sauce, melt the butter in a saucepan over a moderate heat and fry the shallot for 2–3 minutes, or until softened but not brown, stirring constantly.

4 Stir in the maple syrup, rosemary, and port, and bring to the boil. Simmer for 30 seconds, then add the stock and simmer, uncovered, for 3–4 minutes, or until slightly reduced. Add the cherries, and cook for a further 2 minutes to heat them. Season to taste with salt and pepper. Slice the duck and serve with cherry sauce spooned over.

> **CHERRIES**
>
> If fresh cherries are not in season, use frozen or canned cherries instead.

Turkey Milanese

Inspired by the classic veal dish, this features coated cutlets topped with a tomato and artichoke sauce

 serves 4

prep 10 mins • cook 20–25 mins

4 tbsp **plain flour**

salt and freshly ground **black pepper**

4 **turkey breast** cutlets, about 115g (4oz) each

3 tbsp **olive oil**

1 small **onion**, chopped

60ml (2fl oz) **dry white wine**

200g jar **marinated artichoke hearts**, drained

175g (6oz) can **plum tomatoes**, drained weight

few **basil** leaves, torn

1 Combine the flour and ½ tsp each of salt and pepper on a plate. Dip the turkey in the seasoned flour until lightly coated all over, shaking off any excess.

2 Heat 1 tbsp of the oil in a large frying pan over a medium-high heat. Add 2 of the cutlets and fry, turning once, for 2–3 minutes on each side, or until golden brown and cooked through. Remove from the pan and keep warm. Heat another 1 tbsp of oil and repeat with the remaining 2 cutlets.

3 Add the remaining oil to the pan and fry the onion for 4–5 minutes, or until soft. Add the wine and bring the mixture to the boil, stirring often to loosen any brown bits from the bottom of the pan. Stir in the artichokes, tomatoes, and basil, and bring back to the boil. Pour over the cutlets to serve.

● **Good with** buttered tagliatelle or other flat pasta noodles.

● **Leftovers** with its sauce can be served hot on toasted ciabatta with melted provolone cheese.

VARIATION

Veal Milanese

If you would like to try the Italian veal version, simply replace the turkey breasts with the same weight of veal cutlets and continue with the recipe, as above.

Roast Turkey with Cranberry Pistachio Stuffing

The light stuffing is great cooked inside the turkey, but can also be cooked separately

 serves 6-8

 prep 30 mins
• cook 3 hrs 45 mins

 low fat

 freeze the cooked turkey and stuffing for up to 3 months

4.5kg (10lb) oven-ready turkey

15g (½oz) butter

8 streaky bacon rashers

fresh herbs, to garnish (optional)

For the stuffing

45g (1½oz) butter

1 onion, finely chopped

125g (4½oz) fresh white breadcrumbs

2 tbsp finely chopped parsley

115g (4oz) fresh or frozen cranberries, roughly chopped

60g (2oz) pistachio nuts, chopped

salt and freshly ground black pepper

2 egg whites

1-2 tbsp milk, to mix

1 To make the stuffing, melt the butter in a frying pan, add the onion, and fry over a medium heat, stirring occasionally, for 3-4 minutes, or until softened.

2 Remove from the heat and stir in the breadcrumbs, parsley, cranberries, and pistachios. Season to taste with salt and pepper. Leave to cool. Stir in the egg whites with a little milk to make a firm mixture.

3 Preheat the oven to 180°C (350°F/Gas 4). Stuff the neck end of the turkey with enough stuffing to fill the cavity, reserving the rest. Weigh the stuffed turkey and calculate the cooking time of the turkey, allowing 20 minutes per 450g (1lb) plus 20 minutes extra.

4 Brush the melted butter over the turkey skin. Sprinkle with salt and pepper, place in a roasting tin, and cover loosely with foil. Roast the turkey for the calculated time, or until there is no trace of pink in the juices when pierced through the thickest part. Baste occasionally and remove the foil for the last 30-40 minutes of cooking to brown the bird.

5 Roll the remaining stuffing into 8 walnut-sized balls. Stretch the bacon rashers out thinly with the back of a knife, then cut in half crossways. Roll a piece of bacon around each stuffing ball and place on a lightly oiled baking tray.

6 When the turkey is cooked, remove from the oven, cover with foil and leave to rest for at least 20 minutes before carving. Increase the oven temperature to 200°C (400°F/Gas 6), place the stuffing balls in the oven and cook for 15-20 minutes, or until golden brown. Serve the turkey with the stuffing balls and garnish with herbs, if desired.

● **Good with** all the traditional accompaniments, such as roast potatoes, Brussels sprouts, carrots, and gravy.

● **Leftovers** of turkey and stuffing are delicious served cold, with salad or in sandwiches.

> **TURKEY GRAVY**
> Don't throw away the turkey juices; use them to make a delicious gravy with a little flour and stock.

Grilled Poussins

A delicious light lunch cooked under the grill

 serves 4

prep 5 mins • cook 30-35 mins

2 poussins, about 800g (1¾lb) each

2 tbsp butter, melted

1 tbsp lemon juice

1 tbsp Worcestershire sauce

½ tsp dried tarragon, crumbled

½ tsp dried thyme, crumbed

¼ tsp salt

1 Spatchcock each poussin. Cut down each side of the backbone and discard. Turn the bird over, open out, and press down hard on the breastbone to flatten. Preheat the grill to high.

2 Place the melted butter in a bowl and stir in the lemon juice, Worcestershire sauce, herbs, and salt. Place the poussins, skin-side down, on the grill pan rack. Brush the poussins with half the butter mixture and grill 12cm (5in) from the heat source for 18-20 minutes, or until lightly browned on one side and almost tender. Turn over, brush with the remaining butter mixture, and grill for 10-15 minutes, or until they are cooked through and the juices run clear when pierced with a sharp knife.

Spicy Turkey Burgers

A popular snack dish

🍴 serves 4

🕐 prep 10 mins • cook 6 mins

450g (1lb) minced turkey

2 tbsp finely chopped onion

2 tbsp chopped parsley

2 tsp Dijon mustard

2 garlic cloves, finely chopped

60g (2oz) fresh breadcrumbs

1 egg white

salt and freshly ground black pepper

1 tbsp vegetable oil

4 seeded buns

1 large ripe tomato, sliced

2 handfuls of shredded lettuce

1 Mix the turkey, onion, parsley, mustard, garlic, breadcrumbs, and egg white in a bowl, and season to taste with salt and pepper. Form into 4 patties, each 1cm (½in) thick.

2 Heat the oil in a large frying pan. Add the patties and fry for 3–4 minutes on each side, or until browned and cooked through. Meanwhile, toast the buns.

3 Place a turkey patty into each bun, with 1–2 tomato slices and some shredded lettuce.

● **Good with** chunky chips or pickles and potato crisps.

Crispy Roast Duck

Duck is a special-occasion dish in China, and this cooking method makes the most of its sweet, succulent flesh

🍴 serves 4

🕐 prep 1 hr 15 mins, plus drying and resting • cook 1 hr 35 mins

📦 meat hook or kitchen string

1 duck, about 1.8kg (4lb)

1 tsp five-spice powder

3 tbsp oyster sauce

1 tsp salt

For the glaze

3 tbsp honey

1 tbsp dark soy sauce

2 tbsp rice wine or dry sherry

● **Prepare ahead** You can start preparing the duck the day before required, up to the end of step 4, as the recipe requires extra time.

1 Rinse the duck inside and out and pat dry with absorbent kitchen paper. Mix the five-spice powder, oyster sauce, and salt, and spread over and inside the bird.

2 Insert a meat hook through the neck end, or tie string around the neck to hang the duck. Place the duck in a colander in the sink, pour

a kettle of boiling water over it, then pat dry with kitchen paper. Repeat this pouring and drying 5 times.

3 To make the glaze, put the honey, soy sauce, rice wine and 50ml (5fl oz) water in a saucepan and bring to the boil. Reduce the heat, simmer for 10 minutes, or until sticky, then brush the glaze over the duck until thoroughly coated.

4 Hang the duck over a roasting tin or shallow tray in a well-ventilated place and leave for 4–5 hours, or until the skin is dry.

5 Preheat the oven to 230°C (450°F/Gas 8). Place the duck in a roasting tin, breast-side up, and pour 150ml (5fl oz) cold water into the tin. Roast for 20 minutes, reduce the oven to 180°C (350°F/Gas 4), and roast for 1 hour 15 minutes, or until the skin is crisp and golden.

6 Leave the duck to stand for 10 minutes, then joint and arrange the duck on a serving platter. Serve at once.

● **Good with** Chinese pancakes, shredded spring onions, thin batons of cucumber, and hoisin sauce.

Turkey Kebabs

A great dish to barbecue

🍴 makes 6

🕐 prep 20 mins, plus marinating • cook 10–12 mins

❗ soak skewers for 30 minutes

📦 6 wooden skewers

60ml (2fl oz) light soy sauce

2 tbsp olive oil

2 garlic cloves, finely chopped

¾ tsp ground ginger

¼ tsp chilli flakes

675g (1½lb) skinless boneless turkey breasts, cut into 2.5cm (1in) cubes

1 red pepper, deseeded and cut into 2.5cm (1in) pieces

1 green pepper, deseeded and cut into 2.5cm (1in) pieces

1 large courgette, cut into 2.5cm (1in) slices

240ml (8fl oz) plain yogurt

2 tbsp mint, chopped

½ tsp ground cumin

1 Combine the soy sauce, oil, garlic, ginger, and chilli. Add the turkey pieces and toss to coat. Cover, chill, and marinate for at least 1 hour.

2 Thread the turkey, pepper, and courgette onto skewers and brush with any leftover marinade. Grill for 5–6 minutes on each side, or until cooked through.

3 Mix together the yogurt, mint, and cumin, and serve alongside.

Chicken Piri-Piri

Piri-piri sauce is popular in Portugal and South Africa

- 🍴 serves 4
- 🕐 prep 20 mins, plus cooling and marinating • cook 1 hr 15 mins

1 chicken, about 1.5kg (3lb 3oz)

6 fresh red chillies or green chillies

3 garlic cloves

½ tsp dried oregano

2 tsp paprika

120ml (4fl oz) olive oil

4 tbsp red wine vinegar

1 tsp salt

1 Preheat the oven to 190°C (375°F/Gas 5). Cut through the breastbone of the chicken and open it out. Cut off and throw away the wing tips, neck, and parson's nose.

2 Put the chillies on a tray, roast for 15 minutes, then let cool.

3 Remove the stalks from the chillies and discard. Place the chillies with the rest of the ingredients in a pan, and cook over a low heat for 3–5 minutes, stirring frequently. Allow to cool, then blend to a purée.

4 Rub the mixture over the chicken, place in a non-metallic dish, cover, chill, and marinate for at least 1 hour.

5 Preheat the oven to 200°C (400°F/Gas 6). Roast the chicken for 45 minutes, turning once and basting frequently. Serve hot.

Chicken Tikka Masala

An Indian restaurant dish, made popular in Britain

- 🍴 serves 4
- 🕐 prep 20 mins, plus marinating • cook 25 mins
- ❄ freeze for up to 3 months

8 skinless boneless chicken thighs

2 garlic cloves, coarsely chopped

2.5cm (1in) piece of fresh root ginger, coarsely chopped

juice of 1 lime

1 red chilli, deseeded

2 tbsp coarsely chopped coriander leaves, plus extra to garnish

2 tbsp vegetable oil

1 red onion, chopped

1 tsp ground turmeric

1 tsp ground cumin

1 tbsp tomato purée

300ml (10fl oz) double cream

1 tbsp lemon juice

salt and freshly ground black pepper

● **Prepare ahead** The dish can be made 1 day in advance, allowed to cool, covered, and chilled until needed. Reheat gently before serving.

1 Place the chicken in a single layer in a shallow dish. Put the next 5 ingredients and 1 tbsp of the oil in a food processor, process into a paste, and spread over the chicken. Set aside to marinate for 2 hours.

2 Heat the remaining oil in a frying pan, add the onion, and fry until softened and starting to colour. Add the turmeric and cumin and fry gently for 2–3 minutes.

3 Preheat the grill on its highest setting. Lift the chicken from the dish, reserving any marinade left behind, and place on a foil-lined grill rack. Grill for 5 minutes, or until almost cooked and slightly scorched at the edges, turning once.

4 Stir the tomato purée and cream into the frying pan with any leftover marinade. Add the lemon and stir over a medium heat until mixed in. Place the chicken into the pan and baste with the sauce. Simmer for 5 minutes, or until the chicken is cooked through. Season to taste with salt and pepper and serve, sprinkled with coriander.

● **Good with** pilau rice or warm naan bread.

Roast Guinea Fowl with Mustard Sauce

Guinea fowl is less gamey in flavour than grouse

- 🍴 serves 4
- 🕐 prep 40 mins • cook 25 mins

1 tbsp sunflower oil

4 guinea fowl breasts, skin removed

salt and freshly ground black pepper

150ml (5fl oz) vermouth or sherry

150ml (5fl oz) chicken stock

200ml (7fl oz) double cream

2 tsp wholegrain mustard

4–5 sprigs of chives, snipped

1 Preheat the oven to 240°C (475°F/Gas 9). Heat the oil in a frying pan and brown the guinea fowl. Transfer to a roasting tin and season to taste with salt and pepper. Roast for 8–10 minutes, or until the juices run clear when pierced with a knife. Cover and leave to rest for 5 minutes.

2 To make the sauce, bring the vermouth to the boil in a pan, then simmer until reduced by half. Add the stock, return to the boil, then simmer to reduce again. Add the cream and simmer until thick enough to coat the back of a spoon.

3 Whisk the mustard and chives, into the sauce. Season to taste with salt and pepper. Carve the guinea fowl to serve and spoon over the mustard sauce.

Chicken with Chorizo

In Mexico, chorizo is made with fresh pork, but in Spain, the pork is smoked first

 serves 4

 prep 10 mins
• cook 1 hr 10 mins

 freeze for up to 1 month

3 tbsp olive oil

4 skinless chicken legs

250g (9oz) chorizo sausage, cut into bite-sized pieces

1 red onion, thinly sliced

1 tsp ground coriander

1 tsp chopped thyme

1 red pepper, skinned, deseeded, and chopped

1 yellow pepper, skinned, deseeded, and chopped

1 courgette, sliced

2 garlic cloves, crushed

400g can chopped tomatoes

200ml (7fl oz) chicken stock

60ml (2fl oz) dry sherry

freshly ground black pepper

1 **Preheat the oven** to 180°C (350°F/Gas 4). Heat the oil in a large frying pan, add the chicken, and fry for 5–8 minutes, turning frequently, or until browned evenly. Transfer to a casserole dish.

2 **Add the chorizo** to the pan and fry for 2–3 minutes, or until lightly browned, stirring frequently. Remove and add to the casserole. Lower the heat, add the onion to the pan, and fry gently for 5 minutes, or until softened. Add the coriander, fry for 1 minute, then add the thyme, peppers, courgette, and garlic, and fry for 5 minutes.

3 **Add the tomatoes**, stock, and sherry. Season to taste with black pepper, and bring to the boil. Add the mixture into the casserole, cover, and cook in the oven for 40 minutes, or until the chicken is cooked through.

VARIATION

Spicy Chicken Casserole
In step 2, remove the chorizo and add 250g (9oz) chopped new potatoes. In step 3, replace the sherry with a pinch of dried chilli flakes.

Coq au Vin

A French classic that is perfect for entertaining

 serves 4

prep 30 mins
• cook 1 hr 30 mins

large flameproof casserole

freeze for up to 3 months

2 tbsp plain flour

salt and freshly ground black pepper

1 large chicken, jointed

60g (2oz) butter

125g (4½oz) pancetta, cut into thick short strips

2 garlic cloves, crushed

1 carrot, cut into cubes

1 celery stick, roughly chopped

4 tbsp brandy or Cognac

750ml (1¼ pints) red wine, such as Burgundy or Beaujolais

1 bay leaf

4–5 sprigs of thyme

1 tbsp olive oil

450g (1lb) button onions

1 tsp brown sugar

1 tsp red wine vinegar

225g (8oz) small mushrooms

1 **Season the flour** to taste with salt and pepper. Coat the chicken with 1 tbsp of the seasoned flour. Melt half the butter in the casserole, add the chicken, and fry gently until golden brown on all sides.

2 **Add the pancetta**, garlic, carrot, and celery, and fry until softened. Add the remaining flour and cook for 1–2 minutes. Pour in the brandy and wine, stirring to remove any sediment from the bottom of the casserole. Add the bay leaf and thyme, bring to the boil, cover, and simmer for 1 hour.

3 **Meanwhile**, melt the rest of the butter with the olive oil in a frying pan. Add the onions and fry until just brown. Stir in the sugar, vinegar, and 1 tbsp water.

4 **Add the onions** and mushrooms to the chicken, and cook for another 30 minutes, or until the chicken is cooked through and the vegetables are tender.

5 **Transfer the chicken** and vegetables to a hot serving dish. Discard the bay leaf and thyme. Skim off any excess fat and boil the sauce for 3–5 minutes, or until reduced. Pour over the chicken and serve.

● **Prepare ahead** You can make this dish 1 day in advance. Cover and chill, to let the flavours develop.

● **Good with** mashed potatoes and a green vegetable.

Grilled Quail with Ginger Glaze

These quails have a sweet-sour, spicy glaze that's very moreish.
Cook them on a barbecue, under a grill, or on a hot griddle pan

 serves 4

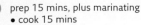 prep 15 mins, plus marinating
• cook 15 mins

 freeze the quail in the marinade
for up to 1 month

8 quails

limes wedges, to serve

For the glaze

1 garlic clove, crushed

1 tbsp finely grated, fresh root ginger

3 tbsp sweet chilli dipping sauce

juice of 1 lime

1 tbsp sesame oil

3 tbsp finely chopped coriander

● **Prepare ahead** Prepare steps
1 and 2, then cover and refrigerate
the quails for up to 2 days.

1 **Using kitchen scissors**, cut
each quail along the backbone,
from the neck end to the parson's
nose. Open the quails, place on to
a cutting board, skin-side up, and
press firmly with your hand to flatten.
Slash the breast skin a couple of times
with a knife to ensure even cooking.

2 **Mix the marinade** ingredients
together with a fork. Brush evenly
over the quails, pressing into the cuts,
and leave to marinate in the fridge for
at least an hour or overnight.

3 **Preheat a grill** to hot. Grill the
quails on a foil-lined grill pan,
turning once, for 12–15 minutes, or
until golden brown and the juices
show no trace of pink when pierced.

4 **Serve hot**, with lime wedges
for squeezing.

VARIATION

Grilled Quail with Hoisin

For a sweet, Chinese barbeque
flavour, replace the chilli sauce with
hoisin sauce and the sesame oil with
1 crushed garlic clove.

Pot-Roasted Partridge with Red Cabbage

Partridge have quite a delicate flavour and are delicious when
pot-roasted, as the flavours become concentrated in the pot

 serves 4

 prep 15 mins • cook 1hr

large flameproof casserole

4 young oven-ready partridges

salt and freshly ground black pepper

30g (1oz) butter

1 tbsp sunflower oil

4 unsmoked lean streaky bacon
rashers, chopped

2 onions, thinly sliced

1 garlic clove, crushed

2 tart dessert apples, cored and
sliced

6 juniper berries, crushed

strip of thinly pared orange zest

175ml (6fl oz) apple juice

450g (1lb) red cabbage, finely
shredded

3 tbsp redcurrant jelly

2 tbsp red wine vinegar

1 **Preheat the oven** to 200°C
(400°F/Gas 6). Season the
partridges all over with salt and
pepper. Melt the butter in the
casserole, and fry the birds quickly,
turning occasionally, until all sides are
browned. Remove from the casserole
and set aside.

2 **Heat the oil** in the casserole,
then stir in the bacon, onions,
and garlic. Cook over a medium heat
for 3–4 minutes, or until the bacon
begins to brown. Add the apples,
juniper berries, orange zest, apple
juice, and cabbage, and bring to the
boil. Cover, reduce the heat, and
simmer for 10 minutes.

3 **Stir in the redcurrant jelly**
and wine vinegar, then place the
partridges on top of the vegetables.
Cover and roast in the oven for
25–30 minutes, or until the meat
is no longer pink.

4 **Remove from the oven** and
allow to stand for 10 minutes
before serving.

Autumn Game Casserole

Mixed game makes a wonderfully rich-flavoured dish. Look for ready-diced packs of meat, which cut down on preparation time

- serves 4
- prep 20 mins
  - cook 1 hr 30 mins
- flameproof casserole
- freeze for up to 3 months

2 tbsp **olive oil**

500g (1lb 2oz) **mixed casserole game**, such as pheasant, partridge, venison, rabbit, and pigeon, diced

1 **onion**, sliced

1 **carrot**, sliced

1 **parsnip**, sliced

1 **fennel bulb**, sliced, leaves reserved

2 tbsp **plain flour**

200ml (7fl oz) **dry cider** or apple juice

200ml (7fl oz) **chicken stock**

250g (9oz) **chestnut mushrooms**, thickly sliced

½ tsp **fennel seeds**

salt and freshly ground **black pepper**

● **Prepare ahead** The casserole can be prepared up to 2 days in advance, then cooled and stored in the refrigerator. Reheat and serve.

1 Preheat the oven to 160°C (325°C/Gas 3). Heat the oil in a flameproof casserole and fry the diced meats, stirring occasionally, for 3–4 minutes, or until lightly browned. Remove and keep hot.

2 Add the onion, carrot, parsnip, and fennel to the pan and fry, stirring occasionally, for 4–5 minutes, or until lightly coloured. Sprinkle in the flour and gradually stir in the cider and stock. Add the mushrooms and fennel seeds, then return the meat to the pan.

3 Season well and bring to the boil. Cover tightly with a lid and place in the oven for 1 hour 20 minutes, or until the meat and vegetables are tender.

4 Sprinkle the casserole with the reserved fennel leaves or chopped parsley, and serve hot.

Roast Quail with Apple and Calvados

Wrapping the quail in pancetta keeps the flesh moist. The apples and calvados add a rich, sweet flavour to the dish

- serves 4
- prep 10 mins
  - cook 25–30 mins
- low fat
- freeze for up to 3 months

8 **quails**

½ tsp freshly grated **nutmeg**

salt and freshly ground **black pepper**

small bunch of **sage** leaves

8 **pancetta** slices

2 crisp **dessert apples**, cored and sliced

15g (½oz) **butter**, melted

2 tsp **demerara sugar**

4 tbsp **calvados** or cider brandy

● **Prepare ahead** Follow step 1, then place the birds into a roasting tin until ready to cook. Cover with cling film and store in the refrigerator for up to 24 hours.

1 Preheat the oven to 200°C (400°F/Gas 6). Season the birds inside and out with the nutmeg, and salt and pepper. Tuck a couple of sage leaves into the cavity, and wrap a strip of pancetta around each bird, tucking the ends underneath.

2 Toss the apples in the butter, sprinkle with the sugar and place in a roasting tin. Arrange the quails on top and roast for 25–30 minutes, turning occasionally, until both the quails and apples are golden brown.

3 Lift the quails and apples on to a warmed serving plate. Stir the calvados into the roasting tin to deglaze, boil for 30 seconds, then spoon over the quails to serve.

● **Good with** roast potatoes and green beans.

Pot-roast Pheasant

Pot-roasting a pheasant retains all its flavour and moistness

 serves 6

 prep 40 mins
• cook 1 hr 40 mins

 large flameproof casserole

2 tbsp olive oil

60g (2oz) butter, chilled

2 pheasants, about 750g (1lb 10oz) each

salt and freshly ground black pepper

250g (8oz) chestnut mushrooms

2 tbsp chopped fresh thyme

1 large onion, finely chopped

100g (3½ oz) rindless streaky bacon, chopped

750ml (1¼ pints) red wine

● **Prepare ahead** The pheasant can be prepared 1 day in advance, covered, and chilled.

1 **Heat half of the oil** and half of the butter in a large frying pan. Brown the pheasants evenly, season with salt and pepper, and place them in the casserole.

2 **Add the mushrooms** and the thyme to the frying pan, and cook for 5 minutes, or until coloured. Add them to the casserole.

3 **Preheat the oven** to 190°C (375°F/ Gas 5). Heat the remaining oil in the pan, then add the onion and bacon, and cook, stirring, for 5 minutes, or until the onion softens. Add the onion, bacon, and wine to the casserole, cover, and roast for 1 hour 30 minutes, or until the pheasants are cooked and a leg pulls away from the bird easily. Strain the liquid from the casserole.

4 **While the meat rests**, skim the fat from the strained juices. Bring to the boil and simmer briskly for 10 minutes, or until reduced by a third. Whisk in the remaining butter to make the sauce glossy. Carve the pheasant, and serve on warmed plates with the hot gravy.

● **Good with** carrot and swede mash, and French beans.

Roast Partridge with Grapes in Sauternes

The fruity Sauternes complements the rich flavour of the game

 serves 6

prep 1 hr, plus standing
• cook 35 mins

6 whole partridges

60g (2oz) butter

12 sage leaves

12 rashers of rindless streaky bacon, or slices of Parma ham

olive oil, for browning

For the sauce

360ml (12fl oz) Sauternes, or other sweet white wine

115g (4oz) white seedless grapes, sliced in half

2 shallots, finely chopped

salt and freshly ground black pepper

30g (1oz) butter, chilled and diced

360ml (12fl oz) chicken stock

● **Prepare ahead** Pour the Sauternes over the grape halves and leave to soak for at least 1 hour.

1 **Cut the breasts** off the partridges. Place a knob of butter and sage leaf on the underside of each partridge breast, then wrap each breast with 1 slice of bacon.

2 **Melt a little olive oil** in a frying pan over a high heat and brown the wrapped partridge breasts on both sides. Place them in a roasting tin and set aside.

3 **Preheat the oven** to 190°C (375°F/Gas 5). To make the sauce, fry the shallots in the tin until softened. Strain the Sauternes into the tin, reserving the grapes. Bring to the boil, simmer for 10 minutes, or until the wine is reduced, then add the stock, and bring back to the boil. When the sauce has reduced again, add the grapes, and simmer gently until ready to serve.

4 **Roast the partridge breasts** for 12 minutes, turning once. Just before serving, bring the sauce back to a gentle simmer, and whisk in the butter. Serve the partridge with the sauce.

VARIATION

Roast Pheasant with Grapes in Sauternes

Replace the partridges with 6 pheasants, using 2 sage leaves and 2 slices of streaky bacon for each. Roast the pheasant breasts for 15 minutes.

Pigeon Breasts en Croûte

If you have never tried cooking pigeon breasts, they are surprisingly easy to prepare

 serves 4

🕐 prep 10 mins, plus marinating • cook 10 mins

8 pigeon breasts

salt and freshly ground black pepper

2 tbsp olive oil

2 shallots, sliced

100g (3½oz) dry-cure bacon lardons

15g (½oz) butter

8 slices of ciabatta, or other rustic bread

2 tbsp Dijon mustard

handful of rocket

For the marinade

60ml (2fl oz) red wine

2 tbsp balsamic vinegar

grated zest and juice of 1 orange

1 Mix the marinade ingredients in a bowl. Add the pigeon breasts, coat evenly, then cover and chill for at least 8 hours.

2 Remove the pigeon from the marinade and season with salt and pepper; reserve the marinade. Heat half the oil in a pan, and fry the shallots and lardons over a moderate heat for 3–4 minutes, or until golden. Remove and keep warm.

3 Preheat the grill on its highest setting. Melt the butter in the pan, add the pigeon breasts, and fry for 4–5 minutes, or until golden, turning once. Brush the bread slices with the remaining oil and grill until golden. Spread each slice with the mustard.

4 Remove the pigeon breasts from the pan, cover with foil, and keep hot. Pour the reserved marinade into the pan, bring to the boil and boil rapidly for 1–2 minutes, to reduce by about half.

5 Divide the rocket between 4 plates and top with the toast. Cut the pigeon breasts in half diagonally, then pile on top with the lardons and shallots. Drizzle with the reduced juices and serve immediately.

Grouse with Garlic Cream Sauce

Young grouse are the best for roasting. Serve one per person

🍴 serves 4

🕐 prep 15 mins • cook 30–35 mins

❄ freeze for up to 3 months

1 garlic bulb

½ tbsp olive oil

4 young oven-ready grouse

salt and freshly ground black pepper

30g (1oz) butter

5 small sprigs of fresh thyme

8 streaky bacon rashers

150ml (5fl oz) dry white wine

250ml (9fl oz) double cream

freshly grated nutmeg

● **Prepare ahead** The sauce can be made in advance, then cooled, covered, and chilled for up to 3 days. If the sauce separates on standing, whisk until smooth.

1 Preheat the oven to 200°C (400°F/Gas 6). Remove the loose outer leaves from the garlic and cut across, about 5mm (¼in) from the top, to expose the flesh. Drizzle with the olive oil and wrap in foil.

2 Season the grouse with salt and pepper, top each with a knob of butter and a sprig of thyme, then wrap each with 2 strips of bacon.

3 Place the grouse and garlic in a roasting tin and roast the grouse for 25–30 minutes, basting halfway through.

4 Remove the grouse from the oven and transfer to a warmed serving platter. Cover with foil to keep warm. Place the roasting tin over a high heat and stir in the wine. Add the last sprig of thyme, and boil until the liquid is reduced by half. Add the cream, return to the boil, stirring, then simmer for 3 minutes, or until reduced. Remove the thyme sprig.

5 Unwrap the garlic and squeeze the softened flesh from the cloves. Mash with a fork, then stir into the creamy sauce in the roasting tin. Adjust the seasoning to taste with salt, pepper, and nutmeg. Serve with the sauce.

● **Good with** roasted cherry tomatoes and mashed potatoes.

Spanish Meatballs

These little veal and pork meatballs, *albóndigas* in Spanish, are also popular served as tapas

🍴 makes 48

🕐 prep 20 mins • cook 1 hr

▣ large flameproof casserole

❄ freeze for up to 3 months

750g (1lb 10oz) minced veal

250g (9oz) minced pork

2 garlic cloves, finely chopped

115g (4oz) parsley, finely chopped

salt and freshly ground black pepper

½ tsp ground nutmeg

5 tbsp dry breadcrumbs

100ml (3½fl oz) milk

2 tbsp light olive oil

3 onions, finely chopped

1 tbsp flour, plus extra for dusting

400ml (14fl oz) red wine or white wine

2 large eggs, beaten

250ml (8fl oz) sunflower oil or

groundnut oil, for frying

2 tbsp chopped parsley, to garnish

● **Prepare ahead** The meatball mixture can be made up to 24 hours in advance, covered, and refrigerated until ready to fry. Cooked meatballs can be made up to 2 days in advance, covered, and refrigerated. Poach the meatballs in the sauce to reheat before serving.

1 **Place the veal**, pork, garlic, and parsley into a bowl, and mix together well. Season with pepper and nutmeg and set aside.

2 **Put the breadcrumbs** in another bowl, pour in the milk, and set aside to soak.

3 **Heat the olive oil** in the casserole over a medium heat, and cook the onions, stirring, for 4–5 minutes, or until softened. Sprinkle in the flour and continue to cook for a further 1 minute. Pour

in the wine, and season to taste with salt and pepper. Bring to a simmer, then reduce the heat and cook for 15 minutes, or until the sauce is reduced. Press the sauce through a sieve and return to the casserole, over a low heat.

4 **Squeeze the excess** milk from the breadcrumbs and add the crumbs to the meat with the eggs and 3 tbsp of the reduced sauce. Mix thoroughly, then roll the mixture into golfball-sized balls, and dust each with a little flour.

5 **Heat the sunflower oil** in a large frying pan. Working in batches, fry the meatballs, turning frequently, for 5 minutes, or until evenly browned. Remove them from the pan, drain on kitchen paper, and transfer to the casserole.

6 **Poach the meatballs** gently in the sauce for 20 minutes, or until the meatballs are no longer pink when cut in half. Serve warm, with the sauce poured over, and garnished with parsley.

● **Good with** crusty bread or with olive herbed mashed potatoes and green beans.

● **Leftovers** can be coarsely chopped, mixed with their sauce, then warmed and used to fill a toasted pitta.

BAKING MEATBALLS

The meatballs can be baked in a roasting tin for 30 minutes in an oven preheated to 180°C (350°F/Gas 4).

Steak au Poivre

This restaurant classic can easily be made at home

🍴 serves 4

🕐 prep 10 mins • cook 12 mins

4 sirloin steaks or fillet steaks, about 225g (8oz) each

½ tsp mustard powder

1–2 tsp black peppercorns or green peppercorns, crushed

2 tbsp sunflower oil

4 tbsp sherry or brandy

150ml (5fl oz) crème fraîche

1 **Trim any excess fat** from the steaks. If using fillet steak, flatten slightly with a meat mallet or rolling pin. Sprinkle with the mustard, then press the peppercorns firmly on both sides of the steaks.

2 **Heat a frying pan** over a high heat, add the oil, and fry the steaks for 2–3 minutes on each side for a rare steak, 4 minutes for medium, and 5–6 minutes for well done. Remove from the pan to rest.

3 **Stir the sherry** into the pan juices, add the crème fraîche, and simmer gently, stirring, for 2–3 minutes, or until just reduced. Serve the steaks with the sauce.

● **Good with** French fries and grilled tomatoes.

Veal Scaloppine

This popular Italian dish uses a classic method to prepare veal

serves 4

prep 10 mins • cook 8 mins

60g (2oz) **plain flour**

salt and freshly ground **black pepper**

4 **veal escalopes**, about 150g (5½oz) each

60g (2oz) **butter**

2 tbsp **olive oil**

60ml (2fl oz) **dry white wine**

250ml (8fl oz) **veal stock** or chicken stock

2 tbsp chopped **flat-leaf parsley**

1 **lime**, cut into wedges, to serve

● **Prepare ahead** The escalopes can be pounded in advance, covered, and refrigerated until needed.

1 **Preheat the oven** to its lowest setting. Season the flour to taste with salt and pepper. Put the veal escalopes between 2 sheets of greaseproof paper and pound them with a rolling pin until they are very thin. Coat both sides of the escalopes with the seasoned flour, then shake off the excess, and set aside.

2 **Melt two-thirds** of the butter with the oil in a large frying pan over a medium heat. Add 2 escalopes and fry for 1–2 minutes on each side, or until golden, pressing down firmly with a spatula to keep the meat as flat as possible. Transfer the escalopes to a plate and keep warm in the oven. Fry the second batch, then remove from the pan and keep warm.

3 **Add the wine** to the pan, increase the heat and bubble for 1 minute. Add the stock and the juices from the plate with the escalopes, and continue bubbling until all the liquid is reduced by half. Stir in the parsley, the remaining butter, and season to taste with salt and pepper.

4 **Place the escalopes** on serving plates and spoon over the pan juices. Serve at once with lime wedges for squeezing over.

● **Good with** sautéed spinach and rice or potatoes.

Swedish Meatballs

Although these are regarded as a Swedish national dish, they are popular in all Scandinavian countries

serves 4

prep 30 mins, plus chilling • cook 20 mins

freeze the meatballs without the sauce, cooked or uncooked, for up to 3 months

60g (2oz) fresh **breadcrumbs**

120ml (4fl oz) **double cream**

60g (2oz) **butter**

1 small **onion**, finely chopped

200g (7oz) lean **minced beef**

200g (7oz) lean **minced lamb**

¼ tsp freshly grated **nutmeg**

1 **egg**, beaten

salt and freshly ground **black pepper**

For the sauce

120ml (4fl oz) **beef stock** or lamb stock

200ml (7fl oz) **double cream**

1 **Put the breadcrumbs** in a bowl, stir in the cream, and leave to soak. Meanwhile, heat 15g (½oz) of butter in a small pan, add the onion, and fry over a low heat until transparent but not brown. Set aside to cool.

2 **Add the beef**, lamb, and nutmeg to the breadcrumbs. Stir in the onion and beaten egg until the mixture is evenly combined. Cover the bowl with cling film and refrigerate for 1 hour.

3 **With damp hands**, shape the meat mixture firmly into golfball-sized balls. Place the meatballs on a large plate, cover with cling film, and chill for 15 minutes.

4 **Melt the remaining** butter in a large frying pan over a medium heat and fry the meatballs in batches, turning gently, for 10 minutes, or until browned and cooked through. Remove with a slotted spoon, and drain on a plate lined with kitchen paper.

5 **To make the sauce**, drain any excess fat from the frying pan, pour in the stock and cream, and stir over a low heat until the sauce bubbles. Simmer for 2 minutes. Serve drizzled over the meatballs.

● **Good with** new potatoes and steamed broccoli.

VARIATION

Chicken and Veal Meatballs
Replace the minced beef with chicken and the minced lamb with turkey for a lighter version of these meatballs.

Meat Loaf

This recipe is great served hot for a weekday family meal,
or cold in a packed lunch or sandwich

 serves 4

 prep 20 mins • cook 30 mins

450g (1lb) loaf tin

sunflower oil, for greasing

225g (8oz) lean minced beef

225g (8oz) minced pork

1 onion, finely chopped

4 tbsp fresh white breadcrumbs

salt and freshly ground black pepper

1 tsp paprika

2 tsp German mustard

2 tbsp chopped parsley

1 egg, beaten

3 hard-boiled eggs, peeled

For the sauce

1 tbsp capers, chopped

3 gherkins, chopped

1 tbsp finely chopped parsley

100g (3½oz) soured cream

● **Prepare ahead** The meatloaf can be prepared up to the end of step 4, covered, and kept in the refrigerator until ready to bake for up to 3 days. The sauce can also be made up to 3 days in advance.

1 **Preheat the oven** to 200°C (400°F/Gas 6). Lightly oil the loaf tin.

2 **Mix together the beef** and pork, onion, breadcrumbs, salt and pepper, paprika, mustard, and parsley. Stir in the beaten egg, then combine all the ingredients together.

3 **Place half the mixture** in the loaf tin, pressing to fill the base evenly. Arrange the hard-boiled eggs down the centre, then top with the remaining meat mixture, smoothing the top so that it is level.

4 **Cover the tin** with foil and bake in the oven for about 30 minutes, until firm. Leave the loaf to stand for 10 minutes before turning out on to a warmed plate.

5 **Meanwhile**, mix together the capers, gherkins, parsley, and soured cream.

6 **Serve the meat loaf** cut into slices, with the sauce spooned over and extra on the side.

● **Good with** a salad of rocket and halved cherry tomatoes.

Hamburgers

Burgers are classic
American fare

 serves 4

 prep 15 mins • cook 10 mins

❄ freeze the uncooked hamburgers for up to 3 months

450g (1lb) lean minced steak

½ onion, very finely chopped

1 egg yolk

salt and freshly ground black pepper

olive oil or sunflower oil

4 sesame seed baps, cut in half and lightly toasted

● **Prepare ahead** The hamburgers can be made a day in advance. Wrap tightly in cling film and chill in the refrigerator overnight.

1 **Place the minced beef** and chopped onions in a mixing bowl, add the egg yolk, season to taste with salt and pepper, and mix well.

2 **Divide the mixture** into 4 equal portions and, using wet hands, shape them into 4 burgers.

3 **Preheat a griddle pan** or grill on its highest setting. Lightly oil the griddle pan and grill the burgers for 3 minutes on each side, or longer if you prefer.

4 **Serve in toasted** sesame buns with your favourite toppings, such as sliced onions, sliced tomatoes, lettuce, pickles, tomato ketchup, mayonnaise, and mustard.

Chinese Chilli Beef Stir-fry

This hot stir-fry is a good choice for lovers of Chinese food who like their dishes spicy rather than sweet and sour

 serves 4

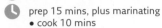 prep 15 mins, plus marinating • cook 10 mins

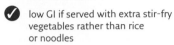 low GI if served with extra stir-fry vegetables rather than rice or noodles

wok

500g (1lb 2oz) **rump steak**, cut into thin strips

3 tbsp **dark soy sauce**

2 tbsp **rice vinegar**

1 tbsp **Chinese five-spice powder**

freshly ground **black pepper**

4 tbsp **vegetable oil**

1 large **red chilli**, deseeded and finely chopped

1 **garlic clove**, peeled and crushed

1 tsp grated, fresh **root ginger**

½ **red pepper**, deseeded and thinly sliced

100g (3½oz) **mangetout**, halved lengthways

100g (3½oz) **tenderstem broccoli**

1 tsp **cornflour**

120ml (4fl oz) **beef stock**

few drops of **toasted sesame oil**

1 **Put the strips** of steak in a bowl with the soy sauce, rice vinegar, and five-spice powder, stirring until coated. Season with black pepper, cover the bowl with cling film, and leave to marinate for several hours, or overnight in the refrigerator.

2 **Heat half the oil** in a wok, add the chilli, garlic, ginger, and red pepper, and stir-fry for 3 minutes. Add the mangetout and broccoli, and stir-fry for 2 minutes. Remove the vegetables and set aside.

3 **Add the rest** of the oil, drain the beef from the marinade (reserving the marinade), and stir-fry over a high heat for 1 minute. Return the vegetables and add the marinade. Stir the cornflour into the stock and gradually pour into the wok. Bring to the boil, stirring, for 1–2 minutes, or until piping hot.

4 **Drizzle over** the sesame oil, and serve at once with boiled rice or egg noodles.

VARIATION

Chicken Chilli Stir-fry
Use the same quantity of chicken and chicken stock instead of the beef and beef stock.

Beef Strogonoff

This classic Russian dish was named after the Strogonov family

serves 4

prep 15 mins • cook 25 mins

700g (1½lb) **fillet steak**, or rump, or sirloin, trimmed

3 tbsp **plain flour**

salt and freshly ground **black pepper**

1 tbsp **paprika**, plus extra for sprinkling

50g (2oz) **butter** or 4 tbsp olive oil

1 **onion**, thinly sliced

225g (8oz) **chestnut mushrooms**, sliced

300ml (10fl oz) **soured cream** or crème fraîche

1 tbsp **French mustard**

lemon juice

1 **Thinly slice the steak** into 5cm (2in) strips. Season the flour with salt, pepper, and paprika then coat the beef strips in the flour. Heat a deep frying pan, put in half the butter or oil, add the onion, and fry over a low heat for 8–10 minutes, or until soft and golden. Add the mushrooms and fry for a few minutes, or until just soft.

2 **Remove the onions** and mushrooms and keep warm. Increase the heat and, when the pan is hot, add the remaining butter, put in the beef strips, and fry briskly, stirring, for 3–4 minutes.

3 **Return the onions** and mushrooms to the pan and season to taste with salt and pepper. Shake the pan over the heat for 1 minute.

4 **Lower the heat**, stir in the cream and mustard, and cook gently for 1 minute; do not allow the cream to come to the boil.

5 **Add lemon juice** to taste and serve immediately.

● **Good with** rice or tagliatelle.

VARIATION

Veal Strogonoff
Omit the onions and use 16 small shallots instead. Use 700g (1½lb) veal fillet instead of the beef. At the end of step 3, pour in 3 tbsp cognac and immediately set alight to it, shaking the pan until the alcohol has burnt itself out.

Balsamic Beef Salad

Colourful and filling, this makes a substantial summer salad

- serves 6
- prep 20 mins
  - cook 1 hr 5 mins

olive oil

600g (1 lb 5oz) **fillet of beef**

2 small **red onions**, cut into wedges

175g (6oz) **cherry tomatoes**

3 tbsp **balsamic vinegar**

2 small **red peppers**

2 good handfuls of **mixed baby salad leaves**

For the dressing

100ml (3½fl oz) **extra virgin olive oil**

3 **garlic cloves**, crushed

1½ tsp **brown sugar**

1 tsp **wholegrain mustard**

2 tsp chopped **oregano** or marjoram

1 small bunch **basil**

salt and freshly ground **black pepper**

1 **Preheat the oven** to 220°C (425°F/Gas 7). Heat a little oil in a frying pan and brown the beef on all sides. Transfer to a roasting dish and roast for 20–30 minutes. Remove from the oven and allow to cool. Reduce the oven temperature to 190°C (375°F/Gas 5).

2 **Place the onions** on a roasting tray and drizzle with olive oil. Roast for 20 minutes, add the cherry tomatoes, and drizzle with a little more oil and 1 tbsp balsamic vinegar. Roast for 10 minutes.

3 **Meanwhile**, quarter and deseed the peppers and place, skin-side up, under a hot grill. Grill until the skin has blackened. Remove from the grill and place in a plastic bag to cool. When cool, remove and discard the charred skin. Slice the peppers into thick strips.

4 **To prepare the dressing**, place the first 6 ingredients in a blender with the remaining balsamic vinegar and blend until smooth, then season to taste with salt and pepper.

5 **Thinly slice the beef**. Place most of the salad leaves in the bottom of a large serving bowl. Add the vegetables and beef then the rest of the leaves. Drizzle some of the dressing over the salad and serve the remainder separately.

Thai Red Beef Curry

Bird's-eye chillies in the curry paste make this dish truly fiery

- serves 4
- prep 20 mins • cook 15 mins

450g (1 lb) **rump steak** or sirloin, thinly sliced along the grain

1 large **garlic clove**, crushed

2–3 tbsp **sunflower oil**

½ **onion**, thinly sliced

1 **red pepper**, deseeded and thinly sliced

200g (7oz) **button mushrooms**, sliced

1½ tbsp **Thai red curry paste**

150g (5½oz) **creamed coconut**, dissolved in 450ml (15fl oz) boiling water

1½ tbsp **Thai fish sauce**

1 tbsp **light soft brown sugar**

100g (3½oz) **spinach leaves**, rinsed and shaken dry

30g (1oz) sweet **basil leaves**, torn

steamed **rice**, to serve

1 **Toss the beef** and garlic in 1 tbsp of the oil. Heat a wok over a high heat, add the beef, and stir-fry for 1 minute, in batches if necessary, until the beef starts to change colour. Remove with a slotted spoon.

2 **Add a little more oil** to the wok, heat until shimmering, then stir-fry the onion and pepper for 2 minutes. Add the mushrooms and cook, stirring for 1–2 minutes, until all the vegetables are tender.

3 **Stir in the curry paste**, coconut, fish sauce, and sugar and bring to the boil, stirring. Reduce the heat, add the beef, spinach, and basil and cook for 3 minutes. Serve hot with steamed rice

THAI RED CURRY PASTE

To make your own curry paste, put 75g (2½oz) chopped shallots, 2 garlic cloves, 8 fresh bird's-eye chillies, a 15cm (6in) piece of lemongrass, a 1cm (½in) piece of galangal, 1 kaffir lime leaf, ½ tsp ground coriander, ¼ tsp fish sauce, ¼ tsp ground cumin, and ½ tsp salt in a blender and process to form a paste. Store in the fridge, in an airtight container, for up to 1 month, or until required. For a less fiery paste, deseed the chillies.

Beef Wellington

Always impressive for a dinner-party main course

 serves 6

prep 45 mins • cook 30–45 mins

1kg (2¼lb) **fillet of beef**, cut from the thick end of the fillet, trimmed of fat

salt and freshly ground **black pepper**

2 tbsp **sunflower oil**

45g (1½oz) **butter**

2 **shallots**, finely chopped

1 **garlic clove**, crushed

250g (9oz) **mixed wild mushrooms**

1 tbsp **brandy** or Madeira

500g packet **ready-made puff pastry**

beaten **egg**, to glaze

1 **Preheat the oven** to 220°C (425°F/Gas 7). Season the meat with salt and pepper. Heat the oil in a large frying pan and fry the beef until browned all over. Place the beef in a roasting tin, roast for 10 minutes, then remove and leave to cool.

2 **Melt the butter** in a pan and fry the shallots and garlic for 2–3 minutes, stirring frequently, until softened. Finely chop the mushrooms, add them to the pan, and cook, stirring, for 4–5 minutes, or until the juices evaporate. Add the brandy, allow to bubble for 30 seconds, then remove from the heat and leave to cool.

3 **Roll out** a third of the pastry to a rectangle about 5cm (2in) larger than the beef. Place on a baking sheet, prick all over with a fork, then bake for 12–15 minutes, or until crisp and golden. Remove and place on a wire rack to cool.

4 **Place the cooked pastry** on a baking sheet, and spread one-third of the mushroom mixture on the centre. Place the beef on top and spread the remaining mushroom mixture over the meat. Roll out the remaining pastry and place it over the beef, tucking in the edges and using beaten egg to seal it to the base.

5 **Brush with egg** to glaze. Make a slit in the top for steam to escape. Bake for 30 minutes for rare, 40 minutes for medium, or 45 minutes for well done. If the pastry starts to become too brown, cover loosely with foil. Remove from the oven and allow to stand for 10 minutes before serving.

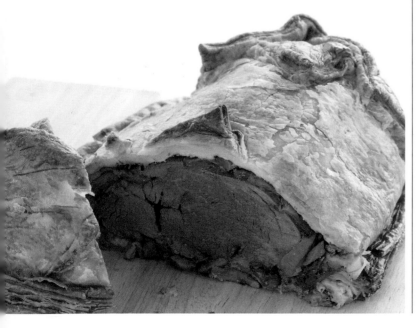

Blanquette de Veau

A simple, delicately flavoured stew

serves 4

prep 15 mins • cook 1½ hrs

large flameproof casserole

675g (1½lb) **veal shoulder** or leg, boned, trimmed, and diced

2 **onions**, roughly chopped

2 **carrots**, peeled and chopped

squeeze of **lemon** juice

1 **bouquet garni** (6 parsley stalks, 1 bay leaf, 1 celery stalk, 5 black peppercorns, and 3 fresh thyme sprigs, tied in muslin)

salt and freshly ground **black pepper**

85g (3oz) **butter**

18 **white pearl onions**

225g (8oz) **brown cap mushrooms**, quartered

2 tbsp **plain white flour**

1 **egg yolk**

2–3 tbsp **single cream**

fresh **parsley**, chopped, to garnish

1 **Put the veal**, onions, carrots, lemon juice, and bouquet garni in the casserole with enough water to cover. Season with salt and pepper. Simmer over a low heat for 1 hour, or until the meat is tender.

2 **Meanwhile**, melt 25g (scant 1oz) of the butter in a frying pan over a medium heat. Add the onions and fry, stirring occasionally, until golden. Add another 25g (scant 1oz) of butter and the mushrooms. Fry for 5 minutes, or until soft, stirring occasionally.

3 **Strain off** the cooking liquid from the veal, reserving 600ml (1 pint). Add the meat and vegetables to the mushrooms and onions, then set aside, and keep warm.

4 **Melt the remaining butter** in a large pan. Add the flour and stir constantly for 1 minute. Remove the pan from the heat and gradually stir in the reserved liquid. Return the pan to the heat and bring the sauce to the boil, stirring, until it thickens.

5 **Adjust the seasoning** to taste, remove the pan from the heat, and let it cool slightly. Beat the egg yolk and cream in a small bowl, then slowly stir it into the sauce. Add the meat and vegetables and reheat, without boiling, for 5 minutes. Season, garnish with parsley, and serve.

Hungarian Goulash

This warming winter stew makes a great main course if you are entertaining, as all the hard work can be done in advance

 serves 4

 prep 25 mins • cook 2½ hrs

 low GI

 freeze, without the soured cream, for up to 3 months

4 tbsp **oil**

900g (2lb) **braising steak**, cut into 2.5cm (1in) cubes

2 large **onions**, thinly sliced

2 **garlic cloves**, crushed

2 **red peppers**, deseeded and chopped

1 tbsp **paprika**, plus extra to garnish

400g can **chopped tomatoes**

2 tbsp **tomato purée**

1 tbsp **plain flour**

300ml (10fl oz) **beef stock**

1 tsp chopped, fresh **thyme**

salt and freshly ground **black pepper**

150ml (5fl oz) **soured cream**

1 **Preheat the oven** to 160°C (325°F/Gas 3).

2 **Heat half** the oil in a large frying pan and brown the meat in batches, transferring to a large casserole as they finish browning.

3 **Add the remaining** oil to the pan, lower the heat and fry the onions, garlic, and peppers until soft. Stir in the paprika and cook for 1 minute, then add the tomatoes and purée. Mix the flour with a little stock until smooth, then pour it into the pan with the rest of the stock. Bring to the boil, stirring often. Add the thyme, season to taste with salt and pepper, then pour the sauce into the casserole.

4 **Cover tightly** and place in the oven for 2 hours, or until the beef is very tender.

5 **To serve**, spoon the goulash into individual bowls and top each serving with a couple spoonfuls of soured cream and sprinkle with a little paprika.

● **Good with** buttered tagliatelle.

VARIATION

With Potato Dumplings
Mix 350g (12oz) of mashed potato in a bowl with 1 beaten egg, 30g (1oz) plain flour, 45g (1½oz) semolina and ½ tsp caraway seeds. The mixture should hold its shape; if not, add flour. Shape into 12 balls and chill for 20 minutes. In a pan of boiling water, simmer for 15 minutes, or until fluffy.

Burgundy Beef

In this classic French casserole, *Boeuf Bourguignon*, long, slow braising ensures the meat becomes tender

 serves 4

 prep 25 mins • cook 2½ hours

 low GI

freeze for up to 3 months

175g (6oz) **streaky bacon rashers**, chopped

1–2 tbsp **oil**

900g (2lb) **braising steak**, cut into 4cm (1½in) cubes

12 small **shallots**

1 tbsp **plain flour**

300ml (10fl oz) **red wine**

300ml (10fl oz) **beef stock**

115g (4oz) **button mushrooms**

1 **bay leaf**

1 tsp **dried herbes de Provence**

salt and freshly ground **black pepper**

4 tbsp fresh **parsley**, chopped

mashed potatoes, to serve

● **Prepare ahead** This dish can be prepared ahead and reheated in a 180°C (350°F/Gas 4) oven for 30 minutes when ready to serve.

1 **Preheat the oven** to 160°C (325°F/Gas 3). Fry the bacon in a non-stick frying pan until lightly browned. Drain on kitchen paper and transfer into a casserole.

2 **Depending on how** much fat is left from the bacon, add a little oil to the pan if necessary so that you have about 2–3 tbsp. Fry the beef in batches over a high heat, transferring to the casserole as they brown.

3 **Reduce the heat** to a medium heat and fry the shallots. Transfer to the casserole and stir the flour into the remaining fat in the frying pan. If the pan is quite dry, mix the flour with a little of the wine or stock. Pour the wine and stock into the frying pan and bring to the boil, stirring constantly until smooth.

4 **Add the mushrooms**, bay leaf and dried herbs. Season to taste with salt and pepper and pour the contents of the pan over the meat and shallots in the casserole. Cover and cook in the oven for 2 hours, or until the meat is very tender.

5 **Serve hot**, sprinkled with chopped parsley.

● **Good with** mashed potatoes, baby carrots and a green vegetable such as broccoli or French beans.

Daube of Beef with Wild Mushrooms

This rich stew benefits from being made a few days before serving so the flavours can develop

serves 6

prep 30 mins • cook 2 hrs

flameproof casserole with a tight-fitting lid

freeze for up to 3 months

2 tbsp **olive oil**

30g (1oz) **butter**

900g (2 lb) **chuck steak**, cut into 7.5cm (3in) pieces

2 tbsp **plain flour**

salt and freshly ground **black pepper**

115g (4oz) rindless **bacon rashers**, chopped

2 small **onions**, finely chopped

3 **garlic cloves**, crushed

1 **celery stalk**, finely chopped

3 **carrots**, diced

1 tbsp chopped fresh or dry **thyme**

900ml (1½pints) **red wine**

2 tbsp **brandy** (optional)

zest and juice of 1 **orange**

175g (6oz) **field mushrooms**

30g (1oz) **dried mushrooms**

1 tbsp **tomato purée**

1 Heat the olive oil and butter in the casserole. Coat the meat in seasoned flour, then brown on all sides in the casserole. Remove the pieces to a warm plate.

2 Fry the bacon, onions, garlic, and celery in the casserole, until lightly coloured. Stir in the beef along with the carrots and thyme. Pour in the red wine, the brandy, and the orange zest and juice; bring to the boil, stirring, then reduce the heat, cover and simmer for 1 hour.

3 Clean and slice the field mushrooms. Put the dried mushrooms in a bowl and pour over boiling water. Leave to soak for 15 minutes, then drain, dry and chop. Stir the mushrooms and the tomato purée into the casserole.

4 Cover and continue to simmer for another 30 minutes, or until the meat is very tender. Serve while still hot.

● **Good with** boiled potatoes, fried bread triangles and a sprinkling of chopped flat-leaf parsley.

● **Leftovers** can be finely chopped and used as a filling for ravioli.

Osso Bucco

This classic, rich veal stew from Milan is flavoured with garlic and salty anchovies

serves 4

prep 15 mins • cook 1¾hrs

Ask the butcher to cut the hind shanks into large chunks

large flameproof casserole

freeze after step 3, once cooled completely, for up to 1 month; thaw completely, then reheat and complete step 4

3 tbsp **plain flour**

salt and freshly ground **black pepper**

4 **veal hind shanks**, cut into 4 cm (1½in) pieces

60g (2oz) **butter**

4 tbsp **olive oil**

4 **garlic cloves**, chopped

½ **onion**, chopped

4 tbsp **tomato purée**

about 120ml (4fl oz) **beef stock** or water

4 tbsp chopped **flat-leaf parsley**

2 **anchovy fillets** in oil, drained and chopped

grated zest of 1 **lemon**

1 Season the flour with salt and pepper, then roll the veal in the flour and shake off any excess.

2 Melt the butter with the oil in a large flameproof casserole. Add the veal, fry for 5 minutes, or until browned on all sides, remove and set aside. Add the garlic and onion to the casserole and fry gently, stirring occasionally, for 5 minutes, or until softened but not browned.

3 Stir in the tomato purée, stock or water and salt and pepper to taste and bring to the boil. Reduce the heat to low, cover the casserole and simmer for 1½ hours, or until the veal is tender. Check as it cooks and add more liquid, if necessary. The gravy should be thick but not stiff.

4 To serve, combine the parsley, anchovies, and lemon zest in a bowl. Stir the mixture into the casserole and serve immediately.

● **Good with** a saffron-flavoured risotto or plain boiled rice.

● **Leftovers** can be made into a ragú to spoon over pasta. Simply shred the meat and add more stock if the sauce is too thick.

● **Prepare ahead** The stew can be made up to the end of step 3, left to cool and chilled for up to 2 days. Reheat gently, then complete step 4.

Steak

A well-cooked steak is delicious, quick, and easy to cook. Tender, juicy steaks are perfectly suited to the quick-cooking techniques of grilling, chargrilling, pan-frying, and barbecuing, so with a little practice a satisfying meal can be on the table in less time it takes to heat a ready meal.

Choosing Steak

Supermarkets and butchers sell many types of steak, varying in price and quality. Only buy steaks that look fresh, with a slightly moist appearance. Any fat around the edge should be white or creamy white.

In hot weather, transport steaks home in an insulated bag, and at all times of the year immediately refrigerate them. Steaks from the supermarket can be left in their tray, but those from the butcher should be taken out of plastic, put on a plate with a lip, and covered with greaseproof paper. Never buy packaged steaks with torn packaging.

Like all raw meat, steaks should be stored at the bottom of the refrigerator so the raw juices do not cross-contaminate other foods. Cook steaks within 3 days of purchasing, or according to the use-by date.

Chilled steaks should be removed from the refrigerator 15 minutes before cooking to return to room temperature, but no longer than that.

What Steak, What Dish?

There are many ways to cook steak, other than for simply serving on its own. Steaks are the main ingredients in recipes as diverse as simple sandwiches to impressive main courses, such as Beef Wellington (p325), but not all steak cuts are suitable for all dishes. Be sure to buy the correct cut for every dish to avoid over- or under-cooking and get the best results.

T-bone Steak Thick and meaty, this is best grilled, pan-fried, or barbecued.

Rump Steak Can be substituted for sirloin steak in most dishes.

Sirloin Steak A less expensive alternative to fillet steak for stir-fries and salads, it can be cut into chunks for steak pies and casseroles. Also very good for barbecuing.

Minute Steak Great in sandwiches, pan-fried with eggs for breakfast, and often used in the classic French dish steak frites.

Fillet Steak Good for quick-cooking dishes, such as Beef Stroganoff (p323) and stir-fries, as well as beef cooked in pastry and beef salads.

MARBLING

The best-quality steaks have thin lines of white fat running through them. This is called marbling.

Marbling adds flavour and helps keep the meat tender. If you are concerned about this small amout of fat, barbecuing, chargrilling, and grilling are the best cooking techniques to use, as the fat melts away during cooking.

Avoid buying meat with yellow marbling, as this can be an indication the meat is old and might be tough.

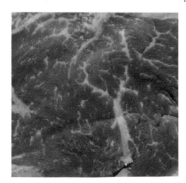

Look for thin lines of white inter-muscular fat when buying steaks. These are an indication of tenderness.

Types of Steak

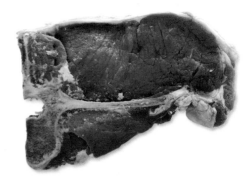

T-bone Steak
Thicker than most steaks, this has a bone left in, which adds extra flavour. Suitable for high-heat quick cooking techniques, and especially good for grilling. Porterhouse is a similar, but thicker, steak.

Rump Steak
Similar to a sirloin (see below), but slightly less tender, so less expensive. The texture can be variable, and the meat is often lean, so it will often require marinating or tenderising.

Sirloin Steak
A moderately expensive, boneless steak with a good flavour and tender texture. This steak is suitable for all cooking techniques.

Minute Steak
Quick pan-frying is the best cooking technique for this very thin, boneless steak. It must be cooked quickly to avoid it becoming tough, hence its name.

Fillet Steak
The most tender and expensive steak, good for celebratory meals. This thick, boneless steak can be chargrilled, grilled, or pan-fried. It also can be barbecued, but other less expensive steaks are more suitable.

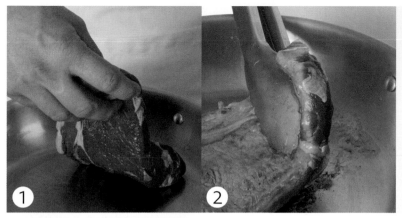

Pan-fry

1 **Heat a heavy** frying pan over a high heat until very hot, but not smoking. Brush the pan with a very thin layer of vegetable oil, put the steak in the pan, and fry for half the time specified below, or in a specific recipe.

2 **Using tongs**, turn the steak over and fry for the remaining time. Use the finger test (below) to determine when the steak is cooked as desired. Remove the steak from the pan, cover with foil, and leave to rest for 5 minutes before serving.

Barbecue

Light the barbecue well in advance so the coals are glowing and ash grey. When ready to cook, brush the steak with vegetable oil, and place it on the rack. Follow the timings below, or in a specific recipe, and use tongs to turn the steak over halfway through the cooking time.

Chargrill

Heat a ridged cast-iron grill pan until it is very hot, but not smoking. Brush the steak with oil before putting it in the pan. Follow the timings below, or in a specific recipe, and use tongs to turn the steak over halfway through the cooking time.

Cooking Steaks to Perfection

The timings below are for barbecuing, chargrilling, or grilling sirloin, rump, and T-bone steaks 4cm (1½in) thick. Timings will vary depending on the type of pan, the exact degree of heat, and the quality and thickness of the meat. Turn the meat after half the specified cooking time.

VERY RARE

Cook until just seared on both sides. The steak feels very soft when pressed, and the interior is reddish purple.
• Cook for 2–3 minutes

RARE

When drops of blood come to the surface, turn the steak over. It feels soft and spongy, and the interior is red.
• Cook for 6–8 minutes

MEDIUM

Turn the steak when drops of juice are first visible. The steak offers resistance when pressed and is pink in the centre.
• Cook for 10–12 minutes

WELL DONE

Turn the steak when drops of juice are clearly visible. The steak feels firm and is uniformly brown throughout.
• Cook for 12–14 minutes

TESTING FOR DONENESS

Take a tip from chefs and use this simple touch test to determine how a steak is cooked. Press the steak to determine how much resistance it has. A very rare steak will feel like the heel of your thumb on a relaxed hand. As you press the tip of your thumb to the tips of your fingers, the heel of your thumb becomes firmer. A rare steak feels like the heel of your thumb when you press your thumb and index together; for medium (below), press your thumb and middle finger together; for well done, press your thumb and little finger together.

Steak

Flavour Boosters for Steak

Good-quality steaks have plenty of flavour, but you can add extra flavour by marinating them before cooking or serving them with flavoured butters or a simple sauce.

Keep a selection of flavoured butters in the refrigerator or freezer for adding instant impact. Simply place a slice of flavoured butter on top of the just-cooked steak, and as it melts the butter and its flavourings mingle with the steak juices.

When a marinade contains an acid ingredient use a non-metallic bowl and don't marinate the steak for longer than 2 hours.

Anchovy Butter
Beat the ingredients together, then roll in greaseproof paper and chill.

60g (2oz) **butter**, softened

2 **anchovy fillets**, finely chopped

½ tbsp grated **lemon** zest

pinch of **cayenne pepper**

black pepper, to taste

Chilli-orange Marinade
Combine all the ingredients in a non-metallic bowl, stirring to dissolve the sugar. Marinate up to 8 hours.

juice of 2 large **oranges**

juice of 1 **lime**

3 **garlic cloves**, crushed

1 tsp **light brown sugar**

a few drops of **Tabasco sauce**

Red Wine Marinade
Combine all the ingredients in a non-metallic bowl. Use any leftover marinade to baste cooking steaks.

500ml (16fl oz) **dry red wine**

3 tbsp **red wine vinegar**

2 **garlic cloves**, crushed

1 strip **lemon** zest

chopped fresh **herbs**, to taste

Mustard Cream Sauce
Combine ingredients, mix, season to taste, and serve alongside steak.

150ml (5fl oz) **soured cream**

4 tbsp **mayonnaise**

1 ½ tbsp **mustard**

½ tsp **horseradish sauce**

¼ tsp **sugar**

salt

Red Wine Sauce
Boil the wine in the pan's cooking juices until reduced by half. Stir in the crème fraîche. Add parsley, season, and serve alongside steak.

200ml (7fl oz) **dry red wine**

150g (5oz) **crème fraîche**

2 tbsp chopped **parsley**

salt and **black pepper**

great with steak

MELTING FLAVOUR

As a slice of fresh herb butter (p236) melts it creates an instant sauce, adding extra flavour to the perfectly grilled steak.

Carrott and Parsnip Purée with Tarragon

This is a flavoursome winter accompaniment

🕐 25 mins   **page 234**

Grilled Vegetables

Serve this Mediterranean-style dish hot or at room temperature with barbecued steaks

🕐 20-30 mins   **page 235**

Potato-Herb Galette

Like a large potato pancake, this grated potato dish can be cut into wedges to serve with steak

🕐 45 mins   **page 241**

Mushrooms in Cream Sauce

Omit the toast and serve these tasty mushrooms alongside steaks

🕐 35 mins   **page 250**

Roast Sweet Potato with Sesame Glaze

These make a colourful change from chips

🕐 1 hr   **page 243**

Chimichurri Sauce

In Argentina, this piquant sauce is always served with barbecued and grilled steaks

🕐 5 mins   **page 282**

Béarnaise Sauce

This traditional French sauce is a classic accompaniment to grilled steaks

🕐 15 mins   **page 359**

Horseradish Sauce

Beef and horseradish is a culinary match that is difficult to better

🕐 10 mins   **page 360**

Steak and Ale Pie

Beer helps to tenderize the beef and imparts a delicious flavour

- serves 4
- prep 20 mins, plus cooling • cook 2 hrs 15 mins
- 1.7 litre (3 pint) pie dish

3 tbsp **plain flour**

salt and freshly ground **black pepper**

675g (1½lb) lean **braising steak**, cut into 2cm (¾in) pieces

3 tbsp **sunflower oil**

1 large **onion**, chopped

1 **garlic clove**, crushed

115g (4oz) **button mushrooms**, halved

175ml (6fl oz) **beef stock**

175ml (6fl oz) **brown ale**

1 **bay leaf**

½ tsp **dried thyme**

1 tbsp **Worcestershire sauce**

1 tbsp **tomato purée**

350g (12oz) ready-made **puff pastry**

beaten **egg** or milk, to glaze

● **Prepare ahead** Make the filling up to 24 hours ahead and keep, covered, in the refrigerator until ready to make the pie.

1 **Season the flour** to taste with salt and pepper. Toss the beef in the flour, shaking off any excess.

2 **Heat 2 tbsp** of the oil in a large non-stick frying pan and fry the steak in batches over a high heat until browned on all sides. Transfer the steak to a large saucepan.

3 **Add the remaining oil** to the frying pan and fry the onion over a medium heat for 5 minutes. Add the garlic and mushrooms and cook for 3–4 minutes, or until beginning to brown, stirring frequently.

4 **Transfer the onion** and mushrooms to the saucepan along with the stock, ale, bay leaf, thyme, Worcestershire sauce, and tomato purée. Bring to the boil, reduce the heat, cover, and simmer gently for 1 hour 30 minutes, or until the meat is tender.

5 **Using a slotted spoon**, transfer the meat and vegetables to the pie dish. Reserve 150ml (5fl oz) of the gravy and pour the rest over the meat mixture. Leave to cool.

6 **Preheat the oven** to 200°C (400°F/Gas 6). Roll out the pastry on a lightly floured surface to a thickness of 3mm (⅛in) and 5cm (2in) larger all round than the dish. Cut a 2cm (¾in) strip from around the pastry, brush the rim of the dish with water, and place the strip on the rim. Brush with water. Place the pastry over the dish and press the pastry edges together to seal; trim off the excess with a knife.

7 **Crimp the pastry edge**. Use the pastry trimmings to decorate, if liked. Brush the pastry with beaten egg and make a hole in the middle for steam to escape. Place on a baking tray and bake for 25 minutes, or until the pastry is puffed and dark golden. Serve immediately, with the reserved gravy served separately.

Chilli con Carne

A Tex-Mex classic

- serves 4–6
- prep 5 mins • cook 50 mins
- freeze for up to 3 months

1 tbsp **olive oil**

1 **onion**, thinly sliced

2 tbsp **chilli sauce**

1 **garlic clove**, crushed

1 tsp **ground cumin**

675g (1½lb) **minced beef**

400g can **red kidney beans**, drained and rinsed

400g can **chopped tomatoes**

salt and freshly ground **black pepper**

soured cream, to serve

1 **Heat the oil** in a large saucepan over a medium heat. Add the onions and fry for 5 minutes, or until softened. Stir in the chilli sauce, garlic, cumin, and beef, and fry for 3 minutes, or until the meat browns, stirring occasionally.

2 **Stir in the kidney beans** and tomatoes and bring to the boil. Reduce the heat, cover, and leave to simmer for 40 minutes, stirring occasionally. Season to taste with salt and pepper and serve with the soured cream.

● **Good with** rice or nachos, and bowls of guacamole and salsa.

Roast Beef

Sunday lunch doesn't come any better than this

 serves 4

prep 20 mins, plus standing • cook 1½–2 hrs

1.5kg (3lb 3oz) **rib of beef**

freshly ground **black pepper**

30g (1oz) **dripping** or white vegetable fat

For the gravy

2 tbsp **plain flour**

450ml (15fl oz) **beef stock**

1 Preheat the oven to 220°C (425°F/Gas 7). Place the beef in a roasting tin, season with plenty of freshly ground black pepper, and spread with the dripping. Roast for 15 minutes.

2 Reduce the heat to 190°C (375°F/Gas 5) and roast for the following cooking times: for rare beef allow 15 minutes per 450g (1lb) plus an extra 15 minutes; for medium rare allow 20 minutes per 450g (1lb) plus 20 minutes; and for well done allow 25 minutes per 450g (1lb) plus 25 minutes. Baste the meat from time to time.

3 Remove the beef from the oven, cover loosely with foil, and set aside in a warm place to rest for 15–20 minutes.

4 To make the gravy, transfer the beef to a carving plate and pour off most of the fat from the roasting tin, leaving 2 tbsp. Place the tin over a medium heat and stir in the flour, scraping the bottom of the tin to incorporate any juices sticking to it. Pour in the stock, stirring or whisking until blended, and bring to the boil, stirring constantly until thickened and smooth. Strain into a warm gravy boat and serve with the beef.

● **Good with** Yorkshire puddings, roast potatoes, and vegetables of your choice.

Beef Salad with Caramelized Walnuts

This works well for a crowd and can be served warm or cold

 serves 6

prep 20 mins • cook 45 mins

4 **beetroots**

olive oil, for drizzling

salt and freshly ground **black pepper**

1kg (2¼lb) **fillet of beef**, trimmed

100g (3½oz) **walnut halves**

1 tbsp **clear honey**

1 tbsp **caster sugar**

175g (6oz) **rocket**

balsamic vinegar, to drizzle

2 tbsp chopped **chives**

For the horseradish cream

½ tbsp fresh **horseradish**, grated

6 tbsp **crème fraîche** or soured cream

1 tbsp **lemon** juice

salt and freshly ground **black pepper**

1 Preheat the oven to 220°C (425°F/Gas 7). Place the beetroot in a roasting tin, drizzle with oil, and season to taste with salt and pepper. Wrap each beetroot in kitchen foil and bake for 40 minutes, or until the beetroot is easily pierced with a knife. Allow to cool, then trim, remove the skin, and cut into eighths.

2 Heat a large frying pan over a high heat. Rub the beef with oil and salt, and coat each side well with coarsely ground black pepper. Sear the beef on both sides, then transfer to a baking dish and roast for 15–20 minutes. If serving cold, allow to cool, wrap tightly in cling film, and chill.

3 Lower the oven to 200°C (400°F/Gas 6). Toss the walnuts in honey, salt, and sugar, and place on a baking tray, spaced evenly apart. Bake for 3 minutes, then remove from the oven and quickly place on to a cool tray.

4 When ready to serve, lightly toss the rocket in oil and vinegar, arrange in a serving bowl, and scatter over the beetroot, walnuts, and chives. Slice the beef thinly and add to the salad.

5 Combine the ingredients for the horseradish cream and serve alongside the salad.

Beef with Walnut Pesto

A great dish for autumn, when fresh walnuts are readily available

🍴 serves 6

🕐 prep 15 mins • cook 4–12 mins

6 beef fillet steaks, about 175g (6oz) each

olive oil, for brushing

For the walnut pesto

100g (3½oz) walnut pieces

50g (1¾oz) grated Parmesan cheese

2 garlic cloves

100ml (3½fl oz) olive oil

30g (1oz) tarragon

30g (1oz) parsley

½ tbsp red wine vinegar

salt and freshly ground black pepper

1 **To make the walnut pesto,** fry the walnuts in a dry frying pan for a few minutes, or until toasted, taking care not to burn them. Allow to cool. Place in a food processor with the other pesto ingredients and pulse until coarsely puréed. Season to taste with salt and pepper.

2 **Preheat a chargrill pan** or the grill. Brush the steaks with a little olive oil and season well with salt and black pepper. Cook them for 2–4 minutes on each side, depending on how you like them. Allow to rest for a few minutes, and serve with a dollop of the walnut pesto on each.

Sauerbraten

This recipe, with its unusual, richly spiced sauce, is based on a traditional German way of marinating and slow-cooking beef, so it's extremely tender

🍴 serves 4–6

🕐 prep 30 mins, plus marinating • cook 2–2¼ hrs

❄ freeze for up to 2 months

1kg (2¼lb) boneless joint of beef, such as topside or rump

2 tbsp sunflower oil

1 onion, sliced

1 celery stick, chopped

1 tbsp plain flour

45g (1½oz) ginger nut biscuits, crushed

salt and freshly ground black pepper

For the marinade

400ml (14fl oz) red wine

150ml (5fl oz) red wine vinegar

2 onions, thinly sliced

1 tbsp light muscovado sugar

½ tsp freshly grated nutmeg

4 whole allspice berries, lightly crushed

4 black peppercorns, lightly crushed

2 bay leaves, crumbled

½ tsp salt

● **Prepare ahead** Steps 1 and 2 should be completed 2–3 days before required.

1 **To make the marinade,** place the wine, vinegar, onions, sugar, nutmeg, allspice, peppercorns, bay leaves, salt, and 150ml (5fl oz) water into a pan. Stir over a high heat until boiling. Remove from the heat and leave to cool completely.

2 **Place the meat** in a bowl that holds the meat snugly and pour enough cooled marinade over the meat to come at least halfway up the sides. Cover and leave to marinate for 2–3 days in a refrigerator, turning the meat over twice each day.

3 **Preheat the oven** to 180°C (350°F/Gas 4). Lift the meat from the marinade, drain well, then pat dry with kitchen paper. Strain the marinade, discard the spices, and reserve the liquid.

4 **Heat the oil** in a large flameproof casserole and brown the meat on all sides. Remove the meat and set aside. Add the onion and celery to the pan and fry, stirring constantly, for 5–6 minutes, or until beginning to brown. Sprinkle the flour over the vegetables and stir over the heat for 1 minute, then stir in 400ml (14fl oz) of the reserved marinade. Stir until boiling.

5 **Place the beef** on top of the vegetables and baste with the liquid. Cover tightly and place in the oven for 2–2¼ hours, or until the meat is tender when tested with a fork.

6 **Lift the meat** onto a warmed serving platter and cover loosely with foil. Strain the cooking liquid, pour it into a saucepan and boil rapidly to reduce to about 300ml (10fl oz). Add the crushed ginger nuts, stirring on the heat until the sauce is smooth. Season to taste with salt and pepper. Slice the meat and serve with a little of the sauce spooned over. Serve the remaining sauce separately.

● **Good with** German Potato Dumplings (p217) and braised red cabbage, or whole roasted potatoes and carrots.

● **Leftovers** can be thinly sliced and piled into rustic bread with braised red cabbage and a little spicy mustard.

Skewered Beef with Lime, Ginger, and Honey

Skewered meats are perfect for barbecues or picnics

🍴 serves 4

🕐 prep 20 mins, plus marinating • cook 4–8 mins

❗ soak wooden skewers in cold water for 30 minutes to prevent burning

▣ wooden skewers

5cm (2in) fresh **root ginger**, peeled

juice of 1 **lime**

1 tbsp **light soy sauce**

1 tbsp **honey**

1 tbsp **olive oil**

3 **spring onions**, roughly chopped

500g (1lb 2oz) **beef fillet** or sirloin, cut into 2.5cm (1in) cubes

16 **cherry tomatoes**

salt and freshly ground **black pepper**

For the avocado cream

1 ripe **avocado**, peeled and stoned

2 **spring onions**, chopped

1 **green chilli**, deseeded and chopped

50g (1¾oz) **cream cheese**

1 **Place the ginger**, lime juice, soy sauce, honey, olive oil, and spring onions into a food processor and process until smooth. Place the beef pieces in a bowl, and pour the marinade over, then cover and leave to marinate for 1–2 hours.

2 **Place the ingredients** for the avocado cream in a blender or food processor, and process until smooth. Season to taste with salt and black pepper.

3 **Preheat a chargrill pan** or a grill until hot. Thread the meat onto the skewers, putting 2 cherry tomatoes on each skewer.

4 **Cook the beef skewers** for 2–4 minutes on each side, or until well-coloured but still pink inside. Season to taste with salt and pepper, and serve with the avocado cream.

● **Leftovers** can be cut into smaller pieces and served cold with salad leaves and the avocado cream, or a fresh vinaigrette.

Roast Fillet of Beef with Redcurrant Jus

A rich, dark sauce, or *jus*, adds plenty of flavour to this dish

🍴 serves 6

🕐 prep 30 mins, plus resting • cook 40 mins–1 hr 10 mins

115g (4oz) **rindless streaky bacon rashers**, finely chopped

600ml (1 pint) **port**

2 tbsp **redcurrant jelly**

150ml (5fl oz) **beef stock**

1 tsp **cornflour**, mixed with 1 tbsp cold water

1kg (2¼lb) **fillet of beef**, in 1 piece

salt and freshly ground **black pepper**

olive oil

● **Prepare ahead** The jus can be made up to 2 days in advance.

1 **Preheat the oven** to 200°C (400°F/Gas 6). Fry the bacon in a non-stick frying pan until crisp. Remove and drain the bacon on kitchen paper. Wipe the frying pan clean and add the port, redcurrant jelly, and stock. Simmer for 5 minutes, or until reduced by a quarter. While still simmering, whisk in the cornflour, and whisk until the sauce is thick and smooth. Return the cooked bacon to the pan; set aside.

2 **Season the beef** with salt and pepper. Heat a frying pan over high heat, add a little olive oil, then brown the beef on all sides. Transfer to a roasting tin and roast for 20 minutes for rare, 40 minutes for medium, or 50 minutes for well done.

3 **When cooked**, allow the meat to rest for 15 minutes before carving, then serve with the sauce spooned over.

● **Good with** potato gratin and a green vegetable, such as asparagus.

VARIATION

Duck Breasts with Redcurrant Jus

Replace the fillet with 6 duck breasts. Use 115g (4oz) pancetta instead of the bacon, and 600ml (1 pint) red wine instead of the port.

Pork and Bean Stew

Otherwise known as *Feijoada*, this is the national dish of Brazil and is made with a variety of meats

 serves 6–8

 prep 15 mins, plus soaking
• cook 1 hr 35 mins

 the beans need to be cooked the day before

500g (1lb 2oz) dried black-eyed beans

2 pig's trotters

250g (9oz) smoked pork ribs

175g (6oz) smoked streaky bacon, left in 1 piece

200g (7oz) can chopped tomatoes

1 tbsp tomato purée

1 bay leaf

salt and freshly ground black pepper

oil, for frying

500g (1lb 2oz) lean pork fillet or steaks

1 small onion, finely chopped

2 garlic cloves, finely chopped

175g (6oz) chorizo sausage, cut into small chunks

1 fresh green chilli, deseeded (optional)

1 orange, cut into wedges, to garnish

3 spring onions, chopped, to garnish

● **Prepare ahead** The stew can be made a day in advance and reheated.

1 **Rinse the beans**, place them in a bowl, and pour over enough cold water to cover. Leave overnight.

2 **Drain the beans** and place in a large saucepan. Cover with fresh water, bring to the boil and boil for 10 minutes, skimming off any scum, then lower the heat, cover and simmer for 1 hour.

3 **Meanwhile**, place the pig's trotters, pork ribs, and streaky bacon in a saucepan with the canned tomatoes and their juice, the tomato

purée, bay leaf, and salt and pepper to taste. Add enough cold water to cover, bring to the boil, skim off any scum, cover, reduce the heat and simmer for 50 minutes.

4 **Drain the cooked beans** and reserve the cooking liquid, then return the beans to the pan. Add the meats with their cooking liquid. Add just enough of the reserved cooking liquid from the beans to cover. Continue to cook, covered, over a low heat, for a further 20 minutes.

5 **Heat 1 tbsp of oil** in a frying pan and brown the pork fillet. Add to the meat and bean mixture and continue to cook for a further 10 minutes, or until the meats are tender and the beans very soft. Wipe out the frying pan, add 1 tbsp of oil and fry the onion and garlic over medium heat for 3–4 minutes, stirring frequently, until soft and translucent. Add the chorizo and chilli, if using, and fry for a further 2 minutes, stirring. Add 2–3 tbsp of the cooked beans to the frying pan and

mash well with the back of a spoon. Add the contents of the frying pan to the meat and beans, stir and cook for a further 10 minutes.

6 **To serve**, remove the larger pieces of meat and cut into smaller pieces. Transfer them and the rest of the meat and bean mixture on to a serving dish and garnish with orange wedges and spring onions. Serve immediately.

● **Good with** plain boiled rice, steamed or fried shredded kale, and a tomato salsa.

VARIATION

Quick Pork and Bean Stew

Instead of using dried beans, use 2 or 3 cans of beans, drained and added to the meat after step 3. This cuts down on preparation time and the need for a second saucepan. Instead of black-eyed beans, black beans, aduki beans, red kidney beans or pinto beans can be used.

Frikadeller

This is a Danish classic, made with chicken instead of veal

 serves 4

 prep 15 mins
• cook 10 mins

 freeze the meatballs, raw or cooked, for up to 3 months

250g (9oz) minced pork

250g (9oz) minced chicken or turkey

1 onion, grated

60g (2oz) fresh white breadcrumbs

5–6 tbsp milk

½ tsp dried thyme

salt and freshly ground black pepper

1 egg, beaten

flour, for dusting

sunflower oil, for shallow frying

1 lemon, cut into wedges, to serve

1 **Add the pork**, chicken, onion, breadcrumbs, milk, and thyme in to a large bowl. Mix together and season with salt and pepper.

2 **Stir in the egg** and a little extra milk, if necessary, to make the mixture soft but not sticky. With lightly floured hands, shape the mixture into 16 small balls.

3 **Heat the oil** in a frying pan and fry the meatballs over a medium heat for 8–10 minutes, turning often, until golden brown.

4 **Drain on kitchen paper**, then serve while still hot, garnished with lemon wedges.

Pork Chops with Green Peppercorn Sauce

These soft, mild peppercorns add a gentle spice to the creamy sauce

 serves 4

prep 10 mins • cook 15 mins

4 lean pork loin chops

salt and freshly ground black pepper

1 tbsp sunflower oil

30g (1oz) butter

1 large shallot, finely chopped

4 tbsp dry sherry

1½ tbsp green peppercorns in brine, rinsed, drained and lightly crushed

150ml (5fl oz) chicken stock

4 tbsp crème fraîche

● **Prepare ahead** The sauce can be made up to 2 days in advance. Reheat gently before serving.

1 **Trim the chops** of excess fat and season with salt and pepper. Heat the oil in a large, heavy frying pan on medium heat and fry the chops for 6–8 minutes on each side, depending on thickness, until golden brown and the juices run clear. Remove from the pan to a warm plate and cover with foil.

2 **To make the sauce**, melt the butter in the pan and fry the shallot over medium heat for 4–5 minutes, stirring often, until soft but not browned. Stir in the sherry and simmer for about 1 minute. Add the peppercorns and stock, bring to the boil and simmer for 2–3 minutes, or until slightly reduced.

3 **Stir in** the crème fraîche, spoon the sauce over the chops and serve immediately.

● **Good with** potato rösti cakes, and steamed green vegetables.

Pork Chops with Blue Cheese Stuffing

This filling is both savoury and sweet and the pecans add a delightful crunchy texture

 serves 4

prep 10 mins • cook 12–16 mins

cocktail sticks

4 lean pork loin chops

1 tbsp olive oil

salt and freshly ground black pepper

For the stuffing

1 dessert apple such as Cox's, peeled and finely diced

100g (3½oz) Roquefort or Stilton, crumbled

45g (1½oz) pecans, chopped

2 spring onions, chopped

1 **Combine the** stuffing ingredients and set aside.

2 **Trim the skin** and excess fat from the pork chops. With a small sharp knife, make a horizontal slit through the fat side of each chop, cutting through the meat almost to the bone to make a pocket.

3 **Evenly divide** the stuffing between the chops, tucking firmly into the pockets. Secure with wooden cocktail sticks.

4 **Preheat the grill** on medium-high. Place the pork chops on a baking sheet, brush with oil, and season with salt and pepper. Grill for 6–8 minutes on each side, depending on thickness, or until golden brown and the juices run clear. Remove the cocktail sticks and serve.

● **Good with** trimmed green beans and new potatoes.

Cassoulet

A hearty bean and meat dish from southwest France

 serves 4-6

 prep 30 mins, plus soaking
• cook 3 hrs 45 mins

 3.5 litre (6 pint) flameproof casserole

350g (12oz) dried haricot beans

1 tbsp olive oil

8 Toulouse sausages

250g (9oz) piece of pancetta or a whole chorizo sausage, cut into small pieces

2 onions, peeled and finely chopped

1 carrot, peeled and chopped

4 garlic cloves, crushed

4 duck legs

1 sprig of thyme, plus ½ tbsp chopped leaves

1 bay leaf

salt and freshly ground black pepper

2 tbsp tomato purée

400g can chopped tomatoes

200ml (7fl oz) white wine

½ day-old baguette

1 tbsp chopped parsley

1 **Place the beans** in a pan, cover with plenty of cold water, bring to the boil, and boil for 10 minutes. Remove from the heat and soak for 2–3 hours, then drain.

2 **Heat the olive oil** in a frying pan and brown the sausages for 7–8 minutes, turning occasionally. Remove from the pan and set aside. Add the pancetta to the pan, and cook for 5 minutes. Remove and set aside with the sausages. Add the onions and carrot, and cook gently for 10 minutes, or until soft. Then add three-quarters of the garlic and cook for 1 minute.

3 **Preheat the oven** to 220°C (425°F/Gas 7). Prick the duck legs all over with a fork and roast for 30 minutes. Remove from the oven. Reserve the duck fat, and reduce the oven to 140°C (275°F/Gas 1).

4 **In a heavy casserole**, layer the ingredients, beginning with half the beans, then onions, carrot, sausages, pancetta, and duck legs, followed by the remaining beans. Push the thyme sprig and bay leaf in among everything and season well with salt and pepper.

5 **Mix together** 900ml (1½ pints) hot water with the tomato purée, tomatoes, and wine, then pour into

the casserole. Cover, and cook in the oven for 3 hours, adding a little extra water if required.

6 **Cut the crusts** off the baguette, then tear the bread into pieces and place in a food processor with the remaining garlic. Process into coarse crumbs. Heat 2 tbsp of the duck fat in a frying pan and fry the crumbs over a medium heat for 7–8 minutes, or until crisp and golden. Drain on kitchen paper and stir in the herbs. Remove the cassoulet from the oven and stir. Sprinkle the breadcrumb topping over in a thick, even layer, and serve.

Pork and Leek Pie

A chunky pie with a crisp crust

 serves 4

prep 25 mins, plus cooling
• cook 1 hr 10 mins

2 tbsp vegetable oil

450g (1lb) lean boneless pork steaks, cut into 2.5cm (1in) cubes

2 leeks, thickly sliced

150g (5½oz) mushrooms, halved

1 tsp thyme leaves

150ml (5fl oz) chicken stock

1 tbsp cornflour, mixed with 1 tbsp water

250ml (8fl oz) apple juice

2 tbsp tomato purée

salt and freshly ground black pepper

250g (9oz) ready-made shortcrust pastry

1 egg, beaten, to glaze

1 **Heat the oil** in a frying pan. Brown the pork, remove, and set aside. Add the vegetables and thyme, and fry for 5 minutes. Add the stock, cornflour, juice, and purée, and bring to the boil, stirring until thickened. Return the pork, season with salt and pepper, and simmer for 25 minutes.

2 **Transfer the pork** and vegetables to a pie dish, reserving the sauce. Roll out the pastry and use to cover the dish, decorating the top with the trimmings. Make a steam hole in the pastry, glaze with the egg, and chill for 30 minutes. Preheat the oven to 200°C (400°F/Gas 6). Bake for 35 minutes, or until the pastry is golden, and serve with the sauce.

Barbecue Spare Ribs

Sticky ribs, popular with adults and children alike

 serves 4

prep 5 mins, plus marinating • cook 1 hr 30 mins

2kg (4½ lb) pork spare ribs

lemon wedges, to serve

sprigs of rosemary, to garnish

For the marinade

6 tbsp mango chutney, sieved

6 tbsp tomato ketchup

6 tbsp white wine vinegar

4 tbsp dark soy sauce

4 tsp garlic purée

2 tbsp chilli sauce

2 tsp smoked paprika

2 x 230g cans chopped tomatoes

100g (3½oz) light soft brown sugar

salt and freshly ground black pepper

1 Combine the marinade ingredients in a non-metallic bowl. Add the ribs and coat well with marinade. Cover, chill, and marinate for at least 30 minutes.

2 Preheat the oven to 190°C (375°F/Gas 5). Place the ribs in a single layer in a roasting tin. Pour over the sauce. Bake, covered with foil, for 1 hour.

3 Baste, then bake, uncovered, for 30 minutes, or until tender. Baste again, then serve with lemon wedges and rosemary sprigs.

Spanish Stew

A filling one-pot meal known as *Cocido* in Spain

 serves 6–8

prep 25 mins • cook 2 hrs 45 mins

4 tbsp olive oil

4 small onions, quartered

2 garlic cloves, sliced

4 thick slices belly pork, about 500g (1lb 2oz) in total

4 chicken thighs, about 300g (10oz) in total

250g (9oz) beef braising steak, cut into 4 slices

175g (6oz) tocino or smoked streaky bacon, cut into 4 pieces

4 small pork spare ribs, 150g (5½oz) in total

100ml (3½fl oz) white wine

175g (6oz) chorizo, cut into 4 pieces

175g (6oz) morcilla (Spanish black pudding)

small ham bone

1 bay leaf

salt and freshly ground black pepper

8 small waxy potatoes

4 carrots, halved lengthways

400g can chickpeas, drained

1 Savoy cabbage or green cabbage heart, quartered

3 tbsp chopped parsley, to garnish

1 Heat 1 tbsp oil in a large saucepan with the onions and garlic and fry for 10 minutes, stirring occasionally. Heat the remaining oil in a frying pan and fry the pork, chicken, beef, tocino, and spare ribs in batches until lightly browned on all sides, then transfer to the pan with the onions.

2 Add the wine into the frying pan, reduce by half, then pour into the saucepan. Add the chorizo, morcilla, ham bone, and bay leaf, season to taste with salt and pepper, then pour in enough cold water to cover. Bring to boil, then simmer, covered, for 1 hour 30 minutes. Add the potatoes and carrots to the pan, continue to cook for 30 minutes, then add the chickpeas and cabbage, and cook for 15 minutes.

3 To serve, remove the bay leaf and ham bone and divide the meat and vegetables between serving plates. Add a few spoonfuls of the hot broth and sprinkle with parsley.

Honey-glazed Gammon

Boiling the ham first makes this joint really moist

 serves 8–10

prep 15 mins • cook 2 hrs

1.5kg (3lb 3oz) boneless gammon joint

1 onion, quartered

2 bay leaves

6 peppercorns

handful of cloves

grated zest and juice of 1 orange

3 tbsp set honey

1 Place the joint in a large saucepan with water to cover. Add the onion, bay leaves, and peppercorns. Bring slowly to the boil, then simmer for 1 hour 30 minutes. Remove from the pan. Allow to cool.

2 Preheat the oven to 200°C (400°F/Gas 6). Using a sharp knife, carefully remove the skin from the ham and discard. Combine the orange zest, honey, and 2 tbsp of the orange juice, then brush the surface of the ham with the mixture. Cut a criss-cross pattern in the fat and push a clove into the centre of each diamond.

3 Place the ham in a roasting tin, bake for 10 minutes, then baste with the glaze. Return to the oven and bake for 20 minutes, or until golden. Allow to rest before carving, and serve.

Lamb Tagine with Couscous

Dried apricots and orange juice, along with cumin, coriander, ginger, and thyme, give this the distinct flavour and aroma of Moroccan cuisine

 serves 4

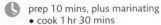 prep 10 mins, plus marinating
• cook 1 hr 30 mins

large flameproof casserole

freeze for up to 1 month; thaw over a low heat and bring to the boil before serving

1 onion, thinly sliced

1 tsp ground coriander

1 tsp ground cumin

1 tsp ground ginger

1 tsp dried thyme

2 tbsp sunflower oil or peanut oil

900g (2lb) boneless lamb, such as shoulder or chump steaks, cut into

2.5cm (1in) cubes

2 tbsp plain flour

300ml (10fl oz) orange juice

600ml (1 pint) chicken stock

120g (4oz) no-soak dried apricots

salt and freshly ground black pepper

mint leaves, to garnish

For the couscous

200g (7oz) quick-cook couscous

salt

● **Prepare ahead** The dish can be cooked up to 2 days in advance.

1 Put the onion, coriander, cumin, ginger, thyme, and 1 tbsp of the oil in a large, non-metallic bowl, then mix in the lamb. Cover and refrigerate for at least 3 hours or overnight to marinate.

2 When ready to cook, preheat the oven to 160°C (325°F/Gas 3). Put the flour in a small bowl and slowly stir in the orange juice until smooth, then set aside.

3 Heat the remaining oil in a large, flameproof casserole over a high heat. Add the lamb mixture and fry, stirring frequently, for 5 minutes, or until browned.

4 Stir the flour mixture into the casserole with the stock. Bring to the boil, stirring, then remove the casserole from the heat, cover and place in the oven for 1 hour.

5 Remove the casserole from the oven. Stir in the apricots, re-cover and return to the oven. Cook for a further 20 minutes, or until the lamb is tender.

6 Meanwhile, put the couscous with salt to taste in a large heatproof bowl and pour over 2.5cm (1in) of boiling water. Cover with a folded tea towel and leave to stand for 10 minutes, or until the grains are tender. Fluff with a fork and keep warm. When the lamb is tender, taste and adjust the seasoning. Sprinkle with mint leaves and serve with the hot couscous.

> TAGINE
> This north-African earthenware cooking pot, traditionally used as a portable oven, is perfect for cooking stews like this. The conical lid acts as a heat retainer and the top is a cool handle. Alternatively, use a casserole with a tight-fitting lid.

Lamb with Blueberries

Blueberries and fresh mint offset the richness of lamb

serves 4

prep 10 mins • cook 8–12 mins

8–12 noisettes of lamb

salt and freshly ground black pepper

2 tbsp olive oil

3 spring onions, chopped

1½ tbsp redcurrant jelly

150ml (5fl oz) lamb stock

150g (5½oz) blueberries

2 tbsp finely chopped mint

1 Season the lamb noisettes with salt and pepper. Heat half the oil in a large, heavy, frying pan and fry the noisettes for 4–6 minutes on each side, or until golden brown but still slightly pink inside. Remove on to a plate and cover with foil.

2 Add the remaining oil to the pan and fry the onions for 2–3 minutes, then stir in the redcurrant jelly and stock. Stir until the jelly is dissolved and the liquid comes to the boil.

3 Add the blueberries and simmer, uncovered, for 2 minutes, then add the mint.

4 Serve the lamb with the sauce spooned over.

Lamb Koftas

Tender minced lamb kebabs with a hint
of Middle Eastern spices

- makes 16
- prep 15 mins, plus chilling • cook 8–10 mins
- soak the skewers in cold water for 30 mins to prevent burning
- 16 wooden skewers

1 slice of **white bread**, crusts removed and torn into small pieces

3 tbsp **milk**

450g (1lb) **minced lamb**

8 sprigs of **coriander**, leaves finely chopped

8 sprigs of **parsley**, leaves finely chopped

1 tbsp **ground cumin**

1 **garlic clove**, crushed

½ tsp **salt**

½ tsp freshly ground **black pepper**

vegetable oil, for brushing

For the sauce

120g (4oz) **cucumber**, deseeded and diced

280g (10oz) **plain yogurt**

● **Prepare ahead** Steps 1, 2 and 3 can be completed up to a day in advance and chilled. The sauce can be made up to 2 days in advance, but if left too long it will become watery.

1 **Put skewers** in hot water and leave to soak. Soak the bread in the milk for 5 minutes.

2 **Put the minced lamb**, coriander, parsley, cumin, garlic, salt, and pepper in a large bowl. Squeeze the milk from the bread and add the bread to the bowl. Mix thoroughly with your hands. Discard the remaining milk.

3 **Using wet hands**, roll 2 tbsp of the mixture into an even sausage shape, then repeat with the remaining mixture to make a total of 16 koftas. Carefully skewer each kofta with a wooden skewer.

4 **Meanwhile**, preheat the grill on its highest setting. Line the grill pan with kitchen foil and lightly brush the grill rack with vegetable oil. Position the rack about 10cm (4in) from the heat.

5 **Put the koftas** on a grill rack in the grill pan and grill, turning frequently, for 8 minutes for slightly pink, or 10 minutes for well done. Mix the cucumber and yogurt with a little salt to taste and serve alongside the cooked koftas.

Braised Lamb

This dish packs plenty of flavour with its tomato, olive, and herb sauce

- serves 6
- prep 20 mins • cook 1½ hrs
- flameproof casserole with a lid
- freeze for up to 1 month

900g (2lb) **lamb leg**, sliced

1 large **onion**, peeled

2 **garlic cloves**, peeled

1 fresh **red chilli** or ½ tsp dried chopped chilli

4 tbsp **olive oil**

120ml (4fl oz) **red wine**

115g (4oz) good quality **black olives**, pitted

400g can **tomatoes**

15g fresh **thyme** or 1 tsp dried thyme

salt and freshly ground **black pepper**

thyme or parsley, to garnish

● **Prepare ahead** The dish can be prepared up to 3 days in advance. Take the dish out of the refrigerator and allow it to come to room temperature, then reheat for 30 minutes, or until piping hot.

1 **Cut each slice** of lamb in half. Place the onion, garlic, and chilli in a food processor and pulse to a coarse paste. Heat the olive oil in a large casserole and brown the meat on both sides, in batches if necessary.

2 **Remove the lamb** to a plate and gently fry the onion mixture for 5 minutes, stirring. Return the lamb to the pan, add the red wine, olives, tomatoes, and thyme and simmer, covered for 1 hour.

3 **Check the lamb** and simmer uncovered for half an hour, or until the lamb is tender. Season to taste with salt and pepper and garnish with freshly chopped herbs.

● **Good with** hot, fluffy couscous.

● **Leftovers** can be coarsely chopped, mixed with some of the sauce, wrapped in filo pastry, and baked to form tasty parcels.

Irish Stew

There are many versions of this dish, with lamb and potatoes, cooked long and slow for maximum flavour and tenderness

- serves 4–6
- prep 20 mins
  - cook 1 hr 40 mins

8 best-end neck of lamb chops, about 750g (1lb 10oz) total weight

800g (1¾lb) onions, sliced

3 carrots, thickly sliced

800g (1¾lb) floury potatoes, peeled and thickly sliced

salt and freshly ground black pepper

large sprig of thyme

1 bay leaf

600ml (1pint) lamb stock or beef stock

Prepare ahead The stew can be made the day before to the end of step 3. Reheat before serving.

1 Preheat the oven to 160°C (325°F/Gas 3).

2 Layer the lamb, onions, carrots, and a third of the potato slices in a large, heavy casserole. Season to taste with salt and pepper between the layers.

3 Tuck the thyme and bay leaf into the ingredients, then top with the remaining potato slices. Pour the stock over, cover, and place in the oven for 1 hour.

4 Remove the lid and return the casserole to the oven for a further 30–40 minutes, or until the top is browned. Serve hot.

Good with a fresh green vegetable, such as spring greens, kale, or broccoli.

Navarin of Lamb

This classic French stew is a complete one-pot meal, traditionally made with young spring vegetables

- serves 4
- prep 30 mins • cook 1½ hrs
- freeze for up to 3 months

15g (½oz) butter

1 tbsp olive oil

900g (2lb) middle neck of lamb, cut into pieces

2 small onions, quartered

1 tbsp plain flour

400ml (14fl oz) lamb stock or beef stock

2 tbsp tomato purée

1 bouquet garni

salt and freshly ground black pepper

300g (10oz) small new potatoes

300g (10oz) small whole carrots

300g (10oz) baby turnips

175g (6oz) French beans

Prepare ahead Follow up to the end of step 2 the day before, then cool, cover, and refrigerate. Bring to the boil, add the vegetables, and continue following the recipe.

1 Melt the butter with the oil in a large flameproof casserole, add the lamb, and fry until brown on all sides. Add the onions and fry gently for 5 minutes, stirring frequently.

2 Sprinkle the flour over the meat and stir well for 2 minutes, or until the pieces are evenly coated. Stir in the stock, then add the tomato purée and bouquet garni, and season to taste with salt and pepper. Bring to the boil, then cover and simmer for 45 minutes.

3 Add the potatoes, carrots, and turnips. Cover and cook for a further 15 minutes, then stir in the beans, cover, and cook for a further 10–15 minutes, or until all the vegetables are tender.

Good with chunks of French bread to soak up the juices.

Leftovers can be stored in the refrigerator, then reheated thoroughly the next day.

Roast Lamb with Flageolets

A perfect Sunday lunch; the beans make a tasty change to the more traditional accompaniment of roast potatoes

- 🍴 serves 4
- 🕐 prep 15 mins
  - cook 1 hr 40 mins

½ leg of **lamb**, about 1.35kg (3lb)

2–3 sprigs **rosemary**

1 tbsp **olive oil**

salt and freshly ground **black pepper**

4 **garlic cloves**, roughly chopped

250g (9oz) **baby plum tomatoes**, halved

410g can **flageolet beans**, drained

1 tbsp **tomato purée**

150ml (5fl oz) **dry white wine**

● **Prepare ahead** The lamb can be prepared and stuffed with the rosemary leaves, ready for roasting, a few hours in advance of cooking.

1 **Preheat the oven** to 180°C (350°F/Gas 4). With a small, sharp knife, make several deep cuts into the skin surface of the lamb. Push a few rosemary leaves into each cut. Place the lamb in a roasting tin, brush with oil, and season with salt and pepper. Roast for 1 hour.

2 **Mix the remaining** rosemary with the garlic, tomatoes, and flageolets. Remove the lamb from the oven and spoon the tomato and bean mixture around it. Mix the tomato purée with the wine and pour over the lamb.

3 **Cover loosely** with foil, then return to the oven for 30–40 minutes, or until the lamb is cooked but the juices are still slightly pink, stirring once. Allow the meat to rest for 10–15 minutes, loosely covered with foil, before carving.

Lamb Kebabs

The secret to melt-in-the-mouth tenderness is a simple but very tasty marinade

- 🍴 serves 4
- 🕐 prep 15 mins, plus marinating
  - cook 10–15 mins
- ✓ low fat, low GI
- 🍢 8 wooden skewers

450g (1lb) **boned leg**, fillet or shoulder of lamb, cut into 2.5cm (1in) cubes

salt and freshly ground **black pepper**

16 **shallots**, blanched

16 **cherry tomatoes**

16 **button mushrooms**

1 **red pepper**, deseeded and cut into square pieces

pitta bread, to serve

salad leaves, to serve

For the marinade

90ml (3fl oz) **olive oil**

juice of 1 **lemon**

1 small **red onion**, finely chopped

1 tbsp **lemon thyme leaves**

1 **Place the lamb** into a large non-metallic dish. Mix the marinade ingredients and pour on to the lamb. Season with salt and pepper, cover, and chill for 2 hours, stirring occasionally. Soak the wooden skewers in cold water.

2 **Remove the meat** and drain, reserving the marinade.

3 **Preheat the grill** to medium. Assemble the kebabs by threading the meat and prepared vegetables on to the skewers. Grill for 10–15 minutes, turning frequently and basting with the marinade.

4 **Serve at once**, with warmed pitta bread and salad leaves.

VARIATION

Curried Lamb Kebabs
Add crushed garlic, chopped coriander, and a pinch of both cumin and curry powder.

Shepherd's Pie

Traditionally a recipe to use meat and potatoes from a Sunday roast, this version is topped with potato and leek mash

 serves 4-6

prep 30 mins • cook 30 mins

750g (1½lb) **minced lamb** or leftover lamb, finely chopped

2 tbsp **sunflower oil**

1 large **onion**, chopped

1 **garlic clove**, crushed

2 **carrots**, sliced

90ml (3fl oz) **dry red wine**

2 tbsp **plain flour**

250ml (8fl oz) **lamb stock** or gravy

1 tbsp **Worcestershire sauce**

2 tbsp chopped **flat-leaf parsley**

1 tbsp **rosemary**, finely crushed

salt and freshly ground **black pepper**

For the potato and leek mash

900g (2lb) **floury potatoes**, such as King Edward, peeled

2 large **leeks**, cut in half lengthways, sliced

60g (2oz) **butter**

150ml (5fl oz) **milk**, warmed

● **Prepare ahead** The pie can be made up to 24 hours in advance and stored in the refrigerator. Ensure the dish is piping hot before serving.

1 **To make the leek mash**, cut the potatoes into large chunks and place in a large saucepan. Cover with water and bring to the boil. Boil for 12 minutes, add the leeks, and cook for a further 5 minutes, or until the potatoes are tender, and drain.

2 **Mash the potatoes** and leeks and return them to a low heat. Stir in the butter and milk, and season to taste with salt and pepper. Preheat the oven to 200°C (400°F/Gas 6).

3 **To make the filling**, if using minced lamb, fry it in a large frying pan over a medium-high heat

for 5 minutes, or until lightly browned. Pour off the fat, remove the meat from the pan and set aside.

4 **In the same pan**, heat the oil. Fry the onion and garlic, stirring for 3-5 minutes, or until softened, then add the carrots. Add the cooked mince or chopped lamb to the pan and stir together.

5 **Add the wine**, increase the heat to high, and cook for 2-3 minutes. Stir in the flour once the wine has evaporated. Stir in the stock, Worcestershire sauce, parsley, and rosemary, and season to taste with salt and pepper. Bring to the boil, then reduce the heat to low, and simmer for 5 minutes.

6 **Spoon the filling** into a large ovenproof dish and top with the mashed potatoes. Place the dish on a baking tray and bake for 30 minutes, or until the mashed potatoes are golden. Leave to rest for 5 minutes, then serve straight from the dish.

● **Good with** a simple green vegetable, such as steamed broccoli or minted peas, served alongside.

VARIATION

Cottage Pie

Virtually the same dish made with beef, rather than lamb. For a cottage pie, follow the recipe above, but use 750g (1½lb) minced beef and replace the carrots with 150g (5½oz) shelled peas, straight from the freezer if frozen, and replace the rosemary with dried thyme. Use the same leek-flavoured topping or omit the leeks and stir 2 tbsp creamed horseradish into the mash instead.

Lamb Cutlets with Herbs and Mustard

An easy summer supper dish

 serves 4

 prep 10 mins, plus marinating • cook 10 mins

6 tbsp chopped **parsley, thyme, mint**, and **marjoram** (if available)

2 **garlic cloves**, chopped

1 tbsp **green peppercorns**, crushed

12 **lamb cutlets**

8 tbsp **olive oil**

juice and zest of 1 **lemon**

2 tsp **Dijon mustard**

sea salt

1 **Mix the herbs**, garlic, and peppercorns. Rub the mixture over the cutlets, pressing down on both sides. Drizzle with olive oil and a little lemon juice, chill, and leave to marinate for at least 2 hours.

2 **Preheat the grill** on its highest setting, then grill the cutlets for 5 minutes on each side, or until the fat is golden and crisp.

3 **Meanwhile**, make the dressing by whisking together 1 tbsp of lemon juice, the lemon zest, mustard, and a pinch of salt. Gradually beat in the remaining oil until the mixture thickens. Serve the cutlets with the dressing drizzled over.

● **Leftovers** can be chopped and stirred into bulghur wheat with more herbs, for a filling tabbouleh.

Honeyed Lamb with Carrot Salsa

This is fresh, healthy, and simple to prepare

 serves 6

prep 20 mins, plus marinating • cook 15 mins

900g (2lb) lamb loin

For the marinade

1 tbsp clear honey

juice of 2 limes

salt and freshly ground black pepper

2 tbsp light soy sauce

1 tbsp chopped rosemary

For the salsa

5 large carrots, peeled and shredded

1 red onion, thinly sliced

1 garlic clove

juice of ½ lemon

1 tbsp pomegranate molasses

1 tbsp chopped mint

4 tbsp olive oil

85g (3oz) toasted sunflower seeds

● **Prepare ahead** The carrot salsa can be made 1 day in advance and chilled. The lamb benefits from being marinated for several hours.

1 **Whisk together** the marinade ingredients, and pour it over the lamb. Leave to marinate for at least 1 hour, or up to 24 hours.

2 **To make the salsa**, combine all the ingredients, except for the sunflower seeds. Season to taste with salt and pepper. Cover with cling film and set aside for 1 hour. Add the sunflower seeds just before serving.

3 **Preheat the oven** to 200°C (400°F/Gas 6). Heat a frying pan on a high heat and fry the lamb until well-browned on all sides. Transfer to a roasting tin and roast for 10 minutes, or until pink. Remove from the oven and allow to rest for 5 minutes.

4 **Carve the loin** into slices and serve on warm plates. Spoon the salsa alongside the lamb.

Quick Lamb Curry

Use leftover lamb for this dish and adjust the amount of curry powder to your taste

 serves 4

 prep 15 mins • cook 25 mins

freeze for up to 3 months

1 onion, quartered

3 garlic cloves, sliced

2.5cm (1in) piece of fresh root ginger, peeled and chopped

2 green peppers, deseeded and quartered

1 green chilli, deseeded

2 tbsp oil

1 tbsp black mustard seeds

1–2 tbsp curry powder

400g can chopped tomatoes

100g (3½ oz) creamed coconut

500g (1lb 2oz) cooked lamb, cut into bite-sized pieces

115g (4oz) frozen peas

salt and freshly ground black pepper

chopped coriander, to garnish

1 **Place the onions**, garlic, ginger, green peppers, and chilli in a blender with 1 tbsp water and blend to a purée.

2 **Heat 1 tbsp oil** in a large saucepan or flameproof casserole, add the mustard seeds and fry, stirring, for 30 seconds, or until they begin to pop. Pour in the onion purée, increase the heat, and allow to bubble, stirring frequently, for 3–5 minutes, or until all the water has evaporated and the purée is thick and fairly dry.

3 **Add the remaining oil** and curry powder, and stir-fry for 30 seconds, then add the tomatoes with their juice, and 75ml (3fl oz) water. Cook for 1 minute, stirring constantly, then add the coconut, and stir until well incorporated.

4 **Add the lamb** and peas and bring back to boiling point, then reduce the heat, cover, and simmer for 10–15 minutes, until heated through. Season to taste with salt and pepper, and serve garnished with chopped coriander.

● **Good with** rice or naan bread, or as part of a feast with other curries.

● **Leftovers** are delicious cut into smaller pieces and served warm as a baked potato topping.

Moussaka

Greece's most famous dish is also a favourite worldwide. Often served in squares cut from a large baking tray, this version makes individual servings

serves 4

prep 30 mins, plus standing • cook 1 hr 30 mins

4 x 8–10cm (3½–4in) ovenproof casserole dishes

freeze for up to 3 months

2 large **aubergines**, cut into 5mm (¼in) slices

salt and freshly ground **black pepper**

5 tbsp **olive oil**

1 large **onion**, chopped

450g (1lb) lean **lamb mince**

100ml (3½fl oz) **red wine**

400g can **chopped tomatoes**

1 tsp **sugar**

100ml (3½fl oz) **lamb stock**

2 tsp **dried oregano**

450g (1lb) **potatoes**, cut into 5mm (¼in) slices

4 tbsp grated **Parmesan cheese**

4 tbsp dried **breadcrumbs**

For the topping

200g (7oz) **Greek strained yogurt**

3 large **eggs**

1 tbsp **cornflour**

115g (4oz) **curd cheese**

60g (2oz) **feta cheese**, crumbled

● **Prepare ahead** The moussaka can be prepared a day in advance, and chilled until ready to reheat.

1 Spread out the aubergine slices on a plate, sprinkle liberally with salt, and leave to stand for 30 minutes. Tip the slices into a colander, rinse thoroughly under cold water, drain, and pat dry.

2 Heat 2 tbsp oil in a large deep frying pan, add the onion, and cook over a low heat, stirring often, until softened. Increase the heat and fry the mince until starting to brown, breaking up any clumps with a spoon.

3 Add the wine, allow to bubble for 1–2 minutes, then add the tomatoes, sugar, stock, and 1 tsp oregano, and season to taste with salt and pepper. Simmer, uncovered, for 30 minutes, or until most of the liquid in the pan has evaporated and the meat sauce is quite thick.

4 Meanwhile, brush the aubergine slices with the remaining oil and grill in batches until softened and golden on both sides. Boil the potato slices in a saucepan of water for 10–15 minutes, or until just tender. Drain.

5 To make the topping, whisk the yogurt, eggs, and cornflour together until smooth, then whisk in the curd and feta.

6 Preheat the oven to 180°C (350°F/Gas 4). Layer the aubergine slices with the meat mixture into the baking dishes, starting with aubergine and finishing with meat. Arrange the potato slices on top in an overlapping layer.

7 Spread over the topping to cover the potatoes completely, scatter with Parmesan, breadcrumbs, and the remaining oregano, and bake for 45 minutes, or until golden brown and bubbling.

VARIATION

Moussaka with Cheese Sauce

If you prefer, instead of the yogurt topping, you can use 450ml (15fl oz) béchamel sauce with 2 handfuls of grated cheese, such as Cheddar, stirred in. Sprinkle with a little extra cheese before baking.

Lamb with Roast Vegetables

A flavoursome dish that is quick and easy to prepare

serves 6

prep 10 mins, plus resting • cook 45 mins

200g (7oz) **red onions**, peeled and quartered

225g (8oz) **baby carrots**, peeled

200g (7oz) **parsnips**, peeled and sliced lengthways

200g (7oz) **new potatoes**, washed

1 **garlic bulb**, separated into cloves, unpeeled

olive oil, for drizzling and frying

balsamic vinegar, for drizzling

salt and freshly ground **black pepper**

600g (1lb 5oz) **lamb loin**, trimmed

1 Preheat the oven to 200°C (400°F/Gas 6). Place the onions, carrots, parsnips, potatoes, and garlic into a roasting tin. Sprinkle with olive oil and balsamic vinegar, and season to taste with salt and pepper. Roast for 35 minutes, or until tender, stirring several times. Remove from the oven and keep warm.

2 Heat a little oil in a pan over a high heat. Brown the lamb on all sides, transfer to a baking tray, and roast for 25 minutes, or until pink. Allow to rest for at least 10 minutes.

3 Slice the lamb and serve with the roasted vegetables alongside.

Lamb Cutlets with Chermoula

Chermoula is a classic, Moroccan spice marinade. Wonderful for grilled meats and fish

🍴 serves 6

🕐 prep 15 mins, plus marinating
• cook 15 mins

12 lamb cutlets, trimmed

4 ripe plum tomatoes, chopped

salt and freshly ground black pepper

1 tbsp balsamic vinegar

For the marinade

1 red onion, finely chopped

2 garlic cloves, crushed

1 tsp ground cumin

¼ tsp smoked paprika

1 tsp ground coriander

grated zest and juice of 1 lemon

120ml (4fl oz) olive oil, plus extra for drizzling

handful of mint, roughly chopped

handful of coriander, chopped

● **Prepare ahead** The meat can be left to marinate for up to 24 hours.

1 Place the trimmed cutlets in a dish. In a mixing bowl, combine the red onion, garlic, cumin, paprika, ground coriander, lemon juice and zest, olive oil, and most of the chopped mint and coriander. Rub the marinade over the lamb and leave to marinate for 30 minutes.

2 Season the chopped tomatoes with salt and pepper, drizzle with a little olive oil, the balsamic vinegar, the remaining coriander, and the mint. Set aside.

3 Preheat the grill on its highest setting. Remove the cutlets from the marinade and grill for 5 minutes each side, or until cooked and crisp.

4 Serve the lamb with the tomato salad alongside.

Warm Lamb Salad with Pomegranate and Walnuts

The meat and dressing can be prepared in advance, making this a great weeknight entertaining dish to serve for friends

🍴 serves 6

🕐 prep 20 mins, plus marinating
• cook 10–15 mins

675g (1½lb) lamb loin fillet

3 handfuls of baby salad leaves

1 head of chicory, separated into leaves

100g (3½oz) walnuts, toasted

1 pomegranate, seeded (optional)

For the marinade

salt and freshly ground black pepper

3 garlic cloves, peeled and crushed

2 tbsp pomegranate molasses

1 tbsp olive oil

pinch of cayenne

few sprigs of thyme

For the vinaigrette

1 shallot, finely chopped

1 tbsp sherry vinegar

1 tbsp pomegranate molasses

2 tbsp walnut oil

2 tbsp olive oil

● **Prepare ahead** As the meat needs marinating for at least 4 hours, or overnight, you can start this recipe the day before you want to cook the lamb.

1 Mix together all the marinade ingredients and smear over the lamb. Cover, chill, and marinate for at least 4 hours.

2 To make the vinaigrette, place the shallots in a bowl, pour over the vinegar and molasses, and leave for 15 minutes. Whisk in the oils, and season to taste with salt and pepper. Set aside.

3 Preheat the oven to 190°C (375°F/Gas 5). Heat a heavy frying pan over a high heat. Brown the fillet on all sides, then transfer to a roasting tin, and roast for 10 minutes, or until pink. Rest the lamb for 15 minutes.

4 Slice the lamb fillet. Serve on a bed of leaves, scattered with walnuts and pomegranate seeds (if using), then drizzle with vinaigrette.

● **Good with** a bowl of Greek yogurt and warmed flatbreads.

Lamb Braised with Green Peas and Preserved Lemons

Similar to a tagine, this dish benefits from being made in advance to allow the flavours to develop

serves 6

prep 15 mins, plus marinating
• cook 1 hr 20 mins

large flameproof casserole

freeze for up to 3 months

15g (½oz) **parsley**, chopped, plus extra to garnish

15g (½oz) **coriander**, chopped, plus extra to garnish

1kg (2¼ lb) **leg of lamb**, cut into slices

2 **onions**, finely chopped

3 **garlic cloves**, chopped

1 tsp grated fresh **root ginger**

9 tbsp **olive oil**

600ml (1 pint) **meat stock**

2 **preserved lemons**, cut into quarters, pulp removed and discarded, zest thinly sliced

450g (1lb) **frozen peas**

1 **lemon**, zest peeled into long, thin strips or cut into wedges, to garnish

🔘 **Prepare ahead** The braised lamb can be made up to 3 days in advance, kept covered in the casserole, and chilled. Cook gently until completely heated through.

1 Combine the parsley, coriander, lamb, onions, garlic, ginger, and olive oil in a large dish and leave to marinate overnight, covered with cling film, in a refrigerator.

2 Remove the lamb, reserving the marinade, and setting it aside. In a hot frying pan, brown the lamb evenly on all sides, then transfer to the casserole, pour over the reserved marinade, add the stock, and bring to the boil. Reduce the heat and simmer, covered, for 1 hour.

3 Add the preserved lemons to the pan, and continue simmering for another 30 minutes, or until the meat is very tender.

4 Adjust the seasoning if necessary, add the peas, and simmer for a further 5 minutes. Serve while still hot with chopped parsley and coriander sprinkled over, and garnish with lemon zest strips or with lemon wedges on the side.

Lamb Brochettes

Stylish lamb skewers

serves 6

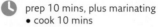
prep 10 mins, plus marinating
• cook 10 mins

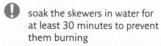
soak the skewers in water for at least 30 minutes to prevent them burning

wooden skewers

2 tbsp **coriander seeds**, toasted

4 **garlic cloves**, crushed

200ml (7fl oz) **olive oil**

2 tsp **clear honey**

1 tsp grated **lemon** zest

salt and freshly ground **black pepper**

1kg (2¼lb) **lamb**, cut into chunks

2 tbsp **red wine vinegar**

6 tbsp chopped **coriander**

5 ripe **tomatoes**, skinned, deseeded and chopped

1 Crush the coriander seeds in a pestle and mortar and stir in half the garlic, 75ml (2½fl oz) olive oil, half the honey, the lemon zest, and pepper to taste. Coat the lamb with the rub, and marinate in a bowl for 2 hours.

2 To make the vinaigrette, whisk the remaining oil, vinegar, and coriander in a bowl, stir in the tomatoes, and set aside.

3 Preheat the grill to high. Skewer the meat, season with salt, and grill for 8 minutes, or until evenly browned. Serve with the tomato vinaigrette.

Slow-cooked Greek Lamb

Roasting lamb is popular during Easter in Greece

serves 4

prep 10 mins • cook 4½–5 hrs

1.35kg (3lb) **leg of lamb**

2 tbsp **olive oil**

3 **garlic cloves**, crushed

1 tsp **ground cinnamon**

1 tsp **dried thyme**

1 tsp **dried oregano** or marjoram

juice of 1 **lemon**

1 tsp freshly ground **black pepper**

1 **onion**, sliced into rings

2 **carrots**, halved lengthways

2 tbsp chopped **parsley**

1 Preheat the oven to 150°C (300°F/Gas 2). Place the lamb in a roasting tin. Mix the oil, garlic, cinnamon, and herbs, and brush over the lamb. Sprinkle with the lemon juice and season to taste with pepper.

2 Half-fill the tin with water, add the onion and carrots. Cook for 3 hours, basting every 30 minutes, and topping up the water if necessary.

3 Cover with foil and cook for another 1½–2 hours, or until the meat comes away from the bone.

4 Remove from the oven, and leave to rest for 20 minutes before serving. Arrange the lamb on a platter with parsley scattered over.

Lamb with Aubergine Purée

Harissa makes a spicy crust for the lamb that goes well with the creamy aubergine

🍴 serves 6

🕐 prep 15 mins, plus marinating • cook 40 mins

900g (2lb) **lamb loin fillet** or noisettes of lamb

2 **aubergines**

2 **garlic cloves**, crushed

2 tbsp **tahini**

120ml (4fl oz) **Greek yogurt**

salt and freshly ground **black pepper**

For the marinade

1 tbsp **harissa**

2 tbsp chopped **mint**, plus extra for garnish

5 tbsp **lemon** juice

3 tbsp **olive oil**

⬤ **Prepare ahead** The aubergine purée can be made 1 day in advance and served at room temperature. The lamb can marinate for up to 24 hours, chilled and covered.

1 Preheat the oven to 220°C (425°F/Gas 7). Place the harissa, mint, 2 tbsp lemon juice, and 1 tbsp olive oil in a bowl. Add the lamb and cover evenly in the marinade. Leave to marinate for at least 30 minutes.

2 Place the aubergines on a baking tray, prick the skin with a fork several times, and bake for 30 minutes, or until the skins have charred. Remove from the oven and, when cool enough to handle, peel away the skins and discard. Place the aubergine flesh into a colander, drain for 15 minutes, then place in a food processor with the garlic, 3 tbsp lemon juice, tahini, and yogurt, and process until smooth. Season to taste with salt and pepper.

3 Remove the lamb from the marinade. Heat a frying pan with 2 tbsp olive oil and brown the lamb on all sides. Roast in the oven for 10 minutes, or longer if desired. Remove, and let rest for 10 minutes.

4 Carve the lamb and serve on warmed plates with the purée. Pour the pan juices over, and sprinkle with chopped mint.

Butterflied Leg of Lamb

Opening out the leg of lamb ensures even marinating and cooking when placed on the barbecue

🍴 serves 8

🕐 prep 15 mins, plus marinating and resting • cook 1 hr

❗ butterfly the leg yourself, or ask your butcher

1.8kg (4lb) **butterflied leg of lamb** (p512)

For the marinade

200ml (7fl oz) **red wine**

90ml (3fl oz) **light soy sauce**

3 **garlic cloves**, crushed

15g (½oz) **mint**, chopped

For the salsa

2 tbsp **olive oil**

1 **garlic clove**, finely chopped

1 fresh **red chilli**, deseeded and finely chopped

1 tbsp **marjoram leaves**

4 fresh **tomatoes**, peeled

2 **red peppers**, grilled, peeled and chopped

salt and freshly ground **black pepper**

2 small **dried chillies**, crumbled

1 Remove any unwanted fat from the lamb with a sharp knife, but leave some on for flavour. Lay the meat flat on a work surface, skin-side down. Make 3 long cuts into the lamb, not quite all the way through: 1 in the centre and 1 on each side of the outside flaps. Place a piece of greaseproof paper over the meat and pound with a rolling pin to level the meat. (This helps it cook evenly.) Place the lamb in a large bowl or dish.

2 Mix the marinade ingredients and pour over the meat. Marinate for at least 2 hours.

3 Heat the olive oil in a saucepan and fry the garlic until it starts to colour. Add the fresh chilli, marjoram leaves, and tomatoes and simmer for 30 minutes, or until the sauce has reduced. Add the peppers and cook for 10 minutes. Season with salt and pepper and crumbled dried chillies. Set aside.

4 Preheat a barbecue or grill to medium-high. Remove the lamb from the marinade and pat dry with kitchen paper. Cook for 30 minutes, turning several times. It should still be pink in the middle. Allow to rest for 15 minutes, then carve. Serve with the salsa alongside.

Steak and Kidney Pudding

A classic old English recipe that is just the dish for hearty appetites

 serves 6-8

prep 30 mins • cook 4 hrs

1.5 litre (2¾ pint) pudding bowl, steamer, or deep pan with a lid

freeze for up to 3 months

For the pastry

350g (12oz) self-raising flour

½ tsp salt

150g (5½ oz) shredded suet

For the filling

675g (1½ lb) lean stewing steak

200g (7oz) ox kidney

3 tbsp plain flour

salt and freshly ground black pepper

1 onion, chopped

150g (5½oz) mushrooms, quartered

2 tbsp Worcestershire sauce

200ml (7fl oz) beef stock

● **Prepare ahead** The pastry can be made up to 1 day in advance, then wrapped and chilled until needed.

1 To make the pastry, sift the flour and salt into a bowl and stir in the suet. Make a well in the centre and stir in just enough cold water to mix to a soft, but not sticky, dough.

2 Trim off any excess fat from the steak and cut the steak and kidney into bite-sized pieces. Season the flour with salt and pepper, then toss the steak and kidney pieces in the flour to coat evenly. Combine with the onion and mushrooms.

3 Roll out two-thirds of the pastry and use to line the pudding bowl. Add the meat mixture, packing closely into the pastry-lined bowl. Sprinkle over the Worcestershire sauce, then add just enough stock to cover three-quarters of the filling.

4 Roll out the remaining pastry to make a lid. Tuck the pastry edges in around the pudding bowl, brush with water, and place the pastry lid on top, pressing to seal.

5 Top the pudding bowl with a round of pleated greaseproof paper, then top with a double layer of pleated foil. Tuck the foil around the rim of the basin firmly, or secure with string if necessary.

6 Place the bowl in the top of a steamer, or on an upturned saucer in a pan of boiling water to come halfway up the sides. Cover and steam for 4 hours, checking the level of water often to ensure it does not boil dry. To serve, remove the foil and paper, run a knife around the edge of the pudding to loosen, then turn out on to a serving plate.

● **Good with** a selection of winter vegetables, such as carrots, cabbage, or leeks.

● **Leftovers** of the filling can be warmed and served over slices of toast for a substantial breakfast dish, or finely chopped and used to fill mini tartlet shells as a tasty appetizer.

Kidneys with Mustard Sauce

This dish makes a tasty lunch, first course, or supper dish

 serves 4

prep 10 mins, plus soaking • cook 10-15 mins

4 lamb's kidneys

30g (1oz) butter

1 tbsp olive oil

1 large onion, finely chopped

2 garlic cloves, crushed

8 chestnut mushrooms, sliced

3 tbsp vermouth or red wine

4 tbsp vegetable stock

2 tsp Dijon mustard

salt and freshly ground black pepper

1 Peel away any skin from the kidneys and cut out the core and membranes. Soak for 5-10 minutes in a little milk or water, then drain and pat dry on kitchen paper.

2 Heat the butter and oil in a frying pan, add the onion, and fry over a medium heat, stirring frequently, for 2-3 minutes. Increase the heat, add the kidneys and garlic, and fry for 2-3 minutes, stirring.

3 Add the mushrooms, fry for a further 2-3 minutes, then add the vermouth and stock and allow to bubble for 1 minute.

4 Reduce the heat, cover, and cook for 4 minutes, or until the kidneys are tender and cooked through. Stir in the mustard and season to taste with salt and pepper.

Sauté of Liver, Bacon, and Onions

Quick to cook, tender calves' liver is the perfect partner to salty bacon and is served here in a rich sauce

🍴 serves 4

🕐 prep 10 mins • cook 10 mins

350g (12oz) **calves' liver**

200g sweet-cured, smoked streaky **bacon** thin-cut rashers

1 tbsp **olive oil**

25g (1oz) **unsalted butter**

4 **shallots**, thinly sliced

120ml (4½fl oz) **vermouth**

1 tsp **Dijon mustard**

dash of **mushroom ketchup** or Worcestershire sauce (optional)

salt and freshly ground **black pepper**

1 Cut the liver and the bacon rashers into strips about 6cm (2¼in) long and 1.5cm (½in) wide. Set aside.

2 Heat half the oil and half the butter in a frying pan over a medium heat, add the shallots, and fry, stirring frequently, for 5 minutes, or until soft and golden. Remove from the pan and reserve.

3 Add the remaining oil and butter to the pan and increase the heat to high. Add the liver and bacon and stir-fry for 3–4 minutes, until the liver is cooked but still slightly pink inside.

4 Return the shallots to the pan, pour in the vermouth, and let it bubble for 1–2 minutes, scraping any bits stuck to the bottom of the pan.

5 Reduce the heat to medium and stir in the mustard and the mushroom ketchup (if using). Serve at once.

⬤ **Good with** smooth, creamy mashed potato and green beans for a tasty supper dish, or served on toasted bread croûtes for a quick dinner party starter.

VARIATION

Lamb's Liver and Bacon
Use the same quantity of lamb's liver, for a more economical version of this recipe. Add a dash of Tabasco sauce for an extra touch of spice.

Braised Oxtail in Wine with Winter Herbs

This wholesome winter dish is best served with a mound of buttery mash

🍴 serves 6

🕐 prep 20 mins • cook 2–3 hrs

❄ freeze for up to 3 months

3 kg (6½ lb) **oxtail**, cut into 225g (8oz) pieces

flour, for dusting

2 tbsp **olive oil**

1 tbsp **clear honey**

2 tbsp chopped **thyme**

2 tbsp chopped **rosemary**

salt and freshly ground **black pepper**

2 **onions**, chopped

1 **fennel bulb**, diced

2 **carrots**, cut into large chunks

2 **garlic cloves**, sliced

2 **red chillies**, finely chopped

750ml bottle full-bodied **red wine**

parsley, chopped, to garnish

⬤ **Prepare ahead** The recipe can be made up to 2 days ahead and chilled. The oxtail benefits from sitting in the juices overnight.

1 Preheat the oven to 150°C (300°F/Gas 2). Toss the oxtail in flour to lightly dust. Heat a large frying pan with the olive oil. Fry the oxtail, browning well on all sides.

2 Remove the oxtail and place in a large casserole. Drizzle the honey over the meat, scatter over the herbs, and season to taste with salt and pepper.

3 Add the vegetables, garlic, and chilli to the frying pan and fry for 6 minutes, or until slightly softened. Add to the oxtail and pour over the wine. Cover tightly and cook for 2–3 hours. The meat should fall away from the bone easily when cooked. Serve garnished with parsley.

Sausages with Butter Beans

This is a satisfying supper dish, great at any time of year but particularly good on a cold winter evening

 serves 4

 prep 10 mins • cook 30 mins

 freeze for up to 3 months

12 thick **pork and herb sausages**

1 tbsp **olive oil**

1 **onion**, sliced

1 **celery stick**, chopped

2 **garlic cloves**, crushed

75ml (2½fl oz) **white wine**

400g can **chopped tomatoes**

3 tbsp **tomato ketchup**

1 tsp **paprika**

salt and freshly ground **black pepper**

400g can **butter beans**

1 tbsp chopped **basil** or parsley, to serve

1 Grill or fry the sausages until browned and cooked through.

2 Meanwhile, heat the oil in a saucepan and gently fry the onion, celery, and garlic, stirring frequently, until soft. Turn up the heat, add the wine and let it bubble for a few moments, then add the canned tomatoes with their juice. Stir in the ketchup and paprika, and season to taste with salt and pepper. Bring to the boil, reduce the heat, and simmer, uncovered, for about 20 minutes, or until thickened and reduced.

3 Stir in the drained butter beans and the cooked sausages, and simmer for a further 10 minutes, then serve immediately, sprinkled with chopped herbs.

⬤ **Good with** creamy mashed potato or a mixture of carrot and potato mash.

⬤ **Leftovers** can be reheated and eaten with crusty bread to mop up the juices.

Black Pudding with Apple

Sweet apples are the perfect partner for savoury, peppery black pudding and bacon. Serve this dish for breakfast or brunch

 serves 4

prep 10 mins • cook 20 mins

3 sweet **eating apples**, peeled, cored and sliced

30g (1oz) **butter**

2 tsp **soft light brown sugar**

vegetable oil, for frying

8 large slices or 16 small slices of **black pudding**

4 **smoked streaky bacon rashers**, cut lengthways into thin strips

100ml (3½fl oz) **cider**

1 Cut each apple slice in half. Melt the butter in a small frying pan, add the apple pieces and sugar and cook over a medium heat, stirring frequently, for 8–10 minutes, or until softened and slightly caramelized. Remove from the heat and set aside.

2 Wipe out the pan, smear the pan with a little oil and fry the black pudding slices, in batches, over a medium-high heat for about 3 minutes on each side, or until slightly crisp. Remove from the pan and keep warm. Fry the bacon strips for 3 minutes, or until cooked through and slightly crisp, stirring frequently. Remove from the pan, increase the heat, and pour in the cider. Allow to bubble until well reduced and syrupy, stirring to incorporate any bits stuck to the bottom of the pan.

3 To serve, place a slice of black pudding on each plate, add a layer of apples, then repeat with the rest of the black pudding and apple. Top with the bacon strips and drizzle with the pan juices.

⬤ **Good with** chutney and granary toast. For a more substantial snack, serve with creamy mashed potato.

VARIATION

Boudin Blanc with Apple

Fry slices of French Boudin blanc sausage instead of the black pudding and add a squeeze of lemon juice to the cooked apples.

Fabada

This simple Spanish spicy sausage and bacon stew is ideal comfort food, and this time-saving version uses canned beans

🍴 serves 4

⏱ prep 5 mins • cook 40 mins

250g (9oz) **morcilla** (Spanish black pudding)

250g (9oz) **chorizo**

250g (9oz) **thick-cut streaky bacon rashers**, tocino, or pancetta

1 tbsp **olive oil**

60ml (2fl oz) **red wine**

2 x 400g cans **white beans**, drained

pinch of **saffron powder**

1 bay leaf

500ml (16fl oz) **chicken stock**

1 **Cut the morcilla**, chorizo, and bacon into large chunks. Heat the oil in a large saucepan, add the sausages and bacon, and fry,

stirring, over a medium-low heat for 2 minutes. Increase the heat, add the wine, and allow it to bubble and reduce for 2–3 minutes.

2 **Stir in the beans**, the saffron, the bay leaf, and just enough chicken stock to cover. Bring to the boil, reduce the heat, cover, and simmer for 30 minutes. Serve hot.

VARIATION

Dried Bean Stew

Soak 500g (1lb 2oz) dried white beans overnight in a large saucepan. Drain the beans and add fresh water to cover. Boil rapidly for 10 minutes, then skim off any froth, lower the heat, cover, and simmer, stirring occasionally for 2–3 hours, or until the beans are tender. Check the water level from time to time, to make sure the beans are just covered.

Sausage, Bacon, and Egg Pie

This pie transports well (so is good for picnics) and can be eaten from your hand just as well as from on a plate

🍴 serves 6-8

⏱ prep 15 mins, plus chilling • cook 50 mins

🍽 20cm (8in) ovenproof pie dish 3.5cm (1½in) deep

For the pastry

350g (12oz) **plain flour**

175g (6oz) **butter**

salt and freshly ground **black pepper**

1½ tbsp **tomato ketchup**

For the filling

450g (1lb) **sausagemeat** or good quality pork sausages, skinned

½ **onion**, finely chopped

pinch of **nutmeg**

pinch of **mace**

1 tbsp **wholegrain mustard**

salt and freshly ground **black pepper**

6 **streaky, rindless bacon rashers**

4 **eggs**

milk, to glaze

● **Prepare ahead** Make the pastry case the day before and chill until ready to use.

1 **Make the pastry** by placing the flour and butter in a food processor and pulsing until the mixture resembles breadcrumbs. Add the seasoning, ketchup, and 5–6 tbsp cold water, and pulse again, until it comes together in a ball. Chill for 30 minutes.

2 **Preheat the oven** to 200°C (400°F/Gas 6). Roll out half of the pastry fairly thinly on a lightly floured surface and line the pie dish.

3 **Mix the sausagemeat** with the onion, nutmeg, mace, and mustard, then season to taste with salt and pepper and spread evenly over the base of the pie crust. Place the bacon over the sausagemeat in lines and crack the eggs over the bacon, leaving them intact if possible, as it looks nice when slicing the pie.

4 **Roll out the remaining** pastry, cover the pie, and pinch the edges to seal. Lightly score a criss-cross pattern on top and brush with a little milk.

5 **Bake the pie** for 20 minutes, then reduce the heat to 180°C (350°F/Gas 4), and bake for another 30 minutes. Cool before serving.

Sausage and Mustard Casserole

Pure winter bliss. Serve it with creamy mashed potato and it will remain a firm favourite

- serves 6
- prep 15 mins • cook 45 mins
- large flameproof casserole

1 tbsp olive oil

12 good quality pork sausages

1 large onion, thinly sliced

225g (8oz) small chestnut mushrooms

1 cooking apple, peeled, cored, and cut into chunks

1 bay leaf

1 tbsp chopped sage

300ml (10fl oz) chicken stock

2 tsp Dijon mustard

1 tsp wholegrain mustard

1 tsp made English mustard

150ml (5fl oz) double cream

salt and freshly ground black pepper

1 **Heat the oil** in the casserole and gently fry the sausages until golden all over. Remove the sausages from the casserole.

2 **Add the onion** and cook until softened. Add the mushrooms and cook for 5 minutes, then stir in the apple, bay leaf, sage, and stock.

3 **Bring to the boil**, then return the sausages to the casserole. Reduce the heat, cover, and cook gently for 20 minutes, stirring often. The apple pieces should break down and thicken the sauce slightly. If they are still holding their shape, mash them with the back of a wooden spoon and stir in.

4 **Mix the mustards** and cream together in a bowl, and season with salt and pepper. Pour into the casserole, increase the heat, and boil gently for 5 minutes, or until the sauce has thickened slightly.

● **Good with** cabbage and creamy mashed potato.

Choucroute Garni

This is a simpler, quicker version of a classic dish from Alsace

- serves 6-8
- prep 30 mins • cook 3 hrs
- large flameproof casserole

3 tbsp goose fat or sunflower oil

250g (9oz) piece smoked gammon, diced

500g (1lb 2oz) pork spare rib, sliced

2 onions, chopped

2 green apples, cored and sliced

1 garlic clove, finely chopped

6 whole black peppercorns, lightly crushed

6 juniper berries, lightly crushed

large sprig of thyme

2 bay leaves

600g jar sauerkraut, thoroughly rinsed and drained

300ml (10fl oz) light beer or Riesling wine

500ml (16fl oz) chicken stock

12 small new potatoes

350g (12oz) smoked sausage, such as bratwurst or fleischwurst, thickly sliced

salt and freshly ground black pepper

parsley, chopped, to garnish

1 **Heat 2 tbsp goose fat** in the casserole and fry the gammon and pork, turning, for 3-4 minutes, or until evenly coloured. Remove the meat and keep warm. Add the onion to the pan and fry for 2-3 minutes.

2 **Add the apples**, garlic, peppercorns, juniper berries, thyme, and bay leaves. Stir in the sauerkraut, return the gammon and pork to the pan, and add the beer and the stock. Place a piece of greaseproof paper on top of the liquid, cover tightly with a lid, and simmer very gently over a very low heat for 2 hours.

3 **Add the potatoes**, pushing them down into the sauerkraut, then cover and cook on a low heat for 50-60 minutes, or until tender.

4 **Meanwhile**, heat the remaining goose fat or oil in a frying pan and fry the sausage quickly until brown, turning once.

5 **Spoon the sauerkraut** mixture on to a large platter and arrange the smoked sausage on top. Season to taste with salt and pepper, sprinkle with parsley, and serve.

Toad in the Hole

This classic British dish is perfect comfort food

 serves 4

 prep 20 mins, plus standing
• cook 40 mins

125g (4½oz) **plain flour**

pinch of **salt**

2 **eggs**

300ml (10fl oz) **milk**

2 tbsp **vegetable oil**

8 **Toulouse sausages**

● **Prepare ahead** The batter can be made up to 24 hours in advance. Keep chilled and whisk briefly just before using.

1 To make the batter, put the flour into a bowl with the salt, make a well in the centre, and add the eggs with a little of the milk. Whisk together, gradually incorporating the flour. Add the remaining milk and whisk to make a smooth batter. Leave to rest for at least 30 minutes.

2 Preheat the oven to 220°C (425°F/Gas 7). Pour the oil into a roasting tin or shallow ovenproof dish. Add the sausages and toss them in the hot oil. Bake the sausages for 5–10 minutes, or until they are just coloured and the fat is very hot.

3 Reduce the oven temperature to 200°C (400°F/Gas 6). Carefully pour the batter around the sausages and return to the oven for a further 30 minutes, or until the batter is risen, golden, and crisp. Serve immediately.

● **Good with** onion gravy, green vegetables, and mustard.

Rabbit Provençale

A French bistro dish that makes the most of this healthy and easy-to-cook meat

serves 4-6

prep 15 mins, plus resting
• cook 1 hr 15 mins

flameproof casserole

2 tbsp **olive oil**

1.25kg (2¾lb) **rabbit**, cut into 10 pieces

100g (3½oz) **pancetta**, chopped

1 **onion**, chopped

4 **garlic** cloves, finely chopped

sprig of **rosemary**, plus extra to garnish

3 **sage** leaves

900g (2lb) **tomatoes**, skinned and crushed

salt and freshly ground **black pepper**

150ml (5fl oz) **dry white wine**

200ml (7fl oz) boiling **water**

1 Heat the oil in the casserole over a medium-high heat and fry the rabbit pieces for 10 minutes, or until browned on all sides. Remove from the pan and drain on kitchen paper. Pour off most of the fat remaining in the pan.

2 Add the pancetta and onion to the pan and cook, stirring, for 5 minutes, or until the pancetta is browned and the onion softened. Add the garlic, stir for 30 seconds, then add the rosemary, sage, and tomatoes, and season to taste with salt and pepper. Cook, stirring frequently, for 10 minutes, or until the tomatoes begin to break up and thicken.

3 Return the rabbit to the pan and add the wine. Stir together and cook over a medium-high heat for 20 minutes, or until the liquid has reduced slightly and the sauce is quite thick. Stir in the boiling water, and add more salt and pepper, if desired. Partially cover, reduce the heat, and simmer, stirring occasionally, for 10-20 minutes, or until the rabbit is very tender.

4 Remove from the heat and rest for at least 10 minutes. Serve, garnished with rosemary.

Roast Venison with Marmalade Gravy

The robust citrus flavours of the sauce complement the rich, gamey flavour of the meat

serves 4

prep 20 mins, plus marinating and resting • cook 40 mins

1.25kg (2¾lb) **haunch of venison**, rolled

1 tbsp **sunflower oil**

3 tbsp **Seville orange marmalade**

For the marinade

300ml (10fl oz) **red wine**

1 tbsp **dark muscovado sugar**

1 tbsp **olive oil**

2 tbsp **orange** juice

1 tbsp **lemon** juice

1 **garlic** clove, crushed

½ tsp **black peppercorns**, crushed

● **Prepare ahead** The venison needs to marinate for 24 hours, or up to 3 days, in advance.

1 Place the venison in a large, non-metallic bowl. Mix together the ingredients for the marinade and pour over the meat, then cover and refrigerate for 24-48 hours.

2 Preheat the oven to 220°C (425°F/Gas 7). Lift the venison from the marinade, pat dry with kitchen paper, and place in a roasting tin. Allow to cool slightly to room temperature for 20 minutes.

3 Roast for 20 minutes, then reduce the oven temperature to 190°C (375°F/Gas 5). Strain the marinade and mix about half of it with the marmalade. Spoon this over the meat, then return the meat to the oven and roast, basting occasionally, for 20 minutes, or until done to your liking. (Venison is generally served medium rare.)

4 Transfer the venison from the oven to a warmed platter, cover loosely with foil, and rest for 10-15 minutes before carving.

5 Meanwhile, skim any excess fat from the juices, then stir in the remaining marinade. Heat until boiling, then boil rapidly for 4-5 minutes to reduce slightly. Serve the gravy with the venison.

● **Good with** lightly steamed seasonal vegetables, such as carrots, asparagus, and green beans.

Rabbit with Honey and Thyme

A readily available meat; most supermarkets now sell packs of rabbit ready to cook

 serves 4

prep 15 mins
• cook 35–40 mins

1 tbsp sunflower oil

15g (½oz) butter

800g (1¾lb) rabbit, diced

1 large onion, sliced

2 garlic cloves, crushed

200ml (7fl oz) dry cider

150ml (5fl oz) chicken stock

small bunch of thyme

salt and freshly ground black pepper

100g (3½oz) dry-cured bacon lardons or streaky bacon rashers, cut into thin strips

2 tbsp clear honey

3 tbsp wholegrain mustard

3 tbsp crème fraîche

1 Heat the oil and butter in a large, heavy frying pan or flameproof casserole and fry the rabbit quickly, until browned on all sides. Add the sliced onion and fry for a further 2–3 minutes.

2 Add the garlic and cook for 30 seconds, stirring constantly. Add the cider, bring to the boil, then stir in the stock. Remove the leaves from the thyme sprigs, discarding any tough stalks, and add to the pan. Season to taste with salt and pepper.

3 Bring back to the boil, then reduce the heat, cover, and simmer gently for 20 minutes, or until the rabbit is tender.

4 Meanwhile, heat a small frying pan, dry-fry the bacon lardons for 2–3 minutes, or until crisp, then drain on kitchen paper.

5 Stir the honey and mustard into the rabbit sauce. Just before serving, add the crème fraîche, and bring to the boil. Serve the rabbit topped with the crisp bacon.

VARIATION

Rabbit with Prunes

Add 200g (7oz) pitted prunes to the pan with the cider, increase the stock to 200ml (7fl oz), and follow the recipe. Add a squeeze of fresh lemon juice to sharpen the flavour at the end of cooking.

Ragout of Venison with Wild Mushrooms

This slowly simmered stew concentrates all the rich flavours of the venison and mushrooms

 serves 4

 prep 15 mins • cook 1¼–2 hrs

flameproof casserole

 freeze for up to 3 months; thaw completely before reheating

1 tbsp olive oil

15g (½oz) butter

4 shallots, sliced

115g (4oz) smoked bacon, diced

600g (1lb 5oz) venison, diced

1 tbsp plain flour

3 tbsp brandy

250g (9oz) wild mushrooms, sliced

250ml (9fl oz) beef stock

1 tbsp tomato purée

1 tbsp Worcestershire sauce

1 tsp dried oregano

salt and freshly ground black pepper

1 Heat the oil and butter in the casserole and fry the shallots and bacon over a medium-high heat, stirring frequently, until beginning to brown.

2 Add the venison and fry for 3–4 minutes, or until browned on all sides, stirring frequently. Stir in the flour, then cook for 1–2 minutes, or until beginning to brown.

3 Add the brandy and stir for 30 seconds, then add the mushrooms and stock. Bring to the boil, stirring often.

4 Stir in the tomato purée, Worcestershire sauce, and oregano, and season to taste with salt and pepper. Reduce the heat to low, cover tightly with a lid, and simmer very gently for 1½–2 hours, or until the venison is tender. (The cooking time will depend on the age of the meat.) Serve hot, straight from the casserole.

● **Good with** pasta, boiled rice, or potatoes.

● **Leftovers** can be reheated the next day. The flavour improves with keeping.

Bread Sauce

This classic sauce is the perfect accompaniment to roast poultry

- makes 500ml (16fl oz)
- prep 15 mins, plus standing • cook 20 mins

25g (scant 1oz) **butter**

1 **onion**, sliced

½ tsp **salt**

150ml (5fl oz) **double cream**

1 **bay leaf**

6 whole **cloves**

75g (2½oz) **white breadcrumbs**

300ml (10fl oz) **milk**

freshly ground **black pepper**

pinch of grated **nutmeg**

● **Prepare ahead** Step 1 can be prepared ahead and left to infuse, or the complete sauce can be made in advance. Cover the surface of the sauce with cling film to prevent a skin forming. Refrigerate for up to 2 days. When ready to use, remove cling film and gently reheat.

1 **Melt the butter** in a small saucepan and add the onion. Cook over a low heat for 4–5 minutes, stirring occasionally. Add the salt, cream, bay leaf, and cloves, and cook for a further 5 minutes. Remove the pan from the heat, and allow to stand for 20 minutes, so the flavours have time to infuse.

2 **Discard the bay leaf** and cloves, then pour the onion mixture into a food processor, and blend to a smooth purée. If you do not have a food processor, very finely chop the onion instead of slicing.

3 **Place the breadcrumbs** and milk in a pan, and bring to the boil. Leave to simmer for 5–10 minutes, stirring occasionally, to make a smooth, thickened sauce. (If you feel the sauce is too thick, then add a little more milk.)

4 **Stir in the onion** purée, season to taste with salt and pepper, then sprinkle with nutmeg.

● **Leftovers** can be turned into a quick savoury snack. Stir in a beaten egg and some grated cheese, pour into a greased ovenproof dish, and bake for 15–20 minutes, or until lightly golden on top.

Cumberland Sauce

This traditional sauce offers just the right combination of sweetness and citrus flavours

- serves 4–6
- prep 10 mins • cook 10–15 mins

1 **lemon**

1 **orange**

1 tsp **mustard powder**

good pinch of **cayenne pepper**

pinch of **salt**

100ml (3½fl oz) **port**

115g (4oz) **redcurrant jelly**

● **Prepare ahead** To serve cold, make up to 2 days ahead, cover, and chill in a refrigerator.

1 **Cut the zest** from half the lemon and half the orange with a potato peeler, taking care not to include the white pith. Cut the zest into very thin slivers. Bring a small saucepan of water to the boil, and blanch the strips for 5 minutes. Drain and run under cold water, to stop them cooking further.

2 **Juice the lemon** and orange, and place the juice in a small pan. Mix in the mustard, cayenne, and salt, and stir until the salt has dissolved. Add the port and redcurrant jelly, bring to the boil, and simmer for 5 minutes, or until the redcurrant jelly has melted.

3 **Strain the sauce** through a sieve into a jug, and stir in the blanched citrus zest. Reheat, if serving hot, or cover and chill if you want to serve it cold.

● **Good with** boiled gammon, deep-fried brie wedges, and vegetarian sausages.

VARIATION

Spicy Cumberland Sauce
For a slightly spicier version, add an extra pinch of cayenne pepper and a pinch each of ground cloves and ground ginger.

Béarnaise Sauce

Created in 1836, this French sauce is great with steak

 serves 4

🕐 prep 10 mins • cook 5 mins

2 small **shallots**, finely chopped

3 tbsp chopped **tarragon**

2 tbsp **white wine vinegar**

2 tbsp **white wine**

1 tsp **peppercorns**, crushed

3 **egg yolks**

200g (7oz) **unsalted butter**, softened and cubed

salt and freshly ground **black pepper**

1 tbsp **lemon juice**

1 Put the shallots, 1 tbsp tarragon, vinegar, wine, and peppercorns in a heavy non-metallic saucepan, and boil for 2 minutes, or until reduced by at least half. Strain through a sieve, and set aside to cool.

2 Put the egg yolks and 1 tbsp water in a heatproof bowl, set over a pan of barely simmering water. The bowl must not touch the water. Whisk in the cooled liquid, then whisk in the butter, a cube at a time, until it has melted and combined. Season to taste with salt, pepper, and lemon juice. Stir in the remaining tarragon, and serve immediately.

Apple Sauce

The flavour of apples contrasts well with rich meats. A family favourite, this sauce goes well with roast pork

 serves 4

🕐 prep 10 mins • cook 15 mins

❄ freeze for up to 3 months

500g (1lb 2oz) **sweet dessert apples**, such as Cox's

150ml (¼ pint) **water**

20g (¾oz) **caster sugar**

juice of ½ **lemon**

½ **cinnamon stick**

pinch of **salt**

30g (1oz) **butter**

1 Peel, core and roughly chop the apples, and place in a heavy saucepan with the water, sugar, lemon, cinnamon, and salt. Cover and cook over a medium heat, shaking the pan occasionally, for 12–15 minutes, or until the apples are tender, but not dried out. Remove the cinnamon stick.

2 Take the pan off the heat and, using a fork, beat in the butter. Serve hot or cold.

⬤ **Good with** roast pork and crackling, fried or grilled black pudding, or potato pancakes.

⬤ **Prepare ahead** This sauce will keep in the refrigerator for up to 3 days.

Cranberry Sauce

A sweet but tangy sauce traditionally served with turkey

 makes 300ml (10fl oz)

🕐 prep 5 mins • cook 15 mins

❄ freeze for up to 2 months

250g (9oz) fresh or frozen **cranberries**

1 small **shallot**, finely chopped

100g (3½oz) **light muscovado sugar**

zest and juice of 1 **orange**

4 tbsp **red wine** or port

⬤ **Prepare ahead** Can be kept refrigerated for up to 1 week.

1 Put the cranberries in a saucepan with the shallot, sugar, orange zest and juice, and red wine. Bring to the boil, stirring, until the sugar has dissolved.

2 Simmer gently for 10–12 minutes, or until the cranberries are beginning to break up.

3 Leave to cool, then transfer to a serving dish or storage jar.

⬤ **Good with** turkey, or other poultry. This sweet sauce can also be served with ice cream.

Sausagemeat Stuffing

Pork and sage is a classic and tasty combination for stuffing

 serves 4

🕐 prep 10 mins • cook 40 mins

❄ freeze for up to 2 months

2 slices **white bread** or brown bread, about 50g (2oz) in total, crusts removed

4 tbsp **stock** or milk

1 **egg**, lightly beaten

2 **shallots**, finely chopped

1 tbsp chopped **sage**, plus whole leaves to garnish

450g (1lb) **pork and apple sausages**, skins removed

salt and freshly ground **black pepper**

fresh **cranberries**, to garnish

● **Prepare ahead** The stuffing can be made up to 24 hours in advance. Cover and chill.

1 Preheat the oven to 180°C (350°F/Gas 4). Tear the bread into pieces and place in a mixing bowl. Sprinkle with the stock and allow to stand for a few minutes. Mash the soggy bread with a fork, then stir in the beaten egg.

2 Add the shallots and sage. Add the sausagemeat to the bowl and season to taste with salt and pepper. Mix until well combined.

3 Press the stuffing mixture into a greased shallow ovenproof dish and bake for 30 minutes.

4 Garnish with cranberries and serve hot.

● **Good with** poultry, or stuffed and cooked inside the bird. (Weigh the bird and calculate the cooking time accordingly.)

● **Leftovers** make great sandwich fillings, with cranberry sauce, tomato chutney, or mustard.

> ### Sausagemeat
> Use the best-quality sausagemeat or sausages you can find. This recipe uses pork and apple sausagemeat but you can use plain pork sausagemeat instead and add 1 small grated apple. This mixture is perfect for stuffing a chicken or turkey, as the fat from the sausagemeat helps to keep the bird moist during cooking.

Horseradish Sauce

This quick and easy sauce is the perfect accompaniment to roast beef or smoked fish

 makes 250ml (8fl oz)

🕐 prep 10 mins

75g (2½oz) fresh **horseradish**, grated

1 tsp made **English mustard**

1 tbsp **white wine vinegar**

1 tsp **caster sugar**

juice of ½ **lemon**

150ml (5fl oz) **double cream**

salt and freshly ground **black pepper**

● **Prepare ahead** Make the sauce a few hours in advance and chill.

1 Put all the ingredients in a large bowl and whisk to a soft peak consistency by hand or with an electric hand whisk. Season to taste with salt and pepper.

2 Spoon into a serving bowl and chill until ready to serve.

Chestnut Stuffing

Chestnuts are a traditional stuffing ingredient, and give this side dish a sweet, nutty flavour

🍴 serves 4–6

🕐 prep 10 mins • cook 30 mins

❄ freeze for up to 2 months

250g (9oz) peeled cooked chestnuts, chopped

1 tbsp olive oil

30g (1oz) butter

1 onion, chopped

75g (2½oz) pancetta, diced

115g (4oz) fresh white breadcrumbs

4 tbsp chopped parsley

salt and freshly ground black pepper

● **Prepare ahead** The stuffing can be made up to 24 hours in advance and refrigerated until ready to cook.

1 **Preheat the oven** to 180°C (350°F/Gas 4). Place the chopped chestnuts in a mixing bowl and set aside.

2 **Heat the oil** and butter in a frying pan over medium heat, add the onion and pancetta, and fry for 5 minutes, or until the onion is soft and the pancetta begins to crisp.

3 **Transfer the contents** of the pan to the bowl with the chestnuts. Add the breadcrumbs and parsley, season with salt and pepper, and mix until well combined.

4 **Press the mixture** into a greased shallow ovenproof dish and bake for 30 minutes.

● **Good with** poultry, or stuffed and cooked inside the bird. (Weigh the bird and calculate the cooking time accordingly.)

VARIATION

Chestnut Stuffing Balls
Add 1 egg, lightly beaten, to the mixture. Form into 8–12 balls, place on a greased baking tray, and bake for 30 minutes.

Cornbread Stuffing

Cornbread gives this recipe its colourful appearance. If you can't find it in the shops, make your own or use white bread instead

🍴 serves 4

🕐 prep 15 mins • cook 45 mins

❄ freeze for up to 2 months

300g (10oz) cornbread, cut into small cubes

60g (2oz) butter

1 small onion, chopped

1 celery stick, chopped

½ red pepper, deseeded and chopped

1 garlic clove, crushed

4 tbsp chopped sage

salt and freshly ground black pepper

1 egg, lightly beaten (optional)

4 tbsp chicken stock

● **Prepare ahead** The stuffing can be made up to 24 hours in advance and refrigerated until ready to cook.

1 **Preheat the oven** to 180°C (350°F/Gas 4). Place the cubes of cornbread on a baking tray and toast in the oven for 15 minutes, or until golden. Allow to cool, then transfer to a mixing bowl.

2 **Melt the butter** in a frying pan, add the onion, celery, and pepper, and fry over medium heat for 5 minutes, or until softened. Add the garlic and fry for a few more seconds.

3 **Transfer the contents** of the pan to the bowl with the bread. Stir in the sage and season to taste with salt and pepper. Add the egg (if using) and the stock, and stir until combined.

4 **Press the mixture** into a greased shallow ovenproof dish and bake for 30 minutes.

● **Good with** roast meats, especially alongside turkey.

● **Leftovers** can be chopped and sprinkled over vegetable dishes as a savoury topping.

CAKES AND DESSERTS

Hot Desserts and Puddings

Sticky Rice
A popular Thai dessert made with short-grain, "glutinous" rice
🕐 40 mins   **page 377**

Cherry Clafoutis
This French favourite can be enjoyed warm or at room temperature
🕐 55 mins –1 hr   **page 377**

Steamed Syrup Pudding
Easy to make and very satisfying to eat, this is a traditional winter treat
🕐 1 hr 50 mins   **page 379**

Chocolate Puddings
A light chocolate sponge with a creamy chocolate centre is a treat for all chocoholics
🕐 30 mins   **page 380**

Tapioca Pudding
Fruit segments and orange juice makes this subtle-flavoured dish far more lively
🕐 40 mins–1 hr   **page 381**

Bread and Butter Pudding
Buttered bread slices baked in a rich custard
🕐 55 mins   **page 382**

Baked Jam Roll
This traditional English pudding is baked for a crisper crust
🕐 40 mins   **page 382**

Sticky Toffee and Banana Pudding
A decadent winter pudding that is quick to prepare
🕐 15 mins   **page 383**

Viennese Apple Strudel
One of the most traditional Austrian desserts, famous for its delicate pastry, and delicious served warm or cold
🕐 1 hr 30 mins   **page 452**

Torrijas
A Spanish version of French toast bathed in a luscious syrup
🕐 25 mins   **page 384**

Cinnamon Pancakes with Apricots and Quark
Small, light-as-air pancakes topped with fruit
🕐 1 hr   **page 384**

Peach Gratin with Muscat Sabayon
Hot peaches topped with a delicate sauce
🕐 45 mins   **page 451**

Pineapple Fritters
Crisp and juicy fried fruit rings
🕐 30 mins   **page 451**

Baked Peaches with Marzipan and Almonds
Fragrant peaches oozing sweet juices

🕐 40 mins   **page 452**

Pears Poached in Wine
Pears gently cooked in red wine and spices, and served warm

🕐 35 mins   **page 453**

Tarte aux Pommes
A two-apple tart. It uses apples that cook down to a purée, and ones that keep their shape

🕐 30 mins   **page 454**

Tart Tatin
This caramelized upside-down apple tart is a French classic

🕐 1 hr 5 mins   **page 456**

Caramelized Autumn Fruits
This is a great way to turn plums and pears into a delicious dessert

🕐 1 hr   **page 458**

Strawberry and Orange Crêpes
Light, melt-in-the-mouth pancakes with a creamy filling make an irresistible dessert

🕐 1 hr   ❄ 3 months   **page 460**

Baked Pears in Marsala
A popular Italian dessert of poached fruit

🕐 1 hr   **page 457**

Blueberry Cobbler
A favourite summer-fruit pudding

🕐 45 mins   **page 458**

Apple Charlotte
A hot fruit dish named for a queen

🕐 1 hr 35 mins   **page 459**

Baked Sharon Fruit with Ratafia Crumbs
Persimmon-like fruit with a crunchy coating

🕐 40 mins   **page 460**

Quick Desserts

Semolina
A warm and comforting milk pudding

🕐 20 mins   **page 379**

Chocolate Puddings
A deliciously light sponge with a rich, creamy chocolate centre

🕐 30 mins   **page 380**

Zabaglione
This classic Italian egg custard can be served warm or cool

🕐 15 mins   **page 380**

Sticky Toffee and Banana Pudding
A scrumptious mix of wintertime flavours

🕐 15 mins   **page 383**

Marzipan Oranges
Perfect little sugary fruits; serve in petits fours cases for an after-dinner treat with coffee

🕐 30 mins   **page 416**

Sweet Lassi
A popular Indian dessert drink of sweetly spiced yogurt

🕐 5 mins   **page 391**

Chocolate Milkshake Float
Rich and creamy, these will delight children of all ages

🕐 10 mins   **page 402**

Pear Gratin
Sophisticated, simple, and foolproof

🕐 15 mins   **page 454**

Bananas Flambéed with Calvados
A fabulous intense dessert

🕐 20 mins   **page 455**

Stewed Plums
At their best in late summer to early autumn, plums are quick to cook

🕐 35 mins   **page 455**

Warm Fruit Compôte
An ideal winter dish when supplies of fresh fruit are limited

🕐 15–20 mins   **page 456**

Grilled Grapefruit
A perfect palette cleanser to finish a meal

🕐 20 mins   **page 461**

Baked Figs with Cinnamon and Honey
A simple-to-prepare stylish dessert

🕐 25 mins   **page 461**

Pear and Grape Salad

Cucumber isn't often added to sweet dishes, but it works perfectly in this exotic fruit salad

🕐 15–20 mins   **page 477**

Pineapple Flambé

Rings of fresh fruit flamed with rum make a smart restaurant-style dessert

🕐 25–30 mins   **page 463**

Honey-baked Apricots with Mascarpone

Canned fruit guarantees an all-year dessert

🕐 20 mins   **page 463**

Melon Cocktail

Your choice of melon balls with a simple sugar syrup and finished with fresh mint

🕐 15 mins   **page 480**

Strawberry Mousse

This speedy dessert is bound to be a favourite with the kids

🕐 15 mins   ❄ 3 months   **page 474**

Eton Mess

A quick indulgent mix of strawberries, cream, and meringue

🕐 10 mins   **page 472**

Mango and Papaya Salad

Light and refreshing fruit flavours in an exotic after dinner salad

🕐 25 mins   **page 481**

Citrus Fruit Salad

Refreshing, colourful, and full of vitamins, this pretty dessert is sunshine in a bowl

🕐 20 mins   **page 484**

Pineapple Milkshake

A fun drink for children, with no need for added sugar

🕐 5 mins   **page 485**

Berries with Citrus Syrup

Juicy seasonal berries are made even more luscious with a sweet lemon-orange syrup

🕐 15 mins   **page 478**

Desserts for a Crowd

Tartuffo
This chocolate truffle cake is rich, dark, and indulgent
🕐 20–25 mins   **page 386**

Vanilla Cheesecake
This rich yet light cheesecake is guaranteed to be a crowd pleaser
🕐 1 hr 15 mins   **page 399**

Black Forest Gâteau
Traditional cherry and chocolate flavoured cake
🕐 1 hr 35 mins ❄ 1 month   **page 414**

Lemon Meringue Pie
This lemon filling topped with vanilla-flavoured meringue is an American family favourite
🕐 1 hr 10 mins –1 hr 20 mins   **page 432**

Panforte
Classic dried fruit and nut cake from Siena, Italy
🕐 1 hr   **page 415**

Angel Food Cake
A light-as-air confection made with egg whites
🕐 1 hr 5 mins–1 hr 15 mins   **page 417**

Chocolate Almond Cake
A dense, moist cake with a rich ganache topping
🕐 55 mins ❄ 1 month   **page 415**

Prune and Almond Tart
A fabulous combination of fruit and nuts
🕐 1 hr 10 mins   **page 427**

Bienenstich
Known as Bee Sting Cake in Germany
🕐 40–45 mins   **page 418**

Blueberry Cream Cheese Tart
Juicy blueberries perfectly complement the creamy filling
🕐 55 mins–1 hr 10 mins   **page 425**

Silesian Poppy Tart
Tarts made with poppy seeds are popular in Eastern Europe
🕐 2 hrs 5 mins   **page 431**

Victoria Sponge Cake
An English classic and time-tested favourite
🕐 40–45 mins ❄ 1 month   **page 413**

Almond and Quince Tart
A tasty almond tart topped with quince cheese
🕐 1 hr 5 mins–1 hr 15 mins   **page 426**

Lemon Cheesecake

A light alternative to cheesecake, especially good for a lunchtime dessert

🕐 1 hr 50 mins   ❄ 3 months   **page 400**

Key Lime Pie

Creamy but tart lime filling in a crumb base

🕐 40-45 mins   **page 429**

Quick Carrot Cake

Always popular, this cake has a hint of spice

🕐 35-40 mins   ❄ 1 month   **page 410**

Chocolate Chiffon Pie

A satisfying contrast between a light, smooth mousse-like filling and a crunchy crumb crust

🕐 45 mins   **page 428**

Almond and Orange Cake

This cake does not need flour or butter, so is great for people on restricted diets

🕐 1 hr 10 mins   **page 411**

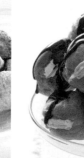

Cannoli

Crisp pastries from Sicily filled with glacé fruits and ricotta cheese

🕐 50 mins   ❄ 3 months   **page 438**

Profiteroles

Light choux pastry buns, filled with cream and drizzled with chocolate sauce

🕐 1 hr   ❄ 3 months   **page 439**

Strawberry Semifreddo

This is Italian ice cream with a twist; texture and sweetness is added by crushed meringues

🕐 20 mins   ❄ 3 months   **page 403**

Marble Cake

The marbled effect is a clever swirl of plain and chocolate batters

🕐 1 hr 30 mins   **page 411**

Lemon Tart

Ever-popular, variations of this tart always appear on restaurant menus

🕐 1 hr 20 mins   **page 431**

Easy Bakes

Madeleines
These little treats were made famous by writer Marcel Proust

🕐 15-20 mins ❄ 1 month **page 414**

Rice Pudding
A rich dish that is all the better for slow cooking

🕐 2 hrs 15 mins-2 hrs 45 mins **page 378**

Steamed Syrup Pudding
A melt-in-the-mouth traditional winter dessert

🕐 1 hr 50 mins **page 379**

Cherry Clafoutis
This French favourite can be enjoyed warm or at room temperature

🕐 1 hr 20 mins – 1 hr 30 mins **page 377**

Baked Jam Roll
A delicious raspberry filling in a crispy crust

🕐 40 mins **page 382**

Sticky Toffee and Banana Pudding
A lovely winter pudding that is quick to make

🕐 15 mins **page 383**

Quindim
This sweet, creamy and very rich dessert is a popular party dish in Brazil

🕐 40-45 mins **page 389**

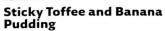

Chocolate Rice Pudding
A Portuguese version that adds chocolate to the classic dish

🕐 50 mins **page 400**

Victoria Sponge Cake
Simple cake layers spread with jam and cream

🕐 40-45 mins ❄ 1 month **page 413**

Vanilla Cheesecake
This rich yet light cheesecake is guaranteed to be a crowd pleaser

🕐 1 hr 15 mins **page 399**

Lemon Poppy Seed Muffins
Quick and easy to make, these muffins are delightful served with brunch or as a teatime treat

🕐 30 mins   **page 422**

French Almond Financiers
So-called because these cakes are said to resemble gold bars

🕐 25–30 mins   ❄ 3 months   **page 412**

Vanilla Cup Cakes
These decorative tea-time treats appeal to adults and children alike

🕐 30–35 mins   **page 419**

Raspberry Cup Cakes
Dainty minicakes that are perfect with after-dinner coffee

🕐 30–35 mins   **page 419**

Chelsea Buns
These sweet and spicy old-fashioned buns are perfect with afternoon tea

🕐 1 hr   **page 421**

Plum Crumble
Fresh fruit with a crunchy pastry topping and some pouring cream

🕐 40–50 mins   ❄ 2 months   **page 453**

Oatmeal Cookies
Great tasting and good for you, too

🕐 30 mins   **page 442**

Flapjacks
Sweet and chewy bars made from just a few storecupboard ingredients

🕐 1 hr   **page 444**

Chocolate Brownies
These walnut and chocolate treats make great snacks at any time

🕐 1 hr 25 mins   **page 445**

Gingerbread Biscuits
These delicious, spicy biscuits are quick and easy to make

🕐 40 mins   **page 445**

Apple Pie
Bramley slices in a flaky pastry case can be served hot or cold

🕐 1 hr 15 mins   **page 450**

Chocolate Muffins
Buttermilk lends a delicious lightness to these chocolatey mini-cakes

🕐 30 mins   **page 423**

Apple Crumble
Sweet dessert apples topped with a baked pastry crust

🕐 1 hr 5 mins   **page 462**

Desserts to Impress

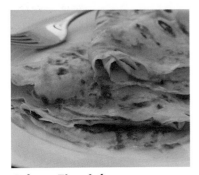

Crêpes Flambé
Crêpes in an orange sauce flamed with brandy

🕐 40 mins–55 mins   ❄ 3 months   **page 376**

Hot Orange Sweet Soufflé
Individual soufflés, flavoured with orange zest

🕐 30–35 mins   ❄ 1 month   **page 383**

Coeur a la Crème
These delicious little puddings are traditionally made in heart-shaped china moulds

🕐 20 mins   **page 385**

Raspberry Charlotte
Make the most of new season fruits with this special summer dessert

🕐 1 hr   **page 387**

Almond and Orange Cake
A carrot purée and almond base makes this a great tasting low calorie treat

🕐 1 hr 10 mins   **page 411**

Classic Pavlova
This is named after the famous Russian ballerina, Anna Pavlova

🕐 1 hr 30 mins   **page 388**

Lemon Meringue Roulade
This traditional filling is given a new twist in this impressive dessert

🕐 45 mins   ❄ 3 months   **page 389**

Floating Islands
Delicious milk-poached meringues swimming in custard

🕐 45 mins   **page 390**

Chocolate Marquise
This rich chocolate pudding has a velvety texture and is delicious served with berries

🕐 15 mins   ❄ 3 months   **page 393**

Lemon and Praline Meringue
Impressive to serve, but easy to make

🕐 2 hrs 5 mins   **page 393**

Paskha
A Russian Easter dish of cheese, candied fruits, and nuts, baked in a flowerpot

🕐 40 mins   **page 392**

Rum Babas
Buttery bakes dipped in syrup and topped with chocolatey cream

🕐 40 mins   ❄ 3 months   **page 420**

Pecan Pie
Crunchy pecan nuts in a syrupy base fill a crispy pastry shell

🕐 1 hr 45 mins   **page 425**

White Chocolate and Mascarpone Tarts
Mini berry-topped tarts are festive summer fare

🕐 25 mins   **page 430**

Red Fruit Medley
This north German dish makes a delicious, not-too-sweet dessert

🕐 15 mins   **page 471**

Sachertorte
A famous Viennese classic, this rich chocolate cake has an apricot jam filling and is coated with a glossy chocolate glaze

🕐 1 hr 25 mins–1 hr 40 mins   ❄ 3 months   **page 416**

Berry Medley
A cocktail of fresh berries coated in a sugar syrup and topped with cream

🕐 15–20 mins   **page 468**

Apple Purée
Served hot, warm, or cold, this is a simple eye-catching dessert

🕐 50–55 mins   **page 459**

Layered Fruit Platter
Spectacular summer fruits served with a rose-petal cream

🕐 15 mins   **page 472**

Pear and Grape Salad
A crisp and refreshing mix of flavours

🕐 15–20 mins   **page 477**

Red Fruit Terrine
All the flavours of summer captured in a stunning terrine

🕐 50 mins   **page 474**

Lychees in Scented Syrup
A refreshing ginger, lime, and star anise-scented fruit dessert

🕐 20 mins   ❄ 2 months   **page 475**

Summer Pudding
This classic British dessert makes the most of juicy and flavourful fresh seasonal fruit

🕐 25–30 mins   **page 476**

Cold Desserts and Puddings

Chocolate Mousse
A favourite with all the family, this creamy, rich, chocolate dessert should be served little and often

🕐 40 mins   **page 385**

Coeur a la Crème
Cheese-based puddings traditionally made in heart-shaped china moulds

🕐 20 mins   **page 385**

Classic Crème Brûlée
French for "burnt cream", this is a sophisticated caramel cream

🕐 1hr 5 mins   **page 392**

Chocolate Marquise
A rich, velvety chocolate pudding with a topping of summer berries

🕐 5 mins ❄ 3 months   **page 393**

Pannacotta with Strawberry Purée
Creamy individual moulded desserts

🕐 20 mins   **page 399**

Vanilla Creams
Chilled baked honey-flavoured vanilla cream topped with saucy cherries

🕐 50 mins   **page 401**

Buttermilk Pannacotta
A traditional Italian dessert of "cooked cream"

🕐 35 mins   **page 401**

Fruit Mousse
Fresh raspberries and blackberries blended with cream and set with gelatine

🕐 40 mins   **page 402**

Double-Chocolate Ice Cream
White chocolate chips in a rich, dark chocolate ice cream

🕐 25 mins ❄ 3 months   **page 405**

Quick Tiramisu
One of Italy's favourite desserts, this quick-to-prepare pudding gets its name, which means "pick-me-up", from the espresso coffee used to flavour the sponge layers

🕐 20 mins   **page 398**

Espresso Granita
A refreshing crystallized coffee-flavoured ice

🕐 10 mins   **page 404**

Vanilla Ice Cream
Creamy home-made ice cream, delicious with fresh berries

🕐 40 mins ❄ 3 months   **page 405**

Orange Sorbet
A lovely, light summer dessert

🕐 25 mins ❄ 3 months   **page 406**

Saffron Kulfi
An Indian iced pudding made from boiled milk

🕐 10 mins ❄ 1 month   **page 406**

Strawberry Ice Cream
Plump strawberries, coconut, rum, and lime flavour this summer favourite

🕐 15 mins ❄ 3 months   **page 407**

Cassata Gelato
This Italian-style ice-cream bombe makes an utterly irresistible dessert

🕐 35 mins ❄ 4 months   **page 407**

Pistachio Ice Cream
A deliciously nutty ice cream

🕐 40–45 mins ❄ 3 months   **page 409**

Mango Sorbet
Scoops of juicy, fragrant mangoes blended with sugar and frozen

🕐 25 mins ❄ 3 months   **page 409**

Passion Fruit Blancmange
A sweet milk pudding with an exotic passion fruit topping

🕐 25 mins   **page 468**

Sparkling Wine Jellies with Passion Fruit
A simple but impressive dessert

🕐 30 mins   **page 471**

Raspberry Soufflé
This fragrant pudding just melts in the mouth

🕐 35 mins ❄ 1 month   **page 470**

Mango and Orange Mousse
Two great fruit flavours blended with cream make for delicious summer-time eating

🕐 40 mins   **page 469**

Peach Melba
Peaches, ice cream, and a raspberry sauce make a diva-like dessert

🕐 45 mins ❄ 6 months   **page 476**

Crêpes Flambé

This twist on a classic French dessert makes a spectacular end to any dinner

serves 4

prep 25-35 mins
• cook 15-20 mins

23cm (9in) crêpe pan

the crêpes can be frozen, interleaved with greaseproof paper, for up to 3 months

For the crêpes

100g (3½oz) plain flour

2 eggs, beaten

sunflower oil or groundnut oil

pinch of salt

250ml (8fl oz) milk

butter, for frying

For the flambé sauce

60g (2oz) unsalted butter

100g (3½oz) maple syrup

juice and grated zest of 2 oranges

4 tbsp brandy or orange liqueur

● **Prepare ahead** Make the crêpes in advance, layering greaseproof paper between each one, then cover with cling film and refrigerate.

1 To make the crêpe batter, put the flour into a large bowl and make a well in the centre. Add the eggs, with oil and salt to taste, and gradually whisk in the milk to make a smooth, thin batter.

2 Heat a 23cm (9in) crêpe pan over a medium heat until hot. Add a knob of butter to coat the base evenly. Ladle in the crêpe batter to cover the base thinly, tilting the pan to spread the batter. Cook for 1-2 minutes, or until the base is golden. Flip the crêpe over and cook for a further minute, or until golden. Fold the crêpe into quarters in the pan, then remove it, set aside, and repeat to make the rest of the crêpes.

3 To prepare the flambé sauce, melt the butter in a separate pan over a medium heat. Add the maple syrup, orange juice, and zest and leave to bubble for 5 minutes, stirring, until the syrup dissolves and the sauce thickens slightly.

4 Add the crêpes one by one into the sauce. Pour the brandy into a clean ladle and tip it into a flame to ignite. Immediately pour the flaming sauce over the crêpes and serve hot.

Lemon and Sugar Crêpes

A favourite treat for breakfast, lunch or tea, these simple pancakes are a family favourite

serves 4

prep 5 mins, plus standing
• cook 10 mins

18cm (7in) crêpe pan

the crêpes can be frozen, interleaved with greaseproof paper, for up to 3 months

115g (4oz) plain flour

¼ tsp salt

1 egg

300ml (10fl oz) milk

about 3 tbsp vegetable oil for frying

lemon wedges and caster sugar, to serve

● **Prepare ahead** The crêpes can be made in advance, layered with greaseproof paper, and wrapped in cling film. Reheat in the oven before topping with lemon juice and sugar.

1 Sift the flour and salt into a large bowl and make a well in the centre. Add the egg and milk and whisk together, gradually drawing in flour from the sides, to make a smooth, thin batter. Slowly add the remaining milk, beating until smooth. Leave to stand for 10 minutes.

2 Preheat the oven to its lowest setting. Heat the crêpe pan over a high heat until hot. Pour in enough vegetable oil to coat the bottom of the pan, swirl around, then pour off the excess.

3 Ladle 3 tbsp of the batter into the centre of the pan and tilt so that it covers the base thinly. Cook the crêpe for 1-2 minutes, or until small bubbles appear. Slide a palette knife underneath and flip over, then continue cooking for 30 seconds, or until golden.

4 Remove and keep warm in the oven. Repeat until all the batter has been used.

5 Serve hot, sprinkled with sugar and lemon juice.

● **Good with** a drizzle of maple syrup, chocolate sauce, or fruit purée instead of the lemon and sugar. These pancakes can also be enjoyed with a whole range of fillings such as stewed fruit or sliced bananas.

Sticky Rice

Also known as "glutinous rice", this short, white-grained rice is used to make a popular Thai dessert

 serves 4

🕐 prep 15 mins, plus soaking overnight • cook 20–25 mins

🍱 bamboo steamer, banana leaves

200g (7oz) **sticky rice**

175ml (6oz) **coconut milk**

30g (1oz) **palm sugar** or soft light brown sugar

2 **mangoes**, peeled, stones removed and diced or sliced

1 **papaya**, deseeded and chopped

juice of 2 **limes**

● **Prepare ahead** Complete step 1 several hours in advance or the night before you cook the rice.

1 Put the rice in a bowl and add enough cold water to cover by 5cm (2in). Leave to soak for several hours or overnight.

2 Drain the rice and transfer to a steamer lined with banana leaves, muslin or another clean, close-weave cloth, spreading out the grains. Steam for 20–25 minutes, or until the rice is tender.

3 Warm the coconut milk and sugar in a saucepan until the sugar dissolves, then mix into the rice. Leave to stand for 15 minutes.

4 To serve, chop 1 mango and cut the other into slices. Place a scoop of rice on a banana leaf, with the fruit on the side. Drizzle with the lime juice.

BANANA LEAVES

These can be bought in Asian stores and should be softened before use by soaking briefly in warm water.

Cherry Clafoutis

This French favourite can be enjoyed warm or at room temperature

 serves 6

🕐 prep 12 mins, plus standing • cook 35–45 mins

🍱 25cm (10 in) flan tin

750g (1lb 10oz) **cherries**

3 tbsp **kirsch**

75g (2½oz) **caster sugar**

butter, for greasing

4 large **eggs**

1 **vanilla pod**, split

100g (3½oz) **plain flour**, sifted

300ml (10fl oz) **milk**

pinch of **salt**

1 Toss the cherries with the kirsch and 2 tbsp of the sugar in a medium-sized bowl, and leave to stand for 30 minutes.

2 Meanwhile, preheat the oven to 200°C (400°F/Gas 6). Butter the flan tin, and set aside.

3 Strain the liquid from the cherries and beat it with the eggs, the seeds from the vanilla pod and the remaining sugar. Slowly beat in the flour, then add the milk and salt and mix to make a smooth batter.

4 Arrange the cherries in the dish, then pour over the batter. Place in the oven and bake for 35–45 minutes, or until the top is browned and the centre is firm to the touch.

5 Dust with sifted icing sugar and allow to cool on a wire rack. Serve warm or at room temperature.

● **Good with** plenty of thick cream or crème fraîche for spooning over, or with vanilla ice cream.

VARIATION

Damson Clafoutis

Substitute damsons or other small plums for the cherries and add more sugar if necessary, to compensate for the tartness of the damsons.

Plum Pudding

So-named because it contains prunes, this is a classic Christmas dish
with butter instead of the traditional beef suet

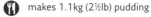 makes 1.1kg (2½lb) pudding

 prep 45 mins, plus soaking
• cook 8-10 hrs

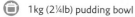 1kg (2¼lb) pudding bowl

❄ freeze for up to 1 year,
or if well sealed, keep for
up to 1 year in a cool place.

85g (3oz) **raisins**

60g (2oz) **currants**

100g (3½oz) **sultanas**

45g (1½oz) **mixed peel**, chopped

115g (4oz) **mixed dried fruit**, such
as figs, dates, and cherries

150ml (5fl oz) **beer**

1 tbsp **whisky** or brandy

finely grated zest and juice of
1 **orange**

finely grated zest and juice of
1 **lemon**

85g (3oz) **pitted prunes**, chopped

150ml (5fl oz) **cold black tea**

1 **dessert apple**, grated

115g (4oz) **butter**, melted, plus extra
for greasing

175g (6oz) **dark soft brown sugar**

1 tbsp **black treacle**

2 **eggs**, beaten

60g (2oz) **self-raising flour**

1 tsp **mixed spice**

115g (4oz) fresh **white
breadcrumbs**

60g (2oz) chopped **almonds**

● **Prepare ahead** The pudding is
best made 1–2 months in advance.
To reheat prior to serving, steam for
1½–2 hours.

1 **Put the first** 9 ingredients into
a large bowl and mix well. Put the
prunes in a small bowl and pour in
the tea. Cover the bowls, then leave
to soak overnight.

2 **Drain the prunes** and discard
the tea. Add the prunes and the
grated apple to the rest of the fruit,
followed by the melted butter, sugar,
treacle, and eggs, stirring well.

3 **Sift in the flour** with the
mixed spice, then stir in the fresh
breadcrumbs and the almonds. Mix
well until all the ingredients are
thoroughly combined.

4 **Grease the pudding bowl**
and pour the mixture into it.
Cover with 2 layers of greaseproof
paper and 1 layer of foil. Tie the layers
to the bowl with string, then put the

bowl into a pan of simmering water
so that it comes at least halfway up
the side of the bowl and steam for
8–10 hours. Check regularly to make
sure that the water level does not
drop too low. Set a timer every hour
or put a marble in the pan so it rattles
when the water level drops.

● **Good with** cream or custard.

> **STEAMING TIP**
> The steaming can be done over 2 or
> 3 days. Steam it for at least 3 hours on
> the first day and then make up the hours
> on following days. The longer the pudding
> is steamed, the darker it will become.

Rice Pudding

A rich dish that is all the better
for slow cooking

🍴 serves 4

⏱ prep 15 mins • cook 2–2½ hrs

🫕 900ml (1½ pint) ovenproof
serving dish

15g (½oz) **butter**, plus extra
for buttering

60g (2oz) **short-grain rice**, such
as Arborio

600ml (1 pint) **full-fat milk**

30g (1oz) **caster sugar**

pinch of **ground cinnamon** or
grated nutmeg

1 **Lightly butter the dish**.
Rinse the rice under cold running
water, then drain well. Pour the rice
and the milk into the dish and leave
to rest for 30 minutes.

2 **Preheat the oven** to 150°C
(300°F/Gas 2). Add the sugar,
stir, then sprinkle the top with
cinnamon or nutmeg and dot with
the butter. Bake for 2–2½ hours, or
until the skin of the rice is golden.

● **Good with** a spoonful of berry
jam or fruit purée.

VARIATION

Turkish Rice Pudding

Cook the rice in boiling water for
5 minutes, drain, then add the milk
and bring to the boil, then simmer for
15 minutes, adding a drop of vanilla
extract. Serve cooled in single servings
with ground cinnamon sprinkled over.

Semolina

This milk pudding is warm and comforting

🍴 serves 4

🕐 prep 5 mins • cook 15 mins

450ml (15fl oz) **milk**

150ml (5fl oz) **double cream**

115g (4oz) **semolina**

85g (3oz) **caster sugar**

3 tbsp **rosewater**

4 tsp **jam**, to serve

1 tbsp **boiling water**

1 **Put the milk** and cream in a saucepan and bring to the boil. Pour in the semolina in a steady stream, stirring all the time. Add the sugar. Bring to the boil and allow to simmer for 3–4 minutes. Keep stirring and, if lumps form, use a whisk to beat them.

2 **Remove from the heat.** If the mixture is too thick, add a little more milk. Pour in the rosewater and mix well.

3 **To serve,** divide the pudding between warm serving bowls. Mix the jam with 1 tbsp boiling water and drizzle over the top.

VARIATION

Baked Semolina

At the end of step 2, transfer the mixture to a buttered baking dish and bake in a moderate oven for 30 minutes, or until lightly browned.

Steamed Syrup Pudding

Easy to make and very satisfying to eat, this is a traditional winter dessert

🍴 serves 4–6

🕐 prep 20 mins • cook 1 hr 30 mins

🍲 900g (2lb) pudding bowl

115g (4oz) **butter**, plus extra for greasing

5 tbsp **golden syrup**

1 tbsp fresh **white breadcrumbs**

115g (4oz) **caster sugar**

finely grated zest of 1 **lemon**

2 **eggs**, beaten

115g (4oz) **self-raising flour**

1 tsp **ground ginger**

60ml (2fl oz) **milk**

1 **Grease the pudding bowl,** then pour in 2 tbsp syrup, and sprinkle the breadcrumbs on top. Fill a large pan, a quarter full with water, and bring to simmering point.

2 **Cream the butter** and sugar together in a mixing bowl until they are light and fluffy. Add the lemon zest, then gradually add the eggs, beating well after each addition.

3 **Sift the flour** with the ginger and fold into the mixture. Add enough milk to make a loose dropping consistency.

4 **Spoon the mixture** carefully into the pudding bowl. Cover with 2 pieces of greaseproof paper and 1 piece of foil and tie these in place with string.

5 **Put the pudding** bowl into the pan of gently simmering water, ensuring the water is not too high up the sides; cover and steam for 1 hour 30 minutes, topping up with boiling water, as necessary.

6 **Just before serving,** warm the remaining golden syrup in a small saucepan and pour over the top of the turned-out pudding.

⬤ **Good with** hot custard, cream, or vanilla ice cream.

Chocolate Puddings

A treat for all chocoholics. These simple-to-make puddings bake until a light sponge surrounds a rich, creamy chocolate centre

 serves 4

prep 10 mins • cook 20 mins

4 x 175ml (6fl oz) dariole moulds or individual pudding basins

45g (1½oz) **butter**, softened, plus extra for greasing

250g (9oz) **dark chocolate**, chopped

115g (4oz) **caster sugar**

4 **eggs**

½ tsp **pure vanilla extract**

45g (1½oz) **plain flour**

pinch of **salt**

● **Prepare ahead** Steps 1 and 2 can be prepared several hours in advance, ready for popping in the oven at the last minute.

1 Generously butter the sides and bottom of the moulds. Cut a piece of greaseproof paper to fit in the bottom of each and put in position, then butter. Set aside. Preheat the oven to 200°C (400°F/Gas 6).

2 Put the chocolate in a heatproof bowl set over a pan of simmering water, without letting the bowl touch the water, and stir for 5 minutes, or until the chocolate is melted and smooth. Set aside.

3 With an electric mixer, beat the butter and sugar until blended and smooth. Beat in the eggs one at a time, beating well after each addition, then add the vanilla. Sift the flour and salt together and gently stir in, then stir in the chocolate. Divide the batter equally between the moulds: the mixture won't fill them to the tops.

4 Put the pudding moulds on a baking tray and bake for 12–15 minutes, or until the sides are set but the centres are still soft when lightly pressed with your fingertips.

5 Put an individual serving plate on top of each pudding, then, wearing oven gloves, invert both so the pudding sits on the serving plate. Remove the lining paper. Serve the puddings hot.

● **Good with** softly whipped double cream or hot custard flavoured with grated orange zest.

● **Leftovers** can be coarsely chopped and spooned over vanilla ice cream with hot fudge sauce to make a special sundae.

CARDAMOM CHOCOLATE

Ring the changes by using some of the more exotically flavoured dark chocolate available – try cardamom and orange, or chilli-flavoured, chocolate, for example.

Zabaglione

This Italian pudding was invented by mistake in the 17th century when wine was poured into egg custard

serves 4

prep 5 mins • cook 10 mins

4 **egg yolks**

4 tbsp **caster sugar**

8 tbsp **Marsala**

finely grated zest of 1 **orange**

8 **sponge fingers** or biscotti, to serve

1 Bring a large saucepan of water to the boil, then lower the heat to simmer.

2 Put the egg yolks, sugar, Marsala, and half the orange zest into a large glass or china bowl and place on top of the pan of simmering water. Start to whisk immediately, using a balloon whisk. Keep whisking for 5–10 minutes, or until the mixture is pale, thick, fluffy, and warmed through.

3 Pour into 4 cocktail glasses and decorate with the remaining orange zest; serve immediately with sponge fingers or biscotti.

Spotted Dick

This classic British suet pudding is also known as Spotted Dog

🍴 serves 4

🕐 prep 15 mins • cook 1½–2 hrs

225g (8oz) self-raising flour, plus extra for dusting

115g (4oz) shredded suet

30g (1oz) fresh white breadcrumbs

85g (3oz) caster sugar

175g (6oz) currants

finely grated zest of 1 lemon

150ml (5fl oz) milk

hot custard, to serve (optional)

● **Prepare ahead** Once mixed, the pudding must be cooked immediately, but it can be kept, cooked, for up to 2 days and reheated before serving.

1 Combine the flour, suet, breadcrumbs, sugar, currants, and lemon zest in a large mixing bowl and mix well. Add 100ml (3½fl oz) milk and mix, using a round-bladed knife. Add more milk, if necessary, to make a dough that is soft but not too wet.

2 On a floured surface, roll the dough into an 18cm (6in) long sausage shape. Take a piece of foil and line with a piece of greaseproof paper. Fold a pleat in it. Put the dough on to the foil and wrap up, folding over the long ends of the foil, to seal. Tie the 2 short ends with string, so that it resembles a cracker.

3 Put the pudding in a steamer and steam for 1½–2 hours, ensuring that it doesn't boil dry.

4 Remove the pudding from the foil and place on a heated serving plate. Serve cut into slices, with custard, if using.

Tapioca Pudding

Fruit segments and orange juice turn this subtly flavoured dish into something far more lively

🍴 serves 4–6

🕐 prep 10 mins • cook 30–50 mins

300g can mandarin oranges in natural juice

220g can pineapple slices in natural juice

450–600ml (15fl oz–1 pint) orange juice

75g (2½oz) tapioca

4 tbsp caster sugar, or to taste

100g (3½oz) Greek-style yogurt or lightly whipped cream (optional)

freshly grated nutmeg or ground cinnamon (optional)

1 Strain the juice from the oranges and pineapple and make up to 600ml (1 pint) with orange juice and set aside. Chop the pineapple into small pieces and set aside with the mandarin segments.

2 Put the tapioca and juice in a saucepan over a high heat and bring to the boil, stirring. The liquid will be very cloudy as it comes up to the boil, but will then clear. Boil gently, stirring often and brushing down the side of the pan with a pastry brush, for 30–50 minutes, or as directed on the packet, until the small "pearls" become translucent and the mixture has thickened and is glossy.

3 Remove the pan from the heat and stir in sugar to taste. Stir the fruit into the pudding, and serve hot. Top with a spoonful of plain yogurt or whipped cream, if desired, and sprinkle with a little nutmeg or cinnamon, if using.

VARIATION

Fruity Tapioca

Cook the tapioca in the juice, allow to cool then stir in the yogurt or cream, followed by the fruit, and chill to make a mousse-like dessert.

Baked Jam Roll

This traditional English pudding was originally steamed in a cloth or shirt sleeve, but baking makes the crust crisper. You can use any jam, but raspberry works particularly well

🍴 serves 4

🕐 prep 10 mins • cook 30 mins

225g (8oz) **self-raising flour**

115g (4oz) **shredded suet**

4–6 tbsp **jam**

1 **egg**, beaten

caster sugar, to sprinkle

custard or **cream**, to serve

1 Preheat the oven to 200°C (400°F/Gas 6) and line a baking tray with greaseproof paper.

2 Put the flour and suet into a mixing bowl and add 100ml (3½fl oz) water. Using a round-bladed knife, mix to a soft but not wet dough. Add more water if necessary.

3 Put the dough on to a floured work surface and roll to a rectangle measuring 18 x 25cm (7 x 10in). Gently warm the jam in a small pan, but do not allow it to get too hot, or it will burn.

4 Spread the pastry with jam and roll up loosely. Put on to the baking tray, seam-side down, then brush with beaten egg and sprinkle with a little caster sugar. Bake in the preheated oven for 30 minutes, or until golden brown and crisp. Serve with custard or cream.

VARIATIONS

Baked Syrup Roll
Make the recipe as above, using 4–6 tbsp golden syrup, in place of the jam.

Baked Marmalade Roll
Make the recipe as above, adding the grated zest of 1 orange to the dough in step 2. Use 4–6 tbsp marmalade, in place of the jam.

Bread and Butter Pudding

Careful cooking in a low oven will produce a pudding with a smooth, velvety texture

🍴 serves 4

🕐 prep 15 mins, plus soaking • cook 40 mins

30g (1oz) **butter**, plus extra to grease

5–6 slices of day-old **bread**, crusts removed, about 175g (6oz) in total

60g (2oz) **raisins**

3 **eggs**

300ml (10fl oz) **full-fat milk**

200ml (7fl oz) **single cream**

60g (2oz) **caster sugar**

1 tsp **pure vanilla extract**

4 tbsp **apricot jam**

2–3 tsp **lemon** juice

● **Prepare ahead** The pudding needs to soak for at least 30 minutes before cooking, but can be left to soak for up to 8 hours.

1 Lightly grease an ovenproof dish with a little butter. Spread the remaining butter on the slices of bread. Cut each slice in half diagonally then in half again to form 4 triangles.

2 Place the raisins in the bottom of the dish and arrange overlapping slices of bread on the top. Beat together the eggs, milk, cream, sugar, and vanilla extract. Carefully pour the mixture over the bread and leave to soak for at least 30 minutes.

3 Preheat the oven to 180°C (350°F/Gas 4). Place the dish in a deep roasting tin and pour boiling water into the tin to a depth of 2.5cm (1in). Bake in the oven for 30–40 minutes, until still slightly moist in the centre, but not runny.

4 Meanwhile, put the jam in a small pan with the lemon juice and 1 tbsp water. Bring to the boil, then push through a sieve. Carefully brush or spoon the sieved jam over the surface of the hot pudding.

VARIATION

Fruity Bread Pudding
Instead of raisins, use different dried fruits. Try chopped apricots, peaches, or mangos; dried blueberries, cherries, or cranberries. You can also use different breads, such as brioche or panettone.

Hot Orange Sweet Soufflé

Hot soufflés are not difficult to make, but they do need a little care. This is a basic sweet soufflé, flavoured with orange zest

 serves 4

 prep 20 mins • cook 12–15 mins

4 small ramekins

freeze, uncooked, in the ramekins for up to 1 month

50g (1¾oz) **butter**, melted

60g (2oz) **caster sugar**, plus extra for dusting

45g (1½oz) **plain flour**

300ml (10fl oz) **milk**

zest of 2 **oranges**, finely grated

2 tbsp **orange juice**

3 **eggs**, separated

1 **egg white**

1 Preheat the oven to 200°C (400°F/Gas 6). Put a baking tray in the oven.

2 Brush the ramekins with melted butter, then dust their insides with sugar, making sure there are no gaps.

3 Add the flour to the remaining melted butter and cook over a low heat for 1 minute. Remove from the heat and gradually add the milk. Return to the heat and bring slowly to the boil, stirring all the time. Simmer for 1–2 minutes, then remove from the heat again and add the orange zest and juice, and all but 1 tsp of the sugar.

4 Add the egg yolks to the sauce, beating in well. Whisk the whites to medium peaks and beat in the remaining 1 tsp of sugar. Mix 1 tbsp of egg whites into the egg yolk mixture to loosen it, then fold in the rest of the egg whites.

5 Pour the mixture into the ramekins, scraping it away from the top of each dish with a small knife. Place on the hot baking tray and bake for 12–15 minutes, or until the puddings are golden and risen, but still a little runny in the centre.

Sticky Toffee and Banana Pudding

A lovely winter pudding that is as fast to prepare as it will be consumed

 serves 6

prep 5 mins • cook 10 mins

115g (4oz) **butter**

115g (4oz) **light muscovado sugar**

200ml (7fl oz) **double cream**

6 tbsp **maple syrup**

225g (8oz) **ginger cake**, sliced

2 large **bananas**

60g (2oz) **pecan nuts**, chopped

● **Prepare ahead** You can assemble the pudding several hours in advance. Toss the bananas in lemon juice first and tuck them under the cake – this will stop them going brown.

1 Preheat the oven to 190°C (375°F/Gas 5). Place the butter, sugar, cream, and maple syrup in a small pan and heat gently, stirring constantly, until smooth.

2 Lightly grease a 20 x 30cm (8 x 12in) ovenproof dish. Arrange the cake and bananas in the dish, pour the sauce over, and scatter the pecans over the top. Bake for 10 minutes, or until the toffee sauce is bubbling.

● **Good with** double cream, custard, or vanilla ice cream.

● **Leftovers** can be reheated and used to top vanilla ice cream, chopped fresh fruit, or slices of cake.

Madeira Cake and Banana Pudding

For a slightly less rich version, replace the ginger cake with 225g (8oz) madeira cake. Madeira is a slightly drier cake, so after you pour the sauce over, leave the mixture to soak for 10 minutes, then complete as above.

Torrijas

In Spain, this version of French toast is usually served as an indulgent pudding rather than as a breakfast dish

serves 4

prep 5 mins, plus standing • cook 20 mins

8 slices 1–2 day-old **baguette**

750ml (1¼ pints) **full-fat milk**

3 tbsp **caster sugar**

1 **cinnamon stick**

200ml (7fl oz) **olive oil**, for frying

3 **eggs**, beaten

4 tbsp **icing sugar**, for dusting

maple syrup, for drizzling

1 Arrange the slices of baguette in a shallow dish. Mix the milk, sugar, and cinnamon in a saucepan. Bring to the boil, stirring constantly, then pour it over the bread. Discard the cinnamon, and leave the bread to stand for 15 minutes, so that it soaks up all the milk.

2 Heat the oil in a frying pan over a medium heat. Using a fork, take a slice of the brioche, coat it in beaten egg, and place it in the frying pan. Repeat with a second slice, as quickly as possible. Fry the slices on both sides until golden, then repeat with the remaining slices, in batches.

3 Drain the fried slices on kitchen paper, arrange on a plate and, when slightly cooled, dust generously with icing sugar, and drizzle with maple syrup. Serve the slices while still warm.

Cinnamon Pancakes with Apricots and Quark

These small, light-as-air pancakes make a delicious brunch

makes 16–20

prep 30 mins • cook 30 mins

250g (9oz) **ripe apricots**, pitted and sliced

juice of 1 **lemon**

115g (4oz) **clear honey**

Quark cheese, to serve

For the pancakes

200g (7oz) **self-raising flour**

30g (1oz) **caster sugar**

½ tsp **ground cinnamon**

2 large **eggs**

200ml (7fl oz) **buttermilk**

60g (2oz) **butter**, melted, plus extra butter for greasing

 Prepare ahead You can make the glazed apricots in advance and reheat them.

1 Place the apricots, lemon juice, and honey in a pan. Simmer gently for a few minutes, or until the apricots have softened

a little, but still hold their shape. Keep warm.

2 To make the pancakes, sift the flour into a bowl and mix in the sugar and cinnamon. Beat the eggs with 4 tbsp of the buttermilk and add to the dry ingredients. Mix, then stir or whisk in the rest of the buttermilk. Stir in the melted butter.

3 Heat a non-stick frying pan and grease with a little butter. Spoon 3 or 4 tbsp of the batter into the pan, well spaced apart, and cook until lightly browned underneath with bubbles appearing on the surface.

4 Flip the pancakes over to brown the other side, then remove from the pan and keep warm in a clean tea towel while you cook the rest of the mixture, making 16–20 pancakes.

5 Serve the pancakes warm with the glazed apricots spooned over the top, and a scoop of Quark cheese alongside.

Chocolate Mousse

For the ultimate chocolate sensation, this is best made with dark chocolate containing at least 70 per cent cocoa solids

- serves 6
- prep 20 mins, plus chilling • cook 20 mins

100g (3½oz) **70 per cent dark chocolate**, broken up

1 tbsp **milk**

2 **eggs**, separated

35g (1¼oz) **caster sugar**

150ml (5fl oz) **double cream**

dark chocolate, plus extra grated or curled to serve

1 **Place the chocolate** and milk in a heatproof bowl over a pan of simmering water. When the chocolate has melted, stir until combined, remove from the heat, and allow to cool slightly.

2 **Place the egg yolks** and sugar in a large bowl and whisk until thick and creamy. Then whisk in the chocolate mixture.

3 **Whip the cream** in a bowl until stiff. Gently fold in the chocolate mixture until combined, taking care not to over mix. Whisk the egg whites until stiff, and gently fold into the chocolate mixture.

4 **Spoon into** individual dishes and refrigerate for at least 2 hours. If you like the mousse soft, take it out of the refrigerator and let it warm to room temperature before serving. Decorate with grated chocolate or chocolate curls, if liked.

● **Good with** biscotti, shortbread, or a little whipped cream.

VARIATION

Light Chocolate Mousse

For a sweeter and lighter taste, make the mousse with 50 per cent dark chocolate or milk chocolate. Top with shavings or curls of white chocolate.

Coeur a la Crème

These delicious little puddings are traditionally made in heart-shaped china moulds

- serves 4
- prep 20 mins, plus draining
- 4 coeur a la crème moulds

225g (8oz) **cottage cheese**, drained and sieved

300ml (10fl oz) **double cream**

60g (2oz) **icing sugar**

1 tsp **pure vanilla extract**

2 **egg whites**

single cream, to serve

fresh berries, to serve

● **Prepare ahead** These little pots need to drain, so it is best to make them 2–3 days in advance. Once made, they will keep chilled for up to 5 days.

1 **Mix the sieved** cottage cheese, cream, sugar, and vanilla extract together. Whisk the egg whites until they form peaks. Fold into the cheese mixture.

2 **Fill the coeur** a la crème moulds with the mixture and cover with cling film. Place in the refrigerator on a wire rack over a plate or tray to drain through the perforated holes, and leave for 2–3 days.

3 **To serve**, carefully invert the puddings on to plates. Serve with single cream and fresh berries.

● **Good with** a sharp, fruity sauce, such as raspberry coulis or a chilled mixed fruit compote.

USING RAMEKINS

Coeur a la crème moulds are available in specialist kitchen shops. You can use ramekins to make this recipe. Line each one with a disc of greaseproof paper cut to fit. Fill the dishes with the mixture and secure a piece of muslin over the top with an elastic band. Turn over on to a wire rack over a plate or tray, and leave for 2–3 days to drain, as above.

Sherry Trifle

Made with raspberries here, this versatile dessert works well with other fruits. Try strawberries, blueberries, or even canned peaches

- serves 4-6
- prep 25 mins, plus cooling and chilling • cook 10 mins
- 1.5 litre (2¾ pint) serving bowl

8 trifle sponge cakes, cut in half lengthways, or 250g (9oz) sponge cake, sliced

115g (4oz) raspberry jam

175g (6oz) raspberries

4 amaretti biscuits, crumbled

100ml (3½fl oz) Amontillado sherry

300ml (10fl oz) double cream

2 tbsp flaked almonds or grated chocolate, to decorate

For the custard

600ml (1 pint) milk

1 vanilla pod

2 tbsp caster sugar, plus 1 tsp for sprinkling

4 egg yolks

● **Prepare ahead** The trifle can be made up to 24 hours in advance, but add the cream and almonds just before serving.

1 To make the custard, pour the milk into a saucepan. Split the vanilla pod in half lengthways, scrape out the seeds, and add them to the milk, along with the sugar. Bring to just below boiling point over a low heat. Meanwhile, whisk the egg yolks in a heatproof bowl.

2 Pour the hot milk over the eggs, whisking continuously until well blended. Wash out the saucepan and half-fill with hot water. Place the pan over low heat with the bowl on top. Stir continuously with a wooden spoon until the mixture coats the back of the spoon. Remove the bowl from the heat and sprinkle the surface with 1 tsp sugar, to help prevent a skin forming, then set aside to cool.

3 Meanwhile, spread the sponge pieces with jam and sandwich together in pairs. Cut each into 2.5cm (1in) pieces and arrange in the bottom of a 1.5 litre (2¾ pint) serving bowl.

4 Add the raspberries, pushing them down into the spaces between the sponges. Sprinkle the amaretti crumbs over in an even layer, then drizzle the sherry evenly all over.

5 When the custard has cooled, spoon it over the cake and fruit and chill in the refrigerator until ready to serve.

6 Before serving, whisk the cream until thickened but not stiff and spoon it over the custard, then sprinkle with almonds.

● **Leftovers** can be served on fruit jelly, ice cream, or as an accompaniment to fruit salad.

VARIATION

Chocolate Banana Trifle
Instead of raspberry jam, use chocolate spread on the trifle sponges. Substitute 1 or 2 sliced bananas for the raspberries. When making the custard, add 200g (7oz) good quality chocolate, broken into pieces, after whisking the hot milk into the eggs. When the mixture is stirred over gentle heat, the chocolate will melt into the custard.

Tartuffo

This chocolate truffle cake is rich, dark, and indulgent

- makes 8 slices
- prep 20-25 mins, plus chilling
- 20cm (8in) springform cake tin

2 egg whites

85g (3oz) caster sugar

250g (9oz) dark chocolate, broken into pieces

300ml (10fl oz) double cream

2 tbsp brandy

6 amaretti biscuits, crushed

icing sugar, to dust

kumquats, to serve (optional)

1 Line the tin with cling film. Place the egg whites and sugar in a heatproof bowl, place over a pan of simmering water, and whisk for 5 minutes, or until thick, pale, and standing in soft peaks.

2 Melt the chocolate in a bowl over a pan of simmering water. Fold the chocolate into the egg mixture until combined. Whip the cream, then fold it in, along with the brandy. Pour into the cake tin and chill for 4-5 hours, or until set.

3 To serve, turn out on to a plate and remove the cling film. Scatter the amaretti biscuits over the top, then dust with icing sugar and serve with the kumquats, if you like.

Raspberry Charlotte

Make the most of the new season's fruits with this special summer dessert

- makes 6 slices
- prep 50 mins, plus chilling • cook 10 mins
- 20cm (8in) cake tin

18–20 sponge fingers, halved

1 vanilla pod

450ml (15fl oz) milk

45g (1½oz) caster sugar

5 egg yolks

15g (½oz) powdered gelatine

250ml (8fl oz) double cream

500g (1lb 2oz) fresh raspberries

icing sugar, for dusting

● **Prepare ahead** Refrigerate, covered, for up to 2 days.

1 Place a disc of greaseproof paper in the bottom of the cake tin. Arrange the sponge fingers, sugar-side out, around the sides of the tin.

2 Put the vanilla pod and milk in a saucepan and slowly bring to the boil. Mix the sugar with the egg yolks, pour the hot milk over the eggs, and mix well. Remove the vanilla pod and pour the custard back into the rinsed-out pan. Put over a low heat and stir until the custard thickens slightly. Sieve into a bowl.

3 Sprinkle the gelatine over 4 tbsp water in a small heatproof dish. Allow it to stand for 5 minutes, then place in a pan of hot water and stir until dissolved. Pour into the custard and mix well. Chill the custard, stirring occasionally, until it thickens. You can speed this up by placing the custard in a tin of iced water, but you must stir frequently.

4 Lightly whip the cream until thick but not too stiff. Fold it into the thickened custard and add half the raspberries. Spoon the mixture carefully into the tin and place in the refrigerator to set completely.

5 Carefully turn out the pudding onto a plate. Arrange the remaining raspberries over the top, and dust with a little icing sugar.

VARIATION

Chocolate Charlotte

Add 175g (6oz) dark chocolate to the milk before adding to the eggs. Omit the vanilla pod and raspberries, and decorate with grated chocolate.

Meringue and Rum Layer Cake

The brown sugar makes the meringue quite chewy and the flavour goes well with rum

- makes 4–6 slices
- prep 1 hr, plus chilling • cook 1 hr 35 mins

For the meringue

85g (3oz) caster sugar

85g (3oz) dark soft muscovado sugar

3 egg whites

For the filling

250g (9oz) mascarpone cheese

30g (1oz) caster sugar

115g (4oz) dark chocolate, chopped

150ml (5fl oz) double cream

3 tbsp rum

85g (3oz) toasted chopped hazelnuts

115g (4oz) can pitted black cherries, drained weight

icing sugar, for dusting

1 Preheat the oven to 130°C (250°F/Gas ½). Draw 3 x 18cm (7in) diameter circles on a piece of greaseproof paper.

2 To make the meringue, mix the sugars together. Whisk the egg whites until very stiff and gradually whisk in the sugar. Divide among the 3 circles and spread flat. Bake for 1½ hours, or until crisp and dry. Transfer to a wire rack to cool.

3 To make the filling, beat the mascarpone and sugar together in a large bowl. Melt the chocolate in a bowl over a pan of simmering water. Allow to cool for 10 minutes.

4 Stir the chocolate into the mascarpone mixture. Whip the cream until it just holds its shape, then add to the mascarpone, along with the rum, nuts, and cherries.

5 Place a meringue circle on a serving plate, spread half the filling over the meringue, and place a second meringue on top. Spread the remaining chocolate mixture over the second meringue and place the last meringue on top. Chill for at least 30 minutes, then dust with icing sugar before serving.

Classic Pavlova

The exact origin of this classic meringue dessert is unknown, but it is named after Russian ballerina Anna Pavlova and credit for inventing it is claimed by both Australia and New Zealand

🍴 makes 6 slices

🕐 prep 15 mins, plus cooling • cook 1hr 15 mins

6 **egg whites**, at room temperature

pinch of **salt**

350g (12oz) **caster sugar**

2 tsp **cornflour**

1 tsp **vinegar**

300ml (10fl oz) **double cream**

strawberries, kiwi fruit, and **passion fruit**, to decorate

● **Prepare ahead** You can make the meringue base up to a week in advance and store it in a dry, airtight tin.

1 Preheat the oven to 180°C (350°F/Gas 4). Line a baking tray with greaseproof paper. Put the egg whites in a large, clean, grease-free bowl with a pinch of salt. Whisk until stiff, then start whisking in the sugar 1 tbsp at a time, whisking well after each addition. Continue whisking until the egg whites are stiff and glossy, then whisk in the cornflour and vinegar.

2 Spoon the meringue on to the baking tray and spread to form a 20cm (8in) circle. Bake for 5 minutes, then reduce the oven to 140°C (275°F/Gas 1) and cook for a further 1 hour and 15 minutes, or until the outside is crisp. Allow it to cool completely before transferring to a serving plate.

3 Whip the cream until it holds its shape, then spoon it onto the meringue base. Decorate with the fruit and serve.

VARIATIONS

Cinnamon Pavlova

Add 2 tbsp ground cinnamon with the cornflour and vinegar. Garnish with whipped cream and strawberries, or in winter with blackberries and sautéed apples.

Nutty Pavlova

Omit the cornflour and vinegar and add 60g (2oz) coarsely ground pistachios or roasted hazelnuts. Top with whipped cream and mango or berries.

Mocha Coffee Pavlova

After whisking the meringue, fold in 3 tbsp cold strong black coffee or coffee essence, to taste. When the meringue is cooked and topped with whipped cream, drizzle 60g (2oz) of melted dark chocolate over it and finish with shavings of dark and white chocolate.

Brown Sugar Meringues

Brown sugar adds a lovely caramel flavour to the meringues

🍴 makes 36 small meringues

🕐 prep 20 mins • cook 1 hr

4 **egg whites**

200g (7oz) **soft brown sugar**

● **Prepare ahead** You can make the meringues up to a week in advance and store it in a dry, airtight tin.

1 Preheat the oven to 130°C (250°F/Gas ½). Whisk the egg whites until stiff in a clean bowl. Whisk in the sugar, 2 tbsp at a time.

2 Line 2 baking trays with greaseproof paper. Using a dessert spoon, place spoonfuls of the meringue mixture on to the trays. Bake for 1 hour, or until crisp on the outside and slightly chewy inside.

● **Good with** whipped double cream as a filling and drizzled with melted dark chocolate.

> **CRISP MERINGUES**
> To make the meringues crisp, turn the oven off and leave them inside until completely cool.

Quindim

This sweet, creamy, and very rich dessert is a popular party dish in Brazil

- serves 4
- prep 15 mins, plus chilling • cook 25-30 mins
- 4 small ramekins

100g (3½ oz) caster sugar

4 egg yolks

2 tbsp grated fresh coconut

60ml (2fl oz) coconut milk

grated fresh coconut, toasted, to serve

1 Preheat the oven to 180°C (350°F/Gas 4). Whisk the sugar and egg yolks in a bowl until light and creamy. Add the fresh coconut and coconut milk, and stir until evenly combined. Spoon into the ramekins.

2 Stand the ramekins in a roasting tin and pour in enough warm water to come halfway up the sides of the dishes.

3 Bake for 25-30 minutes, or until set. Lift the dishes out of the tin, leave to cool and then chill for at least 3-4 hours before serving.

● **Prepare ahead** Make the Quindim several hours ahead or the day before and chill until ready to serve.

Lemon Meringue Roulade

This traditional filling is given a new twist in this impressive dessert

- makes 8 slices
- prep 30 mins • cook 15 mins
- 25 x 35 cm (10 x 14in) shallow baking tin or Swiss roll tin
- freeze for up to 2 months

5 egg whites

225g (8oz) caster sugar

½ tsp white wine vinegar

1 tsp cornflour

½ tsp pure vanilla extract

250ml (8fl oz) double cream

4 tbsp ready-made lemon curd

icing sugar, for dusting

● **Prepare ahead** You can make the meringue up to a week in advance and store it in a dry, airtight tin.

1 Preheat the oven to 180°C (350°F/Gas 4) and line the baking tin with greaseproof paper.

2 Whisk the egg whites until stiff peaks form. Continue whisking at a slower speed and gradually add the caster sugar, a little at a time. Gently fold in the vinegar, cornflour, and vanilla extract.

3 Spread the mixture into the tin and bake in the centre of the oven for 15 minutes. Remove from the oven and allow to cool.

4 Meanwhile, whisk the cream until thick and fold in the lemon curd until blended.

5 Turn the cooled roulade out onto another piece of greaseproof paper and spread the lemon cream evenly over the roulade. Roll the meringue and keep covered and chilled until ready to serve.

Quarkspeise

Easy to make, this simple dessert has a soft texture and can be served with your favourite seasonal fruits

🍴 serves 4

🕐 prep 15 mins, plus chilling

225g (8oz) **Quark cheese** or curd cheese

300ml (10fl oz) **double cream**

2 tbsp **caster sugar**

2 **egg whites**

225g (8oz) **raspberries**

30g (1oz) **icing sugar**

fresh summer berries, to serve

● **Prepare ahead** You can start this dessert the day before, to allow plenty of time for the mixture to drain.

1 **Put the Quark cheese** and cream into a mixing bowl, add the caster sugar, and beat until the mixture is smooth.

2 **Whisk the egg whites** until stiff and, using a large metal spoon, fold into the cheese mixture.

3 **Line a sieve** with muslin and place over a bowl or saucepan to catch the juices. Spoon the creamed mixture into the sieve and press down with the back of a spoon, making sure there are no air pockets. Fold the muslin over the top and place in the refrigerator overnight.

4 **Blend the raspberries** and icing sugar together in a food processor, then sieve to remove the seeds. Open out the muslin and tip the cheese on to a plate. Serve with the raspberry coulis and berries.

> ### MUSLIN LININGS
> The tiny holes in the muslins allow juices to drain slowly. Buy them cut from a roll, to the size you need, or in packs already cut, from all good cookshops.

Floating Islands

In this delicious French dessert, *Iles Flottantes*, meringues poached in milk float on top of vanilla-flavoured custard

🍴 serves 4

🕐 prep 15 mins, plus standing
● cook 30 mins

450ml (15fl oz) **milk**

300ml (10fl oz) **double cream**

175g (6oz) **caster sugar**, plus 2 tsp extra

1 **vanilla pod** (optional)

2 tsp **cornflour**

4 **egg yolks**

1 tsp **pure vanilla extract**

3 **egg whites**

2 tbsp **grated chocolate**, to serve

1 **Place half the milk** in a saucepan with the cream, 2 tsp sugar, and the vanilla pod, if using. Bring to a simmer, remove from the heat, and leave to stand for 30 minutes so the flavours infuse. Remove the vanilla pod.

2 **Put the cornflour** into a bowl and mix in a little cold milk. Pour the infused milk into the bowl, stirring all the time. Put the milk back in the pan and bring to the boil, stirring constantly. Simmer for 2 minutes to cook the cornflour.

3 **Whisk the egg yolks** in a bowl and pour the hot milk over them, whisking all the time. The custard should be thick enough to coat the back of a spoon. If not, place over a gentle heat and, stirring constantly, allow it to thicken. Do not boil or it will curdle. Add the pure vanilla extract at this stage. Pour into a bowl then cover with dampened greaseproof paper to prevent a skin forming, and leave to chill.

4 **Put the remaining milk** and 300ml (10fl oz) water in a deep frying pan, bring to the boil, then reduce the heat so it simmers.

5 **Whisk the egg whites** until they form stiff peaks. Gradually whisk in the rest of the sugar to make the meringue mixture. Carefully place 3 or 4 tbsp of the meringue mixture into the simmering milk and water to cook. Do not put more than 4 at a time into the pan as they will almost double in size. Cook for 1 minute, turning once. Lift out with a slotted spoon and put on a tea towel to drain. Repeat with the remaining meringues, set aside, and let cool.

6 **Divide the custard** between serving dishes and top with 1 or 2 floating islands. Just before serving, sprinkle the islands with the grated chocolate.

Chocolate Bavarian Creams

These little individual puddings are custards, enriched with cream and set with gelatine

🍴 serves 4

🕐 prep 30 mins, plus cooling
● cook 20 mins

🗄 4 dessert moulds or ramekins

200ml (7fl oz) milk

3 egg yolks

85g (3oz) caster sugar

140g (5oz) dark chocolate, finely chopped, plus extra grated, to serve

1½ tsp gelatine

150ml (5fl oz) double cream

whipped cream, to serve

● **Prepare ahead** These puddings will keep in the refrigerator, covered, for up to 3 days, although the gelatine will toughen with keeping and is best eaten on the day.

1 Lightly oil the dessert moulds. Pour the milk in a saucepan and bring to the boiling point. Mix a little of the hot milk with the egg yolks and sugar, then stir into the remaining hot milk, stirring continuously. Cook over a low heat, stirring constantly until it thickens slightly and will coat the back of a wooden spoon. Do not allow it to boil or it will curdle.

2 Pour the custard through a sieve into a bowl and add the chocolate. Stir until the chocolate has melted. Allow to cool.

3 Put 3 tbsp cold water in a small heatproof dish and sprinkle over the gelatine. Leave to soak for 10 minutes, or until spongy in texture. Place the dish in a pan of hot water and stir until dissolved.

4 Stir the gelatine into the cooling custard. Let the custard thicken and stir occasionally until it is on the point of setting. Lightly whip the double cream until it just holds a trail when the whisk is lifted. Fold the cream into the chocolate mixture and pour into the prepared moulds. Place in the refrigerator to set.

5 To serve, dip the base of the moulds very briefly in very hot water and turn out onto a plate. Decorate with grated chocolate. Serve with whipped cream alongside.

Sweet Lassi

There is no better way of cooling down after a fiery curry than with a glass of chilled lassi

🍴 serves 4

🕐 prep 5 mins

500g (1lb 2oz) thick natural yogurt

300ml (10fl oz) milk

few drops of rosewater

1 tbsp caster sugar

4 tbsp crushed ice

few cardamom pods, crushed, to serve

1 Whisk the yogurt, milk, rosewater, and sugar together until evenly combined and foamy, then pour into tall glasses over the crushed ice. Alternatively, put the ingredients into a blender and blend until frothy.

2 Sprinkle a little cardamom over the top of each drink. Serve at once.

VARIATIONS

Salted Lassi

Make this in the same way but omit the rosewater and caster sugar. Rub the rim of each glass with a wedge of lemon or lime and dip in salt until coated. Pour in the drink and serve.

Fruit Lassi

Part or all of the milk can be replaced with an exotic fruit juice such as mango or pineapple. Instead of rosewater, you could use a few drops of vanilla or almond essence.

Classic Crème Brûlée

A classic dessert, its name is French for "burnt cream"

serves 6

prep 20 mins, plus standing • cook 45 mins

6 large ramekins

500ml (16fl oz) **double cream**

1 **vanilla pod**, split in half lengthways

5 **egg yolks**

50g (1¾oz) **caster sugar**

4 tbsp **granulated sugar**

● **Prepare ahead** You can make the puddings, without the brûlée topping, and chill for up to 2 days.

1 **Preheat the oven** to 140°C (275°F/Gas 1). Place the cream in a saucepan and add the vanilla pod. Heat the cream over a low heat until just simmering, then remove from the heat, and set aside to infuse for 1 hour.

2 **Whisk the egg yolks** and caster sugar together in a bowl until well combined. Remove the vanilla pod halves from the cream, and use the tip of a sharp knife to scrape the seeds into the cream.

3 **Whisk the cream** into the egg mixture, then strain through a sieve into a jug. Pour the mixture evenly into 6 ramekins, and place them in a roasting tin half filled with boiling water. Bake for 40 minutes, or until just set. Remove from the tin, cool, and chill.

4 **To serve**, preheat the grill to its highest setting. Sprinkle 2 tsp sugar evenly over the top of each pudding. Grill until the sugar caramelizes, then chill until required.

VARIATIONS

Fruit Brûlée

Put a spoonful of soft berries or cooked fruit (such as apricots or rhubarb) in the bottom of each ramekin before adding the cream.

Chocolate Brûlée

Replace the vanilla pod with 100g (3½oz) grated white or dark chocolate, and stir to melt.

Ginger Brûlée

Replace the vanilla pod with 3 tbsp freshly peeled and grated ginger.

Paskha

This Easter dish from Russia is traditionally made in a tall wooden container, but a new flowerpot is used here

serves 4

prep 40 mins, plus 1–3 days draining

clean new 10cm (4in) flowerpot, muslin

85ml (3fl oz) **double cream**

1 **vanilla pod**, split in half lengthways

1 **egg yolk**

45g (1½oz) **caster sugar**

60g (2oz) **unsalted butter**, softened

350g (12oz) **curd** or ricotta cheese

45g (1½oz) **candied peel**, chopped, plus extra slices to serve

45g (1½oz) **blanched almonds**, chopped

45g (1½oz) **dark chocolate**, chopped

1 **Place the cream** in a small saucepan and scrape the seeds from the vanilla pod into the cream. Heat gently until hot, but not boiling. Beat the egg yolk with the sugar in a bowl, then pour in the cream and mix well. Allow to cool.

2 **Beat the butter** and the cheese together, then beat in the cream mixture. Stir in the candied peel, almonds, and chocolate.

3 **Line the flowerpot** with a double thickness of muslin. Put the mixture into the lined mould and place on a wire rack set over a dish. Refrigerate for 1–3 days to allow the whey to drain out.

4 **When ready to serve**, turn the Paskha out on to a serving dish, and decorate with candied fruit peel slices.

● **Leftovers** can be served cold with hot fudge sauce drizzled over, or cut into chunks and mixed with ice cream or fruit salad.

Lemon and Praline Meringue

Impressive to serve at dinner parties, but quite easy to make

 serves 6

🕐 prep 35 mins • cook 1 hr 30 mins

For the meringue

3 egg whites

pinch of **salt**

175g (6oz) **caster sugar**

For the praline

60g (2oz) **granulated sugar**

60g (2oz) whole **blanched almonds**

pinch of **cream of tartar**

For the filling

150ml (5fl oz) **double cream**

3 tbsp **lemon curd**

85g (3oz) **dark chocolate**

● **Prepare ahead** You can make the meringues and the praline a day in advance, but assemble the pudding at the last minute.

1 **Preheat the oven** to 130°C (250°F/Gas ½) and line a large baking tray with greaseproof paper.

2 **Whisk the egg whites** with the salt, until stiff but not dry. Add 2 tbsp of sugar, and whisk again until smooth and shiny. Continue to add sugar, 1 tbsp at a time, whisking well after each addition. Spoon into a piping bag with a star nozzle attached, and pipe six 10cm (4in) diameter circles on to the baking-parchment lined tray. Bake for 1 hour 30 minutes, or until crisp.

3 **Meanwhile**, make the praline. Oil a baking tray and put the sugar, almonds, and cream of tartar into a small, heavy saucepan. Set the pan over a gentle heat and stir until the sugar dissolves. Boil until the syrup turns golden, then pour out on to the greased baking tray. Leave until completely cold, then coarsely chop.

4 **When ready to serve**, whip the cream until just holding a trail, and fold in the lemon curd. Melt the chocolate in a heatproof bowl over a pan of gently simmering water. Don't allow the bowl to touch the water. Spread each meringue with a little chocolate. Allow to set, then pile the lemon curd cream on top, sprinkle with praline, and serve.

Chocolate Marquise

This very rich chocolate pudding has a velvety texture and is delicious served with tart summer berries

 makes 10–12 slices

🕐 prep 15 mins, plus chilling

 900g (2lb) loaf tin

❄ freeze for up to 3 months

400g (14oz) **dark chocolate**

175g (6oz) **butter**

175g (6oz) **caster sugar**

4 tbsp **cocoa**, plus extra for dusting

6 **egg yolks**

500ml (16fl oz) **double cream**

raspberries, to serve

blueberries, to serve

● **Prepare ahead** You can make this up to 2 days in advance and freeze until required.

1 **Line the loaf tin** with cling film. Put the chocolate, butter, sugar, and cocoa in a saucepan, and melt over a very low heat, stirring.

2 **Put the egg yolks** in a bowl and pour in the melted chocolate, stirring constantly. In a separate bowl, whisk the cream until it just holds a trail. Fold into the chocolate mixture until combined.

3 **Pour into** the prepared tin. Chill in the refrigerator for 2 hours, or until set. Carefully turn out on to a plate, and remove the cling film. Using a hot knife, cut into slices and serve with raspberries, blueberries, and a sprinkling of cocoa.

● **Good with** a big bowl of mixed berries, a fruit salad, or pouring cream.

VARIATION

Individual Chocolate Marquises

You can make pretty individual desserts by spooning the mixture into individual ramekins, and chilling to set. Then pipe whipped cream on top, decorate with a few raspberries, dust with cocoa powder, and serve.

Chocolate

Dark and decadent, luscious, and rich, chocolate is universally adored, and makes undeniably tempting desserts. The impressive-looking ultimate chocolate cake (overleaf) – with its delicious combination of dark and milk chocolate ganache for filling and icing, and milk and plain chocolate curls on top – is surprisingly easy to make.

Choosing Chocolate

There is a staggering selection of chocolate available today, including familiar supermarket brands, organically grown, and those made from Fairtrade sources.

Choosing chocolate first depends on whether it is for eating or for cooking. If it is for eating, the solution is simple: buy what you're in the mood for. Bear in mind, however, plain chocolate will have fewer, if any, additional sweeteners, flavours, or dairy elements that often adds the allure to fancy boxes of chocolate. For cooking, plain chocolate is preferred because of its purity, making it predictable, and not susceptible to uncontrolled variables (such as dairy or cocoa butter replacements) when cooked.

Chocolate is made in countless flavours, styles, and qualities. The quality of chocolate is determined by the percentage of cocoa solids (including cocoa butter) against the additives, such as sugar, milk, and vanilla. A good-quality plain chocolate should contain at least 70 per cent cocoa solids. High-quality chocolate will not shatter, but makes a distinctive, clean snap when broken, and will melt quickly in warmth of your hand. The faster it melts, the higher the cocoa butter content, and the smoother the texture.

STORING TIP

To keep chocolate from melting, and fresh for as long as possible, store it tightly wrapped in its packaging or in cling film. If stored properly, in a cool, dry place, it will keep for 6 months to 1 year. Do not store chocolate for long in the refrigerator, as beads of moisture form on its surface when it comes back to room temperature.

CHOCOLATE FACTS

- All chocolate starts with the cocoa bean *Thobroma cacao*, which translates as "food of the gods".

- Spanish conquistadors introduced chocolate to Europe from Mexico in the 15th century. In fact, the word "chocolate" comes from the *xocolatl*, Aztec for "bitter water", which was an unsweetened chocolate drink spiced with chilli.

- The first chocolate bars were produced in England in the 19th century.

- Couverture chocolate, available with cocoa solids ranging from 32–85 per cent, is the type of chocolate favoured by professional bakers, because of the smooth way it melts and its rich flavour. You will find it in supermarkets and gourmet food shops.

- Cocoa powder is available unsweetened and sweetened, and it is the unsweetened variety that adds an intense chocolate hit to baked goods. Sweetened cocoa powder is best used to flavour milk.

- Never let water come into contact with melted chocolate. The merest drip of water will cause the chocolate to separate and become firm, grainy, and unusable. When melting chocolate, use a bowl that fits snugly over the pan to prevent any water or steam from coming into contact with the chocolate.

- Always use paper piping bags when piping melted chocolate. They are much better to use because they are small and easy to handle, and there is no piping nozzle to clog (which happens in a normal piping bag as the chocolate sets so quickly).

Plus 75 per cent Plain Chocolate
Dark and bitter-tasting, any chocolate with more than 75 per cent cocoa solids listed on the label is best to use for cooking, rather than eating.

Less than 75 per cent Plain Chocolate
This category contains a wide range of styles with at least 35 per cent cocoa solids, although the best quality contains the highest. The finest for eating has 70–75 per cent.

Milk Chocolate
Milk chocolate tastes milder than plain chocolate because it contains extra sugar and milk powder, so is usually saved for eating straight from the foil, but it also makes a great mousse.

White Chocolate
Although not a true chocolate, this is still popular. It is made with cocoa solids, as well as sugar, milk, and vanilla. Excellent for fondues, and for flavouring tarts and cookies.

using chocolate

Chop

Put the chocolate on a cutting board. Work the blade of a chef's knife backwards and forwards over the chocolate until it is as fine or coarse as desired.

Grate

Hold a piece of chocolate firmly against a grater, press down, and rub it down against the holes. Take the piece of chocolate to the top of the grater and repeat until you have as much grated chocolate as required.

Melt

Chop the chocolate into even-sized pieces. Place them in a dry, heatproof bowl over a pan of hot water: the bottom of the bowl must not touch the water. When the chocolate starts to melt, stir until it is smooth.

Shave

Using a vegetable peeler, slowly shave the side of a chocolate bar. The curls, or shavings, will fall from the block. Refrigerate until required.

Pipe Decorations

1 **Draw simple designs** on a piece of paper, then tape a piece of greaseproof paper on top. Make a couple of small paper piping bags. Spoon the melted chocolate into a paper piping bag, then fold over the top to seal. Keep the rest of the chocolate warm.

2 **Using light pressure**, pipe the melted chocolate onto the paper, following the design, letting the chocolate fall evenly from the tip without forcing it. Leave to cool at room temperature, or refrigerate. Once set, use a metal spatula to carefully lift from the paper.

Make Ganache

1 **Melt the chocolate** in a bowl over a pan of simmering water. Remove the pan from the heat and pour in warm cream, stirring together. The cream should not be too hot or it might cause the chocolate to seize and become grainy in texture.

2 **Continue beating** until the 2 ingredients are thoroughly blended. Thorough beating will cause the mixture to cool to a smooth glossy finish.

Make Curls

1 **Pour cooled, melted** chocolate onto a cold work surface. Using a flexible metal spatula, spread the chocolate as thinly as possible, ideally only 1.5mm (1⁄16in) thick, without leaving any holes. If the chocolate is too thick, it will not roll.

2 **When the chocolate** has cooled to the point of setting, mark it in parallel lines the width of a metal scraper. Holding the scraper at 45 degrees, with the blade firmly against the surface, gently push the scraper away from you to produce the curl.

Chocolate

1 **2** **3** **4**

Make Professional Glossy Icing

1 **Make a light, colourless** sugar syrup with 150ml (5fl oz) water with 150g (5oz) sugar. Stir in 300g (10oz) finely chopped dark chocolate until smooth. Heat the mixture to 120°C (225°F). To test, dip your fingers in iced water, then the chocolate, and pull apart – the mixture should form a "thread".

2 **Meanwhile, brush** the cake with 100g (3½oz) apricot jam melted with 4 tbsp water. When the chocolate has reached the correct temperature, remove the pan from the heat and put it on a tea towel; tap the pan to knock out any air bubbles. Ladle warm icing onto the centre of the cake.

3 **Use a warmed metal** spatula to smooth out the icing, using the minimum of strokes, and allowing the excess to flow off the cake on to a sheet of greaseproof paper underneath.

4 **Without disturbing** the cake, tap the rack gently to ensure the icing is even and free of air bubbles. Let stand for 5–10 minutes before moving.

Decadent Chocolate Desserts

Chocolate Mousse
This ultimate chocolate sensation is best when made with dark chocolate
🕐 40 mins **page 385**

White Chocolate and Mascarpone Tarts
White chocolate makes a smooth filling
🕐 45 mins **page 430**

Chocolate Bavarian Creams
These individual puddings are custards, enriched with cream and set with gelatine
🕐 50 mins **page 391**

Chocolate-dipped Fruits
Whatever the season, this decadent treat is perfect to serve with after-dinner drinks
🕐 30 mins **page 470**

Black Forest Gâteau
This rich chocolate cake is from the stunning German region of the same name
🕐 1 hr 35 mins **page 414**

Chocolate Chiffon Pie
The smooth, mousse-like chocolate filling contrasts with the crunchy crumb crust
🕐 45 mins **page 428**

Double-chocolate Ice Cream
For chocolate lovers, this dark chocolate ice cream contains white chocolate chips
🕐 35–40 mins **page 405**

Chocolate Marquise
This very rich chocolate pudding has a velvety texture and is delicious served with berries
🕐 15 mins **page 393**

VERSATILE CHOCOLATE
Easy-to-make chocolate ganache and chocolate curls transform a basic chocolate cake into an extra-special treat.

Milk Chocolate Curls (p395)

Plain Chocolate Curls (p395)

Plain Chocolate Ganache Icing (p395)

Rich Chocolate Sponge Cake (see Black Forest Gâteau sponge recipe on p414)

Milk Chocolate Ganache Filling (p395)

Crème Caramel

A classic French dessert with creamy baked egg custard and a golden caramel top

- serves 4
- prep 20 mins, plus chilling • cook 35–40 mins
- 4 x 200ml (7fl oz) ramekins

175g (6oz) **sugar**

1 **vanilla pod**

600ml (1 pint) **full-fat milk**

4 **eggs**

4 **egg yolks**

60g (2oz) **caster sugar**

1 Preheat the oven to 160°C (325°F/Gas 3). Pour boiling water into the individual ramekins and set aside. Fill a large bowl with cold water. Tip the sugar into a heavy saucepan and place over a low heat, until the sugar has just dissolved. Dip a pastry brush in water and brush the sides of the pan where any sugar crystals form. Increase the heat and boil rapidly, gently swirling the pan until the caramel is a golden-brown colour. Place the base of the pan in the bowl of cold water to rapidly cool to prevent it cooking any further.

2 Working quickly, empty the ramekins and divide the hot caramel between them. Gently swirl the dishes so that the caramel comes halfway up the sides of each ramekin. Set aside to cool.

3 Using a sharp knife, split the vanilla pod and scrape out the seeds; place both the seeds and pod in a saucepan with the milk, and heat until almost boiling. Remove from the heat and discard the pod.

4 Meanwhile, whisk the eggs, egg yolks, and caster sugar together in a large bowl. Pour the warm milk mixture over, whisking to combine, then pour into the ramekins. Place the ramekins in a roasting tin and pour boiling water into the tin to come halfway up the sides of the dishes. Bake for 25–30 minutes, or until just set in the centre. Remove from the tin, cool, then chill until ready to serve.

5 Gently pull the edges of the custard away from the sides of the ramekin using a fingertip. Place a serving plate over the top of the ramekin and invert on to the plate.

VARIATION

Ginger Crème Caramel
Infuse the milk with 2 balls of chopped stem ginger and add 4 tbsp stem ginger syrup to the custard. Serve with ginger snap biscuits.

Quick Tiramisu

One of Italy's favourite desserts, this luscious pudding gets its name, which means "pick-me-up", from the espresso coffee

- serves 4
- prep 20 mins, plus cooling and at least 4 hrs chilling

120ml (4fl oz) **cold espresso coffee**

75ml (2½fl oz) **coffee-flavoured liqueur**

350g (12oz) **mascarpone cheese**

3 tbsp **caster sugar**

360ml (12fl oz) **double cream**

14 **sponge fingers**

cocoa powder, to decorate

coarsely grated **dark chocolate**, to decorate

1 Mix the coffee and liqueur together in a shallow, wide serving bowl and set aside.

2 Put the mascarpone cheese and sugar in a bowl, and beat for a minute or two, until the sugar dissolves. Whip the cream in another bowl until it holds its shape, then fold it into the mascarpone mixture. Put a couple of spoonfuls of the mascarpone mixture in the bottom of a serving dish.

3 Dip and turn 1 sponge finger in the coffee mixture until just soaked, then place it on top of the mascarpone in the dish; repeat with 6 more sponge fingers, placing them side by side in the dish. Cover with half the remaining mascarpone mixture, then soak and layer the remaining sponge fingers. Top with the remaining mascarpone and smooth the surface. Cover the dish with cling film and refrigerate for at least 4 hours.

4 Sprinkle the top with cocoa powder and grated chocolate just before serving.

Vanilla Cheesecake

This rich yet light cheesecake is guaranteed to be a crowd pleaser

🍴 serves 10–12

🕐 prep 20 mins, plus standing and overnight chilling • cook 55 mins

🍲 23cm (9in) springform tin

60g (2oz) butter

225g (8oz) digestive biscuits, finely crushed

1 tbsp demerara sugar

675g (1½lb) full-fat cream cheese, at room temperature

4 eggs, separated

200g (7oz) caster sugar

1 tsp pure vanilla extract

500ml (16fl oz) soured cream

kiwi fruit slices, to garnish

● **Prepare ahead** The biscuit is assembled a day in advance, and chilled until ready to use.

1 Preheat the oven to 180°C (350°F/Gas 4). Lightly grease or line the base of the springform tin with greaseproof paper.

2 Melt the butter in a small saucepan over a medium heat. Add the biscuit crumbs and demerara sugar and stir until blended. Press the crumbs over the base of the tin.

3 Combine the cream cheese, egg yolks, 150g (5½oz) of the caster sugar, and the vanilla in a bowl and beat until blended. In a separate bowl, beat the egg whites until stiff. Fold the egg whites into the cream cheese mixture. Pour the mixture into the tin and smooth the top.

4 Place the tin in the oven and bake for 45 minutes, or until just set in the middle. Remove the tin from the oven and leave it to stand for 10 minutes, or until it sinks back into the tin.

5 Meanwhile, combine the soured cream and remaining sugar in a bowl, and beat until the sugar has dissolved. Pour on top of the cheesecake and smooth the surface. Increase the oven temperature to 240°C (475°F/Gas 9), return the cheesecake to the oven and continue baking for a further 5 minutes. Leave to cool completely on a wire rack, then cover and chill for at least 6 hours. When ready to serve, garnish with slices of kiwi fruit.

Pannacotta with Strawberry Purée

Strawberries are just one of the seasonal fruits that complement this creamy Italian dessert

🍴 serves 4

🕐 prep 5 mins, plus at least 3 hrs chilling

🍲 4 x 150ml (5fl oz) pudding moulds

½ sachet powdered gelatine

300ml (10fl oz) double cream

4 tbsp caster sugar

1 tsp vanilla essence

250g (9oz) strawberries, hulled, plus extra whole strawberries to decorate

● **Prepare ahead** The pannacottas can be made a day in advance and refrigerated in the pots.

1 Pour 2 tbsp water into a small heatproof bowl, sprinkle the gelatine over, and leave to stand for 3–5 minutes, or until it softens and becomes spongy. Quarter-fill a saucepan with water, bring to the boil, then remove the pan from heat. Set the bowl of gelatine in the pan, and leave until the gelatine dissolves, shaking the bowl occasionally.

2 Combine the cream and 2 tbsp sugar in another pan over a medium heat and slowly bring to a simmer, stirring until the sugar has dissolved. Turn off the heat, and stir in the vanilla, then whisk in the gelatine in a slow, steady stream. Strain the vanilla-flavoured cream into the moulds and leave to cool completely. Cover with cling film and chill for at least 3 hours until set.

3 Meanwhile, place the berries in a blender or food processor and blend to make a purée. Stir in 1–2 tbsp sugar to taste, then cover and set aside.

4 To serve, quickly dip the base of each mould in hot water. Working with 1 mould at a time, place a serving plate on top and invert, giving a gentle shake. Lift and remove the mould. Spoon the purée around each pannacotta and decorate with whole strawberries.

Lemon Poppy Seed Cheesecake with Berry Purée

A light alternative to cheesecake, especially good for a lunchtime dessert

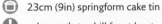 serves 6-8

🕐 prep 20 mins
   • cook 1 hr 30 mins plus cooling

💿 23cm (9in) springform cake tin

❗ cake needs to chill for at least 5 hours before serving

❄ freeze the cheesecake and sauce for up to 3 months

2 lemons

300g (10oz) **cottage cheese**

300g (10oz) **cream cheese**

250ml (8fl oz) **soured cream**

200g (7oz) **caster sugar**

3 tbsp **cornflour**

4 **eggs**

1½ tbsp **poppy seeds**

icing sugar, for dusting

strawberries and raspberries, to decorate

For the purée

250g (8oz) fresh, frozen, or preserved **berries**, such as blackberries, bilberries, raspberries, strawberries,

85g (3oz) **caster sugar**

1 Preheat the oven to 150°C (300°F/Gas 2). Grease and line the cake tin. Grate the zest from the lemons and squeeze the juice. Place the cheeses, soured cream, sugar, cornflour, lemon zest, and two-thirds of the lemon juice into a food processor and process until smooth.

2 Add the eggs and process to combine. Stir in the poppy seeds, pour the mixture into the prepared tin (the mixture should fill half to two-thirds of the tin), and bake for 1 hour 30 minutes, or until the cake is firm.

3 Meanwhile, to make the berry purée, place the berries, sugar, and remaining lemon juice in a food processor and blend until smooth. Chill, covered, until needed.

4 When the cake is done, remove from the oven and run a knife around the edge of the tin to loosen the cake and to stop the surface cracking when cooling. Let it cool in the tin on a wire rack, then chill for at least 5 hours. When ready to serve, remove from the tin, dust with icing sugar, serve with the fresh fruit, and the berry purée.

Chocolate Rice Pudding

Also known as *Arroz Doce*, this is a traditional Portuguese dessert

 serves 4-6

🕐 prep 10 mins • cook 40 mins

500g (1lb 2oz) **short-grain rice**

1 tsp **salt**

900ml (1½ pints) **full-fat milk**

1 tbsp **cocoa powder**

300g (10oz) **caster sugar**

6 **egg yolks**

4 tbsp grated **dark chocolate**

1 Bring 2 litres (3½ pints) water to the boil in a large saucepan. Add the rice and salt, bring back to the boil, reduce the heat, cover, and cook for 10 minutes, then drain.

2 Pour the milk into a saucepan and add the cocoa. Bring to the boil, then add the rice. Reduce the heat and cook, uncovered, for 30 minutes, or until the rice is soft. Add the sugar and stir until dissolved, then remove from the heat and quickly beat in the egg yolks.

3 Divide the rice between individual serving dishes, level the tops, and sprinkle with grated chocolate. Leave to cool, then serve.

VARIATION

Arroz Doce with Lemon and Cinnamon

Omit the cocoa and chocolate. In step 2, add 1 cinnamon stick and the zest of 1 lemon, peeled into strips, to the milk. Before adding the sugar and egg yolks, remove the cinnamon stick and zest. Sprinkle each serving with ¼ tsp ground cinnamon.

Vanilla Creams

Cherries make the perfect topping to vanilla cream

 serves 4

prep 10 mins, plus chilling • cook 40 mins

4 ramekins, or small ovenproof dishes

300ml (10fl oz) double cream

90ml (3fl oz) milk

1 vanilla pod, split

3 egg yolks

1 tbsp clear honey

For the compote

410g can black cherry pie filling

3 tbsp kirsch or brandy

1 **Preheat the oven** to 160°C (325°F/Gas 3). Put the cream, milk, and vanilla pod in a saucepan and bring to simmering point over a low heat. Set aside for 30 minutes.

2 **Whisk the egg yolks** and honey together. Remove the vanilla pod, reheat the cream, whisk into the egg mixture, and pour into the 4 ramekins.

3 **Place the ramekins** on a wire rack in a deep roasting tin, then add water to half-fill the tin. Cover with foil and bake for 25 minutes, or until just set. Leave to cool, then refrigerate for 4 hours.

4 **Place the cherry pie filling** in a pan with the kirsch or brandy and heat gently. Serve the chilled creams with a little of the warmed cherries spooned on top.

Buttermilk Pannacotta

This traditional dessert from the Piedmont region of Italy translates as "cooked cream" due to its smooth consistency

 serves 4

prep 30 mins, plus setting • cook 5 mins

low GI

4 ramekins, or similar individual moulds

For the pannacotta

3 gelatine leaves

200ml (7fl oz) double cream

85g (3oz) caster sugar

1 tsp vanilla essence

500ml (16fl oz) buttermilk

2 tbsp chopped pistachios, to serve

For the sauce

3 tbsp maple syrup

3 tbsp orange juice

225g (8oz) strawberries, halved

● **Prepare ahead** You can make the pannacotta and strawberry sauce up to 24 hours in advance.

1 **To make the pannacotta,** soak the gelatine leaves in cold water for 5 minutes to soften them.

2 **Place the cream** and sugar in a pan, bring to a simmer, stirring, until the sugar dissolves. Remove from the heat and stir in the vanilla.

3 **Squeeze out** the gelatine leaves and stir into the hot cream until melted. Allow to cool slightly, then stir in the buttermilk. Pour into wet ramekins or moulds, allow to cool, then chill until set.

4 **To make the sauce,** put the syrup, orange juice, and strawberries in a pan, and simmer gently for 5 minutes. Remove from the heat and purée in a food processor or blender until smooth. Chill until ready to serve.

5 **Loosen the edges** of the pannacotta and turn out onto serving plates. Pour the strawberry sauce over and scatter with the chopped pistachios.

> **USING GELATINE**
>
> Make sure the gelatine leaves melt completely before adding the buttermilk or the pudding will not set properly.

Strawberry Cheesecake

This no-cook cheesecake takes very little time to make

 serves 8-10

prep 15 mins, plus chilling

20cm (8in) round loose-bottomed flan tin

50g (1¾oz) unsalted butter

100g (3½oz) dark chocolate, broken into pieces

150g (5½oz) digestive biscuits, crushed

400g (14oz) mascarpone cheese

grated zest and juice of 2 limes

2-3 tbsp icing sugar, plus extra for dusting

225g (8oz) strawberries

● **Prepare ahead** The cheesecake can be made up to 24 hours in advance and chilled until required.

1 **Melt the butter** and chocolate in a small saucepan over a very gentle heat, and stir in the biscuit crumbs. Transfer the mixture to the flan tin and press it down firmly and evenly into the tin.

2 **Beat the mascarpone** in a bowl with the lime zest and juice. Stir in the icing sugar, to taste. Spread the cheese mixture over the biscuit base and refrigerate for at least 1 hour.

3 **To serve,** hull and halve the strawberries and arrange them over the cheesecake. Dust with icing sugar and cut into slices.

Chocolate Milkshake Float

Rich and creamy, children will adore this rich and creamy dessert drink, as it is made using their favourite ingredients

🍴 serves 4

🕐 prep 8–10 mins

85g (3oz) milk chocolate, finely chopped, plus extra flaked, to serve

150ml (5fl oz) boiling water

600ml (1 pint) milk

4 scoops chocolate ice cream

4 scoops vanilla ice cream

1 Place the chocolate in a blender or food processor, add the boiling water, and blend until completely smooth.

2 Add the milk and chocolate ice cream and blend again until thick, smooth, and creamy.

3 Pour into 4 glasses and top each with a scoop of vanilla ice cream. Sprinkle with flaked chocolate and serve immediately.

Fruit Mousse

This versatile dessert can be made with other fruit such as mangoes or passionfruit

🍴 serves 6

🕐 prep 40 mins, plus 3 hrs chilling

🍽 6 dessert glasses

2 eggs, separated

75g (2¾oz) caster sugar

60ml (2fl oz) milk

225g (8oz) mix of raspberries and blackberries, plus extra whole blackberries and blueberries, to serve

3 tsp powdered gelatine

300ml (10fl oz) double cream

● **Prepare ahead** Keep covered in the refrigerator for up to 2 days. Top with berries just before serving.

1 Combine the egg yolks, sugar, and milk in a saucepan. Stir over a low heat until slightly thickened, but do not allow to boil. Remove from the heat.

2 Put the raspberries and blackberries into a blender and blend until smooth; push through a sieve to remove pips, and stir into the egg yolk mixture.

3 Sprinkle gelatine over 3 tbsp of cold water in a small bowl and leave to set for 5 minutes, or until spongy. Then put the bowl into a shallow pan of hot water over a low heat, so low that the water is not even simmering. Ensure that the hot water does not go over the side of the bowl and leave for 5 minutes, or until the gelatine has completely dissolved. Remove the gelatine from the pan and set aside to cool.

4 Stir the fruit mixture gently and slowly drizzle the gelatine into it. Whisk the cream until soft peaks form. In a separate bowl, whisk the egg whites into soft peaks. Fold first the cream, and then the egg whites, into the fruit mixture, and pour into the dessert glasses.

5 Chill in the refrigerator for at least 3 hours or overnight, until set. Garnish with a few blackberries and blueberries to serve.

Strawberry Semifreddo

This is Italian ice cream with a twist; texture and sweetness are added by crushed meringues

serves 6-8

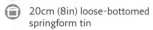
prep 20 mins, plus 6 hrs freezing

20cm (8in) loose-bottomed springform tin

freeze for up to 3 months

225g (8oz) **strawberries**, hulled, plus extra whole strawberries and **redcurrants** to decorate

250ml (8fl oz) **double cream**

50g (1¾oz) **icing sugar**

115g (4oz) **ready-made meringues**, coarsely crushed

3 tbsp **raspberry-flavoured liqueur**

For the coulis

225g (8oz) **strawberries**, hulled

30–50g (1–1¾oz) **icing sugar**

1–2 tsp **lemon juice**, brandy, grappa, or balsamic vinegar

● **Prepare ahead** You can make this dessert the day before.

1 Lightly brush the tin with vegetable oil, line the base with greaseproof paper, and set aside.

2 Purée the strawberries in a blender or food processor. Whip the cream with the icing sugar just until it holds its shape. Fold the strawberry purée and cream together, then fold in the crushed meringues and liqueur. Turn the mixture into the tin, smooth the surface, cover with cling film, and freeze for at least 6 hours or overnight if possible.

3 Meanwhile, make the strawberry coulis. Purée the strawberries in a blender or food processor, then press them through a fine sieve to remove the seeds. Stir 25g (scant 1oz) icing sugar into the purée and taste for sweetness, adding more sugar if necessary. Flavour the coulis with the lemon juice.

4 Just before serving, remove the semifreddo from the tin, peel away the lining paper, and using a warmed knife, cut into slices. Arrange the slices on individual plates, spoon the coulis around the base, and decorate with whole strawberries and redcurrants.

● **Leftovers** can be refrozen for up to 3 months.

Chocolate and Hazelnut Parfaits

These smooth, creamy frozen desserts make a spectacular end to a formal dinner party

serves 4

prep 40 mins, plus 2 hrs freezing

4 x 8cm (3¼in) metal rings

100g (3½oz) **sugar**

3 **egg yolks**

150g (5½oz) **dark chocolate**, melted

200–250g (7–9oz) **hazelnuts**, toasted and finely ground

500ml (16fl oz) **double cream**

● **Prepare ahead** The parfaits can be made up to 12 hours in advance, and stored, covered, in the freezer.

1 Place the sugar with 60ml water (2fl oz) over a low heat, stirring, until the sugar has dissolved. Bring to the boil, brushing any sugar crystals on the inside of the pan with cold water to dissolve. Cook until the syrup reaches the soft ball stage; test for this by placing a drop of the syrup into cold water, and pinching it between your fingers.

2 Whisk together the egg yolks and chocolate. Slowly add the sugar syrup to the egg and chocolate mixture, whisking until thick. Fold in 100g (3½oz) hazelnuts.

3 Whip the cream until it stands in soft peaks. Fold into the chocolate mixture, making sure that all ingredients are thoroughly mixed.

4 Place the metal rings on a baking tray lined with greaseproof paper. Tape parchment collars around the rings, ensuring that they rise 2.5cm (1in) above the rims. Divide the mixture between the rings.

5 Level the surfaces of the parfaits with a knife, then freeze for at least 2 hours, or until firm.

6 When ready to serve, remove the parchment collars, then, working quickly, briefly wrap a hot tea towel around the rings, and gently slide off. Gently press some hazelnuts around the sides of the parfaits, and add a scattering on top.

● **Good with** hot fudge sauce.

Zesty Lemon Granita

Although Italians often eat this on its own as a refreshing sweet treat on a hot day, it makes a delicious dessert after a rich main course

🍴 serves 4

🕐 prep 5–10 mins, plus cooling and at least 4 hrs freezing • cook 5 mins

📦 shallow, freezerproof non-metallic bowl

❄ freeze for up to 1 month

6 lemons

115g (4oz) caster sugar

twists of lemon zest, to decorate

● **Prepare ahead** This whole dish can be prepared a few days in advance; just freeze the serving dishes 1 hour before.

1 **Set the freezer** to its coldest setting and place freezerproof serving bowls or glasses in the freezer. Using a cannelle knife or lemon zester with a v-shaped cutter, thinly pare the zest from 4 of the lemons, and set aside, then grate the zest from the remaining 2 lemons, and set aside, separately.

2 **Dissolve the sugar** in 250ml (8fl oz) of water in a small pan over a medium heat. Increase the heat and bring to the boil, then boil for 5 minutes, or until it turns to a light syrup.

3 **Pour the syrup** into a shallow, freezerproof non-metallic bowl. Stir in the pared lemon zest and set aside to cool completely.

4 **Meanwhile**, squeeze the lemons to make about 250ml (8fl oz) of lemon juice. Remove the pared lemon zest strips from the mixture. Stir in the lemon juice and grated zest.

5 **Transfer to** the freezer for 1–2 hours, or until frozen around the edges and still slightly slushy in the middle. Every 30 minutes or so, use a fork to break up the frozen granita. Continue for 4 hours, or until the mixture has the texture of shaved ice, then leave the granita in the freezer until ready to serve.

● **Good with** a small sweet biscuit served alongside.

● **Leftovers** can be served in sugar cones or mixed with fresh fruit drinks.

Espresso Granita

The texture of granitas should be crystallized, like shaved ice

🍴 serves 4

🕐 prep 5 mins, plus cooling and freezing • cook 5 mins

📦 shallow, freezerproof dish

100g (3½oz) caster sugar

½ tsp pure vanilla extract

300ml (10fl oz) very strong espresso coffee, chilled

● **Prepare ahead** The dish can be made a few days in advance; the serving dishes should be frozen 1 hour before serving.

1 **Set the freezer** to its coldest setting and place freezerproof serving bowls or glasses in the freezer. Dissolve the sugar in 300ml (10fl oz) water in a small saucepan over a medium heat. Increase the heat and bring to the boil, then boil for 5 minutes to make a light syrup.

2 **Pour the syrup** into a shallow, freezerproof dish. Stir in the vanilla and coffee and set aside to cool completely.

3 **Transfer to the freezer.** Every 30 minutes or so, use a fork to break up the frozen chunks. Continue to do this for 4 hours, or until the mixture has the texture of shaved ice, then leave the granita in the freezer until ready to serve.

Vanilla Ice Cream

Nothing beats creamy home-made vanilla ice cream; you'll keep coming back for more

 serves 4

 prep 25 mins, plus freezing • cook 12 mins

 ice cream machine desirable

 freeze for up to 3 months

1 vanilla pod

300ml (10fl oz) milk

3 egg yolks

85g (3oz) caster sugar

300ml (10fl oz) double cream

1 **Split the vanilla pod**, scrape out the seeds, and put the seeds, vanilla pod, and milk into a heavy saucepan and bring almost to the boil. Remove from the heat, cover, and set aside for 30 minutes.

2 **Beat the egg yolks** and sugar in a large bowl. Stir in the infused milk then strain back into the pan. Cook the mixture over a low heat, stirring constantly, until the mixture thickens slightly and just coats the back of a spoon. Do not boil the mixture or the custard will curdle. Pour the mixture back into the bowl and cool completely.

3 **Whisk the cream** into the cooled custard. To freeze the ice cream by hand, pour the mixture into a freezerproof container and freeze for at least 3–4 hours, then whisk to break up any ice crystals. Freeze for a further 2 hours and repeat the process, then freeze until ready to use. To freeze using an ice cream machine, pour the mixture into the prepared freezer bowl and churn according to the manufacturer's instructions. This should take 20–30 minutes. Transfer to a freezerproof container and freeze until needed.

4 **To serve the ice cream**, remove it from the freezer 20–30 minutes prior to scooping.

● **Good with** fresh berries, or ratafia or cantucci biscuits crumbled into the base of the serving glass.

VARIATION

Coffee Ice Cream

Omit the vanilla pod and add 2 tsp of instant coffee powder or granules to the warm milk.

Double-chocolate Ice Cream

With white chocolate chips in a rich, dark chocolate ice cream, this is double-chocolate heaven

 serves 4

 prep 25 mins, plus freezing • cook 12 mins

 ice cream machine desirable

 freeze for up to 3 months

125g (4½oz) dark chocolate, roughly chopped

1 vanilla pod

300ml (10fl oz) milk

3 egg yolks

85g (3oz) caster sugar

300ml (10fl oz) double cream

175g (6oz) white chocolate chips

1 **Split the vanilla pod**, scrape out the seeds, and place both into a heavy pan over a low heat with the milk. Add the chocolate and stir gently until the chocolate has melted. Bring almost to the boil, then remove from the heat, cover, and set aside for 20 minutes.

2 **Beat the egg yolks** and sugar in a large bowl. Stir in the infused milk. then strain back into the saucepan. Cook the mixture over a low heat, stirring constantly until the mixture thickens slightly and coats the back of a spoon. It is important that the mixture does not boil, or it will curdle. Pour the thickened mixture into a bowl and allow it to cool completely.

3 **When the mixture** is cool, whisk in the cream. Pour the mixture into a freezerproof container and freeze for at least 3–4 hours, then stir. Freeze for a further 2 hours and repeat stirring. Stir in the white chocolate chips and freeze until ready to use. Alternatively, use an ice cream machine, and follow the manufacturer's instructions.

4 **Remove the ice cream** from the freezer 10–15 minutes before serving.

Orange Sorbet

Juice-based sorbets are often served in restaurants between courses as a refreshing palate cleanser. They also make a lovely, light summer dessert

- serves 4
- prep 10 mins, plus freezing • cook 15 mins
- ice cream machine desirable
- freeze for up to 3 months

2 large **oranges**

125g (4½oz) **caster sugar**

1 tbsp **orange-flower water**

1 **egg white**

1 Using a vegetable peeler, pare the zest from the oranges, taking care not to include the pith. Place the sugar and 300ml (10fl oz) water into a pan and heat gently until the sugar has dissolved. Add the orange zest and simmer gently for 10 minutes. Allow to cool slightly.

2 Squeeze the juice from the oranges, and add to the sugar mixture. To gain as much juice from your fruit as possible, warm it slightly by rolling it between your hands, or on a work surface, before squeezing.

3 Stir the orange-flower water into the orange syrup, then strain into a shallow container. In a separate, very clean bowl, whisk the egg white to soft peaks, then fold into the orange mixture.

4 If you do not have an ice cream machine, pour the mixture into a freezerproof container and freeze for at least 4 hours, or until almost frozen solid. Mash the mixture with a fork to break up any ice crystals, then freeze until solid. If using an ice cream machine, pour the mixture into the freezer compartment, and churn according to the manufacturer's instructions. Transfer to a freezerproof container and freeze until ready to use.

5 Remove the sorbet from the freezer 15–30 minutes before serving to allow it to soften slightly.

VARIATION

Lemon Sorbet

Replace the oranges with 3 lemons and make as above, omitting the orange-flower water. For a grown-up version, add 75ml (2½fl oz) Campari after you have strained the mixture. This alcoholic sorbet can be stored frozen for only up to 1 month; if you freeze it for any longer, the alcohol will become too strong.

Saffron Kulfi

Kulfi is an iced pudding made from boiled milk, and is eaten all over India. This recipe uses condensed milk for convenience

- serves 6–8
- prep 10 mins, plus freezing
- rubber ice-cube trays
- freeze for up to 1 month

pinch of **saffron threads**

1 tbsp **boiling water**

60g (2oz) **pistachios**

450g can **condensed milk**

300ml (10fl oz) **double cream**

1 Soak the saffron threads in the boiling water in a small bowl for 2 minutes. Chop the pistachios roughly, reserve a few to scatter on the top, then continue with the rest until very finely chopped.

2 Tip the condensed milk into a bowl, and add the nuts. Stir in the saffron threads and liquid.

3 Whip the cream until it holds its shape, then fold it into the milk mixture until well combined. Divide the mixture between the holes in the ice-cube tray, and place in the freezer until frozen. Once completely frozen, place the ice-cube tray in a freezer bag, and store in the freezer until needed.

4 To serve, remove from the freezer, pop the kulfi portions out of the ice-cube tray, and serve on plates, sprinkled with the reserved chopped pistachios.

Strawberry Ice Cream

Rich and creamy, this strawberry ice cream is enhanced with the tropical flavours of coconut, rum, and lime

🍴 serves 4

🕐 prep 15 mins, plus freezing

❄ after the initial freezing, the ice cream can be frozen in an airtight container for up to 3 months

400ml can **coconut milk**

200g (7oz) **white chocolate**, chopped

150g (5½oz) **strawberries**, hulled

4 tbsp **icing sugar**

300ml (10fl oz) **double cream**

2 tbsp **white rum**

finely grated zest and juice of 1 **lime**

lime wedges, to serve

strawberry halves, to serve

1 **Place the coconut milk** and chopped white chocolate into a small saucepan, and heat gently, stirring occasionally, until the chocolate has melted. Set aside and leave to cool slightly.

2 **Place the strawberries** and icing sugar into a food processor and blend to a purée. Whip the cream to soft peaks, and fold into the coconut mixture along with the strawberry purée, white rum, and lime zest and juice.

3 **Pour into** a freezerproof container and freeze for 5–6 hours, breaking up the mixture with a fork every 30 minutes, or until firm. Scoop into balls, and serve with lime wedges and strawberry halves.

Cassata Gelato

This type of Cassata uses one of Italy's favourite ingredients, ice cream, and is utterly irresistible

🍴 serves 6–8

🕐 prep 25 mins, plus 24 hrs freezing • cook 10 mins

🍲 1 x 900ml (1½ pint) and 1 x 600ml (1 pint) mixing bowl or pudding basin

❄ freeze for up to 4 months

175g (6oz) **caster sugar**

4 **egg yolks**

1 tsp **pure vanilla extract**

300ml (10fl oz) **double cream**, lightly whipped

60g (2oz) **glacé cherries**, rinsed and roughly chopped

60g (2oz) **dried apricots**, roughly chopped

60g (2oz) **dried pineapple**, roughly chopped

30g (1oz) shelled **pistachio nuts**, roughly chopped

200g (7oz) fresh **raspberries**

1 **Place the sugar** in a small saucepan together with 120ml (4fl oz) water, and bring to the boil. Boil rapidly for 5 minutes, or until thick and syrupy.

2 **Whisk the egg yolks** with an electric whisk, slowly drizzling in the hot sugar syrup, until the mixture is thick and pale. Fold in the vanilla and whipped cream. Remove a third of the mixture to a separate bowl, and stir in all the dried fruit and nuts. Cover, and chill until required.

3 **Press the raspberries** through a sieve to remove the seeds, then stir the purée into the remaining mixture. Pour into the larger mixing bowl. Place the smaller mixing bowl in the centre of the mixture, and secure in place with tape. (The raspberry mixture will be forced to rise up the sides of the pudding basin.) Freeze for at least 3–4 hours, or until firm.

4 **Remove the tape**, and pour a little hot water into the small bowl to release it. Spoon the dried fruit mixture into the centre, and level the surface. Cover, and freeze overnight.

5 **To serve**, dip the bowl into warm water for a few seconds, then invert on to a serving plate, and remove the bowl. Cut into wedges to serve.

Coffee and Pistachio Parfait

A parfait is a luxuriously smooth ice cream, flavoured with a hot sugar syrup

 serves 8

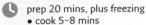 prep 20 mins, plus freezing
• cook 5–8 mins

20cm (8in) square cake tin or plastic container

freeze for up to 3 months

1 vanilla pod

225g (8oz) caster sugar

1 tbsp instant coffee granules

1 tbsp boiling water

6 egg yolks

4 tbsp Marsala

300ml (10fl oz) double cream

150ml (5½ fl oz) Greek yogurt

125g (4½oz) pistachio nuts, shelled and roughly chopped, plus extra to garnish

rose petals, to decorate (optional)

1 **Lightly oil** and line a cake tin. Split the vanilla pod, scrape the seeds into a pan, and add 100ml (3½floz) water. Stir in the sugar and heat gently until the sugar dissolves. Increase the heat and boil rapidly for 2 minutes, or until syrupy. Dissolve the coffee in the boiling water, and stir into the syrup. Set aside.

2 **In a large bowl**, beat the egg yolks and Marsala together with an electric whisk. With the whisk running, add the coffee syrup in a steady stream. Whisk for 6–8 minutes, or until thick and foamy, and at least doubled in size.

3 **Whip the cream**. Fold it into the egg mixture with the Greek yogurt and 85g (3oz) of the nuts. Pour the mixture into the lined cake tin and scatter with the remaining nuts. Freeze for 4 hours, or until firm.

4 **Dip the base of the tin** into a bowl of warm water, then remove the parfait. Cut the parfait into squares. Transfer to a baking tray, lined with greaseproof paper, and return to the freezer until ready to serve.

5 **To serve**, place the parfait on chilled serving plates. Top each square with a scatter of pistachio nuts, and garnish with rose petals, if you like.

Knickerbocker Glory

A childhood favourite, with ice cream, fruit, cream, and sauce. It is traditionally served layered in tall glasses

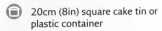 serves 4

prep 15 mins

2 peaches

8 tbsp strawberry ice cream sauce

8 small scoops strawberry ice cream

4 small scoops chocolate ice cream

150ml (5fl oz) double cream, whipped

1 tbsp sugar strands or sugar balls

4 maraschino cherries

wafer biscuits, to serve

1 **Place the peaches** in a pan of boiling water for 30 seconds to loosen the skins. Drain and halve the fruit, discarding the stones, then peel. Cut the flesh into wedges and place a few into the base of 4 tall glasses or sundae dishes. Top with a scoop of strawberry ice cream and a drizzle of strawberry sauce.

2 **Repeat the layering** with the remaining peach slices, strawberry ice cream, and strawberry sauce. Place a scoop of chocolate ice cream on top.

3 **Place a spoonful** of whipped cream to one side of the chocolate ice cream and sprinkle with sugar strands. Decorate with a maraschino cherry and serve each with wafer biscuits.

Mango Sorbet

Juicy, fragrant mangoes make this sorbet a refreshing finish to a summer meal

 serves 4

 prep 15 mins, plus freezing • cook 10 mins

 ice cream machine desirable

 freeze for up to 3 months

2 large **mangoes**

200g (7oz) **caster sugar**

juice of 1 **lemon**

1 **egg white**

1 **Cut the mango** away from each side of the stone. Discard the stone. Make evenly spaced criss-cross cuts into the flesh of the mango halves, then bend each half backwards to separate out the cubes. Cut the flesh from the skin.

2 **Place the mango flesh** in a food processor and process until smooth. Press through a sieve and chill until ready to use.

3 **Pour 300ml (10fl oz)** of water into a saucepan, add the sugar, and heat gently, stirring occasionally. When the sugar has dissolved completely, increase the heat a little and bring to the boil, stirring. Boil for 1 minute, then set aside and allow to cool completely.

4 **Stir the sugar syrup** into the mango purée, then stir in the lemon juice. Whisk the egg whites until soft peaks form, then gently fold into the mango mixture.

5 **Pour the mixture** into a freezerproof container and freeze for at least 4 hours, or until slushy. Mash with a fork to break up any ice crystals. Return to the freezer until solid. Alternatively, pour the mixture into an ice cream machine and churn according to the manufacturer's instructions. Transfer to a freezerproof container and freeze until ready to use.

6 **Transfer the sorbet** to the refrigerator for 15–30 minutes before serving. Scoop into serving dishes and serve.

● **Leftovers** can be blended with fresh mango and banana slices to make a refreshing smoothie.

Pistachio Ice Cream

The seed of an Asian tree, the pistachio nut has a hard outer shell with a distinctive soft green nutty centre

 serves 4

 prep 25–30 mins, plus freezing • cook 12–15 mins

 ice cream machine desirable

❄ freeze for up to 3 months

300ml (10fl oz) **milk**

½ tsp **almond extract**

3 **egg yolks**

85g (3oz) **caster sugar**

few drops of **green food colouring** (optional)

175g (6oz) **pistachio nuts**, shelled and roughly chopped, plus extra to decorate

300ml (10fl oz) **double cream**, lightly whipped

1 **Heat the milk** in a heavy saucepan and bring almost to the boil. Stir in the almond extract.

2 **Beat the egg yolks** and sugar in a large bowl until creamy. Stir in the milk, then strain back into the saucepan. Cook the mixture over a low heat, stirring constantly, until the mixture thickens slightly, or just coats the back of a spoon. Do not boil the mixture or the custard will curdle.

3 **Pour back into** the bowl, stir in the food colouring, if using, and the pistachio nuts, and allow to cool completely. Fold the cream into the cooled custard.

4 **To freeze the ice cream** by hand, pour the mixture into a freezerproof container and freeze for 3–4 hours, then use a fork to break up any ice crystals. Freeze for a further 2 hours and repeat the process. Freeze until ready to serve. To freeze the ice cream in an ice cream machine, pour in the mixture and churn according to the manufacturer's instructions. This should take about 20–30 minutes. Transfer to a freezerproof container and freeze until ready to serve.

5 **Remove the ice cream** from the freezer 15 minutes prior to serving. Serve scoops scattered with chopped pistachios.

Sticky Lemon Cake

The combination of fresh lemon juice and yogurt gives this cake a wonderfully fresh taste and moist texture

- makes 8 slices
- prep 15 mins, plus cooling • cook 40 mins
- 20cm (8in) deep cake tin

175g (6oz) unsalted butter

250g (9oz) caster sugar

2 lemons

3 eggs

75g (2½oz) plain flour

2 tsp baking powder

150g (5½oz) ground almonds

150g (5½oz) natural yogurt

1 **Preheat the oven** to 170°C (325°F/Gas 3). Grease the cake tin and line the base with greaseproof paper. Set aside.

2 **Cream together** the butter and 150g (5½oz) caster sugar in a large bowl. Add the grated zest from both lemons and mix together.

3 **Gradually beat in** the eggs, one at a time. If the mixture shows signs of curdling, add 1 tsp of flour.

4 **Mix the flour**, baking powder, and ground almonds together. Sift into a separate bowl, then fold into the butter and eggs. Stir in the juice of 1 lemon and the yogurt. Pour the mixture into the tin.

5 **Bake for 40 minutes** or until the centre of the cake is just firm to the touch. Do not open the oven door for the first 20 minutes.

6 **Remove the cake** from the oven and leave to cool in the tin.

7 **Heat the remaining sugar** and the juice from the remaining lemon in a saucepan. Pierce the cake several times with a skewer, then drizzle the syrup over the cake. Leave to cool before removing the cake from the tin.

Quick Carrot Cake

Always popular, this cake has a hint of spice

- makes 8 slices
- prep 15 mins, plus cooling • cook 20–25 mins
- 20cm (8in) cake tin

75g (2½oz) wholemeal self-raising flour

1 tsp ground allspice

½ tsp baking powder

½ tsp ground ginger

2 carrots, peeled and coarsely grated

75g (2½oz) soft light brown sugar

50g (1¾oz) sultanas

2 eggs, beaten

3 tbsp fresh orange juice

75g (2½oz) unsalted butter, softened

150g (5½oz) cream cheese

1 tbsp icing sugar

lemon zest, to garnish

1 **Preheat the oven** to 190°C (375°F/Gas 5). Grease the cake tin and line the base. Sift the flour, allspice, baking powder, and ginger into a large bowl, tipping in any bran left in the sieve. Add the carrots, sugar, and sultanas, then stir to mix.

2 **Add the eggs**, 1 tbsp of the orange juice, and the butter. Stir together until well blended.

3 **Stand the prepared tin** on a baking tray, pour in the cake mixture, and level the surface using a palette knife. Bake for 20 minutes, or until a skewer inserted into the centre comes out clean. Let stand in the tin for 10 minutes, to cool.

4 **Run the palette knife** around the sides, invert on to a wire rack, peel off the paper, and leave to cool. Split the cake horizontally for layers.

5 **Meanwhile**, beat the cream cheese with the remaining orange juice and sweeten to taste. Spread the icing in the centre and over the top of the cake and decorate with lemon zest.

Almond and Orange Cake

This cake does not need flour or butter, so is great for people on restricted diets

 makes 8 slices

🕐 prep 10 mins, plus cooling • cook 1 hr

🍰 20cm (8in) deep cake tin

200g (7oz) carrots, peeled

4 large eggs, separated

few drops of pure vanilla extract

1 orange

150g (5½oz) caster sugar

1 tbsp orange juice, or orange- or almond-flavoured liqueur

150g (5½oz) ground almonds

raspberries, to garnish

icing sugar, for dusting

1 **Preheat the oven** to 160°C (325°F/Gas 3). Line the cake tin with greasproof paper.

2 **Cook the carrots** in a little water until tender, then drain, cool slightly, and blend to a purée with the orange juice.

3 **Whisk the egg yolks** in a large bowl with the vanilla and grated orange zest. Gradually add the sugar, whisking until it becomes thick and pale. Fold in the carrot purée and ground almonds.

4 **In a clean, dry bowl**, whisk the egg whites until stiff, then fold them into the yolk mixture. Pour into the prepared cake tin and bake for 1 hour, or until a skewer inserted into the centre comes out clean.

5 **Cool in the tin** for 10 minutes, then transfer the cake to a wire rack and leave to cool completely. Pile on the raspberries and sift icing sugar over the top to serve.

⬤ **Good with** fresh fruit, such as raspberries, blackberries, blueberries, or redcurrants, and a spoonful of Greek yogurt or whipped cream.

Marble Cake

The marbled effect is a clever swirl of plain and chocolate batters

🍴 makes 12 slices

🕐 prep 30 mins, plus cooling • cook 1 hr

🍰 23cm (9in) kugelhopf mould or 35cm x 11cm (14in x 4½in) rectangular tin

300g (10oz) unsalted butter, softened

300g (10oz) caster sugar

few drops of pure vanilla extract

pinch of salt

5 eggs

380g (13oz) plain flour

4 tsp baking powder

4 tbsp milk

20g (¾oz) cocoa powder

icing sugar, for dusting

1 **Preheat the oven** to 180°C (350°F/Gas 4). Grease the kugelhopf mould or rectangular tin.

2 **Place the butter** in a bowl and beat until smooth. Gradually stir in the sugar, vanilla extract, and salt until thickened and smooth. Add the eggs, one at a time, whisking vigorously each time.

3 **Sift the flour** and baking powder into the butter and egg mixture in 2 stages, adding 2 tbsp of the milk in between.

4 **Spoon two-thirds** of the mixture into the prepared tin. Sift the cocoa powder into the rest of the mixture with the remaining milk. Spoon the cocoa version on top of the plain and swirl to create a marbled pattern. Bake for 1 hour, or until risen and golden brown.

5 **Leave to cool** in the tin for 10 minutes, then transfer to a wire rack. Dust with icing sugar.

KUGELHOPF MOULD

Sometimes called a Turk's head or turban pan, a kugelhopf mould is a type of fluted ring mould, with patterns resembling the fabric folds on a turban.

Stollen

This rich, fruity yeast bread, originally from Germany, is traditionally served at Christmas and makes a great alternative to Christmas cake or mince pies

 makes 1 loaf

🕐 prep 35 mins, plus overnight soaking, resting, and rising • cook 50 mins

❄ freeze for up to 1 month; thaw overnight and dust with icing sugar before serving

200g (7oz) raisins

100g (3½oz) currants

100ml (3½fl oz) rum

400g (14oz) plain flour, plus extra for dusting

7g sachet easy-blend dried yeast

60g (2oz) caster sugar

100ml (3½fl oz) milk

few drops of pure vanilla extract

pinch of salt

½ tsp ground mixed spice

2 eggs

175g (6oz) butter, softened

200g (7oz) mixed candied peel

100g (3½oz) ground almonds

icing sugar, for dusting

1 **Put the raisins** and currants into a bowl, pour over the rum, and leave to soak overnight.

2 **The following day**, sift the flour into a large bowl, make a well in the centre, sprinkle in the yeast, and add 1 tsp of the sugar. Gently heat the milk until lukewarm, and pour on top of the yeast. Leave to stand at room temperature for 15 minutes, or until frothy.

3 **Add the rest** of the sugar, the vanilla extract, salt, mixed spice, eggs, and butter. Using a wooden spoon, or hand-mixer with a dough hook, mix, then knead the ingredients together for 5 minutes, or until they form a smooth dough.

4 **Transfer to** a lightly floured work surface. Add the candied peel, soaked raisins and currants, and ground almonds to the dough, kneading for a few minutes, or until evenly incorporated. Return the dough to the bowl, cover with cling film or a damp tea towel, and leave to rise in a warm place until it has doubled in size.

5 **Preheat the oven** to 160°C (325°F/Gas 3). Line a baking tray with greaseproof paper. On a floured surface, roll out the dough to make a 30 x 25cm (12 x 10in) rectangle. Fold 1 long side over, just beyond the middle, then fold over the other long side to overlap the first, curling it over slightly on top to create the stollen shape. Transfer to the baking tray, and put in a warm place to rise again until doubled in size.

6 **Bake in the** oven for 50 minutes, or until risen and pale golden. Transfer to a wire rack to cool completely, then generously dust with icing sugar. Serve cut into thick slices, with or without butter.

⬤ **Good with** other sweet festive treats, such as marzipan sweets, or mince pies.

⬤ **Leftovers** For breakfast, serve the stollen lightly toasted, with butter.

French Almond Financiers

So-called because these cakes are said to resemble gold bars

 makes 12

🕐 prep 15 mins • cook 10-12 mins

📦 12 financier or barquette moulds, or a 12-hole cake tin

❄ freeze for up to 3 months

butter, for greasing

30g (1oz) plain flour, plus extra for dusting

60g (2oz) ground almonds

85g (3oz) icing sugar, sifted

pinch of salt

85g (3oz) unsalted butter

3 egg whites

½ tsp pure vanilla extract

1 **Preheat the oven** to 200°C (400°F/Gas 6). Grease the moulds or cake tin holes well with butter, and dust with flour.

2 **Mix the almonds**, icing sugar, flour, and salt together. Melt the butter, but do not let it get too hot. In a separate, clean bowl, whisk the egg whites until frothy, but not too thick. Add to the almond mixture with the butter and vanilla extract, and fold in.

3 **Half fill the greased** moulds, and bake in the centre of the oven for 10-12 minutes, or until they have risen a little, and are golden and springy to the touch. Allow to cool in the moulds for 5 minutes, then carefully remove and allow to cool completely on a wire rack.

Chocolate Log

A roulade with the classic pairing of dark chocolate and raspberry

 serves 10

prep 30 mins
• cook 15 mins, plus cooling

20cm x 28cm (8 x 11in)
Swiss roll tin

freeze for up to 6 months

3 eggs

85g (3oz) caster sugar

85g (3oz) plain flour

3 tbsp cocoa powder

½ tsp baking powder

icing sugar, for dusting

For the filling and icing

200ml (7fl oz) double cream

140g (5oz) dark chocolate, chopped

3 tbsp raspberry jam

1 Preheat the oven to 180°C (350°F/Gas 4). Line the Swiss roll tin with greaseproof paper.

2 In a large bowl, whisk the eggs with the sugar and 1 tbsp water for 5 minutes, or until pale and light; the mixture should hold a trail. Sift the flour, cocoa powder, and baking powder on to the beaten eggs, then carefully and quickly fold in.

3 Pour the cake mixture into the lined tin, and bake for 12 minutes. It is ready when the top is springy to the touch.

4 Meanwhile, to make the icing, pour the cream into a small saucepan, bring to the boil, then remove from the heat. Add the chopped chocolate, and leave it to melt, stirring occasionally. Allow the mixture to cool and thicken.

5 When the cake is ready, turn it out on to a new piece of greaseproof paper. Peel off the paper from the base of the cake and discard. Roll the sponge up, while still hot, keeping the paper inside. Leave to cool.

6 To assemble the log, carefully unroll the cake, and spread raspberry jam over the surface. Spread a third of the icing over the raspberry jam, and roll it up again. Place the roll on a board, seam-side down. Spread the rest of the icing all over the top, sides, and ends of the cake. Use a fork to create ridges down the length and ends of the cake. Transfer to a serving plate. Just before serving, dust with icing sugar.

Victoria Sponge Cake

An English classic and time-tested favourite

serves 8

prep 20 mins
• cook 20–25 mins

for the best results, have all your ingredients at room temperature

2 x 20cm (8in) sandwich tins

freeze for up to 1 month

175g (6oz) butter

175g (6oz) caster sugar

3 eggs, lightly beaten

175g (6oz) self-raising flour

6–8 tbsp raspberry jam

150ml (5fl oz) double cream

icing sugar, to dust

1 Preheat the oven to 190°C (375°F/Gas 5). Lightly grease and line the bottom of the tins with greaseproof paper.

2 Beat the butter and sugar together until pale and fluffy. It is important to beat the mixture well at this stage to incorporate as much air as possible, which helps prevent the eggs from curdling.

3 Add the eggs a little at a time, beating well after each addition. If the mixture begins to curdle, beat in 1–2 tbsp of the flour. Sift the flour, and fold into the egg mixture using a large metal spoon or a spatula.

4 Divide the mixture equally between the prepared tins, and spread evenly to level the tops. Bake for 20–25 minutes, until pale golden and springy to the touch. Allow the cakes to cool in the tins for 5 minutes, before turning out on to a wire rack. Peel off the lining paper, and allow to cool completely.

5 When the cakes are cool, place one upside down on a serving plate, and spread with the raspberry jam. Lightly whip the cream, until just holding its shape, and spread over the jam. Add the remaining cake, and dust lightly with icing sugar before serving.

VARIATIONS

Banoffee Toffee Cake

Spread 1 layer of the cake with 4 tbsp *dulce de leche* toffee sauce. Toss 1 large, sliced banana in 1 tbsp lemon juice, then place on top, and spread over the double cream, as above. Add the other layer, and dust with cocoa powder.

Lemon Cheesecake

Beat together 175g (6oz) low-fat soft cream cheese, the finely grated zest of 1 lemon, 2 tbsp fresh lemon juice, and 60g (2oz) icing sugar, and fill the sponges. Dust with icing sugar, and decorate with candied lemon zest, if liked.

Black Forest Gâteau

This stunning region of Germany is home to the cuckoo clock, the fairytale castle, and one of our favourite cakes, the Black Forest gateau

- serves 8
- prep 55 mins • cook 40 mins
- 23cm (9in) springform cake tin; piping bag
- freeze for up to 1 month; defrost for 5-6 hours in the fridge

6 eggs

175g (6oz) golden caster sugar

125g (4½oz) plain flour

50g (1¾oz) cocoa powder

1 tsp pure vanilla extract

85g (3oz) butter, melted

600ml (1 pint) double cream

2 x 425g can pitted black cherries

4 tbsp Kirsch

150g (5½oz) dark chocolate, grated

● **Prepare ahead** The cake can be made up to 3 days in advance. Store in the refrigerator until ready to serve.

1 Preheat the oven to 180°C (350°F/Gas 4). Lightly grease and line the bottom of the tin with greaseproof paper. Put the eggs and sugar into a large heatproof bowl, and place over a saucepan filled with simmering water. Don't let the bowl touch the water. Whisk until the mixture is pale and thick, and will hold a trail. Remove from the heat and whisk for another 5 minutes, or until cooled slightly.

2 Sift the flour and cocoa together and fold into the egg mixture using a large metal spoon or a spatula. Fold in the vanilla and butter. Transfer to the prepared tin and level the surface. Bake in the oven for 40 minutes, or until risen and just shrinking away a little from the sides. Turn it out on to a wire rack, discard the lining paper, and cover with a clean cloth. Allow the cake to cool completely.

3 Carefully cut the cake into three layers. Drain 1 can of cherries, placing 6 tbsp of the juice into a bowl with the Kirsch. Roughly chop the drained cherries. Drizzle a third of the Kirsch and cherry syrup over each layer of sponge.

4 Whip the cream until it just holds its shape. Place 1 layer of the cake on to a serving plate. Spread a thin layer of cream over the top of the sponge, and scatter with half the chopped cherries. Repeat with layers and top with the final layer of sponge. Using a palette knife, spread a thin layer of cream around the edges of the cake to cover, and spoon the remaining cream into a piping bag fitted with a star-shaped nozzle.

5 Using a spoon or a palette knife, press the grated chocolate onto the side of the cake. Pipe swirls of cream around the top edge of the cake. Drain the second tin of cherries and use them to fill the centre of the cake. Scatter any remaining chocolate over the piped cream.

Madeleines

These little treats were made famous by writer Marcel Proust

- makes 12
- prep 15-20 mins • cook 10 mins
- madeleine tin or 12-hole bun tins
- freeze for up to 1 month

60g (2oz) butter, melted but not hot, plus extra for greasing

60g (2oz) caster sugar

2 eggs

1 tsp pure vanilla extract

60g (2oz) self-raising flour, sifted

icing sugar, to dust

1 Preheat the oven to 180°C (350°F/Gas 4). Carefully brush the moulds with melted butter and dust with flour.

2 Put the sugar, eggs, and vanilla extract into a mixing bowl and whisk until the mixture is pale, thick, and will hold a trail. This should take 5 minutes with an electric whisk, or slightly longer if you are using a hand whisk.

3 Sift the flour over the top and pour the melted butter down the side of the mixture. Using a large metal spoon, fold them in carefully and quickly, being careful not to knock out any air.

4 Fill the moulds with the mixture and bake in the oven for 10 minutes. Remove from the oven and transfer to a wire rack to cool, before dusting with icing sugar.

Chocolate Almond Cake

A dense, moist cake with a rich ganache topping

 serves 6–8

 prep 30 mins • cook 25 mins

 18cm (7in) loose-bottomed cake tin

 freeze for up to 1 month

plain flour, to dust

115g (4oz) dark chocolate, broken into pieces

115g (4oz) butter, softened

140g (5oz) caster sugar

3 eggs, separated

60g (2oz) ground almonds

30g (1oz) white breadcrumbs

½ tsp baking powder

1 tsp almond extract

1 tbsp brandy or rum (optional)

For the ganache

115g (4oz) plain chocolate

60g (2oz) butter

1 Preheat the oven to 180°C (350°F/Gas 4). Grease the tin and line the bottom of the tin with baking parchment, then dust with plain flour.

2 Place the chocolate pieces in a heatproof bowl over a saucepan of simmering water, melt the chocolate, stirring occasionally. Don't let the bowl touch the water. Set aside.

3 Beat the butter and sugar together until pale and creamy. Add the egg yolks one at a time, beating well after each addition. Beat in the chocolate. Add the almonds, breadcrumbs, baking powder, almond extract, and brandy, if using, and fold in gently with a metal spoon.

4 Whisk the egg whites in a large clean bowl until soft peaks form. Fold into the cake mixture, then spoon into the tin.

5 Bake for 25 minutes, or until a skewer inserted into the centre comes out clean. Remove from the oven and cool on a wire rack.

6 To make the ganache, melt the chocolate and butter together in a bowl over a saucepan of simmering water, stirring to combine. Remove from the heat and cool slightly. Using a palette knife, spread the ganache over the top of the cake. Allow to set.

Panforte

This famous cake from Siena, Italy, dates from the 13th century

 serves 12–16

prep 30 mins • cook 30 mins

20cm (8in) loose-bottomed cake tin

rice paper, for lining

115g (4oz) whole blanched almonds, toasted and roughly chopped

125g (4½oz) hazelnuts, toasted and roughly chopped

200g (7oz) mixed candied orange and lemon peel, chopped

115g (4oz) dried figs, roughly chopped

finely grated zest of 1 lemon

½ tsp ground cinnamon

½ tsp freshly grated nutmeg

¼ tsp ground cloves

¼ tsp ground allspice

75g (2½oz) rice flour or plain flour

30g (1oz) unsalted butter

140g (5oz) caster sugar

4 tbsp clear honey

icing sugar, to dust

● **Prepare ahead** You can make this up to 3 days in advance and store it in an airtight container.

1 Line the base and sides of the cake tin with baking parchment, then put a disc of rice paper on top of the parchment. Preheat the oven to 180°C (350°F/Gas 4).

2 Put the almonds, hazelnuts, candied peel, figs, lemon zest, cinnamon, nutmeg, cloves, allspice, and flour in a large bowl and mix well.

3 Put the butter, caster sugar, and honey in a pan and heat gently until melted. Pour into the fruit and nut mixture and stir to combine. Spoon into the prepared tin and, with damp hands, press down to create a smooth, even layer.

4 Bake for 30 minutes, then remove from the oven, leaving it in the tin to cool and become firm. When completely cold, remove the panforte from the tin. Peel off the parchment but leave the rice paper stuck to the bottom of the cake.

5 Dust heavily with icing sugar and serve cut into small wedges.

Sachertorte

This rich chocolate cake was invented in 1832 by Franz Sacher, a 16-year-old apprentice pastry chef at the court of Prince Klemens von Metternich in Vienna, Austria

- serves 8–12
- prep 40 mins, plus cooling • cook 45–60 mins
- 23cm (9in) round cake tin; piping bag
- freeze, undecorated, for up to 3 months

250g (9oz) **butter**, softened

250g (9oz) **caster sugar**

250g (9oz) **dark chocolate**, melted

½ tsp **pure vanilla extract**

5 **eggs**, separated

250g (9oz) **plain flour**

6–8 tbsp **apricot glaze**, or sieved apricot jam

For the chocolate glaze

300ml (10fl oz) **whipping cream**

200g (7oz) **dark chocolate**, chopped

few drops of **pure vanilla extract**

1 Preheat the oven to 180°C (350°F/Gas 4). Line the cake tin with greaseproof paper.

2 To make the cake, beat together the butter and the sugar until the mixture is light and fluffy, then beat in the chocolate and vanilla extract. Beat in the egg yolks, one at a time, then fold in the plain flour.

3 In a separate, clean large bowl, whisk the egg whites until stiff. Spoon a little of the egg whites into the chocolate mixture, and mix in to lighten it slightly, then carefully fold in the remaining egg whites. Pour the mixture into the lined cake tin and level the surface.

4 Bake the cake in the centre of the oven for 45–60 minutes, or until it feels just firm to the touch in the centre and a skewer inserted into it comes out clean. Remove from the oven, and place the tin on a wire rack. Leave the cake to cool in the tin.

5 To make the chocolate glaze, pour the cream into a small saucepan, and bring it to the boil. Place the chopped chocolate in a bowl, then pour in the cream, and stir until the chocolate melts. Add a few drops of vanilla extract. Leave the chocolate mixture to cool slightly, until it reaches a coating consistency, stirring

occasionally. If the glaze cools too much and becomes too thick, it can be gently re-warmed.

6 Heat the apricot glaze in a small saucepan until runny. Slice the cake in half horizontally, and spread half with a thin layer of the apricot glaze, then sandwich the 2 halves together again. Spread the remaining glaze over the top and sides of the cake.

7 Place the cake on a wire rack over a plate or tray. Reserve 3 tbsp of the glaze. Pour the rest of the glaze over the cake, using a palette knife to spread it evenly over the sides. Any glaze that runs off on to the plate or tray may be re-used. Leave the cake in a cool place until the glaze has set.

8 Beat the reserved glaze briefly, re-warming it slightly if it is very thick, then use it to fill a piping bag fitted with a plain nozzle. Pipe the word "Sacher" across the top of the cake.

Marzipan Oranges

Serve in petits fours cases after dinner with coffee

- makes 6
- prep 30 mins

125g (4½oz) natural almond marzipan

few drops of **orange food colouring**

whole **cloves**, to decorate

1 Mix the marzipan and food colouring in a bowl until combined. Roll 25g (scant 1oz) into a ball and roll over the coarse, star-shaped side of a grater. Push a clove into the top of the orange. Use the blunt edge of a knife to make crease marks around the clove. Repeat.

VARIATIONS

Pear Marzipan Fruits
Colour the marzipan pale green and shape into pears. Cut the cloves in half. Push the star end into the base and use the stick end to create stalks.

Marzipan Bananas
Shape the marzipan into sausage shapes with tapered ends. Bend towards you, then flatten the sides slightly with the back of a knife. Use thinned-down brown paste colouring to paint in a few streaks and marks.

Angel Food Cake

This American cake is similar to a meringue

 serves 8–12

🕐 prep 30 mins, plus cooling • cook 35–45 mins

🍽 1.7 litre (3 pint) ring mould, sugar thermometer

150g (5½oz) plain flour

100g (3½oz) icing sugar

8 egg whites

pinch of cream of tartar

250g (9oz) caster sugar

few drops of almond extract, or vanilla extract

fresh mixed berries, to serve

For the frosting

150g (5½oz) caster sugar

1 egg white

1 **Preheat the oven** to 180°C (350°F/Gas 4). Sift the flour and icing sugar together into a bowl.

2 **Whisk the egg whites** and cream of tartar until stiff, then whisk in the caster sugar, 1 tbsp at a time. Gradually sift over the flour mixture, folding in with a metal spoon. Fold in the almond extract.

3 **Spoon the mixture** gently into the ring mould and level the surface. Place the mould on a baking tray and bake for 35–45 minutes, or until just firm to the touch.

4 **Remove the cake** from the oven, and invert the mould on to a wire rack. Leave the cake to cool, then ease out of the mould.

5 **To make the frosting**, place the caster sugar in a saucepan with 4 tbsp water. Heat gently, stirring, until the sugar dissolves. Boil until the syrup reaches soft-boil stage (114–118°C/238–245°F), or until a little of the syrup forms a soft ball when dropped into very cold water.

6 **Meanwhile**, whisk the egg white until stiff. As soon as the sugar syrup reaches temperature, plunge the base of the pan into cold water to stop the syrup getting any hotter, then pour slowly onto the egg whites, while still whisking, until the frosting holds a stiff peak.

7 **Working quickly**, because the surface will set quite quickly, spread the frosting over the cake with a palette knife, swirling the surface to texture it. Serve with mixed berries.

Celebration Cake

This recipe makes a wonderfully moist, rich fruit cake, ideal for Christmas, a wedding, christening, or birthday

 serves 16

🕐 prep 25 mins, plus overnight soaking • cook 2 hrs 30 mins

🍽 deep 20–25cm (8–10in) square cake tin

200g (7oz) sultanas

400g (14oz) raisins

350g (12oz) prunes, chopped

350g (12oz) glacé cherries

2 small dessert apples, peeled, cored, and finely chopped

600ml (1 pint) cider

4 tsp mixed spice

200g (7oz) unsalted butter, softened

175g (6oz) dark brown sugar

3 eggs, beaten

150g (5½oz) ground almonds

280g (10oz) plain flour

2 tsp baking powder

400g ready-made marzipan icing

3 large egg whites

500g (1lb 2oz) icing sugar

● **Prepare ahead** The day before, cook the fruit in the cider. Leave to cool and store in a cool place.

1 **Place the sultanas**, raisins, prunes, glacé cherries, chopped apple, cider, and spice in a saucepan, bring slowly to simmering point over a medium-low heat, cover, and simmer for 20 minutes, or until most of the liquid has been absorbed.

2 **Remove from** the heat, and leave to rest overnight at room temperature.

3 **Preheat the oven** to 160°C (325°F/Gas 3). Double-line the cake tin with greaseproof paper. In a large bowl, cream the butter and sugar together until pale and fluffy, then add the eggs, a little at a time.

4 **Fold in the fruit** and nuts, then sift the flour and baking powder, and fold into the mixture.

5 **Spoon the mixture** into the prepared tin, cover with foil, and bake for 2½ hours, or until a skewer inserted into the centre of the cake comes out clean. Leave to cool.

6 **Cover with the marzipan** icing. Place the egg whites in a bowl and stir in the icing sugar. Whisk for 10 minutes until stiff, then spread on top of the marzipan. To decorate, make frosted berries by dipping fresh berries in beaten egg white, then in caster sugar, and leaving to dry.

Honey Cake

A sweet cake with a delicate taste of honey

- makes 10–12 slices
- prep 20 mins, plus cooling • cook 1 hr
- 900g (2lb) loaf tin

225g (8oz) **butter**

115g (4oz) **light muscovado sugar**

6 tbsp **clear honey**

4 **eggs**, lightly beaten

450g (1lb) **plain flour**

1½ tsp **baking powder**

1 tsp **ground cinnamon**

For the icing

115g (4oz) **icing sugar**

1 tbsp **clear honey**

1 Preheat the oven to 180°C (350°F/Gas 4). Grease and line the bottom of the loaf tin.

2 Beat the butter and sugar until they are pale and creamy.

Warm the honey in a small pan, then beat into the butter and sugar mixture. Beat in the eggs, a little at a time, beating well after each addition. Add a little flour if the mixture begins to curdle.

3 Sift the flour, baking powder, and cinnamon together, and fold into the cake mixture. Spoon into the prepared loaf tin and level the top. Bake in the centre of the oven for 50–60 minutes. Check after 40 minutes; if the crust is getting too dark, reduce the heat to 160°C (325°F/Gas 3) and cover the crust with a piece of greaseproof paper for the remaining time. The cake is cooked when well risen and if a skewer inserted into the centre comes out clean. Remove from the tin and place on a wire rack to cool completely.

4 Mix the icing sugar with the honey and 1–2 tbsp hot water. Spoon the icing over the top of the cake, allowing it to drizzle down the sides.

Bienenstich

This German recipe is also known as Bee Sting Cake

- makes 8–10 slices
- prep 20 mins, plus rising • cook 20–25 mins
- 20cm (8in) sandwich tin

140g (5oz) **plain flour**

15g (½oz) **butter**, softened

½ tbsp **caster sugar**

1 tsp **fast-action dried yeast**

pinch of **salt**

1 **egg**

1 quantity **crème pâtissière** (p524)

For the glaze

30g (1oz) **butter**

20g (¾oz) **caster sugar**

1 tbsp **clear honey**

1 tbsp **double cream**

30g (1oz) slivered **almonds**

1 tsp **lemon** juice

1 Sift the flour into a bowl. Quickly rub in the butter, then add the sugar, yeast, and salt and mix well. Beat in the egg and add enough water to make a soft dough.

2 Knead on a floured surface for 5–10 minutes, or until smooth, elastic, and shiny. Put in a clean, oiled bowl, cover with cling film, and leave to rise in a warm place for 45–60 minutes, or until doubled in size.

3 Grease the sandwich tin and line with greaseproof paper. Knock back the dough and roll it out into a circle to fit the tin. Push it into the tin and cover with cling film. Leave to rise for 20 minutes.

4 To make the glaze, melt the butter in a small pan, then add the sugar, honey, and cream. Cook over low heat until the sugar has dissolved, then increase the heat and bring to the boil. Allow to simmer for 3 minutes, then remove the pan from the heat and add the almonds and lemon juice. Allow to cool.

5 Preheat the oven to 190°C (375°F/Gas 5). Carefully spread the glaze over the dough, leave to rise for a further 10 minutes, then bake for 20–25 minutes, ensuring it doesn't get too dark on the top. Allow to cool in the tin for 30 minutes, then carefully transfer to a wire rack.

6 Slice the cake in half. Spread a thick layer of crème pâtissière on the bottom half, then place the almond layer on top. Transfer to a serving plate.

Chocolate Cup Cakes

Children will enjoy decorating these with favourite toppings

🍴 makes 18–20

🕐 prep 15 mins • cook 18 mins

🍱 bun tray, paper baking cases

225g (8oz) unsalted butter, softened

225g (8oz) caster sugar

225g (8oz) self-raising flour

1 tsp baking powder

4 eggs

2 tbsp cocoa powder

100g (3½oz) chocolate chips

175g (6oz) plain chocolate

flaked chocolate, to decorate

1 Preheat the oven to 180°C (350°F/Gas 4). Line a bun tray with 18–20 paper baking cases.

2 Place the butter, caster sugar, flour, baking powder, eggs, and cocoa powder in a large mixing bowl and beat with an electric whisk for 2–3 minutes, or until well combined. Stir in the chocolate chips, spoon the mixture into the paper cases, and bake for 18 minutes, or until well risen. Transfer to a wire rack to cool.

3 Melt the chocolate in a bowl over a pan of simmering water, then spoon over the top of the cooled cup cakes. Decorate with flaked chocolate. Leave until set.

Raspberry Cup Cakes

Elegant cakes that are perfect with after-dinner coffee

🍴 makes 18–20

🕐 prep 15 mins • cook 18 mins

🍱 bun tray, paper baking cases

225g (8oz) unsalted butter, softened

225g (8oz) caster sugar

225g (8oz) self-raising flour

1 tsp baking powder

4 eggs

3 tbsp ground almonds

150g (5½oz) raspberries, plus 18–20 extra, to decorate

175g (6oz) white chocolate, plus extra, grated, to decorate

1 Preheat the oven to 180°C (350°F/Gas 4). Line the bun tray with paper baking cases.

2 Place the butter, caster sugar, flour, baking powder, and eggs in a large mixing bowl and beat with an electric hand whisk for 2–3 minutes, or until well combined. Stir in the almonds and raspberries, then spoon the mixture into the paper baking cases and bake for 18 minutes, or until risen and golden brown. Place on a wire rack to cool completely.

3 Put the white chocolate in a bowl and place it over a pan of barely simmering water until the chocolate has melted. Drizzle over the top of the cup cakes. Decorate each one with grated white chocolate and a raspberry.

Vanilla Cup Cakes

Coloured buttercream icing and small decorations transform these simple cup cakes into real family favourites

🍴 makes 18–20

🕐 prep 15 mins • cook 18 mins

🍱 bun tray, paper baking cases, piping bag

225g (8oz) unsalted butter, softened

225g (8oz) caster sugar

225g (8oz) self-raising flour

1 tsp baking powder

4 eggs

1 tsp pure vanilla extract

Buttercream icing (p446), coloured pale pink and yellow

pink metallic balls, to decorate (optional)

1 Preheat the oven to 180°C (350°F/Gas 4). Line a bun tray with 18–20 paper baking cases.

2 Place the butter, sugar, flour, baking powder, eggs, and vanilla extract in a large mixing bowl and beat with an electric whisk for 2–3 minutes, or until well combined. Spoon into the paper baking cases and bake for 18 minutes, or until risen and golden brown. Transfer to a wire rack to cool completely.

3 Pipe a swirl of either pink or yellow icing on top of each cup cake and add a few metallic balls.

Rum Babas

These desserts are perfect to serve at a dinner party, as most of the preparation can be done 1 day in advance – they just need finishing off on the day of serving

makes 4

prep 20 mins, plus rising ● cook 20 mins

4 individual baba tins; piping bag

Freeze the unsoaked babas for up to 3 months

150g (5½oz) strong plain flour

60g (2oz) raisins

1½ tsp fast-action dried yeast

30g (2oz) caster sugar

pinch of salt

2 eggs, lightly beaten

4 tbsp milk, warmed

60g (2oz) butter, melted

300ml (10fl oz) whipping cream

2 tbsp icing sugar

grated chocolate, to serve

For the syrup

125g (4½oz) caster sugar

3 tbsp rum

● **Prepare ahead** You can make the babas and the syrup a day in advance; keep them separate until just before serving.

1 Preheat the oven to 200°C (400°F/Gas 6). Place the flour into a bowl and stir in the raisins, yeast, sugar, and salt. Beat together the egg and milk, and add to the flour mixture. Stir in the melted butter. Beat well for 3–4 minutes, then pour the mixture into well-greased baba tins to half fill them. Place the tins on a baking tray and cover with a sheet of oiled cling film. Leave the tins in a warm place for 30 minutes, or until the mixture has doubled in size and filled the tins.

2 Bake for 10-15 minutes, or until the babas are a light golden colour and just firm to the touch. Allow them to cool in the tins for a few minutes, then turn out on to a wire rack to cool completely.

3 To make the syrup, pour 120fl oz (4fl oz) of water into a saucepan and add the sugar. Place the pan over a gentle heat, stirring constantly until the sugar dissolves. Increase the heat, bring the syrup to the boil, and boil rapidly for 2 minutes. Remove the pan from the heat and leave the syrup to cool. Stir in the rum.

4 Pierce holes over the surface of the babas using a fine skewer, then dip them into the syrup.

5 Just before serving, pour the whipping cream into a bowl, add the icing sugar, then whisk until it forms soft peaks. Put the cream into a piping bag and pipe a swirl into the centre of each baba. Sprinkle a little chocolate over the cream, and serve.

VARIATIONS

Summer Fruit Babas
For a lighter summer variation, fill the centre of the babas with summer berries rather than cream.

Prune and Armagnac Babas
Substitute finely chopped, stoned prunes for the raisins, and use Armagnac instead of rum in the syrup. Scatter a few chopped stoned prunes over the cream instead of the chocolate.

Banana Bread
A moist cake that keeps well

serves 8-10

prep 15 mins ● cook 1-1½hrs

900g (2lb) loaf tin

250g (9oz) self-raising flour

½ tsp baking powder

85g (3oz) butter, plus extra for greasing

150g (5½oz) light muscovado sugar

3 ripe bananas

100ml (3½fl oz) plain yogurt

2 eggs

85g (3oz) walnuts, chopped

● **Prepare ahead** Will keep for up to 1 week in an airtight container.

1 Preheat the oven to 180°C (350°F/Gas 4). Sift the flour and baking powder together into a mixing bowl and rub in the butter until the mixture resembles fine breadcrumbs. Stir in the sugar.

2 Mash the bananas with a fork, then add to the flour with the yogurt, eggs, and walnuts. Beat with a wooden spoon until well combined. Spoon into a greased and lined loaf tin, level the top, then make a slight dip in the centre.

3 Bake for 1-1¼ hours, or until a skewer inserted into the centre comes out clean. Leave to cool in the tin for 5 minutes, then turn out on to a wire rack to cool completely.

Chelsea Buns

These sweet and spicy old-fashioned buns are perfect with afternoon tea

- 🍴 makes 9
- 🕐 prep 30 mins, plus rising and proving • cook 30 mins
- 🍳 23cm (9in) square cake tin
- ❄️ freeze for up to 1 month

280g (10oz) strong white bread flour

½ tsp salt

2 tbsp caster sugar

1 tsp fast-action dried yeast

45g (1½oz) butter

1 egg, lightly beaten

100ml (3½fl oz) tepid milk

115g (4oz) mixed dried fruit

60g (2oz) light muscovado sugar

1 tsp mixed spice

clear honey, to glaze

● **Prepare ahead** Delicious served warm, the buns will also keep for up to 2 days in an airtight container.

1 Mix the flour, salt, caster sugar, and yeast together in a large mixing bowl. Rub in 15g (½oz) of the butter. Make a well in the centre and pour in the beaten egg, followed by the milk. Mix to form a soft pliable dough. Knead for 5 minutes. Place in a lightly oiled bowl and cover with oiled cling film. Leave in a warm place for 1 hour, or until doubled in size.

2 Lightly grease the tin. Tip the dough out on a lightly floured surface and knead briefly. Roll out to a 30 x 23cm (12 x 9in) rectangle.

3 Melt the remaining butter in a saucepan over a low heat, then brush generously on to the surface of the dough, leaving a border along the long edges of the dough. Mix the fruit, muscovado sugar, and spice together and scatter evenly over the melted butter. Roll up the dough from the long edge like a Swiss roll, sealing the end with a little water. Cut the dough into 9 equal pieces. Place the pieces in the tin and space evenly. Cover loosely with oiled cling film and leave to rise until doubled in size.

4 Preheat the oven to 190°C (375°F/Gas 5). Bake the buns for 30 minutes, then brush with a little honey and allow to cool slightly in the tin before transferring to a wire rack to cool. Serve warm or cold.

Cornish Saffron Buns

Saffron gives these fruit buns a light golden colour and a subtle flavour

- 🍴 makes 12
- 🕐 prep 25 mins, plus soaking and rising • cook 25–35 mins
- ❄️ freeze for up to 3 months

large pinch of saffron strands

1 tbsp boiling water

600g (1lb 5oz) strong plain flour

½ tsp salt

125g (4½oz) butter

85g (3oz) caster sugar

7g sachet fast-action dried yeast

1 egg

150ml (5fl oz) milk

200g (7oz) currants

1 Place the saffron into a small dish. Pour over 1 tbsp boiling water and allow the saffron to steep until the water has cooled.

2 Sift the flour and salt into a large bowl, then rub in the butter until the mixture resembles fine breadcrumbs. Stir in the sugar, yeast, and saffron. Beat together the egg, milk, and 100ml (3½fl oz) water, then stir into the flour and mix to form a soft dough.

3 Turn the dough out on to a lightly floured surface and knead for 8–10 minutes, or until smooth and elastic, then knead in the currants.

4 Divide the dough into 12 pieces. Shape each piece into a ball and flatten slightly. Place the balls on an oiled baking tray, and cover loosely with lightly oiled cling film. Leave the buns in a warm place for 30–40 minutes, or until they have doubled in size.

5 Preheat the oven to 220°C (425°F/Gas 7). Bake near the top of the oven for 15–20 minutes, or until the buns are a light golden colour and sound hollow when tapped underneath. Remove the buns from the oven and transfer them to a wire rack to cool. Serve warm or cold.

● **Good with** chilled butter or clotted cream.

● **Leftovers** can be allowed to go a little stale, then used as a base for a trifle or in place of bread in a stuffing.

Apple Muffins

These are best served straight from the oven for breakfast, but are also good in lunchboxes or with afternoon tea

 makes 12

 prep 10 mins • cook 20–25 mins

 12-hole American-style muffin tin; paper cases

1 Golden Delicious apple, peeled and chopped

2 tsp lemon juice

115g (4oz) light demerara sugar, plus extra for sprinkling

200g (7oz) plain flour

85g (3oz) wholemeal flour

4 tsp baking powder

1 tbsp ground mixed spice

½ tsp salt

60g (2oz) pecan nuts, chopped

250ml (8fl oz) milk

4 tbsp sunflower oil

1 egg, beaten

1 **Preheat the oven** to 200°C (400°F/Gas 6). Line a 12-hole American-style muffin tin with paper cases and set aside. Put the apple in a bowl, add the lemon juice, and toss. Add 4 tbsp of the sugar and set aside for 5 minutes.

2 **Meanwhile**, sift the plain and wholemeal flours, baking powder, mixed spice, and salt into a large bowl, tipping in any bran left in the sieve. Stir in the remaining sugar and pecans then make a well in the centre of the dry ingredients.

3 **Beat together the milk**, oil, and egg, then add the apple. Tip the wet ingredients into the centre of the dry ingredients and mix together lightly to make a lumpy batter.

4 **Spoon the mixture** into the paper cases, filling each case three-quarters full. Bake the muffins for 20–25 minutes, or until the tops are peaked and brown. Transfer the muffins to a wire rack and sprinkle with extra sugar. Eat warm or cooled.

 Good with butter when they are still hot.

Lemon Poppy Seed Muffins

Quick and easy to make, these muffins are delightful served with brunch or as a teatime treat

 makes 12

 prep 10 mins • cook 20 mins

 12-hole American-style muffin tin; paper cases

400g (14oz) plain white flour

1½ tsp baking powder

½ tsp baking soda

¼ tsp salt

100g (3½oz) caster sugar

2½ tbsp poppy seeds, black or white

zest of 2 large lemons, finely grated

2 eggs

250ml (8fl oz) soured cream

60g (2oz) butter, melted and cooled

4 tbsp sunflower oil

icing sugar, for dusting

1 **Preheat the oven** to 200°C (400°F/Gas 6). Line a 12-hole American-style muffin tin with paper cases and set aside. Sift the flour, baking powder, baking soda, and salt into a bowl. Stir in sugar, poppy seeds, and lemon zest, then make a well in the centre of the dry ingredients.

2 **In a separate bowl**, beat the eggs. Mix in the soured cream, butter, and oil and pour the mixture into the centre of the dry ingredients. Mix together lightly to make a lumpy batter. Spoon the mixture into the paper cases, filling each case three-quarters full.

3 **Bake the muffins** for 20 minutes, or until well risen and a fine skewer inserted in to the centre comes out clean. Sift icing sugar over the tops while still warm.

Chocolate Muffins

These muffins are sure to fix any chocolate cravings, and the buttermilk lends them a delicious lightness

 makes 12

 prep 10 mins • cook 20 mins

 12-hole American-style muffin tin; paper cases

225g (8oz) **plain flour**

60g (2oz) **cocoa powder**

1 tbsp **baking powder**

pinch of **salt**

115g (4oz) **soft light brown sugar**

150g (5½oz) **chocolate chips**

250ml (8fl oz) **buttermilk**

6 tbsp **sunflower oil**

½ tsp **pure vanilla extract**

2 **eggs**

1 Preheat the oven to 200°C (400°F/Gas 6). Line a 12-hole American-style muffin tin with paper cases and set aside.

2 Sift the flour, cocoa powder, baking powder, and salt into a large bowl. Stir in the sugar and chocolate chips, then make a well in the centre of the dry ingredients.

3 Beat together the buttermilk, oil, vanilla, and eggs and pour the mixture into the centre of the dry ingredients. Mix together lightly to make a lumpy batter. Spoon the mixture into the paper cases, filling each three-quarters full.

4 Bake for 15 minutes, or until well risen and firm to the touch. Immediately transfer the muffins to a wire rack and leave to cool.

Barm Brack

This bread is of Irish origin, where it is sometimes served for Hallowe'en with little charms in it, which are supposed to forecast your luck for the following year. For example, a ring means that you will be getting married

🍴 serves 6–8

🕐 prep 15 mins, plus overnight soaking and proving • cook 50 mins

◉ 20cm (8in) round cake tin

❄ freeze for up to 3 months

500g (1lb 2oz) **mixed dried fruit**

150ml (5fl oz) hot, strong black **tea**

500g (1lb 2oz) **strong plain flour**

60g (2oz) **butter**, plus extra to grease

125g (4½oz) **caster sugar**

1 tsp **ground mixed spice**

7g sachet **fast-action dried yeast**

½ tsp **salt**

150ml (5fl oz) lukewarm **milk**

1 **egg**

beaten **egg**, to glaze

1 Put the dried fruit into a bowl and pour the tea on to the fruit. Stir, then cover the bowl and leave the fruit to soak in and absorb the tea overnight.

2 Put the flour into a bowl and rub in the butter until the mixture resembles fine breadcrumbs. Stir in the sugar, spice, yeast, and salt. Lightly beat together the milk and egg, and add to the flour mixture. If the mixture is too sticky, add a little flour.

3 Turn the dough out on to a lightly floured surface, and knead for 8–10 minutes, or until smooth and elastic. Add the fruit to the dough and knead until the fruit is well mixed, taking care not to knead too much or the soft fruit will start to break down. Depending on the fruit used, it may not have fully absorbed all the tea, and the excess tea may make the dough sticky. If that happens, add a little more flour.

4 Lightly butter the cake tin. Shape the dough into a ball, and press it into the tin. Cover the tin with a piece of oiled cling film, and leave it in a warm place for 40–60 minutes, or until the dough has doubled in size.

5 Preheat the oven to 200°C (400°F/Gas 6). Brush the top of the bread with beaten egg. Bake for 20 minutes. Reduce the temperature to 180°C (350°F/Gas 4) and bake for a further 20–30 minutes, or until it sounds hollow when you take it out of the tin and tap it on the base. If the bread starts to brown too quickly, cover it with a sheet of foil.

6 When the bread is cooked, remove it from the oven and transfer it to a wire rack to cool. Serve the bread warm or cold.

● **Good with** butter and jam

● **Leftovers** can be toasted and served with butter the following day.

Pecan Pie

This sweet, crunchy pie originated in the southern United States, where pecan nuts are widely grown

- 🍴 makes 8 slices
- 🕐 prep 15 mins, plus chilling
  - cook 1 hr 30 mins
- 🍳 23cm (9in) loose-bottomed flan tin; baking beans

375g packet ready-made **sweet dessert pastry**

flour, for dusting

150ml (5fl oz) **maple syrup**

60g (2oz) **butter**

175g (6oz) **light soft brown sugar**

few drops of **pure vanilla extract**

pinch of **salt**

3 **eggs**

200g (7oz) **pecan nuts**

1 Roll the pastry out on a lightly floured surface, then use it to line the flan tin. Trim around the top edge of the tin, and prick the base all over with a fork. Chill for at least 30 minutes.

2 Preheat the oven to 200°C (400°F/Gas 6). Line the pastry case with greaseproof paper, and fill with baking beans. Bake for 10 minutes, then remove the paper and beans, and bake for another 10 minutes, or until pale golden. Remove the pastry case from the oven and reduce the temperature to 180°C (350°F/Gas 4).

3 Pour the maple syrup into a saucepan, and add the butter, sugar, vanilla extract, and salt. Place the pan over a low heat, and stir constantly until the butter has melted, and the sugar dissolved. Remove the pan from the heat, and leave the mixture to cool until it feels just tepid, then beat in the eggs, 1 at a time. Stir in the pecan nuts, then pour the mixture into the pastry case.

4 Bake for 40–50 minutes, or until just set. Cover with a sheet of foil if it is browning too quickly.

5 Remove the pie from the oven, transfer it to a wire rack and leave to cool for 15–20 minutes. Remove from the tin and either serve it warm or leave it on the wire rack to cool completely.

● **Good with** crème fraîche or whipped cream.

Blueberry Cream Cheese Tart

Juicy blueberries perfectly complement the creamy filling

- 🍴 makes 8 slices
- 🕐 prep 25 mins, plus chilling
  - cook 30–45 mins
- 🍳 23cm (9in) loose-bottomed flan tin, baking beans

For the pastry

175g (6oz) **plain flour**

85g (3oz) **butter**, diced

2 tbsp **caster sugar**

1 **egg yolk**

For the filling

115g (4oz) **cream cheese**

60g (2oz) **soured cream**

60g (2oz) **caster sugar**

pinch of grated **nutmeg**

3 **eggs**, beaten

zest of 1 **lemon**

350g (12oz) **blueberries**

icing sugar, to serve

● **Prepare ahead** The tart can be made several days in advance and kept in the refrigerator.

1 Place the flour, butter, and sugar in a food processor, and pulse until it resembles breadcrumbs. Or, rub the butter into the flour with your fingertips until it resembles breadcrumbs, then stir in the sugar.

2 Add the egg yolk and mix to a firm dough. Roll out the pastry on a lightly floured surface and use to line the flan tin. Prick the base with a fork. Chill for at least 30 minutes. Preheat the oven to 200°C (400°F/Gas 6).

3 Line the pastry case with greaseproof paper and fill with baking beans. Bake for 10 minutes, then remove the paper and beans and bake for another 10 minutes, or until pale golden. Remove from the oven and reduce the temperature to 180°C (350°F/Gas 4).

4 Beat together the cream cheese, soured cream, sugar, nutmeg, eggs, and lemon zest until well combined. Pour into the pastry case and scatter the blueberries over the surface. Bake for 25–30 minutes, or until just set. Allow to cool before transferring to a serving plate. Serve warm or cold, dusted with icing sugar.

VARIATION

Raspberry Cream Cheese Pie

Use the same quantity of fresh raspberries in place of the blueberries.

Almond and Quince Tart

Delicious served warm with crème fraîche and a small glass
of vin santo or good sherry for a special occasion

- makes 8 slices
- prep 20 mins, plus chilling • cook 45–55 mins
- 25cm (10in) loose-bottomed fluted flan tin, baking beans

For the pastry

30g (1oz) **ground almonds**

175g (6oz) **plain flour**, plus extra for dusting

1 tbsp **icing sugar**

85g (3oz) **butter**, softened

grated zest of ½ **lemon**

1 **egg yolk**

For the almond filling

200g (7oz) **blanched almonds**

grated zest and juice of 1 **lemon**

grated zest and juice of 1 **orange**

2 tbsp **amaretto liqueur**

200g (7oz) **butter**

100g (3½oz) **icing sugar**

4 **eggs**

For the topping

175g (6oz) **quince cheese** or apricot jam

squeeze of **lemon juice**

icing sugar, for dusting

1 To make the pastry, put the ground almonds, flour, and sugar into a food processor, and pulse briefly to mix. Add the butter, and pulse until the mixture resembles breadcrumbs. Add the lemon zest and egg yolk through the feeder funnel, and process briefly to a smooth dough. Chill for 15 minutes.

2 To make the almond filling, process the blanched almonds in a food processor, until coarsely ground. Add the orange and lemon zests and juices with the amaretto, and process briefly to mix. Pour into a bowl and set aside.

3 Place the butter and sugar in a food processor and process. Add the eggs, 1 at a time, processing briefly to combine. Add this mix to the almond mixture, stir well, and set aside. Roll out the pastry on a lightly floured surface, and use to line the flan tin. If the pastry is difficult to handle, roll it out between 2 sheets of cling film. Chill for 30 minutes.

4 Preheat the oven to 180°C (350°F/Gas 4). Line the pastry case with greaseproof paper and baking beans, and bake blind for 10 minutes. Then remove the paper and beans, and bake for 5 minutes. Cool on a wire rack.

5 Warm the quince cheese in a small saucepan with 1 tbsp water and the lemon juice, stirring until melted. Spread evenly over the base of the tart. Spoon the almond mixture on top. Bake the tart for 30–40 minutes, or until the filling is golden. Leave to cool in the tin for 15 minutes, and then carefully remove to a large serving plate. Dust with icing sugar, and serve warm.

Treacle Tart

A traditional family favourite

- makes 8 slices
- prep 30 mins, plus chilling • cook 30 mins
- 15cm (6in) loose-bottomed fluted flan tin

175g (6oz) **plain flour**, plus extra for dusting

85g (3oz) **butter**, cubed

1 tsp **caster sugar**

1 **egg yolk**

8 tbsp **golden syrup**

zest of 1 **lemon**, finely grated

1 tsp **lemon juice**

pinch of **ground ginger**

4 tbsp fresh **breadcrumbs**

1 Preheat the oven to 190°C (375°F/Gas 5). To make the pastry, sift the flour into a bowl. Add the butter, and rub in with your fingertips, until the mixture resembles coarse breadcrumbs. Add the sugar. Mix the egg yolk with 3 tbsp cold water, and add to the mixture. Combine to form a dough.

2 On a lightly floured surface, roll the pastry into a circle, and use to line the tin. Prick it lightly all over with a fork. Chill for 30 minutes.

3 Warm the syrup in a pan with the lemon zest and juice, but do not allow it to get too hot. Add the ginger. Place the breadcrumbs in the pastry case. Pour the syrup on top.

4 Allow to stand for 5 minutes, then use the pastry trimmings to make a lattice top, if desired. Bake in the oven for 25–30 minutes.

Prune and Almond Tart

A fabulous combination of fruit and nuts

- makes 8 slices
- prep 20 mins, plus chilling • cook 50 mins
- 23cm (9in) loose-bottomed tart tin; baking beans

175g (6oz) **plain flour**, plus extra for dusting

1 tbsp **sugar**

85g (3oz) chilled **butter**

1 small **egg**

200g (7oz) pitted **prunes**

2 tbsp **brandy**

100g (3½oz) **flaked almonds**, toasted

85g (3oz) **caster sugar**

2 **eggs**

1 **egg yolk**

1 tbsp grated **orange** zest

few drops of **almond essence**

30g (1oz) **butter**, softened

120ml (4fl oz) **double cream**

● **Prepare ahead** The tart can be made and chilled 2 days in advance

1 Place the flour, sugar, and butter into a food processor and pulse until it resembles breadcrumbs. Add the egg, and process until the pastry forms a ball. Roll out on a floured surface and use to line the tart tin. Chill for at least 30 minutes.

2 Preheat the oven to 190°C (375°F/Gas 5). Line the pastry case with greaseproof paper and baking beans. Bake for 10 minutes, then take out of the oven. Remove the paper and beans, and bake for a further 5 minutes. Cool on a wire rack.

3 Reduce the oven to 180°C (350°F/Gas 4). Place the prunes in a saucepan, cover with water, and add the brandy. Simmer for 5 minutes, then turn off the heat and set aside. Place half the flaked almonds with the sugar in a food processor, and pulse until finely ground. Add the eggs, egg yolk, orange zest, almond essence, butter, and cream, and process until smooth.

4 Drain the prunes, and cut any large ones in half. Pour the almond cream into the tart, and arrange the prunes on top. Scatter the remaining flaked almonds on top, and bake for 30 minutes, or until just set.

● **Good with** cream or ice cream.

Mince Pies

Making your own mince pies is quick and easy, and they taste much better than shop-bought ones

- makes 18
- prep 20 mins, plus chilling • cook 10–12 mins
- 7.5cm (3in) and 6cm (2½in) biscuit cutters

1 small **cooking apple**

30g (1oz) **butter**, melted

85g (3oz) **sultanas**

85g (3oz) **raisins**

55g (1¾oz) **currants**

45g (1½oz) **mixed peel**, chopped

45g (1½oz) chopped **almonds** or hazelnuts

zest of 1 **lemon**, finely grated

1 tsp **mixed spice**

1 tbsp **brandy** or whisky

30g (1oz) **soft dark brown muscovado sugar**

1 small **banana**

500g packet of **shortcrust pastry**

flour, for dusting

icing sugar, for dusting

● **Prepare ahead** The pies can be baked up to 3 days in advance and stored in an airtight container.

1 Preheat the oven to 190°C (375°F/Gas 5). Grate the apple (including the skin), and place in a large bowl. Add the melted butter, sultanas, raisins, currants, mixed peel, nuts, lemon zest, mixed spice, brandy, and sugar, and mix. Chop the banana into small dice, and add to the bowl. Mix well.

2 Roll out the pastry on a lightly floured surface to a thickness of 2mm (⅛in) and cut out 18 circles using the larger biscuit cutters. Re-roll the pastry, and cut a further 18 smaller circles or shapes.

3 Line patty tins with the larger pastry circles, and place a heaped tsp of mincemeat in each case. Top with the smaller circles or shapes. Chill for 10 minutes, and then bake for 10–12 minutes, or until the pastry is golden. Carefully remove from the tins, and cool on a wire rack. Dust with icing sugar.

Chocolate Chiffon Pie

Rich and indulgent, this pie offers a satisfying contrast between a light, smooth mousse-like filling and a crunchy crumb crust

 makes 8 slices

 prep 30 mins, plus chilling • cook 15 mins

 23cm (9in) loose-bottomed flan tin

For the crumb crust

175g (6oz) digestive biscuits, coarsely broken into pieces

50g (1¾oz) caster sugar

75g (2½oz) butter, melted

1 tsp pure vanilla extract

For the filling

50g (1¾oz) dark chocolate, chopped

150ml (5fl oz) double cream

¼ tsp pure vanilla extract

2 sheets leaf gelatine

3 egg yolks

140g (5oz) caster sugar

pinch of salt

2 egg whites

¼ tsp cream of tartar

To decorate

200ml (7fl oz) double cream

2 tbsp vanilla sugar or sugar

dark chocolate, to decorate

1 Preheat the oven to 190°C (375°F/Gas 5). To make the crust, put the biscuits in a blender or food processor and process until fine crumbs form. Add the sugar and pulse to combine. Pour in the butter and vanilla, and process until blended. Alternatively crush the biscuits in a plastic bag with a rolling pin, then stir in the sugar, butter, and vanilla until combined. Press the crumbs evenly and firmly over the bottom of the flan tin, pressing from the centre outwards. Bake for 8–10 minutes, or until browned at the edge. Transfer to a wire rack, and leave to cool.

2 To make the filling, melt the chocolate in the cream in a saucepan over a low heat, without letting the cream boil, stirring until smooth. Stir in the vanilla. Remove from the heat. Add the gelatine and leave to soak for several minutes, then stir until dissolved.

3 Meanwhile, using an electric mixer, beat the egg yolks with 100g (3½oz) of the sugar until the sugar dissolves and the mixture is thick and creamy. Add the salt, then slowly add the cream mixture, beating for a further 1 minute until the mixture is well blended. Cover the bowl with cling film and chill for 15 minutes, or until the mixture drops from the spoon in a mound.

4 Whisk the egg whites in a large bowl until soft peaks start to form. Sprinkle over the cream of tartar, then add the remaining sugar, 1 tbsp at a time, whisking until stiff peaks form. Set aside. Beat the chilled chocolate mixture for 2 minutes, or until fluffy. Beat in a little of the egg white, then fold in the remainder. Spoon the chocolate mixture into the pie case and smooth the surface.

5 In a separate bowl, whisk the cream for the decoration until it thickens. Sprinkle over the vanilla sugar and continue until stiff. Drop the whipped cream in blobs over the pie's surface, then use a palette knife to spread and swirl the cream. Grate extra dark chocolate over the surface. Chill the decorated pie for at least 2 hours before serving.

Apple and Pear Galette

Sugar-coated fruit in pastry

 makes 8 slices

 prep 40 mins, plus chilling • cook 45 mins

175g (6oz) plain flour, plus extra for dusting

30g (1oz) solid vegetable fat, diced

60g (2oz) butter

3–5 tbsp iced water

For the filling

450g (1lb) Golden Delicious apples

450g (1lb) ripe pears

45g (1½oz) caster sugar

30g (1oz) butter, diced

2 tbsp apricot jam, melted

1 Rub the flour, vegetable fat, and butter together until it resembles coarse crumbs. Add the iced water to form a firm dough. Chill for 30 minutes, wrapped in cling film.

2 Preheat the oven to 220°C (425°F/Gas 7). On a floured surface, roll the pastry to a 38cm (15in) round. Place on a baking tray.

3 Peel and cut the apples and pears into 5mm (¼in) slices, and starting a little way in from the pastry edge, place in concentric circles. Add the sugar and butter and fold the pastry over the edge of the fruit.

4 Bake the galette for 45 minutes, or until the fruit slices are tender. Brush with the jam, cool slightly, and serve warm.

Banana Cream Pie

This traditional American single-crust pie makes a rich and creamy end to any meal

 makes 8 slices

🕐 prep 20 mins, plus chilling • cook 20–25 mins

🍲 23cm (9in) deep pie plate with a flat rim; baking beans

500g packet ready-made **shortcrust pastry**

4 large **egg yolks**

85g (3oz) **caster sugar**

4 tbsp **cornflour**

¼ tsp **salt**

450ml (15fl oz) **full-fat milk**

1 tsp **pure vanilla extract**

3 ripe **bananas**

½ tbsp **lemon juice**

360ml (12fl oz) **whipping cream** or **double cream**

3 tbsp **icing sugar**

⬤ **Prepare ahead** The pastry case can be baked a day in advance and tightly wrapped in kitchen foil.

1 Preheat the oven to 200°C (400°F/Gas 6). Roll out the pastry on a lightly floured surface to a 30cm (12in) circle, use to line the pie plate and trim off the excess. Prick the base all over with a fork.

2 Line the pastry with greaseproof paper, fill with baking beans, and place the plate on a baking tray. Bake for 15 minutes, or until the pastry looks pale golden. Lift off the paper and beans and prick the base again. Return to the oven and bake for a further 5–10 minutes, or until the pastry is golden and dry. Transfer the pie plate to a wire rack and leave to cool completely.

3 Meanwhile, beat the egg yolks, sugar, cornflour, and salt until the sugar dissolves and the mixture is pale yellow. Beat in the milk and vanilla. Transfer the mixture to a saucepan over a medium-high heat and bring to just below the boil, stirring until a smooth, thick custard forms. Reduce the heat and stir for 2 minutes. Strain through a fine sieve into a bowl and leave to cool.

4 Thinly slice the bananas and toss with the lemon juice. Spread them out in the pie case, then top with the custard. Cover the pie with cling film and chill for at least 2 hours.

5 Beat the cream until soft peaks form, then sift over the icing sugar, and continue beating until stiff. Spoon over the custard just before serving.

Key Lime Pie

This pie takes its name from the small limes that come from the Florida Keys, where it originated

 makes 8 slices

🕐 prep 20–25 mins • cook 15–20 mins

🍲 23cm (9in) loose-bottomed flan tin

100g (3½ oz) **butter**

225g (8oz) **digestive biscuits**, crushed

For the filling

5 **limes**, plus 1 extra, cut into thin slices, to decorate

3 large **egg yolks**

400g can **condensed milk**

1 Preheat the oven to 180°C (350°F/Gas 4). Melt the butter in a saucepan over a low heat. Add the digestive biscuit crumbs and stir until well combined. Remove from the heat and tip the mixture into the flan tin, then use the base of a metal spoon to press it evenly and firmly all over the base and sides of the tin. Place on a baking tray and bake for 5–10 minutes.

2 Meanwhile, grate the zest of 3 of the limes into a bowl. Juice all 5 of the limes, and set aside.

3 Place the egg yolks into the bowl with the lime zest, and whisk until the egg has thickened. Pour in the condensed milk and continue whisking for 5 minutes if using an electric whisk, or for 6–7 minutes if whisking by hand. Add the lime juice, and whisk again until it is incorporated. Pour the mixture into the tin and bake for 15–20 minutes, or until it is set.

4 Remove the pie from the oven and leave it to cool completely. Serve the pie decorated with the lime slices.

⬤ **Good with** pouring cream.

VARIATION

Meringue-topped Key Lime Pie

Use the discarded egg whites to make a meringue topping for the pie. Add the topping before you bake the pie.

White Chocolate and Mascarpone Tarts

These pretty little tarts are ideal to serve, piled with fresh summer berries, at dinner parties

- makes 6
- prep 10 mins, plus 20 mins chilling • cook 15 mins, plus 3 hrs setting
- 6 x 10cm (4in) loose-bottomed tart tins, baking beans

For the pastry

250g (9oz) **plain flour**

125g (4½oz) **butter**, chilled

3 tbsp **caster sugar**

1 large **egg**

For the filling

200g (7oz) **white chocolate**

450g (1lb) **mascarpone cheese**

150ml (5fl oz) **double cream**

For the topping

200g (7oz) **strawberries**

200g (7oz) **raspberries**

mint leaves, to decorate

icing sugar, to decorate

1 **Preheat the oven** to 200°C (400°F/Gas 6). To make the pastry, place the flour, butter, and sugar into a food processor and pulse until it resembles breadcrumbs. Add the egg and process until the pastry draws together in a ball.

2 **Roll out the pastry**, line the tart tins with it and chill for 20 minutes.

3 **Line the pastry cases** with greaseproof paper and fill with baking beans. Bake blind for 10 minutes, then remove the paper and beans, and cook for a further 5 minutes. Remove from the oven and cool.

4 **For the filling**, place the white chocolate and 125g (4½oz) of the mascarpone into a heatproof bowl set over simmering water, and stir until melted. Add the remaining mascarpone to the bowl, whisk briskly until smooth, then whisk in the double cream.

5 **Pour the mixture** into the pastry cases and chill for 3 hours, or until softly set. To serve, arrange the berries on top of the tart, and decorate with mint leaves and a sprinkle of icing sugar.

Silesian Poppy Tart

Tarts made with poppy seeds are popular in Eastern Europe

🍴 makes 8 slices

🕐 prep 35 mins, plus cooling
• cook 1 hr 30 mins

▭ 28cm (11in) springform tin

1 litre (1¾ pints) milk

150g (5½ oz) butter

200g (7oz) semolina

200g (7oz) poppy seeds

175g (60oz) caster sugar

1 tsp pure vanilla extract

2 eggs

100g (3½oz) curd cheese

50g (1¾oz) ground almonds

50g (1¾oz) raisins

1 pear, peeled, cored, and grated

icing sugar, for dusting

For the pastry

250g (9oz) plain flour

2 tsp baking powder

125g (4½oz) caster sugar

2–3 drops pure vanilla extract

pinch of salt

1 egg

125g (4½oz) butter, softened

1 **To make the pastry**, sift the flour with the baking powder into a bowl. Add the sugar, vanilla, salt, egg, butter, and a little water. Mix to make a dough, roll into a ball using your hands, and set aside.

2 **Place the milk** and butter in a saucepan and bring to the boil. Gradually stir in the semolina and poppy seeds. Simmer over a low heat for 20 minutes, stirring occasionally, then remove from the heat and allow to cool for 10 minutes.

3 **Preheat the oven** to 180°C (350°F/Gas 4) and grease the base of the tin. Roll out half of the dough and fit it into the base. Roll out the remaining dough into a long strip, and press it to the side of the tin to form an edge 3cm (1¼in) high.

4 **Stir together** the sugar, vanilla, eggs, curd cheese, almonds, and raisins into the cooled poppy seed and semolina mixture. Stir in the pear, pour the mixture evenly into the pastry base, and bake for 1 hour.

5 **Place the tin** onto a wire rack to cool, loosen the edge of the tart with a knife, and remove the ring. Dust with icing sugar before serving.

Lemon Tart

Variations of this ever-popular tart often appear on restaurant menus

🍴 makes 8 slices

🕐 35 mins, plus chilling
• cook 45 mins

▭ 24cm (9in) loose-bottomed tart tin; baking beans

5 eggs

200g (7oz) caster sugar

zest and juice of 4 lemons

250ml (8fl oz) double cream

icing sugar, to serve

lemon zest, to serve

For the pastry

175g (6oz) plain flour, plus extra for dusting

85g (3oz) butter, chilled

45g (1½ oz) caster sugar

1 egg

1 **To make the pastry**, place the flour, butter, and sugar into a food processor and pulse until it resembles breadcrumbs. Add the egg and process until the pastry draws together into a ball.

2 **Roll out the pastry** on a lightly floured surface into a large circle to line the tart tin. Chill for at least 30 minutes.

3 **Beat the eggs** and sugar together until combined. Beat in the lemon zest and juice, then whisk in the cream. Chill for 1 hour.

4 **Preheat the oven** to 190°C (375°F/Gas 5). Line the pastry case with greaseproof paper, fill with baking beans, and bake blind for 10 minutes. Remove the paper and beans, and bake for 5 minutes, or until the base is crisp.

5 **Reduce the oven** to 140°C (275°F/Gas 1). Place the tart tin on a baking tray. Pour in the lemon filling, being careful not to allow the filling to spill over the edges. Bake for 30 minutes, or until just set. Remove from the oven and cool. Serve, dusted with icing sugar and sprinkled with lemon zest over the top.

Lemon Meringue Pie

With the sharpness of the lemon combined with the vanilla-flavoured meringue topping, it is no wonder this pie is an American family favourite

 makes 8 slices

 prep 30 mins, plus cooling • cook 40–50 mins

 23cm (9in) loose-bottomed flan tin; baking beans

400g (14oz) ready-made shortcrust pastry

6 eggs, separated

3 tbsp cornflour

3 tbsp plain flour

400g (14oz) caster sugar

juice of 3 lemons

1 tbsp grated lemon zest

45g (1½oz) butter, diced

½ tsp cream of tartar

½ tsp pure vanilla extract

1 Preheat the oven to 200°C (400°F/Gas 6). Lightly grease the flan tin. Roll out the pastry on a lightly floured surface and use to line the tin.

2 Line the pastry case with greaseproof paper, then fill with baking beans. Place on a baking tray and bake for 10–15 minutes, or until the pastry looks pale golden. Lift off the paper and beans, return to the oven, and bake for 3–5 minutes, or until the pastry is golden and dry. Transfer to a wire rack and leave to cool completely. Reduce the heat to 180°C (350°F/Gas 4).

3 Place the egg yolks in a bowl and lightly beat. Combine the cornflour, flour, and 225g (8oz) of the sugar in a pan. Slowly add 360ml (12fl oz) water and heat gently, stirring, until the sugar dissolves and there are no lumps. Increase the heat slightly and cook, stirring, for 3–5 minutes, or until the mixture starts to thicken.

4 Beat several spoonfuls of the hot mixture into the egg yolks. Pour this mixture into the pan and slowly bring to the boil, stirring constantly. Boil for 3 minutes, then stir in the lemon juice, zest, and butter. Continue boiling for a further 2 minutes, or until the mixture is thick and glossy, stirring constantly and scraping down the side of the pan as necessary. Remove the pan from the heat; cover to keep warm.

5 Whisk the egg whites in a large clean bowl until foamy. Sprinkle over the cream of tartar and whisk. Continue whisking, adding the remaining sugar, 1 tbsp at a time. Add the vanilla with the last tbsp of the sugar, whisking until the meringue is thick and glossy.

6 Pour the lemon filling into the pie case, then top with the meringue, spreading it so it completely covers the filling right up to the pastry edge. Take care not to spill it over the pastry or the tart will be difficult to remove from the tin after baking.

7 Place the pie on a baking tray, place in the oven, and bake for 12–15 minutes, or until the meringue is lightly golden. Place the pie on a wire rack and leave to cool completely before serving.

Citrus Cream Tart

This classic dessert is deliciously fresh and creamy

 makes 8 slices

 prep 20 mins, plus chilling

 1 x 20–25cm (8–10in) loose-bottomed flan tin

115g (4oz) butter, melted

225g (8oz) ginger nut biscuits, crushed

300ml (10fl oz) double cream

2 x 375g cans condensed milk

zest and juice of 4 lemons, plus extra lemon zest, to decorate

zest and juice of 4 limes, plus extra lime zest, to decorate

● **Prepare ahead** The biscuit base can be made up to 24 hours in advance and chilled. The entire tart can be prepared in advance and chilled overnight.

1 Mix the melted butter and crushed biscuits together. Press into the base of the flan tin and chill for at least 1 hour.

2 Put the cream and condensed milk into a food processor. With the machine running, slowly pour in the lemon and lime juices and process until the mixture thickens. Add the lemon and lime zest and process briefly to combine.

3 Spread the mixture evenly over the biscuit base and chill for at least 1 hour.

4 Decorate with lemon and lime zest, and serve.

Spanish Meringue Treats

These thin meringue biscuits are known as "cats' tongues" in Spain

- 🍴 makes 18
- 🕐 prep 20 mins • cook 12 mins
- 🗄 piping bag

175ml (6fl oz) **whipping cream** or double cream

3 tbsp **caster sugar**

1 tsp **vanilla essence**

4 **egg whites**, whisked to soft peaks

150g (5½oz) **plain flour**

● **Prepare ahead** These biscuits can be made several days in advance and stored in an airtight container.

1 Preheat the oven to 190°C (375°F/Gas 5). Beat the cream with the sugar and vanilla essence until it has thickened slightly. Carefully fold in the egg whites. Sprinkle the flour over the mixture, a little at a time, continuing to fold until combined.

2 Lightly grease a baking tray with butter. Using the piping bag, lay down finger-width strips of the mixture, at least 1 finger-width apart, as the mixture will spread during baking. Bake for 10–12 minutes, or until the meringues are golden. The centres should still be gooey. Leave to cool slightly.

3 Using a spatula, carefully lift the meringues off the baking tray and onto a wire rack to cool. Trim, if necessary, while still warm. Serve once the meringues have cooled completely.

● **Good with** a cup of tea, coffee, or hot chocolate. You can also sandwich the biscuits together with chocolate spread.

Kaiserschmarrn

Legend says that this Austrian pancake was created for Emperor Franz Josef. Roughly translated as "Emperor's Mishmash", it is warming and delicious

- 🍴 serves 4
- 🕐 prep 10 mins • cook 10 mins

4 **eggs**

100g (3½oz) **plain flour**

45g (1½oz) **caster sugar**, plus 4 tsp for sprinkling

150ml (5fl oz) **milk**

40g (1½oz) **unsalted butter**

40g (1½oz) **raisins**

icing sugar, to serve

plum preserve, apple preserve, or fruit compote, to serve

1 Separate the eggs and put the yolks, flour, caster sugar, and milk in a bowl. Using a balloon whisk, whisk together to form a smooth batter. In a separate, clean bowl, whisk the whites until stiff and gradually fold into the batter.

2 Melt a quarter of the butter in a non-stick frying pan. When it is foaming, pour a quarter of the batter in the pan and sprinkle a quarter of the raisins over it. Fry over a medium heat for 2–3 minutes, or until the batter is set and brown underneath, then flip over and fry on the other side until golden brown. Set aside. Repeat to make 3 more pancakes.

3 Tear the pancakes into pieces using 2 forks. Put the pieces into a larger frying pan, sprinkle with the extra caster sugar, and cook over a medium heat for 1 minute.

4 Dust with icing sugar and serve with plum preserve.

VARIATION

Kaiserschmarrn with Rum

For a more luxurious dish, soak the raisins in rum before adding them to the pancakes.

Pastry

There is nothing wrong with using packets of ready-made pastry when you want to make a quick tart or pie, but making your own melt-in-the-mouth pastry is very satisfying. Once you master making and using these basic pastries you'll have great scope for expanding your sweet and savoury baking repertoire.

Shortcrust Pastry

For anyone new to pastry-making, this is the recipe to start with. This rich, crisp pastry is easy to make and used for both sweet and savoury dishes, such as these Empanadas (p47). Use shortcrust pastry for:

- Sweet and savoury tarts and tartlets
- Sweet and savoury pies
- Quiches and flans
- Cornish pasties

Baked shortcrust pastry *has a crisp and firm, but light texture.*

Rough Puff Pastry

This flaky, butter-rich pastry is quicker and easier to make than traditional puff pastry, and can be used in any recipe calling for puff pastry, such as this Leek and Cheese Flamiche (p229). Use rough puff pastry in any of the following dishes:

- Meat, fish, and fruit pies
- Fish or meat cooked in pastry
- Vol-au-vents
- Fruit turnovers

Rough puff pastry *dough produces delicate layers of butter-rich pastry.*

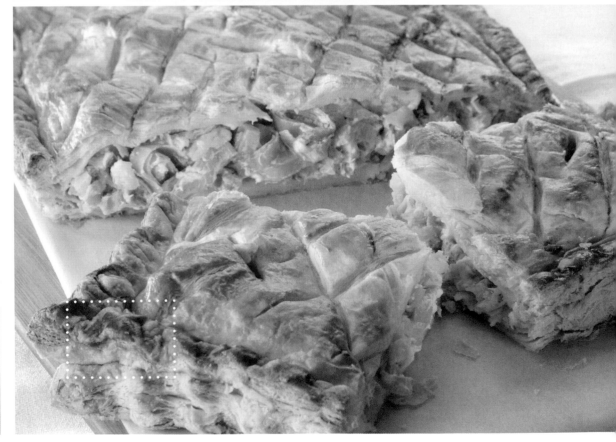

Sweet Shortcrust Pastry

Called *pâte sucrée* in French, this is a basic shortcrust pastry that includes sugar, and is the pastry used for this classic Tarte aux Pommes (p454). Other uses include:

- Sweet tarts and tartlets
- French galettes
- Petits fours

Sweet shortcrust pastry *makes a crisp case for fruit and creamy fillings.*

Choux Pastry

Very easy to make, this pastry bakes into thin, hollow balls that can contain sweet or savoury fillings. Unlike other pastries, choux pastry is too soft to roll out, so it is piped or simply dropped from the spoon onto a baking sheet, which is how these savoury Cheese Puffs (p153) are formed. You also can use it for:

- Profiteroles
- Eclairs
- Gougères
- Croquembouches

Choux pastry *dough bakes to form crisp, hollow balls for filling.*

Pastry

Shortcrust Pastry

1 **Sift 175g (6oz) plain** flour and a pinch of salt into a large bowl. Add 85g (3oz) chilled, diced butter, margarine, or other fat. Lightly stir the butter to coat it in the flour.

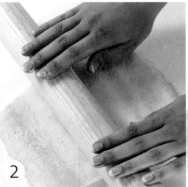

Rough Puff Pastry

1 **Sift 250g (9oz) plain** flour into a bowl. Add 85g (3oz) chilled diced butter and 85g (3oz) chilled diced white vegetable fat, then stir in the flour to coat. Add 150ml (5fl oz) iced water and a squeeze of lemon juice, and stir with a knife to bind.

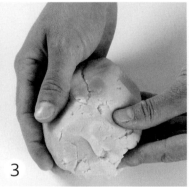

Sweet Shortcrust Pastry

1 **Sift 200g (7oz) plain white** flour and a pinch of salt onto a work surface. Make a well in the centre and add 85g (3oz) soft butter, 4 tbsp caster sugar, and 3 beaten egg yolks. Blend the ingredients in the well together with your fingertips.

Choux Pastry

1 **Bring 240ml (8fl oz) water** and 115g (4oz) diced butter to the boil over a high heat. Remove the pan from the heat and tip in 140g (5oz) plain white flour sifted with 1 tsp salt and 1 tsp sugar all at once and beat until the pastry is smooth.

Tips for Perfect Pastry

- Add chilled water, eggs, and fat straight from the refrigerator.
- Add liquid to the flour and fat mixture gradually. Flours have different absorption rates so you might not need all of it.

- Work quickly. The less you handle the dough the lighter and more delicate the baked pastry will be.
- Refrigerate your pastry dough for at least 30 minutes before rolling out. This makes it easier to roll and

helps prevent dough "shrinking" while baking.
- If at any time the pastry becomes sticky, immediately return it to the refrigerator for 15 minutes, before continuing with the recipe.

- Dust the work surface and rolling pin very lightly with flour when rolling out pastry. If too much extra flour is incorporated at this stage, the baked pastry will be tough.

how to make & use pastry

2 Quickly and lightly rub the fat into the flour with your fingertips until the mixture resembles coarse crumbs. Sprinkle over 2 tbsp iced water. Stir gently to mix.

3 Use your fingers to gather the pastry, and roll it around to form a ball, handling it as little as possible. Wrap the pastry ball in cling film and chill for at least 30 minutes before using.

2 Roll out the dough on a lightly floured surface into a rectangle 3 times as long as it is wide. Fold the top third of the pastry down, then bottom third up, as if folding a letter. Seal the open edges closed with the rolling pin. Wrap in cling film and chill for 15 minutes.

3 With the unfolded edges at the top and bottom, roll and fold the pastry as in step 2. Turn the pastry 90 degrees and repeat the rolling, folding, and turning twice more. Wrap and chill again for at least 30 minutes before using.

2 Using your fingertips, gradually work the sifted flour into the butter mixture until it forms very rough crumbs. If the butter mixture is too sticky and crumbs don't form, work in a little extra flour.

3 Gather the dough into a ball, then knead it very quickly and lightly until it is smooth and pliable. Shape it back into a ball, wrap in cling film, and chill for at least 30 minutes before using.

2 Return the pan to the heat and stir until the dough forms a ball and comes away from the sides of the pan. Quickly remove the pan from the heat.

3 Gradually beat in 4 eggs, one at a time, beating well after each addition. Continue beating until the mixture becomes shiny and drops off the spoon when shaken. It is now ready to use.

Tips for Better Baking

- Preheat the oven to the specified temperature before baking.
- For non-soggy double-crust pies, such as Apple Pie (p450), cut slits in the top crust to let steam escape during baking.
- Very lightly splash the baking tray with water before baking rough puff or puff pastry. The water creates steam in the hot oven, which helps form the many delicate layers.

Savoury Uses

Cheese Straws
Use rough puff or ready-made puff pastry to make these party favourites
🕐 35 mins   **page 55**

Gruyère Tart
A combination of wholemeal and plain flours adds flavour to this shortcrust pastry crust
🕐 1 hr 10 mins   **page 165**

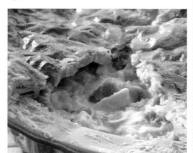

Chicken Pot Pie
Use rough puff pastry in this recipe to give a delightful contrast to the pie's creamy filling
🕐 35 mins   **page 286**

Sweet Uses

Pecan Pie
This American favourite with shortcrust pastry is very rich and filling
🕐 1 hr 45 mins   **page 425**

Lemon Meringue Pie
A creamy lemon filling and light meringue are encased in a shortcrust pastry case
🕐 1 hr 10 mins – 1 hr 20 mins   **page 432**

Profiteroles
A French classic, these cream-filled choux buns are always a popular dessert
🕐 1 hr   **page 439**

WHAT CAN I DO WITH LEFTOVER PASTRY?

- Leftover shortcrust and sweet shortcrust pastry trimmings can be gathered together, shaped into a ball, wrapped in cling film, and refrigerated for up to 3 days, or frozen for up to 6 months.

- Unbaked choux-pastry shapes can be refrigerated for up to 12 hours before filling and baking.

- Unbaked rough puff pastry can be refrigerated for up to 3 days, but it is difficult to re-use trimmings because re-rolling will knock out all the air that forms the layers.

- Rolled and shaped rough puff pastry, such as vol-au-vents, can be frozen for up to 6 months and then baked straight from the freezer, adding 5 minutes to the baking time.

Pastry   437

Cannoli

These crisp pastries filled with glacé fruits and ricotta cheese are a Sicilian speciality

 makes 16

 prep 30 mins, plus cooling
• cook 20 mins

deep-fat fryer or large saucepan half filled with oil; cannoli moulds

freeze the uncooked pastry for up to 3 months

For the pastry

175g (6oz) **plain flour**, plus extra for rolling and dusting

pinch of **salt**

60g (2oz) **butter**

45g (1½oz) **caster sugar**

1 **egg**, beaten

2–3 tbsp **dry white wine** or Marsala

1 **egg white**, lightly beaten

oil, for deep-frying

For the filling

60g (2oz) **dark chocolate**, grated or very finely chopped

350g (12oz) **ricotta cheese**

60g (2oz) **icing sugar**, plus extra to dust

finely grated zest of 1 **orange**

60g (2oz) chopped **glacé fruits** or candied citrus peel

● **Prepare ahead** The pastry can be made several hours in advance and kept chilled. Bring back to room temperature before rolling out.

1 **To make the pastry**, sift the flour and salt into a bowl, and rub in the butter. Stir in the sugar and mix in the beaten egg, and enough wine to make a soft dough. Knead until smooth.

2 **Roll out the pastry** thinly and cut into 16 squares, each measuring roughly 7.5cm (3in). Dust 4 cannoli moulds with flour and wrap a pastry square loosely around each

on the diagonal, dampening the edges with lightly beaten egg white and pressing them together to seal.

3 **Heat the oil** for deep-frying to 180°C (350°F) and deep-fry for 3–4 minutes, or until the pastry is golden and crisp. Drain on a plate lined with kitchen paper, and, when cool enough to handle, carefully twist the metal tubes so you can pull them out of the pastry. Cook 3 more batches in the same way.

4 **To make the filling**, mix together all the ingredients. When the pastry tubes are cold, pipe or spoon the filling into them. Dust with icing sugar to serve.

CANNOLI MOULDS

Although cannoli moulds are available from kitchen stores, short lengths of stainless steel tubing, 15cm (6in) long and 2cm (½in) in diameter, from a hardware shop, work equally well.

Mini Chocolate Nut Pastries

Tasty bite-sized chocolate pastries – the perfect treat

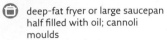 makes 24

prep 25 mins, plus resting
• cook 10–12 mins

115g (4oz) **ground hazelnuts**

2 tbsp **icing sugar**

3 tbsp **amaretto** or almond-flavoured liqueur

75g (2½oz) **dark chocolate**, grated

4 x **filo pastry sheets**, 18 x 30cm (7 x 12in)

3 tbsp **clear honey**, warmed

● **Prepare ahead** The pastries can be made up to 4 hours in advance.

1 **Preheat the oven** to 190°C (375°F/Gas 5). Lightly grease a baking tray. Mix the hazelnuts, 1½ tbsp sugar, amaretto, and chocolate until combined.

2 **Cut out** 24 squares, each 10cm (4in), from the filo. Place some filling in the middle of each square. Brush a little water around the edge, gather the sides around the filling, and pinch into a purse-like shape.

3 **Place the pastries** on the baking tray and bake for 10–12 minutes, or until golden. Brush gently with honey, leave for 5 minutes, then dust with icing sugar. Serve warm or cold.

Profiteroles

These filled choux pastry buns, drizzled with chocolate sauce, are a deliciously decadent dessert

🍴 serves 4

🕐 prep 30 mins, plus cooling
● cook 30 mins

🍳 2 piping bags with a 1cm (½in) plain nozzle and 5mm (¼in) plain nozzle

❄ freeze cooled and unfilled buns in freezer bags or a freezerproof container for up to 3 months; thaw at room temperature for 30 mins before filling and serving

For the choux buns

60g (2oz) plain flour

50g (1¾oz) butter

2 eggs, beaten

For the filling and topping

400ml (14fl oz) double cream

200g (7oz) dark chocolate, broken into pieces

25g (scant 1oz) butter

2 tbsp golden syrup

1 Preheat the oven to 220°C (425°F/ Gas 7). Line 2 large baking trays with greaseproof paper. Sift the flour onto a separate piece of greaseproof paper.

2 Put the butter and 150ml (5fl oz) water into a small saucepan and heat gently until melted. Bring to the boil, remove from the heat, and tip in the flour. Beat quickly with a wooden spoon until the mixture is thick, smooth, and forms a ball in the centre of the saucepan. Cool for 10 minutes.

3 Gradually add the eggs, beating well after each addition. Use enough egg to form a stiff, smooth, and shiny paste. Spoon the mixture into a piping bag fitted with a 1cm (½in) plain nozzle.

4 Pipe walnut-sized rounds, set well apart, on the prepared baking trays. Bake for 20 minutes, or until risen, golden, and crisp. Remove from the oven and make a small slit in the side of each bun to allow the steam to escape. Return to the oven for a further 2 minutes, allow them to crisp, then transfer to a wire rack to cool completely.

5 When ready to serve, pour 100ml (3½fl oz) cream into a saucepan and whip the remainder until just peaking. Pile into a piping bag fitted with a 5mm (¼in) plain nozzle.

6 Add the chocolate, butter, and syrup to the saucepan with the cream and heat very gently until melted, stirring frequently. Meanwhile, pipe cream into each choux bun and pile onto a serving plate or cake stand.

7 When the sauce has melted, mix well, and pour over the choux buns. Serve immediately.

● **Good with** a pile of fresh berry fruits, such as strawberries, raspberries, or blueberries.

VARIATION

Chocolate Eclairs

Instead of piping mounds onto the prepared baking trays, pipe 5cm (2in) lengths and bake as above. You should be able to make 10 eclairs. Allow them to cool, then fill as above, and spread with 150g (5½oz) melted chocolate that has been allowed to cool slightly. Leave to set for a few minutes in the fridge before serving.

Cantucci

From Tuscany, these crisp, twice-baked almond biscuits are ideal for dipping in glasses of vin santo after a meal

🍴 makes 32

🕐 prep 10 mins, plus cooling • cook 40 mins

❄️ freeze for up to 3 months; thaw at room temperature

3 large **eggs**, and 2 large **yolks**, beaten

350g (12oz) **plain white flour**, plus extra for shaping

150g (5½oz) **caster sugar**

150g (5½oz) whole **almonds**, roughly chopped and toasted

2 tsp **baking powder**

finely grated zest of 1 **orange**

● **Prepare ahead** The dough can be prepared up to step 3, covered with cling film and refrigerated for up to 2 days before baking.

1 Preheat the oven to 190°C (375°F/Gas 5) and grease one large baking sheet. Put 2 tbsp of the egg mixture in a separate bowl and set aside.

2 Combine the flour, sugar, almonds, baking powder, and orange zest in a large bowl and stir together. Make a well in the centre and add the eggs, stirring until a dough forms.

3 Shape the dough into a ball, then cut in half. Roll out the dough on a lightly floured surface into 2 logs, each 5cm (2in) wide and 2.5cm (1in) high. Place the logs on the baking sheet, flatten them slightly, and brush the tops with the reserved egg mixture.

4 Bake for 20 minutes, or until lightly browned and the centres are baked through. Remove from the oven and increase the temperature to 200°C (400°F/ Gas 6).

5 Cut the logs diagonally into 1cm (½in) slices. Return the slices to the baking sheet and continue baking for a further 8 minutes, or until golden. Leave the biscuits to cool on the baking sheets for 5 minutes, then transfer to wire racks to cool completely. Store in an airtight container for up to 5 days.

● **Good with** a glass of vin santo for dunking, or with coffee or tea.

● **Leftovers** can be stored in an airtight tin for several days.

Chocolate Chip Cookies

This universal favourite is childsplay to make and a hit with children and adults alike

🍴 makes 45 small cookies

🕐 prep 15 mins • cook 15-20 mins

125g (3½oz) **butter**, softened

125g (3½oz) **light soft brown sugar**

3 tbsp **golden syrup**

1 **egg**

225g (8oz) **self-raising flour**

150g (3½oz) **milk chocolate chips**

1 Preheat the oven to 180°C (350°F/Gas 4) and line baking sheets with greaseproof paper.

2 Cream together the butter and sugar and beat in the golden syrup and egg. Mix in the flour.

3 Place small piles of the mixture on the prepared baking trays, allowing plenty of room for spreading. You can make the cookies as big or as small as you wish. (For a large cookie, use a walnut-sized piece of dough; for a small cookie, use a teaspoon-sized piece.) Press down and decorate each cookie with chocolate chips, pressing them into the dough. Bake for 15-20 minutes, or until golden. Leave on the trays to cool completely.

● **Good with** other party treats for an afternoon tea party, or as part of a packed lunch.

VARIATION

White Chocolate Chip Cookies

Choose white chocolate chips or use bars of white chocolate broken into small pieces instead of the milk chocolate chips.

Shortbread

This popular Scottish bakery classic is an essential for afternoon tea

 makes 10

 prep 15 mins • bake 20 mins

 7.5cm (3 in) fluted cutter

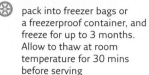 pack into freezer bags or a freezerproof container, and freeze for up to 3 months. Allow to thaw at room temperature for 30 mins before serving

175g (6oz) **unsalted butter**, softened

75g (2½oz) **caster sugar**, plus extra for sprinkling

250g (9oz) **plain flour**, plus extra for dusting

½ tsp **salt**

● **Prepare ahead** Make the shortbread dough up to 24 hours in advance of baking then store, wrapped, in the refrigerator.

1 Preheat the oven to 180°C (350°F/Gas 4). In a large bowl, beat the butter and sugar together until soft and creamy. Add the flour and salt and carefully mix together until well combined and the mixture forms into a firm dough.

2 Turn onto a lightly floured surface and knead gently until smooth. Roll the dough out to a thickness of 5mm (¼in). Using a 7.5cm (3in) round cutter, stamp out 10 rounds.

3 Arrange the shortbread on a large baking tray, spaced slightly apart. Prick the tops with a fork and bake for 20 minutes, or until lightly golden. Sprinkle with sugar and allow them to cool on the baking tray.

● **Good with** a freshly brewed pot of tea.

VARIATION

Chocolate Chip Shortbread

Mix 100g (3½oz) milk or plain chocolate chips into the mixture with the flour and follow the recipe.

Spritzgebäck Biscuits

These delicate, buttery, piped biscuits are based on a traditional type of German cookie that is popular at Christmas time

 makes 45

 prep 45 mins • cook 15 mins

 cookie press or piping bag

380g (13oz) **butter**, softened

250g (9oz) **caster sugar**

few drops of **pure vanilla extract**

pinch of **salt**

500g (1 lb 2oz) **plain flour**, sifted

125g (4½ oz) **ground almonds**

100g (3½ oz) **dark chocolate** or milk chocolate

1 Preheat the oven to 180°C (350°F/Gas 4). Line 2–3 large baking sheets with baking parchment and set aside.

2 Place the butter into a large bowl and beat with a hand mixer or wooden spoon until smooth. Gradually stir in the sugar, vanilla extract, and salt until the mixture is thick and the sugar has completely dissolved. Gradually add two-thirds of the flour, stirring in a little at a time.

3 Add the rest of the flour and ground almonds and knead the mixture briefly on a work surface to make a smooth dough. Shape the dough into rolls and, using a cookie press or piping bag and star nozzle, squeeze 7.5cm (3in) lengths of the dough on to the prepared baking sheets. Bake for 12 minutes, or until lightly golden, and transfer to a wire rack to cool.

4 Melt the chocolate gently in a microwave or in a bowl over a pan of barely simmering water. Dip one end of the cooled biscuits into the melted chocolate, returning to the rack to set. Store in an airtight container for 2–3 days.

VARIATION

Marbled Biscuits

Sift 2 tbsp cocoa powder and mix with 1 tbsp caster sugar. Mix into a third of the dough. When making the rolls for pressing, use two-thirds of light coloured dough and one-third of the chocolate dough and proceed as above.

Raspberry Sables

Originating from Normandy, the name of these rich biscuits comes from the French for "sand", as they have a light, crumbly texture

 makes 12–16

 prep 15 mins, plus chilling ● cook 8–10 mins

 7.5cm (3in) round cutter

 freeze the uncooked dough for up to 1 month

150g (5½oz) **plain flour**, plus extra for dusting

30g (1oz) **ground almonds**

85g (3oz) **icing sugar**

125g (4½oz) **butter**, softened

1 **egg yolk**

½ tsp **almond extract**

raspberry jam

● **Prepare ahead** The biscuit dough will keep for up to 1 week in the refrigerator. The plain, cooked biscuits will keep for several days in an airtight container.

1 **Place all the ingredients**, except the jam, in a food processor, and blend until the mixture forms a soft dough. If you do not have a food processor, beat the sugar, butter, and egg yolk together, then beat in the remaining ingredients (except for the jam) and knead to a soft dough. Wrap in cling film and chill for at least 30 minutes.

2 **Preheat the oven** to 190°C (375°F/Gas 5). Lightly grease 2 baking trays. Roll out the dough on a lightly floured work surface to a thickness of 3mm (⅛in), and cut out rounds with the biscuit cutter. Transfer to the baking trays. Re-roll the dough and cut out rounds until it has all been used. Do not overwork the dough or the biscuits will be tough.

3 **Bake the biscuits** for 8–10 minutes, or until pale golden. Allow to cool slightly on the tray, then transfer to a wire rack to cool completely. To complete, sandwich 2 biscuits together with raspberry jam.

● **Good with** fresh raspberries and a dollop of whipped cream for a delicious dessert.

Oatmeal Cookies

These are a healthier-option biscuit as they are made with sunflower oil rather than butter

 makes 30

prep 10 mins ● cook 20 mins

175g (6oz) **rolled oats**

115g (4oz) **light soft brown sugar**

120ml (4fl oz) **sunflower oil**, plus extra for greasing

1 **egg**, beaten

½ tsp **pure vanilla extract**

● **Prepare ahead** If stored in an airtight container, these cookies will stay crisp for up to 7 days.

1 **Preheat the oven** to 160°C (325°F/Gas 3) and lightly oil 2 baking trays.

2 **Put the oats**, sugar, and oil in a mixing bowl and stir together until combined. Add the beaten egg and vanilla extract, and mix well.

3 **Place small spoonfuls** of mixture onto the baking trays, spacing them apart to allow for spreading. Flatten each slightly with the back of a fork. Bake for 15–18 minutes, or until golden.

4 **Remove the sheets** from the oven and leave for 1–2 minutes, then transfer the cookies to a wire rack to cool completely.

● **Good with** a glass of milk as an after-school snack, or as part of a packed lunch or picnic.

VARIATION

Peanut Butter Cookies

Substitute 1 tbsp of rolled oats with 1 tbsp crunchy peanut butter. Finish and bake as above.

Florentines

These crisp Italian biscuits are packed full of fruit and nuts, and coated with thin layers of luxurious dark chocolate

makes 16–20

prep 20 mins • cook 15–20 mins

60g (2oz) butter

60g (2oz) caster sugar

1 tbsp clear honey

60g (2oz) plain flour

45g (1½oz) chopped mixed peel

45g (1½oz) glacé cherries, finely chopped

45g (1½oz) blanched almonds, finely chopped

1 tsp lemon juice

1 tbsp double cream

175g (6oz) dark chocolate

1 Preheat the oven to 180°C (350°F/Gas 4) and line 2 baking trays with greaseproof paper.

2 Put the butter, sugar, and honey into a small saucepan, and melt gently over a low heat. Then allow to cool until it is just warm. Stir in the next 6 ingredients.

3 Using a teaspoon, drop spoonfuls of the mixture on to the baking trays, leaving space between them for the biscuits to spread.

4 Bake for 10 minutes, or until golden. Do not let them get too dark. Leave them on the baking tray for a few minutes, before lifting them onto a wire rack to cool completely.

5 Break the chocolate up, and put it into a heatproof bowl set over a pan of gently simmering water. Make sure the bowl is not touching the water. Once the chocolate has melted, spread a thin layer of chocolate on the bottom of each biscuit, and place, chocolate-side up, on the wire rack to set. Spread a second layer of chocolate over. Just before they set, make a wavy line in the chocolate with a fork.

> **BAKE TEST**
> To gauge how the mixture is working, test-bake a few florentines. If they are a bit thick, add more honey. If they are too thin, with too many holes, add more flour.

Macaroons

These biscuits are crisp outside and slightly chewy inside. On storing, they tend to dry out – so just give in to temptation

makes 24

prep 10 mins • cook 12–15 mins

2 egg whites

225g (8oz) caster sugar

125g (4½oz) ground almonds

30g (1oz) rice flour

few drops almond extract

24 blanched almonds

6 sheets edible wafer paper

● **Prepare ahead** The macaroons will keep for a few days stored in an airtight container.

1 Preheat the oven to 180°C (350°F/Gas 4). In a large, very clean bowl, whisk the egg whites until stiff, preferably using an electric whisk. Gradually whisk in the sugar, 1 tablespoon at a time, to give a thick, glossy meringue. Fold in the ground almonds, rice flour, and almond extract until well combined.

2 Divide the sheets of edible wafer paper between the 2 baking trays. Place 4 rounded teaspoons of mixture on each piece of edible wafer paper, trying to keep the mixture in rounds, and positioning it on the paper so they are not touching. Place a blanched almond in the centre of each biscuit.

3 Bake the macaroons in the centre of the oven for 12–15 minutes, or until they start to turn a light golden colour.

4 Remove the baking tray from the oven, and slide the wafer papers with the macaroons on to a wire rack. Leave them to cool. When cold, peel the excess paper away from around the base of the macaroons, and store the biscuits in an airtight container until serving.

● **Good with** other teatime treats, such as oatmeal cookies or chocolate-covered florentines.

VARIATION

Hazelnut Macaroons
Substitute ground hazelnuts for ground almonds, and hazelnut essence for almond essence. Place a blanched hazelnut on top of each, instead of a blanched almond. If you can't find hazelnut essence, use a few drops of vanilla extract instead.

Spitzbuben

These melt-in-the-mouth biscuits are a festive treat in Germany, where their name means "little rascals"

- 🍴 makes 9
- 🕐 prep 30 mins • cook 8–10 mins
- 📦 7.5cm (3in) fluted cutter; 2.5cm (1in) plain cutter
- ❄️ freeze the unbaked biscuit dough for up to 1 month

115g (4oz) **butter**, diced

115g (4oz) **caster sugar**

1 large **egg**, beaten

few drops of **pure vanilla extract**

300g (11oz) **plain flour**

pinch of **salt**

raspberry jam or strawberry jam, to decorate

icing sugar, for dusting

1 Beat the butter in a mixing bowl until smooth, then beat in the sugar until creamy. Gradually beat in the egg and vanilla, then sift in the flour and salt, and mix. The dough should be soft, but firm enough to roll. Add more flour if needed for firmness.

2 Preheat the oven to 190°C (375°F/Gas 5). Roll out the dough to 5mm (¼in) thick on a lightly floured surface. Cut out the biscuits using the fluted cutter. Gather up and re-roll the trimmings. You will need 18 rounds in total.

3 Cut a circle from the centre of 9 cookies using the plain cutter. Lift all the cookie rounds onto non-stick baking trays and bake for 8–10 minutes, or until pale golden. Transfer to a wire rack to cool.

4 Spread the biscuits with a little raspberry jam. Dust the cookies with the holes in with icing sugar, and carefully sandwich the cookies together in pairs.

VARIATION

German Butter Cookies

Roll the dough into walnut-sized balls. Press your thumb in the top of each, fill the dip with jam, and press an almond on top. Bake as above.

Tuile Biscuits

These light, crisp biscuits curl up gently as they cool

- 🍴 makes 15
- 🕐 prep 10 mins • cook 30 mins

50g (1¾oz) **butter**, softened

50g (1¾oz) **icing sugar**

1 **egg**

50g (1¾oz) **plain flour**

1 Preheat the oven to 200°C (400°F/Gas 6). Place the butter and icing sugar in a bowl, and cream together until light and fluffy. Beat in the egg and gently fold in the flour.

2 Line a baking tray with greaseproof paper. Place 1–2 tsp of the mixture on the lined sheet and spread it thinly to make a round 6–8cm (2½–3½in) in diameter. Make another 1 or 2 rounds on the sheet. Bake for 5–8 minutes, or until they just start to turn a pale golden colour.

3 Remove the baking tray from the oven and, working quickly, slide a palette knife under the tuiles to release them, then drape them over a rolling pin so that they cool in a curved shape.

4 Repeat the baking and shaping process with the remaining mixture.

TIGHTER CURLS

For more tightly curled biscuits, wrap the tuiles around the oiled handle of a wooden spoon instead of draping them over a rolling pin.

Flapjacks

These chewy bars are simple to make, using only a few storecupboard ingredients

- 🍴 makes 16–20
- 🕐 prep 15 mins, plus cooling • cook 40 mins
- 📦 25cm (10in) square cake tin

225g (8oz) **butter**, plus extra for greasing

225g (8oz) **light soft brown sugar**

2 tbsp **golden syrup**

350g (12oz) **rolled oats**

● **Prepare ahead** Make these a few days in advance and store in an airtight container.

1 Preheat the oven to 150°C (300°F/Gas 2). Lightly grease the square cake tin.

2 Put the butter, sugar, and syrup in a large saucepan and heat over a medium-low heat until the butter has melted. Remove the pan from the heat and stir in the oats.

3 Transfer the mixture to the prepared tin and press down firmly. Bake for 40 minutes, or until evenly golden and just beginning to brown at the edges.

4 Leave to cool for 10 minutes, then cut into 16 squares, or 20 rectangles. Leave in the tin until completely cooled.

Chocolate Brownies

Slightly soft in the centre, these make a tempting teatime treat

🍴 makes 16

🕐 prep 10 mins
• cook 1 hr 15 mins

▢ 20cm (8in) deep square tin; wire rack; serrated knife

50g (1¾oz) **dark chocolate**, chopped

25g (scant 1oz) **butter**

3 **eggs**

1 tbsp **clear honey**

225g (8oz) **soft light brown sugar**

75g (2½oz) **self-raising flour**

175g (6oz) **walnut pieces**

25g (scant 1oz) **white chocolate**, chopped

● **Prepare ahead** The brownies will stay fresh for up to 5 days if tightly wrapped in foil or stored in an airtight container.

1 **Preheat the oven** to 160°C (325°F/Gas 3). Lightly grease or line a 20cm (8in) deep square cake tin with greaseproof paper.

2 **Put the dark chocolate** and butter into a small heatproof bowl over a saucepan of simmering water until melted, stirring occasionally. Don't let the bowl touch the water. Remove the bowl from the pan and set aside to cool slightly.

3 **Beat the eggs**, honey, and brown sugar together, then gradually beat in the melted chocolate mixture. Sift the flour over, add the walnut pieces and white chocolate to the bowl, and gently fold the ingredients together. Pour the mixture into the prepared tin.

4 **Put the tin** in the oven and bake for 30 minutes. Cover loosely with foil and bake for a further 45 minutes. The centre should be a little soft. Leave to cool completely in the tin on a wire rack.

5 **When cold**, invert the brownies on to a board, remove the tin, and cut into squares.

● **Good with** a scoop of vanilla ice cream on top, or try cinnamon or lemon ice cream.

Gingerbread Biscuits

These delicious, fragrant biscuits are quick and easy to make, and popular with everyone

🍴 makes 45

🕐 prep 30 mins, plus cooling
• cook 8–10 mins

▢ biscuit cutters, of your choice, about 7.5cm (3in) in diameter

250g (9oz) **plain flour**

2 tsp **baking powder**

175g (6oz) **caster sugar**

few drops of **pure vanilla extract**

½ tsp **mixed spice**

2 tsp **ground ginger**

100g (3½oz) **clear honey**

1 **egg**, separated

4 tsp **milk**

125g (4½oz) **butter**, softened

125g (4½oz) **ground almonds**

flour, for dusting

chopped **hazelnuts** or almonds, to decorate

1 **Preheat the oven** to 180°C (350°F/Gas 4). Line 2 baking trays with greaseproof paper.

2 **Mix together** the flour and baking powder, and sift into a bowl. Add the sugar, vanilla extract, mixed spice, ginger, honey, egg yolk, milk, butter, and ground almonds. Using a wooden spoon or hand mixer with dough hook, bring the mixture together to form a soft dough, then, using your hands, shape into a ball.

3 **Roll the dough** out thinly on a lightly floured surface to a thickness of 5mm (¼in). Cut out the biscuits using shaped cutters, and place on the baking trays, spaced slightly apart to allow them to spread. Beat the egg white and brush over the biscuits, then sprinkle over the nuts. Bake for 8–10 minutes, or until lightly golden brown.

4 **Remove from the oven** and allow to cool on the tray for 5 minutes, then transfer to a wire rack to cool completely.

Dulce de Leche

An indulgent caramelized milk dessert that is very popular in in Latin America

🍴 serves 8

🕐 prep 5 mins • cook 3¼ hrs

3 litres (5¼ pints) whole milk

600g (1lb 5oz) sugar

3 tbsp white wine vinegar

vanilla ice cream, to serve

1 **Bring the milk** and sugar to the boil in a large saucepan. Reduce to a simmer and add the vinegar; this will separate the milk and sugar.

2 **Simmer for 3 hours**, or until the liquid evaporates, leaving an almost solid toffee. Cool completely and serve with vanilla ice cream.

● **Good with** ice cream, fresh fruit, such as sliced bananas or fruit compotes.

● **Leftovers** can be stirred into slightly softened vanilla ice cream and refrozen. Serve in wafer cones or little cups.

Rich Vanilla Buttercream Icing

This simple recipe can be used to ice cupcakes and sandwich cake layers together

🍴 makes 350g (12oz)

🕐 prep 10 mins

115g (4oz) unsalted butter, at room temperature

2 tbsp milk

1 tsp pure vanilla extract

225g (8oz) icing sugar

● **Prepare ahead** The icing will keep, covered, in the refrigerator for 2 days. If it is too stiff to spread, stir in a little extra milk.

1 **Put the butter**, half the milk, and the vanilla extract in a large mixing bowl and beat until smooth and blended using a hand-held electric mixer.

2 **Sift over** the icing sugar and, with the mixer on a low speed, continue mixing until the icing is smooth and has a spreading consistency. If it is too stiff, beat in a little extra milk.

Chocolate Dessert Sauce

Serve this sauce warm or cold over a variety of desserts. For best results, use a 70 per cent dark chocolate

🍴 makes 300ml (10fl oz)

🕐 prep 5 mins • cook 6–7 mins

225g (8oz) **70 per cent dark chocolate**, broken into pieces

30g (1oz) butter

4 tbsp golden syrup

3 drops pure vanilla extract

● **Prepare ahead** Store the sauce, covered, in the refrigerator for up to 1 week; reheat gently.

1 **Place all the ingredients** along with 2 tbsp water into a small saucepan and heat gently, stirring, for 6–7 minutes, or until smooth and glossy.

● **Good with** ice cream, profiteroles, and poached fruit.

VARIATION

Chocolate and Coffee Dessert Sauce

For a more sophisticated chocolate sauce, add 5–6 tbsp strong black coffee, 2 tbsp brandy, and 1–3 tbsp icing sugar, to taste.

Butterscotch Dessert Sauce

Rich and buttery, this sauce is a big hit with children

🍴 makes 300ml (10fl oz)

🕐 prep 5 mins • cook 5 mins

85g (3oz) butter

115g (4oz) light muscovado sugar

200ml (7fl oz) double cream

● **Prepare ahead** Keep the sauce in an airtight container in the refrigerator for up to 1 week. Reheat gently, a spoonful at a time, so the butter mixes in evenly.

1 **Melt the butter** in a small saucepan. Stir in the sugar and cook over a low heat, stirring occasionally, until the sugar dissolves.

2 **Pour in the cream** and stir until well combined and glossy. Increase the heat and boil gently, whisking, for 2 minutes, or until thickened slightly. Remove from the heat and allow to cool. Serve warm or cold.

● **Good with** ice cream or, for an indulgent dessert, pancakes stacked with whipped cream, sliced bananas, and toasted pecan nuts.

Raspberry Coulis

This quick and easy fruit sauce is an excellent way to add a fresh flavour to all kinds of desserts

🍴 makes 300ml (10fl oz)

🕐 prep 10 mins

❄ freeze for up to 6 months

350g (12oz) fresh **raspberries**

3 tbsp **caster sugar**

2 tsp fresh **orange** juice or lemon juice

1 **Put the raspberries**, sugar, orange juice, and 4 tbsp water in a food processor or blender and process until puréed.

2 **Using a wooden spoon**, push the purée through a fine nylon sieve into a bowl. Taste the coulis and add extra sugar or orange juice to taste, stirring to dissolve the sugar.

3 **Cover the bowl** with cling film and chill until required.

● **Prepare ahead** The sauce can be made up to 2 days in advance and chilled until required.

● **Good with** poached fruit, rich chocolate cake, or drizzled over vanilla ice cream.

Ginger Cream Sauce

Make ordinary fruit into a delicious dessert by dipping in this creamy sauce

🍴 serves 6

🕐 prep 10 mins, plus 1 hr infusing ● cook 45 mins

900ml (1½ pints) **double cream**

125g (4½oz) **caster sugar**

225g (8oz) fresh **root ginger**, peeled and sliced

4 **star anise**

6 **egg yolks**, beaten

five-spice powder, to decorate (optional)

1 **Put the cream** and sugar in a saucepan and heat to just below boiling point. Add the root ginger and star anise and turn off the heat. Cover, and leave the cream to infuse for 1 hour.

2 **Reheat the cream** until just below boiling point. Put the egg yolks in a mixing bowl and strain the cream through a sieve onto the egg yolks. Mix well. Discard the ginger and star anise. Strain the cream and egg mixture back into the pan.

3 **Cook over** a very low heat, stirring constantly, until the sauces thickens. Serve in small pots, decorated with a sprinkle of five-spice powder, if desired.

● **Good with** slices of autumn fruits, such as pears, apples, and figs.

Crème Anglaise

This classic vanilla sauce is wonderful over hot puddings or served cold with berries

🍴 makes 300ml (10fl oz)

🕐 prep 5 mins • cook 10 mins

300ml (10fl oz) **milk**

1 **vanilla pod**, split lengthways

3 **egg yolks**

3 tbsp **caster sugar**

1 tsp **pure vanilla extract** (optional)

● **Prepare ahead** The sauce can be made up to 3 days in advance and refrigerated until required.

1 **Heat the milk** and vanilla pod in a saucepan until nearly boiling. Remove the pan from the heat and leave for 10 minutes, to allow the flavour of the vanilla pod to infuse the milk. Scrape some of the seeds into the milk. Remove the pod, rinse it, and let it dry. When dry, store in an airtight container, as it can be used again.

2 **Meanwhile**, beat the yolks with the caster sugar. Whisk in the hot milk, then return the mixture to the pan.

3 **Place the pan** over a medium-low heat, and simmer, stirring continuously, with a wooden spoon until the sauce is just thick enough to coat the back of the spoon. Do not allow the sauce to boil once the egg yolks are added or the sauce will curdle.

4 **Strain the sauce** through a sieve into a bowl and use as required. If using vanilla extract, add it at this point. If serving cold, stir occasionally to avoid a skin forming.

THICKER CUSTARD

The proportion of egg yolk to milk will affect the thickness of the sauce. The recipe given will produce a sauce with a pouring consistency. If you wish the sauce to be thicker—for using in a trifle, for example—add more yolks.

Crème Pâtissière

This sweet pastry cream is a rich and creamy filling for fruit tarts and choux buns

🍴 makes 300ml (10fl oz)

🕐 prep 10 mins • cook 5 mins

300ml (10fl oz) **milk**

2 **egg yolks**

60g (2oz) **caster sugar**

20g (¾oz) **plain flour**

20g (¾oz) **cornflour**

¼ tsp **pure vanilla extract**

● **Prepare ahead** The crème pâtissière can be made 1 day in advance, covered with cling film, and chilled in a refrigerator until ready to use.

1 **Pour the milk** into a saucepan and heat it to simmering point.

2 **Beat the eggs** and sugar together in a bowl, mix in the flour and cornflour, then pour in the hot milk, and mix well.

3 **Return the mixture** to the pan and bring it slowly to the boil, stirring continuously until it becomes smooth and lump-free. Once the mixture reaches boiling point, reduce the heat, and simmer, stirring for 1–2 minutes, to cook the flour.

4 **Allow it to cool** a little, then stir in the vanilla extract. Use at once, or cover and chill until needed.

Chocolate Custard

This is a rich custard, that both children and adults will enjoy

 makes 350ml (12fl oz)

prep 5 mins, plus cooling • cook 10 mins

300ml (10fl oz) milk

3 egg yolks

5 tbsp caster sugar

½ tsp pure vanilla extract

120g (4oz) dark chocolate, finely chopped

● **Prepare ahead** The sauce can be made 1 day in advance and refrigerated until required. Gradually whisk in a little boiling water and reheat gently.

1 Pour the milk into a saucepan over a medium heat, and heat until small bubbles form on the edge and steam rises. Do not allow the milk to boil.

2 Using an electric mixer, whisk the egg yolks and sugar together until pale yellow and thick. Slowly whisk in the warm milk.

3 Return the mixture to the saucepan and simmer, stirring continuously, over a very low heat until the sauce thickens and coats the back of a spoon. Stir in the vanilla extract, then add the chocolate and stir until it has completely melted.

4 Remove the pan from the heat and strain into a jug or bowl. Serve hot or allow to cool slightly and serve warm.

● **Good with** fresh fruit or poured over sponge cake.

VARIATION

Chocolate-orange Custard

Add 1–2 tbsp finely grated orange zest to the milk in step 1. Leave the milk to infuse for 20 minutes, then strain the milk onto the egg mixture and proceed with the recipe.

Rich Custard

Served warm or cold, this custard tastes great with many different kinds of puddings

 makes 300ml (10fl oz)

prep 10 mins • cook 15 mins

3 egg yolks

2 tbsp caster sugar

½ tsp cornflour

150ml (5fl oz) milk

150ml (5fl oz) double cream

2–3 strips of thinly pared lemon zest

● **Prepare ahead** Can be made up to 2 days in advance, covered, and refrigerated until required.

1 Whisk together the egg yolks, caster sugar, cornflour, and 3 tbsp milk until well blended.

2 Heat the remaining milk, double cream, and lemon zest in a saucepan. Remove from the heat and leave to infuse for 10 minutes. Strain the cream mixture over the egg yolks, whisking continuously. Pour the mixture back into the saucepan, and cook over a low heat, stirring continuously, for 6–8 minutes, or until the mixture is thick enough to coat the back of a spoon. Transfer the custard to a jug and serve.

VARIATION

German-style Vanilla Custard

Omit the lemon zest and replace with 1 split vanilla pod. After the mixture has infused, remove the pod, scrape out the seeds, and return to the cream mixture. Complete the recipe as above. The cleaned pod can be stored in a jar of caster sugar, for at least 2 weeks, to make vanilla sugar.

CUSTARD TIP

To prevent a skin from forming as the custard cools, wet a piece of greaseproof paper and cover the surface.

Apple Pie

A perennial favourite, this version uses ready-made pastry to shorten cooking time

- makes 8 slices
- 25 mins, plus 15 mins chilling • cook 50 mins
- 23cm (9in) deep pie plate with a flat rim and a large bowl

375g (13oz) ready-made **shortcrust pastry**

finely grated zest of 1 **lemon**

2 tbsp fresh **lemon juice**

100g (3½oz) **caster sugar**

4 tbsp **plain flour**

1 tsp **ground mixed spice**

7 **apples**, peeled and thinly sliced

2 tbsp **milk**, to glaze

● **Prepare ahead** Step 1 can be completed a day in advance. Cover the pastry with cling film and chill.

1 Divide the dough into 2 pieces: one piece should be two-thirds of the dough, the other about one-third. On a lightly floured work surface, roll the larger piece into a 30cm (12in) circle and use to line the pie plate, leaving any excess overhang. Cover with cling film and chill for at least 15 minutes. Roll out the remaining dough into a 25cm (10in) circle, place on a plate, cover, and refrigerate.

2 Meanwhile, preheat the oven to 200°C (400°F/Gas 6) with a baking tray inside. Mix the lemon zest and juice, sugar, flour, and mixed spice in a large bowl. Gently toss with the apple slices.

3 Tip the filling into the pie plate. Lightly brush the pastry on the rim of the pie plate with water and place the smaller dough circle on top. Crimp the edges together and cut off the excess pastry. Carefully brush the top of the pastry with milk and cut a few slits.

4 Put the pie on the hot baking tray in the oven. Reduce the temperature to 190°C (375°F/Gas 5) and bake for 50–55 minutes, or until the pastry is golden brown. Leave to stand for 5 minutes, then slice and serve hot.

● **Good with** a scoop of vanilla ice cream or crème Anglaise.

Portuguese Apple Fritters

These light, batter-coated rings contain sweet, soft apple, with the aromatic flavours of aniseed and cinnamon

- makes 20–25
- prep 20 mins, plus resting • cook 15–20 mins
- deep-fat fryer or large saucepan

3 sweet **dessert apples**, such as Golden Delicious, sliced into 3–4mm (⅛in) thick rings

2 tbsp **lemon juice**

4 tbsp **aniseed liqueur**, such as Anis del Mono, Ouzo, or Sambuca

150g (5oz) **caster sugar**

2 **eggs**

150ml (5fl oz) **milk**

75ml (2fl oz) **olive oil**

250g (9oz) **plain flour**

1½ tsp **baking powder**

¼ tsp **ground cinnamon**

vegetable oil, for deep frying

icing sugar, for dusting

1 Peel, core, and thinly slice the apples. Place them in a bowl, sprinkle with the lemon juice, liqueur, and 4 tbsp of the caster sugar. Mix and set aside for 30 minutes.

2 Meanwhile, to make the batter, mix the eggs, milk, and olive oil with the remaining sugar. Sift in the flour, baking powder, and cinnamon and stir well to make a thick, smooth batter. Set aside for 30 minutes, to rest.

3 Heat the oil until a piece of day-old bread sizzles and browns in less than 1 minute. Dip the apple in the batter and fry in batches until golden and crisp. Drain on kitchen paper and serve warm, dusted with icing sugar.

● **Good with** vanilla ice cream, as a dessert, or just as they are with a cup of strong black coffee.

Peach Gratin with Muscat Sabayon

Hot peaches topped with this delicate sauce make a light summer dessert

🍴 serves 4

🕐 prep 20 mins • cook 25 mins

4 peaches

2 figs, quartered (optional)

30g (1oz) vanilla sugar

pinch of ground cardamom

grated zest and juice of 1 lemon

4 egg yolks

60g (2oz) caster sugar

4 tbsp Muscat wine

1 **Preheat the oven** to 200°C (400°F/Gas 6). To peel the peaches, bring a large saucepan of water to the boil and have a bowl of cold water ready. Plunge the peaches into the boiling water for 10–15 seconds, then remove them and place into the cold water. Carefully peel away the skins.

2 **Cut each peach** in half and remove the stone, then cut each half into 3 wedges. Place the wedges, with the fig quarters (if using), in a flameproof dish and sprinkle with the vanilla sugar, cardamom, lemon zest and juice. Bake for 20 minutes.

3 **Meanwhile**, to make the sabayon, place the egg yolks, caster sugar, and wine in a heatproof bowl and place over, but not in, a pan of hot water. Whisk constantly, ideally with an electric whisk, until thickened and frothy.

4 **Preheat the grill** on its highest setting. Pour the sabayon over the fruit, grill for 30 seconds, then serve.

VARIATION

Red Fruits with Muscat Sabayon

Cut 350g (12oz) strawberries in half and place in a flameproof dish with 175g (6oz) raspberries and 175g (6oz) redcurrants or blueberries. Continue with the recipe from step 2. If you have time, the fruits will benefit from 2 hours marinating.

Pineapple Fritters

Crisp and juicy, these hot treats must be served immediately

🍴 serves 4

🕐 prep 20 mins, plus resting • cook 10 mins

1 pineapple, peeled, cored, and sliced into 1.5cm (½in) rings

500ml (16fl oz) sunflower oil, for frying

icing sugar, to serve

For the batter

115g (4oz) plain flour

45g (1½oz) caster sugar

pinch of salt

1 egg

1 egg, separated

150ml (5fl oz) milk

1 **Make the batter** by putting the flour, sugar, and salt in a large mixing bowl. Add the egg, egg yolk, and the milk. Whisk quickly to make a smooth batter.

2 **Whisk the egg white** to form stiff peaks and fold it gently into the batter.

3 **Half fill a large frying pan** with the oil and heat until a piece of day-old bread sizzles and browns in less than 1 minute. Reduce the heat to medium, dip the pineapple slices into the batter, then carefully lower into the oil. Fry for 1–2 minutes, or until golden brown on both sides.

4 **Remove from the pan**, drain on kitchen paper, and sprinkle with icing sugar. Serve immediately.

● **Leftovers** can be cut into pieces and mixed with fresh fruit or vanilla or chocolate icecream.

VARIATION

Banana Fritters

Use 4 bananas, each cut in half lengthways, instead of pineapple.

Viennese Apple Strudel

One of the most traditional Austrian desserts, famous for its delicate pastry, and delicious served warm or cold

🍴 serves 10–12

🕐 prep 50 mins, plus resting
• cook 40 mins

1kg (2¼lb) **dessert apples**, such as Cox or Braeburn

grated zest of ½ **lemon**

3 tbsp **rum**

60g (2oz) **raisins**

100g (3½oz) **caster sugar**

few drops of **pure vanilla extract**

60g (2oz) blanched **almonds**, chopped

4 25 x 45cm (10 x 18in) sheets **filo pastry**, thawed if frozen

60g (2oz) **butter**, melted

60–85g (2–3oz) fresh **breadcrumbs**

icing sugar, for dusting

1 Preheat the oven to 180°C (350°F/Gas 4). Grease a large baking tray. To make the filling, peel, core, and cut the apples into small pieces. Place into a bowl and mix together with the lemon zest, rum, raisins, caster sugar, vanilla extract, and almonds.

2 Place a sheet of filo on a clean work surface and brush with melted butter. Lay another sheet on top and brush with butter. Repeat with the remaining pastry sheets.

3 Sprinkle the breadcrumbs over the pastry, leaving a 2cm (¾in) border. Spoon the filling over the breadcrumbs and fold the edges of the short sides that have been left uncovered over the filling. Roll the pastry, starting from one of the longer sides, and press the ends together tightly. Transfer the strudel onto the baking tray and brush with a little more melted butter.

4 Bake in the oven for 30–40 minutes, brushing the strudel with the remaining melted butter after the first 20 minutes.

5 Remove the strudel from the oven and allow to cool on the baking tray. Sprinkle liberally with icing sugar and serve warm or cold.

● **Good with** whipped cream.

> **PREPARING THE APPLES**
> To ensure your strudel does not turn soggy, choose crisp apples and avoid ones that are too ripe. Also, avoid cutting the apples too small, as they will soften while baking.

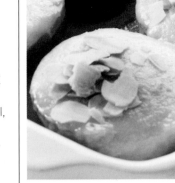

Baked Peaches with Marzipan and Almonds

You cannot beat the fresh, fragrant flavour of ripe, baked peaches oozing sweet juices

🍴 serves 4

🕐 prep 15 mins
• cook 20–25 mins

📦 shallow ovenproof dish

4 ripe **peaches**

60g (2oz) **marzipan**

1–2 tbsp **double cream**

30g (1oz) **flaked almonds**

1 tbsp **clear honey**

2 tbsp **golden caster sugar**

8 tbsp **sweet wine** or Marsala

1 Preheat the oven to 200°C (400°F/Gas 6). Cut the peaches in half and remove the stones. Place in an ovenproof dish in a single layer, cut-side upwards. Mash the marzipan with the cream and spoon into the centre of the peaches. Sprinkle over the flaked almonds and drizzle over the honey.

2 Sprinkle over the caster sugar, pour over the wine, and bake for 20–25 minutes, or until just tender. Remove from the oven, cover, and leave to stand for 5 minutes.

● **Good with** crème fraîche.

Plum Crumble

This popular dessert is quick and easy to make, suitable for both family lunches and dinner parties for friends

🍴 serves 4

🕐 prep 10 mins
• cook 30–40 mins

❄️ freeze for up to 2 months

600g (1lb 5oz) **plums**, stoned and halved

maple syrup or honey, to drizzle

For the crumble

150g (5½oz) **plain flour**

100g (3½oz) **butter**, chilled, and cubed

75g (2½oz) **light soft brown sugar**

60g (2oz) **rolled oats**

⬤ **Prepare ahead** The crumble mix can be made 1 month in advance and kept frozen until ready to use.

1 **Preheat the oven** to 200°C (400°F/Gas 6). To make the crumble topping, place the flour in a large mixing bowl. Rub in the butter with your fingertips until the mixture resembles breadcrumbs. Do not make it too fine or your crumble will have a stodgy top. Stir in the sugar and the oats.

2 **Place the plums** in a medium ovenproof dish, drizzle the maple syrup over, and top with the crumble. Bake for 30–40 minutes, or until the top is golden brown and the plum juices are bubbling.

VARIATION

Rhubarb Crumble

Use 750g (1lb 10oz) rhubarb, cut into 2.5cm (1in) lengths. Generously drizzle the rhubarb with honey and a squeeze of orange juice, then top it with the crumble mix and bake.

Pears Poached in Wine

Wine gives a great depth of flavour to cooked fruit

🍴 serves 4

🕐 prep 5 mins • cook 30 mins

4 firm **pears**

200ml (7floz) **red wine**

50g (2oz) **golden caster sugar**

1 tbsp **lemon juice**

1 **cinnamon stick**

¼ tsp grated **nutmeg**

4 **cloves**

⬤ **Prepare ahead** The pears can be prepared, poached, and chilled up to 3 days in advance.

1 **Peel the pears**, leaving the stalks attached, and cut a small slice from the bottom of each so they will stand up when serving.

2 **Place the wine**, sugar, lemon juice, and spices in a saucepan and heat gently, stirring until the sugar dissolves; then add the pears.

3 **Cover the pan** and simmer gently for 20 minutes, or until the pears are tender, basting often.

4 **Remove the pears** and set aside. Remove the cinnamon stick and discard.

5 **Return the pan** to the heat and boil rapidly until the wine is syrupy and reduced by about one-third. Pour the reduced syrup over the pears.

6 **Serve hot**, or allow to cool in the syrup and chill in a refrigerator before serving.

⬤ **Good with** yogurt, crème fraîche, or ice cream.

VARIATION

Pears in White Wine

Substitute white wine or cider for the red wine; the result will be paler and more golden in colour. Choose a dry white wine or cider, or reduce the amount of sugar in the recipe.

Tarte aux Pommes

This dessert is based on a French classic, using two types of apple:
cooking apples that cook down to a purée, and dessert apples that keep their shape

makes 8 slices

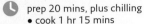
prep 20 mins, plus chilling
• cook 1 hr 15 mins

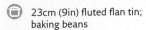
23cm (9in) fluted flan tin;
baking beans

❄ freeze for up to 1 month

375g packet **ready-made sweet pastry**

50g (1¾oz) **butter**

750g (1lb 10oz) **cooking apples**, peeled, cored, and chopped

125g (4½oz) **caster sugar**

finely grated zest and juice of ½ **lemon**

2 tbsp **Calvados** or brandy

2 **dessert apples**

2 tbsp **apricot jam**, sieved

1 Roll the pastry out on a lightly floured surface and line a fluted flan tin. Trim around the top of the tin and prick the pastry base with a fork. Chill the pastry case for at least 30 minutes.

2 Preheat the oven to 200°C (400°F/Gas 6). Line the pastry case with greaseproof paper and fill with baking beans. Bake for 15 minutes. Remove the paper and beans, then return to the oven for a further 5 minutes, or until the pastry is a light golden colour.

3 Melt the butter in a saucepan and add the cooking apples. Cover and cook over low heat, stirring occasionally, for 15 minutes, or until soft and mushy.

4 Push the cooked apple through a sieve to produce a smooth purée, then return it to the

saucepan. Reserve 1 tbsp caster sugar and add the rest to the apple purée, then stir in the lemon zest and Calvados. Return the pan to the heat and simmer, stirring continuously until it thickens.

5 Spoon the purée into the pastry case. Peel, core, and thinly slice the dessert apples and arrange on top of the purée. Brush with the lemon juice and sprinkle with the reserved caster sugar.

6 Bake for 30–35 minutes, or until the apple slices have softened and are starting to turn pale golden.

7 Warm the apricot jam and brush it over the top. Cut into slices and serve.

Pear Gratin

A sophisticated, simple, and foolproof dessert

🍴 serves 4

🕐 prep 10 mins • cook 3–5 mins

4 ripe **Comice pears**

150g (5½oz) **blackberries**

60g (2oz) **walnuts**, roughly chopped

225g (8oz) **mascarpone cheese**

30g (1oz) **dark muscovado sugar**

1 Preheat the grill on its highest setting. Quarter the pears and remove the core. Place them skin-side down into a shallow flameproof dish. Scatter over the blackberries and walnuts.

2 Drop spoonfuls of mascarpone cheese over the pears and sprinkle the sugar on top. Grill for 3–5 minutes, or until the mascarpone is hot and bubbling, and the sugar begins to caramelize.

Good with crisp buttery biscuits.

VARIATION

Pear and Raspberry Gratin

Add 150g (5½oz) raspberries instead of blackberries, and top with a handful of Granola cereal rather than sugar.

Bananas Flambéed with Calvados

The flambéing cooks off the alcohol and concentrates the flavour, making a fabulously intense dessert

 serves 4

prep 10 mins • cook 10 mins

2 oranges

4 ripe bananas

60g (2oz) unsalted butter

85g (3oz) light soft brown sugar

juice of 1 lime

3 tbsp Calvados

double cream, to serve (optional)

1 Remove the zest from half an orange with a potato peeler and chop very finely. Squeeze the juice from both oranges.

2 Peel the bananas and halve lengthways. Melt 45g (1½oz) of the butter in a large non-stick frying pan and fry the banana quickly until lightly coloured on both sides. Remove from the pan, cover, and keep warm.

3 Add the remaining butter to the pan and melt. Sprinkle over the sugar and heat gently, stirring occasionally. Add the lime juice and orange zest and juice to the pan. Cook over a high heat for 2–3 minutes.

4 Add the Calvados and tilt the pan towards the heat if you have a gas hob, or use a match to ignite and cook until the flames burn out. Add the bananas and turn in the sauce to reheat gently.

5 Serve while hot with double cream, if using.

Stewed Plums

At their best in late summer to early autumn, plums are perfect for cooking

 serves 4

 prep 15 mins • cook 20 mins

450g (1lb) ripe red plums, halved and stones removed

85g (3oz) caster sugar

1 star anise

½ cinnamon stick

1 orange

● **Prepare ahead** Can be made up to 2 days in advance. Keep chilled.

1 Place the sugar in a saucepan with 300ml (10fl oz) water, the star anise, and cinnamon. Pare the zest from the orange with a potato peeler, leaving the white pith. Squeeze the juice and add to the pan with the zest. Heat gently until the sugar has dissolved, stirring often.

2 Add the plums and gently stir to coat in the syrup. Simmer gently for 8–15 minutes, depending on the ripeness of your fruit, until tender but still holding their shape. Discard the star anise, cinnamon, and orange zest.

● **Good with** Greek yogurt and clear honey.

VARIATION

Stewed Apricots

Place 450g (1lb) apricots, halved and stoned, into a saucepan. Mix 150ml (5fl oz) cold water, 75g (2½oz) caster sugar, and ½ tsp ground cinnamon and pour it over the fruit. Bring to the boil, cover, and simmer gently over a low heat for 10–15 minutes. Spoon over 4 tbsp extra-thick double cream and stir gently. Scatter with toasted flaked almonds to serve.

Tart Tatin

This caramelized upside-down apple tart is a French classic

 makes 8 slices

prep 30 mins, plus chilling • cook 35 mins

30cm (12in) ovenproof tin or flameproof shallow round dish

For the pastry

150g (5½oz) butter

50g (1¾oz) sugar

225g (8oz) plain flour, plus extra for dusting

1 egg, beaten

For the apple topping

150g (5½oz) butter, softened

200g (7oz) caster sugar

6 large dessert apples, such as Granny Smith's, peeled and quartered

● **Prepare ahead** You can make the pastry up to 24 hours in advance, cover it with cling film and refrigerate.

1 To make the pastry, cream the butter and sugar together until blended. Gradually mix in the flour, then stir in the egg to bind it together. Turn the mixture on to a lightly floured surface and knead until smooth. Wrap in cling film and chill for at least 1 hour.

2 Preheat the oven to 220°C (425°F/Gas 7). For the topping, melt the butter in a 30cm (12in) ovenproof tin over a medium heat. When the butter has melted, add the sugar, stirring occasionally. Increase the heat slightly until the mixture begins to bubble, then continue cooking, stirring occasionally, for 5 minutes, or until it is a light, toffee colour. Remove from the heat.

3 Arrange the apple pieces in the tin, rounded-side down and tightly packed together.

4 Roll out the pastry to form a circle just large enough to fit over the top of the apples. Arrange the pastry neatly on top of the fruit and tuck the edges into the pan. Bake for 30 minutes, or until the pastry is lightly browned and cooked. Allow the tart to stand for 10 minutes before carefully inverting onto a large serving plate. Serve while still warm.

● **Good with** a spoonful of whipped cream, crème fraîche, or ice cream.

VARIATION

Tart aux Poires
This version uses pears instead of apples. Choose 6-8 pears, depending on size. Small pears will produce the best results.

Warm Fruit Compôte

An ideal dish when supplies of fresh fruit are limited

serves 4

prep 10 mins • cook 5-10 mins

30g (1oz) butter

6 prunes, chopped

6 dried apricots, chopped

2 large apples, peeled, cored, and chopped

1 firm pear, peeled, cored, and chopped

1 cinnamon stick

2 tsp sugar

2 tsp lemon juice

yogurt and honey, to serve

● **Prepare ahead** The compôte can be made up to 3 days in advance, covered, and refrigerated.

1 Melt the butter in a heavy saucepan over a medium heat. Add the fruit and cinnamon stick. Cook gently, stirring often, until the fruit has completely softened.

2 Stir in the sugar and heat for a further couple of minutes, or until the sugar has dissolved.

3 Remove the pan from the heat, sprinkle with lemon juice, and serve warm with a spoonful of yogurt and a drizzle of honey.

Stewed Apple with Ginger

This is a delightfully simple pudding for any occasion

serves 4

prep 15 mins • cook 15 mins, plus cooling and chilling

low fat

1.35kg (3lb) sweet dessert apples, such as Cox's Orange Pippins or Braeburn, peeled and thinly sliced

150ml (5fl oz) apple juice

1 tbsp ginger syrup from the jar

3 pieces stem ginger, finely chopped

● **Prepare ahead** The stewed apples can be made in advance and kept in an airtight container in a refrigerator for up to 5 days.

1 Put the apples, juice, and syrup in a medium saucepan and bring to the boil over a medium heat. Lower the heat, cover, and simmer, stirring once or twice, for 15 minutes.

2 Remove the pan from the heat and stir in the finely chopped stem ginger. Allow to cool slightly if serving hot.

● **Good with** a drizzle of fresh cream or mascarpone cheese.

Spiced Baked Apple with Walnuts

This great winter warmer is easy to prepare

🍴 serves 4

🕐 prep 10-15 mins • cook 30 mins

✓ low fat

4 large Golden Delicious apples

splash of lemon juice

85g (3oz) walnuts, halved

1 tbsp raisins

1 tbsp soft light brown sugar

25g (1oz) butter

¼ tsp ground cinnamon

1 Preheat the oven to 180°C (350°F/Gas 4). Carefully cut a 2.5cm (1in) slice from the top of each apple and set aside. Using an apple corer or a small, sharp knife, remove the core from each apple.

2 Put the walnuts, raisins, sugar, butter, and cinnamon into a food processor and pulse several times, to produce a coarse, textured mixture; do not over-process.

3 Fill each apple cavity with the mixture and replace the reserved tops. Arrange the apples in a shallow, ovenproof dish that holds them upright, then fill the pan 1cm (½in) deep with water.

4 Place the dish in the oven and bake for 30 minutes, or until the flesh is tender when pierced with the point of a knife. When slightly cooled, carefully remove the apples from the baking dish, transfer them to serving plates, and serve hot.

● **Good with** large spoonfuls of crème fraîche, custard, or pouring cream.

● **Leftovers** can be reheated and served with cream or custard, or enjoyed cold.

Baked Pears in Marsala

This popular Italian dessert can also be made with other firm fruit, such as plums, peaches, or apricots

🍴 serves 4-6

🕐 prep 10 mins, plus chilling • cook 30-50 mins

6 ripe pears, peeled and halved

100g (3½oz) caster sugar

250ml (8fl oz) dry Marsala

1 tsp pure vanilla extract

1 cinnamon stick

250ml (8fl oz) double or whipping cream

2 tbsp icing sugar

● **Prepare ahead** The dish can be completed a day in advance and gently reheated. The cream can be whipped 1 hour in advance.

1 Preheat the oven to 150°C (300°F/Gas 2). Place the pears in an ovenproof dish, cut-side up, and sprinkle with the sugar, Marsala, and vanilla, then pour in 250ml (8fl oz) water. Add the cinnamon stick.

2 Bake for 30-50 minutes, depending on ripeness, or until tender. Check occasionally and baste with the sugar and Marsala liquid.

3 Meanwhile, in a medium bowl whip the cream, gradually adding the icing sugar until firm peaks form. Serve the pears warm or chilled, in their syrup, with the whipped cream.

● **Good with** sponge fingers or amaretti biscuits.

Baked Apricots in Marsala

Replace the pears with peeled, halved, and stoned apricots, or plums and bake for 20-40 minutes, or until they are tender. If you haven't any Marsala, or if you want a sweeter result, you could use a medium sherry, or port.

Blueberry Cobbler

A classic summer-fruit pudding

 serves 4

prep 15 mins • cook 30 mins

450g (1lb) **blueberries**

2 large **peaches** or 2 eating **apples**, sliced

grated zest of ½ **lemon**

2 tbsp **caster sugar**

For the cobbler

225g (8oz) **self-raising flour**

2 tsp **baking powder**

75g (2½oz) **caster sugar**, plus 1 tbsp for sprinkling

pinch of **salt**

75g (2½oz) **butter**, chilled and diced

1 **egg**

100ml (3½fl oz) **buttermilk**

handful of **flaked almonds**

1 **Preheat the oven** to 190°C (375°F/Gas 5). Spread the blueberries and peaches over the base of a shallow ovenproof dish and sprinkle with lemon zest and sugar.

2 **Sift the flour**, baking powder, caster sugar, and salt into a bowl. Add the butter and work together with your fingers until the mixture resembles breadcrumbs.

3 **Break the egg** into the buttermilk and beat well. Add to the dry ingredients and mix together to form a soft, sticky dough. Drop walnut-sized spoonfuls of the mixture over the top of the fruit, leaving a little space between them. Press them down lightly with your fingers, then sprinkle over the flaked almonds and 1 tbsp of sugar.

4 **Bake for 30 minutes**, or until golden and bubbling, covering it loosely with kitchen foil if it is browning too quickly. It is done when a skewer pushed into the middle comes out clean. Leave to cool briefly before serving.

● **Good with** a spoonful of custard or double cream with each serving.

Caramelized Autumn Fruits

This is a great way to turn autumn fruits into a delicious dessert

 serves 6

 prep 10 mins • cook 20 mins

3 **Granny Smith apples**

3 firm **Conference pears**

4 firm **red plums**

60g (2oz) **butter**

60g (2oz) **caster sugar**

2 tbsp **orange juice** or water

1 **Peel, core, and quarter** the apples and pears. Quarter and stone the plums.

2 **To make the caramel**, heat the butter in a large frying pan over a medium heat. Add the sugar and orange juice and cook, stirring, until the sugar dissolves. Increase the heat and boil until the mixture starts to turn golden brown.

3 **Add the apples** and cook gently, stirring, until they start to soften, then add the pears and cook until softened.

4 **Add the plums** and continue to cook, stirring occasionally, until all the fruit is softened, but not falling apart, and is coated in caramel. Serve warm.

● **Good with** crème fraîche or ice cream, or poured over individual Pavlovas and cream, or with a crème brûlée or home-made shortbread.

VARIATION

Caramelized Summer Fruits

Use summer fruits, such as apricots, peaches, quince, and blackberries, instead of the autumn fruits, to make a tasty summer version.

Apple Charlotte

This hot fruit dish was apparently created for Queen Charlotte

 serves 6-8

🕐 prep 50 mins
• cook 40-45 mins

▣ 23cm (9in) springform cake tin

1.35kg (3lb) **cooking apples**, peeled, cored, and sliced

finely grated zest and juice of 1 **lemon**

85g (3oz) **sultanas**

115g (4oz) **caster sugar**

140g (5oz) **butter**

1 large **loaf of white bread**, unsliced

½ tsp ground **cinnamon**

icing sugar, to dust

1 Place the apples in a large heavy saucepan with the lemon zest and juice, sultanas, and 85g (3oz) of the caster sugar. Cover and cook over a low heat, shaking the pan occasionally, for 8-10 minutes, or until the apples are very tender and beginning to fall apart.

2 Preheat the oven to 190°C (375°F/Gas 5). Melt the butter in a small saucepan and brush a little on the base and sides of the cake tin. Remove the crusts from the bread, then cut the bread into 14 slices. Brush both sides of the bread slices with the butter. Mix together the remaining sugar and the cinnamon, and sprinkle over 1 side of each slice.

3 Use 3 slices of bread to cover the base of the tin, cutting the bread to fit and laying it sugar-side downwards. Cut 8 of the remaining slices in half and use to line the sides of the tin, sugar-side outwards, slightly overlapping them to fit.

4 Spoon the apple mixture into the bread case. Cover with the remaining slices, sugar-side upwards, cutting to fit if necessary. Fold over the bread on the sides of the tin so it slightly overlaps the top of the charlotte. Bake uncovered for 30-35 minutes, or until crisp and golden. Leave to stand in the tin for at least 5 minutes before turning out on a plate. Dust with icing sugar to serve.

Apple Purée

Served hot, warm, or cold, this is the simplest of desserts

 serves 4

🕐 prep 15 mins
• cook 35-40 mins

✓ low fat

1.2kg (2½lb) **cooking apples**

1 tbsp **lemon** juice

100ml (3½fl oz) **apple juice**

75g (2½oz) **caster sugar**

Greek yogurt, to serve (optional)

red dessert apple slices, tossed in lemon juice, to serve (optional)

● **Prepare ahead** Make the purée up to 3 days in advance and refrigerate until ready to serve.

1 Peel, core, and thinly slice the cooking apples and place the slices in a saucepan; toss with the lemon juice, to avoid browning.

2 Add the apple juice and sugar, and place the pan over a medium heat. Bring slowly to the boil, reduce the heat, cover, and simmer for 35-40 minutes, or until the apples are reduced to a pulp, stirring occasionally and breaking up with a wooden spoon.

3 Remove from the heat and allow to cool slightly, then press through a sieve to make a purée.

4 Divide most of the purée between 4 individual glasses, and, if desired, top with Greek yogurt and decorate with the apple slices.

● **Good with** ice cream, cream, or evaporated milk instead of the Greek yogurt.

● **Leftovers** can be served alongside pork chops, or eaten as a snack.

Strawberry and Orange Crêpes

Light, melt-in-the-mouth pancakes with a creamy filling make an irresistible dessert

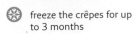
- serves 4
- prep 30 mins, plus standing • cook 30 mins
- freeze the crêpes for up to 3 months

For the crêpes

125g (4½oz) plain flour

pinch of salt

½ tbsp caster sugar

2 eggs, beaten

250ml (8fl oz) milk

30g (1oz) butter, melted, plus extra for frying

For the filling

350g (12oz) strawberries, hulled and sliced

2 oranges, segmented

500g (1lb 2oz) ricotta cheese

1–2 tbsp clear honey

finely grated zest of ½ lemon

1 To make the crêpes, sift the flour and salt into a bowl and stir in the sugar. Make a well in the centre, add the eggs and a little milk, and whisk until smooth. Gradually whisk in the rest of the milk, then the melted butter, and allow to stand for 30 minutes.

2 Heat the frying pan over a medium-high heat. Add a knob of butter and, when foaming, pour in a little batter, swirling it to coat the base of the pan. Cook until golden brown underneath, then flip it over and cook the other side for 1–2 minutes. Slide onto a plate and keep warm. Cook the remaining 7 crêpes in the same way, regreasing the pan as necessary.

3 To make the filling, place half the strawberries and orange segments in a serving bowl and reserve. Sweeten the ricotta with honey to taste and stir in the lemon zest. Spread a little filling over each crêpe, and divide the rest of the strawberries and oranges equally between the crêpes.

4 Fold the crêpes into triangles and serve with the reserved fruit.

Baked Sharon Fruit with Ratafia Crumbs

Sharon fruit is a variety of persimmon. Choose those that are soft, as they need to be slightly overripe

- serves 4
- prep 20 mins • cook 20 mins

4 sharon fruit, stalks removed, halved

30g (1oz) butter

1 tbsp clear honey

85g (3oz) ratafia biscuits, crushed

finely grated zest and juice of 1 large orange

225g (8oz) mascarpone cheese

50g (1¾oz) caster sugar

1 Preheat the oven to 180°C (350°F/Gas 4). Place the sharon fruit in a shallow ovenproof dish, cut-side upwards. Dot the fruit with the butter and drizzle with the honey. Pile the crushed biscuits in the centre of each fruit. Pour the orange juice over and bake for 20 minutes.

2 Meanwhile, mix together the mascarpone, orange zest, and sugar. Chill until ready to serve.

3 Serve the baked fruit hot or warm, with the flavoured mascarpone on the side.

Apple Brown Betty

A "betty" is a baked pudding. This dessert was made popular during colonial American years.

🍴 serves 4

🕐 prep 30 mins
• cook 35–45 mins

🍲 1.2 litre (2 pint) baking dish

85g (3oz) butter

175g (6oz) fresh breadcrumbs

900g (2lb) apples, such as Bramley, Granny Smith, or Golden Delicious

85g (3oz) soft brown sugar

1 tsp ground cinnamon

½ tsp mixed spice

zest of 1 lemon

2 tbsp lemon juice

1 tsp pure vanilla extract

1 Preheat the oven to 180°C (350°F/Gas 4). Melt the butter in a saucepan, add the breadcrumbs, and mix well.

2 Peel, quarter, and core the apples. Cut each quarter into slices and place in a bowl. Add the sugar, cinnamon, mixed spice, lemon zest and juice, and vanilla extract, and mix well.

3 Put half the apple mixture into the baking dish. Cover with half the breadcrumbs, then put in the rest of the apples and top with the remaining breadcrumbs.

4 Bake for 35–45 minutes, checking after 35 minutes. If it is getting too brown, reduce the oven temperature to 160°C (325°F/Gas 3) and cover with greaseproof paper. It is cooked when the crumbs are golden brown and the apples are soft. Serve warm.

⬤ **Good with** double cream, lightly whipped with icing sugar.

Grilled Grapefruit

A perfect palette cleanser to finish a meal

🍴 serves 4

🕐 prep 15 mins • cook 5 mins

🍲 4 flameproof serving dishes

2 pink grapefruit, segmented

2 grapefruit, segmented

2 oranges, segmented

1 egg

2 egg yolks

For the Marsala sabayon

60g (2oz) caster sugar

100ml (3½fl oz) Marsala or sweet sherry

1 Preheat the grill on its highest setting. Arrange the fruit in the dishes. Using an electric whisk, beat the egg and egg yolks together until just beginning to foam.

2 Add the sugar and Marsala and place the bowl over a pan of simmering water. Whisk for 3–4 minutes, or until very thick and foamy. Remove from the heat. Spoon over the fruit and grill for 1 minute, or until the sabayon is golden.

▰ **VARIATION**

Sugar-coated Grapefruit
Sprinkle the fruit with a little demerara sugar instead of the sabayon, and place under the grill for 3–4 minutes.

Baked Figs with Cinnamon and Honey

A simple-to-prepare, but stylish, end to a meal

🍴 serves 4

🕐 prep 2–3 mins • cook 20 mins

6 firm figs

2 tbsp clear honey

2 tbsp brandy or rum

ground cinnamon

1 Preheat the oven to 180°C (350°F/Gas 4). Cut the figs in half and place closely together in a shallow baking dish or roasting tin.

2 Drizzle over the honey and brandy, and sprinkle each fig with a generous pinch of cinnamon.

3 Bake for 20 minutes, or until softened. Check the figs after 10 minutes, as they may differ in ripeness slightly and require different cooking times. Serve warm, or at room temperature.

⬤ **Good with** mascarpone, vanilla ice cream, or crème fraîche.

⬤ **Leftovers** can be chilled and eaten within 2 days.

German Apple Cake

This simple apple cake is made special with a delicious crumbly streusel topping

makes 8 slices

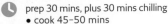
prep 30 mins, plus 30 mins chilling • cook 45–50 mins

20cm (8in) loose-bottomed cake tin

freeze, wrapped, for up to 6 months

2 tart **dessert apples**

175g (6oz) **butter**

175g (6oz) **light muscovado sugar**

finely grated zest of 1 **lemon**

3 **eggs**, lightly beaten

175g (6oz) **self-raising flour**

3 tbsp **milk**

For the streusel topping

115g (4oz) **plain flour**

85g (3oz) **light muscovado sugar**

2 tsp **ground cinnamon**

85g (3oz) **butter**, diced

1 **To make the topping**, put the flour, sugar, and cinnamon in a mixing bowl and rub in the butter to form a ball of dough. Wrap in cling film and chill for 30 minutes.

2 **Preheat the oven** to 190°C (375°F/Gas 5). Grease the cake tin and line with a disc of greaseproof paper. Peel, core, and cut the apples into wedges.

3 **Beat the butter** and sugar until pale and creamy. Add the lemon zest. Beat in the eggs, a little at a time, beating well after each addition. Sift the flour and fold in. Mix in the milk.

4 **Spread half the mixture** in the prepared tin and arrange half the apples in a layer on top. Spread the rest of the mixture over the apples, then add the remaining apples. Coarsely grate the streusel topping and sprinkle evenly on top.

5 **Bake in the centre** of the oven for 45–50 minutes, or until a skewer inserted into the centre comes out clean. Leave the cake in the tin for 10 minutes, then remove from the tin and cool on a wire rack. Serve warm.

Apple Crumble

Sweet dessert apples hold their shape when cooked so are ideal for this popular pudding

serves 4

prep 20 mins • cook 45 mins

500g (1lb 2oz) **sweet dessert apples**, such as Cox's Orange Pippins, peeled, cored, and thinly sliced

1 tbsp **lemon juice**

For the crumble topping

115g (4oz) **plain flour**

75g (2½oz) **butter**

60g (2oz) **rolled oats**

100g (3½oz) **demerara sugar**

1 **Preheat the oven** to 190°C (375°F/Gas 5). Put the apples in an ovenproof dish with the lemon juice and toss until well coated to prevent the apples from browning. Set aside.

2 **To make the crumble** topping, place the flour and butter in a mixing bowl, and rub together until the mixture resembles coarse breadcrumbs. Stir in the oats and sugar.

3 **Place the crumble** mixture on top of the apples, press down gently to level the top, and bake for 45 minutes, or until golden and crisp. Serve hot.

● **Good with** warm custard or chilled pouring cream.

VARIATION

Apple and Blackberry Crumble

Replace 200g (7oz) of the apples with blackberries, and follow the recipe above.

Pineapple Flambé

Rings of fresh pineapple flambéd in rum or brandy make a smart restaurant-style dessert

🍴 serves 4

🕐 prep 15–20 mins
• cook 10 mins

1 pineapple

4 tbsp **dark rum** or brandy

2 tbsp fresh **lime juice**

50g (1¾oz) **salted butter**

50g (1¾oz) **light soft brown sugar**

whipped cream, to serve

ground cinnamon, for dusting

1 **Peel and thinly slice** the pineapple. Cut out the tough core using a small round cutter or the tip of a sharp knife.

2 **Put the pineapple slices** and any pineapple juice into a large frying pan with the rum and lime juice and heat. Light the alcohol by carefully tilting the pan into the gas flame, or by using a match, and allow the flames to die down.

3 **Dot the pineapple** with butter and sprinkle with sugar. Shake the pan while heating gently, until the butter melts, the sugar dissolves, and the mixture thickens to a glaze. Serve with whipped cream and a dusting of ground cinnamon.

⬤ **Good with** mascarpone or ice cream.

VARIATION

Apricot Flambé

Cook 10 apricots, halved and stoned, in 50g (1¾oz) butter for 3–4 minutes, or until softened. Stir in 50g (1¾oz) light brown sugar and the juice of ½ lemon. Heat 4 tbsp apricot brandy in a ladle and ignite; pour over the apricots, and allow the flames to die out before serving.

> **CHOOSING PINEAPPLE**
>
> A fresh pineapple should be an even brown colour. Avoid any with dark patches. It should have a fresh, fragrant aroma; if it does not smell it is not fresh enough. Should you buy one that is not completely ripened, leave it on a windowsill to ripen further in the sun.

Honey-baked Apricots with Mascarpone

This Italian dessert, made here with canned fruit, can be enjoyed all year round

🍴 serves 4

🕐 prep 10 mins • cook 10 mins

410g can **apricots**, drained

3 tbsp **clear honey**

3 tbsp **flaked almonds**

pinch of **ground ginger** or cinnamon

150g (5oz) **mascarpone cheese**, chilled to serve

⬤ **Prepare ahead** The dish can be assembled, ready for baking, several hours in advance.

1 **Preheat the grill** on its highest setting, and lightly butter the bottom and sides of an ovenproof dish large enough to hold all the apricot halves in a single layer.

2 **Put the apricots** in the dish, cut-sides up. Brush with the honey, then scatter over the almonds, and very lightly dust with the ground ginger.

3 **Grill for 10 minutes**, or until the apricots are tender when pierced with the tip of a knife and the almonds are toasted. Serve the apricots hot or cool with the chilled mascarpone on the side.

⬤ **Good with** vanilla ice cream or thick whipped cream instead of the mascarpone.

Jam

It might seem old-fashioned to spend time making jam when shops have such a wide choice, but the best way to make breakfast extra special is to have a jar of home-made jam in the cupboard. These simple steps show you how easy it is to get started.

Choosing Fruit

Making jam is a time-honoured way of preserving seasonal produce. Ideally buy fruit from a loose display so you can select the best. Fruits that feel heavy for their size are likely to contain the most juice. Do not buy any bruised or mouldy fruits, or those that look damp and smell musty.

Storing

Ripe fruit spoils quickly so handle it as little as possible. Remove fruit from any packaging and put it in the refrigerator to slow the ripening process. Or, take advantage of seasonal gluts and freeze fruit for jam-making later in the year. As many fruits collapse when thawed, be sure to label the container with the weight before freezing, so the balance of fruit, sugar, pectin, and acid won't be upset.

Apples
Apples should feel heavy and have a tight, smooth, shiny skin. Apples make excellent jam because of their high pectin levels.

Plums
Tart red plums make excellent jam. Choose plump, round fruits with smooth skins that yield slightly to gentle pressure.

Cranberries
The best cranberries for jam have a bright red colour and look full and round.

Strawberries
The best strawberries are well-shaped, glossy, and red throughout. The hull should be green and fresh looking.

Equipment and Preparation

Assembling your Equipment

If you don't have a preserving pan, use a very large, stainless-steel saucepan deep enough to prevent you being scorched by the boiling jam, with a solid base to distribute heat evenly. A sugar thermometer (see left) clips to the inside of the pan for easy reading to see when jam reaches the setting temperature of 104°C (220°F). If you don't have one, however, follow the recipe and test for a set using the cold plate or flake tests (see far right).

Long-handled spoons prevent you being burnt while stirring and skimming, and using plastic funnels reduces the risk of burning yourself when pouring the hot jam into jars.

Choosing and Sterilizing your Jars

The best jars to use are those with self-sealing lids that form airtight seals, which prevent bacteria from destroying the jam during storage. This is an important consideration for any jams you intend to keep for a long time.

All jars and their closures must be crack-free, clean, and sterilized before being filled with hot jam. Wash all the jars and lids in hot, soapy water and rinse in hot water, or wash in a dishwasher. Put the jars and lids on a wire rack in a large pan, making sure they do not touch each other or the pan's side. Pour in enough boiling water to cover, then boil rapidly for 10 minutes. Using tongs, remove the jars from the water and drain upside-down on clean tea towels. Place the jars on a baking sheet in a preheated 100°C (210°F/Gas low) oven for 15 minutes to dry.

THE SCIENCE BEHIND THE SET

Pectin and acid are two natural substances found in fruits in varying amounts. For a jam to set properly it must contain specific proportions of acid, pectin, and sugar. Pectin is concentrated in fruit skins and cores, and slightly under-ripe fruits contain the most. Slightly under-ripe fruits also contain the most acid, so buy fruits for jam-making just when they are coming into season. Recipes using fruits low in either acid or pectin will include commerical pectin or acid in the form of lemon juice or vinegar.

YIELDS

When making any jam recipe, always treat the quantity it makes as a guideline and be prepared to have a little more or a little less. The actual yield will vary because of several factors, including the size of the fruit, their degree of ripeness, and the size of the pan and the jars.

Gooseberries
Choose gooseberries that are large with a slight tawny blush.

Raspberries
These should look plump and uniformly coloured without any leaves or stems.

Blackberries
Pick or buy blackberries with a deep, dark black-blue hue and that smell fragrant.

Nectarines
The reddish-yellow skin should be smooth and the fruit should feel only slightly firm.

Blueberries
Look for berries that are plump with a blue-grey "bloom". They should feel firm, not soft.

Figs
Choose fruit that feel heavy for their weight and yield slightly when gently pressed. Do not buy any that are soft or smell sour.

Redcurrants
The currants should be uniformly coloured and not bruised or crushed.

How to Make Jam

1 Prepare fruit The first step to making any home-made jam is preparing the fruit. To make the Strawberry Jam (p466) begin by hulling the strawberries. Other fruits, such as apricots, should be prepared as appropriate.

2 Add sugar Put your fruit in the pan, then add all the sugar at once and stir with a wooden spoon over a low heat until it completely dissolves. Bring to a rolling boil. When you think the sugar has dissolved, swirl the spoon in the mixture and check on the back of the spoon that no crystals are visible. If the sugar isn't completely dissolved at this point the jam will be grainy.

3 Skim the surface After testing for a set (see right), keep the pan off the heat and use a large metal spoon to remove any scum from the surface. The jam is now ready to be poured into dry, warm sterilized jars. Leave the jars to cool, then label and date. Jams with an air-tight seal will keep for up to a year in a cool, dark place. They should be refrigerated after opening.

TESTING FOR A SET

Cold Plate Test Put a little of the jam on a chilled plate and leave to cool, then push it gently. If the surface wrinkles, the jam is set. If not, boil a minute longer and re-test.

Flake Test Hold some jam on a wooden spoon above a bowl for a few seconds, then tilt the spoon. The jam should fall off in flakes. If not, boil a minute longer and re-test.

Jam

Strawberry Jam

- makes 7–8 jars
- prep 10 mins • cook 20–25 mins
- large stainless-steel saucepan, large non-metallic bowl, 7–8 x 450g (1lb) dry, warm sterilized jars

2kg (4½lb) **strawberries**

6 tbsp **lemon** juice

1.8kg (4lb) **sugar**

1 Put a small plate in the refrigerator to chill before you begin. Hull the strawberries, weighing them occasionally to determine when you have 1.8kg (4lb) hulled berries. Halve the berries, put them in the non-metallic bowl, and lightly crush with a large fork.

2 Put the crushed berries, accumulated juices, and the lemon juice in a large pan and bring to the boil. Reduce the heat to low and simmer for 5–10 minutes, stirring, or until the berries are soft.

3 Add the sugar and stir over a low heat until it completely dissolves. Increase the heat and boil rapidly for 15 minutes, without stirring, or until the jam reaches the setting point. Remove the pan from the heat and test for a set.

4 With the pan still off the heat, use a large metal spoon to skim the surface. Leave the jam to cool slightly so that a thin skin forms and the berries are evenly distributed throughout. Pour the jam into the prepared jars to within 3mm (⅛in) of the tops and seal. Leave the jam to cool, then label and date the jars. Store in a cool, dark place until ready to use, then refrigerate after opening.

Apricot Jam

- makes 4–5 jars
- prep 15 mins • cook 40 mins
- large stainless-steel saucepan, 4–5 x 450g (1lb) dry, warm sterilized jars

1.35kg (3lb) **apricots**

2 tbsp **lemon** juice

1.35kg (3lb) **sugar**

1 Put a small plate in the refrigerator to chill before you begin. Halve and stone the apricots. Crack a few of the stones with a hammer and take out the kernels; discard the rest. Put the kernels into a heatproof bowl and pour over boiling water to cover. Leave for 1 minute, then transfer to a bowl of cold water. Drain again and rub off the skins with your fingers.

2 Put the apricots, kernels, lemon juice, and 300ml (10fl oz) water into a large stainless-steel pan and bring to the boil. Reduce the heat and simmer, stirring occasionally, for 25 minutes, or until the apricot skins are soft, the fruit is tender, and the mixture reduces by one-third.

3 Add the sugar to the pan and stir until completely dissolved. Increase the heat and bring the mixture to the boil, without stirring, for 10 minutes, or until it reaches the setting point. Remove the pan from the heat and test for a set.

4 With the pan still off the heat, use a large metal spoon to skim the surface and remove the kernels. Immediately pour the jam into the prepared jars to within 3mm (⅛in) of the tops and seal. Leave the jam to cool, then label and date the jars. Store in a cool, dark place until ready to use, then refrigerate after opening.

Blueberry Jam

- makes 7–8 jars
- prep 5 mins, plus standing • cook 15–20 mins
- large stainless-steel saucepan, large non-metallic bowl, 7–8 x 450g (1lb) dry, warm sterilized jars

1.8kg (4lb) **blueberries**

1.35kg (3lb) **sugar**

juice of 2 **lemons**

pinch of **salt**

1 Put the blueberries in a large non-metallic bowl with half the sugar, the lemon juice, and the salt. Stir to mix, then cover and leave to stand at room temperature, without stirring, for 5 hours. Meanwhile, put a small plate in the refrigerator to chill.

2 Pour the contents of the bowl into a large stainless-steel pan over a low heat. Add the remaining sugar and stir until the sugar completely dissolves.

3 Increase the heat and bring the mixture rapidly to the boil, without stirring, then boil for 10–12 minutes, or until it reaches the setting point. Remove the pan from the heat and test for a set.

4 With the pan still off the heat, use a large metal spoon to skim the surface. Leave the jam to cool slightly, then pour it into the prepared jars to within 3mm (⅛in) of the tops and seal. Leave the jam to cool, then label and date the jars. Store in a cool, dark place until ready to use, then refrigerate after opening.

SAFE STORAGE

Once you've made and potted your jam be sure to label the jars clearly with the date. Keep in a cool, dark place, and store in the refrigerator after opening.

Delicious Ways to Use Fruit Jam

Baked Jam Roll

This warm, comforting family favourite tastes great with strawberry or any other fruit jam

🕐 40 mins   **page 382**

Sherry Trifle

Vary this traditional dessert by using a different flavoured fruit jam each time you make it

🕐 35 mins   **page 386**

Victoria Sponge Cake

Always popular for tea, home-made fruit jam and whipped cream make a luscious filling

🕐 40–45 mins   **page 413**

Raspberry Sablés

With a thin layer of jam between butter-rich biscuits, these are irresistible with tea or coffee

🕐 20–25 mins   **page 442**

Passion Fruit Blancmange

This sweet, fruit-flavoured milk pudding is perfect for family lunches or dinner parties with friends

- 🍴 serves 4
- 🕐 prep 15 mins, plus chilling • cook 10 mins
- 🍲 4 x 300ml (10fl oz) blancmange moulds, ramekins, or teacups

85g (3oz) **cornflour**

1 litre (1¾ pints) **milk**

60g (2oz) **caster sugar**

4 **passion fruit**

1 Blend the cornflour with a little of the milk in a medium bowl to make a smooth paste. Place the remaining milk in a large saucepan and bring gently to the boil. Whisk the boiling milk into the cornflour mixture, then return the mixture to the saucepan. Heat gently, stirring continuously, until the mixture comes to boiling point.

Reduce the heat and simmer gently for 5 minutes.

2 Remove the pan from the heat and stir in the sugar. Wet the moulds with a little water.

3 Cut 3 of the passion fruit in half, scoop out the seeds and press through a sieve, reserving the juice. Stir the juice into the mixture, then divide between the moulds. Press a piece of cling film on to the surface of each blancmange and chill in the refrigerator for at least 2 hours, or until set.

4 To serve, dip the base of each mould briefly into hot water and turn out onto individual serving plates. Scoop out the juice and seeds from the remaining passion fruit and spoon over the desserts.

Berry Medley

This cocktail of fresh berries coated in a sugar syrup and topped with a dollop of cream makes a refreshing summer dessert

- 🍴 serves 4
- 🕐 prep 15 mins, plus cooling • cook 2 mins

100g (3½oz) **caster sugar**

finely grated zest and juice of 1 **lemon**

750–800g (1lb 10oz–1¾lb) **strawberries, raspberries,** and **blueberries**

● **Prepare ahead** The fruit should be prepared and chilled at least 1 hour before serving.

1 Pour 300ml (10fl oz) water into a saucepan and add the caster sugar.

2 Place the pan over a medium heat and stir until the sugar crystals dissolve. Increase the heat to bring the syrup to the boil, and boil

rapidly for 1–2 minutes, then remove the pan from the heat.

3 Stir in the lemon zest and juice and leave the syrup to cool.

4 Cut any large strawberries into pieces (if desired). Place the fruit in a bowl and pour over the syrup. Stir the fruit gently so it is all coated in the syrup and then keep the fruit salad chilled until serving.

● **Good with** a dollop of whipped or clotted cream.

VARIATION

Winter Salad

Use sliced apples and segmented oranges. For an exotic version, try papaya and mango and use lime instead of lemon.

Mango and Orange Mousse

A light and refreshing dessert

 serves 4

 prep 40 mins, plus chilling

2 large ripe **mangoes**

finely grated zest and juice of
1 **orange**

60g (2oz) **caster sugar**

2 tsp **powdered gelatine**

pinch of **salt**

1 **egg white**

150ml (5fl oz) **double cream**

1 Halve each mango and remove the stone. Peel away the skin and discard. Set aside 1 quarter of a mango. Cut the remaining mango into chunks, place them into a food processor with the orange juice, and process until smooth. Transfer to a bowl and stir in the orange zest and sugar.

2 Place 3 tbsp water into a small bowl, sprinkle with the gelatine, and leave to soak for 5 minutes. Place the bowl with the gelatine into a larger bowl, half-filled with boiling water, and stir until the gelatine has completely dissolved. Allow to cool slightly, then stir into the mango purée.

3 In a large, clean bowl, add the salt to the egg white and whisk until stiff peaks form. Fold the egg white into the mango mixture.

4 Lightly whip the cream and fold half into the mango mixture. Divide the mixture between 4 dessert glasses and chill for 1 hour, or until the mousse is set.

5 Just before serving, place spoonfuls of the remaining whipped cream on top of the mango mousses and garnish with slices cut from the reserved mango.

Raspberry Soufflé

This light, fragrant pudding just melts in the mouth

- serves 4
- prep 30 mins • cook 5 mins
- 4 ramekins
- open-freeze, undecorated; when frozen, place in a freezer bag, seal, and return to the freezer for up to 1 month

1 tbsp **sunflower oil**

4 tbsp **rosewater**

1 tbsp **powdered gelatine**

350g (12oz) fresh **raspberries**

1 tbsp fresh **lemon juice**

85g (3oz) **icing sugar**, sieved

450ml (15fl oz) **double cream**

4 **egg whites**

mint leaves, to garnish

1 Make 4 double-layered bands of greaseproof paper, large enough to wrap around the outsides of the ramekins and wide enough to sit 5cm (2in) above the rim. Secure with adhesive tape. Brush the inside rim of the paper lightly with oil.

2 Place the rosewater in a small bowl, sprinkle with the gelatine, and leave to soak for 2 minutes, or until it becomes spongy. Set the bowl in a larger bowl half filled with boiling water from the kettle, and stir until the gelatine has dissolved. Remove from the heat and allow to cool slightly.

3 Place all but 8 of the raspberries in a food processor and blend to a purée. Sieve, discarding any pips. Stir in the lemon juice and sugar, then gradually stir in the gelatine. Leave in a cool place until just beginning to set.

4 Whip the cream to soft peaks and fold into the raspberry mixture. In a separate bowl, whisk the egg whites until stiff and gently fold into the raspberry mixture. Pour into the prepared ramekins and chill in the refrigerator until set.

5 Carefully peel off the greaseproof paper from each ramekin. Decorate with the reserved whole raspberries and mint leaves.

- **Leftovers** are delicious spooned between meringues as a filling.

VARIATION

Blackberry Soufflé

Use fresh blackberries in place of the raspberries, taking extra care to remove all of the pips from the purée before adding to the whipped cream.

Chocolate-dipped Fruits

This decadent treat is perfect with after-dinner drinks

- serves 4
- prep 20 mins • cook 10 mins

12 **physalis** (Cape gooseberries)

12 **strawberries**

100g (3½oz) good quality **dark chocolate**

- **Prepare ahead** These can be prepared up to 24 hours in advance and kept refrigerated.

1 Pull back the papery leaves of each physalis to expose the round orange fruit. Leave the stalks on the strawberries. Line a flat tray or plate with greaseproof paper.

2 Break up the chocolate and place it in a heatproof bowl over a pan of barely simmering water and stir occasionally for 8–10 minutes, or until melted and smooth.

3 Holding the fruit by the stalks, dip each fruit into the chocolate and place on the tray. Work quickly, as the chocolate does not take long to set.

4 Chill in the refrigerator until the chocolate is set.

Red Fruit Medley

This north German dish, *Rote Grutze*, translates as "red grits" and makes a delicious, not-too-sweet dessert

🍴 serves 4

🕐 prep 10 mins • cook 5 mins

250g (9oz) **cherries**, pitted

175g (6oz) **raspberries**

150g (5½oz) **redcurrants**

115g (4oz) **blackberries**

115g (4oz) **strawberries**, quartered if large

50g (1¾oz) **golden caster sugar**

2 tbsp **cornflour**

● **Prepare ahead** This dish can be made a day in advance. Before chilling, sprinkle with a little extra sugar to prevent a skin forming, allow to cool, then place in the refrigerator covered with cling film.

1 **Place all the fruit** in a saucepan with 150ml (5fl oz) of water and bring slowly to the boil.

2 **Combine the sugar** and cornflour with 2 tbsp cold water to form a smooth paste. Gradually stir the cornflour paste into the fruit. Cook gently, stirring, until the mixture begins to thicken.

3 **Allow to cool**, then spoon the mixture into individual dishes.

● **Good with** warm custard.

Sparkling Wine Jellies with Passion Fruit

For a special occasion, you may want to use champagne, but any good sparkling wine will do

🍴 serves 6

🕐 prep 20 mins, plus soaking and setting • cook 10 mins

▣ 6 x 200ml (7fl oz) champagne glasses, bowls, or moulds

8 **gelatine** leaves

750ml (1¼ pint) bottle **sparkling wine**

juice of 1 **lemon**

100g (3½oz) **caster sugar**

2 large or 3 small **passion fruit**

rose petals, to garnish

1 **Place the gelatine leaves** in a small bowl, pour over enough cold water to cover, and leave for 10 minutes to soften.

2 **Meanwhile**, pour 110ml (4fl oz) wine into a small pan over low heat. Add the lemon juice and sugar and heat gently, stirring until the sugar is dissolved.

3 **Drain the gelatine**, squeezing out any excess water, add it to the pan, and whisk until dissolved. Allow to cool slightly.

4 **Stir in** the remaining wine and leave to cool completely.

5 **Scoop out the seeds** of the passion fruits and divide between the glasses. Spoon a little jelly into each glass and chill until set.

6 **Divide the remaining** jelly between the glasses and return to the fridge for 2 hours, or until set. Garnish with rose petals and serve.

Layered Fruit Platter

Fresh summer fruits served with a rose-petal cream make this easy-to-prepare summer dessert rather special

 serves 4

prep 15 mins

ensure that the roses have been grown without pesticides or other chemical sprays

1 ripe, baby **pineapple**

1 ripe **mango**, peeled, stoned, and cut into thick wedges

175g (6oz) **strawberries**, halved

1 ripe **fig**, quartered

1 **kiwi fruit**, cut into chunks

2 **passion fruit**, halved

For the rose petal cream

1 red **rose**

150ml (5fl oz) **single cream**

1 tbsp **caster sugar**

1 tbsp **lemon juice**

150ml (5fl oz) **double cream**

pink **rose petals**, to serve

● **Prepare ahead** The rose petal cream can be made up to 24 hours in advance, covered and chilled.

1 Quarter the pineapple lengthways through the green stalk. Run a sharp knife between the flesh and the skin, being careful to keep the shape of the pineapple intact. Slice the pineapple flesh, keeping it in position in the skin.

2 Place crushed ice on a platter and arrange the pineapple and the rest of fruit over it.

3 Remove the red rose petals from the rose, reserve 3 for a garnish, place in a blender with the single cream and sugar, and blend until smooth. Add the lemon juice. Whip the double cream until standing in soft peaks, then whisk in the rose petal cream until soft peaks form again. Transfer to a serving bowl. Add the reserved petals.

4 Scatter the pink rose petals over the fruit and serve the rose petal cream alongside.

● **Leftovers** are perfect for blending with yogurt or fresh fruit juice to make a refreshing drink.

Eton Mess

Culinary legend maintains that this was concocted after a schoolboy dropped a hamper

serves 4

prep 10 mins

350g (12oz) ripe **strawberries**, sliced

2 tbsp **caster sugar**

2 tbsp **orange juice** or orange-flavoured liqueur

300ml (10fl oz) **double cream**

125g (4½oz) ready-baked **meringue nests**

● **Prepare ahead** Steps 1 and 2 can be completed several hours in advance. Assemble the pudding just before serving.

1 Put the strawberries in a bowl, sprinkle over the sugar, add the orange juice, then use a fork to crush the mixture.

2 Whip the cream until stiff peaks begin to form. Crush the meringue nests into small pieces.

3 Stir the meringue into the whipped cream. Top with the berries and the juices, and stir together. Serve immediately.

● **Good with** fresh raspberries and/or blueberries scattered over the top.

Toffee Apples

Bite through the crisp buttery toffee coating to reveal the sweet juicy apple inside

🍴 serves 4

🕐 prep 15 mins • cook 10 mins

📦 wooden lollipop sticks or dowelling rods

4 small **dessert apples**, stalks removed

225g (8oz) **demerara sugar**

25g (scant 1oz) **unsalted butter**

1 tsp **white wine** or cider vinegar

1 tsp **golden syrup**

oil, for greasing

● **Prepare ahead** The apples can be made up to 2 days in advance and stored in a cool, dry place.

1 **Push a wooden stick** firmly into the stalk end of each apple.

2 **Place the remaining** ingredients, apart from the oil, in a heavy saucepan and heat gently until the sugar has dissolved. Boil steadily, without stirring, for 5-10 minutes. Dip a pastry brush into cold water and brush around the edges of the pan occasionally to prevent sugar crystals forming.

3 **Fill a glass** with cold water and drop 1 tsp of the caramel mixture into the water; it should form a ball. If you can roll the ball between your fingertips and it is hard but not brittle, it has reached the "soft crack" stage and is ready to use. Boil for 1 minute more if not, and repeat until ready.

4 **Remove the pan** from the heat. Line a baking tray with lightly oiled non-stick parchment. Dip an apple into the caramel to coat, tilting the pan if necessary, and place the apple upright on the lined baking sheet. Working quickly, repeat with the remaining apples.

5 **Leave until** the apples are completely cold and the toffee has hardened.

Caramel Oranges

This sweet caramel sauce is a perfect match for the sliced fruit

🍴 serves 4

🕐 prep 10 mins, plus standing • cook 15 mins

4 oranges

225g (8oz) **caster sugar**

crème fraîche, to serve

● **Prepare ahead** These can be made up to 2 days in advance and stored in the refrigerator.

1 **Remove the zest** from 1 of the oranges using a potato peeler; take care not to include any of the white pith. Cut the zest into very thin slivers and set aside.

2 **Cut the zest and pith away** from the other oranges. Slice the oranges, arranging them back into the shape of a whole orange, then place the slices in a mixing bowl.

3 **Place the sugar** in a saucepan with 150ml (5fl oz) water. Heat gently until the sugar dissolves. Increase the heat and boil for 8-10 minutes, or until the mixture turns a golden brown colour. As it boils, dip a pastry brush in cold water and brush around the inside of the pan to stop sugar crystals from forming. Slowly add another 150ml (5fl oz) of water to the caramel. Be careful (it will splutter a little), and stir to combine.

4 **Stir in the reserved** orange zest slivers and cook, stirring for 4-5 minutes, or until softened. Pour the syrup over the oranges and leave to stand overnight.

5 **Serve each orange** fanned out on a serving plate with a spoonful of crème fraîche. Drizzle with the caramel syrup.

● **Leftovers** can be chopped and used to top a fresh fruit salad or orange or lemon jelly.

Strawberry Mousse

This speedy dessert is bound to be a favourite with the kids

- serves 4
- prep 15 mins, plus 20 mins chilling
- the mousse can be frozen in individual freezerproof dishes for up to 3 months

450g (1lb) ripe **strawberries**

170g (6oz) can **evaporated milk**, well chilled

30g (1oz) **caster sugar**

200g (7oz) **Greek yogurt**, plus extra to serve

● **Prepare ahead** The mousse can be made several hours in advance.

1 **Slice a strawberry** and set aside for decoration. Divide half the strawberries between 4 dessert glasses and place the remaining strawberries into a food processor and blend to a purée. Push through a sieve to remove the seeds. If you do not have a food processor, mash with a fork before pushing through a sieve.

2 **Using an electric whisk**, whisk the milk in a large bowl until doubled in volume, which will take 6–8 minutes. Whisk in the sugar and stir in the strawberry purée and Greek yogurt until well combined. Spoon the whisked mixture into the glasses and chill for 15–20 minutes.

3 **Serve decorated** with a little extra yogurt and the reserved strawberry slices.

Red Fruit Terrine

All the flavours of summer wrapped up in this stunning red berry terrine

- serves 4-6
- prep 45 mins, plus chilling • cook 5 mins
- 900g (2lb) non-stick loaf tin

75g (2½oz) **caster sugar**

90ml (3fl oz) **elderflower cordial**

juice of 1 **lemon**

2 tbsp **powdered gelatine**

225g (8oz) **raspberries**

115g (4oz) **redcurrants**

140g (5oz) **blueberries**

225g (8oz) ripe **strawberries**, quartered

extra fruit, to decorate

● **Prepare ahead** The terrine can be made a day in advance.

1 **Place the sugar** in a saucepan with 450ml (15fl oz) water. Heat gently until the sugar has dissolved. Bring to the boil and boil the sugar mixture for 1–2 minutes. Cool slightly then stir in the elderflower cordial and the lemon juice.

2 **Place 4 tbsp warm water** into a small bowl and sprinkle over the gelatine. Leave to soak for 2 minutes. Place the bowl in a pan of hot water and stir until the gelatine has dissolved. Stir into the syrup.

3 **Place the non-stick** loaf tin into a roasting tin. Pack crushed ice halfway up the sides of the loaf tin and pour a little water over the ice. Scatter the raspberries into the bottom of the loaf tin and pour over enough elderflower syrup to cover. Allow to set.

4 **Scatter over** the redcurrants and blueberries and pour over enough elderflower syrup to cover. Allow to set. Finally scatter over the strawberries and pour in the remaining syrup. Transfer the roasting tin to the fridge and chill for at least 3 hours, or preferably overnight, until set.

5 **To turn out**, dip the loaf tin into hot water for few seconds and invert onto a plate. Carefully remove the loaf tin. Decorate with extra fruit.

● **Good with** whipped cream, crème fraîche, or lemon-flavoured Greek yogurt.

● **Leftovers** can be used in trifles or sliced and served cold alongside poultry dishes.

Berry Mascarpone Fool

This pretty dessert can be made with any berries of your choice

🍴 serves 4

🕐 prep 15 mins, plus chilling

350g (12oz) **berries**, such as blackberries, raspberries, loganberries, or strawberries

140g (5oz) **caster sugar**

juice of 1 **lemon**

150ml (5fl oz) **double cream**

85g (3oz) **mascarpone cheese**

mint leaves, to decorate (optional)

● **Prepare ahead** The fools will keep overnight in the refrigerator.

1 **Reserve a few berries** for decoration, then purée the remaining berries in a food processor or blender with the sugar, and rub through a fine sieve to remove the seeds. The resulting purée should be quite thick. Add the lemon juice.

2 **Whisk the double cream** until standing in soft peaks. Beat the mascarpone by hand to soften it, and then mix gently together with the cream. Stir half the berry purée through the cream mixture.

3 **Divide the berry purée** among 4 glasses and spoon the cream mixture on top of the purée. Decorate with the reserved berries and a mint leaf, if desired. Chill for several hours before serving.

Fruit Purées

If you do not have a food processor, you can use a stick blender or purée fruits by hand, although it will take a little more effort. Mash the fruits with a fork, then push through a sieve, for a smooth, even texture.

Lychees in Scented Syrup

Fresh lychees in syrup lightly scented with ginger, lime, and a hint of star anise are ideal to round off a spicy Oriental meal

🍴 serves 4

🕐 prep 10 mins • cook 10 mins

✓ low fat

❄ freeze for up to 2 months; thaw at room temperature for 2-3 hours

zest and juice of 1 **lime**

75g (2½oz) golden **caster sugar**

1 **star anise**

600g (1lb 5oz) **lychees**

2 pieces of **stem ginger** in syrup

● **Prepare ahead** Make up to 2 days in advance and store, covered, and chilled, until required.

1 **Place the lime zest** and juice, sugar, star anise, and 150ml (5fl oz) water in a saucepan and heat, gently stirring, until the sugar has dissolved. Increase the heat and boil for 5-10 minutes, or until reduced and syrupy. Remove from the heat.

2 **Meanwhile**, peel the lychees, and remove the stones, if you wish. Place in a serving bowl. Chop the ginger and add to the lychees, with a little of the ginger syrup.

3 **Strain the cooled sugar** syrup through a sieve over the lychees. Allow to cool completely then chill until required. Add the star anise as decoration but do not eat it.

● **Good with** a little single cream, or ice cream.

Strawberries in Scented Syrup

Prepare the syrup as above and allow to cool completely. Pour over quartered or halved strawberries.

Summer Pudding

A classic British dessert made when summer berries are juicy and flavourful

- serves 6
- prep 20–25 mins, plus chilling • cook 5 mins
- 900ml (1½ pint) pudding basin

12 slices **white bread**, crusts removed

125g (4½oz) **blackcurrants**

125g (4½oz) **redcurrants**

150g (5½oz) **caster sugar**

250g (9oz) **mixed berries**, such as strawberries, raspberries, mulberries, and blueberries

● **Prepare ahead** This dish will benefit from being made the day before it is required. It will keep for up to 3 days in the refrigerator.

1 Line the basin with bread slices, beginning with a circle cut to fit the base, then overlapping slices evenly around the side.

2 Lightly cook the currants with the sugar until soft and the juices have run. Stir in the berries and cook for 1 minute, or until just softening.

3 Spoon some of the juices over the bread, then fill the basin with the fruit. Make sure the fruit is packed well into the basin. Cover the fruit with bread, ensuring it is completely covered with an even layer.

4 If there is any juice remaining, spoon this over the top layer of bread. Stand the basin in a dish to catch any overspill of juice. Cover with cling film and place a small plate on top. Put a weight on the plate and chill overnight.

5 Turn out on to a serving plate to serve.

● **Good with** ice cream or cream.

Peach Melba

Auguste Escoffier created this dish for opera singer Dame Nellie Melba when he was head chef of the Savoy Hotel, London

- serves 4
- prep 20 mins • cook 25 mins
- freeze the raspberry sauce for up to 6 months

280g (10oz) **granulated sugar**

4 **peaches**

250g (9oz) **raspberries**

1 tbsp **icing sugar**

squeeze of **lemon** juice

1 tsp **arrowroot**

4 scoops **vanilla ice cream**

1 Put the sugar in a saucepan and add 600ml (1 pint) water. Bring slowly to the boil, ensuring all the sugar has dissolved before it boils. Reduce the heat and simmer for 5 minutes.

2 Meanwhile, dip the peaches in boiling water for 15–30 seconds and peel off the skins. Put the peaches in the syrup and cook over a low heat, turning occasionally, for 15 minutes, or until tender.

3 Put the raspberries, icing sugar, and lemon juice in a saucepan. Mix the arrowroot with a little water and add to the pan. Bring to the boil, then push through a sieve. Taste and add more sugar or lemon juice, if required. Allow the peaches and raspberry sauce to cool, then cut each peach in half and remove the stone.

4 To serve, place a scoop of ice cream in each dish, put 2 peach halves on top, and pour over some of the cold raspberry sauce.

VARIATION

Pear Melba

Although this is not authentic, you can use 4 pears instead of the peaches. Peel the pears, cut each in half, and remove the cores and stalks. Poach, as with the peaches, and serve in the same way.

THICKENING THE SAUCE

Depending on the juiciness of the raspberries, the sauce may be thinner than you'd like. To thicken, mix 1 tsp arrowroot with a little water and add to the sauce.

Pear and Grape Salad

Cucumber is not often added to sweet dishes, but it works perfectly in this exotic fruit salad

🍴 serves 4

🕐 prep 10 mins • cook 5-6 mins

1 cucumber

2 stalks lemongrass

85g (3oz) golden caster sugar

2 ripe red-skinned pears

125g (4½oz) green seedless grapes

125g (4½oz) red seedless grapes

small handful of mint leaves

● **Prepare ahead** The salad can be made up to 2 days in advance, and stored in the refrigerator.

1 Trim the ends from the cucumber. Cut it in half lengthways, scoop out and discard the seeds using a teaspoon, then slice thinly. Remove any tough outer leaves from the lemongrass stalks and discard. Halve lengthways and bash with a rolling pin.

2 Place the lemongrass in a saucepan with the sugar and 200ml (7fl oz) water, and heat gently until the sugar has dissolved. Bring to the boil and boil for 1 minute, then remove from the heat and stir in the cucumber. Allow to cool.

3 Discard the lemongrass. Quarter the pears and discard the cores, then cut the flesh into thin wedges and add to the syrup with the grapes. Scatter over the mint leaves.

● **Good with** plain yogurt or Greek yogurt.

Pears Hélène

This classic dish combines poached pears with a rich chocolate sauce

🍴 serves 4

🕐 prep 10 mins • cook 30 mins

85g (3oz) caster sugar

1 vanilla pod

4 pears

125g (4½oz) dark chocolate, broken into pieces

100ml (3½fl oz) single cream

● **Prepare ahead** The pears and sauce can be kept in a refrigerator, in separate covered containers, for several days. Reheat the sauce gently before assembling the dessert.

1 Place the caster sugar and 300ml (8fl oz) water in a large saucepan and heat gently. Stir until the sugar dissolves. Split open the vanilla pod and add it to the pan. Bring slowly to boiling point, then reduce the heat to a simmer.

2 Peel the pears, leaving the stalks attached, and place in the syrup. Cover and simmer gently for 20 minutes, or until the pears are tender. Remove the pears with a slotted spoon and allow to cool. Remove the vanilla pod (this can be rinsed, dried, and used again) and reserve the poaching syrup.

3 To make the chocolate sauce, melt the chocolate in a bowl over a saucepan of hot water. Place the cream in a small saucepan with 4 tbsp of the poaching syrup. Bring almost to the boil, then remove from the heat. Add the chocolate and stir to form a smooth sauce.

4 Serve immediately, pouring a little of the sauce over the pears and serving the rest separately.

● **Good with** ice cream, or a dollop of whipped cream.

Pineapple with Mint

This fruit platter makes a refreshing end to any meal

 serves 4

 prep 20 mins, plus chilling

✓ low fat

1 large ripe **pineapple**

1 **pomegranate**

finely grated zest and juice of 1 **lime**

25g (scant 1oz) **mint leaves**, chopped

2 tbsp **light soft brown sugar**

● **Prepare ahead** This fruit salad can be made 2–3 hours in advance, and chilled until required.

1 Using a sharp knife, cut away the skin from the pineapple. Cut the flesh into quarters, remove and discard the woody core, and slice thinly. Arrange on a serving plate.

2 Cut the pomegranate in half and remove the seeds, discarding all the membranes. Scatter the seeds over the pineapple slices and pour the lime juice over the fruit.

3 Place the mint in a small bowl, add the lime zest and sugar, and mix well. Scatter evenly over the fruit, then chill in the refrigerator for at least 1 hour. Bring back to room temperature to serve.

● **Good with** softly whipped cream, or thick Greek yogurt.

VARIATION

Pineapple with Chilli

Dissolve 4 tbsp caster sugar in 120ml (4fl oz) water. Add 1 finely diced chilli and bubble for 10 minutes, or until it turns syrupy. Serve poured over the pineapple slices.

Berries with Citrus Syrup

Juicy seasonal berries are made even more luscious with a sweet lemon-orange syrup

🍴 serves 4

🕐 prep 5 mins, plus macerating • cook 10 mins

✓ low fat

500g (1lb 2oz) **mixed red berries**, such as raspberries, strawberries, and redcurrants

125g (4½oz) **caster sugar**

zest of 1 **lemon**, cut into strips

1 tbsp **orange** juice

handful of **mint leaves**

● **Prepare ahead** The dish can be made up to 1 hour in advance.

1 Place the mixed berries in a serving dish and set aside.

2 Mix the sugar with 120ml (4fl oz) water in a heavy-based saucepan. Heat slowly until the sugar has dissolved, stirring occasionally, then increase the heat, and boil for 5 minutes. Remove the pan from the heat and leave to cool, then add the lemon zest and orange juice.

3 Drizzle the syrup over the berries, then add the mint leaves. Leave to macerate for 10 minutes, before serving.

● **Good with** whipped cream or ice cream.

● **Leftovers** can be blended with yogurt, apple juice, or ice to make a delicious fruit smoothie.

Orange and Rosemary Tart

Similar to the classic lemon tart, the rosemary adds a delicate scented flavour to the orange

🍴 makes 6–8 slices

🕐 prep 30 mins, plus chilling
● cook 1 hr

📷 20cm (8in) loose-bottomed flan tin, baking beans

For the pastry

225g (8oz) **plain flour**

115g (4oz) **unsalted butter**, chilled

2 tbsp chopped **rosemary**

2 tbsp **icing sugar**

1 **egg**, lightly beaten

For the filling

500ml (16fl oz) fresh **orange** juice

2 sprigs of fresh **rosemary**

grated zest of 2 **oranges**

175g (6oz) **caster sugar**

4 **eggs**

120ml (4fl oz) **double cream**

orange zest, to decorate (optional)

1 Preheat the oven to 180°C (350°F/Gas 4). To make the pastry, place the flour, butter, and rosemary into a food processor, then pulse briefly until it resembles

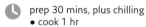

breadcrumbs. Add the sugar and egg, and briefly process until the pastry forms a ball. If a ball does not form, add a little water. Wrap in cling film and chill for 20 minutes.

2 Roll out the pastry and use to line the flan tin. Place a piece of greaseproof paper into the tart case and fill with baking beans. Bake blind for 10 minutes, then remove the paper and beans and bake for 10–15 minutes, or until golden. Reduce the oven temperature to 160°C (325°F/Gas 3).

3 Meanwhile, to make the filling, place the orange juice and rosemary in a pan. Bring to the boil, lower the heat, and simmer until the liquid has thickened and reduced. Allow to cool, strain through a sieve, and discard the rosemary sprigs.

4 Whisk the strained juice, orange zest, sugar, eggs, and cream together until combined, then pour into the baked pastry case. Bake the tart in the centre of the oven for 35 minutes, or until just set. Allow to cool, then chill until required. Serve decorated with orange zest.

Elderflower Jelly with Grapes

Elderflower gives a delicate fragrant flavour to these pretty jellies

🍴 serves 4

🕐 prep 15 mins, plus setting
● cook 5 mins

75ml (2½fl oz) **elderflower cordial**

4 **gelatine leaves**

whipped cream, to serve

seedless green grapes, to serve

● **Prepare ahead** The jelly can be made up to 48 hours in advance, and chilled until needed.

1 Measure 600ml (1 pint) cold water in a jug and stir in the cordial. Place the gelatine leaves in a small bowl, and add 4 tbsp of the

elderflower mixture. Leave to soak for 10 minutes, or until the gelatine is very soft. Place the bowl over a pan of barely simmering water, and stir until the gelatine has completely dissolved.

2 Add the gelatine to the elderflower mixture, and stir well. Pour into 4 glasses, then chill on a tray in a refrigerator for at least 2–3 hours, or until set. Serve the jelly in the glasses, topped with whipped cream and a few grapes.

GELATINE LEAVES

Use gelatine leaves to ensure a clear jelly. They are available in larger supermarkets. Gelatine powder can give a grainy finish.

Melon Cocktail

This colourful dish can be made with any melon, cut into cubes for a casual snack, or cut with a melon baller for a formal event

 serves 4

 prep 15 mins, plus chilling

✔ low fat

melon baller

600g (1lb 5oz) **watermelon**

600g (1lb 5oz) **cantaloupe melon**

600g (1lb 5oz) **honeydew melon**

2–3 tbsp finely shredded **mint leaves**

2 tbsp **honey**

sprig of **mint**, to decorate

● **Prepare ahead** The fruit can be prepared up to 4 hours in advance, and chilled until required.

1 **Using a melon baller**, scoop balls of each melon, or cut into 2cm (¾in) cubes. Place the fruit in a large bowl, add the shredded mint and honey, and toss the mixture gently until the melon is evenly coated with the honey.

2 **Cover and refrigerate** the melon for at least 30 minutes, turning it frequently so the melon soaks up the flavours of the honey and mint.

3 **When ready to serve**, spoon the melon and any juices into individual serving dishes. Decorate each serving with mint.

● **Good with** a rich meal as a light palate-cleansing dessert, or as a refreshing starter or snack.

VARIATION

Exotic Fruit Cocktail
Use one kind of melon and add any variation of cut fruit, such as star fruit, pineapple, kiwi, mango, blueberries, and strawberries.

Autumn Fruit Tart

This is a wonderful recipe to use seasonal fruits

 makes 6 slices

 prep 20 mins, plus chilling ● cook 1 hr

20cm (8in) fluted loose-bottomed flan tin, baking beans

For the pastry

175g (6oz) **plain flour**, plus extra for dusting

1 tbsp **caster sugar**

85g (3oz) **butter**, chilled and diced

1 **egg**

For the filling

4 **dessert apples** or pears

3 large **egg yolks**

4 tbsp **light soft brown sugar**

200ml (7fl oz) **double cream**

1 tsp **pure vanilla extract**

handful of **blackberries**, stoned plums, or blueberries

1 tsp **ground cinnamon**

2 tbsp **caster sugar**

1 **To make the pastry**, place the flour, sugar, and butter in a food processor and process until the mixture resembles breadcrumbs. Add the egg and process until it forms a ball. Roll out and use to line the tin. Prick the pastry several times with a fork, and chill for 30 minutes.

2 **Preheat the oven** to 190°C (375°F/Gas 5). Line the pastry case with greaseproof paper and baking beans, and bake blind for 10 minutes. Remove the paper and beans, bake for 10 minutes, then remove from the oven and leave to cool.

3 **Meanwhile**, peel, core, and thinly slice the apples. Whisk together the egg yolks, brown sugar, cream, and vanilla extract. Arrange the apples and other fruits in the tart shell and pour the cream mixture over. Sprinkle the cinnamon and caster sugar over the top and bake for 40–45 minutes, or until set. Cool in the tin and serve cold.

● **Good with** pouring cream and a few extra berries on the side.

Mango and Papaya Salad

These light and refreshing flavours work well as a dessert, served with Greek yogurt and honey

 serves 4

🕐 prep 15 mins • cook 10 mins

✔ low fat

1 piece **preserved stem ginger**, cut into thin strips

2 tbsp **stem ginger syrup**

2 tbsp **caster sugar**

grated zest and juice of 1 **lemon**

1 **pomegranate**, cut in half, seeds scooped out

1 large ripe **mango**

1 large ripe **papaya fruit**

1 small **ogen melon**

lime wedges, to serve

● **Prepare ahead** The dressing can be made and kept in a refrigerator for up to 2 days in advance. The fruit can be prepared up to 24 hours in advance and chilled until required.

1 Place the ginger, ginger syrup, sugar, and 120ml (4fl oz) of water into a saucepan, and heat gently, stirring occasionally. Bring to the boil, then simmer gently for 5–6 minutes. Remove from the heat, and stir in the lemon zest and juice and the pomegranate seeds.

2 Peel the mangoes and use a sharp knife to cut the flesh away from the stones and slice the mango. Halve, deseed, and peel the papaya, then cut into wedges. Halve and deseed the melon, cut into wedges, and peel, then cut the flesh into bite-sized chunks. Arrange the mango, papaya, and melon on a large serving platter.

3 Pour the pomegranate and ginger dressing over the fruit, and serve with lime wedges to squeeze over.

● **Good with** Greek yogurt or whipped cream.

Apricot Purée

Enjoy this fruit purée for breakfast or dessert

🍴 serves 6

🕐 prep 5 mins, plus cooling • cook 25–30 mins

✔ low fat

❄ freeze for up to 3 months

350g (12oz) **soft dried apricots**

300ml (10fl oz) **orange** juice

Greek yogurt, to serve

muesli or granola, to serve

chopped **pistachio nuts**, to serve

● **Prepare ahead** The purée will keep in a sealed container in the refrigerator for up to 5 days.

1 Put the apricots and orange juice in a small saucepan and bring to the boil over a medium heat. Lower the heat, cover, and simmer for 25–30 minutes, or until very tender.

2 Leave to cool slightly, then transfer the softened fruit into a blender or food processor and blend to a smooth purée. If the mixture has become too thick, add a little more orange juice.

3 Serve warm or cold, layered in dishes with spoonfuls of thick Greek yogurt and muesli. Top with a few pistachio nuts.

VARIATION

Peach Purée

Instead of apricots, use 350g (12oz) dried peaches. The purée also makes a delicious sauce for ice cream, thinned with a little juice or a liqueur.

Pear, Roasted Hazelnut, and Mascarpone Tart

This fruity, rich tart, with its deliciously nutty topping, makes a great pudding for dinner parties

 serves 8

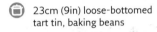 prep 20 mins, plus chilling • cook 50 mins

🍽 23cm (9in) loose-bottomed tart tin, baking beans

For the pastry

150g (5½oz) plain flour, plus extra for dusting

60g (2oz) caster sugar

1 tsp grated lemon zest

60g (2oz) butter, chilled and diced

1 egg

For the filling

125g (4½oz) mascarpone

100g (3½oz) caster sugar, plus extra for sprinkling

1 egg

1 egg yolk

1 tsp pure vanilla extract

2–3 tbsp milk

4 canned pears, sliced

45g (1½oz) roasted hazelnuts, roughly chopped

2 tbsp apricot jam

1 **For the pastry**, place the flour, sugar, and the lemon zest in a food processor. Add the butter and pulse until the mixture resembles breadcrumbs. Add the egg and pulse until the dough gathers in a ball. Transfer to a lightly floured surface and roll out to line the tart tin. Chill for 30 minutes.

2 **Preheat the oven** to 190°C (375°F/Gas 5). Place the tart tin on a baking tray, cover the pastry with greaseproof paper, and fill with baking beans. Bake blind for 10 minutes, remove the paper and beans, and cook for a further 10 minutes. Allow to cool on a wire rack.

3 **Reduce the oven** to 160°C (325°F/Gas 3). Mix the mascarpone, sugar, egg, egg yolk, vanilla extract, and milk together until smooth and pour into the tart shell. Arrange the pears on top, scatter with the roasted hazelnuts, sprinkle with sugar, and bake for 30 minutes, or until just set.

4 **Warm the apricot jam** through by stirring in a little hot water, gently brush it over the tart, and serve cold.

● **Good with** whipped double cream or ice cream.

Red Fruit Smoothie

Smoothies make a healthy breakfast or snack, and are refreshing when the weather is warm

🍽 serves 4

🕐 prep 5 mins

1 banana, broken into pieces

3 tbsp plain yogurt

115g (4oz) frozen mixed red berry fruits

600ml (1 pint) pineapple juice or cloudy apple juice

1 **Place the banana**, yogurt, and berry fruits in a blender or food processor. Pour in the juice and blend until smooth.

2 **To serve**, divide the smoothie between 4 serving glasses.

● **Leftovers** can be chilled in the refrigerator and enjoyed later, adding more ice if desired.

Mixed Berry Smoothie

If you prefer to use fresh fruits, add your choice of raspberries, blackberries, strawberries, redcurrants, blackcurrants, or blueberries, plus 2 or 3 ice cubes. To make a thicker smoothie, add another banana.

Orange Jelly

This jelly is wonderful served after a rich main course, as it is light, refreshing, and not too sweet

- 🍴 serves 4
- 🕐 prep 20 mins, plus soaking and chilling • cook 10 mins
- 📷 4 x 200ml (7fl oz) dessert glasses, serving bowls, or moulds

4 oranges, peeled

850ml (1⅓ pints) orange juice, fresh or bottled

6 gelatine leaves, about 10g (¼oz)

4 tbsp Greek yogurt

● **Prepare ahead** The jellies need to be made at least 2 hours in advance, but can be made up to 48 hours ahead, covered, and chilled.

1 **Using a sharp knife**, cut away all the pith from the oranges. Cut the oranges into segments over a 1-litre measuring jug, so the juice drains into the jug. Divide the segments between the 4 dessert glasses, reserving those from 1 orange to garnish. Add enough orange juice to the jug to make up 900ml (1½ pints).

2 **Place the gelatine** leaves in a small bowl and pour over 50ml of the juice. Leave the gelatine to soak for 10 minutes, or according to the packet instructions, until very soft and gelatinous. Place the bowl over a small pan of simmering water, over a low heat, and stir until the gelatine has dissolved completely.

3 **Pour the gelatine** mixture into the jug and stir well. Pour into the glasses, over the orange segments, dividing the juice equally between the 4 servings.

4 **Place the jellies** in a refrigerator to set for at least 2 hours. When ready to serve, add the reserved orange segments, and a dollop of yogurt to each.

VARIATION

Grapefruit Jelly

Substitute 1 or 2 grapefruits, depending on size, for the oranges, and use grapefruit juice, or a mixture of grapefruit and orange juice.

> **JELLY MOULDS**
> If using jelly moulds, dip the base of each one briefly into hot water so they are easier to turn out on to serving plates.

Caramel Apple and Almond Tart

Almonds and apples are the perfect combination for this sweet pastry dessert

- 🍴 serves 6
- 🕐 prep 20 mins, plus chilling and cooling • cook 45 mins
- 📷 6 x 10cm (4in) loose-bottomed tart tins, baking beans
- ❄ freeze for up to 3 months

For the pastry

250g (9oz) plain flour

125g (4½oz) butter, chilled and diced

2 tbsp caster sugar

1 large egg yolk

For the filling

4 eggs

300ml (10fl oz) soured cream or crème fraîche

2 tbsp maple syrup

115g (4oz) soft light brown sugar

2 tbsp almond liqueur

1 tsp pure vanilla extract

115g (4oz) ground almonds

3 tart dessert apples, such as Granny Smiths, peeled, cored, and sliced

1 tbsp caster sugar

1 **To make the pastry**, place the flour, butter, and caster sugar into a food processor and process until the mixture resembles breadcrumbs. Add the egg yolk and mix briefly to make an even dough, adding a little cold water if it seems too dry. Turn out onto a floured surface, roll out, and use it to line the tart tins. Chill, covered in the refrigerator, for 30 minutes.

2 **Preheat the oven** to 190°C (375°F/Gas 5). Line the pastry cases with greaseproof paper and fill with the baking beans. Bake blind for 10 minutes, then remove the paper and beans and bake for a further 5 minutes. Remove from the oven and leave to cool slightly.

3 **Make the filling** by whisking together all the ingredients, except the caster sugar and apples, until well combined. Pour the mixture into the pastry cases. Arrange the apples on top and dust with the caster sugar. Bake for 20 minutes, or until set. Remove from the oven and leave to cool. Serve cold.

● **Good with** vanilla ice cream and a drizzle of maple syrup.

Rhubarb and Ginger Meringue Cake

The classic combination of rhubarb and ginger makes a tasty filling for this delicious meringue cake

 serves 6–8

prep 30 mins, plus cooling
● cook 1 hr

For the meringues

4 egg whites

pinch of salt

225g (8oz) caster sugar

For the filling

600g (1lb 5oz) rhubarb, chopped

85g (3oz) caster sugar

4 pieces of stem ginger, chopped

½ tsp ground ginger

250ml (8fl oz) double cream

icing sugar, to dust

● **Prepare ahead** Make the meringues up to 1 week in advance; store in an airtight container.

1 Preheat the oven to 180°C (350°F/Gas 4). Place greaseproof paper on 2 baking trays.

2 Whisk the egg whites, the pinch of salt, and 115g (4oz) sugar, in a large, clean bowl until stiff, glossy peaks form. Fold in the rest of the sugar a spoonful at a time.

3 Divide the meringue between the baking trays and spread into 18cm (7in) circles. Bake for 5 minutes, then reduce the oven temperature to 130°C (250°F/Gas ½) and bake for 1 hour. Open the oven door and leave the meringue to cool completely.

4 Meanwhile, put the rhubarb, caster sugar, chopped stem ginger, ground ginger, and water in a large saucepan and cook, covered over a low heat for 20 minutes, or until soft. Allow to cool. If too wet, drain to get rid of some of the liquid, and chill until required.

5 Whip the cream and fold in the rhubarb. Place 1 meringue onto a serving plate, spread it with rhubarb and ginger filling, and top with the remaining meringue. Dust with icing sugar and serve.

Citrus Fruit Salad

Refreshing, colourful, and full of vitamins, this pretty dessert is sunshine on a plate

 serves 4

prep 20 mins

 low fat

3 oranges

1 grapefruit

1 ruby grapefruit

2 clementines or mandarins

juice of 1 lime

1–2 tbsp sugar (optional)

lime zest, to decorate (optional)

● **Prepare ahead** You can assemble the fruit salad up to 24 hours in advance. Cover and refrigerate until needed.

1 Using a small, sharp knife, cut away the skin and all the pith from the oranges and grapefruit. Cutting towards the centre of the fruit, remove each segment from its membrane.

2 Place all the segments in a bowl, squeeze any juice from the membranes into the bowl, and discard the membranes.

3 Peel the clementines and divide into segments. Add to the bowl, then add the lime juice and stir to coat. Sprinkle with sugar to taste (if using), then chill in the refrigerator until ready to serve.

4 Before serving, strain off any excess juice; this can be served separately as a refreshing drink.

● **Leftovers** can be coarsely chopped and served alongside cold duck or chicken as a condiment, or served with plain yogurt as a snack.

VARIATION

Sweet Citrus Salad

Make as above, but replace the 2 grapefruits with 1 pomelo or Ugli fruit. These fruits have a naturally sweeter flavour, so you can omit the sugar entirely.

Pear and Anise Tart with Ginger Crust

Spicy fruit flavours in a cream tart – an ideal winter pudding

serves 6-8

prep 30 mins, plus infusing • cook 45 mins

23cm (9in) loose-bottomed tart tin

freeze for up to 1 month

For the pastry

175g (6oz) **plain flour**, plus extra for dusting

85g (3oz) **butter**, chilled

1 piece of **stem ginger**, drained and sliced, or ½ tsp powdered ginger

1 large **egg yolk**

For the filling

300ml (10fl oz) **double cream**

5 whole **star anise**

30g (1oz) **butter**

30g (1oz) **soft brown sugar** or muscovado sugar

4 **conference pears**, peeled, cored, and thinly sliced

3 **egg yolks**

60g (2oz) **caster sugar**

1 To make the pastry, place the flour and butter in a food processor, and process until it resembles breadcrumbs. Add the ginger, then the egg yolk, and process until the pastry comes together into a ball and is evenly combined.

2 Lightly grease the tart tin. Roll the pastry out onto a floured surface, use it to line the tin, then refrigerate while you make the filling.

3 Place the cream and star anise in a small pan over a low heat, until nearly boiling, then remove from heat, cover the pan, and leave to infuse for at least 1 hour.

4 Melt the butter in a frying pan, add the brown sugar, and stir, until melted. Add the pears and allow to caramelize for 5 minutes.

5 Preheat the oven to 190°C (375°F/Gas 5), and place a baking tray in the oven. Remove the star anise from the cream, and whisk in the egg yolks and sugar.

6 Remove the pastry case from the fridge. Arrange the pears and caramel sauce over the base, then pour the cream mixture over. Place on the baking tray in the oven and bake for 25–30 minutes, or until golden and set. Serve cold.

Mango and Lime Smoothie

This drink makes a refreshing start to the day, and the lime gives a little hidden "kick"

serves 4

prep 5 mins

2 **mangoes**, peeled, stoned, and chopped

2 **bananas**, chopped

200ml (7fl oz) **orange** juice

juice of 1 **lime**

4 tbsp **natural yogurt**

1 Place all the ingredients into a blender, or use a stick blender, and blend until smooth. Serve immediately.

● **Good with** muffins, for a feel-good breakfast.

Passion Fruit Smoothie

Make the smoothie as above, but replace the orange juice with 200ml (7fl oz) pineapple juice. Omit the lime; instead, add the pulp of 2 passion fruit.

Pineapple Milkshake

A fun drink for children, with no need for added sugar

serves 2

prep 5 mins

2 ripe **bananas**, chopped

150ml (5fl oz) **milk**, chilled

2 **pineapple rings** from a can, chopped

2-3 tbsp **pineapple juice**, from the can

1 scoop **vanilla ice cream**

1 Place all the ingredients in a blender, or use a stick blender, and blend to a smooth milkshake. Serve in tall glasses, adding ice if the drink is not cold enough.

Techniques Eggs

Separate

Many recipes call for either yolks or whites. Smell your eggs first to be sure they are fresh, or use the floating test on p140

1 Break the shell of a cold egg by tapping it against the rim of the bowl. Insert your fingers into the break and gently pry the two halves apart. Some of the white will escape into the bowl.

2 Gently shift the yolk back and forth between the shell halves, allowing the white to fall into the bowl. Take care to keep the yolk intact. Place the yolk into another bowl and set aside. Remove any shells that may have fallen into the bowl.

Whisk Egg Whites

For the best results, use a copper bowl and a balloon whisk

1 Place the egg whites in the bowl and begin whisking slowly, using a small range of motion.

2 Continue whisking steadily, using larger strokes, until the whites have lost their translucency and start to foam.

3 Incorporating as much air as possible, increase your speed and range of motion until the whites have mounted to the desired degree and are stiff but not dry.

4 Test by lifting the whisk; the peaks should be firm but glossy and the tips should hang.

Poach

Use your freshest eggs, as they have thicker whites and are less likely to be dispersed when poached

1 Crack an egg onto a small plate, being careful not to break the yolk, then slide it into a pan of gently boiling water with vinegar (see "Poaching Water").

2 Using a slotted spoon, gently lift the white over the yolk until set. Repeat with remaining eggs. Adjust the heat to a gentle boil and poach for 3–5 minutes, or until the whites are completely set.

3 Place the eggs in another pan of gently simmering salted water for 30 seconds to remove the taste of the vinegar. Then drain the eggs briefly on a clean towel or with a slotted spoon.

POACHING WATER

In the boiling water, add 1 tsp of white vinegar to every litre (1¾ pints) of water. This will help the egg white to coagulate rather than form streamers. Do not add salt, as it will discourage coagulation. If you wish to remove any leftover vinegar-taste, plunge the poached eggs into a separate pan of gently simmering, salted water.

Boil

Despite the name, eggs must be simmered – never boiled. If a green ring appears, it is the result of overcooking (or an old egg)

For Soft-boiled

The whites will be set and the yolks runny. Use a pan large enough to hold the eggs in a single layer. Cover them with at least 5cm (2in) of cold water and set the pan over high heat. Bring the water to the boil, then lower to a simmer for 2–3 minutes.

For Hard-boiled

Both the whites and the yolks will be set. Continue to simmer for 10 minutes from the boil. Once the eggs have cooked, place the pan under a stream of cold running water to stop the cooking process. Peel away and discard the shells when cool enough to handle.

Scramble

Scramble as you like, whether you prefer your curds large, small, or completely scrambled in traditional French-style

1 Crack the eggs into a bowl, making sure to remove any fallen shell. With a fork, break the yolks and beat the eggs. Season with salt and freshly ground black pepper.

2 Heat a non-stick pan over medium heat, then melt a knob of butter to lightly coat the base. When the butter has melted but not yet browned, pour in the beaten eggs.

3 Using a wooden spoon, pull the setting egg from the edges into the centre to cook the raw egg. For larger curdles, let the egg set longer before scrambling.

For creamier eggs, add a little milk when beating the eggs in step 1, or add a little cream just before the eggs are finished.

Make a Classic Omelette

A 3-egg omelette is easiest to handle; any more than 6 eggs will be more difficult

1 Beat and season the eggs. Heat a non-stick frying pan over a moderate heat and melt a knob of butter. Add the eggs, tilting the pan so the eggs can spread evenly.

2 Stir the eggs with a fork to distribute the eggs evenly. Stop stirring the eggs just as soon as they are set. Fold the side of the omelette nearest to you halfway over itself.

3 Sharply tap the handle of the pan to encourage the other side of the omelette to curl over and slide to the edge of the pan.

4 Tilt the pan over a serving plate, so that the omelette falls seam side down. Serve immediately.

Techniques Fruit and Nuts

Make Lemon-zest Julienne

These strips are used in a large variety of recipes as flavourings and garnishes. Choose lemons that are unwaxed

1 Using a peeler, remove strips of the zest with as little of the bitter pith as possible.

2 If pith remains, use a sharp knife to slice it off by running your knife along the peel away from you. Using a rocking motion with your knife, slice the peel into strips.

Peel and Prepare Apples

Choose apples that are sweet-smelling, firm, and unbruised. The skin should be taut and unbroken

Core and Peel

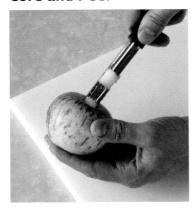

1 Core an apple by pushing a corer straight into the stalk of the apple and through to the bottom. Twist and loosen the core, then pull it out with the corer.

2 Using a peeler or small paring knife, gently remove the skin of the apple by making a circular path around the body from top to bottom.

Make Rings

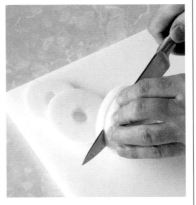

Place the cored apple on its side and hold it steady against a clean cutting board. Using a sharp knife, slice down through the apple. Repeat making slices of even thickness.

Chop

After slicing, stack the rings, a few at a time. Slice down through the pile, then repeat crossways in the opposite direction, making pieces of about the same size.

Segment Citrus Fruit

Segmenting citrus fruit ensures clean and precise wedges for a more attractive garnish

1 With a sharp knife, cut off the top and bottom of the fruit so it can stand upright. Holding it firmly, slice down and around the flesh, following the contour of the skin. Try to remove as much of the white pith as possible.

2 Slice along the lines of the membrane, which separates each slice. Repeat slicing between each membrane.

Prepare a Mango

Cutting halves alongside the fibrous stone and "hedgehogging" the mango is the cleanest way to remove the flesh

1 **Standing the mango** on its side, cut the mango by running your knife just to one side of the stone; repeat the cut on the other side, so that a single slice remains with the stone encased.

2 **With the halves** flesh-side up, cut the flesh into strips lengthways then crossways, cutting to, but not through, the skin. Invert the skin so that the flesh is exposed. Run your knife along the skin to remove the segments.

Cut Pineapple

Best when fresh, preparing pineapple is simple. Take care when handling the sharp outer skin

Make Rings

1 **With a sharp knife**, cut the top and the base from the pineapple. Stand the pineapple upright and cut along the contour of the flesh, removing the skin in long strips from top to bottom.

2 **To make the rings**, turn the pineapple sideways and slice. Use a round cutter to remove the centre of each ring.

Make Wedges

1 **Quarter the fruit**, then cut lengthways to remove the core at the centre of each piece. Beginning at the plume end, cut between the flesh and the skin.

2 **Cut the flesh crossways** against the skin, making slices of even width. Repeat, cutting the other quarters into slices.

Peel Soft Fruit

Removing the skin from peaches and nectarines is necessary for many desserts, sauces, and purées

1 **Starting at the base**, make a cut crossways around the middle, just through the skin. Then repeat the cut in the other direction so that the skin is quartered in wedges.

2 **Place the fruit** into a heatproof bowl and pour over boiling water from a kettle. Remove the fruit from the water with a slotted spoon and transfer it to a separate bowl filled with cold water. When the fruit is cool enough to handle, remove it from the water and carefully pull the skin from the flesh with your fingers.

Poach Fruit

Choose firm fruits for poaching that are not too ripe, as these will hold their shape better

Poaching Stone Fruit in Sugar Syrup

1 **To simmering sugar syrup**, add the fruits once the stones have been removed and the bodies halved. Make sure the fruits are completely submerged in the syrup.

2 **Poach the fruits** for 10–15 minutes, or until tender and remove them with a slotted spoon. Boil the syrup until it is slightly reduced, strain, then pour over the fruit to serve.

Poaching Pears in Wine

1 **Heat red wine** with flavourings – such as fresh citrus peels, whole cinnamon sticks, fresh ginger, or vanilla beans – and sugar until the sugar dissolves. Add the prepared pears and bring the wine slowly to a simmer. Poach for 15–25 minutes or until tender.

2 **Remove from the heat** and let the pears cool in the liquid. Once cool, remove the pears with a slotted spoon and bring the liquid to a simmer. When slightly reduced, serve the sauce with the fruit.

Make a Sauce for Crêpes

This sauce is best when coating sweet crêpes while still warm. For a flambé sauce, see p376

1 **In a large frying pan**, heat 2 tbsp orange or lemon juice with 1 tbsp sugar and a kob of butter over a low heat. Simmer the sauce for 5 minutes, or until slightly thickened.

2 **Place the crêpes** into the pan one at a time, coating evenly with the sauce.

3 **Fold the crêpe in half**, then in half again and transfer immediately to a plate. Repeat with the remaining crêpes.

For Flambéing

For impressive presentation, setting a flame to the crêpes is always exciting. Gently warm the liquor and brandy in a pan. Remove from the heat and set alight, being careful to keep the pan away from your body. Immediately, pour the sauce over the crêpes. When the flames have died down, serve the crêpes.

Peel Chestnuts

Choose chestnuts that are heavy with smooth, shiny shells

BLANCHING CHESTNUTS

Instead of grilling or deep-frying the chestnuts to split their shells, they can also be blanched. Place the chestnuts in a saucepan with plenty of cold water to cover them and bring to the boil. When the shells split, drain the chestnuts on kitchen paper and peel when cool enough to handle.

1 Using a small, sharp knife, carefully pierce the top of each chestnut to keep it from rupturing when heated.

2 Grill or deep-fry the chestnuts for about 3 minutes, or until their shells split. When they are cool enough to handle, remove both the inner and outer shells.

3 Coarsely chop the flesh with a sharp knife if you wish to use them for stuffing.

Prepare Almonds

Just as easily as buying your almonds already prepared, you can blanch, flake, and chop them yourself

1 To blanch, place the almonds in a bowl and pour over enough boiling water to cover them. Leave for 1 minute, then drain.

2 To peel, pinch each almond with your fingers to remove the skin. Alternatively, the nuts can be rubbed between kitchen paper to remove the skins.

3 To flake, use a large, sharp knife to cut the almonds into slices of the desired thickness. To make thin slivers, carefully slice the almonds lengthways.

4 To chop, use a large, sharp knife to cut pieces of desired size – coarse or fine. Use your knuckles to guide your knife through the almonds as you chop.

Shell Walnuts and Pecans

Walnuts and pecans are often used in salads and desserts

Use a nutcracker. The inner skin is difficult to peel away, but fine to eat. Take extra care to keep your fingers out of the way of the nutcracker.

Skin Pistachios

Inside the hard, tan shell is the pale, green nut

Place the pistachios in a saucepan with plenty of cold water to cover them and bring to the boil. When the skins split, place the pistachios between two clean kitchen towels and rub the skins off.

Nuts   493

Techniques Grains and Pasta

Soak and Cook Rice by Absorption

Throughout Asia, this is the most common way to cook rice. Always be sure to soak and rinse the rice before cooking

1 Put the rice and water or stock into a large saucepan. Over moderate heat, bring to the boil, stir once and lower the heat to simmer uncovered for 10–12 minutes, or until all the liquid is absorbed.

2 Remove the saucepan from the heat and cover with a fitted lid with a clean, folded towel in between. Leave the rice to steam, without removing the lid, for 20 minutes.

3 Remove the folded towel and replace the lid. Leave the rice to sit for 5 minutes, covered. Fluff the rice with a fork and serve.

Make Basic Risotto

The best risotto is made from the combination of rich, well-flavoured stock and constant stirring

1 Heat the stock in saucepan to a gentle simmer. In a separate, large pan, heat the oil and butter. When the butter is melted, add the onion and cook until softened, but not brown. Stir in the rice, coating the grains in the butter and oil.

2 Add the wine, bring to a gentle boil, and stir until absorbed. Add one ladle of simmering stock and stir until it is absorbed. Repeat, adding one ladle of stock at a time, stirring constantly for 25 minutes, or until the rice is tender but not mushy.

3 Stir in a little more butter and some Parmesan cheese. Season to taste with salt and pepper and remove from the heat. Leave the risotto to rest, covered, for 2 minutes before serving.

Risotto should be creamy but with distinguishably separate grains of rice, and never mushy. Use short-medium grains, as these will swell, but still maintain their individual shape. Use any fish, shellfish, meat, chicken, or vegetable stock to embellish the flavour.

Make Soft and Grilled Polenta

A staple of Italian cooking, polenta is one of the most versatile grains

For Soft Polenta

1 **Bring a large pan** of salted water to the boil. Gradually pour in the polenta, whisking quickly and continuously to ensure there are no lumps and the mixture is smooth.

2 **Reduce the heat** to low and continue cooking for 40–45 minutes, or until coming away from the edge of the pan, whisking occasionally. Stir in butter, Parmesan cheese, and season to taste.

For Grilled Polenta

1 **Make soft polenta**, but without the butter and cheese. Once thickened, pour it onto a greased baking tray, spread with a spatula, then leave it to set. (Keep up to 4 days, chilled and covered.)

2 **When ready to use**, turn the tray out onto a board. Cut the polenta into the desired shapes and sizes. Brush the pieces with olive oil, then grill on a hot, ridged grill pan for about 3–5 minutes on each side.

Cook Dried Pasta

Dried pasta is essential to have in your storecupboard, as it can form the basis of many quick dishes

1 **Bring a large pan** of salted water to the boil and gently pour in the pasta.

2 **Boil uncovered**, following the recommended cook time on the packet, or until *al dente* when tasted.

3 **Drain the pasta through** a colander, shaking it gently to remove any excess water.

> **TEST PASTA FOR *AL DENTE***
>
> Al Dente is the Italian phrase for "to the tooth", which describes the texture of the pasta as tender but just cooked so a little resistance remains. The best test for this is by taste, not packet instructions.

Boil Noodles

Noodles need to be soaked in hot water or boiled for a few minutes before using

1 **To boil egg**, wheat, or buckwheat noodles, bring a large saucepan of water to the boil. Add the noodles, allow the water to return to the boil, then cook until the noodles are softened and flexible, about 2 minutes.

2 **Drain the noodles** in a colander and place them under cold, running water. Toss the noodles with a little oil to prevent them from sticking, then proceed with the desired recipe.

Techniques Vegetables

Steam

This is a healthy way to prepare vegetables, but if over-steamed the vegetables will lose their vibrant colour and flavour

1 **Bring about 2½cm (1in)** of water to the boil in the bottom pan of a steamer. Place the vegetables in the upper basket and position it above the bottom pan.

2 **When the steam rises**, cover the pan with a fitted lid and cook until the vegetables are just tender.

Stir-fry

This low-fat cooking method uses very little oil so the vegetables retain their natural flavours and take hardly any time to cook

1 **When the wok (or pan)** is hot, add sunflower, rapeseed, or groundnut oil, tilting the pan to spread the oil around the base of the wok. When very hot, toss in garlic, ginger, chilli, or spring onions.

2 **Add the desired vegetables** and use a spatula to toss continually. If using meat, add it before the vegetables, using a more delayed toss to allow the meat to sit and cook for a few seconds.

3 **Some vegetables**, such as broccoli, are best when steamed for just a few minutes longer. Add a couple of tbsp of water and cover the wok until vegetables are just tender and still crisp.

STIR-FRYING TIPS

For best results, cut the vegetables to approximately the same size. Vegetables or meats that take longest to cook should be added first. Season to taste with salt, pepper, soy sauce, Chinese hot sauce, or chilli flakes.

Cut Carrot Batonnets

Batonnets are 5mm (¼in) wide and 5–6cm (2–2½in) long. Any long, straight vegetable can be cut to this shape

1 **Peel each carrot** and cut in half crossways. Set a mandolin blade to a 5mm (¼in) thickness. Hold the mandolin steady with one hand and press the carrot firmly with the palm of the other, taking care to keep your fingers clear of the blade. Slice each carrot up and down a few times until the slices are the right thickness and uniform.

2 **Stack the slices** in the order in which they fell and square them off by cutting the rounded sides with a sharp knife. Slice the carrot lengthways into strips of equal width.

Peel and Dice an Onion

Once an onion is halved, it can be sliced or diced. This technique is for quick dicing, which helps prevent your eyes from watering

1 **Using a sharp chef's knife**, cut the onion lengthways in half and peel off the skin, leaving the root to hold the layers together.

2 **Lay one half** cut-side down. Make a few slices into the onion horizontally, cutting up to but not through the root.

3 **With the forward tip** of your knife, slice down through the layers vertically, cutting as close to the root as possible.

4 **Cut across** the vertical slices to produce an even dice. Use the root to hold the onion steady, then discard when all the onion is diced.

Wash and Cut Leeks Julienne

The mildest of the onion family, julienned leeks are wonderful in soups and sauces

1 **With a sharp knife**, trim off the root end and some of the dark, green leaf top. Cut the leek in half lengthways and gently spread the layers apart. Rinse the leek under cold running water and gently shake off any excess water.

2 **For julienne**, cut off all the green part of the leek, then cut it crossways to the desired length. Lay each section cut-side down and slice it into strips about 3mm (⅛in) wide.

Peel and Chop Garlic

Garlic is essential to many recipes and peeling it is easy once you know how

1 **Place each garlic clove** flat on a cutting board. Place a large knife blade on top and pound it with the palm of your hand.

2 **Discard the skin** and cut off the ends of each clove.

3 **Slice the clove** into slivers lengthways, then cut across into tiny chunks. Collect the pieces into a pile and chop again for finer pieces.

Choosing Garlic

Pre-peeled garlic is convenient if you plan to use it within a few days, but buying it fresh and preparing it yourself is easy. Choose fresh bulbs that are firm and compact. The skin should be smoothly attached to the base of the bulb, not tattered or frayed. Although garlic keeps for up to 2 months in a cool, dark and dry place, be sure to check that the cloves are still firm and free of sprouts. Never store garlic in a refrigerator.

Peel and Deseed Tomatoes

Before using tomatoes for sauces or soups they must be peeled and deseeded

1 **Remove the green stem**, score an "X" in the skin of each tomato, at the base, then immerse it in a pan of boiling water for 20 seconds, or until the skin loosens.

2 **With a slotted spoon**, remove the tomato from the boiling water and place it into a bowl of iced water to cool.

3 **When cool enough** to handle, use a paring knife to peel away the loosened skin.

4 **Cut each tomato** in half and gently squeeze out the seeds over a bowl and discard.

Prepare Broccoli

How to separate broccoli florets from the main stalks

1 **Lay the broccoli** stalk flat on a clean cutting board and remove the thick portion of the stalk.

2 **To remove the florets**, slide the knife between the smaller stalks through the head. Rinse the florets with cold water and drain.

Prepare Cauliflower

How to separate cauliflower florets from the main stalks

1 **Lay the head** of cauliflower on a cutting board with the stalk facing up. Cut off the large stalk and remove any leaves.

2 **Using a small paring knife**, carefully cut the florets from the centre. Rinse the florets with cold water and drain.

Trim Greens

Before cutting and cooking hearty greens of Swiss chard, kale, and spring greens, you must trim them

1 **Discard all limp** and discoloured leaves. Slice each leaf along both sides of the centre rib, then remove it and discard.

2 **Working with a few leaves** at a time, roll them loosely into a bunch. Cut across the roll to the desired width, making strips.

Stone and Remove Avocado Flesh

The flesh of an avocado is rich and luxurious once you peel the skin and remove the stone

1 With a chef's knife, slice straight into the avocado, cutting all the way around the stone.

2 Gently twist the halves in opposite directions and separate.

3 Strike the cutting edge of your knife into the stone and lift the knife (wiggling if necessary) to remove it from the avocado.

4 Use a wooden spoon to carefully release the stone from your knife and discard.

5 Quarter the avocado and use a paring knife to peel away and discard the skin.

6 To dice an avocado, cut it into neat slices lengthways, then repeat crossways to the desired size.

Alternatively, you can slice an avocado. Halve and remove the stone, then use a spatula to remove the flesh from the skin, kept whole if possible. Place on a cutting board and cut into slices or wedges. Rub the flesh with lemon to prevent browning.

Trim Asparagus

For tender, less fibrous asparagus, trim and peel the spear

1 With a sharp knife, cut the hard ends from the spears. Alternatively, snap the bottoms of the asparagus spears.

2 Rotating the spear, use a vegetable peeler to remove a thin layer of skin from all sides.

Prepare Artichokes

Artichokes can be served whole with the leaves or trimmed to expose the heart

To Serve Whole

1 Holding the stalk to steady the artichoke, cut the tough tips off with strong kitchen scissors.

2 Use a chef's knife to cut the stalk from the base.

3 Cut off the pointed tip and pull away any dark outer leaves.

> ### PREVENT BROWNING
> Once artichokes are cut and exposed to oxygen, their leaves and hearts will begin to turn brown. To prevent this, rub the cut side of a fresh lemon onto the exposed flesh of the artichoke.

To Serve the Hearts

1 Cut or pull away all of the leaves from the artichoke, then cut the stalk from the base.

2 With a sharp knife, cut off the soft middle cone of leaves just above the hairy choke.

3 Rub the exposed flesh with fresh lemon juice to reduce browning. Trim away the bottom leaves with a paring knife.

4 The hairy choke can be removed if you plan to cut the heart into pieces for cooking.

Bake Beetroot

This technique is often used for baking potatoes, but is a wonderful method for roots and tubers

1 Preheat the oven to 200°C (400°F/Gas 6). Cut off the stalks, wash and dry the beets, then salt and wrap them individually in foil.

2 Place the beetroots in a shallow roasting tin and bake them in the oven for 45 minutes, or until tender when pierced with a knife.

3 Once cool enough to handle, peel away the skin of the beetroots with a paring knife. Be careful, as the juice will stain easily.

4 Rinse and slice the beetroots. Serve the slices arranged on a platter, seasoned to taste with salt, pepper, olive oil, and lemon juice.

Prepare Bell Peppers

Red, green, orange, and yellow peppers add brilliant colour and sweetness to stir-frys, and distinctive flavour to many dishes

1 Place the pepper on its side and cut off the top and bottom. Stand the pepper on one of the cut ends and slice it in half lengthways. Remove the core and seeds.

2 Open each section and lay them flat on the cutting board. Using a sideways motion, remove the remaining pale, fleshy ribs.

3 Cut the peppers into smaller sections, following the divisions of the pepper. Chop according to the preparation of your dish.

For stuffing and roasting, cut around the stalk and remove with the core attached. Rinse away the stray seeds and dry.

Roast and Peel Peppers

Roasting peppers makes removing their skins easy and enhances the flavour and sweetness of the flesh

1 Hold the pepper over an open flame to char the skin. Rotate the pepper and char each side evenly.

2 Put each pepper into a plastic bag and seal tightly. Set the bag aside and allow the skins to loosen.

3 When the peppers have cooled completely, use your fingers to peel away the charred skin.

4 Pull off the stalk, keeping the core attached if possible. Discard seeds and slice the flesh into strips.

Deseed and Cut Chillies

Chillies contain capsaicin, which gives off a fiery heat

1 Cut the chilli lengthways in half. Using the tip of your knife, scrape out the seeds and remove the membrane and stem.

2 Flatten each chilli half with the palm of your hand and slice lengthways into strips.

3 For dice, hold the strips firmly together and slice crossways to make equal-size pieces.

Safety Tip

Once you have touched the seeds and inner membranes of hot chillies, never touch your eyes or nose, as they will burn painfully. Wash your hands immediately after preparing the hot chillies, or alternatively, wear gloves.

Peel Squash

Squashes and pumpkins have hard, thick skins, which must be peeled; the flesh is usually cubed or cut into chunks

1 Holding the squash firmly on a cutting board, use a chef's knife to cut the squash lengthways in half, working from the stalk end to the core end.

2 Using a spoon, remove the seeds and fibres from each squash half and discard.

3 Use a vegetable peeler or knife to remove the skin. Cut the squash into pieces or chunks.

Rehydrate Dried Mushrooms

Preserving mushrooms by drying them intensifies their flavour when they are rehydrated and used

1 To rehydrate dried mushrooms, place the mushrooms – either wild or cultivated – into a bowl of hot water. Allow them to soak for at least 15 minutes.

2 Remove the mushrooms with a slotted spoon from the soaking liquid. If you plan to use the soaking liquid in your recipe, strain the liquid through a coffee filter or muslin to remove any sand or grit.

Make Deep-fried Crisps

Any vegetable with a high starch content, such as potatoes, sweet potatoes, or parsnips, can be sliced thinly and deep fried

1 Preheat the oil or deep fryer to 160°C (325°F). Meanwhile, using a mandolin or knife, slice the peeled potatoes thinly.

2 When the oil is hot, add a batch of potatoes, using a frying basket to lower them into the oil.

3 Fry for about 2 minutes, or until crisp and golden brown on both sides. Lift the crisps out of the oil and drain briefly on kitchen paper.

4 While still warm, season the crisps with salt to taste.

Core and Shred Cabbage

Shredded cabbage is used in many recipes, but the vibrant purple variation makes a particularly attractive side dish

1 Hold the head of cabbage firmly on the cutting board and use a sharp knife to cut it in half, straight through the stalk end.

2 Cut the halves again through the stalk lengthways and slice out the core from each quarter.

3 Working with each quarter at a time, place the wedge cut-side down. Cut across the cabbage, creating shreds.

Remove Sweetcorn Kernels

One of the sweetest vegetables, nothing is better than using fresh sweetcorn rather than tinned or frozen

1 Remove the husks and all the silk thread from the corn-on-the-cob. Rinse the husked corn under cold running water.

2 Place the blunt end on the cutting board. Use a sharp chef's knife and slice straight down the cob. Rotate the cob and repeat.

3 To extract the "milk", hold the cob upright in a bowl and use your knife to scrape down the side. Rotate the corn and repeat.

Chop Herbs

Chop fresh herbs just before using to release their flavour and aroma

1 Strip the leaves from stems and gather them together in a tight pile. With basil leaves (shown), layer the leaves and roll them gently.

2 Using a large, sharp knife, slice through the herbs, holding them together with your other hand.

3 Gather the herbs into a pile and chop through the herbs using a rocking motion. Gather and repeat to achieve the desired size.

Techniques Fish and Shellfish

Gut Fish

You can gut fish through the stomach (for stuffing and filleting) or through the gills (for poaching whole and cutting into steaks)

Through the Stomach

1 **On a clean work surface,** place the fish on its side. Holding it firmly, make a shallow incision in the underside from just before the fin to the head. Any fish knife, small chef's knife, or sharp kitchen scissors will work well for this.

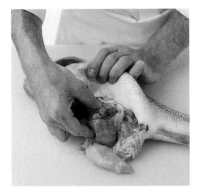

2 **Remove the guts** using your hands, and cut off the gills, taking care not to cut yourself, as they can be very sharp.

3 **Rinse the entire cavity** with cold, running water to remove any remaining blood or guts. Use kitchen paper to pat the fish dry. The fish can now be scaled and trimmed.

Through the Gills

1 **Carefully hook** your index finger under the gills to lift them from the base of the head. Using sharp kitchen scissors or a fish knife, cut off the gills and discard.

2 **Put your fingers** through the hole formed by the removed gills and pull out the guts.

3 **Using scissors,** make a small slit in the stomach at the ventral (anal) opening. Use your fingers to pull out any remaining guts. Rinse with cold, running water. The fish can now be scaled and trimmed.

Scale and Trim Fish

Use either a fish scaler or the blade of a chef's knife to scrape off the scales if you plan to serve the fish with its skin

1 **Lay the fish** on top of a clean work surface. Holding the fish by the tail, scrape the scales off using strokes towards the head.

2 **Using kitchen scissors,** remove the dorsal (back) fin, the belly fins, and the two on either side of the head.

Fillet and Skin a Fish

There is no need to scale a fish beforehand if you plan to skin the fish fillets

1 **Gut the fish** through the stomach, then use a large chef's knife to cut into the head at an angle, just behind the gills, until you reach the backbone. Cut the fish down the length of one side of the backbone, turn the fish over, and repeat the cut on the other side of the backbone.

2 **Place the fillet**, skin-side down onto a clean work surface. Insert a fish knife into the flesh of the fish near the tail end. Turn the blade at an angle almost parallel to the skin and cut off the flesh, while holding the skin taut.

Bone a Flat Fish

Popular flat fish varieties include flounder, sole, turbot, and brill

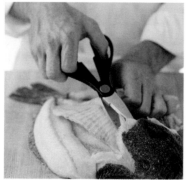

> ### SKINNING A FLAT FISH
> To hold the shape of the fish, the white-skinned side is left attached. The dark side, however, can be removed. Place the fish white-side up and make a small cut at the tail end between the dark skin and the flesh. Keep the blade of your knife flat against the skin and, while holding the skin taut with the other hand, cut the flesh neatly away.

1 **Place the fish** dark-side up and cut just to, but not through, the backbone from head to tail. Working from the incision, cut away the flesh one half at a time, so the backbone is exposed with two fillets laid open. Slide your blade under the backbone to cut away the flesh.

2 **Use kitchen scissors** to snip the backbone from the head and tail ends of the fish, then make a cut through the middle of the backbone.

3 **Lift the backbone pieces** from the flesh and discard. Before stuffing, be sure to check for and remove any remaining bones.

Bone a Round Fish

Once gutted, scaled, and trimmed, a round fish can be boned through the stomach and stuffed for cooking

1 **Open the fish** by making an incision from the tail to the head. Using the blade of your knife, loosen the backbone (transverse bones) on the top side, then turn the fish over to loosen the other side.

2 **Using kitchen scissors**, snip the backbone from the head and tail ends. Starting at the tail, peel the bones away from the flesh and discard. Before stuffing, be sure to check for and remove any remaining bones left in the flesh.

Bake *en Papillote*

The term *en papillote* is French for "in a paper bag". What is cooked inside remains moist and can be kept sealed to serve

1 Cut a heart shape 5cm (2in) longer than the fish out of greaseproof paper. Brush the paper with oil and place a piece of fish onto one half of the heart with herbs and vegetables. Drizzle with white wine.

2 Fold over the other half of the paper and twist the edges to seal the parcel. Repeat for the other pieces of fish. Place the parcels on a baking sheet and bake at 180°C (350°F/Gas 4) for 15–20 minutes.

Remove the Meat from a Crab

Shown below is a common European crab, but the Dungeness crab is prepared much in the same way

1 On a chopping board, place the cooked crab on its back and firmly twist the claws and legs to break them from the body.

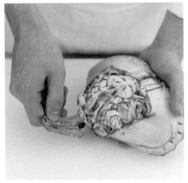

2 On the underside of the body, lift the triangular tail flap (the apron), twist it off and discard.

3 Break and separate the central section from the shell. Lift off the shell and remove any white meat from it using a teaspoon or fork.

4 Use your fingers to remove the gills (dead man's fingers) from the central body and discard. Remove the intestines from either the shell or the body and discard.

5 Crack with your hands or use a large knife to cut the central body into large sections. Using a lobster pick or skewer, dislodge all the white meat and reserve in a bowl. Remove and discard any remaining pieces of the membrane.

6 Remove the soft brown meat from the shell using a teaspoon and reserve with the white meat (there is no brown meat in Dungeness crab). Remove and discard the head sac. If there is any roe in the shell, it too can be reserved.

7 To crack the shell on each leg, use the blunt side of a heavy knife. Remove the meat in one piece using a lobster pick. Reserve with the white meat.

8 With shellfish crackers or a nutcracker, break the shell of the claws. Remove the white meat to be served and discard any bits of remaining membrane.

Prepare Mussels

Mussels must be scrubbed and de-bearded before use

1 **In the sink**, scrub the mussels under cold, running water. Rinse away grit or sand and remove any barnacles with a small, sharp knife. Discard any mussels that are open.

2 **To remove the "beard"**, pinch the dark stringy piece between your fingers, pull it away from the mussel and discard.

Open Scallops

Scallops are bought out of the shell or closed

1 **Hold the scallop firmly**, flat-side up, and insert a thin, flexible knife, keeping the blade close to the top shell of the scallop, and sever the muscle.

2 **Run your knife** along the bottom shell to detach the scallop. Cut away and discard the fringe-like membrane. Rinse the scallop and coral before using.

Open Oysters

As for shucking oysters, the technique is perfected with practice. Use a towel to protect your hand from the oysters' sharp shells

1 **Holding the oyster** flat in a towel will help prevent the deliciously briny liquid from spilling out. Insert the tip of an oyster knife into the hinge to open the shell. Keep the blade close to the top of the shell so the oyster is not damaged. Cut the muscle and lift off the top shell.

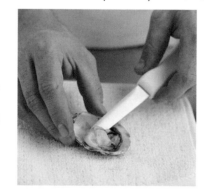

2 **Detach the oyster** from the bottom shell by carefully sliding the blade of your knife beneath the oyster. The oysters can be served raw on the half shell (but be sure to scrub the shells thoroughly before opening), or removed and cooked.

Open Clams

Clams must be cleaned well, as they tend to be very sandy

 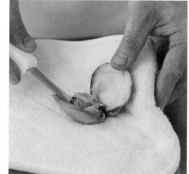

1 **Discard any open clams**. Place the clam in a towel to protect fingers, then insert the knife tip and twist to force the shells apart.

2 **Sever the muscle** and release the clam. If using soft-shell clams, remove and discard the dark membrane before serving.

Peel and Devein Prawns

Remove the veins of large prawns, as they are gritty

1 **Remove the head** and legs by pulling them off with your fingers, then peel away the shells, saving them for stock, if you like.

2 **Using the tip** of a paring knife or cocktail stick, hook the vein where the head was and gently pull it away from the body.

Techniques Meat

Joint a Chicken

Poultry are often left whole for roasting, poaching, and slow-cooking in a pot. For other methods, cut them into 4 or 8 pieces

Remove the Wishbone
Using a sharp knife, scrape the flesh away from the wishbone, then use your fingers to twist and lift it free.

1 Remove the wishbone, then place the bird breast-side up onto a cutting board. Using a sharp knife, cut down and through the thigh joint to separate the leg from the rest of the body.

2 Bend the leg back to dislodge the leg joint. When the ball is free from the socket, you will hear a pop.

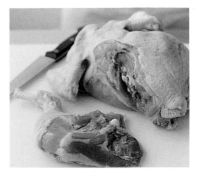

3 Use your knife to cut any meat or skin that is still attached to the body. Repeat to remove the other leg. Each leg can be further divided into a thigh and a drumstick.

4 Fully extend one wing, then use sharp poultry shears to cut off the winglet at the middle joint. Repeat to remove the other winglet.

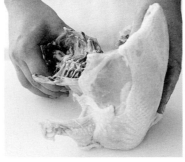

5 Using your hands, firmly grasp the backbone and break it from the crown (the 2 breasts and wings on the bone).

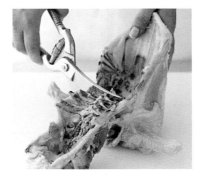

6 Using poultry shears, cut the lower end of the backbone from the remaining body.

7 Starting at the neck, use poultry shears to cut all the way through the backbone to separate the breasts.

8 The chicken is now cut into 4 pieces. Any leftover bones (such as the backbone) can be used to flavour chicken stock.

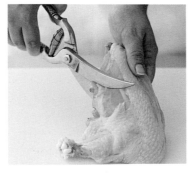

9 Use poultry shears to cut each breast in half diagonally, producing one breast and one wing. Repeat to separate the other breast from the wing.

10 Cut each leg through the knee joint, above the drumstick that connects to the thigh, and cut through to separate. Now, there is one drumstick and one thigh. Repeat to separate the other leg.

11 The chicken is now cut into 8 pieces.

Bone Poultry

For quickly braised dishes or recipes that call for poultry to be flattened, the bones must first be removed

Detach the Breast

1 **Using poultry shears**, work from the thickest wing end of the breast toward the narrowest end and cut away the ribs and the backbone.

2 **Using a sharp knife**, follow the contour of the breastbone to cut the flesh neatly off the bone.

> ### POULTRY TOOLS
>
> A boning knife is essential for removing the flesh from the bones. The blade is thin and short, which gives most of its control to the tip as it works all angles and cuts through flesh and ligaments. Choose one with a slightly flexible blade. Never cut onto the bone or you will blunt the tip. Poultry shears are also an invaluable tool when jointing and boning poultry pieces. The curved blades and long handles give the shears more power to cut through ribcages and backbones. Use poultry shears to cut through rather than around bones. Choose a pair that are comfortable to hold and easy to clean.

Bone a Leg

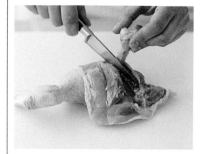

1 **Place the leg skin-side** down on a cutting board. Using a sharp knife, cut the flesh away from the start of the thigh bone. Continue cutting to expose the bone.

2 **With the same technique**, start from the knuckle and cut down the length of the drumstick.

3 **Lift the bones up** from the central knuckle joint. Using short strokes with the tip of your knife, remove the 2 bones from the flesh.

Bone a Thigh

1 **Place the thigh skin-side** down on a cutting board. Using a small, sharp knife, cut away the flesh to expose the thigh bone.

2 **Cut an incision** through the flesh, following the contour of the exposed bone. Cut around the bone to cut it completely free from the flesh and discard or use for stock.

Bone a Drumstick

1 **Starting in the middle** of the drumstick, insert the tip of your knife until you locate the bone. Slice along the bone in both directions to expose it fully.

2 **Open the flesh** and neatly cut around the bone to free it completely from the flesh and discard, or use to flavour stock.

Spatchcock a Bird

Ideal for grilling, this preparation for small poultry flattens the bird to ensure even cooking

1 Place the bird breast-side down on a sturdy cutting board. Using poultry shears, cut along both sides of the backbone, remove it completely, and discard or use for stock. Open the bird and turn it over.

2 Using the heel of one hand and the other hand to stabilize, press down firmly to crush the breastbone. Once flattened, use a sharp knife to cut slits into the legs and thighs to ensure even cooking.

3 Carefully push one metal skewer diagonally through the left leg to the right wing, then a second skewer through the right leg to the left wing.

4 The bird can now be brushed with a marinade if desired, then grilled or roasted in the oven.

Marinate Chicken

Using a marinade will produce more tender and flavourful chicken

Mix the ingredients of your marinade in a bowl. In a separate bowl, large enough to hold the chicken in a single layer, coat the chicken with the marinade, turning the pieces to coat the other side. Cover the bowl with cling film and chill in the refrigerator for an hour, or more, depending on the marinade and the time available.

NOTE

Marinating poultry can have two purposes. If using an **acid-based marinade** (such as red wine or vinegar), it will break down tough proteins and tenderise the meat. Leave poultry to marinate in an acid-based marinade for no longer than 1 hour.

Oil-based marinades mixed with aromatics (such as garlic, chilli or ginger) are used for the sole purpose of flavouring the meat. Marinating time for an oil-based mixture can be up to 4 hours.

Stuff a Chicken Breast

Avoid the temptation to overstuff the chicken breasts, as the likelihood of messy leakage will be higher

1 Using a sharp knife, cut a pocket about 4cm (1½in) deep into the side of the breast fillet. Make your cut so that both sides of the pocket are of even thickness, which will ensure even cooking.

2 Gently press the filling into the pocket and close the flesh back together. Secure with a cocktail stick. Rolling the stuffed fillet in a crumb coating before cooking will help seal the pocket.

Breading Meat

This technique is used most commonly for chicken, but also works nicely for pork

1 **Place each fillet** between 2 pieces of cling film, then pound them with a rolling pin until the fillets have increased in size and reached an even thickness.

2 **Remove the cling film** and season the fillets to taste with salt, pepper, and freshly chopped herbs. Dip the seasoned fillets into beaten egg, coating each side evenly.

3 **Turn the fillets** in breadcrumbs, pressing an even coat to both sides. Repeat the process with the remaining fillets.

Frying Heat 1cm (½in) of oil in a frying pan until hot and fry the fillets for 4–5 minutes on each side until cooked through. Drain on kitchen paper.

Carve Poultry

All white-fleshed poultry, including turkey and poussin, can be carved using this technique

1 **Once the bird has rested**, place it breast-side up on a cutting board. Staying close to the body of the bird, cut down through each leg at the joint, then in half to separate the drumstick from the thigh. Repeat with the other leg.

2 **Hold the bird steady** with a carving fork, and slice downwards and lengthways along one side of the breastbone to remove the breast meat. Repeat the slice on the other side of the breastbone.

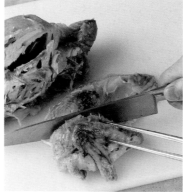

3 **Cut the breast pieces** in half on a slight diagonal, leaving a good portion of breast meat attached to the wing. Repeat separating the breast and wing of the other side.

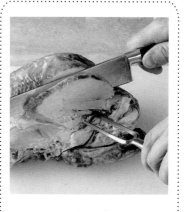

Carve the Breast Meat
To slice the breast meat from the body, hold the bird steady with a fork and make a horizontal cut under the breast meat above the wing. Cut all the way to the breastbone. Carve neat, even slices from the breast, keeping your knife parallel to the rib cage. Repeat slicing on the other side.

Butterfly a Leg of Lamb

The leg consists of 3 bones: the pelvic, which is the broadest, then the thigh and shank

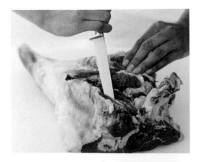

1 **Place the lamb** on a cutting board, fleshiest-side down. Locate the pelvis at the widest end of the leg and hold it firmly while using a sharp, long-bladed knife to cut around and expose the leg bone.

4 **When you reach** the bottom of the leg, cut through the sinew and tendons to release the bone completely from the flesh. All 3 bones (the pelvis, thigh and shank) should come away in one piece.

2 **Make an incision** from the pelvis to the bottom of the leg, cutting through the flesh just to the bone. Using short strokes (to prevent tearing the meat), work your knife closely around the leg bone, releasing it from the flesh.

5 **Open out the leg** so that the meat lies flat on the cutting board. With short strokes, make cuts downward through the thick meaty pieces on either side.

3 **Keeping close to the bone**, continue using short strokes down the length of the leg. Cut away the flesh from around the ball and socket joint and also from the shank.

6 **Open out the flesh** of the butterflied leg. If there are areas that are thicker than others, cut thin fillets from the thick piece and fold it over a thin area. This is helpful for more even cooking.

Bone a Saddle of Lamb

Once the bones are removed, the whole saddle of meat is perfect for stuffing

1 **Using a sharp knife**, cut away the membrane covering the fatty side of the saddle, then turn it over on to a cutting board. Working from the centre, use short strokes to cut off the 2 fillets from either side of the backbone and reserve, to cook alongside the saddle.

2 **Loosen the outside edge** of one side of the backbone using short, slicing strokes. Working from the side edge toward the centre, release the side of the backbone. Repeat with the other side.

3 **Starting at one end**, use short, slicing strokes to cut under and around the backbone. As the bone is released from the flesh, lift it away and cut beneath it.

4 **Work from the centre**, outwards, to cut away the meat and fat from the outer flaps. When the flaps are clean, square off the edges. Turn the saddle over, lightly score through the fat of the other side and cook as desired.

Roast a Rib of Beef

This classic takes little effort to prepare but leaves a lasting impression when cooked to perfection

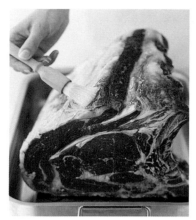

1 **Remove the meat** from the refrigerator in advance to allow it to come to room temperature. Preheat the oven to 230°C (450°F/Gas 8). Brush with oil and scatter over fresh herbs, such as thyme or rosemary. Alternatively, make multiple cuts into the fat and stick slivers of garlic and herbs inside. Position the meat, rib-side down, in a roasting tin and place in the oven.

2 **After 20 minutes**, reduce the oven temperature to 160°C (325°F/Gas 3), then continue roasting for the calculated amount of time (approximately 2 hours or more, depending on the size), basting occasionally. The most accurate way to test for doneness is by inserting a meat thermometer (50°C/120°F for medium rare). Before carving, leave the roast to stand for 15–20 minutes, covered with kitchen foil.

Carve Roast Beef

It is important to let your roast rest for 20–30 minutes so the meat relaxes and retains its flavourful juices

1 **Place the roast** on a cutting board with the ends of the ribs facing up. Holding the meat steady with a carving fork, use a sawing action to cut downwards against the sides of the bones.

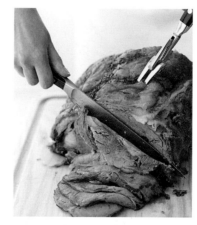

2 **Remove the bones** and position the meat fat-side up on the cutting board. With a sawing action, cut downwards, across the grain of the meat, into slices of your desired thickness. Reserve the pan juices to make a gravy.

Grill Steaks

Tender, prime cuts of meat are suitable for cooking under the grill, on a barbecue, or on a ridged cast-iron grill pan

1 **Heat the grill pan** (alternatively a grill or a barbecue) over a high heat. Brush both sides of the steaks with oil and season with salt and freshly ground black pepper.

2 **When the grill pan** is very hot, place the steaks diagonally across the ridges. Cook for 1 minute, then rotate the steaks 45 degrees and cook for another 1–2 minutes. Flip the steaks over and repeat the crossing grill marks on the other side. Remove the steaks from the grill pan and allow to rest before serving.

Make Hamburgers

Always use good quality minced meat from your butcher to avoid dry or rubbery burgers

BETTER BURGERS

Make ordinary burgers into something exquisite by adding veal, pork, lamb, sausage meat or even foie gras to your minced beef. Also try adding chopped onion or shallots and a combination of fresh herbs, such as thyme or parsley. Always season with salt and freshly ground black pepper.

1 **Place the minced meat** in a bowl, with shallots, breadcrumbs, and herbs if you wish. Season with salt and freshly ground black pepper and mix together with your hands.

2 **Divide the meat** into even pieces and roll each out into a ball. Flatten the balls slightly and chill for at least 30 minutes before grilling. Chilling allows the meat to firm and helps it stay together while cooking.

3 **Heat the grill pan** over a medium-high heat. When hot, place the burgers on the pan and cook for 6–7 minutes, turning once. Check the centre of one burger to be sure it is cooked through.

Boil and Glaze a Ham

Boiling a ham or gammon (the hind legs of a pig) will remove any extra saltiness left from the brine it was cured in

To Boil

1 **Place the ham** in a large bowl, cover with cold water, and leave it to soak in the refrigerator for at least 24 hours to dilute the salty brine.

2 **Remove the ham** and rinse it with cold running water. Place it in a large saucepan; cover with cold water, and bring to the boil. Allow to boil for 5 minutes, or until the scum rises to the surface. Drain, rinse again, and return to a clean pan. Add the stock and other flavouring ingredients. Bring to the boil, then simmer over a very low heat for 2½ hours, covered. After cooking, the meat will be very tender.

To Glaze

1 **Boil the ham**. Using a sharp knife, score the fat into a diamond-shaped pattern, which will allow the glaze to penetrate and flavour the meat.

2 **Warm a glaze** of brown sugar and English mustard until it is melted, then spread it evenly over the fat so that the glaze falls into the cuts. Roast the ham following your recipe, covered loosely with kitchen foil. Remove the foil for the last 30 minutes of roasting, to brown the top of the ham.

Make a Perfect Crackling

Do not baste the crackling when roasting the pork, or the crackling will not be crisp

1 Using a very sharp knife, score the rind of a pork shoulder widthways, working from the centre, outward. Repeat for the other end.

2 Massage the rind liberally with sea salt, then rub the entire shoulder with a little oil. Roast the meat according to your recipe.

3 When finished resting, hold the meat with a carving fork and cut just beneath the crackling. Lift away the crackling in one piece.

4 Using kitchen scissors or a sharp knife, cut the crackling crossways in half. Serve alongside the roasted meat.

Prepare Kidneys

A 500g (1lb 2oz) veal kidney will serve 4 people

1 Using your hands, gently pull away and discard the fat (suet) that surrounds the whole kidney.

2 Lay the kidney upside down, with the fatty core facing up. With the point of a sharp knife cut around the core, remove, and discard.

3 Now that the membrane is released, use your fingers to peel it from the kidney and discard.

4 Using a sharp knife, cut the kidney into pieces following the natural curves of the lobes. Prepare the kidneys as desired.

Deglaze a Roasting Tin

The drippings and meat juices that remain on the bottom of your roasting tin provide rich flavour for making gravy

1 Pour all but about 2 tbsp of the fat from the roasting tin, leaving the juices and sediments. Bring the juices to a low simmer, then whisk in 2 tbsp of plain flour.

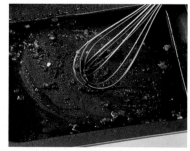

2 Using a kitchen towel, hold the tin at an angle so all the juices collect in one corner. Briskly whisk, being sure to scrape the bottom and the sides of the tin.

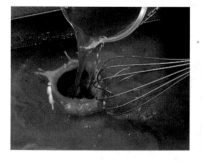

3 Gradually add stock, making a thick paste at first, then slowly thinning it with the stock. Continue whisking until smooth and bring the gravy to a simmer. Season to taste.

THE PERFECT GRAVY

To ensure a smooth, lump-free gravy, it is important to whisk continuously. For a thicker gravy, add less stock, and for a thinner one, add more. Add a splash of red wine before adding the stock, or flavour with a little Worcestershire sauce. Season to taste, although it may not need much salt.

Techniques Sauces

Make Hollandaise
A well-made hollandaise sauce should be light, somewhat tart, and just fluffy

1 In a small, heavy saucepan bring 2 tbsp vinegar, 2 tbsp water, and 1 tbsp of lightly crushed, white peppercorns to the boil. Reduce the heat and simmer for 1 minute, or until the mixture has reduced by one-third.

2 Remove from the heat and leave to stand until the liquid has chilled completely. Strain the liquid into a heatproof bowl, add 4 egg yolks, and whisk.

3 Place the bowl over a pan of simmering water. (The water should be filled to just below the bottom of the bowl.) Whisk the mixture for 5–6 minutes, or until the sauce thickens and is creamy and smooth in texture.

4 Place the bowl onto a dampened tea towel (to prevent slipping and burning). In a thin stream, slowly pour in 250g (9oz) of clarified butter and whisk until the sauce has thickened and become glossy and smooth.

5 Gently whisk in the juice of half a lemon, then season to taste with salt, freshly ground white pepper and cayenne pepper. Serve immediately. This recipe will make 600ml (1 pint).

Make a Classic Vinaigrette
A good vinaigrette depends on a careful balance of ingredients: the flavour should be complemented by the acidity but never overwhelmed

> ### VINAIGRETTE VARIATIONS
> A simple variation to this classic recipe is to use the juice of 1 lemon, or good quality balsamic or rice wine vinegar, instead. Or, add fresh herbs or fruit. A few great flavour additions are shallots, garlic, and truffles. Try different combinations like orange and rosemary, honey and ginger, or lemon and paprika.

1 In a clean bowl, combine 2 tsp Dijon mustard, 2 tbsp good-quality vinegar (balsamic, champagne, or white wine) and freshly ground black pepper.

2 Gradually whisk in 120ml (4fl oz) of extra virgin olive oil, until completely emulsified. Adjust the seasoning if necessary.

3 Serve as a salad dressing or in place of a heavier sauce for fish, poultry, or pasta. This recipe will make 150ml (5fl oz) of dressing.

Make Mayonnaise

Emulsified sauces turn out better when all ingredients are brought to room temperature before using

1 Gently whisk together 2 egg yolks, 1 tsp Dijon mustard and 2 tsp white wine vinegar into a mixing bowl. Add a pinch of salt and freshly ground black or white pepper, depending on taste.

2 Place the mixing bowl on a dampened kitchen towel (to prevent slipping) and gradually add 300ml (10fl oz) of sunflower or canola oil – beginning with one drop at a time, then to a drizzle – whisking continuously.

3 As the sauce begins to thicken, add the oil in a steady stream and continue whisking to keep the emulsion stable.

4 When all the oil has been incorporated and the mayonnaise is smooth and thick, whisk in 2 tsp of fresh lemon juice and adjust the seasoning to taste. This recipe makes 360ml (12fl oz).

Save Curdled Mayonnaise

1 Curdling can happen for many reasons: the egg yolks or the oil were too cold when combined, the mixing bowl was not clean, the oil was added too hastily, or too much oil was added. You will know your mayonnaise has curdled or split when the mixture separates into coagulated flecks of egg and oil.

2 The mayonnaise can easily be saved. Simply place 1 egg yolk into a clean mixing bowl, and very slowly, add in the curdled mayonnaise, whisking continuously.

3 Continue whisking until the curdled mixture is completely smooth and incorporated.

MAYONNAISE-BASED SAUCES

Classic mayonnaise is the base for many emulsified sauces.

To make **aioli**, add 4 crushed garlic cloves to the egg yolks, then continue following the recipe. Serve as a dip for vegetables or with fish.

To make **rouille**, add a pinch of saffron and ¼ tsp of cayenne pepper to the finished aioli (above). Serve with the Mediterranean fish soup, bouillabaisse.

To make **Tartare sauce**, add 1 tsp Dijon mustard, 25g (scant 1oz) finely chopped gherkins, 25g (scant 1oz) rinsed and chopped capers, 2 tbsp chopped chervil, and 2 finely chopped shallots to the finished mayonnaise. Serve with fish and chips.

Make Béchamel Sauce

Endlessly versatile, béchamel (the king of white sauces) has been used for many years in European cooking

1 **Stud 4 whole cloves** into a small onion, halved. Place them into a saucepan with 600ml (1 pint) of full-fat milk and 1 bay leaf. Bring almost to the boil, then reduce the heat and simmer for 4–5 minutes. Allow the milk to cool completely while it infuses.

2 **Melt 45g (1½oz)** of unsalted butter over a low heat in a separate pan. Add 45g (1½oz) of flour and cook gently for about 30 seconds, stirring the mixture into a pale roux with a wooden spoon.

3 **Remove the pan** from the heat. Strain in the milk mixture and whisk vigorously until the sauce is smooth. Return the pan to a medium heat, still whisking continuously, for 4–5 minutes, or until the sauce comes to the boil.

4 **Reduce the heat,** and simmer for 5 minutes, or until smooth, thickened, and glossy. Season to taste with salt, white pepper, and nutmeg; this recipe makes 600ml (1 pint).

Clarify Butter

The butter fat and milk solids separate when gently heated, making them great for sauces and higher-temperature cooking

1 **Cut the butter** into cubes and place them into a saucepan over a low heat. Keep watch over the butter so that it does not burn, as this will destroy the fresh flavour.

2 **When the milk solids** have separated from the fat, skim off any froth and remove from the heat. Carefully pour the clarified butter into a bowl, trying to keep the milk solids in the pan. Remove any impurities from the surface and use as desired.

Make Fresh Tomato Sauce

With just a few other ingredients, tomatoes make a great sauce for pasta, poultry, seafood, meat, and vegetables

1 **In a saucepan** over low heat, place 25g (scant 1oz) of unsalted butter, 2 chopped shallots, 1tbsp olive oil, 1 bay leaf, and 3 crushed garlic cloves. Stir, cover and sweat the ingredients for 5–6 minutes.

2 **Chop and deseed** 1kg (2¼lb) of ripe plum tomatoes and add them to the pan with 2 tbsp tomato purée and 1tbsp sugar. Cook for 5 minutes, stirring, then add 250ml (8fl oz) of water and bring to the boil.

3 **Reduce the heat** and simmer for 30 minutes, then season to taste with salt and pepper. Using a ladle, press the sauce through a sieve. Heat the sauce again before serving. This recipe makes 600ml (1 pint).

> **SAUCE VARIATIONS**
>
> For a heartier, rustic sauce, remove the bay leaf but do not press the sauce through a sieve. Add fresh thyme before serving. Also try adding freshly chopped basil or oregano. If you would like to add a spicy kick to your sauce, add a chopped hot chilli or hot chilli-pepper flakes.

Make Stock

A home-made stock is one of the most valuable ingredients you can have in your kitchen

Chicken Stock

1 **Add either raw chicken** bones, the whole carcass, or the bones and scraps from a cooked chicken into a large stockpot with carrots, celery, onions, and a bouquet garni of fresh herbs.

2 **Cover with water** and bring to the boil. Reduce the heat and simmer for 2–3 hours, skimming frequently. Ladle the stock through a fine sieve and season to taste. Let cool and refrigerate for up to 3 days.

3 **After the stock** has been refrigerated, the congealed fat can easily be lifted from the surface with a slotted spoon.

Quick Skimming Fold a double-thick kitchen towel and pass it through the surface of the hot stock; the kitchen towel will absorb the fat.

Fish Stock

1 **Using a sharp knife**, cut the fish bones and trimmings into equal-sized pieces. Place them in a bowl of cold, salted water to dégorge, or remove any extra blood. Drain and place the bones and trimmings into a large stockpot.

2 **Cut carrots**, celery, and onion into pieces of equal size and add them (and any other flavourings you wish to add) into the pan with the fish. Cover with water, raise the heat, and bring to the boil.

3 **Once the stock** reaches the boil, lower the heat, and simmer for 20 minutes (any longer and the stock will start to become bitter). Skim off the scum that rises to the surface with a slotted spoon.

4 **Ladle the stock** through a fine sieve, pressing the solids against the sieve with the ladle to extract any extra liquid. Season to taste with salt and freshly ground black pepper, let cool, and refrigerate for up to 3 days.

Vegetable Stock

1 **Place chopped carrots**, celery, onion and a bouquet garni into a large stockpot. Cover with water and bring to the boil. Reduce the heat and simmer the stock for up to 1 hour.

2 **Ladle the stock** through a fine sieve, pressing the vegetables against the sieve to extract any extra liquid. Season to taste with salt and freshly ground black pepper, let cool, and refrigerate for up to 3 days.

Techniques Baking

Prepare and Line a Cake Tin

Greasing, flouring, or lining your tin ensures that baked layers turn out cleanly and easily

1 Melt unsalted butter (unless your recipe states otherwise) and use a pastry brush to apply a thin, even layer over the bottom and sides of the tin, making sure to brush butter into the corners, if applicable.

2 Sprinkle a small amount of flour into the tin. Shake the pan so the flour coats the bottom and rotate the tin to coat the sides. Turn the tin upside down and tap the centre to remove the excess flour.

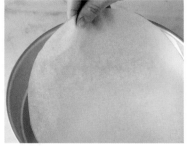

3 Or, if using a paper liner, instead of flouring, place a fitted piece of greaseproof paper directly on to the greased bottom.

Parchment Lining To create the liner, stand the tin on the parchment and draw around the base with a pencil. Cut out just inside the pencil line.

Make Pastry

Once rested, pastry dough can be used straight away or stored for up to two days in a refrigerator, wrapped tightly in cling film

By Hand

1 Mix 375g (13oz) of unsalted, room temperature butter, with 1 egg yolk and 1½ tsp of salt. In another bowl, mix 2 tsp sugar with 100ml (3½fl oz) milk, then gradually stir it into the butter mixture.

2 Sift 500g (1lb 2oz) of plain flour into a bowl, then gradually stir it into the butter. When all the flour is added, continue mixing with a wooden spoon or gently combine the ingredients with your hands.

3 Dust a work surface with flour and turn out the dough. Using the palm of your hand, lightly knead the pastry until it forms a soft, moist dough. This recipe will make 1kg (2¼lb) of pastry.

4 Shape the dough into a ball, wrap it in cling film, and refrigerate for at least 2 hours. Allowing the gluten and flour to relax during chilling will prevent the dough from shrinking when in the hot oven.

In a Food Processor

1 Fit the metal blade into the food processor. Tip in the butter, salt, egg yolk, sugar, and milk and process until smooth. Sift the flour into a separate bowl, then gradually add it into the food processor.

2 Using the pulse button, process the mixture until it just starts to come together and stop when the pastry has formed a ball. Wrap in cling film and refrigerate for at least 2 hours.

Bake Pastry Blind

Pastry must be pre-cooked if its filling will not be baked or baked only for a short time

1 Once the pastry is fitted in the tin, prick the bottom with a fork. This will allow trapped air to escape during baking.

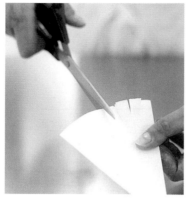

2 Cut out a circle of baking parchment, just slightly larger than the tin. Fold the parchment in half 3 times to make a triangular shape and clip the edges at regular intervals with scissors.

3 Place the parchment circle into the tin and fill it with an even layer of ceramic or metal baking beans. Bake at 180°C (350°F/ Gas 4) for 15–20 minutes.

4 When cool enough to handle, remove the beans and parchment. For fully baked pastry, return the pastry to the oven for a further 5–8 minutes, or until golden.

Trim Decorate Pastry

Before baking pies and tarts, remove excess pastry, and decorate the edges for a finished look

Trim

Roll the pastry out, then press it gently into the bottom of the tin and against the sides. Firmly roll a rolling pin over the top of the tin to trim off the excess pastry.

Forked Edge

Using a fork, press the dough to the rim of the plate. Repeat around the edge in even intervals.

Rope Edge

Pinch the dough between your thumb and the knuckle of your index finger, then place your thumb in the groove left by the index finger and pinch as before. Repeat around the edge.

Fluted Edge

Push one index finger against the outside edge of the rim and pinch the pastry with the other index finger and thumb to form a ruffle. Repeat around the edge, leaving an even gap between each ruffle.

Make a Pizza Base

Rolling and turning the dough often is important are order to achieve a thin, even crust. For a basic pizza dough recipe, see p98

1 Form a well in the centre of the flour and add the liquid ingredients into it, gradually bringing the flour into the centre.

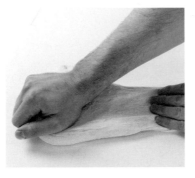

2 Knead the dough for 10 minutes, or until smooth. Set the dough aside in a bowl, cover with cling film and allow to rise.

3 When the dough has doubled in size, turn it out onto a floured surface. Working from the centre, outward, roll the dough in to a circle. Flip the dough and repeat.

4 Carefully transfer the dough to a lightly oiled and floured baking tray. Pinch the edges with your thumb and index finger to make a small rim.

Mix and Knead Yeast Dough

Dough should be well combined and kneaded to a silken and elastic finish

1 Place the flour and other dry ingredients into a large bowl. Make a well in the centre and gradually add the liquid ingredients.

2 Using your fingers, mix the wet and dry ingredients together, digging into the bottom of the bowl and pressing the dough between your fingers to make sure all the liquid has been incorporated into the flour. The dough should be soft but not sticky.

3 When ready to knead, turn the dough onto a floured surface and, with oiled fingers, fold it in half towards you.

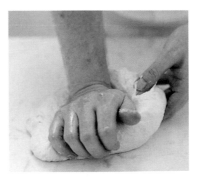

4 Using the heel of your hand, gently but firmly press down and away through the centre to stretch and knead the dough.

5 Lift and rotate the dough a quarter turn. Repeat the folding, pressing and rotating 10–12 times.

6 Let the dough rest, as directed in your recipe, then continue kneading. Each kneading will require less oil and produce a more elastic dough.

Seal and Glaze Pastry

A variety of ingredients can be used to seal in moisture or produce a glossy finish for pastry

Fruit Tarts

Apply a melted jelly, jam, or light caramel over the fruit when you remove the tart from the oven to give the fruit a lustrous appearance.

Turnovers

For turnovers, brush with an egg wash (1 egg yolk, 1 tbsp water and a pinch of salt) before baking to give the turnovers a rich, golden colour and glossy glaze.

Pie Edges

Pie edges can be sealed with beaten egg white and the tops made glossy by brushing with beaten egg.

Cooked Tart

For a cooked tart thinly glaze the base of a cooked tart shell with melted dark or white chocolate and allow to set to stop the base from softening once filled.

Make Brioche Dough

Since the dough is very sticky, use an electric mixer. See p70 for ingredient quantities

1 Pour the flour into the bowl of an electric mixer. Add instant dried yeast and caster sugar. Using the dough hook attachment, mix on medium speed and gradually add the milk and eggs. Mix until smooth, then add the remaining eggs, one at a time, until fully incorporated.

2 Once the dough is mixed and begins to come away from the edges of the bowl, add salt and unsalted butter (at room temperature and cut into pieces). Continue mixing until the dough comes away from the edges again.

3 When the dough is mixed and smooth, remove it from the mixing bowl and transfer it to another large bowl. Cover with cling film and leave it to sit at room temperature for 2–3 hours, or until it doubles in size. The risen dough will be very sticky.

4 On a lightly floured work surface, deflate the dough back to its original size by punching it down with your fist. Return the dough to the bowl and cover it with cling film. Place it in a refrigerator and let it rise for 1¼ hours. Deflate once more, then shape into balls and bake.

Make Blinis

For serving with spreads or smoked fish, these yeasted pancakes are perfect little appetizers. For blini quantities and recipe see p44

1 Mix the yeast and liquid together in a mixing bowl, then stir in the sifted flours and salt until the batter is smooth and well combined. Beat in the melted butter and egg yolk. In a separate bowl, whisk the egg white until soft peaks form. Fold the egg white gently into the batter.

2 Heat a heavy, non-stick pan, then spoon small discs of the batter on the pan and leave to cook, undisturbed until the edges brown, and bubbles appear on the surface. Flip the blinis, and cook for 2–3 minutes longer, or until the second side is golden. Transfer to a plate and cover. Add more batter and repeat.

Techniques Cakes and Desserts

Whip Cream

Depending on your recipe, you can whip to soft or stiff peaks. Chill the whisk, bowl, and cream beforehand

1 **Remove the cream** from the refrigerator and let it reach the temperature of 5°C (40°F). Start whipping slowly with about 2 strokes per second (or the lowest speed on an electric mixer) until the cream begins to thicken. Increase the whipping to a moderate speed for soft peaks.

2 **For stiff peaks**, continue beating the cream. Test by lifting the beaters to see if the cream retains its shape.

Pipe

For more than just cream, a bag and nozzle can be used to pipe meringue, pastry, and sorbet

1 **Place the nozzle** in the bag then give it a twist to seal and prevent leakage.

2 **Holding the bag** just above the nozzle with one hand, fold the top of the bag over with your other hand, creating a "collar", and begin spooning in the cream.

3 **Continue filling**, until the bag is three-quarters full. Twist the top of the bag to clear any air pockets. The cream should be just visible in the tip of the nozzle.

4 **Holding the twisted end** of the bag taut in one hand, use your other hand to gently press the filling to start a steady flow and direct the nozzle as desired.

Make Crème Pâtissière

This pastry cream is the classic, custard-style filing for profiteroles, éclairs, and the famous Gâteau St. Honoré

1 **In a heavy saucepan** over low heat, bring 250ml (8fl oz) full-fat milk, 25g (scant 1oz) cornflower, the seeds and pods of 2 vanilla pods, and 30g (1oz) sugar to the boil, whisking.

2 **Meanwhile**, whisk 3 egg yolks with 30g (1oz) of sugar in a bowl. Continue whisking and slowly pour in the hot milk. Transfer to the pan and whisk until just to the boil, then remove from heat.

3 **Immediately place** the whole saucepan into a bowl of iced water and remove the vanilla pods. While it chills, cut 25g (scant 1oz) of butter at room temperature into pieces.

4 **Once the sauce** has cooled, add the cut butter pieces and briskly whisk them into the sauce until it is smooth and glossy. Best when used right away, this recipe will make 300ml (10fl oz).

Test Setting Point for Jam

The night before making jam, clean, destem, and mix berries with sugar

Using a wooden spoon, scoop up some of the jam. Hold the jam above the bowl for a few seconds, allowing it to cool. Tilt the spoon at an angle – the jam should fall in a flake rather than a stream.

Place a little of the jam on to a cool plate. Allow it to cool, then push it to the side, using your finger. If the surface wrinkles, the jam is ready.

Make Fruit Crumble

Adding a crumble to fresh fruit makes a quick and easy dessert. For fruit crumble recipes, see p453 and 462

SUCCESSFUL CRUMBLE TOPPING

A perfect crumble topping should be made of coarse crumbs. Anything finer will mean the topping will have a cake-like texture rather than a rough crumble. Make sure the butter is chilled and your hands are as cool as possible. Run your hands under cold water if they start getting too hot, or put the whole bowl in a refrigerator for a few minutes to allow the mixture to chill.

Once made, the topping can be tipped into a freezer bag and frozen until ready to use. There is no need to defrost before using and this also stops the crumble mixture clumping together when baking.

1 Rub unsalted butter into plain flour until it resembles chunky breadcrumbs. Add sugar and oats and mix together.

2 Cut fresh fruit to line the bottom of an ovenproof dish. Spoon over the crumble mixture and bake until golden and crisp.

Steam Sponge Puddings

A steamed sponge differs from a baked one in that it is moister and quite heavy. For ingredient quantities and recipe, see p379

1 Mix a good quality fruit preserve with dry sherry and some chopped, dried fruit. Stir them together in the bottom of the pudding basin.

2 Spoon in the sponge mixture over the preserves. Pleat the wax paper and place it over the top of the basin. Secure it firmly around the outer rim of the bowl with string.

3 To keep out the steam, cover the wax paper with pleated kitchen foil. Secure the foil to the outer rim and place the pudding in a steamer over boiling water.

4 Remove the pudding from the steamer. When cool enough to handle, remove the foil and paper. Cover the top with a plate, invert, then lift the basin off the pudding. Serve with Crème Anglaise.

Make Ice Cream

For ice cream ingredient quantities and recipes, see pp403–409

VARIATIONS ON VANILLA

The greatness of vanilla is that it pairs well with almost everything. Add fresh or frozen fruit when processing the mixture to make strawberry or peach ice cream. Chop your favourite chocolate and add it with 2 tbsp of cocoa powder. Or try adding some instant coffee, a little sugar and some almonds.

1 Prepare a batch of Crème Anglaise (see p405) and cool in a bowl set over a separate bowl of ice. Stir the mixture continuously to prevent a skin forming on the surface.

2 Continue to stir the mixture to ensure a smooth texture. Fold in 240ml (8oz) of double cream, and stir gently until the two mixtures are completely combined.

3 Pour the custard mixture into a sorbetière, or ice cream churn. Continue churning or processing until thick and smooth, then place in a container and freeze until firm.

Make Granita

A frozen combination of a full-flavoured syrup and water (or red or white wine) is light and refreshing after any meal

1 Make a syrup of sugar, fruit juice, water, and/or wine over low heat. Bring slowly to the boil, reduce the heat and simmer for 2–3 minutes, stirring. Remove from the heat, let cool, then pour the liquid into a shallow baking tray and freeze. When half-frozen, use a fork to break up the frozen chunks. Repeat once or twice, to break up the crystals, until evenly frozen.

2 Remove the granita from the freezer 5–10 minutes before serving, to thaw slightly. Use a spoon to scrape up the frozen granita and serve in pre-chilled glasses.

Make a Soufflé Omelette

This dessert omelette is made by folding stiffly whisked egg whites with the yolk and grilling for just a moment

1 Separate 2 eggs. Beat the yolks with 1 tbsp of caster sugar, 1 tbsp water and ¼ tsp of vanilla extract. Whisk the whites until stiff, then stir in a small amount of the yolk mixture into the whites. When incorporated, carefully fold the remaining yolks into the mixture.

2 Heat a flat frying pan over moderate heat, then melt enough butter to lightly cover the bottom of the pan. Pour in the eggs and cook until set and the bottom is just beginning to brown. Place under a hot grill until the top is golden. Quickly add a sweet filling, fold over, and serve immediately.

Make Lacy Crêpes

Making these crepes involves two essential points: the right temperature and the perfect batter. See p376 for ingredient quantities

1 Heat a little clarified butter in a crêpe pan and pour off any excess. Holding the pan at an angle, pour in a little of the batter.

2 Tilt and swirl the pan as you pour in more batter to thinly and evenly coat the base of the pan.

3 When the crêpe has cooked to a pale gold underneath, use a long spatula to loosen and flip the crêpe back into the pan.

4 Cook until the second side is golden. Place on baking parchment with a layer between each finished crêpe. Continue cooking the rest of the batter.

Fold Crêpes

Traditionally, crêpes are folded in fans, but other folded variations are just as attractive

Fill crêpes with about 1 tsp of sweet fruit preserves, cooked fruit or chocolate sauce. Fold as desired and eat immediately.

Fans

To fold fans, fold one half of the crêpe over the other, then repeat the fold in half again.

Pannequets

To fold pannequets, or squares, fold opposite sides inward to meet in the centre. Then bring the top and bottom together at the centre. Serve with the folded-side down.

Cigarettes

To fold cigarettes, or rolls, fold opposite sides inward to meet in the centre. Starting from one end, roll the crêpe, taking care not to roll too tightly, as the filling will squeeze out.

Making Choux Paste

Choux is a soft paste and rises into a crisp, airy and light case during cooking. For ingredient quantities, see p439

1 In a saucepan, heat the butter and the water until the butter melts. Increase the heat and bring to the full boil. Tip in the flour, remove from the heat and stir vigorously.

2 When a smooth paste develops, return to the heat. The paste will dry out a little and form a ball. The dough should begin to pull away from the side of the pan.

3 Remove from the heat again and gradually beat in the eggs, trying to incorporate as much air as possible when stirring.

4 Continue stirring until the paste is very smooth. The paste is now ready to be shaped.

Shaping Choux Paste

Choux in any shape is perfect for filling with chocolate or crème patissière

Choux Buns

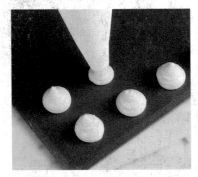

1 Pipe neat and uniform globes on to a lined baking sheet, pressing the nozzle gently into the paste at the end of each globe to avoid forming a peak. Allow plenty of space between each one.

2 If peaks should form, dip a fork in a little beaten egg to gently flatten them. Lightly brush the buns with beaten egg, using a pastry brush, then bake.

3 When the buns are cooked, they should be puffed and golden. Make a small slit in each of the buns to allow the steam to escape, then cool on a wire rack.

4 When cool, cut a small split in the base of each bun. Fill by piping cream or chocolate through the split using a large, plain nozzle.

Choux Fingers

Using a plain nozzle, pipe the choux paste in strips, making each "finger" identical in length. Bake, pierce and cool on a wire rack. Split in half, pipe flavoured mousse onto the base. Replace the top and repeat for the other fingers.

Choux Rings

Mark out circles of your chosen size on a baking sheet, using a circular cutter dusted with flour. These templates will ensure uniform ring sizes. Following the circles, pipe choux rings using an appropriately sized ring nozzle. Bake the rings, pierce and cool on a wire rack. Split the rings in half, fill with cream, and replace the tops.

Make Sponge Cakes

A light Génoise sponge is perfect with simple cream or preserves. Add butter for a firmer sponge that will support the weight of the fruit

1 Preheat the oven to 190°C (375°F/Gas 5) and line the bottom of a springform cake tin with greaseproof paper. Sift 200g (8oz) plain flour and set aside. Place a heatproof bowl over boiling water, making sure the water does not touch the bowl. Place 6 eggs, 20g (¾oz) honey, and a little salt into the bowl, and using an electric mixer whisk at a moderate speed until the mixture is a creamy, pale yellow, doubled in size.

2 Remove the bowl from the heat and whisk at a high speed until the mixture is cooled and thick. Add grated zest of ½ lemon, set the speed to low and continue whisking for 15 minutes to stabilize the eggs. Using a spatula, gradually fold the sifted flour into the mixture. Stir a few tbsp of the mixture into 60g (2¼oz) melted unsalted butter, then quickly combine the two, taking care not to lose any volume.

3 Pour the mixture into the prepared cake tin, smooth the top and place it into the oven. Reduce the heat to 175°C (350°F/Gas 4) and bake for 30–40 minutes, or until golden brown and springy to the touch. Remove from the oven and leave to cool in the pan for 10 minutes. Cut around the edges of the cake, then release the springform. Peel away the paper lining and leave to cool on a wire rack.

4 To cut layers, place the cake on a firm and level surface. Place one hand firmly on top to steady the cake and using a sharp, long-bladed, serrated knife, gently make an even guideline around the cake. Following your guideline, cut through the layer completely. Using a long spatula, carefully lift the layer, set aside and fill the cake. If desired, multiple layers can be made, depending on the size of the cake.

Roll a Sponge Roulade

A roulade is less likely to tear if filled and rolled while it is still warm

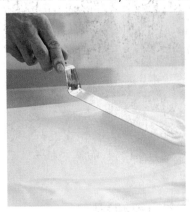

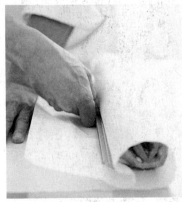

1 Make the mixture for the sponge cake, taking care to fold in the egg white mixture very gently so that none of the volume is lost.

2 Turn the mixture out onto the lined baking tray and spread evenly to the edge using a spatula. Bake until golden and springy to the touch. Sprinkle with a little caster sugar and place a clean piece of baking parchment on top. Carefully turn out the cake.

3 Slowly peel away the bottom layer of parchment paper, taking care not to tear the cake. Spread with your desired filling and roll, using the second piece of parchment to support the roulade with a little gentle pressure.

4 Fold one half of the paper completely over the roulade. With the roulade in the centre of the fold, hold the bottom half and push a ruler against the roll with your free hand. This will tighten and shape the roulade evenly. Remove the paper, cover and trim the ends to serve.

Make French Meringue

This meringue will be caramelized and crunchy on the outside and soft and yielding inside. For ingredient quantities, see p388

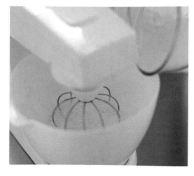

1 **In a large mixing bowl**, whisk together the egg whites, half of the sugar, and the vanilla seeds at a moderate speed.

2 **Continue whisking** until the mixture becomes smooth, shiny, and firm.

3 **Using a rubber spatula**, gradually fold the rest of the sugar into the egg mixture, taking care not to lose any of the volume.

4 **Shape then bake** the meringue so that the centre is just golden. Turn off the oven. Prop the oven door open and leave to dry for at least 8 hours or overnight.

Shape Meringue

Using a pastry bag with different tops, meringue can be formed into many shapes and sizes, or applied as a topping to a tart

For discs or layers, onto a baking tray lined with parchment and using a pastry bag with a star tip, pipe the meringue in a spiral beginning in the centre and moving outward. Bake for 1 hour 20 minutes, then let dry.

For shells, using a pastry bag with a round tip, pipe the meringue in equal-sized globes and bake for 1 hour 10 minutes, then let dry.

For fingers, using a pastry bag with a round tip, pipe the meringue in to thin, even sticks, and dust with icing sugar. Bake for 30–35 minutes, then let dry.

To cover a tart, using a pastry bag with a star tip, pipe the meringue over the surface of the tart in attractive peaks. Dust with icing sugar and place under a hot grill for a few minutes, or until golden brown.

Use Leaf Gelatine

Whether you are using gelatine in leaf or powder form, it must first be soaked in a little cold water

1 **Soak 3 leaves** (equal to about 1½ tsp of powdered gelatine) in a bowl covered in cold water, for at least 10 minutes. After soaking, squeeze out as much liquid from the leaves as possible before using.

2 **Bring 3 tbsp of water** just to the boil in a small saucepan. Remove the pan from the heat and stir in the gelatine until dissolved. Use as your recipe instructs.

Make Caramel

To help prevent the sugar from crystallizing, add some liquid glucose (available at your local chemist)

Make Syrup

1 **Combine 150ml (5fl oz)** of water, 330g (12oz) caster sugar, and 120g (4oz) liquid glucose in a heavy saucepan over a low heat, stirring often with a wooden spoon. Use a wet pastry brush to wipe down the side of the pan to prevent the sugar from crystallizing. Once the sugar has dissolved, bring the liquid to the boil.

2 **When the caramel** becomes golden brown in colour and is just thick enough to coat the back of a teaspoon, stop the cooking at once by plunging the entire pan into a large bowl of iced water. This recipe makes 500ml (17fl oz).

Make Sauce

Remove the pan from the iced water after a minute, but while the syrup is still warm. Whisk in a knob of softened butter and softly whipped cream or crème fraîche to your taste. Whisk until the sauce is thick, slightly sticky, and smooth. Return the pan to a low heat, and bring to a gentle boil, or until the sauce temperature reaches 103°C (217°F).

Measure the temperature of the caramel accurately, by using a sugar thermometer.

Prepare Chocolate

Chill the chocolate before cutting and grating, as the warmth of your hands will quickly melt it

Chop

For chopping, use your hands to break the chocolate into small pieces, then chill the pieces in the freezer for a few minutes. Place the chilled chocolate on a cutting board. Using a sharp knife, hold the tip down with your other hand and chop, using a rocking motion.

Grate

For grating, rub chilled chocolate against the face of the grater, using the widest holes. Once the chocolate begins to melt, stick it back in the freezer. Once re-hardened, continue grating until you have enough.

Melt

To melt chocolate, bring a pan of water to the boil, then reduce the heat to low. Place the chopped chocolate in a heatproof bowl and set it over the gently simmering water. Allow the chocolate to melt, then stir with a wooden spoon until it is smooth and the consistency is even.

Make Curls

For curls, spread soft or melted chocolate onto a cool marble surface. Use the blade of a chef's knife to scrape the chocolate into curls.

Index

Acknowledgments

For Carroll & Brown Limited

Project Manager Chrissie Lloyd
Project Editor Chrissa Yee
Managing Art Editor John Casey

Commissioning Editor Susie Johns
Senior Editor Helen Barker-Benfield
Recipe Editor Jacqueline Bellefontaine
Editors Louise Coe, Beverly LeBlanc, Kate Pollard, Wanda Allardice,
Rhona Kyle, Lucy Jessop, Ian Wood, Michele Clarke

Art Directors Anne Fisher, Denise Brown, Luis Peral-Aranda,
Tracy Stewart-Murray, Ruth Hope
Designers Emily Cook, Richard Walsh, Paul Stradling, Oliver Keen
Technical Advisor George Taylor

Food Stylists Teresa Goldfinch, Wendy Strang, Sarah Lee, Liz Cambio, Lizzie Harris,
Marie-Ange Lapierre, Jane Oliver, Brian Brooke, Sam Squire, Madeleine Cameron,
Katie Giovanni, Liz Franklin, Patricia Dunbar, Viv Gill, Lorna Brash, Tonia George

Photographers Carole Tuff, Tony Cambio, William Shaw, Stuart West, David Munns,
David Murray, Adrian Heapy, Nigel Gibson, Kieran Watson, Roddy Paine,
Gavin Sawyer, Ian O'Leary

Recipe Developers Christine France, Caroline Marson, Lorna Brash, Clare Lewis,
Catherine Atkinson, Liz Ashworth, Jacqueline Bellefontaine, Beverly LeBlanc, Susie Johns,
Tomaz Zaleski, Helen Barker-Benfield, Wendy Sweetzer, Kathryn Hawkins,
Fiona Burrell, Sue McMahon, Viv Gill, Nicky Sanderson de la Peña,
and Victoria Blashford-Snell

Proofreader John Skermer
Index Marie Lorimer

Thanks also to **Denby Pottery** for use of their products for photography
and to Jonathan Worth for hand modelling

Editor-in-Chief
Victoria Blashford-Snell first began cooking in pubs and restaurants in Bath and
Wiltshire. As a result of her zest for travel, she developed an imaginative variety of tastes,
from the Mediterranean to the Great Barrier Reef to the Himalayas. Today she runs
a successful catering business and teaches regular cookery courses in the UK.

Victoria has written several popular cookbooks, including *Canapés* and *Diva Cooking*, and has
co-authored six *Books for Cooks* cookbooks. She has also presented 30 programmes for
Carlton Food Network, UK, and appears regularly on several food shows in the US and Canada.

Useful Information

Oven Temperature Equivalents

CELSIUS	FAHRENHEIT	GAS	DESCRIPTION
110°C	225°F	¼	Cool
120°C	250°F	½	Cool
140°C	275°F	1	Very Low
150°C	300°F	2	Very Low
170°C	325°F	3	Low
180°C	350°F	4	Moderate
190°C	375°F	5	Moderately Hot
200°C	400°F	6	Hot
220°C	425°F	7	Hot
230°C	450°F	8	Very Hot

Volume Equivalents

METRIC	IMPERIAL	METRIC	IMPERIAL
25ml	1fl oz	200ml	7fl oz (⅓ pint)
50ml	2fl oz	225ml	8fl oz
75ml	2fl oz	250ml	9fl oz
100ml	3fl oz	300ml	10fl oz (½ pint)
125ml	4fl oz	350ml	12fl oz
150ml	5fl oz (¼ pint)	400ml	14fl oz
175ml	6fl oz	500ml	18fl oz

Refrigerator and Freezer Storage Guide

FOOD	REFRIGERATOR	FREEZER
Raw poultry, fish, and meat (small pieces)	2-3 days	3-6 months
Raw minced beef and poultry	1-2 days	3 months
Cooked whole roasts or whole poultry	2-3 days	9 months
Cooked poultry pieces	1-2 days	1 month (6 months in stock or gravy)
Bread	-	3 months
Ice cream	-	1-2 months
Soups and stews	2-3 days	1-3 months
Casseroles	2-3 days	2-4 weeks
Biscuits	-	6-8 months